A DICTIONARY OF BATTLES

A Dictionary of Battles 1816–1976 by Brigadier Peter Young with Brigadier Michael Calvert, also published by New English Library, is a companion volume (Volume IV of a series) to this book.

A DICTIONARY
OF BATTLES

1715–1815

Brigadier Michael Calvert, DSO

with Brigadier Peter Young, DSO, MC

MAYFLOWER BOOKS
NEW YORK

Copyright January, 1979 by Brigadier Michael
Calvert

All rights reserved under International and Pan
American Copyright Convention. Published
in the United States by Mayflower Books,
Inc., 575 Lexington Avenue, New York City 10022.

Originally published in England by The New
English Library, Barnard's Inn, Holborn,
London, EC1N 2JR.

Library of Congress Cataloging in Publication
Data
Young, Peder.
   Dictionary of battles.

   Bibliography: p.
   Includes index.
   1. Battles—Dictionaries.
   2. Military history—Dictionaries.
I. Calvert, Michael, joint author.
II. Title.
D25.A2Y68 1979   904'.7   78–23518

FIRST AMERICAN EDITION 1979

ISBN: 0 8317 2261 4

Printed in Great Britain by Thomson Litho Ltd,
East Kilbride, Scotland
Bound by Hunter and Foulis, Edinburgh,
Scotland.

Contents

Author's Preface

The purpose of this *Dictionary of Battles* is to list and describe within certain geographical limits, which are separated into sections, all the essential military and naval battles and engagements of the period. Volume III covers the period 1715–1815, during which more major wars were fought all over the world between European powers than ever before. In fact this period has been named by some historians as the Second Hundred Years' War.

As these conflicts are listed in alphabetical, and not chronological, order, we have endeavoured to treat each entry as an individual entity. Cross-references to other entries within each section are indicated in parentheses either by the names in small capitals or by the abbreviation qv or qqv. However, in general, to avoid needless complexities, cross-references to battles placed in different sections are not given.

Scope of the entries
The length of an entry does not necessarily reflect the scale of the battle or the numbers engaged, and it should be noted that some quite small engagements had more far-reaching historical and geopolitical results than others of greater intensity. Moreover, on occasions, some of the smaller engagements illustrated greater military skill than certain thoughtless head-on clashes ordered by unintelligent generals.

Our chief aim has been to record the names of all battles which a historian, tactician, student or writer might wish to investigate. In this context some of the lesser known conflicts may arouse greater interest than the more familiar ones. Certainly many of those who have studied Volume IV (1816 to 1976), the first book in this series that has been published, have told us that they found the more obscure battles and campaigns the most interesting parts of the *Dictionary*.

In the headnote to each entry we have given first the name of the battle (with any alternative name in brackets); second its location within present-day boundaries; next the name of the war or campaign; and lastly the date on which it took place according to the new-style (Gregorian) calendar. (In certain cases we have had difficulty in identifying the combatants. For instance, in the '15 and '45 campaigns (of the eighteenth century) in Scotland, English and Scots fought on either side, so we have identified the participants as Hanoverians and Jacobites—which may not please all their adherents.) We then state briefly the forces engaged, coupled with the full name and rank of the commanders, and give an estimate of the strengths of the opposing forces, culled from the most reliable sources. There follows a brief analytical description of the battle itself, covering some of the more interesting tactics involved and the casualties suffered. We complete the entry with the result of the contest and consequences (if any) of the engagement.

With some minor battles, or in cases where little information is available, yet which we felt merited inclusion, we have compressed the different aspects of the action into one or two paragraphs.

Believing as we do that there is no such thing as a 'definitive' book on any subject, least of all on battles and wars where the victor tends to write history for the glorification of his own side, we have done our best to write a balanced and fair description of each conflict. Researchers can follow up our brief outlines with deeper study if they wish further to try and find the truth. For so often truth is a many-sided diamond and we each usually see only one facet of it.

Campaigns
In certain, but not all, instances where the origin of individual battles is obscure, we have included an entry for the campaign as a whole in which the narrative links up more than one battle and, we hope, clarifies for the reader its place in history.

Insurrections
We have recorded a number of the more important insurrections, guerrilla actions and, in a few cases, riots which have influenced the military situation. This especially applies to the Peninsular War section where guerrillas played such an important part. A number of their actions are quite rightly, in my opinion, listed on a par with more well-known battles with which they rank in military importance, although they are often neglected by some historians.

Sea battles and ship-to-ship engagements

All well-known sea battles have been recorded in the same manner as the land battles, in language to which naval experts will not take exception and which we hope that the layman too will understand. A number of the more significant ship-to-ship actions have also been described, but pressure of space would not allow us to register every such engagement. Inevitably, because of their geographical locations, it has sometimes been difficult to decide in which section of the *Dictionary* they should be placed.

We have converted certain early French naval ranks such as *chef d'escadre* and *lieutenant-général* into their British and American equivalents of rear-admiral and vice-admiral respectively for ease of recognition, as is customary in works of this nature.

Ranks and titles

The naming of the correct rank and titles of the participant commanders, varying as they do from battle to battle as they won promotion and further honours, has been a recurrent headache to us as we sought to hit on an acceptable and yet not too elongated nomenclature. While we cannot compete with *Debrett* or the *Almanach de Gotha* in this respect, we have attempted none the less to identify correctly the rank and title held by a commander at the time of the battle in question without adding a great rigmarole of names to which some commanders are or were entitled but which are not central to the purpose of this dictionary. However, we have not attempted to translate Arabic, Turkish, Mongolian, or even early Scottish, ranks (such as chief of a clan) into any equivalent modern military rank.

Nomenclature

The Westernised spelling of Eastern names changes from country to country and era to era much more than most people realise. The transliteration of Arabic, Moslem, Indian, Chinese, Cyrillic and Glogolitic names into the Roman alphabet has never been consistent among historians.

In this volume we have opted (as we shall in Volume II where this factor is even more significant) for the better-known methods of spelling Arabic names, well aware that, for instance, the accepted spelling of Arabic names can be quite different in the Iberian Peninsula to that in the Middle East or North Africa. Where there is likely to be confusion we have provided an alternative spelling in parenthesis.

There is too this persistent problem for the compiler: the considerable variations in spelling of the names of commanders. The spelling in the earliest sources closest to the time of action, especially of Indian and Arabic names and titles, is often totally at variance with more modern versions. We have therefore tried to strike a reasonable balance.

Casualties and numbers engaged

Anyone who has fought in a war or taken part in the forefront of a battle will be aware that a commander never does know exactly how many troops he has under command at any one time. There are always officers and men coming and going, men recovering from wounds and rejoining their units, reinforcements arriving or being diverted, men deserting before battle, and other unknown factors which militate against exactitude. The ration strength is just as likely to be as inexact as any other estimate. Some historians try to give figures to the last digit, but their quantities are largely based on guesswork. So, in giving the strengths of forces engaged, we have rounded off the numbers in most cases in order to give a comparative estimate between the strengths of each side, which is really all that the tactician wants to know.

Similarly, calculations of casualties vary widely. Nowadays some nations automatically grant pensions to anyone wounded and this, naturally, increases the proportion of wounded to killed very considerably, as efficient regimental clerks and quartermasters record men with mere scratches as 'wounded' so that they can qualify for a pension.

Victors usually exaggerate the number of vanquished killed, and in Euro-Asian conflicts a new factor has crept in whereby European armies tend to record the so-called 'graves' of their enemies in order to inflate their own estimates of casualties inflicted and boost reports of their success. 'Body counts' became a feature of American reporting which distorted the estimates of the numbers of enemy alive and dead. The resultant false statistics often affected overall strategy when believed by politicians and civil servants.

There are always a number of deserters, camp followers, semi-warlike bands and hangers-on roaming around every theatre of war. This confuses the issue and makes it impossible to gauge accurately the exact total of casualties in even the most disciplined army. So again we have rounded off figures to the nearest zero or two. Also we have not entered into the arcane controversy as to whether one should say 'killed *and* wounded' or 'killed *or* wounded' and have used both phrases indiscriminately.

Index

A selective index of battles, personalities and ships (including map references) is provided for cross-reference purposes.

Sources

Under the guidance of the co-authors, the entries in this dictionary have been compiled by a team of researchers, each of whom is qualified in his own particular subject. The co-authors themselves also made substantial contributions to certain sections. Our policy has been not necessarily to make each contributor adopt one particular style, since we felt that some variations in phraseology and approach would add to the readability of the volume. In Volume IV we noted only a comparatively small selection of the main sources consulted. This suggested to certain readers that only a few sources were used. Yet most contributors, as they compiled their accounts, examined at least five sources for their material. Their results were re-examined and, where necessary, redrafted by myself as General Editor and then co-ordinated to avoid inconsistencies by the Consultant Editor of New English Library, Michael Levien, the whole concept being under the original authorship and final overall vetting of Brigadier Peter Young. Thus each entry was subject to careful scrutiny before reaching the proof stage.

In compiling the facts about a battle we have certainly not relied on one source alone. For instance, in a battle between, say, the British and French in Spain, in which Portuguese units were also engaged, we have consulted not only British accounts, but French, Spanish and Portuguese sources as well. Many service officers have been brought up on hagiographic regimental histories written by authors commissioned to do so by the regiments concerned, and not surprisingly such writers have said what they think will please their paymasters. This is also true of 'official' biographies of commanders. Rarely do they tell the whole truth, 'warts and all', the writers considering that their chief duty is to glorify their subject for the benefit of his family who have commissioned them, and to overlook his blemishes. Consequently a reader will often dismiss an impartial account as 'wrong', judging it purely from the standpoint of a biased or distorted one.

In this volume the wars which have had the most one-sided and partial popular accounts, which must be held suspect, are the War of 1812, the wars in the Indian peninsula, the Peninsular War and Waterloo.

Interrelationship of the four volumes

We decided to start with Volume IV and work backwards. But this has inevitably led to insoluble problems. Battles have often been fought again and again on the same locations. So if a battle is recorded in Volume IV as Acre V, Basra III, or Cairo IV, and we find as we go back in history that there are more such actions than we previously calculated, or originally intended to include, we are in a predicament.

Similarly in Volume IV we at first tried to record the dates of birth and death of each commander mentioned for identification purposes, but found it impossible to obtain such data from behind the Iron Curtain, certainly in the time available. So we decided to scrap this very useful aid to the historian. Yet, as we go back in history we find that it is more and more necessary to record such data in order to identify commanders of the same, or similar, names. To avoid confusion in the matter of identification we have given the full name of certain commanders (sometimes with a whole string of forenames), cumbersome as the practice may be.

Maps

A number of maps showing the location of battles are incorporated at the beginning of each section for the various wars and campaigns listed within that section. These outline maps have been kept as simple as possible, with coastlines and rivers drawn in to judge comparative distances, and modern boundaries included only when necessary. They should be sufficient for the reader to locate a battle and reidentify its position on a modern or historical atlas.

Conclusion

A dictionary of any sort, like a language, should be a living entity. The co-authors hope that this first edition of the four volumes will be the basis for future editions, in which can be added new material and further information that the researcher may require.

BRIGADIER MICHAEL CALVERT,
DSO, MA, C Eng, MICE, FR Hist S
London, 1977

Acknowledgements

The authors of this volume of *Dictionary of Battles* wish to take the opportunity of acknowledging and thanking the many contributors who have worked so hard in research to ensure accuracy in their compilation of the various sections. They include Stephen Clissold, OBE, who, besides overseas posts, worked for many years at the Foreign Office Library; Evan Davies, now lecturing in history at the Britannia Royal Naval College, Dartmouth; Ian Walker, MBE, formerly of the Foreign Office; Leslie Clinton-Robinson, MBE; Alison Michelli; James East, MA, lecturer in history who, besides making many other contributions, carried out the indexing; Captain A. P. W. Northey, RN, CBE, DSC, Yeoman Usher of the Black Rod; and our special assistants, Tony Calvert and Michael Clarke, who helped keep the production machinery going as well as checking items of research.

We have also to thank Ann Walker of Home Types Ltd and her indefatigible team of typists.

Special acknowledgement must be made to Michael Levien, our consultant editor, who co-ordinated all the entries and checked one with another to ensure uniformity in addition to carrying out invaluable and massive editorial work on the typescripts and to Martin Noble, Hardcover editor for NEL, who co-ordinated things at this end.

Richard Natkiel of *The Economist* has again drawn a fine selection of maps showing the locations of all the battles in the campaigns with dates. In no other publication to date will be found such a wide and detailed presentation of geo-military knowledge of this period.

We have also to thank the Librarians of the Royal United Services Institution for Defence Studies, the Ministry of Defence, the Royal Naval College, Greenwich, the National Army Museum, the Imperial War Museum, the British Museum, and various municipal libraries, especially those of Kensington, Chelsea and Westminister, without whose help we could not have completed our task.

List of Maps

SECTION ONE

GREAT BRITAIN AND EUROPE

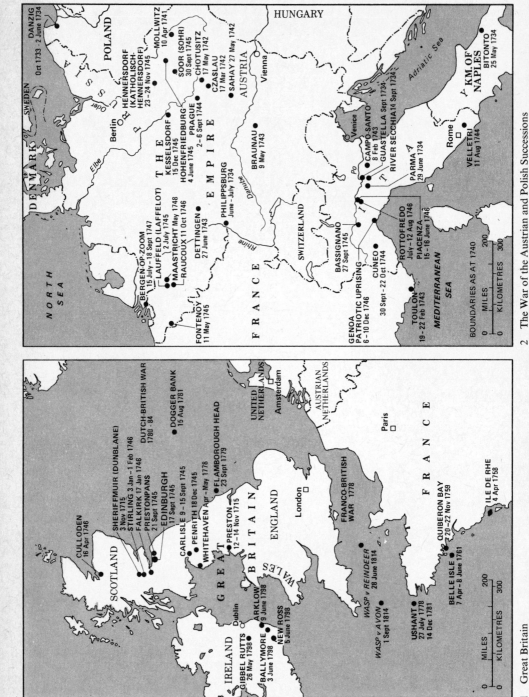

1 Great Britain

2 The War of the Austrian and Polish Successions

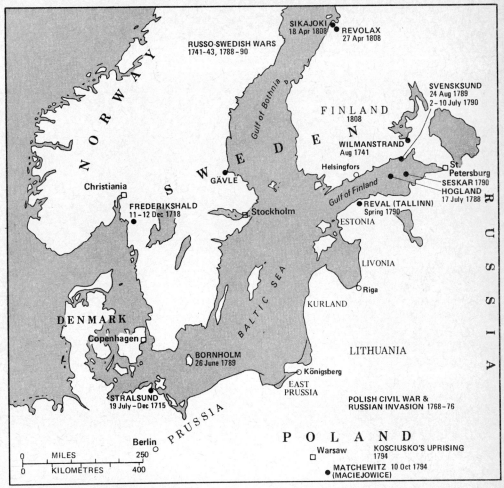

3 Northern Europe: Miscellaneous Battles

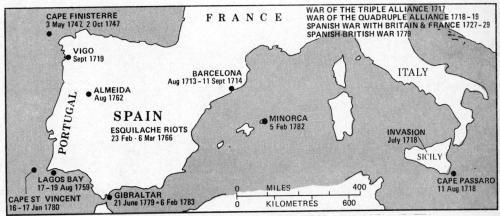

4 Southern Europe: The War of the Triple Alliance, 1717; The War of the Quadruple Alliance, 1718–19; Spanish Wars with Britain and France, 1727–9; The Spanish-British War, 1779

4

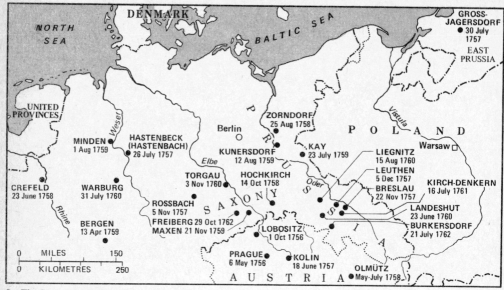

5 The Seven Years' War: Central Europe

6 The Ottoman Wars

ALMEIDA (Portugal)   Seven Years' War/Portuguese Campaign   August 1762
Spain, allied to France in the Family Compact, entered the Seven Years' War (qv) and invaded Portugal, England's ally and traditional target of Spanish ambitions. In May 1762 a Spanish army crossed the frontier, seized several fortresses and in August, with the help of French units, forced the capitulation of Almeida with its 4,000-strong garrison. An expeditionary force of 7,000 men had meanwhile arrived from England and helped the Portuguese to hold the line of the Tagus, barring the Spaniards' advance on Lisbon and repulsing them at Villa Velha.

ARKLOW (Co Wicklow, Eire)   Irish Rebellion   9 June 1798
Fought between the Militia and Volunteers under Major-General the Hon Francis Needham and the insurgents under Billy Byrne, Edward Fitzgerald and Father Michael Murphy.
Strength: Chiefly Militia and Yeomanry 1,600; Rebels 20,000–30,000.
  The insurgents attacked the town of Arklow, which was defended by the Militia and Volunteers. Thanks to Needham's skill and courage the poorly armed insurgents were defeated, Dublin was saved, and the back of the rebellion was broken. Father Murphy, who was among those leading the attack on the barricade with great intrepidity, was shot, and his death greatly discomforted his followers. His head was struck off and, by order of Lord Mountnorris, his body was burnt.

AUSTRIAN SUCCESSION (PRAGMATIC SANCTION), WAR OF THE   Spanish Campaigns 1741–8
Conflict between the major European powers followed the death of the Emperor Charles VI who, under a provision known as the Pragmatic Sanction, wished the succession to pass to his daughter Maria Theresa. The rival claims of Charles Albert of Bavaria were supported by France and Spain against Austria, Prussia, England and Sardinia, which supported Maria Theresa.
  Within this wider conflict, the hostilities between Spain and England started during the War of Jenkins' Ear were further extended (e.g. to Florida). Spain also aimed to recover Gibraltar and Minorca.
  Spain's main effort was made in Italy, where she hoped to regain her former possessions ceded under the Treaty of Utrecht. After fighting some inconclusive engagements the Spanish commander Montemar was replaced by General Count John de Gages, who attacked the Austrians at Campo-Santo (qv) but was driven back southwards until, on 11 August 1744, he made a successful stand at Velletri (qv). A French army, meanwhile, had crossed the Alps into N Italy but, failing to take the key fortress of Cuneo (qv), was forced to withdraw. During 1745, strengthened by the adhesion of Genoa, the Franco-Spanish forces made some advances. Savoy, which had sided with Austria, was defeated at Bassignano (qv) in September 1745, and Milan was entered. Weakened, however, by disease and dissension, the Allies suffered disaster at Piacenza (qv), which ended Spain's hopes of regaining her possessions in Italy.

SUMMARY OF THE CAMPAIGNS
First Silesian War 1740–2: Frederick the Great of Prussia invaded Silesia, an Austrian possession, and told Maria Theresa he would support her and her husband's claim to the Imperial throne of the Habsburg Empire. The Empress refused. In 1741 Bavaria, France (unofficially), Saxony, Savoy and Sweden all joined the Prussians, while England and Holland allied themselves with the Austrians. After campaigns in Silesia and Bohemia, Maria Theresa ceded Silesia to Frederick, and Prussia left the war for the time being.
Bohemia and S Germany 1742–3: Two years of campaigning in Bavaria, Bohemia and S Germany culminated in an official French declaration of war. In the north a French army was set to invade England with Prince Charles (the Young Pretender), who intended to depose George II. The British navy, assisted by the weather, foiled the attempt.
Second Silesian War 1744–5: Frederick of Prussia rejoined the war in alliance with France and invaded Bohemia, but he was forced to retreat owing to the prompt action of Austria and the inaction of his ally, France. The war ended when Maximilian Joseph succeeded Charles VII as Elector of Bavaria and renounced his claim to the Austrian throne. Austria, Saxony, England and Holland had formed a Quadruple Alliance against France, Prussia and Bavaria, but the French in the north were cut off from the Prussians in the south. In Flanders, the French were successful, overrunning the whole country after the Battle of Fontenoy (qv), while in the south Frederick also gained a string of successes, forcing Maria Theresa to make peace, recognising his possession of Silesia while he in turn recognised the election of her husband, Francis Stephen, as Emperor.
The Netherlands 1746–8: French operations in the Austrian Netherlands and Holland were largely

successful but made no difference to the outcome of the war when peace came in 1748 and most conquests were restored.

Italy 1741–8: There were initial Austrian successes in Italy, but the provinces gained were ultimately given up to the French. The war ended with most of the Duchy of Milan, however, still in Austrian hands.

Naval Operations: Naval operations took place mostly between the French, Spanish and British, in which the British gained the more important victories.

AUSTRO-RUSSIAN-TURKISH WAR   1736–9

The conflict grew out of the War of the Polish Succession (qv) when France persuaded Turkey to enter the war against her traditional enemies, Austria and Russia. Turkey remained out of the European war until she had concluded peace with the Persians. By this time the War of the Polish Succession was also over and a new war resulted when Russia opened hostilities by invading Turkish and Tartar lands north of the Black Sea. Austria, having a secret treaty with Russia, entered the war the following year. Operations were conducted in the Ukraine, the Balkans and Moldavia and the Russians gained the upper hand. Their Austrian allies, alarmed at their success, concluded the Treaty of Belgrade with the Turks. Austria's withdrawal forced Russia to make peace as well and the war ended with the Treaty of Nissa, signed on 3 October 1739.

AUSTRO-VENETIAN-TURKISH WAR   1716–18

The Austrians joined Venice in the conflict against Turkey, which was ultimately settled in terms unfavourable to the latter. Meanwhile Hungary, which supported the Ottomans, staged an insurrection under the leadership of Francis Rákózy II against the Austrian Emperor Charles VI. The stratagem was a complete failure (see BELGRADE I).

AZOV (near Rostov-on-Don, USSR)   Austro-Russian-Turkish War   1 July 1735

Fought between the Russians under General Count Petr Lacy and the Turks.

The Russians took the opportunity while the Turkish main forces were at war with Nadir Shah (Efchar), the Shah Kouli Khan of Persia, to seize territory in the Black Sea area. General Lacy besieged Azov (on the NE corner of the Sea of Azov), and it succumbed on 1 July 1736, but he lost so many men from battle and disease that he abandoned this fortress after its capture and retired into Russia.

However, this predatory action was the flashpoint which started the Austro-Russian-Turkish war.

BALLYMORE (Co Wexford)   Irish Rebellion   3 June 1798

Fought between the British under Colonel Walpole and the Rebels under Father Murphy.

Strength: Royal troops 500; Rebels 14,000 pikemen.

During their march on Enniscorthy, the Royal troops were surprised and overwhelmed by a rebel force. Walpole was among those killed, the main part of his force being cut to pieces.

After this success the Rebels took to plunder and drink, and, having been dispersed by General Johnson, left behind 2,600 of their number–either killed, wounded or drunk.

BARCELONA (Spain)   War of the Spanish Succession   August 1713–11 September 1714

Although the Treaty of Utrecht put an end to the War of the Spanish Succession and confirmed the Bourbon dynasty in possession of the Spanish throne, the Catalans continued to resist.

Barcelona organised its defence under General Antonio de Villaroel, who had some 12,000 men under his command. The forces of Philip V and his French allies, numbering 20,000, proved insufficient to invest the city effectively. Reinforcements were sent from Flanders and Sicily. The besiegers made little headway during the winter of 1713/14. Louis XIV's general, the Duke of Berwick, then took command and the blockade by sea was strengthened. The defenders continued to make sorties and rejected calls to surrender. On 11 September 1714 Berwick ordered a general assault, which the defenders, reduced to 8,000 men, were unable to resist.

The fall of Barcelona ended Catalan resistance and established Philip V's centralised government throughout Spain.

BASSIGNANO (N Italy)   War of the Austrian Succession   27 September 1745

Fought between the French, Spanish, Neapolitans and Genoese under General Jean-Baptiste-François Desmarets, Marquis de Maillebois, of France, and General Count John de Gages of Spain, and the Sardinians and a detachment of Austrians under General Count Johann Lobkowitz of Austria.

Genoa joined the French and Spanish in their effort to break the Austrian hold over Italy. On 27 September 1745 the combined forces of the French, Spanish, Neapolitans and Genoese met a mixed army of Sardinians and Austrians at Bassignano and decisively defeated them. Following this victory they went on to capture Alessandria and other Austrian-held fortresses in the valley of the river Po.

BELGRADE (BEOGRAD) I (Yugoslavia)   Austro-Ottoman War   16 August 1717
Charles VI of Austria (who had himself been captured by the Turks a few years earlier) was alarmed at the Turkish expansion in the Balkans. When the Turks under the Grand Vizier Ali Kumurji occupied Greek Morea (qv) and drove out the Venetians, Charles decided in 1716 to ally himself with Venice and declared war on the Ottoman Empire.

Prince Eugène of Savoy, at the head of the Imperial forces, having defeated the Turks at Peterwardein (qv) and captured Temesvar (qv), after which the whole Banat (Romania) fell into his hands, proceeded in July 1717 to besiege Belgrade (Beograd) with 20,000 men. The garrison was 30,000 strong. Before the Austrians could assault the city a relief force of 150,000 under the Grand Vizier, Khalil Pasha, arrived.

Eugène, as usual, took the initiative. While a small detachment of his army repulsed a sortie from the city, he advanced at night and threw his main army at the Turkish entrenchments. Eugène's right wing fared badly and was, for a time, cut off from the main army, but Eugène led his reserve to its rescue, being himself wounded in the assault. Meanwhile the Austrian main thrust had achieved surprise and successfully driven the Turks out of their positions. Belgrade surrendered on 21 August.

The Austrians lost 5,500 men, including Marshal Hauben. The Turkish losses in men and material were immense and included 20,000 men, 131 bronze cannon, 35 mortars and their whole reserve of powder and projectiles.

The Sublime Porte, recognising its weakness, concluded a peace at Passarowitz on 21 July 1718 in which it ceded to the Emperor Belgrade, Temesvar, Wallachia as far as the Aluta, and a portion of Serbia, but retained the Morea (Peleponnisos).

BELGRADE (BEOGRAD) II (Yugoslavia)   Austro-Russian-Turkish War   July 1738–September 1739
Fought between the Austrians under Field-Marshal Count George Oliver von Wallis and General Suckow (fortress commander), and the Turks under Elvias Mohammed Pasha and the former Grand Vizier and Governor of Bosnia, Ali Pasha.
Strength: Austrians (initially) 15,000 garrison + 10,000 field army; Turks 150,000 (maximum).

After Wallis had been overwhelmed at Kroszka (qv) in July 1738 he shut himself up with the remains of his army with the garrison of the huge, well-provisioned fortress of Belgrade (Beograd). The main armies of the Turks were, at that time, heavily engaged with the victorious Russian Marshal Count Burkhardt Christoph von Münnich, (see UKRAINE CAMPAIGNS OF COUNT MÜNNICH) who repeatedly beat them and pulverised their army at Khotin, during which he captured much of the Grand Vizier's siege train.

Owing to this lack of heavy siege weapons the Turks, although making repeated assaults on the fortress during its thirteen months' investment, could not hope to reduce it. The Emperor Charles VI instructed both Wallis and the Imperial Plenipotentiary, Marshal Count Wilhelm Reinhardt von Neipperg, to make peace overtures to the Grand Vizier, Elvias Mohammed Pasha.

After protracted negotiations, the Treaty of Belgrade was signed on 18 September 1739, by the terms of which Belgrade was handed over to the Turks (see also VALIEVO). On that day Suckow's garrison, reduced now to 9,000 effectives owing to sickness and casualties, marched out with colours flying, having first razed the outer fortifications with explosives according to the terms of the treaty.

Wallis and Neipperg were made the scapegoats for the failures of the Emperor's ill-prepared armies and Charles died, broken-hearted, six months later.

BELGRADE (Beograd) III (Yugoslavia)   Ottoman Wars   8 October 1789
The Turks held Belgrade (Beograd) against the Austrians, under General Baron Gideon Ernst von Laudon, who sought the reduction of the town. After a brief siege, the town surrendered on 8 October 1789.

This operation was part of a co-ordinated advance into Moldavia, Wallachia and Bosnia, the success of which enabled the Russian-Austrian alliance to penetrate deeper into Turkey. Belgrade was returned to Turkey in exchange for part of Bosnia by the Treaty of Sistova (1791).

BELLEISLE (Quiberon Bay, France)   Seven Years' War   7 April–8 June 1761
Fought between the British naval and military forces commanded by Commodore Augustus Keppel and
General Hodgson, and the French garrison of Belleisle, commanded by General Saint Croix.
Strength: British 8,000 + fleet convoy; French 3,000.
Aim: The British destruction of the French Admiral de la Clue's and Marshal Hubert de Conflan's fleets in
1759 had put an end to the chances of the French reinforcing their overseas possessions effectively. The
French naval ports from Dunkirk round to Marseilles were littered with the wrecks of their squadrons and
Quiberon Bay (qv) had become to all intents and purposes a British fleet anchorage where the sailors grew
vegetables and sunbathed on the numerous islets, as the Royal Navy imposed their tight blockade of the
French coast. However, a French garrison still held out on the island of Belleisle off the mouth of the
Loire. The British Prime Minister, William Pitt, whose aim it was to destroy totally all vestige of French
sea-power, ordered the capture of the island.
Battle: On 7 April 1761 Keppel anchored his ships off Belleisle. Hodgson embarked his men in flat-
bottomed small craft, and endeavoured to storm Port St André at the east end of the island. The British
were repulsed, and those who landed overpowered, their casualties being 500 men killed, wounded or
taken prisoner. Two weeks later, the British commanders tried again, and several assaults were made and
repulsed by the French. Eventually a feint attack by the British succeeded and compelled the French to
retire into the fortifications of Palais. After strong gales had delayed him, Hodgson managed to land
artillery. On 13 May the British stormed the French entrenchments, compelling the French to retire into
the citadel. On 7 June Saint Croix capitulated. British casualties were 700 killed and wounded, while in
contrast French casualties were very few.
    On 8 June 1761, Saint Croix was granted the honours of war, he and his garrison marching out of the
citadel in full-dress uniform and being repatriated to France.

BENDER (BENDERY, TIGHINA) I (USSR)   Russo-Ottoman Wars   1738
From the Ukraine, Marshal Count Burkhardt von Münnich marched on Moldavia. Attempting to cross
the Dniester, at Bender (Bendery, Tighina), however, he was repulsed and forced to retreat, leaving a large
portion of his army dead from battle, disease and starvation (see UKRAINE CAMPAIGNS OF COUNT MÜNNICH).

BENDER (BENDERY, TIGHINA) II (USSR)   Russo-Ottoman Wars   August–October 1769
After the defeat of the main Turkish army on the river Dniester (qv) General Count Peter Rumiantsev
(Romanzov), who had taken over command of the Russian armies invading the Balkans from Prince
Alexander Galitzin, sent one of his generals, Count Nikolai Repnin, to reduce the fortress of Ismail; and
another, Count Nikita Panin, to take the more important stronghold of Bender (Bendery, Tighina), while
he advanced with his main army into Bessarabia. After a siege of three months Repnin captured Bender
and, according to Russian custom when fighting the Turks, massacred the garrison of 3,500 men.

BERGEN (Hesse, W Germany)   Seven Years' War   13 April 1759
Fought between the French under Marshal Victor François, Duc de Broglie, and the Prussians,
Brunswickers and British under Field-Marshal Ferdinand, Duke of Brunswick.
Strength: French 70,000; Prussians/Brunswickers/British 35,000.
Aim: The Prussians strove to drive the French back over their frontiers.
Battle: The French had moved up the Main valley, where they occupied Bergen–10 miles NE of
Frankfurt-on-Main. Meanwhile Ferdinand marched with an Allied army of Prussians, German and
British to engage them. Finding the French already in possession of Bergen, Ferdinand attacked the
garrison on 13 April, only to be sharply repulsed. The Allies suffered more casualties than the French, who
strengthened their frontier.
Result: Ferdinand was forced to retire northward to the Wesel River, while the French captured the
bridges across the Wesel at Minden (qv), occupying a position too strong for direct attack.

BERGEN-OP-ZOOM (N Brabant, Holland)   War of the Austrian Succession   15 July–18 September
1747
General Count Ulrich von Löwendahl, commanding a French corps, laid siege to Bergen-op-Zoom with
its British/Dutch garrison.
Strength: French 25,000; British/Dutch 4,500.
    Marshal Comte Maurice de Saxe, after his victory at Lauffeld (qv), detached a corps under von

Löwendahl to invest Bergen-op-Zoom, an important strategic link on the Scheldt estuary in the W Netherlands. The Anglo-Dutch garrison resisted the French attacks and made a number of sorties, causing heavy casualties among the French. On 17 September the French made a surprise assault on the fortifications, successfully penetrating the walls and, after heavy fighting, capturing the city. On the following day the garrison surrendered. The French sustained 22,000 casualties, and the Anglo-Dutch forces 4,000. A Scottish brigade serving with the Dutch lost 1,120 men out of a strength of 1,450.

BITONTO (Apulia, Italy)   War of the Polish Succession/Italian Campaign   25 May 1734
Fought between Spanish troops under the Count of Montemar and the Infante Don Carlos (later Charles III of Spain), and the Austrians and their allies under General Otto von Traun.
Strength: Spanish 12,000; Austrians/Allies 9,000.
Aim: The aim of the Spanish was to take advantage of the hostilities between France and Austria during the War of the Polish Succession (qv) in order to regain previous Spanish possessions in Italy.
Battle: After a 40,000-strong Spanish army had occupied Naples, part of this force marched east to meet the enemy who had moved up from their base in Taranto to occupy strong positions round Bitonto. Montemar divided his forces into seven columns, four of them cavalry and three infantry and sappers. The Spanish cavalry engaged the enemy horse which were holding the left flank, routed them, and drove them back to Bari. The Austrian infantry resisted stubbornly but were forced back on Bitonto, where they surrendered. Austrian and Allied lost 8,000 dead, wounded and prisoners, in contrast to the Spanish 3,000.
Result: The Spanish victory led to the surrender of the fortresses of Pescara and Gaeta, followed by that of Capua, where General Traun was holding out, and consolidated Spain's hold on the Kingdom of Naples.

BORNHOLM (Baltic Sea, Denmark)   Russo-Swedish War   26 June 1789
Fought between a Russian fleet under Admiral Chitchakov and a Swedish invasion flotilla of flat-bottomed boats with naval escort under Admiral Count Karl August Ehrensvärd.
   The Russians, supplemented by a considerable number of British naval officers with experience of war, broke up a Swedish invasion fleet between the islands of Bornholm and Götland, which subsequently sought refuge to the north in the harbour of Karlskrona.
   However, Ehrensvärd soon set sail again to meet his fate at Svensksund I (qv) in the Gulf of Finland.

BRAUNAU (Austrian-W German frontier)   War of the Austrian Succession   9 May 1743
A three-pronged invasion of Bavaria by the Austrians under Marshal Prince Charles of Lorraine, General Prince Johann Lobkowitz of Austria and Count Ludwig von Khevenhüller found the Bavarians under Marshal Count Friedrich von Seckendorf, aided by the French, undecided as to what course to adopt.
Strength: Austrians 50,000; French 10,000 infantry and cavalry, Bavarians 20,000.
Battle: The Austrians under Khevenhüller advancing from Salzburg found the Bavarians and French entrenched on the outskirts of Braunau. Khevenhüller attacked the Allied centre and flanks but made little headway until a squadron of Austrian hussars dismounted and stormed a hill from which Allied artillery fire had held up the Austrians. Once this strongpoint had been taken the enemy dispersed and retreated through Braunau and across the Inn River. Austrian casualties were 1,500 killed and wounded, while the Allied forces lost 2,000 men killed and wounded and had 2,000 men captured.
Result: As a result of this defeat the Elector of Bavaria decided to quit his capital, Munich, and retreated to Augsburg, capital of Swabia, 38 miles NW of Munich.

BRESLAU (WROCLAW) (Poland)   Seven Years' War   22 November 1757
In 1757 Prussia was assailed from both the west and the south. While Frederick the Great stopped the French thrust at Rossbach (qv) the Austrians under Marshal Prince Charles of Lorraine and Field-Marshal Count Leopold von Daun advanced up the Oder valley, masking the fortress of Schweidnitz (Swidnica) until they reached the outskirts of Breslau (Wroclaw). Here a Prussian army of 20,000 under Duke Wilhelm von Brunswick-Bevern had drawn up beneath the city walls to bar the Austrian's path. Charles, with 60,000 men, defeated the Prussians and drove them back through Breslau, where they left a garrison of 6,000. Two days later he took the city and the fortress of Schweidnitz. Casualties sustained by the Prussians were 5,000 killed and wounded plus 3,600 captured, including Brunswick-Bevern, and 80 guns. Austrian losses were 8,000 men.
   Frederick at once marched back into Silesia to unite the remnants of Wilhelm's army with his own and check the Austrian advance.

BUCHAREST (BUKAREST, BUCARESTI) (Romania)   Ottoman Wars   1771
After the occupation of Moldavia and Wallachia in the autumn of 1771 (see PRUTH), operations died down apart from guerrilla action by the Turks against the Russian lines of communication.

In the spring of 1771 Field-Marshal Count Peter Rumiantsev (Romanzov) decided to capture Bucharest (Bukarest, Bucaresti), which was held by the Janissary commander, Mousson Oglon, and was the nub of the resistance throughout the area. After a stubborn defence the Turks were defeated, the city entered and the customary loot, rape, pillage and arson by the Russian army took place.

BURKERSDORF (BURKATÖW) (Silesia, Poland)   Seven Years' War   21 July 1762
Fought between the Prussians under Frederick the Great and the Austrians under Field-Marshal Count Leopold von Daun.
Strength: Prussians 25,000; Austrians 25,000.

After the costly fight at Torgau (qv) in Silesia the Prussian and Austrian armies met again in an inconclusive struggle at Burkersdorf (Burkatöw), where Frederick's superior tactics drove the Austrians from the field. There were few casualties on both sides.

Both armies were now war-weary and exhausted, but this engagement helped Frederick to improve his control over Silesia.

CAMPO-SANTO (N Italy)   Austro-Spanish War   8 February 1743
Fought between the Spanish under General Count John de Gages and the Austrians and Piedmontese under Marshal Otto von Traun.
Aim: Spain had sent an expeditionary army to Italy in an attempt to regain her former possessions there.
Battle: The Spanish army marched from Bologna and crossed the Panaro River by Campo-Santo with the aim of surprising the Austrians. The latter, who held good positions along the Finale-Modena road, brought up six cavalry regiments which fell upon the Spaniards' right flank. The infantry held them until their cavalry came up and drove them back. The Spaniards were slow to follow up this success, and when the infantry finally advanced they encountered strong reinforcements. Some Spanish units, in the confusion and failing light, turned their fire on each other. They were driven back over the Panaro and pursued to the fortresses of Bologna, Ferrara and Marca de Ancona, where they tried to reform. Spanish casualties numbered 4,000 men, while Austrian and Piedmontese lost 2,000 men.
Result: The remnants of the Spanish army, reduced to about 6,000 men, finally fell back to the Kingdom of Naples.

CAPE FINISTERRE I (NW coast of Spain)   War of the Austrian Succession   3 May 1747
Admiral Lord Anson, commanding a British squadron, fought the French under Admiral de la Jonquière.
Strength: British 14 ships of the line, including the flagship *Prince George* (90); French 9 ships of the line + 26 armed merchantmen carrying troops.
Battle: Knowing the movements of the French through a superbly organised British intelligence system, Admiral Anson sailed from Spithead on 9 April 1747, and cruised in the Bay of Biscay searching for the French. Early on 3 May 1747 he sighted the French 25 miles NW of Cape Finisterre. De la Jonquière took up line of battle ahead of his main force while he ordered the troop carriers to escape to the westward. On seeing the French fleet making a break for it in the darkening evening, Anson signalled a 'general chase', ordering each of his leading ships to attack the first enemy ship she caught, cripple her and press on to the next, leaving the cripple to be finished off by his slower ships. After a sharp, running engagement of only three hours Anson had taken the entire French squadron of 12 ships, including *'Invincible'* (74) and *Sérieux* (64).

Anson then pursued the convoy and captured 6 of them, the remaining 20 merchantmen escaping in the darkness. Anson stated later that it was the superiority of British gunnery and discipline which mainly accounted for Jonquière's defeat. No ships were lost by the British, while French losses were 9 men-of-war and 6 merchantmen plus 3,000 prisoners.
Result: Anson's victory prevented badly needed aid and supplies from reaching the French West Indian colonies. It was the first decisive naval victory of the war.

CAPE FINISTERRE II (NW coast of Spain)   War of the Austrian Succession   2 October 1747
Rear-Admiral Sir Edward Hawke, commanding a British western squadron, fought Admiral de l'Etenduère, in command of a French squadron.

Strength: British 14 ships of the line + 1 60-gun East Indiaman; French 8 ships of the line + convoy of more than 200 merchantmen.

Aim: Through their intelligence system which had infiltrated the French navy the Admiralty became aware that a large French convoy was assembling in the Basque Roads with the intention of reinforcing their garrisons in the West Indies. On 5 September 1747 the Admiralty ordered Rear-Admiral Sir Edward Hawke to patrol between Ushant and Cape Finisterre in order to intercept it. Hawke sailed to and fro but could find no trace of the French, who in fact did not sail from Ile-de-Aix until 6 October 1747.

Battle: Some fourteen days later, on 20 October 1747, Hawke intercepted the French off Finisterre and moved to engage, ordering the same tactics of 'general chase' which Admiral Anson had so successfully developed in May (FINISTERRE I). De l'Etenduère ordered his convoy to scatter, while he moved to engage the British and balk their purpose. Outnumbered and outgunned, Admiral de l'Etenduère fought for more than nine hours, but by nightfall Hawke had taken 6 of the French squadron (3 74s, 2 64s and a 50) and only the flagship *Tonnant* (80) and *Intrepide* (74) managed to make Brest safely, though badly damaged. The French lost 6 ships of the line. The British lost no ships, but lost 598 killed and wounded.

Result: Through his sacrifice and long, staunch fight, de l'Etenduère succeeded in defeating the British purpose, as all the French convoy of 200 ships escaped.

CAPE PASSARO (Sicily)   War of the Quadruple Alliance   11 August 1718
Fought between a British fleet of 21 vessels under Vice-Admiral Sir George Byng and a Spanish fleet under Admiral Don Antonio Castañeta.

Strength: British 21 ships; Spanish 29 ships.

Vice-Admiral Byng sighted the Spanish squadron in the Straits of Messina. Byng sent 4 of his fastest ships, *Kent, Superbe, Grafton* and *Oxford*, to overtake the Spanish fleet which had retired in a long, straggling line. The chase went on through the night, and it was not until next morning, off Cape Passaro, that the British ships came up with the sternmost Spaniards and opened fire. The action resolved itself into a series of single-ship combats in which the Spanish ships were overpowered in turn by greatly superior seamanship. However, casualties were heavy on both sides. The Spaniards lost 15 ships, sunk or captured. Admiral Castañeta was taken prisoner, but died of his wounds.

Note should be taken that this was the first engagement in which the word 'chase' was used to describe the tactical method of waging a sea-battle.

CAPE ST VINCENT II ('THE MOONLIGHT VICTORY') (SW Portugal)   American War of Independence   16/17 January 1780
An allied French and Spanish force besieged Gibraltar (qv) for the latter part of the American Revolution. On 29 December Admiral Sir George Rodney left England with 36 warships escorting a large convoy of transports to relieve the garrison. Off Cape St Vincent on the SW coast of Portugal the English met 11 Spanish warships under Don Juan de Langara. The Spaniards believed Rodney's force was merely a convoy and made no move until it was too late. At 4pm on 16 January Rodney attacked, taking 4 of the enemy including their flagship, and sinking 3 more, the fight continuing throughout a dark and stormy night lit by the intermittent beams of a fitful moon.

Rodney suffered no losses and went on to relieve Gibraltar, taking the captured vessels with him.

CARLISLE (Cumbria, England)   Jacobite Rebellion (the 'Forty-five')   9–15 September 1745
The garrison was commanded by Lt-Colonel Durand, a regular officer, and the siege undertaken by the Jacobite army under Prince Charles Edward Stuart on its march into England. The fortifications of both town and castle were in disrepair, and the defenders were a regular garrison of 80 invalids, a master gunner and 4 gunners, reinforced by 500 foot and 70 horse of the Militia, who did not like serving under a regular officer.

The first challenge to surrender was made on 9 September, and ignored by the town authorities who were hoping for assistance from Field-Marshal Sir George Wade, whose army was centred at Newcastle. This was not forthcoming, and the siege and blockade began on the 12th. Three days later both town and castle capitulated.

Carlisle remained in Jacobite hands under a garrison of 100 men while Prince Charles continued his march through Manchester to Derby. On his return to Scotland he left a garrison of 400 men under John Hamilton. The castle was bombarded by the Duke of Cumberland's artillery on 29 December, and surrendered on the 30th.

CHESME (CESME, TCHESME, TSHESHME) (Anatolian coast, Turkey) Russo-Ottoman Wars   7–8 July 1770
Fought between the Russian navy commanded by Admiral Alexei Orlov and Vice-Admiral John Elphinston and a Turkish fleet under Hassan Bey (see also MOREA).
Strength: Russians 20 ships (including 9 ships of the line); Turks 14 ships of the line, several frigates + a vast number of transports and storeships, totalling over 200 in the port of Chesmé.

On 6 July the hostile fleets met between the islands of Scio and Natolia in the channel between the island of Chios and the mainland. A desultory combat followed, lasting for four hours until the flagships of the two admirals were blown up, nearly all being killed or drowned. The Turks, alarmed at the explosion, retired in great disorder to their home port of Chesmé in the mainland opposite Chios, although the Russian losses were greater than theirs.

Next morning, Rear-Admiral Elphinston, a Scotsman in Russian pay, taking advantage of this retreat, appeared with his Russian squadron of 4 ships of the line, several frigates and some smaller vessels before the port and sent in 2 fire-ships under Lieutenants Dugdale and Mackenzie. The Turks thought that they were renegades seeking sanctuary and welcomed them. However, the pretended deserters, having entered without difficulty, put their grappling hooks on to the nearest of the rows of tied-up ships and soon phosphorous fire, rockets, pitch and flame were belching over the Turkish fleet engulfing all their vessels, powder and cannon until all were consumed, except for one 64-gun ship of the line and a few galleys.

The Dardanelles were not defended and Elphinston wanted to take advantage of his success to force the Straits and capture Constantinople. But his more cautious commander-in-chief, Admiral Orlov, refused and instead laid siege to Lemnos (qv), allowing time for the French general and diplomat, Baron François de Tott, who had been sent by Louis XVI to assist the Turks, to fortify the Straits. In a few days Tott had improvised a seemingly impregnable system of defence, complete with mounted batteries, fire-ships and an army of 30,000 to man the fortification.

The Russians had missed their one chance in 200 years of attacking and capturing Constantinople, but this remarkable naval campaign (although assisted by the British) was a startling reminder to the Western powers of Russian potentiality and interest in the Mediterranean.

One of Elphinston's captains, Samuel Greig, has erroneously been given credit for this action–it was an exaggeration that possibly arose as a result of his later celebrity when commanding the Russian fleet in the Swedish war in the Baltic (see HOGLAND).

CHOTIN (CHOCIM, CHOCZIM, CHOTYN, HOTIN) (USSR)   June–September 1769
Fought between a Russian army under Prince Alexander Galitzin and later Field-Marshal Count Peter Rumiantsev (Romanzov) and the Turks under the Grand Vizier, Emir Pasha, and Ignatius Potocki, a Polish Patriot.
Strength: Russians 65,000; Turks varying from 20,000 to 60,000.
Aim: Galitzin, collecting an army of 65,000 at Podolia (Podolskij), was ordered by Catherine the Great to capture the city of Chotin on the river Dniester and then to occupy Moldavia.
Battle: In July Galitzin passed the Dniester and made an unsuccessful attack on the fortress of Chotin, which was defended by Potocki. Emir Pasha was, meanwhile, moving the Sultan's army from Constantinople to the Danube. The two armies met on the Dniester, where the Turks were decisively defeated. Galitzin again invested Chotin but Potocki's continued resistance gave Emir Pasha time to recover and come to his assistance. The Grand Vizier had been given orders by the Sultan to move in order to encircle the Russian army. Emir Pasha, however, tried a direct assault on the Russians and was again defeated and his army dispersed. Consequently his head soon adorned the gate of the Serai and he was succeeded by Moldowandji as Grand Vizier.

Moldowandji placed two pontoon bridges over the Dniester and attacked the entrenched armies of the Russians on the north bank. The river suddenly rose in autumn flood and a mass of Turkish soldiers, fearing they would be cut off, fled across the bridges, which gave way, causing thousands to drown and leaving 6,000 men isolated on the north bank. These were soon destroyed by the Russians, and Chotin was evacuated.
Result: Rumiantsev, who had taken over from Galitzin who had resigned, went on to occupy Moldavia and Wallachia, so that the Russian objective was achieved.

CHOTUSITZ (Bohemia, Czechoslovakia)   War of the Austrian Succession   17 May 1742
The Prussians, commanded by Frederick the Great and Prince Leopold of Anhalt-Dessau, fought an Austrian army led by Marshal Prince Charles of Lorraine.

Strength: Prussians 30,000; Austrians 30,000.

Aim: Prince Charles, although without his allies, hoped to defeat the Prussians in Silesia where he had followed Frederick's army retreating from Moravia.

Battle: The place of action was a small village in flat country with ponds, marsh and quagmires on the west and a large river, the Dobrowa, on the eastern flank. Prince Charles assaulted the Prussians with strong cavalry attacks, which they withstood. Then Frederick enticed the Austrian horsemen into the marshy ground south of the Elbe where the Prussian infantry trapped them and made a series of counter-attacks. The Austrians withdrew their forces as best they could, retreating some 15 to 20 miles. Frederick's efforts to rejuvenate his cavalry wearied by a long campaign had paid off. The Prussians lost 4,100 dead and wounded plus 700 men captured. The Austrians lost 3,000 dead and wounded, and in addition 3,500 were captured or missing. They also lost 17 cannon.

Result: The Austrians did not achieve their objective.

Frederick the Great did not pursue his beaten enemy as energetically as he might have done, as he had achieved enough to make Empress Maria Theresa look favourably on his terms of peace. Moreover, he did not wish the French left alone with the only powerful army in central Europe.

CREFELD (KREFELD) (N Rhine-Westphalia. W Germany)   Seven Years' War   23 June 1758

Fought between Field-Marshal Ferdinand, Duke of Brunswick, leading a mixed army of Hanoverians, Hessians and Brunswickers, and a French force commanded by Louis de Bourbon-Condé, Comte de Clermont.

Strength: Hanoverians/Hessians/Brunswickers 32,000; French 50,000.

Battle: Duke Ferdinand forced the retreat of the French in the Rhine valley, until de Clermont endeavoured to make a stand at Crefeld. The Duke's army struck the left flank of the French, routing them and causing comparatively heavy losses. The combined German army lost 1,800 killed and wounded, while the French casualties were 5,200 killed and wounded plus 3,000 prisoners.

Result: The French first retreated to Neuss, about 12 miles from Crefeld, and 5 miles across the Rhine from Düsseldorf. Then, on 28 June 1758, de Clermont moved on to the outskirts of Cologne, fearing a Prussian advance into the Netherlands.

CRIMEA I (USSR)   Austro-Russian-Turkish War   1737

In the operations in 1737 the Russian army, reinforced by 40,000 recruits, divided into two. One army, under the command of Count Burkhardt von Münnich, proceeded to Otchakov (near Odessa) (see UKRAINE CAMPAIGNS OF COUNT MÜNNICH); while the other, under Marshal Count Petr Lacy, invaded the Crimea.

Although Lacy overran the Crimea, his ill-equipped and badly supported army lost 30,000 dead out of 53,000 mainly from disease, starvation and desertion. The Tartars fought in a guerrilla fashion and picked off all those who strayed. The army finally mutinied and retreated back to the Russian Ukraine.

CRIMEA II (USSR)   Russo-Ottoman Wars   1771

The Russian advance into the Crimea (see RUSSO-OTTOMAN WARS [1768–74]) had been suspended when Field-Marshal Count Peter Rumiantzev (Romanzov) had been switched to the Balkans to take Prince Alexander Galitzin's place after his resignation. Russian attempts to capture Trebizond and operate with the Georgians in the Caucasus had been unsuccessful. But early in 1771 Prince Vasili Michailovich Dolgoruki advanced into the Crimea and, in a series of actions against the Tartars, conquered the whole peninsula, proclaimed its independence under Muscovite sovereignty and installed Sherim Bey as Pasha. This was a very neat operation.

CULLODEN (Inverness-shire, Scotland)   Jacobite Rebellion (the 'Forty-five')   16 April 1746

Fought between the Jacobite army led by Prince Charles Edward Stuart and the pro-Hanoverian army under Prince William Augustus, Duke of Cumberland.

Strength: Jacobites: the Jacobites had in the area some 8,000 men, but could muster only 5,000 in the battle-line. The front line consisted of 3,000 men under the Duke of Perth, with Lord George Murray commanding the right, and Lord Ogilvy the left. The Jacobite artillery was ill-manned and ineffectually supplied; Hanoverians: the front line consisted of 7 regiments, totalling 3,700 men; the second line, under Major-General John Huske, 6 regiments with 1 in reserve; the third was composed of Highland irregular troops. The first and second lines were supported by dragoons on the wings. The army totalled 9,000 men.

Aim: The British army under its new commander, with greatly increased numbers and artillery manned by experienced gunners, sought to destroy the Jacobite forces which had retreated to Inverness.

Battle: The Jacobites, hastily drawn up on unsuitable ground (the fault both of the Prince and of his Adjutant-General, John William O'Sullivan), were ill-fed, poorly armed, and exhausted and dispirited after an abortive attempt to launch a surprise attack the previous night.

After an ineffective artillery attack by the Jacobites, the British put up a devastating barrage of fire which, with the Prince failing to order either an advance or a retreat, resulted in heavy casualties and much demoralisation. This forced Charles's centre and right to make a desperate charge, unsupported by the Macdonalds on the left. They succeeded in breaking through the British front line, but were mown down by the fire from the second, which had been drawn up three deep for just this purpose. Cumberland's dragoons then charged, overcame the Jacobite left wing, and outflanked their right, finally routing the Jacobite second line. The whole Jacobite army thereupon fled, pursued by the Hanoverian cavalry. The Hanoverians lost 50 dead and 250 wounded, compared with the Jacobite losses of 1,200 men killed and wounded. In addition 500 Jacobites were taken prisoner, including 200 Frenchmen.

Result: This total defeat ended the Jacobite Rebellion. Prince Charles, a fugitive for five months, escaped finally to France on 20 September 1746.

CUNEO (CONI) (Italy)   War of the Austrian Succession   30 September–22 October 1744

Fought between the Sardinian and Austrian armies, under Charles Emmanuel I, King of Sardinia, and General Prince Johann Lobkowitz of Austria, and a Franco-Spanish army under Prince Louis de Conti of France and Philip, Infante of Spain.

Strength: Austrians/Sardinians 40,000; French/Spanish 40,000.

The French and Spanish allies had laid siege to Cuneo, 70 miles west of Genoa. Charles Emmanuel I and Prince Lobkowitz marched to relieve the city. On 30 September 1744 the Austro-Sardinian army attacked the Franco-Spanish force at Madonna del Olmo on the outskirts of Cuneo. In a sharp encounter the Sardinian King was forced to retreat. Conti, unable to implement his initial success, running short of supplies, and impeded by the interference of Philip, was forced to give up the siege on 22 October and retreat into France. The French and Spanish lost 8,000 killed and wounded; the Austrian and Sardinian 5,000 killed and wounded.

The year closed with the forces of Sardinia and Austria encamped in positions which split the French and Spanish forces in Italy into two separate regions.

CZASLAU (Bohemia, Czechoslovakia)   War of the Austrian Succession   17 March 1742

Fought between the Prussians, commanded by Frederick the Great, and the Austrians, commanded by Marshal Prince Charles of Lorraine.

Strength: Prussians 30,000; Austrians 50,000.

Aim: The Prussians were moving across Moravia and Bohemia with the intention of relieving Marshal Duc de Broglie's French force in the vicinity of Prague.

Battle: Frederick, having received intelligence that Broglie planned to cut off his communications from his supply trains, drew up his army in order of battle at Czaslau, 40 miles SE of Prague, at 3am and waited for the approaching Austrians. A general engagement began at 8am. The Austrians drove the Prussians back, and began to plunder the baggage and supply trains. The Prussians re-formed, renewed the engagement and drove the Austrians off the battlefield. The Austrians lost 5,000 men killed or wounded, with 1,200 captured and 18 pieces of artillery lost. General Pallant was killed and some standards also lost. The Prussians lost 3,000 men killed and wounded. General Werdick was killed and 5 standards were lost.

Result: The immediate Prussian objective was achieved, the Austrians retreating in good order to the camp at Wilonow, behind Czaslau.

DANZIG (GDANSK) I (Poland)   War of the Polish Succession   October 1733–2 June 1734

The first engagement of the war took place when a Russian army of 30,000 under Marshal Count Burkhardt von Münnich, aided by 10,000 Saxons, besieged Danzig (Gdansk), at the mouth of the Vistula. The garrison was commanded by Stanislas Leszczynski (Lescinski), King of Poland. Although the French managed once to relieve the town by sea, putting in 2,200 men, the garrison was forced to capitulate on 2 June 1734.

Stanislas escaped by sea disguised as a sailor.

DETTINGEN (Bavaria, W Germany)   War of the Austrian Succession   27 June 1743
King George II of England, commanding an Anglo-Austro-Hanoverian and Hessian army, fought the French and Bavarians led by the Marshal Adrien Maurice, Duc de Noailles, and General Louis, Duc de Gramont.
Strength: Allies 40,000; French/Bavarians 60,000 (of which only 20,000 to 30,000 in action).
Aim: The Allied army advanced into the west of Germany in an endeavour to drive a wedge between the French and Bavarian forces.
Battle: The French opened the action by bringing the Allied left, anchored on to the south bank of the Main River, under artillery fire. George II re-formed his army to face the river, which gave de Gramont the idea of emerging from his concealed position and launching a cavalry attack. This failed to upset George II, who turned his troops again and marched through the bogs and marsh until he came face to face with the advancing French infantry. The English contingent led by their monarch poured a deadly fire into the French infantry, which then retreated in panic and disorder behind their own cavalry which now also came under heavy fire. George II was at his best urging on his troops in person, sighting artillery pieces and, regardless of risk, pushing ahead of his subjects, sword in hand. The French cavalry crumbled and retreated hastily. This caused panic among the French infantry, which fled, many drowning in their efforts to swim across the Main. The Allies lost 2,400 men; and the French and Bavarian 6,000 killed and wounded, many perishing in the Main River.
Result: The Allied victory resulted in a French withdrawal over the Rhine. This battle was the last occasion in which a King of England led his troops personally into action.

DNIESTER (Moldavia, USSR)   Ottoman Wars   9 September 1769
A Russian force under Field-Marshal Count Peter Rumiantzev (Romanzov), encamped on the Dniester north of Bender, were attacked by the Turks under Ali Moldovani Pasha, who crossed the river in front of their opponents and launched a fierce attack. After a bitter fight, the Turks were defeated and forced to withdraw. The Russians went on to seize Jassy (Iasa) and then to occupy Moldavia and Wallachia.

DOGGER BANK (North Sea)   Dutch-British War   15 August 1781
In 1780 the Dutch government was persuaded by the loquacious New England politician, Adam Smith, to recognise American independence. So in December Britain declared war on Holland. The entry of Holland into the war meant that the British navy had to patrol the North Sea, which stretched the capability of the fleet to the utmost, as now all the maritime powers of Europe joined in the 'Armed Neutrality' were against Britain.

The only engagement between the two countries took place when Vice-Admiral Sir Hyde Parker with 7 warships and 6 frigates, convoying some 200 merchantment from the Baltic, met a Dutch squadron of similar size commanded by Admiral Johann Zoutman taking a convoy to the Baltic. Parker ordered his merchantmen to make for England and then bore down on his enemy, line abreast. He reserved his fire until his ships, turning together, formed line alongside the Dutch fleet which had also formed a well-ordered line of battle. Parker laid his flagship alongside Zoutman's *Admiraal de Ruyter*. After three hours savage fighting, in which both sides suffered heavy losses, the Dutch managed to bear away and take their convoy to Texel, leaving Parker's squadron too badly damaged to follow them. One Dutch ship, *Hollandia*, foundered. Dutch losses were 142 men killed and 403 wounded; and British, 109 killed and 362 wounded.

Parker, after criticising the Admiralty for dispatching him with such a small force, resigned his commission.

DUNBLANE   see SHERIFFMUIR

DUTCH-BRITISH WAR   1780–4
Holland was persuaded in 1780 to recognise American independence. Clandestine trade between the two countries followed, forcing Britain to declare war on Holland on 20 December 1780. Apart from engaging in one naval action on the Dogger Bank (qv), Britain took over a number of Dutch islands and trading stations in the East and West Indies which were useful to her fleet and trade.

EDINBURGH (Scotland)   Jacobite Rebellion (the 'Forty-five')   17 September 1745
The Jacobite army, led by Prince Charles Edward Stuart, had left Perth on 11 September 1745 to march to

the capital. Edinburgh Castle was commanded by the eighty-five-year-old Lt-General Joshua Guest, while decisions regarding the defence of the town were in the hands of the Lord Provost, Archibald Stewart.

With the approach of the Prince's army, some show of resistance was offered by two regiments of dragoons supported by the Edinburgh Regiment and the Town Guard. But with the ignominious flight of the dragoons from Coltbridge all hope of resistance was lost. The Lord Provost, therefore, receiving a summons to surrender on the 16th, dispatched a deputation from the Council to open negotiations. The next day a second deputation, unsuccessfully requesting more time to consider the position, returned to Edinburgh, covertly followed by a detachment of Highlanders under Donald Cameron Lochiel and John William O'Sullivan, who rushed the opened gates and disarmed the volunteer guard. By the next morning the whole town was in Jacobite hands. On the same day the Prince set up his headquarters in Holyrood Palace, to which he was to return for six weeks after his victory at Prestonpans (qv).

During the first week of October Prince Charles attempted a blockade of the castle, but Guest gave covering fire while his men made sorties to collect provisions. Recognising that the damage to the town was injuring his popularity, the Prince called off the blockade. The town itself was retaken for the Hanoverians by Lt-General Roger Handasyde within a few days of the Jacobite army's crossing the border into England.

ESQUILACHE RIOTS (Spain) 23 February–6 March 1766

Serious riots in Madrid and other Spanish cities were sparked off on 23 February 1766 by a decree initiated by Charles III's unpopular Italian minister, the Marquis of Esquilache, forbidding the wearing of the traditional long Spanish cloak and broad-brimmed round hat. The underlying causes were discontent over food shortages and high prices, resentment at foreign influence at court, and dislike of other reforms arbitrarily imposed by the Minister. The riots culminated on 1 March with the presentation to the King of a petition embodying the popular demands. Order was restored on 6 March with the resignation of Esquilache and with royal promises–not all of them honoured–to remedy other abuses.

FALKIRK (Stirlingshire, Scotland) Jacobite Rebellion (the 'Forty-five') 17 January 1746

Fought between the Jacobite army under Prince Charles Edward Stuart and the pro-Hanoverian army under Lt-General Henry Hawley.

Aim: Hawley led his army out from Edinburgh to relieve Stirling, which was under siege by the Jacobites.
Strength: The Hanoverian army consisted of 8,500 men, comprising 12 battalions of infantry and 3 regiments of dragoons, together with artillery. The Jacobites had 8,000 men, including cavalry and artillery.
Battle: Hawley's underestimate of Murray's tactical skill and of the Highlanders' ability to withstand a cavalry charge proved disastrous. After a feint to the north the Jacobite army appeared unexpectedly on the high ground to the SW, forcing a hasty realignment of the Hanoverian forces. In the ensuing battle the 13th and 14th Dragoons on the Hanoverian left wing fled, pursued by MacDonald of Glengarry's and MacDonald of Clanranald's men who, incapable of restraint, were lost to the battle. The Hanoverian centre and right, after driving back the clansmen, were able to make an orderly retreat as a result in part of Major-General John Huske's competence and in part of a failure of command by Prince Charles.

After a battle lasting twenty minutes the Hanoverians had lost 300 killed and wounded, and 100 captured. The Jacobites lost 50 killed, 80 wounded and 1–Major Macdonald of Tiendrish–taken prisoner. He was subsequently hanged at Edinburgh.
Result: The Hanoverians retired, in some confusion, to Linlithgow, the Jacobites to Falkirk, from where they took up once more the siege of Stirling.

Despite this success, Prince Charles's fortunes were declining. After failing to take Stirling Castle he was persuaded by his commanding officers that he had no alternative but to retreat to the Highlands, where three months later, at Culloden (qv), he was finally defeated.

FINLAND 1808

Fought between the Russians under Prince Mikhail Barclay de Tolly and the Swedes.

By the Treaty of Tilsit (7 November 1807), Napoleon and Alexander I of Russia contracted an alliance, following which they demanded that Sweden end her coalition with England. Sweden refused to declare war on England and in February the Russians invaded Finland.

Following inconclusive warfare, the Swedes evacuated Finland in December and, by the Treaty of Frederikshavn (September 1809), ceded Finland to Russia along with the Aäland Islands.

FLAMBOROUGH HEAD (Yorkshire, England)   American War of Independence   23 September 1779

In Brest, the American Commander John Paul Jones, after capturing a number of prizes in the Irish Sea in 1778 including the British sloop *Drake*, bombarding Whitehaven in his frigate *Ranger*, and forcing the Earl of Selkirk to give him dinner, obtained in 1779 a rebuilt Indiaman which he named *Bonhomme Richard*. With this vessel he again sailed for the east coast of England. Off Flamborough Head he encountered 2 English frigates, *Serapis* (44) and *Countess of Scarborough*. The main action was fought between *Bonhomme Richard* and *Serapis*, although the treachery of one of his captains hampered Jones. The American vessel, mounting 42 guns, was lashed on to *Serapis*, enabling the crew to fire into the British ship from the rigging. Captain Richard Pearson demanded Jones's surrender when *Bonhomme Richard* caught fire, but Jones refused and the struggle continued until after dark when, dismasted and set alight by an explosion caused by an American grenade, *Serapis* finally surrendered. Jones transferred his crew to the British ship. *Bonhomme Richard* sank the following day. This is one of the few naval engagements in which a victorious captain lost his own ship and returned to port in a captured vessel.

This British defeat was made worse in that it was witnessed by thousands of spectators who flocked to the cliffs between Scarborough and Bridlington, to see a British frigate of superior guns being beaten by the legendary John Paul Jones. His fame spread through Britain and Europe, war insurance rates rocketed and it was even found necessary to convoy the Belfast linen trade. The guerrilla actions of Paul Jones and similar privateers interrupted Britain's communications with America, gained munitions, stores and clothing for the Patriot forces, and lowered the prestige of Britain on the continent. It was upon their legendary conflicts and courageous example that the tradition of the US navy was founded.

John Paul Jones went on to become a Russian admiral under Catherine the Great and took part in her Ottoman campaign in the Black Sea in the period 1787–92 at the Battles of Liman and Ochakov (qqv).

FOCSANI (FOKSHANI) (Moldavia, E Romania)   Russo-Ottoman Wars   31 July 1789

Fought between the Turks under Yusuf Pasha and an allied Russo-Austrian army under Field-Marshal Count Suvorov and Friedrich Josias, Prince of Saxe-Coburg.

Strength: Turks 55,000; Russians/Austrians 40,000.

Aim: The Allied army sought to drive the Turks southward out of Moldavia and Wallachia.

Battle: Forty thousand Russians and Austrians, driven hard by Suvorov from Belat (Bîrlad) after a rapid advance, crossed the river Purna and stormed the Turkish fortified camp at Focsani (Fokshani), taking the Turks completely by surprise. Within one hour, at a loss of only 800 men, the Allies overran the camp, driving the Turkish infantry out in complete disorder while their cavalry galloped away. Suvorov's men pursued the Turks 'with great impetuosity and vehement zeal' so that all the baggage stores and artillery totalling 70 pieces of cannon and 100 standards were captured. The Turks lost about 4,000 dead on the battlefield and many more dispersed over the countryside.

Suvorov remained in Moldavia, while the Turks under the Grand Vizier collected a new army to march into Wallachia, where the Austrians under the Prince of Saxe-Coburg had taken up a position at Martinesti (qv) on the river Rimnik (qv).

FONTENOY (Hainaut, Belgium)   War of the Austrian Succession   11 May 1745

The French under Marshal Comte Maurice de Saxe fought an Anglo-Dutch-Austrian army led by Prince William Augustus, Duke of Cumberland, son of George II of England.

Strength: French 70,000 men with 70 guns; Allies 53,000 men with 80 guns.

Aim: In 1745 the French concentrated their efforts in the Netherlands, where an army of 70,000 lay siege to Tournai. The French force was commanded by Comte Maurice de Saxe, who had with him Louis XV and the Dauphin. The Allies sent an army to relieve Tournai, in the province of Hainaut. This force of 50,000 men under the Duke of Cumberland was made up of English, Dutch, Hanoverians and Austrians. Saxe, leaving 18,000 men to prosecute the siege, deployed 52,000 at Fontenoy, 5 miles SE of the city, in order to block the Allied advance.

Battle: Saxe's position ran from the Scheldt to the Gavrain wood and was protected to the front by three redoubts which poured enfilading fire into the Allied ranks and for two hours halted the Allied attack. After some inconclusive skirmishing, Cumberland decided to smash through the French line and massed a body of 15,000 foot which was deployed in three lines–English in the first two and Hanoverians in the third. The formation advanced under cover of further skirmishing and passed between one of the redoubts and Fontenoy. The commanders then paused to dress their ranks and salute the French before continuing a relentless advance which smashed through the surprised French front line. Saxe, who had been carried to the field on a litter, suffering from dropsy, was forced to take to his horse. He swiftly established a second line which poured fire into the Allied ranks and halted their advance. The Irish Guards, Stuart supporters in exile, were conspicuous in the French line. The arrival of artillery and cavalry eventually smashed the Allied formation, from which survivors made good their retreat while repulsing French efforts to pursue. Cumberland withdrew in good order after dark, having lost over 7,000 killed. French losses were 7,200 killed or wounded.

This was the last battle of this war in which the English participated, for they were recalled shortly afterwards to deal with the '45 Rebellion in Scotland of Prince Charles Edward Stuart (Bonnie Prince Charlie) which Saxe had instigated for this very purpose.

FRANCO-BRITISH WAR   1778
The French recognition of the United States of America led her to lend active support to the Americans and to a declaration of war, on 17 June 1778, against Britain.

In the protracted operations against the British government the Revolutionaries had fought on long enough and with sufficient zeal and effectiveness to gain this support, without which their chances of victory were slim indeed. By 1780 most of the maritime countries of Europe, including Russia, Sweden, Holland, Spain and Portugal were actively assisting the Revolutionaries against their rival, Britain, which ensured her defeat on the N American continent.

FREDERIKSHALD (HALDEN) (SE Norway)   Great Northern War   11/12 December 1718
Having rebuilt his country's military strength, Charles XII of Sweden raised an army of 25,000 and invaded Norway, then held by Denmark. Early in December 1718 he besieged the fortress of Frederikshald (Halden). On the night of 11/12 December, while he was inspecting the front lines of the siege works, he was shot dead through the eye by a musket-ball–presumably fired by a Danish soldier, although a French officer (Colonel Maigret), who was present, thought it was an assassination. The Swedes at once raised the siege.

Charles was succeeded by his sister, Ulrica Eleanora, and her husband, Frederick I of Hesse-Cassel. They concluded the Treaty of Nystad on 30 August 1721 which ended the war. Russia, which received the territories of Karelia, Estonia and an area around Vyborg, now became the dominant power in northern Europe.

FREIBURG (Saxony, E Germany)   Seven Years' War   29 October 1762
The Prussians, under Prince Henry Ludwig, brother of Frederick the Great, and General Friedrich Wilhelm von Seydlitz, fought the Austro-Saxon force commanded by Marshal Serbelloni.
Strength: Prussians 30,000; Austrians/Saxons 40,000.

Both sides were at the point of exhaustion when this relatively minor action took place. The Prussians attacked and drove the Austro-Saxon force back. Von Seydlitz, with his usual initiative, led the infantry at a stage where his cavalry could not charge. Only minor casualties were sustained by both sides.

This action ended the war. A treaty of peace between Austria and Prussia was signed at Hubertusburg on 15 February 1763, by which the Prussians remained in possession of Silesia, while Saxony stayed within the Austrian Empire.

GÄVLE (GEFLE) (Sweden)   Russo-Swedish War   1721
After hostilities between Sweden and Russia had been renewed in 1719, the Czar, Peter the Great, sent his fleet on raiding expeditions along the Swedish coast, in which Stockholm itself was threatened. A British fleet under Vice-Admiral Sir John Norris was sent to the Baltic, ostensibly to keep the peace, but without clear orders as to its role. The plundering of the whole coast of Sweden continued until June 1721 and culminated, under the eyes of Admiral Norris, in the ravaging by Admiral Golitsin of the coast between Gävle (Gefle) and Umea in the Gulf of Bothnia and the burning of four small towns, nineteen villages, eighty houses belonging to nobles, and the destruction of twelve ironworks. Golitsin also destroyed a number of ships and carried away with him 4 warships.

After these depredations the Swedes concluded the Treaty of Nystad, ending twenty-one years of war, on 10 September 1721, in which they lost most of their S Baltic possessions. Peter, having destroyed much of the manufacturing capability of the Swedes, lured their artisans away in order to build a new industrial Russia.

GENOA I (Italy)   Patriotic Rising   6–10 December 1746
The Austrian garrison at Genoa under General Botta was attacked by the inhabitants of the town on 6 December and, after five days of street fighting, was driven out with the loss of 5,000 men. Although the Genoese briefly re-established communications with their old allies, the French, the Austrians besieged the town early the following year. But a French army under Marshal Belleisle advanced across the Maritime Alps and, in July 1747, relieved the staunch citizens of Genoa. But Genoa, from then on, had to rely on France to maintain her unstable independence.

GIBBEL RUTTS (Co Kildare, Eire)   Irish Rebellion   26 May 1798
Fought between the Regulars under Sir James Duff and the Irish Rebels.
   Duff attacked the Rebel camp on the Curragh at the point of the bayonet, and dispersed it with a loss to the Rebels of 350 killed.

GIBRALTAR (W Mediterranean)   American War of Independence   21 June 1779–6 February 1783
Gibraltar, captured in 1704 during the War of the Spanish Succession, had been retained by England under the Treaty of Utrecht (1713). An attempt to recover it was made in February 1727 by a mixed force of Spaniards and mercenaries commanded by the Count of Las Torres. The siege was raised the following June after the Spaniards had suffered 1,450 killed and wounded and the British little more than 300.
   A more determined attempt to conquer the Rock was made in June 1779. The first phase was confined to a sea blockade under Admiral Barcelo and a gradual build-up of Spanish forces under General Alvarez Sotomayor which, by September, numbered 7,000. The Governor, General George Eliot (Lord Heathfield), had 4,000 British and 1,300 Hanoverians under his command. When supplies ran short during the winter of this year, Admiral Sir George Rodney set out with 22 ships of the line and 14 frigates to escort a large convoy of supply ships past the principal French and Spanish naval bases to revictual the garrison. After a fight with a Spanish squadron of 11 ships of the line off Cape St Vincent (qv) on 16/17 January 1780, the convoy reached the Gut of Gibraltar and resupplied the garrison for another year. Operations continued to be confined to an exchange of gunfire, attempts to tighten or to break the blockade, and occasional sorties, as in November 1781 when the Spanish batteries at La Linea were spiked.
   Following the capture of Menorca (qv) from the British, Spanish and French units, commanded by the Duc de Crillon, arrived to reinforce the attackers, who now numbered 30,000. At sea, the Toulon squadron was expected, to make a total of 44 ships of the line plus smaller warships. Floating batteries, claimed to be non-inflammable and unsinkable, mounting 140 36-pounders and manned by 5,200 officers and men, were also brought into service. In September 1782 a general attack was opened and the floating batteries went into action, only to be destroyed by red-hot shot with the loss of nearly 2,000 Allied lives. A loose blockade was maintained, but through relentless pressure applied by the Prime Minister, Lord Shelburne, on an Admiralty which kept insisting on the grave risks to British naval commitments elsewhere in the Atlantic and Mediterranean if Gibraltar was given priority, a supreme effort was launched to relieve the garrison.
   On 11 September 1782 a convoy of the East India trading fleet accompanied by 50 more supply ships and an escort of 34 ships of the line and a number of frigates set out from Portsmouth under the command of Admiral Lord Howe in *Victory*. Further convoys joined the fleet, now 186 strong, as it entered the Atlantic. On 11 October the fleet, still completely intact, sailed into the Gut of Gibraltar. A Spanish Fleet under Admiral Don José de Cordóva of 49 ships of the line was anchored off Algeciras but made no move to intercept.
   By the time the siege was lifted early in February 1783 the British casualties amounted to 350 killed, more than 500 lost through disease, and over 1,000 more wounded. But this long and staunch defence of Gibraltar did much to boost British morale in a difficult time. The Rock became a symbol of British power and invincibility.

GLADSMUIR   see PRESTONPANS

GROSS-JÄGERSDORF (E Germany)   Seven Years' War   30 July 1757
Prussia was threatened from the east by a Russian army of 90,000 sent against the country by the Czarina Elizabeth and under the command of Marshal Count Stepan Apraxin. A Prussian army of 30,000 under General Hans von Lehwald tried to block their advance. The outnumbered Prussians were defeated at Gross-Jägersdorf and the road to Berlin lay open.

Apraxin was unable to take advantage of the situation, however, for his supply lines broke down and part of his army mutinied, forcing him to retreat into Russia.

GUASTELLA (Italy)   War of the Polish Succession   September 1734
The French, under Marshals de Coigny and Duc de Broglie, having beaten the Austrians at Parma pursued them to Guastella, where the Prince of Württemberg had taken up a position. After a fierce contest the French won and Württemberg was slain, but such were the French casualties that their army was rendered inoperable for some weeks.

HASTENBECK (HASTENBACH) (Lower Saxony, W Germany)   Seven Years' War   26 July 1757
Prince William Augustus, Duke of Cumberland, with an army of Hanoverians, Hessians and Brunswickers totalling 36,000 men, took up a position at Hastenbeck (Hastenbach) on the Weser, 3 miles SE of Hamelin (Hameln), to protect Hanover from invasion by the French. A force of 74,000 under Louis le Tellier, Marquis de Courtanvaux (later Duc d'Estrées), marched into the province and attacked the defending army. After a fierce but confused struggle, during which both commanders believed they had lost, Cumberland's left was turned, his principal battery lost, and he conceded victory by withdrawing in good order to Stade on the Elbe, where the Hanoverians had placed their archives and their treasury. He had lost 1,200 men.
Six weeks later, on 6 September, Cumberland signed the Convention of Kloster-Zeven, dissolving his army and abandoning Hanover and Brunswick to the French. Prussia now stood in great danger from this quarter. George II, disgusted at the convention for which he was in fact chiefly responsible, said openly at court: 'Here is my son who has ruined me and disgraced himself' (Walpole). The Duke thereupon resigned his military appointments; which was perhaps just as well, for though a capable officer, he had grown corpulent and was troubled by an old wound in his leg.

HENNERSDORF (KATHOLISCH-HENNERSDORF) (Lusatia, Saxony, E Germany)   Seven Years' War   23–4 November 1745
Fought between the Prussians, under Frederick the Great and General Hans von Ziethen, and the Austrians and Saxons under Marshal Prince Charles of Lorraine and Marshal Count Rutowski.
Strength: Prussians 35,000–40,000; Austrians/Saxons 40,000.
Aim: The Austrian command led by Charles of Lorraine had devised a two-pronged plan of attack with the aim of taking Frankfurt-am-der-Oder. The Saxons under Rutowski were to march on Brandenburg from the west and south, while Charles of Lorraine was to come in from the SE. Frederick the Great was well aware of the enemy plan, having been told of it by Rudenskjöld, the Swedish Envoy at Berlin, a personal friend of his. It was Brühl, the Saxon Minister, while entertaining the Swedish Envoy at a lively and alcoholic dinner, who had first divulged the particulars of the Allied plan.
Battle: Charles of Lorraine began his march on 20 November and, by nightfall on the 23rd, his army was struggling along 20 miles of ground near the Neisse and Quiess Rivers, without a thought of any difficulty ahead. On 23 November Frederick made his move. By evening he was across the Quiess at Naumburg with 35,000 men, while General Hans von Ziethen's cavalry were already in action. At Hennersdorf (Katholisch-Hennersdorf), a village 2 miles long, Ziethen routed the Saxon cavalry and infantry, and all but annihilated them. Against the Prussian casualties of 1,000 men the Austrians and Saxons had 9,000 killed and wounded, plus 1,000 men and 4 large guns captured.
Result: The forces of Charles of Lorraine having been cut in two, they retreated in disorder back to Bohemia, leaving the towns of Gorlitz and Zittau to surrender. Their baggage and supply trains were captured by the Prussian cavalry. Charles eventually managed to re-form his beaten army at Aussig in Bohemia. He then moved slowly down the Elbe to join Marshal Rutowski.

HOCHKIRCH (Upper Lusatia, Saxony, E Germany)   Seven Years' War   14 October 1758
Fought between the Prussians under Frederick the Great and the Austrians under Marshal Count Leopold von Daun.
Strength: Prussians 37,000; Austrians 90,000.
Aim: Frederick's aim was to relieve the army commanded by his brother, Prince Henry of Prussia, which was threatened by the Austrians near Dresden.
Battle: Von Daun's superior Austrian forces surprised the Prussian army by surrounding it at night and attacking at dawn. General Hans von Ziethen and his cavalry managed to open a route through the

Austrian lines along which the Prussians were able to retreat, thus avoiding total defeat. The Prussians lost 10,000 killed, wounded and taken prisoner, plus 101 guns. The Austrian casualties totalled 8,000 killed and wounded.

Result: Frederick the Great had lost 100,000 experienced troops in this campaign. Although he could still raise a force of 150,000 men, the fighting spirit among his forces was diminishing and their experience now lacking.

HOGLAND (Gulf of Finland)   Russo-Swedish War   17 July 1788
Fought between a Swedish fleet under Duke Charles of Sudermania and a Russian fleet under Admiral Samuel Greig.
Strength: Swedish 15 ships of the line + 5 frigates; Russians 17 ships of the line + 7 frigates.
Gustavus III of Sweden decided to march against St Petersburg (Petrograd/Leningrad) by way of Vyborg on the Russo-Finnish border. The first objective was the small fortress of Friedrichsham (Fredericks-hamn), with the army supported by the Swedish fleet. However, just before war was declared on 22 June 1789, Duke Charles, with 15 ships of the line and 5 frigates, gave chase to 3 Russian warships. A Russian fleet appeared under Admiral Greig, a Scotsman, which outnumbered the Swedish fleet by 2 ships of the line and 2 frigates.

The battle took place off the island of Hogland in the Gulf of Finland on 17 July, both sides losing one ship of the line; but the Swedish fleet was compelled to run for safety to the harbour of Sveaborg (Helsinki), where they remained blockaded by the Russians for the whole of the campaign.

The Russian fleet was not so strong as Charles had supposed as, just before it was to sail, Catherine the Great had given command of one ship to the famous US captain, John Paul Jones, whereat all the British officers in the Russian fleet, including many of the captains, signified their intention to quit the squadron, so that 8 ships were left without officers. Catherine was forced to withdraw the 'pirate captain' Paul Jones and sent him ostensibly to the Black Sea; but she finally got rid of him altogether.

HOHENFRIEDBURG (DOBROMIERZ) (Wroclaw, Poland)   War of the Austrian Succession   4 June 1745
Fought between the Prussians commanded by Frederick the Great and the Austro-Saxon army of Marshal Prince Charles of Lorraine.
Strength: Prussians 60,000; Austrians/Saxons 80,000.
Frederick, determined to prevent Empress Maria Theresa from reclaiming Silesia, took his army to Frankenstein in S Silesia, while Prince Charles of Lorraine concentrated his forces at Landshut in the west, threatening Breslau. Charles then moved his army into two camps, the Austrians at Hohenfriedburg, the Saxons at Striegau (Strzegom).

The Prussians marched at dawn, first attacking the Saxon camp at Striegau, surprising them and routing them. Frederick then turned on the Austrians, and after a brisk engagement, put them to flight. At 8am the battle was over. The Austro-Saxons lost 9,000 killed and wounded, plus 7,000 men including 4 generals captured, and had 66 guns taken. The Prussians lost less than 2,000 killed and wounded.

As the Austrian and Saxons fled into Bohemia, Frederick pursued with about half his army, leaving the rest to cope with Austrian and Hungarian pandours (guerrilla forces) in the south. After three months of inconclusive movements along the Upper Elbe River, Frederick began withdrawing to Silesia with Charles of Lorraine, who had reorganised and reinforced his beaten armies, following him but avoiding battle. Frederick halted at Soor (qv).

ILE DE RHE (off La Rochelle, W France)   Seven Years' War   4 April 1758
A French convoy of 40 ships, protected by 5 warships and 6 frigates, set sail from Rochefort (near La Rochelle) bound for Louisbourg, Nova Scotia, and was attacked by a British squadron of 7 ships of the line and 3 frigates under Admiral Sir Edward Hawke. All the French ships were driven ashore on the Ile de Rhé, and as Hawke reported in his dispatch, 'At 5 next morning [5 April] I saw them all aground, almost dry, about 5 or 6 miles distance from us . . . many of the merchants and several of the ships of war were on their broadsides.'

ISMAIL (IZMAIL) (USSR/Romania border)   Russo-Ottoman Wars   March–22 December 1790
The fortress of Ismail (Izmail), controlling one of the mouths of the Danube, had been under desultory siege by Field-Marshal Prince Grigori Potëmkin for seven months.

Potëmkin had an augury that the town would fall within three days. He immediately summoned Field-Marshal Count Alexander Suvorov and ordered him to take it at all costs. Suvorov issued two summons for surrender on 21 December, threatening the garrison with the fate of Ochakov (see KINBURN) to no avail.

At 4am the next day Suvorov started the storming of the fortress. After great slaughter the walls were mounted at 8 o'clock and the struggle continued in the streets where every house became a redoubt, the Tartars of the Crimea, in league with the Turks, being the prime movers in the defence. In the market square 4,000 of them fought for four hours until none was left. Suvorov now opened a passage for his cavalry and the massacre of the garrison continued until 4pm. At last, in the evening, the attacking Russians got the message which had sustained them in their murderous assault. Suvorov gave the signal that as a reward for their valour the garrison and inhabitants of the town of Ismail was at the disposal of the Russian army for loot, rapine and slaughter as they wished for three days and nights. Upwards of 43,000 Turkish soldiers were killed and about 90,000 women, children and civilians slaughtered or taken as booty. The Russians lost 15,000 in their blind assault.

This victory consolidated Russian control of the mouth of the Danube. Two French émigrés, the Duc de Richelieu and the Comte de Langeron, were present at this Russian triumph and General Mikhail Kutusov, Napoleon's opponent in 1812, led the sixth assault.

KAGUL (KARKUL) (USSR)   Russo-Ottoman Wars   3 August 1770
General Count Peter Rumiantsev (Romanzov) had been directed to operate in the Crimea area (see RUSSO-OTTOMAN WARS [1768–74]) while Prince Alexander Galitzin made the main thrust over the Danube at Chotin (qv). As Rumiantsev's 17,000-strong army advanced he was faced with a Turkish force of 50,000 to his front and a mainly irregular cavalry force of 35,000 Tartars to his rear. Rumiantsev boldly attacked the Turks who, at that initial period of the war, were ill-trained, and defeated them decisively, capturing all their baggage and artillery. Turning on the Tartars with the same rapidity and momentum, Rumiantsev drove them back into the Crimea. He then followed the Russian retreat to the Danube and forced the line of the river Pruth (qv) two months later.

At this time Prince Galitzin, disgusted at the behaviour of Catherine's current favourite, Count Gregory Orlov, resigned his command, so that the remainder of the Balkan campaign was conducted by Rumiantzev.

KAY (E Germany-Polish border)   Seven Years' War   23 July 1759
Fought between the Russians commanded by Count Peter Soltikov and the Prussians led by General Richard von Wedell.
Strength: Russians 70,000; Prussians 26,000.

The Russians, advancing from Posen to the Oder River with the intention of taking Frankfurt, were intercepted by the Prussians led by von Wedell at Kay, a small hamlet west of Züllichau. Von Wedell rashly attacked the large Russian force, was badly beaten and forced to retreat across the Oder. The Russians lost 500 killed and wounded; the Prussians 6,000 killed, wounded or captured.

The Russians continued their advance on Frankfurt and took possession of the city.

KESSELSDORF (E Germany)   War of the Austrian Succession   15 December 1745
The second, northern, prong of the Austro-Saxon attack directed on Berlin was led by Marshal Count Rutowski with his mainly Saxon army. To halt him, a Prussian army under Leopold I of Anhalt-Dessau advanced up the left bank of the Elbe from Magdeburg. The two armies met at Kesselsdorf, 10 miles west of Dresden, on 15 December. The Prussian attack routed the Saxon army and repulsed the invasion.

This action was the last of a series of Prussian victories in the Second Silesian War (1744–5) and, with the withdrawal of the English army to deal with the Scottish rebellion, coupled with Marshal Comte Maurice de Saxe's victories in Flanders, caused Maria Theresa to sue for peace. In the Treaty of Dresden that followed she recognised Frederick II of Prussia's conquest of Silesia, while he agreed to the election of her husband as Emperor.

KINBURN (or OCHAKOV) (USSR)   Russo-Ottoman Wars   17 May 1787
Fought between the Russians, under Field-Marshal Count Alexander Suvorov and Prince of Nassau-Siegen, and the Turkish army and fleet under Osman Pasha and Hassan el Ghasi.

Aim: Kinburn was a small fortress occupied by the Russians and situated on a promontory opposite Ochakov (qv), in and around which the Turkish army was stationed. Suvorov's object was to prevent the Turkish fleet landing an infantry division on the Kinburn promontory.
Battle: Suvorov erected a battery to cannonade the Turkish fleet from land as it was attacked by the Russian fleet. He allowed the Turks to disembark 6,000–7,000 men on the promontory. He then sent four regiments of Cossacks to attack them and himself led two battalions with fixed bayonets to charge them, and wiped the lot out including the wounded. As Nassau-Siegen attacked the Turkish fleet, Suvorov opened up with his shore battery and destroyed three-quarters of the Turkish ships.
Result: The immediate Russian objective was achieved.

This was the opening round of the war. Nothing much happened during the remainder of 1787 and the greater part of 1788 except for fleet action by John Paul Jones and others against the Turks (see LIMAN). The Russian army meanwhile started its advance down the Black Sea coast, although Ochakov was still under siege. Suvorov was wounded during the siege.

KIRCH-DENKERN (Poland)   Seven Years' War   16 July 1761
Fought between the Prussians under Field-Marshal Ferdinand, Duke of Brunswick and the French under Marshal Charles, Duc de Soubise, and Marshal Victor François, Duc de Broglie.

The Prussians held a strong position in and around the village of Kirch-Denkern, near Wroclaw, which the French attacked. Heavy fighting took place and the French were repulsed with loss, suffering 4,000 killed and wounded. Prussians casualties numbered 1,000 men.

Although his enemy failed in their attack this battle did little to enhance the fortunes of Frederick I's army. The Austrians under Marshal Baron Gideon von Laudon and the Russians under General Alexander Buturlin went on to cut Frederick off from Prussia by moving to Liegnitz. Frederick retreated to the fortified camp of Bunzewitz (Czechoslovakia), 20 miles east of Glatz.

KOLIN (Bohemia, Czechoslovakia)   Seven Years' War   18 June 1757
Fought between the Austrians under Field-Marshal Count Leopold von Daun and the Prussians under Frederick the Great.
Strength: Austrians 60,000 with 145 guns; Prussians 34,000 with 50 guns.
Aim: The Prussians were besieging Prague. The Austrians advanced to relieve the city.
Battle: Frederick the Great endeavoured to foil the advancing Austrians by moving across their front and striking their right flank. The Prussians, not advancing with their usual speed because of the great heat of the day, gave von Daun time to reinforce his right. Although the Prussians attacked with vigour, heavy fire from the Austrians repulsed them. Frederick then ordered Prince Maurice of Anhalt-Dessau to lead his reserve into attack, but this force was unable to penetrate the Austrian centre. The Austrians, being far superior in strength in both men and guns, inflicted heavy losses on the Prussians, forcing their infantry to retreat on all sectors of the front. The Austrians lost 8,000 killed and wounded. The Prussians had 8,000 killed and wounded, 6,000 taken prisoner, and lost 45 guns.
Result: Frederick the Great was forced to drop the siege of Prague and leave Bohemia.

KOSCIUSKO'S POLISH UPRISING   1794
When Catherine the Great of Russia decided to partition Poland a second time in 1794 the Poles made Tadeusz (Thaddeus) Andrzej Bonawentura Kosciusko, who was born in Lithuania and had served with distinction with the Americans in their War of Independence, their dictator. By 1792 Kosciusko had already made his name in Poland when, with 5,000 men, he had held a Russian army of 18,000 at bay for five days at Dubienka.

On appointment as leader of the Polish Patriots Kosciusko immediately took the offensive and, with 4,000 troops and 2,000 peasants armed with agricultural implements, defeated a Russian force of 7,000 at Raclawice on 3 April 1794. When the insurrection spread to all the occupied parts of Poland on 18 April, 2,000 Russians were put to the sword.

Both Russia and Prussia invaded the rump of the country with 25,000 men and 179 guns under Prince Frederick William of Prussia and 65,000 men and 74 guns under the Russian General Fersen. Soon Kosciusko's army of 35,000 men and 200 guns was besieged in Warsaw. Between 26 August and 6 September the Poles withstood two assaults. The invaders had then to dissipate their forces around Poland to try to subdue the guerrillas who were attacking their communications and the siege was temporarily lifted.

However, on 10 October 1794, Kosciusko was caught at Maciejowice with only 7,000 men by General Fersen with 16,000 Russians and was decisively defeated. Kosciusko was captured and, with his enthusiasm and military skill extinguished, Warsaw capitulated, Polish resistance collapsed and the remainder of Poland was partitioned between Russia, Prussia and Austria. Austria received Cracow, Prussia Warsaw, while the lion's share of the territory was swallowed by Russia which now had a permanent claim in central Europe.

KOSTLIJU (SHUMLA, SHUMEN, KOLAROVGRAD) (Bulgaria)   Russo-Ottoman War   July 1774
Fought between the Turks under the Grand Vizier Muhsinzade and the Russians under Field-Marshal Count Alexander Suvorov.

Since the initial Russian victories at the beginning of the war the Turks had worn down the Czarina's armies by 'harassing' warfare, a form of guerrilla warfare by regular troops to which the Russians, with their inefficient communications from the Dniester to the Danube, were particularly susceptible. Even Field-Marshal Count Peter Rumiantsev (Romanzov) had, in 1773, been driven back into Bessarabia after defeats at Roskana and Rushchuk in Bulgaria. With both countries exhausted by this long war, Catherine II sent the forty-five-year-old Suvorov, who had done so well against Pugachëv (PUGACHËV'S PEASANT UPRISING, to bring the Turks to battle. An advance element of 25,000 Turks was defeated by General Soltikov, the remnants falling back to join the Grand Vizier's army, increasing it to a total of 60,000 men.

Driving south with his usual impetus, Suvorov with 50,000 men managed to catch a portion of this Turkish army crossing a tributary of the Danube and defeated them, driving the rest into the fortress of Shumla where they were blockaded. The ignominious defeat of the Turkish Grand Vizier was the last straw.

This was to be the last battle of the campaign. The new Sultan, Abdul-Hamid, had not the warlike spirit of his doughty predecessor, Mustapha III. At the Treaty of Kutchuk-Kainardji, the Turks, quite unnecessarily as the Russians were exhausted, surrendered much of the northern coast of the Black Sea to Russian suzerainty as well as making concessions in Bessarabia and elsewhere. Russia's economic, military and maritime power was thus greatly increased.

KROSZKA (KROTZKA) (Yugoslavia)   Austro-Russian-Turkish War   23 July 1739
Fought between the Austrians under Field Marshal Count George von Wallis and the Turks under the Grand Vizier, Al-Haji Mohammed.

Russia had declared war on Turkey. The Austrians pretended to mediate but secretly amassed an army on the frontier and prepared to give Russia aid. The Austrians invaded in 1737 and were beaten at Banyaluka and Valievo (qv) and had to evacuate Bosnia. In Serbia they did no better and were forced back across the Danube by the Turks. The Turks were beaten at Konieh but retook Semendria, Mahadia and Orsova.

On 23 July 1739, after a fifteen-hour battle, Count Wallis was put to flight by Al-Haji Mohammed at Kroszka. Belgrade (BEGRADE II) was invested three days later.

The Turks had not been so successful against the Russians (see UKRAINE CAMPAIGNS OF COUNT MÜNNICH) and on 18 September a Treaty of Belgrade was signed, ending the war.

KUNERSDORF (E Germany)   Seven Years' War   12 August 1759
Fought between the Prussians, under Frederick the Great and the Russians under Count Peter Saltykov (Soltikov), and the Austrians under Count Hadik von Futak and Marshal Baron Gideon von Laudon.

A Russian army of 55,000 under Saltykov joined the Austrian force of 35,000 under von Futak and von Laudon despite the efforts of Frederick to prevent this junction. The Allies entrenched themselves in a strong position in sandhills flanked by woodland. With 50,000 men, Frederick attempted a double envelopment of the Allied force which had the Russians on the Prussians' right and the Austrians on their left flank. The Prussian force became disorganised and disorientated in the heavily wooded and broken ground and the attack became uncoordinated, and so was delivered piecemeal. On the right, the Prussians succeeded in driving the Russians out of their entrenchments and capturing 180 guns with the aid of General Friedrich Wilhelm von Seydlitz's cavalry. Against Seydlitz's advice, Frederick decided to press on with the attack on the left flank. There, although unsupported by the Russians, the Austrians held off, and finally after six hours of fighting, threw back the Prussian attack. Frederick lost over 20,000 men and 178 guns in this, his worst defeat. The Allies lost 15,700.

Frederick considered abdication and he did temporarily resign his command, for his army was now reduced to 3,000 men. The Allies, however, were too weak and too divided to press home the advantage they had gained and eventually lack of supplies forced the Russians to return home and the alliance was broken.

LAGOS BAY (off the coast of Portugal)   Seven Years' War   17–19 August 1759
Fought between a British fleet under Admiral Edward Boscawen and a French fleet led by Admiral de la Clue Sabran.
   In order to begin the invasion of Scotland, which Marshal Comte Maurice de Saxe planned in order to scare the British back from the continent where they had been too successful, a fleet of 12 ships under Admiral de la Clue Sabran left Toulon for Brest on 15 August. On 17 August they passed Gibraltar, where a British fleet was refitting. An English frigate sighted the fleet and a squadron of 7 ships under Admiral Boscawen (who was in his flagship *Namur*) put to sea at once. Five French ships broke away and fled to Cadiz. But Admiral de la Clue Sabran was determined to press on up the coast. At 10am on 18 August Boscawen caught up with the remainder off Lagos and engaged them in a running battle. *Namur* engaged the French flagship *Océan* and was disabled. Boscawen shifted his flag to *Newark*. Two French ships, *Souverain* and *Guernier*, escaped west into the Atlantic. Of the remainder, *Centaure* (74) engaged the English for five hours to enable the others to get away. Finally *Centaure* struck her colours, but only when she was a wreck and her captain and half her crew killed. De la Clue Sabran ran *Océan* ashore in Lagos Bay and the remainder of the French fleet anchored under the Portuguese guns. However, though Portugal was neutral, Boscawen went in after them. *Océan* and *Redoubtable* were set on fire, and *Modeste* and *Témeraire* were taken as prizes.
   All French hopes of a combination of the Brest (Atlantic) and the Toulon (Mediteranean) fleets had now to be abandoned, and new plans for an invasion had to be considered.

LANDESHUT (KAMIENNA GÓRA) (Silesia, E Germany)   Seven Years' War   23 June 1760
Fought between the Austrians led by Field-Marshal Baron Gideon von Laudon and the Prussians commanded by Baron Heinrich de la Motte-Fouqué.
   In Silesia, an Austrian army under von Laudon seized the Prussian fortress of Landeshut (Kamienna Góra) in the Sudetic Mountains. The Prussian force of 13,000 under Motte-Fouqué was ordered to recapture the stronghold but, when the attempt was made, the Prussians were repulsed by a force of 31,000 Austrians. As a result the Prussian army was practically annihilated.
   Frederick then marched to Silesia himself.

LAUFFELD (LAFFELOT) (NE Belgium)   War of the Austrian Succession   2 July 1745
Fought between the French under Marshal Comte Maurice de Saxe and a British-Dutch-Hanoverian-Austrian army led by William Augustus, Duke of Cumberland, and Marshal Count Leopold von Daun.
Strength: French 30,000 (at Lauffeld) + 12,000 (de Saxe); Allies 90,000.
   The Allies had cut off and isolated a French force of 30,000 at the village of Lauffeld (Laffelot), west of Maastricht. De Saxe marched a relieving force 50 miles in two days against the Allies and on 2 July 1745 he attacked them. Three times the French took the village, but each time the Allies managed to recapture it by counter-attacks. About noon the French drove the British centre in, defeat was imminent, but then Colonel Sir John Ligonier and his British cavalry charged, allowing the British infantry and the other Allied forces to withdraw in good order, leaving the French in possession of Lauffeld. The French lost 14,000 killed and wounded and the Allied 6,000 killed and wounded, of which 2,000 were British.
   De Saxe had won the engagement, but at a cost. He now sent a French force under Count Ulrich von Lowendal to lay siege to Bergen-op-Zoom (qv) on the Schelde River in the W Netherlands, while he took his main army to isolate Maastricht (qv) before the armies settled down for the winter.

LEMNOS (LIMNOS) (N Aegean Sea)   Russo-Ottoman Wars   July 1770–April 1771
Fought between a Russian fleet and marines under Admiral Alexei Orlov and the Turkish garrison of Lemnos (Limnos) coupled with a relieving naval force under Hassan Bey.
   After the main Turkish fleet in the Aegean had been annihilated by the fire-ships of Vice-Admiral John Elphinston at Chesmé (qv), the Russian Admiral Orlov, instead of quickly forcing the Dardanelles and attacking Constantinople as Elphinston wished, decided to lay siege to the island of Lemnos. This desultory affair lasted through the winter until in April 1771 Hassan Bey, 'the crocodile of the sea', decided

on a surprise attack. He concealed 4,000 picked volunteers in galleys and, without artillery and relying entirely on surprise, landed and overcame the besiegers, the remnants of whom fled to their ships. Hassan Bey was rewarded with the title of Kapudan Pasha for this exploit.

All hope of the Russians forcing the Dardanelles evaporated after this defeat.

LEUTHEN (Silesia, E Germany)   Seven Years' War   5 December 1757
Fought between the Prussians under Frederick the Great and the Austrians under Marshal Prince Charles of Lorraine and Marshal Count Leopold von Daun.
Aim: To meet the Austrian threat in the south Frederick marched hastily to Liegnitz (Legnica), where he met the survivors of the defeat at Breslau (qv). With 36,000 men he now took the offensive, intending to liberate the city. Meanwhile Charles of Lorraine and von Daun, with 80,000 men, were deployed along a 5-mile front running north-south to the west of Breslau. The right flank was anchored on a marsh, the left on the Schweidnitz (Swidnica) River. Both wings were protected by cavalry and the Austrian reserve lay behind the left wing in expectation that Frederick would try to envelop that more exposed flank which was his usual tactic.
Battle: Frederick, meanwhile, advanced over undulating ground and made as if to attack the right wing with four columns, two of infantry and two of cavalry. When his columns were concealed by a dip in the land, however, he changed direction and marched on the Austrian left while his opponent Charles prepared for the main weight of the attack to fall on his right and, consequently, moved his reserve to that wing. While one column of Prussian cavalry feinted against the Austrian right, the three remaining columns attacked on the left. The assault opened with the bombardment by 10 fortress cannon on the abatis behind which the Austrians were formed up. This onslaught shattered their fortifications. The Austrian left was deployed so that their wing was refused. Frederick advanced in echelon in two lines so that the Prussians had great numerical superiority at the point of contact. The attack threw the Austrians back and a Prussian cavalry charge by General Hans von Zeithen drove them in on to the centre. The Austrian cavalry attempted to counter-attack but were caught by the rear of the Prussian charge and scattered. The Austrian right was then attacked and broken. Only nightfall enabled the Austrians to withdraw across the Schweidnitz to Breslau. Their losses were 20,000 captured, 6,750 killed or wounded and 116 guns and 51 colours taken. The Prussians lost 6,150 killed or wounded. Breslau fell five days later.
Result: The Battle of Leuthen was one of Frederick's greatest victories and showed his complete tactical mastery in the field and the superb disciplined drill of his men in the battle-line.

LIEGNITZ (LEGNICA) (Silesia, E Germany)   Seven Years' War   15 August 1760
Fought between the Prussians under Frederick the Great and the Austrians under Marshal Count Leopold von Daun and Marshal Baron Gideon von Laudon.

With 30,000 men Frederick the Great marched into Silesia, reaching Liegnitz (Legnica) on 15 August. Here, he found two Austrian armies under von Daun and von Laudon and a Russian force under General Czernichev closing in around him. Overnight, Frederick began to retreat along the only road open to him, that to Parchwitz. At the same time, von Laudon's force moved to block the road. The two armies clashed near Liegnitz and the Prussians succeeded in cutting their way out of the encirclement, leaving 10,000 Austrian casualties and taking 82 guns. The Russians were then tricked into retiring north, while Frederick also marched north towards Berlin by a different route.

LIMAN (USSR)   Ottoman Wars   17/27 June 1788
Fought between the Russian Black Sea fleet commanded by Admirals John Paul Jones and Prince of Nassau-Siegen and a Turkish fleet under Hassan el Ghasi.
Aim: The Russians, in alliance with the Austrians, were attempting to drive back the Turks, especially after their encroachments in the Caucusus and pressure in the Balkans.
Battle: On 17 June Nassau-Siegen's flotilla was the first to contact the Turkish fleet and it was only Paul Jones's intervention that saved him from disaster. The Russians attacked again on 27 June led by Paul Jones, took the Turks by surprise and effectively wiped them out as a fighting force, since they lost 15 ships, 3,000 men killed and 1,600 prisoners to the Russians' 1 ship lost, 18 men killed and 67 wounded.
Result: This victory opened the way to a Russian advance over the river Dnieper and south towards the Danube.

LOBOSITZ (LOVOCIZE) (Bohemia, Czechoslovakia)   Seven Years' War   1 October 1756
Fought between Prussians and Hanoverians under Frederick the Great and an Austrian force commanded
   by Marshal Maximilian von Browne.
Strength: Prussians/Hanoverians 70,000; Austrians 30,000 + 18,000 Saxons at Pirna.
Aim: The Austrians sought to go to the aid of their Saxon allies under siege at Pirna on the Elbe River.
Battle: The adversaries met in battle in the Erzgebirge Mountains in a heavy morning fog which split the
engagement into a number of uncoordinated battalion-strength struggles. The superior discipline and
morale of the Prussians was the major cause of the defeat of the Austrians. Both sides suffered 3,000
casualties.
Result: This battle led to the surrender of the Saxons at Pirna on 15 October 1756, and their impressment
into the Prussian army by Frederick the Great.

MAASTRICHT (Limburg, Netherlands)   War of the Austrian Succession   May 1748
Fought between the French, commanded by Marshal Comte Maurice de Saxe, and the Hanoverian,
Austrian, Dutch and British armies led by the Prince of Orange and Prince William Augustus, Duke of
Cumberland.
Strength: French 40,000; Allies 70,000.
   At the close of operations in 1747 and with the armies in winter quarters Marshal Comte de Saxe had
isolated Maastricht with his main army. He resumed operations in the spring of 1748. While a Russian
army marched across Germany to join the Allies in the Netherlands, the unwieldy coalition of Allied
forces proved unable to master the resourceful and brilliant de Saxe who attacked and took Maastricht on
7 May 1748. French casualties were 4,000 killed and wounded; Allied casualties, 5,000 killed and
wounded.
   The garrison at Maastricht was granted the honour of war and marched out to join the other forces of
the Duke of Cumberland.
   This victory ended all further operations of any importance and, on 18 October 1748, the Treaty of Aix-
la-Chapelle (Aachen) was signed. The treaty again recognised the Prussian possession of Silesia, the
Pragmatic Sanction in Austria, and the rights of the House of Hanover to the Electorate of Hanover and
the British throne. Parma, Guastella and Placentia in Italy were ceded to Don Philip of Spain.

MARTINESTI (Romania)   Ottoman Wars   23 September 1789
Fought between Turks under Osman Pasha and an allied Russo-Austrian army under Friedrich Josias,
Prince of Saxe-Coburg and Field-Marshal Count Alexander Suvorov.
Strength: Turks 70,000; Russians/Austrians 27,000.
Aim: The Turks, who had superior numbers, were determined to drive the Austrians out of north
Wallachia. But Saxe-Coburg had written to Suvorov for help, as he was outnumbered.
Battle: Suvorov, who received Saxe-Coburg's letter on 16 September, immediately gave orders to march,
so that when Osman Pasha drew his huge army up to attack at Martinesti, 50 miles NE of Galati (Galatz),
he found the Russians facing his right wing and the Austrians in the centre and left, with plenty of artillery.
The Turkish cavalry attempted an encirclement of the Russian flank but were driven off. Then Suvorov, to
whom Saxe-Coburg had ceded overall command, anxious to seize the initiative, ordered a general frontal
attack, after first driving the Turks out of some awkward positions in woods on the flanks. The Russians
and Austrians attacked with great ferocity and, after a long hard battle, won a complete victory, the Turks
eventually fleeing in disorder. The booty captured was immense. Ten thousand Turks were killed and
wounded, while 8,000 were drowned trying to cross the Rimnik (qv), the victorious Allies losing but 617
men killed and wounded.
Result: The Turkish objective was not achieved.

MATCHEWITZ (MACIEJOWICE) (Lublin, Poland)   First Polish Rising   10 October 1794
Fought between the Russians under Baron de Fersen and the Poles under Thaddeus Kosciusko.
Strength: Russians 16,000; Poles 7,000.
   After a fierce fight, the Poles, many of whom were only armed with scythes and pikes, were totally
defeated with a loss of 4,000 dead. Kosciusko was severely wounded.
   The Polish uprising, which had started at the Battle of Raclawice on 3 April 1794, collapsed. Kosciusko
had previously volunteered and taken part in the American Revolution. On the third partition of Poland
the following year, the ancient Polish nation disappeared, and Russia had a foothold in central Europe.

MATCHIN (E Bulgaria)   Ottoman Wars   10 July 1791
Fought between the Turks under Yusuf Pasha and the Russians under General Prince Nikolai Repnin.
Strength: Turks 100,000; Russians 40,000.
Aim: The Russians aimed to exploit the Allied victories at Focsani, Martinesti and Rimnik (qqv).
Battle: Although the Turkish right wing did not hold, the perseverance of the left and centre left the result in doubt until General Mikhail Kutusov led a charge of the Russian left which drove the Turks back and defeated them with heavy loss.
Result: Further withdrawal of Turkish forces to the south. This defeat led to the Treaty of Jassy, concluded on 9 January 1792 between Russia and Turkey, in which Russia acquired the fortress of Ochakov (see KINBURN), the surrounding territory from the Dniester River to the Bug, and the protectorate of Georgia.

MAXEN (E Germany)   Seven Years' War   21 November 1759
Fought between the Austrians under Marshal Count Leopold von Daun and the Prussians under General Friedrich von Finck.
Strength: Austrians 42,000; Prussians 12,000.
   Von Finck had been sent with a small force by Frederick the Great to reconnoitre the Austrian defences of Dresden. The Austrians lured von Finck on to Maxen, 10 miles south of Dresden, surrounded his forces and, after two days, compelled him to surrender. The Austrians sustained 300 casualties, killed and wounded. Prussians losses numbered 12,000, mostly prisoners and included 17 generals, plus 17 guns.
   Von Daun failed to follow up this success. As the campaigning season was ending both sides retired and encamped for the winter. Von Finck was later court-martialled, convicted and imprisoned by Frederick the Great for dereliction of duty.

MINDEN (Lower Saxony, W Germany)   Seven Years' War   1 August 1759
Fought between the Prussians, Hanoverians and British under Field-Marshal Ferdinand, Duke of Brunswick and the French commanded by the Marquis Louis de Contades.
Aim: A French army of 60,000 under the Marquis de Contades moved north to threaten the Prussian ally, Hanover. To block their advance, the Duke of Brunswick concentrated a hastily gathered army of 45,000 English, Prussians and Hanoverians at Minden on the river Wesel. The French had 170 guns to the Allied total of 187.
Battle: With part of his army Ferdinand feinted towards the French right and, when Contades moved his whole strength to meet the threat, launched his main attack in eight columns on the centre. The advance was delayed by bad weather which enabled the French to re-form and meet the Allied attack in good order. The French were gaining the upper hand when the British infantry, followed by the Hanoverians, attacked the French cavalry, which were placed in the centre of the line and protected by artillery. This attack had resulted largely from misunderstood orders but it was effective. The Allied infantry beat back an attempted cavalry counter-attack by a bayonet-charge and then went on to drive through the centre of the French line. Seeing this success, Brunswick ordered the British cavalry under General Lord George Sackville with his fourteen squadrons (five regiments) of British and Hanoverian cavalry to charge the French. Sackville refused in spite of various attempts by aides-de-camp to induce him to do so. The result was that the French, although defeated, were able to withdraw in good order, having lost 7,086 killed, wounded and captured, as well as 43 guns and 17 colours. Allied losses were 2,762, most of whom were British.
Result: The victory saved Hanover. The French retired to the Rhine, followed by Ferdinand. Sackville was court-martialled and dismissed from the army, only to appear twenty years later as Lord George Germain as Secretary of State for the Colonies in Lord North's régime, which was most responsible for the loss by Britain of her American colonies.

MINORCA (MENORCA) (Balearic Islands, Spain)   Spanish-English War   5 February 1782
Minorca, captured by the English in the War of the Spanish Succession and retained under the Treaty of Utrecht (1713), was seized by the French in 1756, retaken by the English, and attacked again by a mixed Franco-Spanish force in 1781. The expedition, which sailed from Cadiz on 20 July under the command of the Duke of Crillon, comprised 7,464 men and 50 warships.
   The troops landed in the Bay of Mezquita and occupied Mahon, the capital, but the Governor, General James Murray with 700 men, continued to hold out in the fortress of San Felipe. On 24 October the

expeditionary force was reinforced by four regiments of French infantry. The garrison resisted for six months, but sickness and battle casualties forced Murray to surrender on 5 February 1782.

The island was recaptured, without offering resistance, in 1798, but returned to Spain under the Treaty of Amiens (1802).

MOLLWITZ (Wroclaw, Poland)   War of the Austrian Succession/First Silesian War   10 April 1741
In 1740 Frederick the Great invaded Silesia at the head of 30,000 men. The following year, Maria Theresa sent an army of 20,000 under Marshal Count Wilhelm Reinhardt von Neipperg to eject the invaders. At Mollwitz, 7 miles east of Brieg, Frederick with 20,000 men and 60 guns met the equal force of Neipperg who, however, had only 18 guns. Frederick also had numerical superiority in infantry. Neipperg brought on the battle, which was fought with snow on the ground, though the action was begun by a Prussian artillery bombardment. An Austrian cavalry charge swept the Prussian right wing, mainly cavalry, off the field, Frederick with it. Command of the Prussian infantry was exercised by Count Kurt von Schwerin, and when the victorious Austrian cavalry tried to ride down these infantry they were halted by quick and accurate musket-fire. Five Austrian charges were halted and then the Prussian infantry advanced, firing twice as fast as the Austrians. Neipperg's left wing was outflanked and the whole line rolled up. The Austrians withdrew under cover of darkness, leaving 5,000 dead, wounded and captured. Prussian losses were 2,500.

The well-drilled and disciplined Prussian infantry won the day by their staunchness and accuracy of fire. Frederick never again left the field of battle.

'MOONLIGHT VICTORY, THE'   see CAPE ST VINCENT I

MOREA (PELOPONNISOS) (Greece)   RUSSO-OTTOMAN WARS   1769–70
Fought between Greek Patriots supported by a Russian navy under Admiral Alexei Orlov and the Turkish and Albanian counter-insurgency forces.

The year 1769 had been a good one for Catherine of Russia, as her forces had been victorious on land with General Count Peter Rumiantsev (Romanzov) crossing the Dniester, capturing Jassy, capital of Bessarabia, and his generals Prince Nikolai Repnin and Count Nikita Panin besieging and successfully assaulting the fortresses of Ismail and Bender (BENDER II) respectively. Rumiantsev then advanced and occupied Bucharest (qv), while other armies crossed the Kuban and into the Caucusus.

Catherine, however, not satisfied with her successes on land, decided to use sea-power to attempt to drive the Turks right out of Europe by supporting her army's advance from the north, with a flanking movement through the Mediterranean and Aegean from the south. In autumn 1769 she sent three squadrons (12 ships) of men-of-war under Admiral Orlov from Kronstadt in the Baltic through the English Channel, Bay of Biscay and Mediterranean to land at Navarino on the Morea (Peloponnisos) peninsular to generate and stimulate a revolt of her co-religionists against the Turks.

A typical unbridled revolutionary warfare started with, first, the Greeks butchering the Turks, and the Turks in turn bringing forth their own fierce co-religionists, the Albanians, who retaliated in kind, with Ali Bey the Governor of Egypt, who had also taken the opportunity of Turkish weakness to rebel, trying to join the Russians and adding to the confusion. The Turks, past masters over the centuries at counter-insurgency, quickly scotched the revolt on Morea accompanied by great and indiscriminate slaughter.

Britain was supporting Russia, and many of her naval officers had trained her marines and were serving in her Mediterranean squadron, one of whom, the Scotsman Vice-Admiral John Elphinston, commanded a squadron of 4 ships of the line, several frigates and some smaller vessels. It was Elphinston's aim to force the Dardanelles which were not at that time defended. A naval battle became inevitable and this took place at Chesmé (qv) between the island of Chios and the Anatolian coast on 7–8 July 1770.

NETHERLANDS CIVIL WAR   1785–7
Fought between the pro-French Patriot Party and the troops of the States-General under Stadholder William V. No major actions were fought. Order was restored when William called Prussian troops in during 1787.

NEW ROSS (Co Leinster, Eire)   Irish Rebellion   5 June 1798
Fought between the Irish Rebels under Father Roche and Bagenal Harvey, and the British regulars under General Johnstone.

Strength: Rebels 30,000; Regulars 1,400.

Regulars posted in New Ross, Wexford, were attacked by the Rebels who gained the centre of the town before being driven out by a bayonet-charge and then totally routed. Rebel losses were 2,600 killed.

OCHAKOV (USSR)   Russo-Ottoman Wars   November–16 December 1788
Fought between the Russians under Field-Marshal Count Alexander Suvorov and the Turkish garrison of Ochakov.
Strength: Russians 40,000; Turks 20,000.
Aim: Field-Marshal Prince Grigori Potëmkin ordered Suvorov to conduct the siege of Ochakov which stood in the way of a Russian advance into Moldavia and Wallachia.
Battle: The siege started late in the year and the Russians, owing to bad administration, suffered severely from lack of supplies, cold and disease. The city was encircled on the Black Sea side by a lagoon, called a Liman. By December this was sufficiently frozen for Suvorov to order an advance across it. Regiment after regiment attacked across the ice, suffering terrible slaughter until, on 16 December 1788, Ochakov was stormed. Potëmkin ordered a slaughter of the garrison, and in the subsequent massacre 20,000 Turks were killed. Russian casualties from shot and disease, totalled 15,000, including 4,000 on the final assault.
Result: The Russian objective was achieved. Subsequently each Russian soldier received a medal, and Potëmkin was given 100,000 roubles from Catherine the Great, since much booty had been seized.
(See also KINBURN)

OLMÜTZ (OLOMUC) (Moravia, Czechoslovakia)   Seven Years' War   May–July 1758
Fought between the Prussians under Frederick the Great and the Austrians commanded by Marshal Count Leopold von Daun.
Strength: Prussians 40,000; Austrians 36,000.

Frederick the Great, knowing that he had nothing to fear as yet from the Russians, opened his summer campaign by marching on Olmütz (Olomuc), and laying siege to this strongly fortified arsenal. He was almost at once in difficulties. He had insufficient troops to surround and invest the fortress, and all his supplies and munitions had to be brought up from Niesse, 90 miles away. Moreover, a great deal of the road between Niesse and Olmütz lay over rough and hilly country, infested by Austrian cavalry and inhabited by a population devoted to the Austrian throne, which made it difficult for the Prussians to procure good intelligence.

Von Daun with his 36,000 Austrians hung on the skirts of the Prussian invaders, evaded battle, while harassing the supply lines and, at the same time, managed to reinforce Olmütz with both troops and supplies. In late June a Prussian convoy of food and ammunition, comprising some 3,500 wagons with some 7,000 troops as escort, set out from Niesse. Von Daun's troops attacked the convoy and were twice repulsed. On the third and main attack von Daun and Marshal-Baron Gideon von Laudon ambushed the convoy and destroyed or captured a great part of it. Some 250 wagons out of 3,500 managed to straggle through to the Prussians at Olmütz, but in spite of this Frederick was forced to raise the siege. The Prussians lost 4,500 killed and wounded (though most of this total figure was made up of prisoners), and in addition they lost more than 3,000 wagons of supplies. In contrast, the Austrian lost 400 killed or wounded.

On 1 July Frederick, perceiving that his attempt to lay siege on Olmütz was a failure, extricated his army and, in dispersed groups, they made their way back to Königsgrätz. Von Daun followed and encamped near Königsgrätz, but did not attack.

PARMA (N Italy)   War of the Polish Succession   29 June 1734
Fought between a Franco-Piedmontese army under Marshal François Coigny and an Austrian army led by Field-Marshal Count Claudius de Mercy.
Strength: French/Piedmontese 30,000; Austrians 30,000.

The war which had opened with the Russians invading E Europe had shifted to Italy in 1734 as the Austrians, Russia's ally, directed their main operations against France, Spain and Savoy. The Austrians were engaged by the French at Parma. The Austrian army suffered from lack of direction from Vienna, and leadership in the field, as Field-Marshal de Mercy was killed early in the action. The Austrians attempted four assaults on the French, but were repulsed by the French who inflicted heavy losses on their adversaries, although they too suffered high casualties. The Franco-Piedmontese lost 6,000 killed and wounded; and the Austrians 6,300 killed and wounded.

As a result, the French were able to force the Austrians to give up Milan and the Po valley, while the Spaniards drove them out of the Neapolitan provinces by the end of 1735. By the Treaty of Vienna 1738 Austria recovered Milan, but lost Naples and Sicily to Charles IV of Spain.

PENRITH (Cumbria, England)   Jacobite Rebellion (the 'Forty-five')   18 December 1745
Fought between Prince Charles Edward Stuart's rearguard (MacDonald of Glengarry's regiment), commanded by Lord George Murray, with MacPherson of Cluny's and Stewart of Ardshiel's regiments under the Duke of Perth, and detachments of three dragoon regiments of Prince William Augustus, the Duke of Cumberland's pursuing army.
Aim: Although Murray was under orders not to engage the enemy, on learning from a prisoner taken at Clifton that Cumberland was only a mile away with a 4,000-strong army, he judged it expedient to try delaying tactics with the 1,000 men at his disposal.
Battle: The battle took place after nightfall. Murray's right wing met with little opposition, and overran some of Cumberland's pickets. But his left wing met stiff but brief opposition by a party of dragoons. Finally the dragoons retreated to Cumberland's main force on the moor, and Murray was able to break off his attack and to join Prince Charles at Penrith on his return journey to Carlisle and Scotland. As to casualties, some dozen were killed and twice this number wounded on each side.
Result: This heavy skirmish checked Cumberland's pursuit of the Jacobite army, enabling the latter to continue their retreat in safety.

PETERWARDEIN (PETROVARADIN) (Vojvodina, Yugoslavia)   Ottoman Wars   5 August 1716
After the entry of Austria into the Venetian-Ottoman conflict, Prince Eugène of Savoy took 60,000 men, veterans of the War of the Spanish Succession, into the field to meet the Turkish force of 110,000 men and 164 guns, led by Darnad Ali Pasha. The experienced Austrians routed the Turks at Peterwardein (Petrovaradin), killing or wounding 20,000, and capturing 50 colours and all their guns. Austrian losses were 3,000 killed and 2,000 wounded.
The victors now turned their attention to Belgrade (BELGRADE I).

PHILIPPSBURG (Baden Württemberg, W Germany)   War of the Polish Succession   June–July 1734
In the only significant engagement along the Rhine, Philippsburg, a fortress east of the Rhine and near Karlsruhe, was besieged by a French army under the Duke of Berwick. An Austrian relief force under Prince Eugène of Savoy was unable to get through, being blocked by General Comte Maurice de Saxe.
16,000 Russian troops, the first ever seen in W Europe, joined Eugène, but his force was too cosmopolitan to achieve any worthwhile results. In July, Berwick's French troops attacked again, and although Berwick was killed (cut in two by a cannon-ball), his troops went on to capture Philippsburg in July 1834.
At the time of his defeat Prince Eugène was in his seventy-third year. This was his last battle and he died two years later, having fought over 200 battles.

PIACENZA (TREBBIA) (N Italy)   War of the Austrian Succession/Franco-Spanish Campaign in Italy   15/16 June 1746
Fought between a Spanish expeditionary army, commanded by the Count of Gages and the Infante Don Felipe, together with the French under the Marshal Jean Marquis de Maillebois, against Austria and her allies under General Prince Joseph Wenzel von Lichtenstein and Charles Emmanuel of Sardinia.
Aim: The Spaniards, with the help of France, aimed to recover their former possessions in Italy.
Battle: The Franco-Spanish forces were on the retreat before an enemy counter-offensive. After evacuating Parma, they attempted to hold Piacenza (Trebbia), Alto Monferrato and the line of the Nura River. Lichtenstein, after suffering a slight reverse at Codogno, launched an attack on Piacenza, held by Don Felipe's Spaniards. Maillebois came to his aid and a fierce twenty-four-hour battle on the shores of the Trebbia River ensued. This resulted in the rout of the Franco-Spanish forces. Maillebois and Don Felipe escaped and reached safety beyond the river Po. The French and Spanish lost 5,000 dead and wounded, and 2,000 prisoners, while the Austrians lost only 1,000 killed and wounded.
Result: This was one of the gravest defeats ever suffered by Spain at this time. News of it caused the death of Philip V and the collapse of his dreams for regaining Spain's Italian possessions.

POLISH CIVIL WAR AND RUSSIAN INVASION   1768–76
The pro-Russian government in Poland was unpopular with a group of dissident noblemen who organised themselves into the 'Confederation of the Bar' and, with the aid of the French General Charles-François Dumouriez, attempted to lead an armed insurrection against Russian religious and political aggression. Russian armed support of the Polish government was largely responsible for the failure of the movement. However, this rebellion led, in 1772, to the first partition of Poland between Frederick the Great of Prussia and Russia with guerrilla warfare continuing throughout the land, which culminated, after the second partition in 1793, with a national uprising under Tadeusz (Thaddeus) Kosciusko (see KOSCIUSKO'S POLISH UPRISING).

POLISH SUCCESSION, WAR OF THE   Italian Campaign   1734–5
Although not directly concerned with the dispute, in which France and Austria supported rival claimants to the Polish throne, Spain was allied to France and took the opportunity of pressing her claims against Austria in Italy. Following the success of the Austrians at the Battle of Parma (qv) (June 1734) and of the French at Luzzara (19 September 1734), the Spaniards won a victory over the Austrians at Bitonto (qv) which consolidated their hold over the Kingdom of Naples.

'POTATO WAR, THE'   see PRUSSIAN WAR OF THE BAVARIAN SUCCESSION

PRAGUE I (Czechoslovakia)   War of the Austrian Succession   2–6 September 1744
Fought between the Prussians under Frederick the Great and the Austrians led by Marshal Prince Charles of Lorraine.
Strength: Prussians 80,000; Austrians 20,000.
   Believing that Charles of Lorraine would soon begin an invasion from Austria with the intention of regaining Silesia, Frederick the Great entered into an alliance with Louis XV of France in August 1744, and then dispatched his armies of 80,000 men in three columns through Saxony, Silesia and Lusatia into Bohemia, converged on Prague, overwhelmed the defenders and forced their surrender in five days. Prussian casualties amounted to 6,000 killed and wounded. Austrian casualties numbered 4,000 killed and wounded, and in addition 16,000 men were captured.
   Once in possession of Prague, Frederick marched his army south on Budweis, where he was in a position to threaten the Danube valley and Vienna.

PRAGUE II (Czechoslovakia)   Seven Years' War   6 May 1756
Fought between the Prussians, under the command of Frederick the Great, and the Austrians led by Marshal Prince Charles of Lorraine.
Strength: Prussians 65,000 with 82 guns; Austrians 70,000 with 59 guns.
Aim: The Prussian aim was to capture Prague.
Battle: In a fierce and bloody struggle on the outskirts of Prague, Frederick sent his troops against the Austrians but was repulsed. Changing his tactics, Frederick then sent his cavalry to attack the right wing of the Austrians. As the latter tried to check this move, Frederick threw columns of troops into a gap in the Austrian centre and succeeded in splitting their army into two, sending them reeling back to Prague. The Prussians sustained casualties of 13,200 killed and wounded, while 14,000 Austrians were killed, wounded and captured.
Result: Frederick managed to penetrate part of the city and laid Prague under siege (see KOLIN).

PRESTON (Lancashire, England)   Jacobite Rebellion   12–14 November 1715
Fought between a mixed force of English and Scottish Jacobites under Major-General Thomas Forster, recently commissioned by John Erskine, Earl of Mar (Bobbing John), and a pro-Hanoverian army under Lt-General Sir Charles Wills and Lt-General Sir George Carpenter.
Aim: General Forster and Lord Derwentwater, supported by cavalry from the Scottish Lowlands under Lord Kenmure, and a force of Highland infantry under Brigadier Mackintosh, entered Preston on 10 November, to be joined by a number of local Jacobite adherents. It was their intention to advance on Manchester, where they had hope of further support, when the English army under General Wills trapped them in the town.
Strength: Jacobites: the English cavalry under Forster and the Scottish under Kenmure had joined forces with Brigadier Mackintosh's infantry at Kelso on 22 October; the combined forces amounted to 1,400

infantry and 600 cavalry. Of these, some 500 of Mackintosh's men deserted before the advance into England. The remainder were joined by another 200 at Preston. Total: 1,700 men; Hanoverians: Wills had under his command 6 cavalry and 1 infantry regiments. General Carpenter brought up 500 of his dragoons and was joined by a number of local supporters. Total: 2,000 men.

Battle: On hearing of the advance of the English army (on the night of 11 November) Forster and his advisers decided against defending the approach to the town over the Ribble, and concentrated on building 4 barricades in the centre of the town itself; of these, 3 were protected by 2 cannon each. On 12 November Wills directed attacks against 2 of there barricades but was repulsed. However the next day, with the arrival of General Carpenter's force, a full-scale investment of the town was undertaken. General Forster, with insufficient ammunition to withstand a siege and no hope of relief, opened negotiations for surrender. These were concluded on the following morning, and the Hanoverians entered the town in two detachments to receive the formal surrender of the Jacobites in the market-place. The Jacobites lost 17 men killed and 1,500 taken prisoner; while the Hanoverians lost 70 men killed and had the same number wounded.

Result: This battle brought to an end the Jacobite rising in the south.

PRESTONPANS (E Lothian, Scotland) Jacobite Rebellion (the 'Forty-five') 21 September 1745

In this, the first major battle of the 'Forty-five', the pro-Hanoverian army was commanded by Lt-General Sir John Cope, and the Jacobite army by Prince Charles Edward Stuart. However, as the Prince was persuaded by his commanders to remain in the rear of the battle-line, his troops were led by Lord George Murray.

Strength: Hanoverians 2,300 (including the 13th and 14th Dragoons which had already been routed from Coltbridge) with 6 pieces of artillery (manned by completely inexperienced gunners); Jacobites 2,500 without artillery.

Aim: Prince Charles, after raising his standard at Glenfinnan on 19 August, had evaded Cope's army at Inverness and marched south to Edinburgh, pursued by the Hanoverian army which now caught up with him.

Battle: The first charge by the Jacobites routed the entire Hanoverian army. In a battle lasting some six minutes the losses were: Hanoverians: 300 men killed, 500 wounded and 1,500 captured; Jacobites: 30 killed and 70 wounded.

Result: This victory enabled Prince Charles to spend six weeks in Edinburgh, recruiting more troops, and welcoming French and Irish officers with money, ammunition and 6 Swedish field-guns, in preparation for his march into England.

The engagement is known also as the Battle of Gladsmuir.

PRUSSIAN 'WAR' OF THE BAVARIAN SUCCESSION ('THE POTATO WAR') 1777–9

This bloodless war resulted from a clash which arose on the death of the Elector Maximilian III when Austria and Prussia selected different candidates to succeed him. Frederick the Great marched into Bohemia in 1778 and an Austrian army did likewise. They did nothing for two years and finally dispersed when the Treaty of Teschen was signed on 13 May 1779. As there were no battles, neither side took any prisoners, and their only booty when the armies returned to their respective countries was a crop of potatoes filched from Bohemia. Hence the descriptive term used ever since in the Prussian army–'The Potato War'.

PRUTH, THE (Romania) Russo-Ottoman Wars 2 September–October 1770

After Prince Alexander Galitzin resigned (see KAGUL) the Russian advance into Moldavia and Wallachia was commanded by Field-Marshal Count Peter Rumiantsev (Romanzov). Galitzin's own efforts to advance had twice been repulsed. But Rumiantsev, after defeating the Turks at Kagul and clearing away the Tartars from his rear, collected a well-balanced force of 60,000 men and in September 1770 advanced to the east bank of the River Pruth, a northern tributary of the Danube.

The main Turkish army, 120,000 strong under Halil Bey, was drawn up in three lines of entrenchments along the Pruth, but it covered a long front so that there were gaps between, giving the appearance of separate fortresses, not mutually supporting. By concentrating and tackling each fortified area in turn, Rumiantsev defeated the Turks in detail and cleared the line of the river. He then advanced through Moldavia and into Wallachia.

Military operations died down for the winter and, apart from the occupation of Bucharest (qv), were not resumed again in great intensity until 1773, the Turks meanwhile carrying out a debilitating and successful guerrilla campaign against the Russian communications.

PUGACHËV'S PEASANT UPRISING (SE USSR)   1773–4
Fought between Cossacks and Russian peasants led by Yemelyan I Pugachëv and Catherine the Great's Imperial Army under Field-Marshal Count Alexander Suvorov.

Pugachëv's original aim was to found an independent Cossack state in the S Urals. To win support Pugachëv, who was illiterate 'but an extremely bold and determined man' (Catherine's description written to Voltaire), claimed to be Catherine's assassinated husband, Czar Peter III, who had returned to free his people from bondage.

The revolt spread rapidly and extended well beyond Cossack country until Pugachëv's army of serfs swept across SE Russia, overrunning army garrisons and killing landlords and nobles, until in the winter of 1773–4 they reached within 120 miles of Moscow. By then Pugachëv could count on a total of 15,000 armed men. Catherine's army was engaged in fighting the Turks (1768–74), but once Suvorov had inflicted a crushing defeat on the Turks at Kostliju (qv) and Shumla and the Turks had sued for peace, Catherine could concentrate her army on counter-insurgency operations.

As the pressure on him by Suvorov's battle-experienced troops increased, Pugachëv retreated towards the Volga, destroying everything as he went. This scorched-earth policy lost him his popularity: he was betrayed by his own lieutenants in return for their lives and was captured. He was then brought to Moscow, exhibited in a cage to show that he was not the late Czar and eventually beheaded.

The Empress and her minister took vengeance on the peasants in the area of insurrection, resulting in thousands of deaths. The Empress summed up Pugachëv in these words: 'No one since Tamerlane has done more harm that he has.'

QUADRUPLE ALLIANCE War of the   Operations in Spain, Italy and the Mediterranean   1718–19
The Quadruple Alliance developed out of the Triple Alliance (qv), after Austria had joined the coalition of England, France and Holland against Spain.

The moving spirit on the Spanish side was Philip's powerful Italian minister Cardinal Alberoni, whose plans included an alliance with Russia, Turkey and Sweden against Austria, and the removal of Philip of Orléans as Regent of France in order to permit Philip V to ascend the French throne. These ambitious designs came to nothing. In the Mediterranean, Spain's initial success in Sardinia and Sicily (qv) was nullified by the destruction of the Spanish fleet off Cape Passaro (qv), which enabled the Austrians to reoccupy the island. In Spain itself a French army under the Duke of Berwick crossed the Pyrenees, occupied San Sebastián and ravaged the northern provinces, while a British force occupied Vigo (qv) and other points in Galicia.

Alberoni fell from power, and Philip was forced to renounce his claims to the French throne, to Sardinia and to Sicily, and to his former possessions in Italy, though the dukedoms of Parma, Piacenza and Tuscany were allowed later to revert to his son (later Charles III of Spain).

QUIBERON BAY (NW France)   Seven Years' War   20–2 November 1759
Fought between a British fleet under Admiral Sir Edward Hawke and the French under Admiral Marquis de Conflans.
Strength: British 23 ships of the line; French 21 ships of the line.
Aim: Admiral de Conflans commanded a French fleet gathered with a view to covering the invasion of Scotland.
Battle: Sir Edward Hawke with his fleet had been keeping watch on the French since January, but on 9 November a wild gale blew Hawke back to Torbay. De Conflans took the opportunity to sail for Quiberon Bay, where he intended to pick up a number of flat-bottomed vessels and 18,000 troops for the invasion attempt. British secret intelligence advised Hawke of the French move. He put to sea with 23 ships and on 20 November sighted de Conflans (in *Soleil Royal*) off Quiberon Bay. Conflans, realising that in the open seas his squadron would be no match for Hawke's more powerful, better trained and experienced crews, took up a defensive position in the rock-strewn Quiberon Bay. The weather was stormy, visibility bad, the coast rocky and with dangerous tidal races, but at about 10am on 20 November Hawke in *Royal George* signalled his fleet to follow him and engage the enemy.

With the gale rising and the wind shifting to the NW the French fleet was thrown into disorder. In a rock-strewn area 5 miles long and 6 miles wide, hemmed in by surf-covered islands and shoals, thousands of spectators gathered to see close on 50 storm-tossed ships of the line fight each other as best they could in an area where there was no room for manoeuvre as the grey November skies were still further darkened by the smoke from guns and burning ships. Squall after squall added to the confusion.

By 5pm in the gathering gloom the wind came again more northerly, obliging the French fleet to wear. More and more British ships poured into the bay and fighting continued in the darkness. By dawn 5 French ships had been sunk or wrecked, while of the British fleet *Resolution* and *Essex* were being destroyed by the waves on the Four Shoal.

On 22 November the weather moderated and Hawke sent in crews to burn *Soleil Royal* and *Héros*. One division of the French fleet had escaped out of the bay, but the remainder (7 ships) were hemmed in the Villaine River, where they were duly watched by the British fleet for the next twelve months. Constant grinding and pounding on the shallow river bottom eventually broke their backs. Altogether the French lost 7 ships sunk or captured, plus 7 ships which were later wrecked and 2,000 sailors killed or captured. The British had 2 ships wrecked and lost 270 sailors.

Result : The victory at Quiberon Bay put an end to French ideas of invading Britain, and extinguished the waning hopes of the Jacobites. The House of Hanover and the Protestant succession was made secure and for generations Britain was bound to remain stubbornly Protestant and opposed to all forms of 'Popery'.

RAUCOUX (ROCAUX, ROUCAUX) (Liège, Belgium)   War of the Austrian Succession   11 October 1746

Fought between the French led by Marshal Comte Maurice de Saxe, and Austro-Dutch forces commanded by Marshal Prince Charles of Lorraine.

Strength : French 120,000; Austrians/Dutch 80,000.

Aim : The French under de Saxe had taken Antwerp and were sweeping through the region between Brussels and the Meuse (Maas) River. Charles of Lorraine sought by a major effort to stop the French.

Battle : Served with good intelligence, an arm to which he always gave the highest priority, de Saxe learned of the approach of the army of Charles of Lorraine, and moved his forces to Raucoux (Rocaux, Roucaux), where he met the enemy. On 11 October 1746 the French attacked and decisively defeated the Austro-Dutch forces, pursuing them to the Meuse. French casualties numbered 5,000 killed and wounded; and Austro-Dutch casualties were 5,000 killed and wounded.

Result : The Austro-Dutch objective was not achieved. Both armies now went into winter quarters, camping on opposite banks of the Meuse River.

REVAL (TALLIN) (USSR)   Russo-Swedish War   spring 1790

Fought between a Swedish fleet under the Duke of Sudermania and the Russian garrison and fleet under Admiral Chitchakov.

Aim : The Swedish fleet sought to reduce the port of Reval (Tallin) by sea.

Battle : The Swedish fleet attacked Reval but Russian shore batteries and the fleet under Admiral Chitchakov drove them off with considerable loss.

Result : The battle proved a prelude to the maritime campaign culminating in Svensksund II (qv) with a fleet rehabilitated by Gustavus III, after the defeat at Svensksund I (qv) in 1789.

REVOLAX (S Finland)   Russo-Swedish Wars   27 April 1808

Fought between the Russians under General Bonlatov and the Swedes under General Klingspar.

Strength : Russians 4,000; Swedes 8,000.

Aim : The Swedes sought to ambush the Russians.

Battle : Klinspar surprised an isolated Russian column and surrounded it. The Russians tried to cut their way out, but fewer than 1,000 men succeeded in escaping. Bonlatov fell in the battle.

Result : The Swedish objective was achieved.

RIMNIK (RIMNICU SARAT, RIMNITZ) (E Romania)   Russo-Ottoman Wars   22 September 1789

Fought between a Turkish army under the Grand Vizier and a Russo-Austrian army under the Prince of Saxe-Coburg and Field-Marshal Count Alexander Suvorov.

Strength : Turks 60,000; Russians/Austrians 25,000.

Aim : The Allied army sought to put to rout the Turkish army.

Battle: After Martinesti (qv) the Allies chased and attacked the Turks as they crossed the Rimnik (Rimnitz, Rimnicu Sãrat) River, some 50 miles east of Galati (Galatz), and more or less wiped out the Sultan's troops. The whole army was killed, captured or dispersed, and 8,000 were drowned in the Rimnik. This was, in effect, a pursuit after a victory carried out with intense ferocity, driven on by the insatiable Suvorov.

Result: The Turkish Sultan, Abdul-Hamid, died, crushed by defeat. His successor, Selim III, signed a peace treaty at Jassy, three years later, which left the Turks' European territories extending only as far as the Dniester River. Catherine the Great rewarded Count Suvorov with the title Count Rimniksky.

ROSSBACH (Saxony-Anhalt, E Germany)   Seven Years' War   5 November 1757

Fought between the Austrians, commanded by Prince Joseph of Saxe-Hildburghausen, and the French, commanded by Marshal Prince Charles de Soubise against the Prussians and Hanoverians under their Emperor, Frederick the Great.

Strength: Austrians/French 64,000 with 80 guns; Prussians/Hanoverians 21,000.

Aim: Frederick had taken up a position opposite the French and Austrians to cover their objective, Saxony. The latter, who were greatly superior in numbers and guns, aimed to turn the Prussian left flank and continue their advance into Saxony.

Battle: Frederick, aware of the Allied intention to encircle his left flank, made a move to withdraw east of Rossbach. When the Allies closed in they met strong Prussian artillery and infantry fire. Then the Prussian and Hanoverian cavalry under Friedrich Wilhelm von Seydlitz charge the Allied right flank and threw it into confusion. Frederick then launched his main force at the Allied centre. The superior discipline, drill and *esprit de corps* of the Prussians prevailed and the Allies were routed. The Austro-French forces sustained casualties of 3,000 dead and wounded, and had 5,000 prisoners taken. Prussian and Hanoverian casualties numbered 500 men.

Result: The Austro-French army failed in their objective. Frederick was now able to move quickly to Silesia, where the Austrians were threatening Breslau (qv).

ROTTOFREDO (Piacenza, Italy)   War of the Austrian Succession   July 1746–12 August 1746

Fought between the Austrians under General Prince Joseph Wenzel von Lichtenstein and the French under Marshal Marquis de Maillebois.

Strength: Austrians 30,000; French 26,000.

The Austrians had been pursuing the retreat of the French in Italy throughout July and early August of 1746. On 12 August the rearguard was attacked by the Austrians and, after a violent struggle, was defeated with heavy losses. The Austrians suffered 4,000 killed and wounded, the French 8,000 killed, wounded and captured, plus 19 guns taken.

This defeat led to the surrender of the 8,000 French garrison of Piacenza (qv) to the Austro-Sardinian forces.

RUSSO-OTTOMAN WARS   4 October 1768–74; 1787–92

War of 1768–74

Russia had been stirring up trouble and subversion throughout the Turkish Empire including supporting revolts in Montenegro, Georgia, Crimea, Bessarabia and Greece. The Turks were still engaged in a war with the Persians, but when the Russians actually invaded Bessarabia in hot pursuit of some fugitive Poles, on 4 October 1768 Sultan Mustapha declared war.

Both sides were slow to react. However, in 1769 Catherine ordered a general invasion. Prince Alexander Galitzin, with an army of 65,000, was directed to the fortress of Chotin (qv) and on to occupy Moldavia. Field-Marshal Count Peter Rumiantsev (Romanzov) was sent to Azov and Taganrog. A third army of 11,000 men was sent to occupy Poland to prevent her aiding the Turks. A fourth army under Major-General Medem advanced from Tsaritsin (Volgograd) into the Karbada and the Kuban. A fifth army under General Gottlieb Heinrich Todleben was directed on Tiflis (Tibilisi) in the central Caucasus to attack Erzurum and Trebizond (Trabzon) in Turkey in concert with the Christian Georgian princes. At the same time money, arms, ammunition and officers were sent to the Bosnians and Montenegrins to encourage them to revolt. After initial successes on land Catherine sent a fleet through the Mediterranean to stir up trouble in Morea (qv) and threaten the Dardanelles (see LEMNOS).

Egypt, Tripolitania, Syria and Algiers also revolted. But in spite of defeats and enormous casualties, such was the resilience of the Turks and their enlightened Sultan Mustapha III, that from 1771 to 1773 the war turned in their favour. Although Ottoman domination in the Crimea was destroyed, the Russians were temporarily chased beyond the Danube. Ali Bey of Egypt was defeated at Cairo and the remaining revolts were put down with skilled counter-insurgency methods at which the Turks were adept.

But in spite of a revolt by the Don Cossacks under Yemelyan Pugachëv (PUGACHËV'S PEASANT UPRISING)–who were, in turn, helped by the Turks–which was suppressed with the utmost ferocity by Field-Marchal Count Alexander Suvorov, under this same ferocious commander Russia made a recovery in the Balkans just in time for her to benefit by the eventual peace treaty.

But Mustapha III died on 21 September 1774. His brother, Abdul-Hamid, who succeeded him (in January 1774, when he was too ill to rule), after suffering defeats at Kostliju (qv)–at the hands of Suvorov–and elsewhere in the Balkans, signed the Treaty of Kutchuk-Kainardji on 17 July 1774, whereby the Turks gave up the fortress of Kinburn (qv), Kertch and Yenikale (qv) in the Crimea, and yielded to the Russians in Bessarabia and in the Kuban. Finally the Turks had to agree to concede what was a consummate victory for the Russians: Catherine was now permitted to possess a Black Sea fleet with bases. Austria, on hearing the terms of the treaty, claimed and gained Bukovina.

This was considered to mark the beginning of the dissolution of the Turkish Empire, at least in Europe. But it was a long time dying.

War of 1787–92

Russian encroachments on Georgia and demands that Turkey should cede that province and Bessarabia led to war. The Austrians joined the Russians and the combined armies were ultimately successful on land after forcing the Turks to withdraw to the Danube. At sea, the notable American raider John Paul Jones fought with the Russian fleet (see KINBURN and LIMAN) which gained the upper hand. A revolt in Morea, Greece, hampered Turkish operations in 1790 and the war ended with the Treaty of Jassy, wherein Jassy and Moldavia were returned to Turkey but Russia kept all conquered territory east of the Dniester.

RUSSO-PERSIAN WARS   1804–13

This long conflict resulted from the Russian annexation of Georgia in 1800. The country had previously been under the suzerainty of Persia and her efforts to support the anti-Russian factions led to armed conflict. The course of events was as follows:

1804: The Russian army under General Sisianov met the Persians under their able commander Prince Abbas Mirza in the inconclusive three-day Battle of Echmiaozin. During that year Shah Fath Ali provided Abbas Mirza with strong reinforcements which enabled him to relieve Erivan and compel the Russians to raise the siege.

1812: On 31 October the Russians surprised and routed the Persians under Abbas Mirza on the Aras River in the Battle of Aslanduz.

1813: By the Treaty of Gulistan signed on 12 October the Persians ceded Georgia and other trans-Caucasian provinces, including Baku, to Russia.

RUSSO-SWEDISH WAR   1741–3

Russia supported Austria in the War of Succession, and Sweden, prompted by France, joined the other side hoping to avenge the defeats sustained in the Great Northern War. The conclusion of the Turkish war released substantial Russian forces; and Sweden, whose army was initially only about 15,000 strong, was utterly defeated and forced to make peace, ceding part of Finland as far as the river Kyemmene to Russia at the Treaty of Abo on 7 August 1743.

RUSSO-SWEDISH (-DANISH) WAR   1788–90

In order to forestall any possible moves against his country by Russian or Prussian forces, Gustavus III, King of Sweden, invaded Russian Finland in 1788. Daring moves by land and sea at first brought success to the Swedes, and the Russians, already at war with Turkey thanks to Catherine II's policies, became concerned. The Swedes were finally repulsed at Svataipol (Sebastopol) and then, following an alliance contracted with the Russians, Denmark attacked Sweden, further hampering them.

On 24 August 1789 the first naval battle of Svenskund (SVENSKUND I) was fought. The Swedish fleet under Admiral Count Karl Ehrensvärd was pitted against a Russian fleet under Admiral Krose (Kruze). The Swedes were decisively defeated with a loss of 33 ships, and Ehrensvärd was dismissed. On 2–9 July

1790 a second battle was fought (SVENSKUND II). Gustavus had completely rebuilt his navy which was under the command of the Duke of Sudermania. The Swedes attacked in single file in a narrow channel. The attack was successful until a powder ship exploded and the Swedish line collapsed, forcing the fleet to take refuge in the then Swedish-held fortress of Sveaborg (Helsinki). On 9 July the Swedish fleet put to sea once more. The Russians advanced on them in crescent formation, but Swedish gunners blew holes in the Russian line and the 195 Swedish vessels destroyed the Russian navy of 151 ships piecemeal, in one of the great naval fights of Scandinavian history. The Russians lost 53 ships sunk or captured, largely through the poor leadership of Prince of Nassau-Siegen, an adventurer in Russian service. Vice-Admiral (William) Sidney Smith, a Briton serving with the Swedes, played an outstanding part in the battle.

On 15 August 1790 the Treaty of Verela (Wereloe) was signed, restoring the *status quo ante*.

SAHAY (Czechoslovakia)   War of the Austrian Succession   27 May 1742
Fought between the French, commanded by Marshal Duc de Broglie, and the Austrians, led by General Prince Johann Lobkowitz.
Strength: French 20,000; Austrians 10,000.
   Lobkowitz had established a camp of 10,000 men at Sahay, near Budweis, to cover the approaches to Prague, 65 miles to the south. De Broglie, made aware of this fact, advanced on the camp. The Austrians had been forewarned and had brought up artillery. The engagement began at about 6pm and lasted until darkness stopped further action. Lobkowitz, suspecting the French intended to cut his lines of communication to Budweis, retreated, leaving the French to occupy Sahay. Each side lost about 400 men killed and wounded.

SECCHIA, RIVER (Modena, Italy)   War of the Polish Succession   14 September 1734
After the Battle of Guastella (qv), the French, having suffered severely, moved to the banks of the river Secchia, near Modena, to rest and recuperate.
   An Austrian force under Count Koningsegg moved silently by night and surprised the French while still in bivouac. The French, under Marshal Duc de Broglie, were routed: 5,000 prisoners, 100 guns and all their stores, baggage and ammunition were taken.

SESKAR (Gulf of Finland)   Russo-Swedish War   1790
Fought between the Swedish fleet under the Duke of Sudermania and a Russian squadron under Admiral Krose (Kruze).
Aim: The Russians sought to cripple the Swedish fleet.
Battle: In a battle lasting from dawn until after nightfall, the Swedes were totally defeated.
Result: The Swedish fleet was severely weakened.

SEVEN YEARS' WAR   1756–63
The war, also called the Third Silesian War, was prompted by Prussia's increasing power and territorial gains under Frederick the Great. Austria, France, Russia, Sweden and Saxony formed a coalition to curb Frederick who was joined by England, since the latter was already at war with France in North America. Spain joined the coalition in 1761.
   In a war fought mainly in E Europe, the Allies were ultimately defeated after seven years of fighting, and the *status quo ante* was restored. Frederick retained Silesia, still a bone of contention.
   The war established Frederick as one of the great military leaders in history. His superiority on land laid the foundations for the unification of Germany. At sea, the English also gained mastery, consolidating the beginning of their empire at the expense of the French.

SHERIFFMUIR (Perthshire, Scotland)   Jacobite Rebellion   13 November 1715
Fought between the Jacobite army under John Erskine, Earl of Mar, and the pro-Hanoverian army under John Campbell, Duke of Argyll.
Strength: Jacobites: The first line consisted of 10 battalions of infantry; the second of 5, supported by the Gordons and the Mackenzies. Both lines were protected on the flanks by cavalry. Total: 8,000 men; Hanoverians: The first line had 6 battalions with 3 cavalry squadrons on each wing; the second, 2 infantry divisions with 1 cavalry squadron on each wing. Total: 3,300 men.
Aim: After raising the Stuart Royal Standard at Braemar in the central Highlands of Scotland on 6 September, Mar had retired to Perth to collect an army. In this he was successful but, recognising the

necessity of leading this army into action if they were not to drift home again, he marched south on 10 November in the hope of defeating Argyll and joining up with the Lowland Jacobites.
Battle: Sheriffmuir is famous for its indecisive result, the left wing of each army being driven off the field of battle. In the centre the Hanoverians gained some advantage by a flanking movement, but both the main armies disengaged in fair order. Some 500 men were killed and wounded on each side. This engagement is also known as the Battle of Dunblane.
Result: Though the Earl of Mar still had his army intact, he had been prevented from marching south, and now faced the gradual disintegration of his forces. The day before the battle Inverness had been retaken by the Hanoverians, and the defeat at Preston (qv) put an end to any hopes of success farther south. The arrival of the Chevalier de St George did nothing to inspire his waning cause, and on 4 February 1716 he and Mar set sail for France.

SICILY, INVASION OF (Italy)   War of the Triple Alliance   July 1718
In July 1718, following the successful occupation by the Spanish of Sardinia a 30,000-strong Spanish expeditionary force under the Marquis of Lede invaded Sicily, with the aim of using it as a base for operation against S Italy. The Spaniards captured Messina but, early in August, an Austrian force of 3,000, landed by a British fleet, blockaded the city and in October 1719 captured it.
On 26 August 1718 the Spanish fleet was destroyed by Vice-Admiral Sir George Byng's squadron off Cape Passaro (qv).

SIKAJOKI (S Finland)   Russo-Swedish Wars   18 April 1808
Fought between the Russians under General Frederick William Buxhoevden and the Swedes under General Klingspar.
Aim: The Swedes sought to expel the Russians from Finland.
Battle: The Russians moved out on to the ice at the mouth of the Sikajoki river with the aim of outflanking the Swedes. At the same time they attacked from the front. Both assaults were repulsed after eight hours of fighting, Klingspar taking the offensive and driving the Russians from the field. The Russians sustained heavy losses. Swedish losses were 1,000 killed and wounded.
Result: Despite the Swedish victory, Finland was ceded to Russia in 1809.

SOOR (SOHR) (Bohemia, Czechoslovakia)   War of the Austrian Succession   30 September 1745
The Austrians and Saxons, commanded by Marshal Prince Charles of Lorraine, brother-in-law of Empress Maria Theresa, fought the Prussians under Frederick the Great.
Strength: Austrians/Saxons 40,000; Prussians 20,000.
Aim: The Prussians had inflicted a major defeat on the Austrians at Hohenfriedberg (qv) on 4 June 1745, but the Empress Maria Theresa still had ambitions to reclaim Silesia and sent Charles of Lorraine to overcome the Prussians.
Battle: The Austrians surprised the Prussian army encamped in the valley near the village of Soor (Sohr) and managed to encircle it completely. Frederick, with his highly trained men who could fire two volleys to every shot fired at them, managed to form his army into a single strong thrust at one point in the Austrian circle and to break through. Prince Charles was thus forced to retreat. The Austrians lost 800 killed, 2,780 wounded, 3,000 captured and 22 guns. The Saxons lost 755 killed, wounded or captured. Prussian casualties were 900 killed, 2,700 wounded and 300 missing.
Result: This Austrian defeat did not deter the Empress Maria Theresa. She sent reinforcements to Charles, and sent another Austrian army to join a Saxon force in W Saxony. The two forces marched towards Berlin. Frederick then marched from Silesia into Saxony, forcing Charles of Lorraine to halt and face eastward to counter Frederick's move.

SPANISH-BRITISH WAR   1779
Following France, on 21 June 1779 Spain entered into the Anglo-American conflict, but she did not recognise the independence of the United States because of her own colonies in N America which would be affected. As it turned out this decision to declare war on Britain, without obtaining the friendship of the embryonic United States, which was to be a boon to France during the next 160 years, initiated a long period of Spanish decline.

SPANISH WAR WITH BRITAIN AND FRANCE   1727–9

This Spanish war with Britain and France, in which hardly any blood was shed, was the result of the refusal by France and Britain to allow Spain to claim the Italian duchies granted her in the Treaty of The Hague (1720). The Spaniards besieged Gibraltar and there were some naval engagements in the West Indies. Hostilities were over by May 1727 and negotiations began on March 1728. By the Treaty of Seville, signed in 1729, Spain's claim to the Italian duchies was recognised and Britain's possession of Gibraltar was confirmed.

STIRLING (Stirlingshire, Scotland)   Jacobite Rebellion (the 'Forty-five')   3 January–1 February 1746

Encouraged by the acquisition of a train of artillery (brought from France by Lord John Drummond), Prince Charles Edward Stuart decided to invest Stirling Castle which was held for the Government by Major-General William Blakeney.

The town, defended by 500 Militia and Volunteers, fell immediately, but the castle presented more difficulty. The Jacobite artillery commander, Colonel James Grant, held that there was only one practical site for the artillery. As the use of this site would endanger the town, the proposal drove the townspeople to strong protest. A second site, on Gowan Hill to the north of the castle, was proposed by Chevalier Mirabel de Gordon, a French artillery officer, and to this inept suggestion the Prince acquiesced.

The siege was temporarily interrupted by the arrival of Lt-General Henry Hawley with his Hanoverian army. Leaving 1,000 men at Stirling under the Duke of Perth, Prince Charles met and defeated Hawley at Falkirk (qv) on the 17th, and returned to the siege. On the 18th the garrison commander rejected a call to surrender and, eleven days later, three of Gordon's batteries on Gowan Hill opened fire. Half an hour later, under withering return fire from the superior guns in the castle, they were abandoned.

Three days later (1 February) the Jacobite army began its retreat to Inverness, leaving a holding garrison in the town of Stirling itself.

STRALSUND (E Germany)   Great Northern War   19 July–December 1715

Returning to Sweden after a long absence, Charles XII of Sweden sought to rebuild the military strength of the country. In July 1715 the Baltic port of Stralsund in Pomerania with a garrison of 9,000 was besieged by 36,000 men under Frederick William of Prussia and Frederick IV of Denmark. The Allies also captured the island of Rügen which commanded the town. Charles decided to retake the position but his attack was beaten off, the whole of his assault force being killed or captured and he himself being seriously wounded. On 10 October the Allies captured the outworks of the town and by 20 October the place was no longer deemed defensible. Charles escaped to Sweden by boat and in December 1715 the garrison surrendered.

SVENSKSUND I (USSR-Finnish border)   Russo-Swedish War   24 August 1789

Fought between a Swedish fleet under Admiral Count Karl Ehrensvärd and a Russian fleet under Prince Charles Nassau-Siegen and Admiral Krose (Kruze).

Gustavus III of Sweden, in spite of setbacks, was still intent on advancing along the southern coast of Finland and attacking St Petersburg (Leningrad). While his army attacked (and was repulsed) at Friedrichsham (Frederikshamn) between Kotka and Vyborg, the Swedish fleet sailed into the Svensksund (Suenske Sound) with an assault force in flat-bottomed boats. A Russian fleet under Nassau-Siegen and Krose attacked and destroyed 33 Swedish vessels. Ehrensvärd managed to withdraw the greater part of his invasion force but, on 1 September, was again attacked at Högsfoz and both the navy and army were forced to retreat, although the latter settled down in winter quarters on the frontiers of Russia.

SVENSKSUND II (USSR-Finnish border)   Russo-Swedish War   2–10 July 1790

In the spring of 1790 Gustavus III of Sweden was determined to persist in his attempts to capture Catherine the Great's capital, St Petersburg (Leningrad). After a successful naval engagement in the Gulf of Finland on 15 May and after making two unsuccessful assaults on the fortress of Friederichsham (Frederikshamn) on 17–18 May, he reached Vyborg on 2 June 1790 and disembarked a division of troops at Blörke, 40 miles west of St Petersburg.

Two Russian fleets awaited him, one at Kronstadt and the other in Revel. He ordered Duke Charles of Sudermania, commanding his naval forces, to prevent the junction of the two Russian fleets. The Swedish fleet consisted of 19 ships of the line, 27 frigates and a large number of gunboats and galleys totalling in all 2,000 guns. However, on 6 June when the Duke of Sudermania's fleet entered Vyborg sound, the two

Russian fleets under Prince Charles Nassau-Siegen and Admiral Chitchakov totalling 30 ships of the line and 18 frigates, formed junction and blockaded the sound.

By the end of June the Swedish fleet in the Bay of Vyborg was reduced to extremities. Some, including Duke Charles, counselled capitulation. But eventually Duke Charles decided to try to break out. This he did on 3 July. Owing to Chitchakov's neglect, the Swedes brought the blockading Russian fleet to an engagement, but at the cost of 7 ships of the line, 3 frigates, 30 galleys and gunboats, and 6,500 soldiers on board, including most of the Swedish Royal Guard. While the larger ships had tried to reach the open sea, the galleys and gunboats took refuge in the Suenske Sound (Svensksund, to the west of Vyborg Sound) which was protected by rocky reefs. On 9 July Nassau-Siegen decided to pursue these ships into these dangerous waters where by now the Swedish fleet, which still had 195 ships to the Russian 151, had re-formed into crescent formation to protect their sanctuary. As the Russians entered the sound they were destroyed piecemeal by superior gunnery from ships protected by rocks from direct assault. The battle continued on into 10 July. Altogether 55 Russian ships were captured and more were destroyed, while 14,000 Russians were killed or captured.

This was the greatest sea fight and naval victory in Scandinavian history. The French Revolution having broken out meanwhile, Gustavus decided not to pursue his advantage and made peace with Russia at the Treaty of Varela (Ivereloe) on the Kyemmene River on 15 August 1790.

TEMESVAR (TIMISOARA) (Banat, W Romania)   Austro-Turkish War   August–October 1716
Fought between the Austrians under Prince Eugène of Savoy and the Turks under the Grand Vizier Ali Kumurji.

After winning the decisive Battle of Peterwardein (qv) Prince Eugène turned on the last Turkish stronghold in Hungary, Temesvar (Timisoara) and, after a brief siege of six weeks, overcame the garrison. He then advanced on Belgrade (BELGRADE I).

TORGAU (Saxony-Anhalt, E Germany)   Seven Years' War   3 November 1760
Fought between Frederick the Great of Prussia and Marshal Leopold von Daun of Austria.
Strength: Prussians 45,000; Austrians 64,000.
Aim: Frederick the Great marched to relieve Berlin, his capital, which had been seized by the Austrians and Russians, but the latter left Berlin and moved to Torgau. Frederick intended to send half his force around the Austrian right and attack their rear while General Hans von Ziethen, with the other half of the Prussians, was to attack the Austrian front.
Battle: The Prussians, under Frederick, moving to the attack became confused and disorganised as a result of bad weather and faulty timing, giving the Austrians time to re-group. A small Austrian force had attracted the attention of Ziethen and he opened fire prematurely. Frederick, believing this was the main assault, sent his own troops in piecemeal against the Austrian rear. All Frederick's attacks were repulsed and he committed his reserves to action. As nightfall came Ziethen at last reached his intended position and attacked. Frederick, thereupon, managed to renew his attacks in the dark. The Austrian front collapsed; von Daun retreated and crossed the Elbe. The Prussians lost 13,000 killed and wounded; while the Austrians had 4,200 killed and wounded, as well as 7,000 prisoners taken.
Result: Winter was at hand and both adversaries were exhausted. Thus, the campaign ended. Frederick regained Saxony.

TOULON (France)   War of the Austrian Succession   19–22 February 1743
Fought between a French fleet commanded by Admiral de la Bruyère de Court, together with a Spanish fleet, and an English fleet commanded by Vice-Admiral Thomas Matthews.
Strength: French 15 ships, Spanish 12 ships; British 27 ships of the line + 8 frigates.

Late in 1742 an English fleet blockaded Toulon after Admiral Matthews had chased a Spanish squadron of 12 ships into the harbour, where they joined a French flotilla of 15 ships. Four months later, on 19 February 1743, the combined fleets came out to sea. After a three-day chase Matthews came up with the enemy and ordered the signal for line of battle. Matthews then abandoned the line of battle himself and bore down on the enemy's rear. The ships of his own division stationed immediately ahead and astern followed his example, but all his other ships fell into a state of complete confusion and the battle, lasting six hours, was inconclusive. The ambiguous orders, the inadequacy of the signalling system, plus the disobedience and dissension among senior officers (particularly Vice-Admiral Richard Lestock), was mainly responsible for the unsuccessful action. The Franco-Spanish Allies inflicted heavier casualties and greater damage on the English than they suffered themselves, although they lost 1 ship to Captain Edward Hawke.

For two days more the fleets remained in sight of each other, but Matthews then abandoned the chase, claiming that he did not want to leave the coasts of France and Italy unprotected. Subsequently Matthews, Lestock and 4 captains were court-martialled. Matthews and his captains were found guilty and cashiered, but Lestock was acquitted–much to the astonishment and perplexity of the Service.

TRIPLE ALLIANCE, WAR OF THE   1717
The Triple Alliance was formed between England, France and Holland against Spain, whose King, Philip V, aspired to regain Spain's former possessions in Italy and the Mediterranean and also to succeed to the French throne.

After a Spanish expeditionary army had attacked the Austrian forces in Sardinia and Sicily (qv), Austria joined the anti-Spanish coalition, thus converting it into a Quadruple Alliance (qv).

TURKO-RUSSIAN WAR   1806–12
A dispute between the two countries over Wallachia, Moldavia and Bessarabia was inflamed by the French Ambassador to the Porte.
1806: On 6 November Turkey declared war and Russian troops immediately invaded Wallachia and Moldavia.
1807: In February and March Britain intervened. Vice-Admiral Sir John Duckworth took a British fleet through the Dardanelles, forcing a passage after a fierce action with the Turkish forts. Vice-Admiral Sir (William) Sidney Smith, in command of the rear division, took a prominent part in the action. Duckworth delivered a twenty-four-hour ultimatum to Turkey, ordering her to make peace with Russia and to dismiss the French Ambassador. Sultan Selim III resisted the ultimatum and the population of Constantinople lined 1,000 guns along the sea-wall. The British fleet suffered some damage before Duckworth withdrew into the Mediterranean, being mauled once again as he passed through the Dardanelles. On 30 June a Russian fleet under Admiral Dmitri Seniavin defeated a slightly bigger Turkish fleet in the Battle of Lemnos. In August there was an armistice, largely due to the mediation of Napoleon at Tilsit. Russian forces drew back from Wallachia and Moldavia. The Turks retired to Adrianople (Edirne).
1809–12: During these years there was sporadic warfare in which Russia generally gained the upper hand.

On 28 May 1812 the Treaty of Bucharest (Bucaresti) was signed under British mediation. Bessarabia was given to Russia, but Wallachia and Moldavia remained Turkish. The Russians were able to reinforce their forces opposing the French invasion.

UKRAINE CAMPAIGNS OF COUNT MÜNNICH   Austro-Russian-Turkish War   1737–8
Fought between the Russians under Marshal Count Burkhardt von Münnich and the Turks under overall command of the Grand Vizier, Al-Haji Mohammed.

In 1737 Count Münnich advanced towards the Euxine River, and laid siege to and captured the fortress of Ochakov on the Black Sea. Then, owing to disagreements with his allies, the Austrians, he ceased active operations for the year while many of his men died of disease or were picked off by Tartar guerrillas. Münnich withdrew for the winter.

In 1738 Münnich again crossed the Bug River and, in an effort to invade Moldavia, was defeated at Bender I (qv) on the Dniester River. Through lack of organised supplies he was again forced to retire, losing most of his artillery.

In 1739 Münnich, collecting a well-found army of 68,000 at Kiev, crossed the Bug, met an army of 90,000 Turks in a pitched battle at Khotin (Stavutshan, Stavuchany) on 17 August and decisively defeated them. Pursuing his defeated enemy Münnich captured Jassy, the capital of Moldavia, and was preparing to advance south through Wallachia when the Austrians, whose Emperor Charles VI was sick, and whose armies had been beaten at Banyaluka and Valievo, became alarmed at these Russian successes, and started peace negotiations with the Turks, which resulted in the Treaty of Belgrade between Austria and Turkey on 18 September 1739.

The Turkish army, which had been successfully fighting the Austrians, was now available to strike at Münnich's right flank. This forced the Russians to make peace at the Treaty of Nissa on 3 October 1739, wherein they surrendered all their conquests save the fortress of Azov. The Russians also were forced to agree, under British pressure supporting the Sultan, not to build a Black Sea fleet. This ended the Austro-Russian-Turkish War.

USHANT (OUESSANT) I (off coast of France)   War of the American Revolution   27 July 1778
A British fleet of 30 sail under Admiral Lord Keppel met a French force of equal strength under Admiral Count d'Orvilliers off the Coast of Brittany, 70 miles to the west of Ushant (Ouessant). After an inconclusive fight which lasted all day both sides drew off to repair damage. No ships were lost.

In this the first naval battle of the war between France and England the tactic of the French ships was to fire at their opponents' masts and rigging with the result that the British ships were so damaged that they could not tack, and the French could sail away. The high standard of French seamanship and discipline had come as a disagreeable surprise to their enemies. Owing to public indignation at the failure of the British fleet Keppel was tried by court-martial but acquitted. The court found that the charge was 'malicious and ill-founded' and that Keppel had behaved as 'a judicious, brave and experienced officer'.

USHANT (OUESSANT) II (off coast of France)   War of the American Revolution   14 December 1781
On 14 December 1781 Admiral Comte de Guichen sailed from Brest with 21 ships of the line to escort a large convoy of merchantmen and transports across the Atlantic. One hundred and fifty miles off Ushant, Rear-Admiral Richard Kempenfeldt in *Victory*, who was maintaining the blockade of the French ports with 11 ships of the line, appeared through the foggy haze in such a position where he felt he could, by sailing astern of de Guichen's fleet, cut off the merchantmen and destroy many of them. This he did while de Guichen's fleet was out of range. Next morning, on seeing the size of the French fleet, Kempenfeldt thought it prudent to sail for England with his numerous prizes, for which he was criticised.

VALIEVO (VALJEVO) (Yugoslavia)   Austro-Russian-Turkish War   1737
Fought between the Austrians under Marshal Count Friedrich von Seckendorf and the Turks under the Grand Vizier, Al-Haji Mohammed.

At the same time as the Austrians were ostensibly acting as peace-makers to negotiate an end to the war between Russia and Turkey, they amassed armies on the Turkish frontiers and invaded Serbia, Bosnia and Wallachia. In Bosnia the Austrians under von Seckendorf, with 26,000 infantry, 15,000 cavalry and 3,000 local irregulars, were hopelessly beaten by 30,000 battle-trained Ottomans and Janisseries at Valievo (Valjevo) and Banyaluka in the autumn of 1737, and were driven ignominiously back over their frontiers.

After further defeats at Konieh and Kroszka (qv), and in spite of Fabian tactics by Count Lothar Konigsegg-Rothenfels, the Austrians were beaten all along the line. After protracted negotiations (see also BELGRADE II) a peace was patched up at Belgrade on 18 September 1739 in which the Austrians gave up Belgrade, which had been originally captured by Prince Eugène (BELGRADE I), and also Serbia, Austrian Wallachia and the fortresses of Orsova and Shabatz.

At the start of the war Austria had over 275 generals and 20 highly paid field-marshals, but the administration and readiness for war had been completely neglected. By injecting an unprepared army into somebody else's war the Emperor Charles VI had lost all the advantages painfully gained by Prince Eugène of Savoy in the previous war with the Turks, culminating in the Treaty of Passarowitz in 1718.

VELLETRI (central Italy)   War of the Austrian Succession   11 August 1744
Fought between the Austrians, under General Prince Johann Lobkowitz and Marshal Count Maximilian von Browne and a Spanish-Neapolitan army commanded by King Charles IV of the Kingdom of the Two Sicilies and General Count John de Gages.
Strength: Austrians 6,000; Spanish/Neapolitans 6,000.
Aim: The Austrians were trying to break the stalemate in the hostilities by carrying out a surprise raid on the Allied camp with the object of taking Charles IV prisoner.
Battle: Von Browne led an élite detachment through the Alban hills from San Gennaro to the outskirts of Velletri, 20 miles south of Rome. Browne was able to approach the town through the wild countryside without creating a reaction from the enemy sentries. In one of the ironies of war, von Browne first came up against two Spanish regiments of Irishmen like himself. A fierce mêlée took place at the southern entrance to Velletri, which gave Charles IV time to escape from the town. The Austrians managed to penetrate into Velletri, but there Croatian irregulars decided to engage in plundering the town. This gave time for some of the Allied officers to rally their troops in a square in the north of the town, and to order the rest of their forces, which were outside Velletri, to close in on the town from the west.

Von Browne had ascertained that the steep slopes would not allow his cavalry to circle round to the northern gates of Velletri so that he could take the Allied forces in the rear. His troops engaged in the street fighting inside the town were doing badly, so von Browne decided he would withdraw with what booty his

troops had collected, and with his wounded and prisoners he retreated to San Gennaro. The Austrians lost 500 killed and wounded. The Spanish-Neapolitan forces had 2,000 men killed and wounded, plus 600 captured.
Result: The Austrians did not succeed in their objective.

VIGO (Galicia, Spain)   War of the Quadruple Alliance   September 1719
In September 1719, while Spain was fighting England's partners in the Quadruple Alliance (qv) in Italy, a British expeditionary force of 4,000 troops under Major-General Lord Cobham was sent from England against NW Spain (Galicia). Cobham's plan had been to attack Corunna (La Coruña), but finding the fortifications there too strong, he sailed on to Vigo which he invested and captured.

After a short occupation of this port and other towns in Galicia, the expedition returned home with a quantity of captured stores and arms which had been intended for the Jacobite Rebellion in Scotland.

WARBURG (N Rhine-Westphalia, W Germany)   Seven Years' War   31 July 1760
Fought between the Prussians under Field-Marshal Prince Ferdinand, Duke of Brunswick, supported by British cavalry under John Manners, Marquis of Granby, and the French under Chevalier de Muy.

Prince Ferdinand of Brunswick continued to guard W Prussia against French attacks. He was aided by a contingent of British cavalry under the Marquis of Granby, the successor to the incompetent and cowardly Lord George Sackville who had refused to charge at Minden (qv). A new French threat emerged in the summer of 1760 when a force of 30,000 men under de Muy advanced once more on Hanover. In slightly superior force, the Prussians met their attackers at Warburg, where the French were defeated. This victory was mainly achieved by the competent performance of the British cavalry led by Granby, which enveloped both French flanks and forced then to retreat with the loss of 3,000 casualties including 1,500 prisoners and 10 guns.

Thus the British cavalry regained their reputation lost at Minden. The French were then driven back to the Rhine.

WHITEHAVEN (Cumbria, England)   American War of Independence   April–May 1778
Fought between the British and John Paul Jones in USS *Ranger*.

The American naval raider John Paul Jones in *Ranger* entered the Irish Sea in order to prey upon British shipping. After securing a number of prizes, including the British sloop *Drake*, Paul Jones raided the port of Whitehaven on the Cumbrian coast. Finding no worthwhile prizes, he landed and spiked the guns of the fort. Not since the Dutch raided Sheerness in 1667 had an English seaport suffered such indignity.

Paul Jones sailed on to St Mary's Island in the Solway Firth and, on 23 April, occupied the Earl of Selkirk's residence.

Jones then sailed with his prizes to Brest from where he put out again in command of a squadron to continue his guerrilla attacks on British shipping (see FLAMBOROUGH HEAD).
Result: The fame of Paul Jones spread quickly throughout the British Isles and the Continent. War insurance rates rose to unprecedented heights. Never before or since have the British Isles been so alarmed and harassed as by the depredations of these American cruisers and privateers around their coasts.

WILMANSTRAND (VILMANSTRAND, LAPEENRANTA) (Lake Salmaa, SE Finland)   Russo-Swedish War   August 1741
A Russian army of 10,000 under Marshal Count Petr Lacy defeated 6,000 Swedes, inflicting casualties of 3,300 killed and wounded, and taking 1,300 prisoners. The victors lost 2,400 killed or wounded.

After this battle the fortress of Wilmanstrand (Vilmanstrand, Lapeenranta) at once surrendered to the Russians, but the Swedes collected an army of such superior numbers that no further progress was made by Lacy throughout the rest of the campaign. A peace treaty was signed two years later which moved the Russian frontier north to the Kyemmene River.

YENIKALE, GULF OF (Black Sea)   Ottoman Wars   July 1790
Fought between the Turkish fleet and the Russian fleet under Admiral Vladimir Ouschakov.
Aim: Each fleet sought to reduce the other.
Battle: An extended, fierce battle ended when both sides drew off without any decisive result.

ZORNDORF (Zielona Gora, Poland)   Seven Years' War   25 August 1758
Fought between a Prussian-Hanoverian army led by Frederick the Great and a Russian army commanded by Count William Fermor which was threatening Prussia.
Strength: Prussians/Hanoverians 36,000; Russians 40,000.

Frederick, using his favourite oblique attack approach, crossed the entire Russian front and struck their right flank. The Russians repulsed the attack by General Friedrich Wilhelm von Seydlitz, commanding the Prussian cavalry, crossed the supposedly impassable marshy ground and charged one of the three Russian irregular square formations. Frederick then shifted his attack to the new Russian right flank but was again repulsed. Von Seydlitz, re-forming his cavalry, again rode against the Russian infantry, parts of which he put to flight with heavy loss. The battle, in effect, was won by von Seydlitz's cavalry. The Prussian-Hanoverian army sustained 13,500 casualties to the Russian losses of 21,000 men.

The Russians retreated to Kaliningrad (Königsberg), thus ending their threat to Prussia.

SECTION TWO
SOUTHERN ASIA

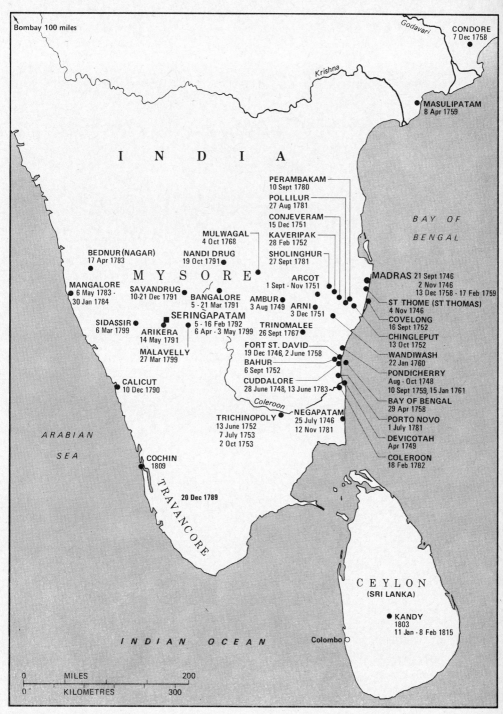

Bombay 100 miles

I N D I A

Godavari

CONDORE
7 Dec 1758

Krishna

MASULIPATAM
8 Apr 1759

BAY OF
BENGAL

PERAMBAKAM
10 Sept 1780

POLLILUR
27 Aug 1781

CONJEVERAM
15 Dec 1751

MULWAGAL
4 Oct 1768

KAVERIPAK
28 Feb 1752

BEDNUR (NAGAR)
17 Apr 1783

NANDI DRUG
19 Oct 1791

SHOLINGHUR
27 Sept 1781

M Y S O R E

ARCOT
1 Sept - Nov 1751

MADRAS 21 Sept 1746
2 Nov 1746
13 Dec 1758 - 17 Feb 1759

MANGALORE
6 May 1783 -
30 Jan 1784

SAVANDRUG
10-21 Dec 1791

BANGALORE
5 - 21 Mar 1791

AMBUR
3 Aug 1749

ARNI
3 Dec 1751

ST THOME (ST THOMAS)
4 Nov 1746

COVELONG
16 Sept 1752

SIDASSIR
6 Mar 1799

SERINGAPATAM
5 - 16 Feb 1792
6 Apr - 3 May 1799

ARIKERA
14 May 1791

TRINOMALEE
26 Sept 1767

CHINGLEPUT
13 Oct 1752

WANDIWASH
22 Jan 1760

MALAVELLY
27 Mar 1799

FORT ST. DAVID
19 Dec 1746, 2 June 1758

PONDICHERRY
Aug - Oct 1748
10 Sept 1759, 15 Jan 1761

BAHUR
6 Sept 1752

CALICUT
10 Dec 1790

CUDDALORE
28 June 1748, 13 June 1783

BAY OF BENGAL
29 Apr 1758

Coleroon

NEGAPATAM
25 July 1746
12 Nov 1781

PORTO NOVO
1 July 1781

TRICHINOPOLY
13 June 1752
7 July 1753
2 Oct 1753

DEVICOTAH
Apr 1749

COLEROON
18 Feb 1782

A R A B I A N
S E A

COCHIN
1809

T R A V A N C O R E

20 Dec 1789

C E Y L O N
(SRI LANKA)

I N D I A N   O C E A N

Colombo

KANDY
1803
11 Jan - 8 Feb 1815

0   MILES   200

0   KILOMETRES   300

7   Southern India

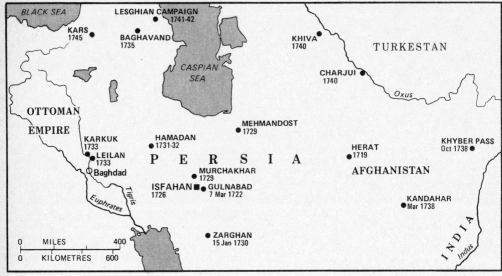

8   Persia

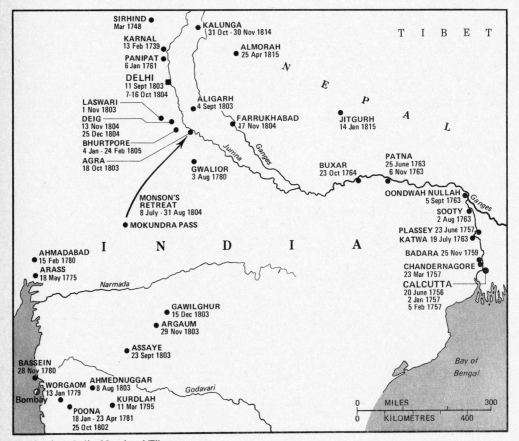

9   Northern India, Nepal and Tibet

AGRA (Uttar Pradesh, India)   Second Mahratta War   18 October 1803
Fought between the British under General Gerard Lake and the Mahratta forces of Doulut Rao Scindia of Gwalior.
Strength: British 10,500 cavalry and infantry; Mahrattas 4,500 (fortress garrison) + 3,200 (troops occupying the town) + 26 guns.
Aim: After the occupation of Delhi (DELHI I), on 24 September Lake marched on Agra, being reinforced on the way by cavalry and infantry units previously detached, and on 4 October encamped on the south side of the town. He then found that the town itself was occupied by seven battalions of Mahratta infantry with 26 guns, which it was necessary to deal with before the fortress itself, commanded by George Hessing, an adventurer of Dutch extraction, could be besieged.
Battle: On 10 October Lake made two separate attacks, each with three battalions of sepoys, on the town and the ravines before it, driving off the enemy with a loss of 600 men and their 26 guns. This was not easily achieved, however, and the British casualties totalled 228 killed and wounded. Two days later the remainder of the seven battalions, some 2,500 men, surrendered. Lake then turned his attention to the fort itself, opening fire with one of his batteries on 17 October with such effect that the garrison surrendered the following day, and the British were in possession of Agra.
Result: The capture of this great fortress town greatly enhanced British prestige in India. Enormous quantities of stores were taken and a very large sum of money in the treasury was seized as prize-money. Another practical result was the newly acquired friendship of the powerful Raja of Bhurtpore, who brought with him a contingent of 5,000 horse.

AHMADABAD (Gujarat, India)   First Mahratta War   15 February 1780
Fought between the British under Brigadier-General Thomas Goddard and the garrison of Ahmadabad under a Brahmin commandant.
Strength: British 1,000 European infantry + 100 European gunners + 4,800 sepoys + 1,000 native cavalry; Mahrattas 6,000 Arab and Sindi infantry + 2,000 Mahratta horse.
Aim: Following the humiliating Treaty of Worgaom (qv) the Governor-General, Warren Hastings, ordered Colonel Goddard, in command of the Bengali troops sent to the assistance of the Bombay government, to proceed as quickly as possible to the west coast. He reached the port of Surat in Gujarat on 26 February 1779 and entered into negotiations with Futteh Singh, the Gaekwar of Baroda, one of the Mahratta princes. The Gaekwar, however, persistently evaded a definite agreement and on New Year's Day 1780 Goddard, now promoted Brigadier-General, moved north to capture Dubhoy, not far from Baroda. This successful operation finally persuaded the Gaekwar to conclude a defensive and offensive alliance with the British, and secured the province of Gujarat. Goddard now moved rapidly northwards to besiege the city of Ahmadabad.
Battle: The walls of Ahmadabad were of immense extent and extremely strong. On 12 February Goddard opened a battery of siege guns and after a heavy cannonade effected a breach on the following day. An assault party of volunteers from the Bombay Division commanded by Lt-Colonel James Hartley stormed the breach but met with stiff resistance. However, having suffered 300 casualties, the garrison surrendered on 15 February. Hearing that the Mahratta chiefs Mahadaji Scindia and Tookaji Holkar had crossed the river Nerbudda with some 22,000 horse, Goddard at once turned back southwards to meet them. Then followed a series of indecisive engagements in which, however, Goddard held the Mahrattas steadily at bay.
Result: The onset of the rainy season in May put an end to the campaign and Goddard retired to the river Nerbudda area to canton his troops, having successfully held Gujarat against further Mahratta intervention.

AHMEDNUGGAR (AHMADNAGAR) (Maharashtra, India)   Second Mahratta War   8 August 1803
Fought between the British under Major-General Arthur Wellesley and the garrison of Ahmednuggar (Ahmadnagar).
Strength: British 1,600 European infantry and cavalry + 200 gunners + 1,400 native cavalry + 8,000 sepoys + 5,000 Mysorean and Mahratta horse; Mahrattas 2,000 (town garrison) + 1,400 (fortress garrison).
Aim: After the declaration of war against the Mahratta Confederacy, on 6 August 1803, Wellesley decided as a first step in the offensive against the Mahratta chief Doulut Rao Scindia of Gwalior to capture his hill fortress of Ahmednuggar, considered amongst the strongest in India, about 60 miles NE of Poona.

Battle: On 8 August Wellesley commenced operations by ordering three divisions from his line of march to attack the outer defence walls around the *pettah*, or fortified native town, which were obstinately defended by a body of Arab mercenaries and one of Scindia's regular battalions, supported by cavalry. The walls were, however, stormed the same day at three separate points and the *pettah* secured. Of this engagement a Mahratta chief is reported to have said: 'These English are a strange people and their General a wonderful man. They came here in the morning, looked at the fortified wall, walked over it, killed all the garrison, and returned to breakfast.' Two days later Wellesley opened up a battery of 4 18-pounders on the fortress, and on 12 August, after a continuous cannonade, the Killidar commanding the fort garrison surrendered, being allowed to march out with his 1,400 troops with full honours of war. The total casualties sustained by the British in this action amounted to 79 Europeans and 62 sepoys killed and wounded.

Result: Within a matter of three days, Wellesley had secured a firm strategic base with an abundance of supplies for his drive into the interior, at the same time cutting off the northern Mahratta chiefs from their southern allies.

ALIGARH (Uttar Pradesh, India)   Second Mahratta War   4 September 1803
Fought between the British under General Gerard Lake and the Mahratta garrison under Colonel Pierre Cuillier Pedron.
Strength: British 1,200 European cavalry + 600 European infantry + 4,500 native cavalry + 8,000 sepoys + 65 guns; Mahrattas 35,000 (field forces) + 2,500 (garrison) with 73 guns.
Aim: While Major-General Arthur Wellesley was conducting a successful campaign against the joint armies of Doulut Rao Scindia of Gwalior and Rughuji Bhonsla, Raja of Berar, in the Deccan, General Lake with his headquarters at Cawnpore (Kanpur) was taking the field against Scindia's main army in the north. Trained and commanded by a French mercenary Pierre Cuillier Pedron, this army consisted of some 35,000 men, including 20,000 horse and a very large artillery train. On 29 August 1802 Lake's force entered Mahratta territory and marched on the fortress of Aligarh, before which Pedron had concentrated his whole army. On Lake's approach, however, he retired to Agra, leaving instructions to the garrison commander, Colonel Pedron, to defend the fortress to the last.
Battle: At dawn on the morning of 4 September the assault party, commanded by Colonel William Monson and consisting of four companies of the 76th Highlanders, supported by two sepoy battalions, approached the causeway to the main gate of the fort, covered by heavy fire from 2 batteries. This was the only means of access to the fort, which was surrounded by a ditch 100 feet wide with 10 feet of water. Initial attempts at scaling the ramparts were unsuccessful, but eventually the main gate was blown in by the Highlanders, who then fought their way through the fortress against deadly converging fire of grape and musketry until it was taken. Of the garrison, over 2,000 perished on the bayonet or by drowning in the ditch while attempting to escape. British casualties amounted to 55 killed and 205 wounded.
Result: After leaving a sepoy battalion to garrison Aligarh, Lake marched on 7 September towards Delhi. The same day Pedron and several other of his French officers offered to surrender to Lake, asking for safe conduct to Lucknow, which was willingly granted. The senior French officer remaining with the Mahrattas was then Louis Bourquien, who took over command of Scindia's army.

ALMORAH (Nepal)   Gurkha War   25 April 1815
Fought between a British force under Colonel Jasper Nicolls and the Gurkha garrison of Almorah.
Strength: British 2,200 sepoys + 1,000 irregular levies + 10 guns; Gurkhas 4,000.
Aim: In an attempt to increase pressure on the Gurkhas in this difficult and frustrating campaign Lord Moira, the Governor-General of India, raised a strong force of levies in Rohilkhand (Uttar Pradesh) under 2 British officers for an attack upon the province of Kumaon. By the end of March the force had penetrated deep into the heart of the province. The following month, reinforced by a contingent of native infantry under Colonel Jasper Nicolls, the column, which now had artillery support, advanced to the walls of the important town of Almorah.
Battle: On the night of 25 April Nicolls's troops were attacked by a strong force of Gurkhas, but managed to repulse them with some loss. The town was then bombarded at close range, after which the British infantry assaulted and carried the heights and then the town itself. The Governor formally surrendered the following day.
Result: A treaty of capitulation was then signed providing for the surrender of the entire province of Kumaon to the British and the withdrawal of all Gurkha troops to east of the Kali River, the present

western frontier of Nepal. This defeat proved a major disaster for Gurkha arms and profoundly affected their morale. Shortly afterwards Major-General Sir David Ochterlony signally defeated the Gurkha Commander-in-Chief, Umur Singh Thapa, at Malaon. Thousands of his troops deserted to the British and were formed into the first Gurkha battalions in the British army. In February 1816 Ochterlony was appointed to command the main invasion force, now 20,000 strong in four brigades, with its objective, Katmandu. Forcing his way through the Churia Ghati Pass he reached Makwanpur, where on 27 February 1816, the last and decisive battle of the war was fought.

In February 1817, after the successful conclusion of the Gurkha War, the Governor-General Lord Moira was created Marquess of Hastings, a vote of thanks for his services having been passed a few days previously in both Houses of Parliament.

AMBUR (AMOOR) (Andhra Pradesh, India)   Second Carnatic War   3 August 1749
Fought between the combined armies of Muzaffar Jang, Viceroy of the Deccan, Chanda Sahib and a French contingent under the Marquis de Bussy-Castelnau, and the army of Anwar-ud-Din, Nawab of the Carnatic.
Strength: Deccan army 30,000 + French 2,400 (400 Europeans + 2,000 sepoys) + Chanda Sahib's force 3,500 native troops; Carnatic army 20,000.
Aim: In spite of the peace Treaty of Aix-la-Chapelle between France and Britain which terminated the War of the Austrian Succession, hostilities continued between the two East India Companies which took opposing sides in internal Indian politics. Following the death in 1748 of the Nizam-ul-Mulk, the Mogul Emperor's Viceroy in the Deccan in central India, his grandson Muzaffar Jang had been appointed Nizam instead of his father Nasir Jang. At the same time one of his Hindu supporters, Chanda Sahib, had laid claims to the Nawabship of the Carnatic and was supported by the French. On the other hand the British East India Company supported the incumbents, Nasir Jang and Anwar-ud-Din, as Nizam and Nawab respectively.
Battle: After a closely fought battle the army of Anwar-ud-Din proved quite incapable of withstanding the disciplined onslaught of the French infantry and was signally defeated, the Nawab himself being slain on the field.
Result: Chanda Sahib now became the *de facto* Nawab of the Carnatic and took up residence in his capital of Arcot. The Nizam showed his gratitude to his French allies by making substantial grants of land around Pondicherry. Mohammed Ali, the second son of the former Nawab, had retreated to Trichinopoly, the capital of the state of Tanjore, and hastily prepared the great natural fortress for the siege he knew to be only a matter of time.

ARASS (Gujarat, India)   First Mahratta War   18 May 1775
Fought between the British under Lt-Colonel Thomas Keating and a Mahratta force under Hari Punt Phurkay.
Strength: British 800 Europeans + 1,800 sepoys + 20,000 Indian levies; Mahrattas 30,000 horse and foot.
Aim: In March 1775 an undertaking was entered into by the Bombay Presidency to support the claims of Ragonath Rao (better known as Ragobah) to be acknowledged as Peshwa of Poona, the titular head of the Mahratta Confederacy of States in central India. In return, Ragobah agreed to the payment of large subsidies and to cede the port of Bassein and the island of Salsette near Bombay to the East India Company in perpetuity. Ragobah was, however, opposed by two powerful Mahratta chiefs, Mahadaji Scindia of Gwalier and Tookaji Holkar of Indore. A force under Lt-Colonel Keating was accordingly dispatched to his assistance from Bombay by sea, disembarking at Cambay in Gujarat on 17 March. After joining forces with Ragobah and his motley host of some 20,000 men, Keating decided to march northwards to Ahmadabad (qv).
Battle: On the morning of 18 May the army was advancing towards the village of Arass when 6 guns suddenly opened fire on the rear from a grove on the left of the road, while a large body of Mahratta foot was seen approaching from the same area. Keating at once halted the column, silenced the enemy artillery with his own 4 rear guns and drove back the advancing force. However, 2 of the Mahratta guns were not withdrawn with the rest, and Captain Myers was detailed to lead two companies of Europeans and one of sepoys up a sandy lane where the guns were posted. The Mahrattas now blocked the lane behind the British with 2 elephants and launched continuous cavalry attacks until both grenadiers and sepoys were seized with panic and fled back to the main body, which however remained unshaken. Keating handled his

artillery with great skill and eventually drove back the enemy with heavy loss. The action, however, cost him 272 killed and wounded including 11 officers, while the Mahratta losses exceeded 1,000 men.
Result: This victory greatly discouraged the Mahrattas who made no further attempt to hinder Keating's progress. He marched on to Dubhoy, some 20 miles SE of Baroda, where a temporary peace was arranged with Futteh Singh, the Gaekwar of Baroda, who had been one of Ragobah's chief opponents.

ARCOT (Tamil Nadu, India)   Second Carnatic War   1 September/November 1751
Fought between the British under Captain Robert Clive and an Indian army under Raja Sahib with a French contingent commanded by M. De Saussey.
Strength: British 200 Europeans + 300 sepoys + 3 field pieces and 2 18-pounders; Indians 10,000 cavalry and infantry + French 150.
Aim: In July 1751 an Indian force of some 8,000 men under Chanda Sahib, the French nominee for the Nawabship of the Carnatic, with a French contingent, besieged the town of Trichinopoly, about 200 miles SW of Madras, where Mohammed Ali, son of the former Nawab, was trapped together with a British force 1,600 strong. To relieve the pressure on Trichinopoly by a bold diversion, Captain Robert Clive seized the fortress of Arcot, Chanda Sahib's capital 64 miles SW of Madras. On arriving in the town on 20 September Clive found that the garrison of 1,100 had marched out the previous night on learning of his approach. Clive then repaired the defences of the fort and made every preparation to resist a siege. When Chanda Sahib heard of the capture of his capital, he dispatched a force of some 10,000 men under his son Raja Sahib to recover it.
Battle: On 4 October Raja Sahib's force entered the town of Arcot and began the investment of the fort. On the very next day Clive made a bold sally towards the palace which Raja Sahib had made his headquarters, but he was driven back with the loss of 33 killed and wounded. From then on Clive and his men, reduced by sickness to 120 Europeans and 200 sepoys, were closely besieged, the enemy cutting off the water supply from outside. Fortunately the garrison was not short of food and managed to hold out for fifty days.

In the meantime Governor Saunders at Fort St David had persuaded the redoubtable Mahratta chieftain Morari Rao, with a force of 6,000 cavalry, to move to the aid of the beleaguered garrison. On learning of this, Raja Sahib decided on a final assault and on 24 November the enemy troops swarmed up to the breach in the walls of the fort while a herd of elephants with iron headplates was brought forward to batter down the gates. When, however, they came within range of musket-fire the elephants stampeded, trampling down the Indians urging them on. Another assault across the moat led by the sepoy commander Abdul Codah Khan was repelled with enemy losses of some 400, including the leader. On the following day Raja Sahib raised the siege and marched away, abandoning several guns and large quantities of stores and ammunition.
Result: Although the cost in casualties during the fifty-day siege had been heavy, it was not a high price to pay for the re-establishment of British prestige in India, and created a tradition of British invincibility on which the future Indian Empire was to be built.

ARGAUM (ARGAON) (Maharashtra, India)   Second Mahratta War   29 November 1803
Fought between the British under Major-General Arthur Wellesley and the combined Mahratta forces of Doulut Rao Scindia of Gwalior and Rughuji Bhonsla, Raja of Berar, commanded by his brother Manu Bapu.
Strength: British 11,000; Mahrattas 10,000 infantry + 25,000 cavalry.
Aim: After his overwhelming victory at Assaye (qv) Wellesley joined forces with Colonel James Stevenson's corps at Parterley, 6 miles north of the river Purna, during the afternoon of 29 November 1803. Only 5 miles to the north, on a flat plain in front of the village of Argaum (Argaon), Wellesley observed a large concentration of Mahratta horse and infantry, and immediately decided to attack.
Battle: Advancing through shoulder-high corn, the British columns were able to come within striking distance of the Mahrattas before they were observed. They were then greeted by an intense artillery bombardment from 50 guns, when two sepoy battalions broke and fled. Wellesley perceived what had happened and immediately rode up to the retreating troops and succeeded in rallying them. He then drew up his infantry in a single line with the cavalry in reserve and advanced on the enemy. At this stage the column was attacked by a large body of Arab mercenaries, but after a short sharp struggle with the 74th and 78th Highlanders they were beaten back with casualties of some 600 killed and wounded. After two cavalry attacks on the extremities of the British line had been repulsed, the whole Mahratta force then gave way and fled the field, leaving 38 guns behind. The cavalry under Colonel St Leger pursued the fleeing

enemy far into the night under the light of the moon, inflicting some 3,000 casualties and capturing all their elephants and baggage. Wellesley's casualties were only 362 killed and wounded, including 162 Europeans. After the battle was over Wellesley said of the panic retreat of the sepoys: 'If I had not been there to rally them and restore the battle, we should have lost the day.'

Result: Halting at Ellichpoor, about 40 miles NE of Argaum, to establish a hospital for the wounded, Wellesley then pressed on with his whole force towards the hill fortress of Gawilghur (qv), where the defeated army of Argaum had taken refuge.

ARIKERA (Karnataka, India)   Third Mysore War   14 May 1791
Fought between the British under Lord Cornwallis, the Governor-General of India, and the Mysoreans under Tipu Sultan.

Strength: British 23,000 Europeans and sepoys + 10,000 cavalry (Nizam's forces); Mysoreans 20,000 horse and foot.

Aim: After the capture of Bangalore (qv) Cornwallis joined forces with a contingent of 10,000 horse provided by the Nizam of Hyderabad and, on 3 May, marched towards Tipu's capital, Seringapatam. In the meantime General Sir Robert Abercrombie, advancing from Bombay with a force of nine battalions, passed through Coorg into Mysore and encamped at Periapatam, some 40 miles west of Seringapatam, awaiting further orders from Cornwallis. The main British force took the southern route through Kankanhalli to avoid Tipu's entrenched position at Chennapatna but, on arriving at Arikera, 9 miles south of Seringapatam, they found the ford across the river Cauvery impassable. Cornwallis then decided to stage a night attack against the Mysore army which Tipu had withdrawn to an extremely strong position in front of the city.

Battle: At 11 pm on 14 May a force of six European and twelve sepoy battalions, together with 1,000 cavalry and 36 bullock-drawn field guns, led by Cornwallis himself, set off to make a wide detour northward and turn the enemy's left flank by a surprise night attack. Unfortunately for this force a tremendous thunderstorm with torrential rain broke just before it set out, and column after column lost its way, until eventually the attack had to be called off. At first light, appreciating the threat to his flank, Tipu sent one of his commanders, Qamar-ud-Din, with a strong force to occupy a range of low hills which would protect his flank. However, a force of five battalions, led by Colonel Maxwell, drove the Mysoreans from the hills. Tipu now retreated into the safety of Seringapatam, having lost some 2,000 men in the engagement. British casualties amounted to 500 killed and wounded.

Result: As it was now too late in the season to undertake a major siege Cornwallis was reluctantly obliged to destroy the whole of his battering train and heavy baggage and retreat in easy stages to Bangalore, at the same time sending a message to Abercrombie to return to Bombay. Plans were then made for the final campaign to take place the following year.

ARNI (Tamil Nadu, India)   Second Carnatic War   3 December 1751
Fought between a British force under Captain Robert Clive, supported by Mahratta horse under Buzangara, and an Indian/French force under Raja Sahib.

Strength: British 200 Europeans + 700 sepoys + 600 Mahratta cavalry; Indians 3,000 native levies + French 300 Europeans + 1,500 sepoys.

Aim: Following the siege of Arcot (qv) Clive decided to take immediate action to drive the forces of Raja Sahib out of the surrounding country. Leaving a small garrison in Arcot he marched towards the great fortress of Vellore, some 20 miles to the SW, where Raja Sahib had entrenched his forces. Hearing that he had moved out to join a French reinforcement on its way from Pondicherry, Clive thereupon marched rapidly by night to encounter the enemy before they could return to Vellore.

Battle: The two armies met on the morning of 3 December 1751 near the town of Arni, about 20 miles south of Arcot. Clive placed his European troops and artillery on an eminence facing the enemy across swampy paddy-fields. In the village on the right he placed his sepoys with the Mahratta horse in a palm grove on the left. The enemy advanced at noon, but owing to the swampy nature of the fields could not bring up their artillery except along a narrow causeway near the village. Here they were enfiladed by Clive's sepoys and prevented from making any further progress. A contingent of French troops with the artillery now attempted to advance under cover of a *choultry* (open shelter for travellers) and were attacked and dispersed by Clive's sepoys, as a result of which the enemy sepoys and horse alike retired. The Mahrattas chased the retreating cavalry and Clive advanced with his infantry and field pieces along the causeway in pursuit of the main body of the Indian forces now scattering in flight, leaving most of their baggage. Two hundred of the enemy were killed, including 50 French, whereas the British lost no Europeans and only 8 sepoys and 50 Mahrattas. Seven hundred French-trained sepoys surrendered and were enrolled in the British forces.

Result: Raja Sahib's army scattered in groups of 20 or 30 and the French did not stop until they reached the fortress of Gingee, half-way to Pondicherry. Arni was Clive's first victory in a set battle in the field and he won it through his skill in placing his men and artillery.

ASSAYE (Maharashtra, India)   Second Mahratta War   23 September 1803
Fought between the British army under Major-General Arthur Wellesley and the combined Mahratta forces of Doulut Rao Scindia of Gwalior and Rughuji Bhonsla, Raja of Berar, trained by the French General de Boigne.

Strength: British 350 European cavalry + 1,200 European infantry + 160 European artillery + 1,250 native (Madras) cavalry + 4,000 sepoys + 22 guns + 5,000 Mysore and Mahratta horse (Peshwa's army); Mahrattas 30,000 cavalry + 10,500 infantry + 100 guns.

Aim: After the reduction of Ahmednuggar (qv), the hill fortress stronghold of Scindia, Wellesley marched northwards with the intention of bringing the Mahratta armies of Scindia and the Bhonsla to battle. After crossing the great river Godavery, he learned that the enemy had joined forces in the neighbourhood of Bokerdun, and it was then agreed between Wellesley and his second in command, Colonel James Stevenson, that their respective corps should proceed by separate passes through the mountains, converging on the evening of 24 September. However, on 23 September, before Stevenson had emerged from the hills, Wellesley discovered that the whole of the Mahratta force was only 6 miles away from his position, drawn up in a vast array between Bokerdun on the left and the village of Assaye on the right, on the opposite banks of the swollen river Kaitna. In spite of the fact that his men had already marched 24 miles that day, Wellesley decided to attack at once with his own troops, without waiting for Stevenson.

Battle: Having fortunately discovered an unsuspected ford across the Kaitna, Wellesley brought the whole of his force safely across and formed them up in three lines, with the cavalry in the rear, in the narrow tongue of land, only 1 mile wide, between the Kaitna and its tributary the Juah, which flowed behind Assaye. As he did so the French-trained Mahratta infantry changed their front with great and unexpected precision to face the British. Wellesley ordered an immediate advance in the face of most devastating fire from the enemy's 100 guns. However, there was no resisting the infantry's attack and the Mahratta gunners were cut down at their posts. Some feigned dead until the British had swept over them, after which they rose and, turning their guns about, fired on their backs, only to be shot down or bayoneted in their turn.

Meanwhile the attack by the 74th Highlanders came to a halt in the face of terrific artillery and musket-fire, and they were then attacked by hordes of Mahratta horse on both flanks. At this stage Wellesley ordered his cavalry under Colonel Maxwell to advance, and the 19th Light Dragoons, together with the 4th, 5th and 7th Madras Native Cavalry, rode through the Highlanders' ranks to sweep the Mahratta horse before them, and then forced the supporting infantry to break and flee across the river Juah behind them. The tide had now turned, and Wellesley, who had had two horses killed under him, ordered the 78th Highlanders, supported by the native cavalry, to head a fresh attack on Assaye, driving the enemy out at the point of the bayonet. In the meantime the British cavalry caused the remaining Mahratta infantry brigade under its German Commander, Pohlmann, to retire, Maxwell being killed in the process. Scindia and the Bhonsla had long since left the field.

In this fiercely fought contest, the Mahrattas suffered casualties of 1,200 killed and 4,800 wounded, together with the loss of 98 guns and all their stores and equipment. British casualties were 1,584 killed and wounded, 650 of them Europeans. The Mysore and Maharatta horse from the Peshwa's army attached to the British force, whose loyalty was suspect, took no part in the action. Wellesley, later as Duke of Wellington, was to observe that this battle was 'the bloodiest for the numbers that I ever saw'.

Result: The following evening Colonel Stevenson came up with his troops and at once proceeded in pursuit of the retreating enemy, and in October captured the important city of Burhanpur and the fort of Asirgarh. On 29 December Wellesley and Stevenson joined forced once more at Parterley, 6 miles north of the river Purna, a tributary of the Taptee, with the intention of proceeding against the Mahratta fortress of Gawilghur (qv).

BADARA (West Bengal, India)   Bengal Wars   25 November 1759
Fought between the British under Colonel Francis Forde and the Dutch under their commander M. Roussel.

Strength: British 320 Europeans + 50 European cavalry + 800 sepoys + 100 native cavalry; Dutch 700 Europeans + 800 Malays (expeditionary force) + 150 Europeans (garrison).

Aim: Jealous of British successes in Bengal, the Dutch decided to send troops from Batavia to reinforce their settlement at Chinsura on the river Hooghly. On their arrival in the Bay of Bengal in October 1759 Mir Jafar, the Nawab of Bengal, feeling antagonised by his subjection to Clive and the Council of the East India Company, decided to act in concert with the Dutch for the overthrow of the British. In the second week in November the Dutch seized some small Company vessels and burned the British Agent's house at Fulta, south of Calcutta, after which they stood up the river.

Battle: On 24 November Forde, with 100 men of the 101st Foot and 400 sepoys with 4 guns, reached Chandernagore on his march north towards Chinsura, where he found the way barred by a party of 120 Dutch and 300 sepoys with 4 guns. Forde launched an immediate attack and drove the Dutch from their positions, capturing all their guns. That evening Forde received reinforcements in readiness to deal with the Dutch and Malay troops landed from the river. Early on the morning of 25 November Forde took up a position midway between Chinsura and Chandernagore, with the village of Badara on his right and a broad deep ravine protecting his front. At 10am the Dutch advanced to the attack, but were thrown into confusion by intense musketry and cannon fire from the ravine. Forde then counter-attacked with his cavalry, whereupon the entire Dutch force turned and fled. Of the Dutch over 100 were killed and 350 captured, while 200 Malays were killed and as many wounded. British casualties did not exceed 30 killed and wounded.

While this highly successful land action was in progress, Clive's armed East Indiamen under Captain Wilson attacked the Dutch squadron, 3 against 7, capturing 6 of them on the spot, the seventh falling an easy prey to 2 British men-of-war down-river.

Result: This decisive action sealed the fate of the Dutch in India. Their settlers at Chinsura sued abjectly not only for mercy but for protection and were never again a threat to the British in Bengal. The Dutch government disavowed the action of their fleet and paid compensation for the damage done.

BAGHAVAND (USSR)   Persian Wars   1735
Fought between the Persians under Nadir Kuli Beg and the Turks under Abdulla Köprulu.
Strength: Persians 30,000; Turks 80,000.
Aim: The Ottoman Sultan Mahmud refused to ratify the peace treaty entered into between Nadir and Ahmed Pasha, the Governor of Baghdad, after the Turkish defeat at Leilan (qv) in 1733, and a fresh army had been dispatched into the field under Abdulla Köprulu. In the meantime Nadir had entered into an alliance with Russia whereby Baku and Derbent, previously occupied by the Russians, were returned to Persia. This achieved, Nadir invaded Turkey and besieged Tiflis, Erivan and Ganja with the design of forcing the Turkish leader into a general engagement. This move was successful and Abdulla quitted his entrenched camp at Kars in Armenia and advanced on Erivan (Yerevan).
Battle: The Persians had retired to a chosen position on the plains of Baghavand, where they were attacked in force by the Turks. Although inferior in numbers the Persians gained a complete victory. The Turks were outmanoeuvred and outfought, and after sustaining crushing losses fled the field, the Ottoman Commander being among the slain.
Result: Nadir now occupied the three towns of Tiflis, Erivan and Ganja without further opposition and the Sultan agreed to ratify the Treaty of Baghdad, as a result of which Persia recovered part of her lost western provinces.

The following year, on the death of the infant Shah Abbas III, Nadir was unanimously elected to the throne and in 1736 was crowned with much splendour as Shah of Persia. His acceptance of the throne was subject, however, to the condition that the nation would abandon the Shia doctrine introduced by the now defunct Safavi dynasty and return to Sunni orthodoxy.

BAHUR (BEHOOR) (Tamil Nadu, India)   Second Carnatic War   6 September 1752
Fought between the British under Major Stringer Lawrence and a French force under M. Kerjean.
Strength: British 400 Europeans + 1,700 sepoys + 400 native cavalry; French 500 Europeans + 1,500 sepoys + 500 native cavalry + 8 guns.
Aim: Following the capture of Trichinopoly (TRICHINOPOLY I) in June 1752 the British Governor, Thomas Saunders, decided to attack the fortress of Gingee, situated some 40 miles NW of Fort St David and a symbol of French military strength in the Carnatic. The force detailed for the purpose was, however, defeated with heavy loss by a French contingent under M. Kerjean, nephew of the French Governor-

General, the Marquis Joseph-François Dupleix. After this success Kerjean proceeded to blockade Fort St David and cut its communications with Trichinopoly. On learning of this move, Stringer Lawrence at once marched to intercept the French, taking up a position close to the village of Bahur (Behoor) 2 miles inland from Fort St David.

Battle: At dawn on 6 September Lawrence marched off to attack the French, who were now encamped about 2 miles from the village of Bahur. The British advanced firing, platoon after platoon, but the French never wavered until bayonets crossed and fierce, hand-to-hand fighting ensued. When, however, a company of the élite British Grenadiers forced their way through the centre the French flung down their arms and fled, after sustaining heavy losses. M. Kerjean himself with 115 officers and men were taken prisoner. British casualties were 4 officers and 78 men killed or wounded.

Result: In spite of this signal victory, Lawrence did not consider it prudent to venture on further operations until he could ascertain whether the fickle Mahrattas would finally attach themselves to the French or to the British.

BANGALORE (Karnataka, India)   Third Mysore War   5–21 March 1791
Fought between the British invasion force commanded by the Governor-General of India, Lord Cornwallis, and the Mysorean garrison.
Strength: British 19,000; Mysoreans 8,000 (fort) + 9,000 (town).
Aim: During most of 1790 abortive attempts were made by a British force of some 15,000 men, commanded by Major-General William Medows, to gain a decisive victory against the massive armies of Tipu Sultan, the 'Tiger of Mysore', reputed to be in the region of 88,000 horse and foot. Tipu, however, proved elusive and, after a series of minor successes on both sides, the resultant stalemate decided Lord Cornwallis to take over command of the army himself. Concentrating his force at Vellout, 18 miles west of Madras, he proceeded straight up the E Ghats by the Mugli Pass and, by 21 February, his entire army of some 19,000 men was encamped at Palamnair on the Mysore plateau without having fired a shot. On 5 March Cornwallis arrived before Bangalore and laid siege to the town.
Battle: Bangalore consisted of a fort and a *pettah*, or fortified native town, adjoining it. The fort proper was strongly built with 26 round towers surrounded by a ditch. The town, situated to the north of the fort, was enclosed by a rampart and redoubts. Leaving garrisons in each, Tipu had retired to a position 6 miles to the west with the remainder of his force. Cornwallis decided to carry the town first and accordingly, at dawn on 7 March with the 36th Foot and a battalion of sepoys, launched the attack. Within two hours most of the town was in the possession of the British. Tipu then detached 6,000 men to reinforce the town garrison. Some desperate fighting ensued until eventually the streets were cleared with the bayonet, the Mysoreans sustaining casualties of some 2,000 killed and wounded. British casualties amounted to only 130.

Now constantly harassed by Tipu's field force, Cornwallis decided that the fort must be assaulted without further delay. So, on the night of 21 March, in bright moonlight, the fort was stormed by the 36th and 72nd Foot. Over 1,000 Mysoreans were killed in the attack, while the total British casualties during the entire siege operations were fewer than 500. Large quantities of military stores were captured in the fort and also quantities of invaluable forage in the town.
Result: Cornwallis had now obtained a secure base for his advance on Tipu's capital, Seringapatam (SERINGAPATAM I). He marched NE to contact the force of 10,000 horse provided by the Nizam of Hyderabad and commanded by Raja Tejwant. The combined armies then returned to Bangalore and prepared for the final stages of the campaign. In the meantime Tipu had taken up a defensive position at Chennapatna, half-way to the capital.

BASSEIN (Maharashtra, India)   First Mahratta War   28 November–11 December 1780
Fought between the British army under Brigadier-General Thomas Goddard and Mahratta forces under Ramchunder Gunnesh.
Strength: British (Goddard's force) 120 European gunners + 200 European infantry + 2,000 sepoys + 700 native cavalry + (Hartley's force) 400 Europeans + 2,600 sepoys + 100 native cavalry + 100 gunners; Mahrattas 2,000 (garrison) + 20,000 horse and foot (field force).
Aim: After five years of indecisive campaigning against the forces of the Mahratta Confederacy in central India, the Governor-General, Warren Hastings, decided that an attempt must be made to obtain some solid advantage from this costly and interminable war. General Goddard was accordingly instructed to besiege Bassein, the Mahratta port north of Bombay. At the same time Lt-Colonel James Hartley with one

under-strength European battalion and four sepoy battalions was ordered to cover the besieging force and drive out the enemy outposts.

Battle: On 28 November 1780 Goddard opened his trenches before Bassein with a siege battery of 24-pounders and a battery of 20 mortars, concentrating on the north face of the town. While this bombardment was proceeding, Hartley with great skill kept the Mahratta hordes from relieving the beleaguered garrison. Gradually he was forced back to Doogaur, 9 miles east of Bassein. Here, at bay, he finally turned, having been reinforced with two battalions under Major Hopkins, and after three days' fierce fighting, repulsed the enemy with heavy loss. Realising that their rescue was now impossible, the garrison surrendered on 11 December, with the loss to the besiegers of only 13 men.

Result: While this campaign on the west coast was at last achieving some degree of success, a disastrous defeat had been inflicted on the British by Haider Ali, the ruler of Mysore, near Madras in the Carnatic. The Bengal government therefore ordered Goddard to conclude peace with the Mahrattas immediately the expected overtures were made by the Peshwa at Poona (see POONA I).

BAY OF BENGAL (SE India)   Third Carnatic War   29 April 1758
Naval battle fought between the British under Rear-Admiral Sir George Pocock and a French squadron under Rear-Admiral Comte Anne-Antoine d'Aché.

Strength: British 7 ships; French 9 ships.

Aim: On 28 April 1758 a fleet of 12 French sail appeared off Fort St David on the Coromandel coast under Rear-Admiral D'Aché, carrying a regiment of infantry and 50 gunners together with Comte Thomas-Arthur Lally de Tollendal, an officer who had been with the Irish Brigade in the French army and had now been appointed to the supreme command of the French forces in India. Lally's instructions from Versailles were first to besiege Fort St David, so he sailed with 3 ships of the squadron on to Pondicherry, the main French base in the Carnatic, to give the necessary orders, while d'Aché stood out to sea.

Battle: A British squadron under Commodore Charles Steevens had reached Madras some five weeks before d'Aché appeared, and this joined Admiral Pocock's squadron in the river Hooghly. The combined fleet then sailed with 7 ships of the line to intercept the French, coming in sight of them on the morning of 29 April off Cuddalore. Although the engagement that followed was indecisive, it was decidedly to the disadvantage of the French, who suffered casualties of 600 men killed or wounded, and 1 of their ships of the line was so badly damaged that it had to be run ashore and abandoned. The British lost little over 100 men, but their rigging was so badly cut up that they could not pursue the French.

Result: The British squadron returned to Madras to refit while the French anchored some 20 miles north of Pondicherry in the roadstead at Alumparva.

BEDNUR (Karnataka, India)   Second Mysore War   17 April 1783
Fought between a British Force from the Bombay Presidency under Brigadier-General Richard Matthews and the Mysoreans under Tipu Sultan.

Strength: British 3,000 (including 73rd Highlanders); Mysoreans 140,000 horse and foot.

Aim: While the main activity in the war had been concentrated in the Carnatic, military action sponsored by the Bombay Presidency in the west had also been undertaken, but with less spectacular results. In January 1783 a force under General Matthews was dispatched south by sea to Cundapore, with orders to capture the large and prosperous Mysorean provincial capital of Bednur, which had been seized by Haider Ali in 1763. After they had successfully overcome a massive series of defensive positions *en route*, overtures were made by the Governor of Bednur, Shaik Ayaz, for the surrender of the town, which Matthews then occupied without further resistance. His total casualties in this enterprise were no more than 50 killed and wounded. On 9 March Mangalore was also occupied by a British garrison. By this time, however, Tipu Sultan had slowly begun to make his way westwards from the Carnatic.

Battle: On 17 April Tipu arrived before Bednur, dividing his huge army into two columns, one of which was used to cut off Matthews's communications with the coast, while the other invested the town. Matthews now had only some 1,600 effectives, having used the remainder for garrison troops in outlying stations. The outer line of defences of the town was too extensive to be held by the limited number of defenders and was carried at the first assault, the garrison being forced to retreat into the citadel. There for ten days a desperate defence was put up against hopeless odds, Matthews being compelled to surrender on 3 May, his troops to be allowed to withdraw unmolested to Bombay. Tipu, however, was infuriated to find the treasury bare, and ordered the entire garrison to be put in irons and marched off as prisoners to the dungeons of Seringapatam.

Result: After taking Bednur, Tipu marched on to recapture Mangalore (qv). The unfortunate Matthews was to die in Seringapatam shortly afterwards, probably through eating poisoned food.

BHURTPORE (BHARATPUR) (Madhya Pradesh, India) Second Mahratta War 4 January–24 February 1805
Fought between the British under General Gerard Lake and the garrison and field troops of Jaswunt Rao Holkar Maharaja of Indore.
Strength: British (after reinforcements) 1,500 European infantry + 7,500 sepoys + 1,600 European cavalry+1,400 native cavalry+400 horse artillery+6 18-pounder siege guns and 8 brass mortars; Mahrattas/Jats 8,000 garrison infantry + Mahrattas 20,000 Holkar's cavalry + Indians 8,000 Amir Khan's horse and foot + 4 guns.
Aim: After the reduction of Deig in November 1804 (DEIG I) General Lake proceeded to the investment of Bhurtpore (Bharatpur), 34 miles west of Agra, the massive fortress town of Holkar's ally, Ranjit Singh, Raja of Bhurtpore. The town itself was 8 miles in circumference and surrounded by a very high strong wall with numerous bastions mounting guns and encircled by a wide, deep ditch which was flooded on Lake's approach. The citadel at the eastern end of the town rose to a height of 114 feet and was immensely strong. Outside the walls the garrison was supported by hordes of roving cavalry under direct command of Holkar and his ally, Amir Khan of Tonk, with a strong force of irregular horse and infantry with artillery support.
Battle: On 7 January Lake, who had concentrated the whole of his force opposite the SW angle of the town, opened fire with his 18-pounder battery, and two days later a breach was made and declared practicable. That night the first of four desperate attempts at assaulting the town was launched, using the 22nd, 75th and 76th Foot with three sepoy battalions in support, and this was repelled with great slaughter. On 21 January a second breach was effected and a determined daytime assault fared no better, being repulsed with heavy losses. Then followed a lull in the siege operations until on 10 February the force was augmented by a Bombay Division under Major-General Jones, including the 65th and 86th Foot and four sepoy battalions. On 19 February the third assault took place, but its effect was largely destroyed by two determined sorties by the garrison; it was also marked by a panic refusal on the part of one European storming party to follow its officers, and the attack was relinquished. The next day the fourth and final assault, led by Colonel William Monson, took place, the storming parties consisting mainly of the fresh Bombay Division, but after a bold and determined effort to scale the fortress walls, the attackers were driven back under tremendous fire.
     All told, the British casualties in these fruitless operations amounted to 3,203 killed and wounded. On 24 February Lake formally raised the siege and drew off his army 6 miles to the NE. During the course of the siege, Lake's forces and their supply convoys had been constantly harassed by the cavalry of Holkar and his partisan ally, Amir Khan, both of whom had, however, been roughly handled and suffered severe losses.
Result: The main cause of this costly failure was undoubtedly Lake's serious deficiency in heavy siege cannon and also lack of skilled engineers, and no amount of gallantry on the part of the assault troops could compensate for these defects. For years afterwards the British were to be taunted with the jibe 'Go and take Bhurtpore!' It was not, however, until 1825 that the defeat was avenged, when General Lord Combermere captured the fortress, but on that occasion he had an army of some 27,000 men with a siege train of 102 guns, a force many times greater than Lake's. During the remainder of 1805 Lake continued his pursuit of the remnants of Holkar's army into the Punjab, until on 24 December a peace treaty was signed which, ironically enough, restored all Holkar's dominions intact. After some years of excessive indulgence in brandy, the Mahratta chieftain died in 1811, three years after Lake's own death on his return to England.

BLACK MANGO TREE, THE BATTLE OF THE   see PANIPAT

BUXAR (BAKSAR) (Bihar, India) Bengal Wars 23 October 1764
Fought between the British under Major Hector Munro and the Imperial Mogul forces led by Shuja-ud-Daula, the Nawab of Oudh.
Strength: British 1,000 Europeans (including 101st and 103rd Foot) + 5,300 sepoys + 900 native cavalry + 28 guns; Mogul army 45,000 + 5,000 Durani (Afghan) horse + 194 guns.
Aim: After the capture of Patna in November 1763 (PATNA II) Mir Kasim retreated with his army to Oudh,

where he entered into an alliance with the Emperor Shah Alam and Shuja-ud-Daula, the ambitious Nawab of Oudh. In March 1764 the united armies of the three parties marched to Benares and crossed the Ganges. On 3 May the Imperial forces launched an attack on a strong British force before Patna, but they were beaten off and retreated to Buxar (Baksar), 77 miles west of Patna. In August 1764 the British force came under command of Major Munro, who was immediately faced with a mutiny among his sepoy battalions, quelled by blowing 24 of the ringleaders from the gun-mouth. Having re-established discipline, Munro reorganised his forces and proceeded to Buxar. Meanwhile dissension in the Allied army led to the eventual expulsion of Mir Kasim and the whole force came under the command of the Nawab of Oudh. *Battle:* On 22 October 1764 the advancing British came in sight of the enemy's strongly entrenched position at Buxar. Early the following morning they were astonished to see the whole army of Shuja-ud-Daula moving out of its entrenchments with the object of giving battle on the plain. Munro then drew up his force in two lines, with the reserve midway between them to meet the onslaught. Action commenced when a large body of Durani horse charged down on Munro's left flank, to be met with furious musket-fire and dispersed. A key point in the enemy's position was a grove held by a large force of cavalry and infantry with several guns and this was attacked and carried with the bayonet, 27 guns being captured. The retreating troops were driven across the front of the enemy's centre, causing great confusion. Following another abortive cavalry attack by 6,000 horse the whole Imperial army commenced to withdraw: Munro then ordered a general advance, sweeping the enemy from their position and also from the fortified village of Buxar. To bar pursuit Shuja-ud-Daula ordered the destruction of a bridge of boats across a stream behind the position, and in the ensuing panic elephants, camels and men were crushed to death in the quagmire. Allied casualties were over 2,000 dead and a larger number wounded, while several thousands perished in the nullah. Large quantities of stores and 167 guns were captured. Of the Europeans, 11 officers and 92 men were killed or wounded; and of the sepoys, 250 were killed, 435 wounded and 85 missing.
Result: After this crushing defeat Shuja-ud-Daula's army gradually disintegrated and eventually, on 26 May 1765, he gave himself up to the British. Robert Clive, now Baron Clive of Plassey and Governor of Bengal, was magnanimous and with the nominal approval of the Emperor Shah Alam, with whom friendly relations had now been resumed, reinstated the Nawab as sovereign ruler of Oudh. He stipulated, however, that British garrisons should be maintained at Allahabad, Chunar, Benares and Lucknow.

CALCUTTA I (W Bengal, India)   Bengal wars   20 June 1756

Fought between a British garrison, under Captain Minchin and the Governor Roger Drake, and the Bengali army under Siraj-ud-Daula, Nawab of Bengal.
Strength: British 515; Bengalis 50,000 + French gunners 200.
Aim: On his death in 1756 Alivardi Khan, the Nawab of Bengal, was succeeded by his grand-nephew Siraj-ud-Daula. Difficulties soon arose between the East India Company in the settlement at Calcutta and the new Nawab, who feared the Europeans would interfere in the government of Bengal. Accordingly as a pretext he ordered Governor Roger Drake to dismantle the fortifications of the settlement at Fort William. On the latter's refusal to do so, Siraj-ud-Daula occupied the subordinate British factory at Kasimbazar, some 140 miles up-river from Calcutta. With his army supported by a strong artillery group of Frenchmen commanded by the mercenary Marquis de St Jacques, the Nawab then marched on Calcutta. The defences of the settlement had been seriously neglected and reserves of arms and ammunition were quite inadequate. Of the British troops available, 70 out of a total of 280 were sick and unable to bear arms. Two companies of Militia were hastily mobilised and it was decided to concentrate on a defensive line round the European houses near the fort.
Battle: The first attack by 4,000 of the Nawab's men, backed by the fire of 6 guns, against a redoubt defended by 25 men under Ensign Piccard was repulsed with considerable loss to the attackers. On the morning of 18 June, however, after setting fire to large areas of the city, the Nawab's troops, together with 7,000 professional looters, infiltrated the city and, occupying many of the houses facing the fort, poured in constant fire from small arms and captured cannon. By midday on 19 June the defenders had been forced to withdraw into the fort itself, with some 2,000 Eurasian civilians. The decision was made to evacuate the fort and take to the ships lying off-shore in the Hooghly, among the first to embark being Governor Drake and Captain Minchin. The ships then pulled down the river and eventually anchored at Fulta. This left only 170 of the defenders still in the fort, and they chose the city magistrate, John Zephaniah Holwell, as their leader. The men continued to fight on with desperate gallantry and it was only when their effective numbers had been reduced to 14 that Holwell decided to surrender. Despite the smallness of the defending

force, the casualties they inflicted on the Bengalis were said to have amounted to 7,000 killed and wounded.

Result: There now followed the horror of what came to be known as the 'Black Hole of Calcutta'. It was touched off when some of the European soldiers who were drunk began to assault their native guards, and to prevent further trouble the Nawab ordered that all the prisoners be confined in a cell in the barracks for the night. He probably did not realise that this cell–known as the 'Black Hole'–measured only 18 feet long by 14 feet wide and that it had only two small air-holes. In this room 146 prisoners, including 1 woman and 12 wounded officers, were confined to spend one of the hottest nights of the Bengal summer. When the door was opened at 6 o'clock the next morning only 23 persons, including Holwell himself, staggered out alive.

After renaming Calcutta 'Alinagar' and erecting a mosque inside the fort precincts, the Nawab left the city and returned to his capital of Murshidabad.

CALCUTTA II (W Bengal, India)   Bengal Wars   2 January 1757
Fought between the British forces under Lt-Colonel Robert Clive, supported by Vice-Admiral Charles Watson, and a Bengali garrison under the Governor, Manik Chand.
Strength: British 528 infantry + 250 39th Foot (as marines) + 940 sepoys + 109 artillerymen + 160 lascars (camp followers); Bengalis 2,000 cavalry + 1,500 infantry.
Aim: The relief expedition for the recapture of Calcutta sailed from Madras on 16 October 1756. Five British ships under the command of Vice-Admiral Watson and 6 Company transports carried the European soldiers and sepoys, together with three companies of King's troops of the 39th Foot, later the Dorsetshire Regiment, the first British regular unit in India, these latter serving as marines. The intention was not so much to exact retribution from Siraj-ud-Daula, the Nawab of Bengal, as to force him to agree to a settlement favourable to the East India Company.

Unfortunately for the British the fleet was dispersed by monsoon gales and only 5 vessels, including Watson's flagship *Kent*, had arrived at Fulta, 50 miles up the river Hooghly, by 15 December. After an unsatisfactory exchange of letters between Clive and the Nawab it was decided to commence offensive operations with the forces available by attacking the fort at Budge-Budge on the banks of the river half-way between Fulta and Calcutta.
Battle: On 28 December Clive with some 500 men and 2 field pieces landed and took the road to Calcutta in order to ambush the garrison of Budge-Budge if it withdrew following the planned naval bombardment from the river-front the next day. The troops made an exhausting night march through deep swamp and jungle and at 10 o'clock the following morning were resting when suddenly without warning they were attacked by Manik Chand with a force of over 3,000 horse and foot. After a skirmish lasting over an hour, in which the Bengalis lost 150 killed to the British casualties of 18 killed and wounded, Manik Chand drew off his forces and returned in haste to Calcutta. Following this encounter it was decided to postpone the attack on the fort until the next morning, but the issue was decided that night when a drunken sailor named Strahan took it into his head to storm the fort himself. Rushing alone through a breach in the walls he cried, 'The place is mine'. Fortunately for him the garrison had been slipping away in the darkness and, hearing his shouts, his comrades hastened to his support and in no time the fort was taken.

The squadron then moved up-river on the 20-mile journey to Calcutta and at dawn on 2 January 1757 Clive landed again. Joining up with the sepoys he advanced on the city. As the ships approached Fort William they came under fire from Manik Chand's batteries, but these were soon silenced. As Clive's force approached, the garrison fled and the city was reoccupied without bloodshed.
Result: Drake and his council were now reinstalled once more in Calcutta, little more than six months since they had left it so ignominiously. The city had been heavily plundered by the Nawab's army and was now almost completely in ruins and the fort severely damaged.

CALCUTTA III (W Bengal, India)   Bengal Wars   5 February 1757
Fought between a British force under Colonel Robert Clive and the army of the Siraj-ud-Daula, Nawab of Bengal.
Strength: British 470 European infantry + 70 gunners + 600 sailors (gun-haulers) + 800 sepoys + 6 field pieces and 1 howitzer; Bengalis 22,000 infantry + 18,000 cavalry + 40 guns.
Aim: After the reoccupation of Calcutta the Council of the East India Company formally declared war on the Nawab of Bengal. It was then decided to recapture the town of Hooghly before the Nawab could advance from Murshidabad. Accordingly a contingent of some 650 men taken up the river by the British

navy occupied the town after the garrison of 2,000 had fled. On hearing this the Nawab at once marched southward with his army and by 2 February 1757 had encamped to the east of Calcutta.

Battle: At dawn on 5 February Clive and his troops were approaching the Bengali camp when a thick fog descended so that it was impossible to see more than a few yards. Thus shrouded from view Clive's force was able to march through the long straggling camp causing havoc by firing on both sides. They were then attacked by 300 of the Nawab's élite Persian horse guards who were practically annihilated by the British musket-fire. Suddenly the fog lifted and in the morning sunlight Clive's troops became a perfect target for the Nawab's cannon and parties of attacking horsemen. Eventually, however, they managed to reach a bridge spanning the so-called Mahratta Ditch defending the approaches to Calcutta and crossed to the safety of Fort William. British casualties were 57 killed and 137 wounded, whereas the Nawab's were much more considerable, 1,300 of his troops being killed or wounded as well as 500 horses lost.

Result: Although this affair could hardly be accounted a victory for Clive, it frightened Siraj-ud-Daula sufficiently into agreeing to sign a treaty promising to pay compensation to the Company and to restore all privileges previously enjoyed by the British. He then retired with his army to Murshidabad. His decision was probably influenced by the disturbing news that Ahmed Shah Abdali, the Shah of Afghanistan, was advancing with his hordes of horsemen towards Bengal.

CALICUT (KOZHIKADE) (Kerala, India)   Third Mysore War   10 December 1790
Fought between a British contingent commanded by Colonel James Hartley and a Mysorean force under Tipu Sultan's general, Hussein Ali.

Strength: British 600 Europeans + 1,900 sepoys; Mysoreans 9,000.

Aim: The British objective was to eliminate the Mysorean hold over the Malabar coastal strip.

Battle: The Mysorean force had taken up a strong defensive position in a ploughed field in front of Calicut (Kozhikade) on the Malabar coast. Hartley attacked and carried the position with the loss of only 52 men. The Mysorean casualties amounted to 1,000 killed and wounded plus 900 prisoners, including their commander Hussein Ali.

Result: Four days after this spirited victory, General Sir Robert Abercrombie appeared before the town of Cannamore with a force from Bombay. The town was reduced within twenty-four hours and Abercrombie followed up this success with the occupation of the entire provice of Malabar.

CHANDERNAGORE (W Bengal, India)   Bengal Wars   23 March 1757
Fought between the British under Colonel Robert Clive, with naval support commanded by Vice-Admiral Charles Watson, and a French garrison under the Governor M. Renault.

Strength: British 700 European infantry + 1,600 sepoys; French 237 European infantry + 220 European sailors + 167 sepoys + 170 Eurasian infantry and gunners + 2,000 Bengalis (loaned by the Nawab of Bengal).

Aim: After the recapture of Calcutta (CALCUTTA III) the East India Company proposed to present Siraj-ud-Daula, the Nawab of Bengal, with demands for compensation for the immense damage done by his plundering army and sent an envoy to his camp near Murshidabad for this purpose. Before taking further positive action to enforce their demands, however, Clive and Watson decided that they could not run the risk of the Nawab's being supported by the European troops in the French settlement at Chandernagore on the banks of the Hooghly, 20 miles north of Calcutta. It was accordingly decided to capture the fort and eliminate the French threat, on the added grounds too that Britain and France were now officially at war in Europe.

Battle: Clive's troops marched northwards from Calcutta on 8 March and four days later the naval squadron under Admiral Watson proceeded up the Hooghly. On the following day Clive summoned the French Governor Renault to surrender. Receiving no reply Clive then attacked the town from the west side, occupying a number of outposts, whereupon the Nawab's contingent decided to desert. By 15 March the French were obliged to abandon the town and retire into Fort d'Orléans on the river side. By 19 March the British squadron had arrived and, after some difficulty, HMS *Kent* and *Tyger* slipped past the French boom. They then commenced to bombard the fort whose guns, however, inflicted considerable damage among the ships. After three hours the guns of the fort were silenced and the French Commander surrendered. The casualties of both contestants were about the same, 200 men, the heaviest on the British side being sustained by the navy.

Result: The capture of Chandernagore destroyed French influence in Bengal and, as Clive put it, dealt 'an unexpressable blow to the French Company'.

CHARJUI (CHARDZHOU) (USSR)   Persian Wars   1740
Fought between the Persians under Nadir Shah and the Uzbegs under Abdul Fayz Khan, King of
Bukhara.
Strength: Persians 50,000; Uzbegs 30,000
Aim: After his successful invasion of India, Nadir spent the rest of 1739 in an expedition into Sind (Scinde,
Pakistan) to establish his authority in this newly acquired province. He then turned his attention to the
Uzbegs of Bukhara (USSR) and Khiva (USSR). From both countries hordes of raiders annually ravaged
Khorasan in N Persia and the punitive campaign which was planned against them was organised from
Balkh (USSR), where large quantities of grain had been collected. These supplies were loaded on to boats
and the Persian army marched NW on both banks of the river Oxus (Amu Darya) to Charjui
(Chardzhou), where a bridge of boats was constructed across the river.
Battle: Realising that he was quite unable to resist Nadir's veteran forces, Abdul Fayz Khan submitted
without a fight and surrendered himself at the camp of Nadir.
Result: Nadir restored Abdul Fayz to the throne of Bukhara on condition that the Oxus should constitute
the boundary of Persia. One result of this campaign was that 8,000 Uzbegs were enlisted into the Persian
army.

CHINGLEPUT (Tamil Nadu, India)   Second Carnatic War   13 October 1752
Fought between the British under Captain Robert Clive and the French garrison of Chingleput.
Strength: British 200 Europeans + 500 sepoys + 4 24-pounder siege guns; French 40 Europeans + 500
sepoys + 15 guns.
Aim: Following the capture of the fortress of Covelong (qv) in mid-September Clive decided to proceed
immediately to the investment of the immensely strong fortress of Chingleput, 30 miles inland from the
coast.
Battle: Arriving outside the walls of the fort, Clive set up his battery of siege guns and after a four days'
cannonade succeeded in breaching the walls. The terror inspired by Clive's name among his adversaries
was such that this success was sufficient to induce the French Commander to offer to surrender on
condition that the garrison be allowed to march out with the honours of war, to which request Clive was
quite happy to accede.
Result: As a result of the reduction of Covelong and Chingleput, large areas of the country north of the
Paliar River to Arcot came under British influence, and to quote the words of Major Stringer Lawrence:
'Clive had driven one more nail into the coffin of French hopes and ambitions.'

COCHIN (Kerala, India)   Rebellion in Travancore   1809
Fought between the Travancoreans and the British.
    The Raja of Travancore was bound, under the terms of several treaties, to maintain a force of subsidiary
troops, staffed by English officers, to be at the disposal of the East India Company. Differences arose
between the Raja and the British and a plot to assassinate the British Resident and expel all British
garrisons in S India was discovered. The subsidiary force was full of discontent, having been under the
influence of the Prime Minister of the state who was anti-British. The force was reinforced by the general
commanding the Malabar coast.
    The Residency at Cochin was attacked by a strong group which was, however, repulsed by the small
garrison. The revolt continued and a movement of all troops from the south became necessary. At
Palamcottah, a British column met the Travancoreans in a sharp skirmish, out of which the British
emerged victors. Only one other clash occurred when the British were again successful.
    The approach of large British forces finally persuaded the Raja to comply with the terms of the treaty
and his dissident Prime Minister was dismissed.

COLEROON (Tamil Nadu, India)   Second Mysore War   18 February 1782
Fought between a British force under Colonel John Brathwaite and a Mysorean army under Tipu Sultan
with French support under Major Henri Lally.
Strength: British 60 Europeans + 1,600 sepoys; Mysoreans 13,000 horse and foot + French 400 cavalry.
    After his reverses at the hands of General Sir Eyre Coote in the operations during 1781, Haider Ali
abandoned many of his posts in the Carnatic and retired with his main forces to Mysore. Then suddenly
the tide of British successes was stemmed by a considerable disaster.

Battle: Colonel Brathwaite, while encamped a few miles south of the river Coleroon, was surprised by a large Mysorean column under Tipu Sultan, Haider Ali's heir. Tipu's large host hemmed in the British, and although Brathwaite's position was strong and he put up a desperate resistance against overwhelming odds, Lally's final cavalry charge broke through the British ranks and they were compelled to surrender. With one exception, every British officer present was either killed or wounded, but at least one-third of Brathwaite's force made good their escape.

Result: Although this success was not in itself a sufficient reason to cause Haider Ali to alter his plan of campaign, the arrival of a large contingent of French troops, brought with the French fleet under Admiral Pierre André de Suffren, materially altered the whole military situation to Haider's advantage. In the meantime Colonel Brathwaite and his surviving officers were imprisoned in the dungeons in Tipu Sultan's capital of Seringapatam.

CONDORE (Andhra Pradesh, India) Third Carnatic War 7 December 1758
Fought between a British expeditionary force from Bengal under Lt-Colonel Francis Forde, allied with a native force under Raja Anundaraz, and the French under the Marquis de Conflans.

Strength: 500 Europeans + 100 lascars + 2,000 sepoys + 7 field guns and 11 battery cannon + 500 Indian horse + 5,000 Indian foot; French 500 Europeans + 6,000 sepoys + 36 guns and mortars.

Aim: Hoping to take advantage of the Marquis de Bussy-Castelnau's withdrawal from the Deccan to aid Comte Thomas-Arthur Lally de Tollendal in his operations against Madras, Robert Clive, now Governor of Bengal, decided to ship a force from Calcutta under Lt-Colonel Francis Forde to act in concert with Raja Anundaraz, a ruler in the Northern Sirkars who had revolted against the French and seized Vizagapatam (Vishakhapatnam). On 20 October 1758 the expedition reached that port and then marched SW to join with Anundaraz's troops near Cossimcotah.

Battle: On 3 December the British force in conjunction with the native levies of Raja Anundaraz came in sight of Conflan's force encamped near Peddapore, 40 miles north of Rajahmundry, astride the highroad to the south. Three days later Forde advanced to within 4 miles of the French position which, however, he found too strong to be attacked frontally and so decided to outflank it by occupying the village of Condore, 3 miles distant. At 8am on the morning of 9 December when Forde was preparing to pitch camp on the plain before Condore, Conflans was seen approaching at a rapid pace with his entire force. Forde immediately formed his line with the British 101st and 102nd Foot, flanked by 6 guns in the centre, with wings on either side each of 900 sepoys. He then disposed his centre at the rear of a field of maize, which quite concealed the British troops. At a range of 1,000 yards the French opened fire with 30 pieces, to which Ford could only reply with 8 guns. The French then advanced to attack the sepoy battalion on the left, not having observed the British infantry concealed behind the maize field. At the crucial moment Forde ordered the British battalion to advance across the path of the French who were taken completely by surprise. The French broke and fled, but Anundaraz's cavalry refused to pursue them at a time when they could have played a major part in their destruction. The whole British force then advanced to the French camp where the remnants of the French battalion had rallied in a deep hollow with guns in support, but they fled on seeing the British guns come forward. French casualties in killed, wounded and captured amounted to 14 officers and 163 men, 30 cannon and the whole of their baggage. British casualties amounted to 40 Europeans and 200 sepoys killed and wounded.

Result: On the following day the British advanced to Rajahmundry, 40 miles south and occupied the fort without opposition Forde then decided to follow up his success with an advance on Masulipatam (qv).

CONJEVERAM (Tamil Nadu, India) Second Carnatic War 15 December 1751
Fought between the British under Captain Robert Clive and the French under a Portuguese soldier of fortune known as La Volonté.

Strength: British 200 Europeans + 700 sepoys + 600 Mahratta cavalry; French 300 Europeans + 400 sepoys.

Aim: After his success at Arni (qv) Clive was urged by Thomas Saunders, Governor of Madras, to attack Conjeveram, 40 miles to the NE, which was now held by a detachment of French who were disrupting communications between Arcot and Madras. They had also captured a party of English sick and wounded officers and soldiers and were reported to be treating them with great cruelty.

Battle: Clive arrived at Conjeveram accompanied by the Mahratta horse under their chieftain Buzangara on 15 December 1751. The enemy held the great temple which was surrounded by inner and outer walls and strongly fortified. La Volonté refused to surrender, threatening that if the British did not withdraw he

would hang the 2 officers in the captured party, Lieutenants Revell and Glass. Clive ignored the threat and the following day his cannon commenced to batter the massive temple walls. Although the French had no guns they maintained fierce musket-fire, causing several casualties. After two days of bombardment the walls began to crumble. At this stage Revell was forced to mount the breach in the hope that his presence there would halt the British fire, but he was quickly brought down by the intervention of Moden Sahib, Chanda Sahib's Governor of Conjeveram who was secretly in league with the British and their nominee for the Nawabship of the Carnatic, Mohammed Ali. That night La Volonté and his garrison slipped quietly away, leaving all the prisoners behind unharmed.
Result: After taking possession of the great temple the British destroyed its defences and then abandoned it. Having looted Conjeveram the Mahrattas, under Buzangara, left for Trichinopoly. Without their support Clive decided to send most of his force back to support the garrison at Arcot. He himself returned to Madras to be welcomed as a hero.

COVELONG (Tamil Nadu, India)   Second Carnatic War   16 September 1752
Fought between the British under Captain Robert Clive and the French garrison of Covelong.
Strength: British 200 European recruits + 500 sepoys + 4 24-pounder siege guns; French 50 Europeans + 300 sepoys.
Aim: Although the surrender of Trichinopoly to the British on 13 June 1752 (TRICHONOPOLY I) considerably reduced French influence on the Coromandel coast, the French Governor-General at Pondicherry, the Marquis Joseph-François Dupleix, continued his efforts to regain lost ground by intense political intrigue. It was accordingly decided by the British Governor at Fort St David, Thomas Saunders, that the two fortresses of Covelong and Chingleput (qv)–some 30 miles south of Madras–which were still under French control, must be reduced. Clive was ordered to carry out this task.
Battle: With his force of raw recruits, both British and Indian, Clive set out from Madras on 15 September 1752 for Covelong, a walled fortress on the coast to the south. On arriving before it Clive occupied a stretch of gardens a short distance from the fort and set up a battery. A steady bombardment was then opened up on the ramparts. Shattered by the effect of the siege guns, the Garrison Commander surrendered. On taking possession of the fort Clive found 50 guns captured by the French from Madras in the siege of 1746. The following morning a French relief force from Chingleput was ambushed and the Commanding Officer, 20 European soldiers, 250 sepoys and 2 guns were captured.
Result: The most remarkable feature of this engagement was the way in which Clive was able to weld the new recruits fresh from England as well as the Indians into a disciplined fighting force. At first, according to one report, they even ran away at the sound of their own fire, one of them disappearing altogether, to be found the next day hiding at the bottom of a well.

CUDDALORE I (Tamil Nadu, India)   First Carnatic War   28 June 1748
Fought between the British garrison under Major Stringer Lawrence and a French force from Pondicherry, the main French base in the Carnatic.
Strength: British 600 Europeans + 400 sepoys; French 800 Europeans + 1,000 sepoys.
Aim: After making several abortive attempts to capture Fort St David (qv) which, following the fall of Madras in October 1746, had become the main British base on the Coromandel coast, the French Governor-General, the Marquis Joseph-François Dupleix, decided to turn his attention to Cuddalore, a fortified British station 2 miles to the south.
Battle: Dupleix's intention was to surprise Cuddalore by night and with this aim in view he arranged for his troops to be concealed in some hills about 3 miles from the station until the time came for the attack. Lawrence, who had full intelligence of the plan, ostentatiously removed the garrison and guns from Cuddalore to Fort St David in full view of the French during the day but sent them back after dark with considerable reinforcements. At midnight the French advanced to the walls of the fort, but no sooner had they planted their scaling ladders than they were met with a withering fire of musketry and grape. Most of them flung down their arms without firing a shot, and all fled back to Pondicherry.
Result: This was the first direct brush between French and English troops in India and ended in the complete discomfiture of the former, and proved a setback to Dupleix's ambitions to achieve supremacy in the Carnatic.

CUDDALORE II (Tamil Nadu, India)   Second Mysore War   13 June 1783
Fought between the British, under General Sir James Stuart, and the Mysorean forces outside Cuddalore under Tipu Sultan together with the garrison under General the Marquis de Bussy-Castelnau.

Strength: British 1,660 Europeans + 8,340 sepoys + 1,000 native cavalry; French 3,000 Europeans + 3,000 sepoys + Mysoreans 3,000 infantry + 2,000 cavalry.

Aim: After the death of Haider Ali on 7 December 1782, his son Tipu Sultan (Tippoo Sahib), the celebrated 'Tiger of Mysore', was proclaimed ruler in his place, and continued operations against the British in conjunction with his French allies. In April 1783 the Madras authorities decided to recover Cuddalore, the port on the Coromandel coast used by the French squadron of Admiral Pierre André de Suffren as a base, to which he had transported de Bussy and his reinforcements. Accordingly a force under General Sir James Stuart, with supplies for twenty-five days, set off southwards from Madras. On 7 June he took up position 2 miles south of the fort of Cuddalore, with his right near the sea and his left on the Bandipollam hills.

Battle: On the night of 7 June the French moved out of the fort and occupied an entrenched position about 2 miles from the British. On 12 June, after all his stores had been landed, Stuart determined to attack. Accordingly, the following morning Lt-Colonel Kelly with the 102nd Foot and three sepoy battalions circumvented the Bandipollam hills and captured a battery of enemy guns which were then turned on Tipu's infantry, speedily dispersing them. A general advance against the French entrenchments was, however, repulsed with heavy loss, and desperate fighting ensued. Lt-Colonel Stuart of the 71st Foot managed to occupy one of the French redoubts and during the night the French retired within the fortress, leaving 13 guns in British hands. British casualties were heavy, numbering 1,000 killed and wounded, while the French casualties did not exceed 500. Among the French captured during this action was a certain Sergeant Bernadotte, subsequently a Marshal of France and the future King Charles XIV of Sweden.

The same evening Admiral Suffren's squadron of 15 sail reappeared off the port and was engaged by the British Admiral Sir Edward Hughes with his fleet of 18 ships. An indecisive action followed in which each side lost about 500 men. Hughes however retired to Madras, leaving Suffren in command of the seas.

Result: On 28 June 1783 news came that peace had been declared in Europe between England and France. A convention was then concluded between Stuart and de Bussy under which it was agreed that a period of four months should be allowed for the belligerents to accede to the peace treaty. Stuart was shortly afterwards dismissed from the service of the East India Company for persistent insubordination, and Suffren sailed home to France with a sense of failure. The British were then left to deal with Tipu Sultan alone.

DEIG (DIG) I (Uttar Pradesh, India)   Second Mahratta War   13 November 1804
Fought between the British under Major-General John Henry Fraser and the Mahratta forces of Jaswunt Rao Holkar, Maharaja of Indore.

Strength: British 900 European infantry + 4,200 sepoys + 700 cavalry; Mahrattas 14,000 infantry + 3,000 cavalry + 162 guns.

Aim: Having failed to capture Delhi (DELHI II), Holkar sent back his infantry by a circuitous route through the hills to Deig (Dig), a strong fortress belonging to his ally Ranjit Singh, Raja of Bhurtpore, while he retired northwards along the river Jumna towards Panipat. General Gerard Lake, commanding all British troops in the north, decided to follow Holkar himself with most of his cavalry, allocating the bulk of his infantry, field artillery and two regiments of native cavalry to his Divisional Commander, Major-General Fraser, for the reduction of the town and fortress of Deig.

Battle: Fraser found the Mahrattas drawn up outside the fortress walls in a strong position, their left protected by a morass near the fort itself and their right by a village on a height, bristling with guns. At 3am on 13 November Fraser gave the order to advance and the village was speedily carried. He then placed himself at the head of the 76th Foot and charged down the hill on the nearest line of guns. Unfortunately for him at this early stage in the battle a cannon-ball carried away one of his legs. The command now devolved on Colonel William Monson, who immediately led the 76th and 101st Foot with two sepoy battalions against the enemy lines, capturing battery after battery, and driving all before them. Hundreds of the fleeing Mahrattas perished in the morass or drowned in the ditch surrounding the fortress, while others crowded inside under cover of fire from the fort guns. A large body of the enemy infantry at the southern end of the morass were next attacked and, after fierce fighting, dispersed and scattered in all directions. Mahratta casualties numbered over 2,000 men and 87 of their guns were captured. Of the British 6 officers were killed, including General Fraser, who died a few days later, and 17 wounded; 244 European other ranks and 373 native soldiers were killed or wounded.

Result: Of this engagement General Lake said afterwards: 'I have reason to believe that the affair of the 13th was a very near business. The personal courage of Monson alone saved it.' This was a generous acknowledgment of the fact that Monson had by this action more than redeemed the disgrace of the retreat from the Mokundra Pass (qv). After the victory Monson retired to Mathura to await the arrival of the siege train from Agra before proceeding to the investment of the fortress of Deig itself.

DEIG (DIG) II (Uttar Pradesh, India)   Second Mahratta War   25 December 1804
Fought between the British under General Gerard Lake and the Mahratta garrison of Jaswunt Rao Holkar, Maharaja of Indore.
Strength: British 1,000 European cavalry + 2,000 native cavalry + 900 European infantry + 7,000 sepoys + 10 siege guns and 4 mortars; Mahrattas 8,000.
Aim: On 20 November Lake's cavalry left Farrukhabad (qv) after their successful encounter with Holkar's forces and, crossing the river Jumna, linked up with Colonel William Monson's troops near Mathura. On 1 December Lake then advanced southwards to invest Deig (Dig), the fortress town belonging to the former British ally, the Raja of Bhurtpore, who had now treacherously espoused the cause of Holkar.
Battle: On 10 December the siege train arrived from Agra, and three days later Lake's entire force moved forward and encamped on the western side of the fortress. The town of Deig was defended by a strong mud wall with a deep ditch on all sides except at the SW angle where the defences were continued to a rocky eminence known as the Shah Bourj. By 20 December a battery of heavy guns made a practicable breach in the walls of the Shah Bourj defences. Late on the night of 23 December three storming parties, commanded by Colonel Macrae, assaulted these defences, taking them after heavy fighting, after which the main walls of the town were speedily carried in the face of intense musket-fire. Preparations were then made for the final assault on the citadel, but the enemy evacuated it during the ensuing night. By Christmas morning, 1804, the whole town and fortress of Deig were in Lake's possession, together with most of Holkar's remaining artillery and huge stores of grain and considerable treasure in specie. British casualties in the siege were comparatively light, totalling 43 killed and 184 wounded.
Result: Having repaired the defences of Deig, Lake marched SE on 28 December towards the fortress of Bhurtpore (qv), for the last major action of the campaign.

DELHI I (Haryana, India)   Second Mahratta War   11 September 1803
Fought between the British under General Gerard Lake and the Mahratta army under the French General Louis Bourquien.
Strength: British 1,000 cavalry + 3,500 infantry; Mahrattas 6,000 cavalry + 13,000 infantry.
Aim: After the capture of the Mahratta hill fortress of Aligarh (qv), Lake marched towards Delhi, which he aimed to capture, arriving within 6 miles to the east of the city on 10 September. He then received intelligence that Bourquien had crossed the river Jumna in the night and that the whole Mahratta force was drawn up on rising ground with the river to their rear.
Battle: Bourquien opened the action with heavy artillery fire, whereupon Lake ordered his cavalry back, hoping to lure the enemy from their lines. This feint was successful and the cavalry, galloping away to both flanks, revealed the British line of battalions advancing, with the 76th Foot on the right. The advance was maintained under tremendous fire until within 100 yards of the enemy, when Lake gave the order to fire a volley and charge. The British dashed forward, supported now by the cavalry and the 'galloper guns', the forerunner of horse artillery developed by Lake. The Mahrattas broke and fled in all directions and many were driven into the river. Mahratta casualties amounted to some 3,000 men, and 68 of their guns were captured. British casualties totalled 478 killed, wounded and missing, and of these 137 belonged to the 76th Highlanders.
Result: This victory enabled Lake to occupy Delhi and brought the entire country between the Jumna and the Ganges under British control. On 14 September Bourquien and 4 other French officers surrendered, and were sent down to Calcutta. On 16 September Lake was welcomed by the Mogul Emperor Shah Alam II, now old and blind, who was to die three years later at the age of eighty-three, having, as Fortescue says, 'lived to see the occupants of a few small factories become masters of India'.

DELHI II (Haryana, India)   Second Mahratta War   7–16 October 1804
Fought between the British garrison of Delhi, commanded by Colonel David Ochterlony, and the army of Jaswunt Rao Holkar, Maharaja of Indore, commanded by Bapaji Scindia.
Strength: British 800 sepoys + 1,200 local levies; Mahrattas 19,000 + 160 guns.
Aim: After the disaster of Monson's Retreat (see MOKUNDRA PASS), Holkar continued his victorious march

towards Delhi, which he hoped to capture and with it the person of the Mogul Emperor Shah Alam II. In the meantime, on 22 September, General Gerard Lake, the Commander-in-Chief, concentrated his forces at Agra and marched northwards to relieve Delhi.

Battle: On 7 October Holkar's army invested the city, whose defences were in a very dilapidated condition, and set up batteries against the SW wall. A determined sortie by the garrison was highly successful and the sepoys spiked all the enemy's guns with small cost to themselves. On 14 October the Mahrattas made an assault on the Lahore Gate, which was beaten off with considerable loss to the attackers. Finally, on the approach of General Lake, the Mahrattas raised the siege and retired. The garrison was so small that it had to be on constant duty during the whole nine days of the siege of the city, whose walls were 10 miles in circumference.

Result: After the failure of his attempt on Delhi, Holkar divided his forces, sending back his infantry through the hills to Deig (see DEIG I and II), a strong fortress belonging to his ally the Raja of Bhurtpore, while he moved with his cavalry up the river Jumna to Panipat. Leaving Major-General John Henry Fraser with a force at Delhi to deal with Holkar's infantry, Lake himself led the pursuit of the Mahratta leader with the remainder of his cavalry, with some infantry support.

DEVICOTAH (DEVI KOTAL) (Tamil Nadu, India)   Second Carnatic War   April 1749
Fought between the British under Major Stringer Lawrence and the forces of Partab Singh, Raja of Tanjore.

Strength: British 800 Europeans + 1,500 sepoys; Tanjorines 20,000.

Aim: Alarmed at the expansionist activities of the French in India, the British decided to espouse the cause of the deposed Raja Sauhojee of the State of Tanjore some 30 miles south of Fort St David on the Coromandel coast. It was agreed to send troops to reinstate Sauhojee in return for the grant of the fort of Devicotah (Devi Kotal) at the mouth of the Coleroon River. The first expedition which set out in March 1749 under Captain James Cope was a complete failure; a cyclone scattered the artillery and baggage train and the troops were compelled to retreat with heavy losses. To redeem this failure all available forces at Fort St David under the command of Stringer Lawrence, with Captain Robert Clive as a Company Commander, landed at the mouth of the Coleroon on an island close to Devicotah, together with heavy artillery.

Battle: Lawrence first subjected the fort to a three-day bombardment, by which time a breach had been blasted in the walls. However, this was protected by a narrow but swift-flowing river. At this stage Clive asked to lead the assault and with a force of 30 British soldiers and 200 sepoys crossed the stream towards the enemy's entrenchments. There they came under constant attack by bodies of Tanjorine cavalry. Forming a small square, the British fought back desperately until only Clive and 3 men were left standing. At this stage Lawrence arrived with the main force and dispersed the cavalry. At the head of his sepoys Clive now stormed the breach and the fort was taken.

Result: This victory was very timely, coming as a morale-booster in the face of recent French successes. The sequel, however, was not one of the most creditable in the annals of the East India Company. Instead of continuing to aid the deposed Raja, negotiations were entered into with Partab Singh, as a result of which, in return for a promise of the cession of Devicotah, Sauhojee was pensioned off.

FARRUKHABAD (Uttar Pradesh, India)   Second Mahratta War   17 November 1804
Fought between the British under General Gerard Lake and the Mahrattas under Jaswunt Rao Holkar, Maharaja of Indore.

Strength: British 200 European infantry + 1,800 sepoys + 1,000 European cavalry + 1,500 native cavalry; Mahrattas 60,000 cavalry.

Aim: After his failure to capture Delhi (see DELHI II), Holkar divided his forces, sending his infantry through the hills to the fortress of Deig (qv), while he led his cavalry northwards along the Jumna River in a series of pillaging raids. Lake similarly divided his forces, sending Major-General John Henry Fraser with the bulk of the infantry to invest Deig, while he personally took his cavalry with some infantry support in pursuit of Holkar.

Battle: After a prolonged pursuit, Lake's force came on 16 November to the village of Aligunge, which had been plundered by Holkar's troops and was still burning. Here he learned that Holkar was now at Farrukhabad, 36 miles east, a sufficient distance away for him to judge himself safe for the night. At 9pm that evening Lake's cavalry and horse artillery rode off in bright moonlight towards Farrukhabad. Dawn was just breaking when they come upon the Mahratta camp with its still sleeping inmates quite unaware of their approach until the 'galloper guns' opened fire. Led by the 8th Light Dragoons, the cavalry then swept down on the camp, inflicting severe losses on the helpless enemy. More than 3,000 Mahrattas were killed in the fray and the fleeing enemy horse were pursued for over 10 miles. British casualties were only 28 men killed and wounded. Early in the battle, Holkar had galloped off with a few followers, leaving his hapless force leaderless, and he did not draw rein until he had crossed the river Kali, 18 miles away.

Result: This action completely destroyed Holkar's cavalry as a fighting force. Lake's achievement had indeed been remarkable; between the time of leaving Delhi on 31 October and the surprise attack at Farrukhabad he had marched 350 miles. In the twenty-four hours preceding the action he had marched 70 miles, attacking the enemy without a halt and then pursuing the defeated Mahrattas. Almost immediately afterwards he turned south again to join forces with Colonel William Monson for the siege of Deig.

FORT ST DAVID I (Tamil Nadu, India)   First Carnatic War   19 December 1746
Fought between the British garrison at Fort St David, supported by a force of Indian cavalry under Maphuze Khan and Mohammed Ali, sons of the Nawab of the Carnatic, and a French force under General de Bury.
Strength: British 200 Europeans + 100 sepoys + 2,000 Indian cavalry; French 900 Europeans + 700 sepoys + 6 guns and 6 mortars.
Aim: After the fall of Madras, Fort St David, 12 miles south of the French base at Pondicherry, became the rallying-point of the British on the Coromandel coast. The fort though small was the strongest the British possessed in India. The French intended to invest the fort.
Battle: On 19 December 1746 de Bury crossed the river Pennar and took up a position in a walled garden about 1½ miles from Fort St David. Here the French, who had posted neither picquets nor sentries, were suddenly attacked by the Indian cavalry force sent by Anwar-ud-Din, Nawab of the Carnatic, at the request of the British, under the command of his two sons. Fortunately for de Bury his artillery stood firm, although his infantry fled in panic, and saved the force from annihilation. After sustaining casualties of 132 killed and wounded the French retreated to their base at Ariancopang, near Pondicherry.
Result: The following month a squadron of French ships arrived on the coast and with this display of force behind him the Governor-General at Pondicherry, the Marquis Joseph-François Dupleix, reopened negotiations with Anwar-Ud-Din and persuaded him with a gift of £15,000 to conclude peace with the French and withdraw his troops from Fort St David. In May 1757 the French made a second attempt to invest the fort but were again foiled, this time by the arrival of a British squadron under Admiral Griffen in the roadstead.

FORT ST DAVID II (Tamil Nadu, India)   Third Carnatic War   2 June 1758
Fought between the British garrison at Fort St David, under Major Polier, and the French under Comte Thomas-Arthur Lally de Tollendal.
Strength: British 350 Europeans + 250 European sailors + 1,600 sepoys; French 2,500 Europeans + 2,500 sepoys.
Aim: On 29 April a force of 1,000 French with 1,000 sepoys arrived before Fort St David from Pondicherry, the main French base in the Carnatic, and exchanged shots with the garrison. On 1 May Lally de Tollendal sent a detached force under Comte d'Estaing against the town of Cuddalore, a few miles to the south, which was garrisoned by five companies of sepoys only. Three days later they capitulated. On 6 May the French squadron commanded by Admiral Comte Anne-Antoine d'Aché anchored before Fort St David, landing the troops on board, and the French then proceeded to erect their first battery for their proposed siege.
Battle: Polier made the grave mistake of attempting to defend several outworks with inadequate forces instead of destroying them and retiring within the main fortress. Lally was therefore able to drive the defenders from these outworks piecemeal. His successes scared the British sepoys into wholesale desertion until finally, on 2 June, although the fort had not been breached, the garrison capitulated.
Result: Lally's great objective was achieved and he followed up his success by the capture of Fort Devicotah (Devi Kotal) at the mouth of the Coleroon River. The authorities in Madras were now thoroughly alarmed and called in all the scattered garrisons in the Carnatic as a precaution against the day when Madras itself might be invested.

GAWILGHUR (Maharashtra, India)   Second Mahratta War   15 December 1803
Fought between the British force under Major-General Arthur Wellesley and the Mahratta garrison of troops of Rughuji Bhonsla, Raja of Berar.

Strength: British 10,500; Mahrattas 4,000.

Aim: Following the British victory over the combined Mahratta forces of Scindia of Gwalior and the Bhonsla at Argaum (qv) on 29 November, Wellesley marched with his whole force to Gawilghur, the hill fortress where the defeated infantry of the Bhonsla had taken refuge. Situated on a lofty mountain between the headwaters of the rivers Taptee and Purna, some 170 miles NE of Aurangabad, the fort itself was divided into two distinct parts, a main citadel fronting to the south and an outer fort covering the approach from the north. The fortress, long considered impregnable, was approached by three extremely difficult roads. In fact, as Wellesley himself remarked, the greatest problem in attacking Gawilghur was to approach it at all.

Battle: The main assault was entrusted to the division commanded by Wellesley's second in command, Colonel James Stevenson. Having dragged heavy siege ordance and stores over mountainous approaches for four days, 2 batteries of 9 guns were erected on the night of 12 December in front of the north face. At the same time Wellesley's troops mounted a battery of 4 guns near the southern gate. By the night of 14 December practicable breaches had been made and the outer fort was taken by storm. The main citadel was assaulted by the light company of the Scots Brigade and the 94th Foot on the following day, and in a very short time the British were in full possession of Gawilghur, with casualties of only 14 killed and 112 wounded.

Result: Following this final blow, a peace treaty, the Treaty of Deogaom, was concluded with the Bhonsla, under which he ceded the provinces of Kullack and Berar and renounced all claims on the territories of the Nizam of Hyderabad. A similar treaty with Scindia of Gwalior had to await the outcome of the campaign waged during this same period by General Lake in the north, culminating in the victory at Laswari (qv).

GOLDEN ROCK   see TRICHINOPOLY (TIRUCHCHIRAPALLI) II

GULNABAD (Iran)   Persian Wars   7 March 1722
Fought between the Afghan invading army under Mahmud Khan and the Persians under Rustum Khan.
Strength: Afghans 20,000 with 100 swivel guns mounted on camels; Persians 20,000 infantry + 30,000 cavalry + 24 guns.

Aim: In the winter of 1721 Mahmud Khan, the son of Mir Vais and now the independent ruler of Kandahar, invaded Persia and marched on the capital Isfahan where Shah Husain unsuccessfully attempted to buy him off with £30,000. It was then decided to take the field against the invaders and a Persian army commanded by Rustum Khan, the General of the Royal Guards, marched towards the Afghans' prepared position at Gulnabad, a village 11 miles from Isfahan.

Battle: The battle opened with a charge by the Persian right which was partly successful. At the same time the Arab cavalry, under its leader the Vali (Regent) of Arabia, turned the enemy's left flank and fell on the Afghan camp which was then plundered, the Arabs taking no further part in the fighting. The Afghans then opened up with their swivel guns, causing great havoc among the Persian left wing, which soon broke and fled. The pursuing Afghans wheeled on the rear of the Persian artillery, cutting the gunners to pieces. The guns were then turned on the Persian infantry which also broke and fled the field, having incurred no more than 2,000 casualties.

Result: By this crushing defeat the military power of the Persian Safavi dynasty was destroyed and the Persian army never again faced the Afghans in the field. After taking Farrahabad and Julfa, Mahmud Khan proceeded to invest Isfahan, which was eventually starved into submission. Shah Husain then surrendered to the conqueror and an Afghan dynasty ruled in Persia.

GWALIOR (Madhya Pradesh, India)   First Mahratta War   3 August 1780
Fought between a British force under Captain William Popham and the Mahratta army under Mahadaji Scindia of Gwalior.
Strength: British 400 Europeans + 2,000 sepoys; Mahrattas 20,000 (field force) + 2,000 (garrison).

Aim: Following the repudiation of the Convention of Worgaom by the Governor-General of India, Warren Hastings, and the capture of Ahmadabad (qv) by Brigadier-General Thomas Goddard's force in Gujarat in February 1780, it was decided to stage a diversion in the Gohud area south of Agra to cause as much trouble as possible to the Mahratta chief, Mahadaji Scindia. A force of 2,400, hastily improvised out of drafts for Goddard's army and commanded by Captain Popham, was dispatched for this purpose, with the approval of the Commander-in-Chief in Bengal, General Sir Eyre Coote.

Battle: Popham crossed the river Jumna in February 1780 and promptly attacked and defeated a body of Mahrattas near Gohud. He then turned against Lahar, about 50 miles west of Kalpi, successfully carrying the fort by storm with the loss of little more than 100 men. Finally, Popham carried out the feat which has caused his name to live in Indian military history–the capture of Gwalior. This rock fortress was deemed impregnable, owing to its lofty, isolated position and sheer scarped walls. On the night of 3 August, however, by skilful use of rope ladders, Popham carried 20 Europeans and 1,200 sepoys up the cliff-face and then over a wall 30 feet high into the heart of the fortress. The astonished garrison surrendered without firing a shot and Gwalior was captured without the loss of a single man. As Fortescue says: 'There is no more memorable feat in our Indian military history for skill and daring.'

Result: In spite of this inspiring victory, operations against the Mahrattas had been indecisive and unsatisfactory on the whole, and at the end of the rainy season the Bengal government decided to improve the position if possible by the capture of the Mahratta-held port of Bassein (qv), a few miles north of Bombay.

HAMADAN (Iran)   Persian Wars   1731–2
Fought between the Persians under Nadir Kuli Beg and the Turks.
Strength: Persians 20,000; Turks 30,000.
Aim: After the expulsion of the Afghan invaders from Persia Nadir Kuli Beg, as Commander-in-Chief of the Shah's forces, turned his attention to the Turks. The position was serious, as the whole of Azarbaijan and most of Iraq were in the possession of the Sultan. Defeating a Turkish army near Hamadan, 200 miles west of Teheran, he regained both provinces, and was besieging Erivan (Yerevan, Armenia) when news came of a rebellion in Khorasan inspired by the Abdali Afghans of Herat. Raising the siege he immediately marched 1,400 miles eastwards, defeating the Abdalis and capturing Herat early in 1732. In his absence Shah Tahmasp II rashly decided to take the field in person against the Turks.
Battle: Tahmasp marched to Erivan, which he invested without success. Forced to retreat he was defeated by a Turkish army at Korijan near Hamadan, with heavy losses.
Result: Having lost all the territories regained by Nadir, Tahmasp concluded a treaty with the Turks by which the river Aras became the boundary of Persia and large areas to the NW of the country were ceded to the Turks. On his return to Isfahan, Nadir repudiated the treaty and deposed Tahmasp, setting up Tahmasp's infant son as a puppet Shah, Abbas III, with himself as Regent. He then sent an envoy to Constantinople with the message 'Restore the provinces of Persia or prepare for war'.

HERAT (Afghanistan)   Persian Wars   1719
Fought between the Persians under Safi Kuli Khan and the Afghans under Asadullah Khan.
Strength: Persians 30,000; Afghans 15,000.
Aim: Inspired by the success of Mir Vais, ruler of the Ghilzai Afghans, in throwing off the Persian yoke in Kandahar, Asadullah Khan, Chief of the Abdali Afghans, declared Herat independent and joined the Uzbegs in plundering raids on Khorasan in N Persia. To meet these incursions a Persian army, commanded by Safi Kuli Khan, marched on Herat.
Battle: Asadullah with an army of only 15,000 decided to engage the superior Persian forces and attacked. The battle was hotly contested until by mistake the Persian artillery fired on their own cavalry. Fearing treachery the whole army was thrown into confusion and the Afghans, seizing their chance, made a decisive charge to win the day, Safi himself being captured. Persian casualties were high, being estimated at 10,000, and they lost all their artillery and baggage. Afghan casualties were about 3,000 men.
Result: By this victory the Abdali Afghans won their freedom and henceforth constituted an independent state on the NE frontier of Persia.

ISFAHAN (ISPAHAN) (Iran)   Persian Wars   1726
Fought between the Afghan army under Shah Ashraf and the Turks under Ahmed Pasha.
Strength: Afghans 20,000 with 40 swivel guns mounted on camels; Turks 60,000 with 70 guns.
Aim: In 1725 Mahmud Khan, the Afghan ruler of Persia, was murdered by his followers. The previous year under the Treaty of Constantinople Russia and Turkey had agreed on a subdivision of N and W Persia. Turkey, already having occupied Tiflis in Georgia (USSR), now captured Hamadan, Erivan (Yerevan) and Tabriz. Mahmud's successor Ashraf had sent an embassy to Constantinople to negotiate a settlement, but on its failure war was declared and a Turkish army advanced on Isfahan (Ispahan).
Battle: Taking the offensive Shah Ashraf attacked and cut to pieces a detached body of Turks 2,000

strong, which caused Ahmed Pasha to halt and set up an entrenched position. At this stage the Afghans dispatched 4 mullahs to see the Turkish leader and endeavour to sow dissension among the invaders. So successful were they that a large contingent of Turks deserted. This determined Ahmed Pasha to force a general engagement without further delay. The Afghans, however, fought superbly, routing the Turkish forces and killing 12,000 in the course of the battle. The victor refused to allow any pursuit of the enemy and released all his prisoners, a political move to suit his own purposes.

Result: A treaty was concluded in 1727 by which Ashraf acknowledged the Sultan of Turkey as Caliph and was in turn recognised as Shah of Persia. The provinces held by Turkey were all ceded to the Sultan, Persia thus being dismembered.

JITGURGH (Nepál)   Gurkha War   14 January 1815
Fought between a British column under Major-General John Sullivan Wood and the Gurkhas under Umur Singh Thapa.
Strength: British 500 Europeans + 4,000 sepoys + 3 guns; Gurkhas 1,200
Aim: After the declaration of war in November 1815 by Lord Moira, Governor-General of India, against the Gurkhas, because of their continual depredations in disputed territories in N India, four invasion columns entered Nepal through separate passes with the ultimate objective of converging on the capital, Katmandu. One of these columns, commanded by General Wood and consisting of the 17th Foot with the remainder native cavalry and infantry, left their base at Gorakhpur (Uttar Pradesh) to advance to Palpa on the river Kali, thus severing the main line of communication between Katmandu and the large Gurkha forces in the west under command of Umur Singh Thapa, the principal Gurkha general. During Wood's advance, it was suggested to him by a native agent, who subsequently proved treacherous, that he should first carry a fortified stockade at the mouth of the pass leading to Palpa.
Battle: The stockade was about 10 miles from his base and Wood, taking twenty-one companies to attack it from the front, with a further seven companies for an assault on the left, marched for some 7 miles through thick jungle. He had been assured by the guide that the stockade was in open country beyond the jungle, but was suddenly fired on while still in dense forest. He then ordered eight companies of the 17th Foot, together with two sepoy companies, to attack in front while two more companies of the 17th made for a hill which commanded the stockade. Resistance was tenacious and, judging that the stockade would in any case be untenable, Wood withdrew his forces, having sustained over 130 casualties. The Gurkha casualties were probably greater but, as the British had retreated, the Gurkhas claimed a victory.
Result: This engagement was to be the pattern of many other similar ones in this fiercely fought war. In this particular case it had results beyond the expectation of the Gurkhas, as its outcome made Wood decide that his force was insufficient to take the offensive in the hills. He accordingly fortified Lotan, and rested on the defensive. Gurkha aggressive tactics succeeded in paralysing the progress not only of Wood's column but also of that of Major-General Marley, leading the main invasion column against Butwal and Katmandu, advancing from Patna to the east of Wood's line of approach. This precipitated an event almost unprecedented in the history of the British army: Marley, having already suffered several reverses and feeling the situation becoming altogether beyond his control, rode out of his camp before daylight on 10 February 1815 and vanished. Although relieved of his command by the Governor-General, Marley, who turned up later, was not dismissed by the army, his desertion being considered the result of a severe nervous breakdown. He died a full general in 1842.

KALUNGA (Nepal)   Gurkha War   31 October–30 November 1814
Fought between a British column under Major-General Rollo Gillespie and the Gurkha garrison at Kalunga under Bulbhader Singh.
Strength: British 300 Europeans + 2,200 sepoys + 8 guns; Gurkhas 600 with 6 guns.
Aim: During the early part of the nineteenth century the Gurkhas under a very able leader, Umur Singh Thapa, had extended their dominion as far westward as the river Sutlej and, by 1814, had descended southwards in repeated raids into disputed territory on the Indian border. In November 1814, after repeated protests which were treated by the Gurkhas with contempt, Lord Moira, the Governor-General of India, issued a formal declaration of war. The campaign, which was to take place in largely unknown mountainous terrain, began with an advance on four fronts simultaneously, with the prime objective of defeating Umur Singh's main force in the Rupar area on the Sutlej, and ultimately of occupying the Nepalese capital, Katmandu. This initial attempt to reduce the garrison of the fort at Kalunga in the Dehra Dun region situated on the summit of an almost inaccessible mountain peak, was the first important engagement of the war.

Battle: During the afternoon of 30 October Gillespie brought up his force to a plateau about 800 yards from Kalunga and 400 feet below it on the other side of a deep ravine. During the night batteries of 12-pounders and 6-pounders with some mortars were brought up by elephants and, before daybreak, three columns moved out to attack the fort from the north, east and south. Gillespie planned to lead an assault from the west. In the first attack from the west, dismounted cavalry of the 8th Light Dragoons, together with infantry of the 53rd Foot, managed to overrun a stockade lying between them and the fort, but were subsequently repulsed with the loss of 225 officers and men, including General Gillespie who was shot through the heart while spurring his men on. The command then devolved on Colonel Mawbey, who decided to await the arrival of heavy siege guns from Delhi before proceeding. By 27 November a practicable breach had been effected but the subsequent assault was again repulsed with heavy losses, no fewer than 480 men being killed or wounded. Mawbey continued to shell the fort for three days, after which the 70 survivors of the garrison, including the redoubtable Bulbhader Singh, who had put up a most heroic defence, managed to escape. The British then occupied the fort and, in the subsequent pursuit, caught up with and killed about 50 of the fleeing garrison.

Result: This costly victory made the British realise the quality of the Gurkha troops they were fighting, and many equally stubbornly fought actions were to follow. The fall of Kalunga, however, did have its effect upon Gurkha morale, as they then evacuated a similar fort at Bairat without resistance, giving the British command of the whole Dehra Dun area, and of the main east-west passes.

KANDAHAR (Afghanistan)   Persian Wars   March 1738

Fought between the Persian invading force under Nadir Shah and the Afghan garrison under Husain Khan.

Strength: Persians 80,000 infantry + 30,000 cavalry; Afghans 30,000.

Aim: When Nadir Shah came to the throne of Persia after the death of the infant Shah Abbas III in 1736 he determined to recover the former provinces of Persia and restore her previous frontiers. In accordance with this policy he led a large army into Afghanistan against the stronghold of Kandahar, which was governed by Husain Khan, the brother of Mahmud Khan—the former conqueror of Persia. Realising he was quite unable to meet Nadir's army in the field Husain shut himself up in the city which was strongly fortified, fully provisioned and manned by a large garrison.

Battle: Nadir considered the city too strong to besiege without heavy guns which he lacked and decided on a blockade. He constructed a line of towers round the city 28 miles in circumference, each manned by infantry with muskets. After an abortive twelve-month siege, however, he decided on more aggressive tactics and his Bakhtiari tribesmen dragged guns up on to a number of towers commanding the city, which was then at his mercy. Kandahar now surrendered and Husain fled to the province of Mazanderan, where he was eventually captured.

Result: Nadir treated the Afghan garrison with great moderation and enlisted some 4,000 of them into his army. While the protracted siege had been carried on, smaller Persian columns had been engaged in recovering the former Persian provinces of Balkh and Baluchistan (now in Pakistan). By the capture of Kandahar, however, Nadir had secured a firm base for the invasion of Mogul India which he had been seriously planning during the long months of the siege.

KANDYAN WAR I (Sri Lanka)   1803

Fought between the British under Major-General Hay Macdowall and the forces of the Kandyan King, Sri Wikrama Raja Sinha.

Strength: British (Macdowall's force) 700 European infantry + 1,000 Ceylon infantry + 200 Bengal artillery + (Barbutt's force) 500 European infantry + 1,000 Malay infantry + 100 Madras artillery; Kandyans 10,000–50,000 estimated.

Aim: In 1803 the Governor of Ceylon (Sri Lanka), the Hon Frederick North, (later Earl of Guilford), having failed in his efforts to persuade the Kandyan King to accept British suzerainty, decided, with the connivance of Pilima Talauva, the Adigar or Chief Minister, to install a suitable pretender to the throne, one Muttuswamy. An expedition was accordingly launched with this end in view in January, using two converging forces, one commanded by Major-General Macdowall setting out from Colombo on the west coast and the other under Colonel Barbutt from Trincomalee on the east.

Battle: The active opposition encountered by both columns in their advance on the Kandyan capital was negligible, the difficult terrain proving their greatest obstacle. On 21 February the two joined forces and entered the city of Kandy, which had been evacuated by the King and the whole population. The royal treasure and everything of value had been taken, ammunition dumps had been blown up and several of the main buildings were in flames. Muttuswamy was formally installed as King in an empty capital.

The British force, now completely isolated and in difficulties over food supplies and suffering from disease, gradually disintegrated, and Macdowall himself was obliged to retire to Colombo on account of ill-health. A large part of each column returned to their respective bases, leaving a garrison of some 300 Europeans and 700 native infantry in the capital, soon considerably reduced by disease and the guerrilla attacks of the Kandyans hiding in the jungle. On 24 June 1803 the remnants of the British force, on orders from the Governor, started a withdrawal from the city, taking Muttuswamy with them, when they were attacked by the Kandyans and massacred practically to a man.

Result: This campaign proved positively that the mountainous terrain of the Ceylon interior, with its lack of roads, impenetrable jungle and deep gorges, together with its malarious climate, could not be held by inadequately supplied European troops against Sinhalese guerrilla activities.

Encouraged by the result of his tactics, Sri Wikrama now took the offensive and carried out a number of attacks against British-held bases on the coast, but with little success. In September 1804 a campaign organised by the new military commander, Lt-General David Wemyss, using small columns converging on the capital from different routes, was planned and then called off. Unfortunately for them the main column of 72 men of the 19th Foot with 240 Malays and sepoys, commanded by Captain Arthur Johnston, did not receive notice of the cancellation, and set off from Batticaloa. After incredible hardships the force managed to reach Kandy, once again evacuated, and stayed there for only fifty-six hours. They then retreated, harassed by large bodies of Kandyans, eventually reaching Trincomalee on 19 October, with casualties of 69 men killed and wounded, only to be informed that the whole operation had been countermanded before they had started.

KANDYAN WAR II (Sri Lanka) 11 January–8 February 1815
Fought between the British under Lt-General Sir Robert Brownrigg and the army of the Kandyan King, Sri Wikrama Raja Sinha, commanded by Molligoda.
Strength: 900 European infantry + 1,800 (Ceylon Regiment); Kandyans 10,000.
Aim: In March 1811 Lt-General Sir Robert Brownrigg was appointed Governor and Commander-in-Chief of Ceylon (Sri Lanka) and endeavoured to establish close relationships with the court of the Kandyan King. The latter was unpopular with his chieftains and, having executed his former Adigar or Chief Minister, Pilima Talauva, in 1812, he became increasingly autocratic and tyrannical, and was responsible for the mutilation of a number of British traders taken in Kandyan territory and accused of spying. When in January 1815 the King's forces chased a band of insurgents across the border into British territory, Brownrigg took this as a *casus belli* and two days later ordered the invasion of Kandy, and a state of war was proclaimed.
Battle: This expedition was much more carefully planned than the disastrous fiasco of 1803 (see KANDYAN WAR I), both from the tactical and logistic points of view. In a carefully co-ordinated operation, a series of eight small columns marching along five different routes were to draw a noose around the inner Kandyan mountain stronghold, seizing all the main passes and cutting off enemy retreat roads. On 8 February, as the net drew inexorably closer, Molligoda, the King's General, surrendered to the British, and six days later Brownrigg entered a deserted Kandy, the King having fled with his wives. On 18 February he was found hiding in the mountains and apprehended.
Result: Thus after a forty-day campaign 2,357 years of Sinhalese independence was at an end. On 2 March, in the Audience Hall of the Royal Palace in Kandy, Brownrigg received the submission of the chieftains, and the Kandyan provinces were formally ceded to the British under a convention signed a week later, so that British sovereignty now extended over the whole of Ceylon.

Sri Wikrama, described by one source as a handsome, lusty man not unlike Henry VIII in appearance, was exiled to Madras, where he lived in comfortable circumstances until 1832, when he died of dropsy at the age of fifty-two.

KARKUK (Iraq) Persian Wars 1733
Fought between the Persians under Nadir Kuli Beg and the Turks under Topal Osman.
Strength: Persians 30,000; Turks 60,000.
Aim: Nadir, acting as Regent, denounced the treaty entered into by Shah Tahmasp II in 1731, whereby large areas of NW Persia had been ceded to the Ottoman Sultan Mahmud, and war was declared between the two powers. The campaign opened with the siege of Baghdad, whose defender, Ahmed Pasha, was

determined to offer desperate resistance. The situation was entirely changed, however, by the arrival of a powerful Turkish army commanded by Topal Osman. Nadir unwisely divided his forces, leaving 12,000 men to occupy the trenches before Baghdad and marching north to meet the Turks at Karkuk, near Samarra, about 50 miles from the capital.

Battle: The ensuing battle was one of the fiercest fought between the two nations. At first the Persians gained an advantage in defeating the Turkish horse, but the flight of the cavalry left the formidable Ottoman infantry, whose advance restored the position. Gradually the battle went against the smaller forces of the Persians and Nadir twice had his horse shot under him. After eight hours of desperate fighting the Persian army was completely routed. The news quickly reached Baghdad, whereupon the garrison sallied out and annihilated the isolated Persian division. The main army fled in disorder and was not re-formed until it reached Hamadan, 200 miles to the east.

Result: Although Nadir's position was now extremely critical after this disaster, his reputation was such that recruits flocked to his standard and in less than three months he was ready once again to take the field with a powerful and well-equipped army.

KARNAL (Haryana, India)   Persian Wars   13 February 1739
Fought between the Persian invading army under Nadir Shah and the Mogul armies commanded by Mohammed Shah.

Strength: Persians 100,000; Indians 80,000.

Aim: Thoroughly alarmed by the rapid advance of the Persian forces into India, the Emperor Mohammed Shah, collecting what troops he could, marched to the plain of Karnal on the right bank of the river Jumna, 60 miles due north of Delhi. Here he formed an entrenched camp and awaited the invaders. In the meantime he received reinforcements of 30,000 men under Saadat Khan, the Persian-descended Viceroy of Oudh, who urged immediate action to prevent the army breaking up through lack of supplies.

Battle: The battle started when Saadat Khan led his troops out to drive off a detached force of 6,000 Kurds engaged in pillaging. On both sides reinforcements were now hurried up and the engagement became general. Nadir employed his customary tactics of ambush with success and Saadat was defeated and taken prisoner. Fire-balls were then used to stampede the enemy's elephants, causing panic among the Indian troops, and after a further advance by Nadir's forces the Indian army was completely routed. The battle lasted less than two hours, during which upwards of 20,000 Indians were slain and an equal number taken captive.

Result: Mohammed Shah surrendered and was well treated by the conqueror–they were both Turkomen, said Nadir, who then marched in triumph to Delhi. Here he was entertained in the most sumptuous manner by the Emperor, who handed over to him the amassed wealth of his ancestors including the fabulous Peacock Throne and the famous *Kohi nur* (Koh-i-noor) diamond. The total value of the spoils was estimated at £87 million. By this short campaign Nadir had struck a blow that resounded throughout the world. He wisely realised, however, that to hold Delhi was beyond his powers, and so, replacing Mohammed Shah on the throne, he recrossed the Indus and marched back to Kabul with his immense treasure, having now recovered all the provinces which had once formed part of the Persian Empire.

KARS (Turkey)   Persian Wars   1745
Fought between the Persian army under Nadir Shah and the Turks under Yakan Mohammed Pasha.

Strength: Persians 80,000; Turks 100,000 cavalry + 40,000 infantry.

Aim: Encouraged by the internal strife in Persia following Nadir Shah's disastrous Lesghian campaign (qv), Turkey decided to risk another trial of strength and for a time desultory warfare took place mostly in the area of Mosul (Iraq), the Persians suffering considerable casualties in their abortive assaults. Finally in 1745 a large Turkish army under Yakan Mohammed Pasha advanced from Kars in Turkey prepared to do battle.

Battle: The Turkish leader advancing at the head of his vast army halted close to the Persian positions and fortified his camp. The next day the two armies met and after a series of combats extending over four days the Persians gained a decisive victory. The Turks were driven headlong back to their camp, where they murdered their general and fled in complete disorder. Nadir captured the whole of the enemy's artillery and stores and many thousand Turks were killed or made prisoner.

Result: After this brilliant victory a peace treaty was agreed between the two nations, under which the boundaries which existed between them in the days of the Sultan Murad IV in the previous century were to be re-established.

This was the last great victory of Nadir Shah who, having completely alienated his subjects by his increasingly bloodthirsty acts, was assassinated during a campaign against the Kurds in 1747 by Salah Khan, the captain of his bodyguard. With his death the empire he had created was all too soon to fall apart in civil war.

KATWA (CUTWA) (W Bengal, India)   Bengal Wars   19 July 1763
Fought between the British under Major Thomas Adams and Mir Kasim's Bengali army under Mohammed Taki Khan.
Strength: British 850 Europeans + 1,500 sepoys + 12 guns; Bengalis 5,000 infantry + 4,000 cavalry + 25 guns.
Aim: After the annihilation of the British garrison at Patna in June 1763 (PATNA I), Mir Kasim wrote to the Council of the East India Company at Calcutta repudiating certain concessions he had granted on being installed as Nawab of Bengal. The Council thereupon deposed him and reinstated the aging Mir Jafar in his former position as ruler. Major Adams, the senior British officer in Bengal, was instructed to proceed to Murshidabad to enforce the order. Adams crossed the river Bagiruttee at Agurdeep and on 19th July encountered a strong contingent of Mir Kasim's army occupying an entrenched position opposite the fort at Katwa.
Battle: The action began with an advance of Adams's cavalry to screen the movement of his infantry. Mohammed Taki met the attack with his best troops, supported by a rocket battery, and forced the British cavalry to retreat. The British infantry, however, continued its steady advance despite furious attacks by the enemy. At the height of the battle Mohammed Taki placed himself at the head of a chosen corps of Afghan cavalry for a supreme effort against Adams's right flank. At their approach a company of sepoys concealed in jungle rose and poured a volley into the galloping mass. Mohammed Taki fell, shot through the head, whereupon the Afghans turned and fled. This was the signal for the entire Bengali army to give way, leaving 8 guns and a mass of stores behind them. At the same time a British detachment on the other side of the river captured the fort at Katwa with 17 cannon. The Bengalis had been dispersed with great slaughter, whereas British casualties amounted to only 32 killed and wounded.
Result: On 25 July Adams occupied Murshidabad, into which Mir Jafar was escorted with due ceremony to the great satisfaction of the mass of the populace.

KAVERIPAK (COVREPAUK) (Tamil Nadu, India)   Second Carnatic War   28 February 1752
Fought between the British under Captain Robert Clive and a joint Indian/French force under Raja Sahib.
Strength: British 380 Europeans + 1,300 sepoys + 120 cavalry + 6 guns; Indians/French 400 Europeans + 2,000 sepoys + 2,000 native cavalry + 9 guns.
Aim: After Clive's return to Madras following the French defeat at Conjeveram (qv) Raja Sahib, the son of Chanda Sahib, the French-aligned contender for the Nawabship of the Carnatic, proceeded to collect his scattered army and, aided and abetted by the French, ravaged the country to the west of Madras. On instructions from the British Governor, Thomas Saunders, Clive quickly recruited 500 sepoys, and reinforced by a party of 100 Europeans lately arrived from Bengal and a detachment from Arcot, he marched on towards Conjeveram, where it was reported that Raja Sahib had regrouped his forces and was strongly entrenched.
Battle: When the British reached Conjeveram they found that Raja Sahib had left his camp and moved on. At dusk on 28 February Clive's force was approaching the village of Kaveripak (Covrepauk), 16 miles NW from Conjeveram, when his advanced guard was surprised by sudden fire from 9 field guns on its right flank. Clive had unwittingly stumbled into an enemy ambush and was trapped. He immediately ordered his men into a dry watercourse on the left side of the road. The enemy artillery continued to pour in fire from a mango grove on the right where the French were stationed with a body of infantry in support. Raja Sahib's main force now advanced towards the British over open ground to the left of the road, but they were kept at a distance by heavy musket-fire and by 2 field pieces firing across the watercourse. For three hours until night fell the artillery duel continued, neither side giving way. Clive then sent a Portuguese half-caste subedar (company officer) to reconnoitre a side-road which led to the rear of the French battery. The way was reported clear and Clive immediately ordered Ensign William Keene to take a detachment of 200 Europeans and several companies of sepoys to go round, guided by Subedar Shawlum. The detachment got to within 50 yards of the enemy without discovery, and when they opened fire they took the French completely by surprise. The French abandoned their guns and fled, closely followed by the rest of Raja

Sahib's force. The French losses were 350 killed. British casualties numbered only 40 Europeans and 30 sepoys killed and as many wounded.
Result: Kaveripak was a decisive victory which greatly enhanced the reputation of the British and resulted in the destruction of the army built up by Raja Sahib and the French Governor-General, Marquis Joseph-François Dupleix, and it was now finally disbanded. Unlike Clive's previous successes it brought considerable territorial gains, and the whole of the Arcot country was now clear of the enemy.

KHIVA (USSR)   Persian Wars   1740
Fought between the Persian forces under Nadir Shah and the Uzbeg army of the Khan of Khiva.
Strength: Persians 50,000; Uzbegs 30,000.
Aim: After subduing Bukhara at the battle of Charjui (qv) Nadir proceeded to carry out his plans for the conquest of Khiva, the other centre of the marauding forces constantly ravaging the northern provinces of Persia.
Battle: The Turkomen forces carried out a surprise raid and nearly succeeded in capturing the bridge of boats thrown across the river Oxus (Amu Darya) at Charjui and destroying the convoy of grain on which the Persian army depended for its very existence in this campaign. However, by forced marches Nadir managed to forestall the attack, and after a desperately hard-fought engagement won the day. Hearing that Ilbars Khan, the ruler of Khiva, was in the fort of Jayuk, Nadir invested the place and forced the Khan to surrender.
Result: No mercy was shown to Ilbars Khan, who had put to death Nadir's envoys, and he was executed with all his advisers. From Khiva Nadir then marched to Meshed, which he had made his capital and where he celebrated his victories. Nadir Shah was now at the zenith of his fame and power.

KHYBER PASS (Afghanistan-Pakistan)   Persian Wars   October 1738
Fought between the Persians under Nadir Shah and a Mogul army.
Strength: Persians 100,000; Moguls 20,000.
Aim: Nadir had notified Mohammed Shah, the Mogul Emperor of India, of his Afghan campaign and had requested that no fugitives be allowed asylum across the frontier. Nevertheless, fugitives frequently escaped to Ghazni and Kabul, at that time the capital of the Indian province of E Afghanistan, and it was evident that proper orders to prevent this had not been given either in error or on purpose. Nadir used this fact as a *casus belli* and with a large force marched north from Kandahar to Kabul, capturing Ghazni on the way. After a determined defence under its Commandant, Shir Khan, Kabul was ultimately taken in June 1738 with enormous booty and most of its defenders put to the sword. Then, leaving a garrison in the city, Nadir turned towards the Punjab.
Battle: In order to avoid the tribesmen massing in the western end of the Khyber Pass who had blocked the defiles with felled trees, Nadir crossed the mountain range by the nearby Tsatsobi Pass (which Alexander is reputed to have used) into what is now the North-West Frontier Province of Pakistan. He then turned round to attack the rear of a strong Mogul force massed at the eastern end of the Khyber Pass and completely routed them.
Result: Nadir now advanced rapidly into India, seizing Peshawar and Lahore and crossing the river Indus at Attock.

KURDLAH (Maharashtra, India)   Mahratta Wars   11 March 1795
Fought between the armies of the Mahratta Confederacy under the Peshwa, Madhao Rao II, with Puresham Bhow as Commander-in-Chief, and the army of the Nizam of Hyderabad, commanded by the Nizam and his Vizier, Mushir-ul-Mulk.
Strength: Mahratta armies 130,000 horse and foot + 10,000 Pindari irregulars + 150 guns; Nizam's forces 110,000 horse and foot.
Aim: For a number of years the Mahratta Confederacy had maintained territorial claims against Nizam Ali of Hyderabad which he had ignored or evaded, at the same time submitting counter-claims for reparations for inroads by Mahratta marauders. It was eventually decided that only an armed confrontation would resolve the differences and the Nizam advanced towards the Mahratta frontier in the direction of Kurdlah, descending the Mohree Ghat. The Mahratta forces, consisting of contingents provided by all the main chieftains, the Peshwa himself, Doulut Rao Scindia of Gwalior, Rughuji Bhonsla of Berar and Tukaji Holkar of Indore and others, now converged on Poona and marched to meet the invader.

Battle: The Nizam's troops were at first successful and a charge of Pathan horsemen drove thousands of the Mahrattas precipitately from the field. However, when the Mogul infantry supported by cavalry were advancing they were assailed by a shower of rockets and the fire of 35 cannon judiciously placed by Scindia's French Commander, Colonel Pierre Cuillier Perron. After confused night fighting, the Nizam sought refuge within the walls of Kurdlah, a small fort surrounded by hills. Now only about one-tenth of his original troops remained and the next morning the Mahrattas arrived and invested the fort. After two days' siege the Nizam surrendered on 15 March. In spite of the large numbers of troops and guns involved fewer than 200 men were lost on either side in this affray.

Result: Under the peace terms that followed, the Nizam was obliged to surrender the person of his Vizier, Mushir-ul-Mulk, regarded by the Mahrattas as their real enemy, and to make large territorial concessions as well as pay heavy financial indemnities. This major victory assured Mahratta supremacy in central India for some years to come.

LASWARI (Rajasthan, India)   Second Mahratta War   1 November 1803
Fought between the British under General Gerard Lake and the Mahratta army of Doulut Rao Scindia of Gwalior, commanded by one Abaji.

Strength: British 1,500 European cavalry + 600 European infantry + 2,500 native cavalry + 3,400 sepoys; Mahrattas 9,000 infantry + 4,000–5,000 cavalry.

Aim: After capturing the fortress town of Agra (qv), Lake turned his attention to the last remaining Mahratta force, some 14,000 strong and well equipped with artillery, the flower of Scindia's army, now operating in Jaipur country. On 27 October he marched westwards and then four days later, intent on overtaking the now retreating enemy, he set off in pursuit with his three cavalry brigades, leaving the infantry and guns to follow. The Mahrattas flooded the roadways by cutting the embankment of a large reservoir, thus impeding his advance. They then took up a strong position between the villages of Laswari and Mohaulpore, their 72 guns linked by chains, concealed from view by a broad strip of high grass.

Battle: At dawn on 1 November Lake himself led his three cavalry brigades to the attack, but although they charged the Mahratta gunners and supporting infantry with great gallantry, their efforts were unavailing and at length Lake recalled them to await the arrival of the infantry and artillery. In the meantime the enemy were able to recover their guns and re-form around the village of Mohaulpore on their right. At 11am the 76th Highlanders and four sepoy battalions appeared after a gruelling march of 25 miles. Resting the men for an hour, Lake then decided to attack the Mahratta right with his infantry, supported by two cavalry brigades, while the third brigade threatened the enemy's left. Lake's horse-drawn artillery, the 'galloping guns', were brought forward in two groups to menace the Mahratta front. The infantry advance was, however, halted by intense artillery fire which inflicted heavy losses and at this critical moment Abaji flung his cavalry against them, only to be repulsed. Lake now ordered the 29th Light Dragoons to counter-charge, but at this point his horse was shot under him. The next moment his son, Lt-Colonel George Lake, who had offered the General his mount, was severely wounded. The cavalry now dashed forward with irresistible force and all the guns were carried. The Mahrattas still continued fighting with desperate valour until they had been driven in turn from every position in the field. The Mahratta casualties were enormous–7,000 being killed, wounded or dispersed–a mere 2,000 were left to become prisoners. British casualties were considerable, totalling 834, including 82 Europeans killed and 248 wounded, the cavalry losing 453 horses. Lake reported of this battle: 'I never was in so severe a business in my life or anything like it ... these fellows fought like devils, or rather like heroes.'

Result: As one authority put it, the Battle of Laswari 'was the fairest, most equally matched, and the most hotly-contested battle ever fought between the British and the natives of India'. It dealt a decisive blow to the aspirations of Scindia and decided him to accept the peace terms offered by the Governor-General, Marquess Wellesley. On 30 December 1803 the Treaty of Surji Arjengaon was signed, under which Scindia ceded to the British all his territories between the Jumna and the Ganges, and several other districts and forts.

Now that the power of both Scindia and the Bhonsla had been broken, there remained only one major Mahratta prince to deal with, Jaswunt Rao Holkar of Indore.

LEILAN (Iraq)   Persian Wars   1733
Fought between the Persians under Nadir Kuli Beg and the Turks under Topal Osman.

Strength: Persians 50,000; Turks 30,000.

Aim: After the brilliant Turkish victory at Karkuk (qv) Topal Osman became the victim of jealous intrigues in Constantinople, as a result of which both pay and reinforcements for his army were withheld. Consequently he was in a position of marked inferiority at the opening of the new campaign against the Persians in 1733. He sent his cavalry forward to meet the advancing Persians at Leilan near Karkuk on the river Tigris, about 50 miles north of Baghdad.

Battle: As in the previous battle at Karkuk earlier in the year the Turks were unable to withstand the onslaught of the stronger Persian cavalry, but on this occasion in their flight they also swept away the infantry with them. Topal Osman, who was a cripple and was carried in a litter, was killed and the Turkish army routed.

Result: After this signal victory Nadir marched on Baghdad, where he concluded a treaty of peace with the Governor Ahmed Pasha.

LESGHIAN CAMPAIGN (USSR)   Persian Wars   1741–2
Fought between the Persian army under Nadir Shah and the Lesghian tribesmen of Daghestan (USSR).
Strength: Persians 30,000; Lesghians 15,000.
Aim: During the Indian campaign of Nadir Shah the savage Lesghian tribesmen, who inhabited the inaccessible mountain country of Daghestan, carried out raids in the settled districts of N Persia, in one of which they killed Ibrahim Khan, the only brother of the Shah. In 1741 Nadir embarked on a punitive expedition against the Lesghians, with some initial success. Then, posting a force of 8,000 men to keep open his communications, he led the main body of his army deeper and deeper into the densely wooded mountains against the elusive tribesmen.
Battle: The Lesghians, employing true guerrilla tactics, seized the opportunity presented by Nadir's over-extended forces and attacked both the main body and the connecting force simultaneously, inflicting heavy losses. Nadir continued to fight on desperately, but eventually lack of supplies forced him to retreat to Derbent (USSR) on the western shores of the Caspian Sea, where his shattered and nearly starving army was supplied by ship from the port of Astrakhan.
Result: This disastrous campaign had the effect of encouraging Nadir's many enemies and resulted in the outbreak in 1743–4 of three rebellions in Shirwan, Fars and Astrabad–all of which were, however, crushed with great severity.

MADRAS I (Tamil Nadu, India)   First Carnatic War   21 September 1746
Fought between the British garrison under Governor Nicholas Morse and a French force commanded by Admiral Comte Bertrand Mahé de la Bourdonnais.
Stength: British 200 Europeans; French 1,100 Europeans + 400 sepoys.
Aim: After the naval engagement at Negapatam in July 1746 (NEGAPATAM I), which gave the French freedom of the seas in the Bay of Bengal, preparations went ahead at Pondicherry for the siege of Madras. Governor Morse had appealed to Anwar-ud-Din, Nawab of the Carnatic, to fulfil his pledge to ensure neutrality within his domains–but to no effect. The only part of Madras capable of being defended was the European settlement of Fort St George, with a garrison of only 200 untrained soldiers under the command of a seventy-two-year-old Swede, Peter Eckman. Although 200 cannon were mounted round the walls no one in the garrison knew how to fire them. On 29 August the French squadron under Bourdonnais appeared before Madras, bombarded it for a time as part of a softening-up process, and after creating considerable panic sailed away again.
Battle: On 14 September the French fleet reappeared off Madras and landed a force of European troops with native auxiliaries and set up batteries. Fort St George was then subjected to a short bombardment from two sides; one cannon ball burst open the door of a liquor store and the garrison decided to drown their sorrows instead of fighting. Faced by hysterical calls from the populace to end the fighting, Morse agreed to surrender, although only 6 men had been killed. Among those captured was a young writer aged twenty-one named Robert Clive who, together with a companion, disguised himself as a native clerk and made good his escape to Fort St David, 12 miles south of Pondicherry.
Result: A dispute now arose between the French Governor-General, the Marquis Joseph-François Dupleix, and Bourdonnais as to the future of Madras, the former saying he had promised it to the Nawab in return for his neutrality, while the latter wished to return it to the British for ransom. However, on 14 October monsoon gales destroyed 4 of the French ships and damaged the remainder. As soon as they were repaired Bourdonnais sailed from Indian waters never to return, and Dupleix took possession of Madras in the name of France.

MADRAS II (Tamil Nadu, India)   First Carnatic War   2 November 1746
Fought between the French garrison of Madras under the command of M. D'Espréménil and the army of
the Nawab of the Carnatic commanded by his son Maphuze Khan.
Strength: French 400 Europeans + 2 guns; Indians 10,000.
Aim: With the withdrawal of Admiral Comte Bertrand Mahé de Bourdonnais from the Bay of Bengal in
October 1746 (see MADRAS I), the French Governor-General at Pondicherry, Marquis Joseph-François
Dupleix, found himself with a force of 3,000 trained European soldiers at his disposal. This was a useful
accession of strength as he was faced with a demand from Anwar-ud-Din, the Nawab of the Carnatic, that
Madras—now captured by the French—should be delivered up to him as promised. Growing suspicious at
the long delay the Nawab dispatched his son Maphuze Khan with a force of some 10,000 to invest the town.
Dupleix sent orders to D'Espréménil, the officer in command of the garrison, to hold the town at all costs.
Battle: D'Espréménil decided that his best ploy was to take the offensive in spite of the apparently
overwhelming odds, and he made a sortie with 400 of the garrison and 2 field pieces. Seeing this
insignificant force drawn up outside the town the Indian cavalry swept down *en masse* upon the motionless
troops. Then, moving as if on parade, the French opened their ranks and their 2 guns poured fire on the
advancing columns. Seventy of the Indian cavalry rolled in the dust and the rest were so seized with panic
that the whole force fled, abandoning their camp to the victors.
Result: This short action provided a great object lesson for European forces in Indian warfare and
demonstrated the incomparable advantage of their superior fire-power. Their artillery was capable of
firing up to 15 rounds a minute, which utterly confounded the Indians with their obsolete cannon whose
normal rate of fire was no more than 4 shots in an hour.

MADRAS III (Tamil Nadu, India)   Third Carnatic War   13 December 1758–17 February 1759
Fought between the British garrison under Colonel Stringer Lawrence and the French army from
Pondicherry under Comte Thomas-Arthur Lally de Tollendal.
Strength: British 1,750 Europeans + 2,200 sepoys; French 2,300 Europeans + 5,000 sepoys.
Aim: Determined on an all-out effort to drive the British from Madras and the Coromandel coast, Comte
Lally de Tollendal, recently appointed Supreme French Commander in S India, decided to recall the
Marquis Charles-Joseph de Bussy-Castelnau with his armed forces from the court of the Nizam Salabat
Jang and the administration of the Deccan, thus seriously jeopardising French political influence in the
whole area. Lally, however, considered the risk worth the effort to oust the British, and at the end of
November 1758 the French force started on its march to Madras.
Battle: By 13 December Lally's whole force was encamped in the plain about 1 mile to the SW of Fort St
George. Nearer approach to the fort was barred by two rivers, the Triplicane and the North, so Lally
passed round to the other side of the fort, the British evacuating the outer posts before him as he advanced.
He then established himself in the Black Town on the NW Front of Fort St George. On 14 December
Colonel Draper, commanding the 79th Regiment, led a sortie in force with about 600 men into the Black
Town. It was, however, none too successful and the troops were fortunate to be able to re-enter the fort in
safety, having lost 200 men killed and captured, the French losses being about the same. Lally now began
to erect siege batteries which, on 2 January 1759, opened fire on the fort. The bombardment continued
throughout the month, but with very little effect. On 7 February Major John Caillaud brought a number
of reinforcements, including 2,000 horse provided by the Raja of Tanjore, to swell the garrison of the
inland fort of Chingleput, foolishly bypassed by Lally on his approach to Madras. Realising too late this
menace to his rear, Lally detached a force 900 Europeans, 1,200 sepoys and 500 native horse with 8 field
pieces to reduce Chingleput, but after a fierce struggle the French were repulsed with heavy loss. Lally's
position was now becoming desperate and the arrival of Admiral Sir George Pocock's squadron in the
roads on 16 February tipped the scales against him. On the following day Lally gave up the siege on which
he had staked so much and was in full retreat to Arcot, leaving 52 guns and all his stores and ammunition
behind. The garrison's casualties amounted to 33 officers, 580 Europeans and 300 sepoys killed or
wounded.
Result: So ended the siege of Madras, the last large-scale offensive operation of the French against their
British rivals in India.

MALAVELLY (Karnataka, India)   Fourth Mysore War   27 March 1799
Fought between the main British force under Lt-Colonel George Harris and the Mysorean army of Tipu
Sultan.

Strength: British 21,000 + (Nizam of Hyderabad's force) 16,000; Mysoreans 6,000.

Aim: Early in March 1799 General Harris marched from Vellore with the intention of investing Seringapatam. At Ambur he was joined by a well-equipped contingent from Hyderabad of some 16,000 horse and foot, reinforced by the 33rd Foot, all under the command of Colonel Arthur Wellesley, brother of the Governor-General, Lord Mornington. In support from the west, the Bombay Presidency sent up a force of some 6,000 under Lt-General James Stuart. After reaching Bangalore, Harris chose the same route to Seringapatam, via Kankanhalli, as Cornwallis had done seven years previously (see SERINGA-PATAM I), Tipu learning that the British were taking the southern road, marched to intercept them near the Maddur River.

Battle: Mysorean cavalry, with strong infantry and artillery support, attacked the British as they advanced out of thick jungle near the large village of Malavelly. On the north flank the Mysorean horse were thrown into confusion by a charge of cavalry under Major-General Floyd, while to the south the Hyderabad contingent under Colonel Wellesley repulsed an attack by 2,000 enemy infantry advancing in column, the 33rd Foot dispersing them with a determined bayonet-charge. As the Mysorean infantry fled before this onslaught they were cut down by the British cavalry. Total enemy losses amounted to about 1,000. British losses were slight.

Result: Ten days later Harris crossed the river Cauvery at Sosile, 15 miles from Seringapatam (see SERINGAPATAM II), and advanced on the city.

MANGALORE (Karnataka, India)   Second Mysore War   6 May 1783–30 January 1784
Fought between the British garrison under Major John Campbell and the Mysorean army of Tipu Sultan, with French support under M. de Cossigny.

Strength: British 600 Europeans (73rd Foot) + 1,400 sepoys; Mysoreans 140,000 horse and foot + French 400.

Aim: Following the occupation of Bednur (qv) by a British force under Brigadier-General Richard Matthews, the coastal town of Mangalore, Mysore's main outlet to the sea, was occupied by a detached force under Major Campbell. After the capture of Bednur by Tipu Sultan on 3 May, the latter immediately sent a force against Mangalore in the hope that the mere news of the disaster would induce the garrison to surrender. Much to his astonishment, however, the Mysorean detachment was attacked on 6 May by Campbell 12 miles from the fort and defeated with the loss of all its artillery. Tipu thereupon marched against Mangalore with his whole army. A summons to surrender was refused and the siege began.

Battle: In a short time the walls of the fortress were breached and in ruins, but the fierce attacks of the assailants were invariably repulsed with heavy losses. After fifty-six days of open-trench warfare, Campbell received a letter from the French Commander with the Mysore army informing him of the cessation of hostilities in the Carnatic, following the conclusion of peace in Europe. Tipu was consequently compelled to agree to an armistice, one article of which stipulated for the supply of the garrison with victuals. This provision was not honoured and, despite the peace negotiations currently taking place between the British and Tipu, the latter openly renewed the siege. At last the garrison, reduced to half by scurvy and starvation, surrendered on 30 January 1784, on condition that they would be transported to Tellicherry, farther south on the Malabar coast. Here, worn out by his exertions and weakened by sickness and starvation, Major Campbell died in the following March.

Result: After long and protracted negotiations between Tipu Sultan and commisioners sent by the Governor of Madras, Lord Macartney, peace terms were eventually agreed, and on 11 March 1784 the Second Mysore War came formally to an end. Under this Treaty of Mangalore there was to be mutual restitution of territories and prisoners and Tipu agreed to renounce all claims to the Carnatic. Thus four years of war for the mastery of S India came to an end.

MASULIPATAM (MACHILIPATNAM (Andhra Pradesh, India)   Third Carnatic War   8 April 1759
Fought between a British Force under Lt-Colonel Francis Forde, with Indian levies under Raja Anundaraz, and the French garrison commanded by the Marquis de Conflans.

Strength: 346 Europeans + 1,400 sepoys + 500 Indian cavalry + 5,000 Indian foot; French 600 Europeans + 2,000 sepoys.

Aim: After his victory at Condore (qv) Forde hoped to make a quick advance against Masulipatam (Machilipatnam), the most important town and centre of French influence in the Northern Sirkars. However, it was some time before he was able to obtain the funds promised by his ally Raja Anundaraz, and it was not until 28 January 1759 that Forde was able to resume his march. Conflans had not been idle in the meantime, and had set up garrisons in Narsapore and Concal, two outlying strongholds to the north of Masulipatam, and it was necessary to reduce them before proceeding to the main objective. At last on 6 March he came within sight of the town.

Battle: On the landward side Masulipatam was surrounded everywhere by a heavy swamp, the road to the town being carried on a causeway to the main gate on the NW front, but Forde managed to find some solid ground on sandhills to the east of the fort. During the next eighteen days siege guns landed from ships were erected and on 25 March the batteries opened up a heavy and continuous fire until three of the fort's bastions had been breached. Forde now heard the alarming news that Salabat Jang, the Viceroy of the Deccan, whose jurisdiction included the Northern Sirkars, was approaching with a relief force of some 40,000 men. He therefore determined to storm the fort without further delay. During the whole of the daylight hours of 7 April the British gunners maintained a fierce fire, and then at midnight three assault parties went in simultaneously, two demonstrations in force as feints against the main gate and the SW corner of the fort, while the main attack was delivered against the Chameleon bastion on the NE front. After a series of fierce engagements the main bastions were all taken. Conflans, at his wit's end and concluding his position to be hopeless, surrendered, over 500 European troops and 2,000 sepoys laying down their arms. Thus the British were masters of Masulipatam with casualties of 86 Europeans and 200 sepoys killed and wounded.

Result: After this daring and spectacular victory, achieved when Forde had only two days' artillery ammunition left, Salabat Jang quickly consented to open negotiations and finally concluded a treaty granting the British 80 miles of coastline and undertaking not to entertain French troops again in the Deccan. Thus French influence at the court of Hyderabad was replaced by British–as Clive had anticipated, with his customary opportunism.

MEHMANDOST (Iran)   Persian Wars   1729

Fought between Persian forces under Shah Tahmasp II, aided by Nadir Kuli Beg, a Khorasan chieftain, and the Afghans under Ashraf Shah.

Strength: Persians 15,000; Afghans 30,000.

Aim: Following the conquest of Persia by the Afghan Mahmud Khan, Tahmasp Mirza, the son and heir of the deposed Shah Husain, had broken out of Isfahan with 600 followers and set up court in Farrahabad in Mazanderan in N Persia. Here he was joined by Nadir Kuli Beg with 5,000 Kurdish tribesmen. As a preliminary to the recovery of Persia from the Afghan invader, Nadir, who was destined to achieve fame as the last of the great Asiatic conquerors, persuaded the young Shah to march into Khorasan, where the cities of Meshed and Herat were occupied. Realising that the position was now reaching serious proportions, Mahmud's successor Ashraf marched northwards and met the Persian forces at Damghan on the river Mehmandost.

Battle: The Afghans immediately charged but made no impression on the veterans trained by Nadir whose musket- and artillery fire inflicted heavy losses. Asraf now detached two columns to make a circuit to right and left of the Persian forces while he attacked in front. These attacks were beaten off with ease and Nadir then ordered a general advance which completely broke the Afghans already discouraged by the death of their leader's standard-bearer. They fled in panic from the field until reaching Teheran 200 miles away.

Result: The defeated Afghan army retired to Isfahan where Ashraf endeavoured to reorganise his forces for the next phase of operations.

MOKUNDRA PASS (MONSON'S RETREAT) (Madhya Pradesh, India)   Second Mahratta War   8 July–31 August 1804

Fought between a British/Indian force under Colonel William Monson and the Mahratta army of Jaswunt Rao Holkar, Maharaja of Indore.

Strength: British/Indians 3,000 sepoys + 3,000 irregular native cavalry; Mahrattas 60,000 cavalry + 15,000 infantry.

Aim: After the defeat of the combined armies of Doulut Rao Scindia and Rughuji Bhonsla, the only important Mahratta prince who remained unconquered was Jaswunt Rao Holkar, a high-spirited, ambitious and ruthless leader who was openly antagonistic to British rule. Known to be conspiring with Scindia to induce the latter to join with him against the British, he had murdered 3 English officers serving with his forces and then openly plundered the territories of the Raja of Jaipur, who was under British protection. On 16 April 1804 the Governor-General of India, Marquess Wellesley, ordered General Gerard Lake, the Commander-in-Chief, to commence hostilities.

Lake marched from his headquarters at Cawnpore (Kanpur) towards Jaipur, sending on in advance a detachment of three sepoy battalions under Colonel Monson. On the appearance of this force, Holkar retreated rapidly southwards, followed by Monson, now reinforced to five and a half battalions and accompanied by a contingent of Scindia's cavalry, commanded by Bapaji Scindia now on the side of the British. Monson finally took up a position south of the Mokundra Pass, some 70 miles to the north of Ujjein. Here on 7 July he received intelligence that Holkar was crossing the Chambal River with all his army some 25 miles distant.

Battle: Although Monson's first instinct was to advance, he realised that he had only two days' supplies for his troops. In spite of remonstrances from all his subordinate commanders, he took what was to prove a most disastrous decision to retire to the Mokundra Pass, which he intended to hold as a defensive position. This proved impossible to hold, however, and the retreat was continued, harassed by Holkar's cavalry and horse artillery. By 16 July Monson had been obliged to abandon all his guns, and later at the crossing of the river Nala all the baggage had to be sacrificed. On 14 August, at Rampura, the now starving force was reinforced by two sepoy battalions and some irregular horse sent by General Lake, but no supplies. Monson, now thoroughly dispirited, ordered the retreat to Kushalghur, and on the march was attacked by Holkar's cavalry, one of his sepoy battalions being practically annihilated.

The rest of the story was one of continuous attacks, heroic stands and heavy losses sustained against overwhelming numbers. By dawn on 31 August the survivors, exhausted and starving, reached the safety of Agra. Of the British officers with the force, 14 had been killed, 2 were missing and 5 wounded, while of the five and a half sepoy battalions, little more than one half were left. It was one of the heaviest disasters which had up to then befallen the British in India.

Result: Although General Arthur Wellesley pronounced the event to be the 'greatest disaster and most disgraceful to our character that had ever occurred', it is generally regarded that the main responsibility for the débâcle lay with General Lake for sending too small a force for the task entrusted to it and not seeing that it was properly supplied. This fact he was later to acknowledge personally, saying: '. . . all blame ought to fall upon me for detaching the force in the first place'. However, the result was a great boost to Mahratta morale and Holkar pursued his victorious march towards Delhi (see DELHI II). General Lake now gave orders for his troops to march from their cantonments and assemble at Agra.

MONSON'S RETREAT   see MOKUNDRA PASS

MULWAGAL (Karnataka, India)   First Mysore War   4 October 1768
Fought between a British force under Colonel Wood and the Mysorean army of Haider Ali.
Strength: British 600 Europeans + 4,400 sepoys; Mysoreans 40,000 infantry + 25,000 cavalry.
Aim: During the course of the year 1768 the desultory and indecisive campaign between the forces of the Madras Presidency commanded by Colonel Joseph Smith supported by a division under Colonel Wood, and the Mysorean army continued with no great advantage to either side. Forts and villages were taken and retaken but very few large-scale operations took place. At last, in September, Haider Ali considered his prospects of ultimate victory so doubtful that he offered to cede the whole of the Baramahal Province to the British together with an indemnity of £100,000 as the price of peace, which the Madras Council foolishly rejected. Haider then took the field again and recaptured the strong and important fort of Mulwagal in the E Ghats, a few miles NE of Colar, and a vital post in the British lines of communications to Madras. On 3 October Wood advanced on the fort in an attempt to retake it.
Battle: After a strong attack on the lower fort, the British advanced towards the summit but were beaten back with some loss. On the following day Haider pushed forward a few light troops to tempt Wood into a second advance. Wood fell into the trap and the two companies pursuing the enemy suddenly found themselves facing Haider's whole army. Wood formed his troops into a hollow square and fought his way back to the main body, now deployed in a rock-strewn area of open ground. The British were now steadily pressed back by vastly superior numbers and in danger of annihilation. At this stage Captain Brooke, who had been left near the fortress with four companies of sepoys and 2 guns to guard the baggage, collected every single man and climbed to the top of a hill with his guns manned by wounded gunners. Here he opened a heavy fire of grape on Haider's left flank while his men shouted 'Huzza! Huzza! Smith, Smith!' The very name 'Smith' seemed to strike terror among the Mysoreans, and the enemy started to fall back imagining the arrival of reinforcements under the redoubtable British Commander-in-Chief. Wood seized the opportunity to re-form, and although Haider made a succession of attacks on discovering the trick, he was repulsed each time and at nightfall withdrew, having lost at least 1,000 men. British casualties

amounted to over 230 killed and wounded. Three days after this action Smith did in fact arrive with his column from Colar, and Haider retreated towards his headquarters at Bangalore.

Result: The same pattern of warfare continued into early 1769, with the advantage gradually accruing to Haider Ali, until the Madras Council decided to make overtures for peace. Negotiations were, however, fruitless and were broken off in March. Haider then resolved to bring matters to a head, and with a chosen corps of 6,000 cavalry and 200 infantry, marched 130 miles in eighty-four hours to appear suddenly at the gates of Madras. By 29 March the outskirts of the city were in his hands, and he then demanded that the Governor should send a particular council member, one Josias du Pré, to discuss the terms of peace. Smith's forces following up Haider were ordered to remain 25 miles distant while the talks proceeded.

The subsequent Treaty of Madras, concluded on 2 April 1769, provided for the mutual restitution of all captured territories and prisoners, with the engagement that each party should assist the other in the event of invasion by a third party. Thus ended, somewhat ingloriously, the First Mysore War.

MURCHAKHAR (Iran)   Persian Wars   1729
Fought between the Persian army under Nadir Kuli Beg and the Afghans under Ashraf Shah.
Strength: Persians 20,000; Afghans 15,000.
Aim: After the crushing defeat of his forces at Mehmandost (qv) Ashraf retired to Isfahan and collected all the families and property of the Afghans into the fort there. Then, taking up an entrenched position at Murchakhar 36 miles north of Isfahan, he prepared to fight a decisive battle for his throne.
Battle: The Persian forces under Nadir had marched south from Teheran collecting numerous recruits on the way. The Afghan position was found to be a strong one, but Nadir's tribesmen, encouraged by their previous successes, carried all before them. After losing about 4,000 men the Afghans broke and fled back to Isfahan. There they feverishly prepared for flight and, evacuating the capital, they retreated to Shiraz, 250 miles to the south. The helpless captive Shah Husain was put to death by Ashraf before he departed.
Result: Three days after this decisive victory Nadir entered the capital, to be followed shortly after by Shah Tahmasp II.

NANDI DRUG (Karnataka, India)   Third Mysore War   19 October 1791
Fought between the British army, commanded by Lord Cornwallis, Governor-General of India, and the Mysorean garrison at Nandi Drug.
Strength: British 1,000; Mysoreans 2,000.
Aim: Cornwallis decided on the capture of the fortress of Nandi Drug, situated on the summit of a granite mountain some 36 miles north of Bangalore which lay athwart the line of communications between his army at Bangalore and the Nizam of Hyderabad's troops.
Battle: The fortress was only accessible from one side. Major Gowdie was detailed to lead the assaulting force, and guns had to be dragged up the mountain pass with the help of elephants before it was possible for the siege to begin. Cornwallis, impatient for results and considering progress altogether too slow, moved out of Bangalore with a large force, hoping to intimidate the garrison into surrender. As the mere presence of his troops did not produce the desired effect, it was finally decided to take the place by storm, using the flank companies of the 36th and 71st Foot, with 102nd Foot in support. The garrison put up some resistance but were soon overcome, at a cost of not more than 2 British killed and 28 wounded.
Result: By the capture of this formidable fortress, Cornwallis secured his line of communications with Hyderabad in readiness for the final campaign to be opened the following year.

NEGAPATAM (NAGAPATTINAM) I (Tamil Nadu, India)   First Carnatic War   25 July 1746
Fought between a British naval squadron under Commodore Edward Peyton and a French fleet under Admiral Comte Bertrand Mahé de la Bourdonnais.
Strength: British 7 ships of the line; French 8 ships of the line.
Aim: In 1745 a British squadron under Commodore Curtis Bennett arrived in the Bay of Bengal, and in the absence of the French fleet which had been recalled to France, completely dominated the area. Fearing an attack on Pondicherry, the main French base in the Carnatic, the Governor-General the Marquis Joseph-François Dupleix, appealed for protection to Anwar-ud-Din, Nawab of the Carnatic and nominal overlord of both British and French. The Nawab accordingly warned the British Governor in Madras that he would not countenance any attack on French possessions on the Coromandel coast. At the same time Dupleix sent an urgent plea for help to Admiral de la Bourdonnais, commanding the French naval forces

at Mauritius. In July 1746 the Admiral duly arrived at Pondicherry with a squadron of 8 ships, carrying 1,200 troops.

Battle: On 25 July a naval action took place near Negapatam (Nagapattinam), off the coast of Tanjore, between the French squadron and the British fleet now under command of Commodore Peyton following the death of Bennett from fever. The British were completely outmanoeuvred by Bourdonnais, suffering damage which forced Peyton to retire. He then set sail for Trincomalee in Ceylon for repairs, leaving the French in command of the seas.

Result: As a result of the British defeat the French were able to proceed to invest Madras without fear of naval interference.

NEGAPATAM (NAGAPATTINAM) II (Tamil Nadu, India)   Second Mysore War   12 November 1781

Fought between the British under General Sir Hector Munro and the Negapatam (Nagapattinam) garrison of Haider Ali's Mysore troops.

Strength: British 4,000 (combined naval, army and marine force); Mysoreans 8,000.

Aim: On the outbreak of war between England and Holland in 1781, Haider Ali, the dictator of Mysore, already at war with the British, agreed to cede to the Dutch the British-held district of Nagore on the Coromandel coast and to protect on their behalf the nearby settlement of Negapatam. It was accordingly decided to besiege Negapatam and General Sir Hector Munro was placed at the head of a joint naval and military task force which was successfully landed at Nagore on 21 October 1781.

Battle: Munro proceeded south with his joint force to Negapatam. There a chain of 5 redoubts which covered the town on the northern side was carried by storm against greatly superior numbers, and nine days after the trenches had been opened the Mysoreans surrendered. Large quantities of naval and military stores were captured.

Result: The reduction of Negapatam deprived the French of the principal station for the troops expected to arrive shortly from France and resulted in the evacuation by Haider Ali of all the positions he held in that area.

OONDWAH NULLAH (Bihar, India)   Bengal Wars   5 September 1763

Fought between the British under Major Thomas Adams and the Bengali forces under Mir Kasim, former Nawab of Bengal.

Strength: British 1,000 Europeans + 4,000 sepoys + 12 guns; Bengalis 30,000 with 100 guns.

Aim: After defeating the army of the deposed Nawab of Bengal, Mir Kasim, at Sooty (qv), Adams marched up the southern bank of the Ganges, pitching camp within 4 miles of the Bengali entrenchments at the famous pass of Oondwah Nullah, a position of extraordinary strength 5 miles south of Rajmahal. Across the gorge a formidable line of entrenchments had been constructed with ramparts 60 feet wide and 10 feet high protected by a ditch 60 feet wide and 12 feet deep in water. Batteries were placed at intervals with more than 100 cannon in all. About a mile in rear ran an old line of works along the steep-banked rivulet known as the Oondwah Nullah, crossed by only one stone bridge and strongly guarded. Almost the entire front of the entrenchments between the hills and the Ganges was covered by a deep morass.

Battle: After a month's hard work, Adams set up a battery of siege guns and on 3 September opened fire on the ramparts, with little success. Fortunately for the British, a European soldier who had deserted from the East India Company's service came over from the enemy's camp and offered to point out a ford through the morass if he were promised a pardon. A force of 1,000 men with scaling ladders under Captain James Irving was accordingly detailed to cross the morass and take the fortified hill on the Bengali right, which was duly accomplished under cover of darkness. At the same time a column under Captain Moran attacked the small breach in the wall near the main gate. Beset in the dark from two points at once the bewildered Bengalis turned and fled in confusion for the stone bridge over the nullah, only to be mown down by the defenders who had instructions to shoot all fugitives. In the general panic which followed, hundreds were drowned in the Ganges, but the great mass plunged into the nullah itself which was choked with dead; in all several thousands of the Bengali force were killed. Adam's casualties were light, only 21 Europeans being killed and wounded, and 102 sepoys killed and wounded. Large numbers of prisoners were taken, together with a vast quantity of stores.

Result: Following this brilliant victory, Adams advanced on Monghyr, Mir Kasim's capital, which was captured on 11 October, Mir Kasim having fled to Patna. After making arrangements to convert Monghyr into an advanced base for operations, Adams pressed on relentlessly to Patna (see PATNA II).

PANIPAT (Haryana, India)   Afghan Wars   6 January 1761
Fought between the Afghan and Rohilla army under Ahmed Shah Durani, Shah of Afghanistan, and the forces of the Mahratta Confederacy commanded by Sedasheo Rao Bhao (known as 'The Bhao') and Wiswas Rao, son of the Peshwa, the hereditary ruler of the Mahrattas.
Strength: Afghans/Rohillas 41,800 cavalry + 38,000 infantry + 15,000 Indian horse + 70 guns; Mahrattas 55,000 cavalry + 15,000 irregular horse + 15,000 infantry + 300 guns and rockets.
Aim: Four times between 1748 and 1756 Ahmed Shah Durani, with his hordes of Afghan horsemen and long trains of artillery, had invaded India, leaving a trail of desolation behind. At last in despair the Mogul Emperor Alamgir II and his Vizier Shabab-ud-Din appealed to the Mahrattas to rally round the Empire of India against the northern invaders. The chiefs of the Mahratta Confederacy, conceiving this to be their opportunity to achieve hegemony over the whole of Hindustan, eagerly responded and advanced in force from their states in the Deccan as far as the river Indus, in which they had long sworn to water their horses. Before long, however, Ahmed Shah once more appeared at the head of a formidable army and the Mahrattas were forced to retreat. Ahmed now secured promises of Moslem support from the Rohillas of Rohilkhand in N Oudh and also from Shuja-ud-Daula, Nawab of Oudh, and the combined force gathered at Karnal. In the meantime the Mahrattas, having plundered Delhi, proceeded to Panipat, 50 miles to the north of the capital, where they entrenched themselves. The Afghans now crossed the Jumna and after several skirmishes with the enemy set up their own entrenchments. For nearly three months thereafter the two armies watched each other, during which time each side became increasingly straitened for food supplies, although the Mahrattas suffered much the greater hardship. At last in desperation the Mahrattas decided to leave their entrenched camp and confront the invaders in the field.
Battle: Before daybreak on the morning of 6 January 1761 the Mahrattas set forth from their camp, advancing slowly and regularly with their artillery in front. They then commenced hostilities by a general discharge of their guns all along the line, followed by a determined attack with their well-disciplined infantry under Ibrahim Khan Gardi against the Rohillas in the Afghan centre, who were broken with great slaughter. Headed by the Bhao and Wiswas Rao the main body then charged the Afghan centre and the Duranis were forced to give ground. At this critical stage Ahmed ordered up his reserve and at the same time commanded a division on his left to wheel and take the enemy in the flank. The Mahrattas resisted gallantly, but when their leader Wiswas Rao was mortally wounded they finally broke and fled. The pursuit was relentless, continuing in every direction for up to 20 miles, and great numbers of prisoners were butchered in cold blood. The total number of slain, including the masses of fleeing camp followers, was said to have amounted to nearly 200,000, and almost all the great Mahratta chiefs were killed or wounded. The wreck of the once great army retired beyond the river Nerbudda far to the south, and shortly after receiving news of the disaster the Peshwa died of the shock.
Result: Panipat, known as 'the Battle of the Black Mango Tree' after the ancient tree which stood in the plain, is one of the decisive battles of history. Their crushing defeat threw back Mahratta power for over thirty years, enabling the British to consolidate their position in both Bengal and Madras.
   After the battle Ahmed Shah entered Delhi and declared Ali Jauhar Emperor with the title of Shah Alam (King of the World), securing to himself the whole of the Mogul provinces in Afghanistan and the Punjab. He then returned with his victorious army to Kandahar and never afterwards took any share in the affairs of India.

PATNA I (Bihar, India)   Bengal Wars   25 June 1763
Fought between a British force under Mr Ellis and Captain Carstairs and Bengali columns commanded by Maskarian and Samru.
Strength: British 300 European infantry + 2,500 sepoys; Bengalis 10,000.
Aim: In 1760 Mir Jafar, the ageing Nawab of Bengal, abdicated to be superseded by his son-in-law Mir Mohammed Kasim, an energetic and ambitious ruler. Clive was now in England and Mir Kasim considered the East India Company was ruthlessly exploiting the resources of his country. He therefore determined to risk another clash with the British and raised a large and well-trained army, including many recruits from the warlike northern tribes, officered by European mercenaries, including a German called Reinhardt who assumed the name of Samru and an Armenian called Maskarian as Brigade Commanders. Anticipating trouble, Mir Kasim removed his capital from Murshidabad to Monghyr, half-way between Calcutta and Benares, but it was in Patna where hostilities actually started.
Battle: Mr Ellis, the East India Company agent in Patna, had been incensed by Mir Kasim's attempt to counter abuses by abolishing customs dues. Without asking Calcutta for authority, he placed himself and

the head of the garrison troops at the factory just outside the city and at dawn on 25 June 1763 made a surprise attack, scaling the walls, and within a few hours the city was captured. Ellis then made the fatal mistake of allowing his men to loot, and while they had run free and were widely dispersed they were surprised by a Bengali column under Maskarian and driven out of the city. The majority of the force then regrouped behind the factory, but their defence was short-lived. The next day they crossed the Ganges in an attempt to escape but were pursued by the Bengalis, now reinforced by Samru's Brigade, and forced to surrender. Those not killed were led back in chains to Patna, including Ellis, and thrown into gaol.
Result: Encouraged by this victory, Mir Kasim's forces sacked the Company's factory at Kasimbazar and captured the town of Dacca.

PATNA II (Bihar, India)   Bengal Wars   6 November 1763
Fought between the British under Major Thomas Adams and the garrison at Patna under Mir Kasim.
Strength: British 800 Europeans + 3,500 sepoys + 12 guns; Bengalis 6,000.
Aim: After his defeat at Oondwah Nullah (qv) and the subsequent fall of Monghyr, Mir Kasim now fulfilled his threat against the British prisoners captured in the engagement at Patna in June 1763 (PATNA I). He ordered Samru–the name assumed by his German commander Reinhardt–to surround the gaol and call out the 150 British officers and men, whereupon they were brutally massacred. The only one allowed to escape was a Dr Fullerton, on account of medical treatment he had accorded Mir Kasim. The latter then withdrew to a distance of 20 miles from the city ready for a further flight if necessary.
    On 28 October Adams encamped on the eastern side of Patna, a fortified city of considerable strength, its northern face abutting on the river and the three other sides protected by thick ramparts and a wide and deep ditch. His aim was to retake the city.
Battle: By 5 November Adams's siege guns had made two practicable breaches in the outer walls and before dawn the following morning two storming parties moved forward to the attack. After desperate hand-to-hand fighting on the ramparts the attackers forced the defenders back and opened the eastern gate, allowing the main body to rush in. Further resistance was overcome by a determined bayonet-charge and the city was captured. Bengali losses were considerable, about 2,000 being killed in the fighting and 500 burned to death in a building in which they had taken refuge. British casualties were 146 killed and wounded.
Result: As soon as Patna had been placed in a state of defence, Adams set off again in his relentless pursuit of Mir Kasim, who still had 30,000 men in the field. He abandoned the chase, however, at the river Karamnassa, which marked the boundary between Bihar and Oudh, pending instructions from the Council of the East India Company in Calcutta. This was Adams's last campaign as he died soon afterwards in Calcutta at the age of thirty-four. When news of his victorious campaign reached England, Adams was promoted Brigadier-General, but had already been dead some months.

PERAMBAKAM (Tamil Nadu, India)   Second Mysore War   10 September 1780
Fought between a British force under Lt-Colonel William Baillie and the Mysore armies under Haider Ali and Tipu Sultan, and a French contingent under Major Henri Lally.
Strength: British 400 Europeans + 3,400 sepoys; Mysoreans 55,000 infantry + 28,000 cavalry + 7,000 rocket gunners + French 400.
Aim: After the intervention of France in 1778 in the American War of Independence on the side of the Colonists, the British attacked French possessions in India, taking Pondicherry on the east coast and Mahé on the west. This latter seizure incensed Haider Ali, the ruler of Mysore, since it adjoined his conquests on the Malabar coast and he consequently decided to side with the French and declare war on the British. In July 1780 Haider, with his son and heir Tipu Sultan (Tippoo Sahib), swept down through the Changama Pass on the Carnatic with a well-organised army of some 90,000 troops, burning and pillaging on the way. The British forces under General Sir Hector Munro, the hero of Buxar (qv), were dispersed in various locations and immediate orders were given for their concentration at Conjeveram, 42 miles inland from Madras.
Battle: A force of 2,800 men, including 400 Europeans, under Colonel Baillie set out from Guntur on the river Kistnah to rendezvous at Conjeveram as instructed. On 25 August Baillie reached the river Kortalaiyer and encamped on the north side. Owing to sudden rains, the river rose overnight and Baillie was unable to cross until 3 September, allowing Haider plenty of time to detach his son Tipu Sultan with 5,000 foot, 6,000 horse and 18 guns to intercept the British. On 6 September Baillie reached Perambakam, where he was attacked by Tipu who, however, withdrew after heavy losses. Tipu then appealed to his

father for reinforcements, which were sent at once. At the same time Munro, pinned down at Conjeveram, had managed to send Baillie 1,000 men under Colonel Fletcher, raising his total force to about 3,700. On the morning of 10 September, while on the march, Baillie's force was attacked by the combined armies of Tipu, Lally and Haider, who had decided to join his son. Resistance was heroic and it was only after the British square had been broken by the fanatical charge of 1,000 Mysore horse that Baillie was compelled to surrender. By the time the slaughter had ended–reputedly at the intervention of Haider's French staff–36 out of 86 European officers had been killed, and the remaining 50 taken prisoner. Altogether 250 prisoners were taken and the rest of the force killed or scattered.

Result: This affray was the worst disaster suffered by British arms in India up to that time and Munro was obliged to make a rapid and undignified retreat back to Marmalong, 4 miles south of Madras, after a disastrous campaign of twenty-one days. Madras was now without troops and open to attack by Haider, who was only prevented from following up his success because the greater part of his army was still engaged in besieging Wandiwash, and fortunately for the British he allowed this fact to cloud his judgement and missed an opportunity which would not recur. The unfortunate Colonel Baillie was to die in prison in Seringapatam two years later.

PLASSEY (PALASI) (W Bengal, India)   Bengal Wars   23 June 1757
Fought between the British under Colonel Robert Clive and the army of Siraj-ud-Daula, Nawab of Bengal.

Strength: British 613 European infantry + 171 gunners + 2,100 sepoys + 91 topasses (Eurasian camp followers) + 10 field pieces and 2 howitzers; Bengalis 35,000 infantry + 15,000 Pathan cavalry + French 50 gunners with 53 guns (mostly heavy).

Aim: After the capture of Chandernagore (qv) Clive wrote to Siraj-ud-Daula urging him to force the French to give up their remaining settlements in Bengal; but the Nawab proved intransigent. About this time news reached Clive of a palace conspiracy to replace the Nawab by Mir Jafar, the Paymaster-General of the Bengali army. Siraj-ud-Daula became suspicious and, instead of withdrawing all his troops to Murshidabad as promised, he left half in his fortified camp at Plassey (Palasi), 20 miles to the south. Clive thereupon decided to confront the Nawab's army at Plassey, taking a gamble that the divisions commanded by Mir Jafar and his fellow conspirator Rai Durlabh would defect to the British.

Battle: At dusk on 22 June, having received a letter from Mir Jafar promising his support, Clive with his main force left Katwa and crossed to the left bank of the Hooghly, reaching Plassey in the early hours. The troops then occupied a mango grove known as the Laksha Bagh which formed a good line of defence, with a hunting lodge on the left known as Plassey House which Clive made his headquarters. At dawn on 23 June the Nawab's army emerged from its camp about a mile to the north, advancing in three divisions which fanned out to encircle and outflank the British force. Clive now ordered his troops to advance out of the mango grove, the Europeans in the centre flanked by the sepoys on either side. A heavy and continuous artillery barrage then ensued and after an hour Clive was forced to withdraw his men back into the grove. At noon, however, rain began to fall in torrents, soaking the ammunition of the Bengalis whose fire then slackened.

Thinking the British had suffered likewise, a body of the Nawab's horse under Mir Madan advanced, only to be met with a deadly fire of grape, the British having covered their ammunition with tarpaulins against the rain. A shell from a 6-pounder mortally wounded Mir Madan, and the death of his most loyal commander greatly distressed the Nawab. Sending for Mir Jafar he begged him to defend 'his life and honour', but was told that it was too late to attack that day. He was advised, furthermore, that the troops should be recalled and that he himself should retire to his capital. Acting on this counsel the Nawab mounted his fastest camel and with an escort of 2,000 horse returned to Murshidabad. Seeing the Nawab's troops withdrawing Clive called up his reserves and ordered a general advance. After a fierce rearguard action the Bengali forces broke and fled, leaving the British in possession of their entrenched camp, baggage and stores. The fleeing enemy were pursued for about 6 miles, but without cavalry the British could go no farther. Plassey was a comparatively bloodless battle. The Nawab out of his vast force only lost 500 men and the British casualties amounted to only 13 Europeans and 50 sepoys killed or wounded. The issue of the battle had in fact been decided by the treachery of Mir Jafar and the other conspirators.

Result: After this spectacular victory, the British troops proceeded to Daudpur. On the following morning Mir Jafar arrived for consultations with Clive, after which he hurried on to Murshidabad. On 29 June with an escort of 500 troops Clive entered the city as a conqueror, the streets being lined with people. Mir Jafar was now formally installed as Nawab of Bengal, Orissa and Bihar and under a treaty with the British he agreed to pay the sum of £3 million as compensation for the damage and losses sustained at Calcutta (see CALCUTTA I and II).

Two days earlier Siraj-ud-Daula, accompanied by his favourite wife, had left the city in disguise. On 2 July, however, he was recognised by a fakir near Rajmahal and was apprehended and returned to Murshidabad as a prisoner. He was then stabbed to death at the instigation of Mir Jafar and his bleeding corpse paraded through the streets on an elephant. He was only twenty years old.

On his return to England in 1760 Clive 'the heaven-born general' as Pitt called him, was given an Irish peerage and created Baron Clive of Plassey.

POLLILUR (Tamil Nadu, India)   Second Mysore War   27 August 1781
Fought between the British under General Sir Eyre Coote and the Mysorean army under Haider Ali.
Strength: British 2,000 Europeans + 10,000 sepoys + 300 artillerymen + 500 native cavalry; Mysoreans 80,000 horse and foot.
Aim: After his victory at Porto Novo (qv) Coote marched northward, picking up reinforcements of ten sepoy battalions and two companies of artillery on the way. On 26 August 1781 he reached Perambakam (qv), scene of Lt-Colonel William Baillie's overwhelming defeat twelve months before. Haider Ali's forces were drawn up in the same encampment near the village of Pollilur as during that previous action, the superstitious Mohammedan having been assured by his astrologers that this would ensure certain victory. On the following morning, despite the fact that visibility was extremely limited because of clouds of dust raised by strong winds, Coote decided to go straight in to the attack.
Battle: Coote first occupied a thick grove to the left of his line of march as a vantage-point. The advance of the main body of his force, led by General Sir Hector Munro, ran into enfilading fire from Tipu Sultan's advance detachment, but succeeded in finding a good position for its guns and forced Tipu to retire. Haider's artillery was now concentrating heavy fire on the British position in the grove, following this up with strong infantry attacks. As the day wore on, the wind died down, giving a better view of the field of battle, and Coote now ordered a brigade advance on the village of Pollilur, which speedily drove out the enemy, and then raked the whole of Haider's line with artillery fire. The Mysore army hastened to retreat, leaving Coote at nightfall in command of the field, although the combat had actually come to an end with little advantage to either side. British casualties amounted to 53 killed and 370 wounded, including Brigadier James Stuart, who lost his left leg below the knee. Haider Ali's casualties, mainly the result of artillery fire, amounted to 2,000 killed and wounded.
Result: Following this indecisive action Coote returned to Madras, where he resigned his command as a protest at the futility of maintaining an army in the field which was virtually incapable of movement for lack of transport.

PONDICHERRY (PUDUCHCHERI) I (Tamil Nadu, India)   First Carnatic War   August–October 1748
Fought between a combined British naval and military force commanded by Admiral Edward Boscawen and the French garrison at Pondicherry (Puduchcheri) under the Governor-General the Marquis Joseph-François Dupleix.
Strength: British 2,900 European infantry + 800 marines + 80 gunners + 2,000 sepoys; French 1,800 Europeans + 3,000 sepoys.
Aim: When the news reached England of the fall of Madras in September 1746 (MADRAS I) the East India Company asked for help from the British government. A powerful squadron of men-of-war and transports under the command of Admiral Boscawen was accordingly dispatched, and it arrived off Fort St David in August 1748 with over 2,000 regular troops on board. Shortly after his arrival Boscawen set out with a combined services force to besiege Pondicherry. In the meantime Dupleix had strengthened the defences of the city and also added a strong fort at Ariancopang, about 2 miles to the south.
Battle: Boscawen decided it was essential to capture the fort at Ariancopang before investing Pondicherry itself, but his engineers proved slow and inefficient. A cavalry sortie against the trenches of the naval brigade spread panic among the troops who rushed back to their camp, leaving Major Stringer Lawrence, the most experienced officer in the expedition, to be taken prisoner. Accident then came to the aid of the British when a magazine blew up in the fort, causing heavy casualties, whereupon the garrison withdrew into Pondicherry. Boscawen then moved forward and opened trenches against the NW corner of the town. A further sortie by the French was this time repulsed with great loss and M. Paradis, the ablest of the French engineer officers, was killed. At last, early in October, 2 batteries opened fire on the town, only to

be answered by twice as formidable a fire from the guns of the besieged. The fire of the British batteries continued for three days with little result and a supporting naval bombardment proved equally ineffectual. On 11 October Boscawen decided to raise the siege, as the rainy season had set in and the British trenches were flooded. The force then retreated, leaving 1,000 European dead behind.
Result: This highly unsatisfactory enterprise proved a great blow to British influence and prestige in India. Eleven days had been wasted in the quite unnecessary operations before Ariancopang, and the engineers proved completely incompetent in the placing of their batteries. All these shortcomings were carefully noted by a young ensign who accompanied the expedition, named Robert Clive, who was in due course to accomplish the downfall of Dupleix.

A few months later news reached India of the peace Treaty of Aix-la-Chapelle, as a result of which Madras was handed back to the British in exchange for Cape Breton in N America. However, neither the French nor British were prepared to accept the *status quo* and their struggle for supremacy in India was to continue for many years to come.

PONDICHERRY (PUDUCHCHERI) II (Tamil Nadu, India)   Third Carnatic War   10 September 1759
Fought between a British naval squadron commanded by Rear-Admiral Sir George Pocock and a French squadron under Rear-Admiral Comte Anne-Antoine d'Aché.
Strength: British 10 ships; French 11 ships.
Aim: After the failure of Comte Thomas-Arthur Lally de Tollendal to capture Madras earlier in 1759, (MADRAS II), a number of minor engagements took place in the Carnatic between the British and French. Admiral Pocock cruised off Pondicherry (Puduchcheri) in anticipation of the eventual return to the Bay of Bengal of the French fleet under Admiral d'Aché.
Battle: On 10 September D'Aché arrived with 11 ships of the line and was immediately engaged by Pocock, flying his flag in *Yarmouth*. The action was severe but ended inconclusively, although the French ships were so badly damaged that they retired to the roads at Pondicherry.
Result: Admiral d'Aché was so chagrined by his continual failure to defeat the British at sea after three successive actions, that he decided to return to Mauritius despite strong protests from Lally. With his departure went the last hope for the French forces in India. Pocock returned to England, to be succeeded by Rear-Admiral Charles Steevens.

PONDICHERRY (PUDUCHCHERI) III (Tamil Nadu, India)   Third Carnatic War   15 January 1761
Fought between the British under Colonel Eyre Coote, with naval support under Rear-Admiral Charles Steevens, and the French garrison at Pondicherry (Puduchcheri) under Comte Thomas-Arthur Lally de Tollendal.
Strength: British 2,500 Europeans + 3,500 sepoys + 1,200 Indian cavalry + naval support; French 2,000 Europeans + 1,000 sepoys + Mysoreans 8,000 horse and foot.
Aim: After his major defeat at Wandiwash (qv) Lally retreated to Pondicherry, the main French base on the Coromandel coast. He called in all French garrisons from Trichinopoly and other scattered stations in the area and entered into an agreement with Haider Ali, then Commander of the Mysore forces, for the services of 8,000 men, although they subsequently withdrew without taking part in the battle. Despite strong opposition from the civil authorities, Lally resolved to fight to the end.
Battle: On 2 September 1760 Coote's force was reinforced by further East India Company troops, together with half a regiment of Morris's Highlanders, the 89th Foot. Three men-of-war also came with the transports raising the squadron before Pondicherry to 17 sail. At this stage Lally made a daring attack on the British camp which miscarried and, despite their conspicuous gallantry, his troops were repulsed. On the last day of 1760 a sudden hurricane burst over the town and harbour, sinking 3 British ships with all hands and driving 3 ashore. The siege works set up by Coote were also destroyed. However, the surviving ships continued the blockade and the siege works were repaired and pushed forward, and the bombardment resumed. On 15 January the garrison, being on the brink of starvation, surrendered. A few weeks sufficed to reduce the few isolated fortresses still held by French garrisons and on 5 April 1761 the white flag of the Bourbons ceased to fly in India.
Result: Thus after some fifteen years of continual struggle between French and British for empire in the East, the British were left supreme in India. Under the terms of the Peace of Paris in 1763, which ended the Seven Year's War, Pondicherry was in fact restored to France, but it never again became a menace to

British influence. On his return to France, Lally was arraigned for treason for having surrendered Pondicherry, and in 1766 was beheaded.

Although at this length of time France's treatment to her potential empire-builders in India such as Dupleix and Lally seems to have been unjustifiably harsh, the moralistic condemnation meted out by eighteenth-century Britain to her much more successful counterparts, Clive and Warren Hastings, is even more difficult to defend.

POONA I (Maharashtra, India)   First Mahratta War   18 January–23 April 1781
Fought between the British under Brigadier-General Thomas Goddard and the Mahrattas under their chiefs, Hari Punt Phurkay, Puresham (Paraeshram) Bhow and Tookaji Holkar.
Strength: British 650 Europeans + 4,700 sepoys + 800 native cavalry; Mahrattas 56,000 horse and foot.
Aim: After the capture of Bassein (qv) in December 1780 Goddard had been instructed to conclude peace with the Mahrattas as soon as the expected overtures were received from the Peshwa at Poona. Goddard considered that a military threat to the Mahratta capital itself would hasten matters and prove effective in bringing the Mahratta chiefs to a speedy decision. He therefore advanced from Bombay towards the passes. The Mahratta Commander, Hari Punt Phurkay, at once fell back slowly on Poona, leaving a strong guard at the Bore Ghat and at the same time detaching a force of 12,000 men to cut Goddard's rear communications with Bombay.
Battle: On 8 February 1781 Goddard's advance party of Bengali troops under Colonel Parker forced the pass at the Bore Ghat and pushed on to Khandalleh. At this stage, however, Goddard's progress towards Poona came to a halt through lack of troops. On two occasions convoys escorted by sepoy battalions had been subjected to heavy attacks by Mahratta horse while on their way to the British forward camp. Goddard was at last forced to accept the advice of the Bombay government to stand on the defensive and send his Madras sepoys back east where they were now urgently wanted. The subsequent retreat to Bombay, begun in April, nearly proved disastrous, Goddard's force being constantly harried by three separate bodies of the enemy, totalling some 56,000 men. After continuous heavy fighting he eventually reached the coast at Panwelly having suffered casualties of 466 men killed and wounded, including 18 European officers.
Result: To counteract this abortive operation, a more successful diversion led by Colonel Camac took place about the same time in Malwa, to the north, resulting in the Mahratta chieftain Mahadaji Scindia suing for peace. Eventually, on 17 May 1782, the Peace of Salbai was concluded, under which large areas were returned to the Mahrattas and the British finally abandoned the cause of Ragobah as Peshwa. However, they had no alternative, as the Governor-General considered it essential to be free to concentrate on the main contest with Haider Ali of Mysore and the French in the Carnatic.

POONA II (Maharashtra, India)   Second Mahratta War   25 October 1802
Fought between the army of Jaswunt Rao Holkar, Maharaja of Indore, and the combined forces of Baji Rao, the Peshwa of Poona, and Doulut Rao Scindia of Gwalior, commanded by Sewdashio Bhow Bhaskur.
Strength: Holkar's army 8,000 infantry (with British officers) + 5,000 irregular infantry + 25,000 cavalry; Peshwa's Scindia's forces 6,000 infantry (with British officers) + 4,000 irregular infantry + 25,000 cavalry.
Aim: Since 1798, internal dissensions had brought the Mahratta Confederacy into confusion. The ambitious Jaswunt Rao Holkar took advantage of the position to invade and ravage the territories of his rival Doulut Rao Scindia, who then combined his forces with those of the Peshwa, Baji Rao, to repel Holkar's rapid advance on Poona, the Mahratta capital.
Battle: The action, which took place near Poona itself, started on the morning of 25 October 1802 with a brisk cannonade which was kept up on both sides for three hours. At first the battle between the opposing cavalry forces was evenly contested, until a final charge led by Holkar himself routed Scindia's horse. In the meantime, six of Scindia's infantry battalions had given way, but the remaining four stood their ground with great determination. Eventually, however, they were overcome by Holkar's relentless cavalry charges. His victory was now complete and the whole of the enemy's guns, baggage and stores fell into his hands.
Result: Baji Rao fled to the coast, where he embarked on a British ship and was conveyed to the port of Bassein, north of Bombay. On 31 December 1802 he signed the Treaty of Bassein, whereby he placed himself under the protection of the British government and concluded a defensive and offensive alliance.

On 13 May 1803 the Peshwa was escorted back to his capital by a British force commanded by Major-General Arthur Wellesley, brother of the Governor-General, the Marquess Wellesley, and was restored with great ceremony to the masnud (throne). General Wellesley was now instructed to take all steps 'to restore the tranquillity of the Deccan' by negotiation, if possible, but otherwise by force of arms. On 6 August 1803 negotiations with the Mahratta chieftains, Doulut Rao Scindia of Gwalior and Rughji Bhonsla, Raja of Nagpur and Berar, broke down and the Second Mahratta War became inevitable.

PORTO NOVO (Tamil Nadu, India)   Second Mysore War   1 July 1781
Fought between the British under General Sir Eyre Coote and the Mysore army under Haider Ali.
Strength: British 2,000 Europeans + 5,000 sepoys + 500 native cavalry + 48 guns; Mysoreans 80,000 horse and foot.
Aim: On the news of Colonel William Baillie's disastrous defeat at Perambakam (qv), General Sir Eyre Coote was called from Bengal to take command of the British troops in the Carnatic in place of General Sir Hector Munro. Haider Ali had taken Arcot and a number of other British posts and on 17 January 1781 Coote marched southwards from Madras, relying for his supplies on a flotilla of small vessels which followed his movements along the coast. Coote's design was to relieve various beleaguered garrisons and draw Haider Ali after him by threatening Pondicherry. This tactic was successful and, abandoning his sieges, the Mysore chief followed southwards. No action, however, took place for the next five months as Coote, through lack of supplies, was obliged to remain inactive at Cuddalore. Then, in June, Coote was informed that Haider was busy fortifying a strong position 3 miles north of the British camp, near Porto Novo.
Battle: In the early morning of 1 July Coote, leaving his camp baggage under heavy guard, marched to an extensive plain crowded with enemy cavalry. He then formed his force into two columns and continued his advance. Then the swarms of horsemen on the plain melted away, revealing a large semicircle of entrenchments and batteries covering the line of advance. Coote had observed that though Haider's left rested on the sea, a chain of sandhills had been left undefended, and leading a column through this area unobserved, he turned the enemy's entrenched position. At the same time the main divisions under General Sir Hector Munro and Brigadier James Stuart advanced against Haider's centre, their progress fiercely contested. At this stage, Haider ordered a general advance of his massed cavalry. At the moment, however, of giving the order for the attack, the cavalry commander Mir Sahib was killed by a round shot, while simultaneously the closely packed squadrons were raked by fire from a British schooner standing close in to shore. The cavalry, leaderless, panicked and fled. Haider was now persuaded by the Mysorean leaders to leave the field, and his whole army then steadily retreated. Coote judged himself too weak in cavalry to pursue. British casualties were slight, being little more than 300 killed and wounded, whereas Mysore casualties amounted to 3,000 killed and 6,000 wounded.
Result: Although Coote had not succeeded in destroying Haider Ali's army or taking any prisoners or guns, there is no doubt that this victory was the salvation of the British in S India. The battle thwarted the aggressive schemes of the Mysorean ruler and forced him to act on the defensive, paving the way after his death in December 1782 for the destruction of the warlike state he had created.

ST THOME (ST THOMAS) (Tamil Nadu, India)   First Carnatic War   4 November 1746
Fought between a French force commanded by M. Paradis and the army of Anwar-ud-Din, Nawab of the Carnatic, commanded by his son Maphuze Khan.
Strength: French 230 Europeans + 730 sepoys; Indians 10,000.
Aim: After the humiliating defeat of the Nawab's army at the hands of the French garrison of Madras on 2 November 1746 (MADRAS II), Maphuze Khan marched on St Thomé (St Thomas), some 4 miles to the south, to intercept a French force under the command of a Swiss officer named Paradis on its way from Pondicherry to relieve Madras.
Battle: On 4 November the French found their way barred by an army of some 10,000 Indians supported by artillery and drawn up on the far bank of a river. Knowing the river to be fordable Paradis unhesitatingly led his men across it and straight upon the enemy. After firing 1 volley the French charged with the bayonet. The effect of this bold move was to transform the Nawab's army into a disorganised rabble which turned and fled headlong into the town of St Thomé, only to be jammed in hopeless confusion in the narrow streets. The French continued to pour volley after volley into the struggling mass. A contingent from Madras, *en route* to join forces with Paradis, attacked the fugitives in the rear and completed the rout.

Result: The French Governor-General at Pondicherry, the Marquis Joseph-François Dupleix, now appointed Paradis to the chief command in Madras and issued a proclamation that the town belonged to the French by right of conquest.

The most important result of this victory was the realisation that a small, well-trained and disciplined European force was more than a match for native armies in spite of their seemingly overwhelming strength. Both for the French and the British in their turn this was a discovery of momentous significance which was to transform the balance of power in India.

SAVANDRUG (SAVANDURGA) (Karnataka, India)   Third Mysore War   10–21 December 1791
Fought between a British column under Colonel Stuart and the Mysorean garrison at Savandrug (Savandurga).
Strength: British 4,000; Mysoreans 2,000.
Aim: The British objective was the massive hill fortress of Savandrug, the 'Rock of Death', lying about 20 miles NW of Bangalore, the headquarters of the British forces under the Governor-General Lord Cornwallis. Rising to a height of 900 feet from precipitous ravines covered with thick jungle, its base was some 8 miles round and, at the top, the rock split into two with a citadel on each peak.
Battle: After hard effort the British cut a road through the jungle and dragged heavy guns up the mountain. On 17 December 2 batteries opened fire and, after a two-day bombardment, opened a breach in the wall on the eastern hill. On the night of 21 December the assault part, consisting of flank companies of the 52nd and 76th Foot, supported by the 71st and 72nd Foot and two sepoy companies, rushed the breach, while the band of the 52nd played 'Britons, Strike Home'. However, there was no opposition to strike home on, for the garrison had fled in panic and both forts were taken with the cost to the British of 1 man wounded. Of the garrison about 100 were killed and others met their death when they fell over the precipices endeavouring to escape.
Result: By the capture of this hill fortress, considered impregnable, the northern route which Cornwallis intended to follow in his projected advance on Seringapatam in the following year's campaign, was cleared.

SERINGAPATAM (SRIRANGAPATAM) I (Karnataka, India)   5–16 February 1792
Fought between the combined British and Indian armies under Lord Cornwallis, the Governor-General of India, and the Mysorean garrison under Tipu Sultan.
Strength: British (Cornwallis's force) 6,000 Europeans + 16,000 sepoys + 46 field guns, 4 howitzers, 36 mortars and siege guns + (Nizam of Hyderabad's force) 18,000 cavalry + Mahrattas 12,000 (under Hari Punt) + (Abercrombie's force) 3,000 Europeans + 6,000 sepoys + 14 guns; Mysoreans 40,000 infantry + 5,000 cavalry + 100 field guns and 300 mounted guns.
Aim: This was the final reckoning between the British, commanded by Lord Cornwallis, and the forces of Tipu Sultan, the notorious 'Tiger of Mysore', now defending his island capital of Seringapatam (Srirangapatam). The campaign of 1792 started on 26 January when Cornwallis left Bangalore, passing by Savandrug (qv), where he was joined by the Nizam of Hyderabad's cavalry and a Mahratta contingent. The combined armies reached the outskirts of Seringapatam on 5 February, and encamped 4 miles north of the city at French Rocks. Meanwhile a supporting force of 9,000 men under General Sir Robert Abercrombie had set out from Tellichery on the Malabar coast with a battering train of 14 heavy guns and was now approaching from the west. However, after reconnoitring the defences, Cornwallis decided to attack in three divisions on the evening of 6 February without waiting for Abercrombie's column to appear.
Battle: The total force used in the assault, comprisng infantry only, amounted to about 8,700 men; the right column was commanded by Major-General William Medows with 3,300 men, the left column was under Colonel Maxwell with 1,700 men, and the centre with the remainder under Cornwallis himself. All columns moved off at 8.30pm under a full moon and met with considerable resistance until the outlying works were taken, including all the redoubts commanding the town. The action now took on the form of the siege of an embattled city, although Tipu continued to direct counter-attacks against the troops now occupying most of the island of Seringapatam itself. Many of Tipu's forces had by now deserted, including the entire corps of Ahmadis, some 10,000 strong, who formed the centre of his battle-line. On 16 February the arrival of General Abercrombie's force completed the investment of Tipu's citadel on the southern side, and caused him to agree to treat. In the siege operations the defenders lost over 4,000 men and 86

guns–a total of 800 guns in all had been captured in the whole campaign. British casualties amounted to 535 men killed and wounded.

Result: A peace treaty was signed on 19 March 1792 under which the British obtained suzerainty over the whole of spice-bearing Malabar as well as the province of Coorg, and control of the Baramahal region of SE Mysore. In addition, Tipu agreed to pay large indemnities, release all prisoners and deliver up 2 of his sons as hostages. The whole campaign had been well organised and decisively executed and as the historian Fortescue remarked: 'Cornwallis showed a nerve, audacity and swiftness in action which entitle him to high rank among commanders.' However, the story of Tipu Sultan, or Tippoo Sahib as he was known to many admiring English at home, was not yet over, and it was not until the end of the century that the final tragedy was to be enacted (see SERINGAPATAM II).

SERINGAPATAM (SRIRANGAPATAM) II (Karnataka, India)   Fourth Mysore War   6 April–3 May 1799

Fought between a British invasion force under Lt-General George Harris and the Mysorean garrison under Tipu Sultan.

Strength: British (Harris's force) 21,000+(Stuart's force) 6,000+47 siege guns+(Nizam of Hyderabad's force) 16,000; Mysoreans 14,000 (fort)+8,000 (entrenchments)+14,000 cavalry (outside the city).

Aim: Early in March 1799 Lt-General Harris marched from Vellore to conquer Mysore. At Ambur he was joined by a well-equipped contingent from Hyderabad of some 16,000 horse and foot, reinforced by the 33rd Foot, and under the overall command of Colonel Arthur Wellesley, brother of the Governor-General, Lord Mornington. In support from the Bombay Presidency came a force of 6,000 under the command of Lt-General James Stuart. After reaching Bangalore, Harris proceeded towards Seringa-patam (Srirangapatam) by the south road via Kankanhalli, and after repulsing a determined attack by Tipu at Malavelly (qv) reached a position some 3 miles SW of the capital by 5 April.

Battle: The defences of Seringapatam had been strengthened to some extent since the last siege in 1792, but many of the fortifications were still unfinished. By 14 April Stuart's force had arrived and was detailed to cover the north bank of the river. Early on 22 April his position was fiercely attacked by some 6,000 Mysorean infantry, but they were repulsed with heavy losses to the attackers. By 2 May batteries had been brought into position and they effected a large breach in the wall near the NW bastion. On 4 May an assault party of 2,500 Europeans and 1,800 sepoys led by General David Baird (once a prisoner in Tipu's dungeons) stormed through the breach under furious musket-fire. The defenders were routed and, in the course of the fighting, Tipu Sultan, the 'Tiger of Mysore', was slain, his dead body being recovered from beneath a pile of corpses. Mysorean casualties were estimated at 6,000 killed and wounded, while British casualties amounted to 1,464.

Result: Colonel Arthur Wellesley was appointed Military Governor of Seringapatam with the task of restoring order in the sacked city. The total value of the specie, jewels and other stores not already looted by the soldiery amounted to some £2 million, about half of which was treated as prize-money. The Commander-in-Chief's share came to some £142,000. In December 1799, Lord Mornington, the Governor-General, was created a Marquess for his services.

So far as Tipu Sultan, or Tippoo Sahib as he was popularly called, was concerned, he became for many years a legendary figure in Britain and the hero of many a romantic story.

SHOLINGHUR (Tamil Nadu, India)   Second Mysore War   27 September 1781

Fought between the British under General Sir Eyre Coote and the Mysorean army under Haider Ali.

Strength: British 2,000 Europeans + 8,000 sepoys + 300 artillerymen + 500 native cavalry + 48 guns; Mysoreans 70,000 horse and foot with 70 guns.

Aim: Having been persuaded by the Madras authorities to withdraw the resignation he had tendered after Pollilur (qv), Coote again took to the field against Haider Ali in September 1781, his main objective being the relief of the British garrison besieged in Vellore. On the march he received intelligence that Haider was at Sholinghur, about 30 miles due west of Tripassore, holding a strong position to bar the British approach to Vellore.

Battle: Early in the morning of 27 September Coote espied the Mysore army established 3 miles from his position. He then drew up his force as usual in two lines and advanced in that formation against the enemy, whose main body was sited behind the crest of a long ridge with its front protected by swampy rice fields. Haider had ordered his hordes of cavalry to harass Coote's flanks and charge in on the slightest sign of

disorder. When they did so, however, they were mown down by musket-fire and eventually retired after suffering heavy losses. At the same time the battalions in the British second line had been exposed to a succession of furious attacks by a separate corps commanded by Haider's son Tipu Sultan. They held their ground, however, and Tipu was obliged to draw off his troops and retire to the main body. By midnight the whole of the British force was encamped on the ground which Haider had occupied. British casualties were fewer than 100 killed and wounded, whereas the Mysore casualties were reckoned to exceed 5,000 men.
Result: A number of minor engagements followed and in late October Coote was able to relieve Vellore. However, on 22 November, he returned to Madras just as the monsoon was breaking, with his army half-starved owing to the inefficient supply arrangements of the Madras Council.

SIDASSIR (SIDDESVARA) (Karnataka, India)   Fourth Mysore War   6 March 1799
Fought between the advance guard of Lt-General James Stuart's force under Lt-Colonel Montrésor and the Mysorean army under Tipu Sultan.
Strength: British 2,000; Mysoreans 12,000.
Aim: Tipu Sultan, the 'Tiger of Mysore', had again been intriguing with the French against the British position in S India and a letter of encouragement is on record from Napoleon Bonaparte from his own headquarters in Cairo addressed to 'our greatest friend Tippoo Saib'. The new Governor-General, Lord Mornington, decided on 3 February 1799 to invade Mysore with his main force commanded by Lt-General George Harris, the Commander-in-Chief of the Madras Presidency, supported by a column from the Bombay army under General Stuart.
Battle: The Mysoreans attacked the advance guard of Stuart's force which had occupied an observation-post on Sidassir Hill just inside Coorg and engaged them for six hours. The main frontal attack was supported by large parties of the enemy who had crept up during the night on Montrésor's flanks. The British had almost run out of ammunition when the main force arrived and drove the Mysoreans back. The enemy losses amounted to some 2,000 including their leader Mohammed Raza, Tipu's cousin, known as the 'Binky Nabob' because of his sinister reputation as an incendiarist, *benki* being Canarese for 'fire'. British casualties in this action were 143 killed and wounded.
Result: On 11 March Tipu retreated towards Seringapatam to regroup.

SIRHIND (Punjab, India)   Afghan Wars   March 1748
Fought between the Afghans, under Ahmed Shah Durani, and the Mogul army under Prince Ahmed and the Vizier, Kamr-u-Din Khan.
Strength: Afghans 15,000; Moguls 40,000.
Aim: On the assassination of Nadir Shah in June 1747, Ahmed Khan Durani, son of the hereditary chief of the Abdali tribe of Afghans based on Herat, who was one of Nadir's most trusted generals, seized control of most of the region now known as Afghanistan. With a force of 10,000 cavalry under his command and in control of a large part of Nadir's treasure he had no difficulty in obtaining the support of the tribes and was crowned Shah in Kandahar. Realising the increasing weakness of the Mogul Empire he made several major invasions into India during the course of his reign of twenty-six years and annexed most of the western provinces of the dying Empire. His first invasion in 1748, however, was far from being successful. The Viceroy of the Punjab was in revolt against Delhi and Ahmed was able to occupy Lahore with little opposition. He marched towards the river Sutlej, where the fords were occupied by a large Mogul army sent from Delhi to bar his approach.
Battle: Ahmed and his force made the crossing of the Sutlej where no ford existed, leaving the Mogul army in his rear, and captured Sirhind, where the Mogul baggage and stores had been left. Not only did he seize the stores but he also found a number of guns which he had previously lacked. This intrepid move caused the enemy to halt and hastily entrench their position. Despite the fact that the Mogul Vizier was killed by a cannon-ball while at prayers in his tent, his army continued to repel the Duranis' savage and repeated attacks for ten days. When a last desperate attack on the entrenchments was beaten off with heavy losses, the Afghan army accepted defeat and retreated under cover of night.
Result: Ahmed Shah now returned to Afghanistan, after persuading the new Viceroy of the Punjab to engage to pay him tribute. Shortly afterwards the Emperor Mohammed Shah died, to be succeeded by the son who had commanded the Mogul army at Sirhind and who now bore the same name and title as the Afghan monarch he had defeated.

SOOTY (Bihar, India)   Bengal Wars   2 August 1763
Fought between the British under Major Thomas Adams and the Bengali army of Mir Kasim.
Strength: British 730 European infantry + 150 European cavalry + 120 European gunners + 4,000 sepoys + 10 guns; Bengalis 10,000 infantry + 20,000 cavalry + 200 European gunners with 20 guns.
Aim: After installing Mir Jafar as Nawab in Murshidabad Adams continued his march, having been reinforced, following the right bank of the river Bagiruttee towards Mir Kasim's main defensive position at Sooty, about 35 miles to the NW, manned by his most disciplined troops. At dawn on 2 August 1763 Adams came upon the enemy on the plains of Gheria, Mir Kasim having confidently left his strongly entrenched position to meet the advancing British force.
Battle: Action commenced shortly after 8am with an artillery duel, during which both armies advanced slowly, Adams keeping his flanks close to the river Bagiruttee on his right and the river Banslee on his left. After coming under devastating musket-fire the Bengalis released a body of cavalry to attack the British left, which they did with considerable success, almost annihilating a battalion of sepoys. At the same time the British centre was dangerously assailed both in front and rear, whereupon Adams brought up the 101st Foot and a reserve sepoy battalion and restored the position. The British line then re-formed and a determined bayonet-charge caused the whole of Mir Kasim's host to give way, only the rocket troop striving unavailingly to stem the advance. Pressing hard on the heels of the fugitives Adams drove them beyond their entrenchments at Sooty before they could rally to defend them. The Bengali camp with 23 guns and vast quantities of stores and 150 boats laden with ammunition were captured. The Bengalis left 2,000 dead and wounded on the field, and British casualties were not light–numbering 102 Europeans killed or wounded, and 280 sepoys killed or wounded.
Result: One of the hardest fought actions in the history of British India, this victory was nevertheless inconclusive and after clearing the entrenchments Adams marched towards the stronghold where Mir Kasim had decided to make his final stand at Oondwa Nullah (qv).

SUGAR LOAF ROCK   see TRICHINOPOLY (TIRUCHCHIRAPALLI) III

TRAVANCORE (Kerala, India)   Third Mysore War   20 December 1789
Fought between the Mysorean army under Tipu Sultan and the Travancorean forces of the Dharma Raja of Travancore.
Strength: Mysoreans 15,000; Travancoreans 50,000.
Aim: In mid-December 1789 Tipu Sultan (Tippoo Sahib), the 'Tiger of Mysore', marched from Coimbatore in S Mysore towards the Travancore Lines, a strong defensive position dividing the northern part of the state of Travancore from Malabar. He then sent an ultimatum to the Raja who returned an evasive answer to the effect that he wished to consult his British allies.
Battle: Tipu then attacked the Lines at night. Having destroyed part of the ramparts, the advance party were on their way to open the main gate when the garrison counter-attacked. The Mysoreans were forced back, causing confusion among the advancing main body, and resulting in their complete rout with considerable loss.
Result: This unprovoked attack, although unsuccessful, decided the Governor-General of India, Lord Cornwallis, to concert action with the Mahratta Confederacy and the Nizam of Hyderabad against Tipu. While negotiations were being pursued, Tipu again attacked the Travancore Lines and, in May 1790, was successful, overrunning the whole of the state. His action precipitated the Third Mysore War.

TRICHINOPOLY (TIRUCHCHIRAPALLI) I (Tamil Nadu, India)   Second Carnatic War   13 June 1752
Fought between a British force under Major Stringer Lawrence and a French/Indian force under Jacques Law and Chanda Sahib besieging Trichinopoly (Tiruchchirapalli).
Strength: British 400 Europeans + 1,100 sepoys + 8 guns + Mysoreans, Mahrattas and Tanjorines 20,000 cavalry + 80,000 infantry; French 900 Europeans + 2,000 sepoys + 30,000 Indian levies.
Aim: The French forces besieging Trichinopoly were under Jacques Law, who had proved an incompetent commander, and little progress had been made in investing the town where Mohammed Ali, the British protégé for the Nawabship of the Carnatic, together with a British contingent of some 1,600 strong under the Swiss Captain Rudolph de Gingens, were beleagured. The British authorities in Madras, heartened by Clive's successes, particularly at Kaveripack (qv), decided to send an expedition for the relief of the town before more French help could arrive from Europe. Commanded by Stringer Lawrence, with Clive as

second in command and supported by a native force of some 100,000 under the Regent of Mysore, the relief set out from Fort St David on 28 May 1752.

Battle: Trichinopoly is situated on the south bank of the river Cauvery, which at this point is divided from an arm of the river Coleroon by the long narrow island of Srirangam. The town itself was surmounted by a great rock fortress and the island contained 2 defended temples. Lawrence's troops, supported by the Mysorean force, advanced across the plain towards Trichinopoly in the face of heavy enemy fire, but after a fierce artillery duel Law allowed them to enter the town unhindered. Then, unnerved by a night attack which failed, Law retired to the island of Srirangam. At this stage Clive proposed that the British force be divided into two bodies—one to cross to the north bank of the Coleroon in order to sever French communications with Pondicherry, and the other to remain on the south bank of the Cauvery. On the night of 17 April Clive took 400 British, 700 sepoys and 4,000 Mahratta and Tanjorine horse with 6 field guns to the village of Samiaveram, about 9 miles north of the island. From this base he repulsed a relieving force from Pondicherry but very nearly lost his life in a subsequent daring night ambush. A heavy bombardment of Chanda Sahib's camp near the large temple on Srirangam caused great confusion and resulted in the desertion of large numbers to Clive. On 18 May Lawrence moved into Srirangam and brought up his battery cannon. Realising he had now no hope of being relieved, Law surrendered on 13 June. As a result, 800 French troops and 2,000 sepoys became prisoners of war, and 41 guns were captured.

Result: A few days later Chanda Sahib was assassinated by order of the Tanjore chief and his head sent to Mohammed Ali, now formally proclaimed Nawab of the Carnatic.

The fall of Trichinopoly was the final blow to the French Governor-General, the Marquis Joseph-François Dupleix, and thereafter French influence in India entered on a period of decline. When news of the loss of the town reached France, Dupleix was recalled in 1754—dying nine years later in great poverty.

TRICHINOPOLY (TIRUCHCHIRAPALLI) II (GOLDEN ROCK) (Tamil Nadu, India)   Second Carnatic War   7 July 1753

Fought between the British garrison at Trichinopoly (Tiruchchirapalli) under Major Stringer Lawrence and Captain John Dalton, and a French/Indian army under M. Astruc.

Strength: British 500 Europeans + 2,000 sepoys + 3,000 native cavalry; French 450 Europeans + 2,500 sepoys + Indians 8,000 Mysore horse + 3,000 Mahratta horse + 15,000 native infantry.

Aim: After the capture of Trichinopoly from the French in June 1752 (TRICHINOPOLY I), a British garrison of 2,200 under Captain John Dalton had been left in the town. Owing to the indefatigable intrigues of the French Governor-General, the Marquis Joseph-François Dupleix, the Mysore and Mahratta forces which had assisted the British in the siege had now openly attached themselves to the French cause. After vainly attempting to bring the French to action in the field Lawrence decided to march straight to Trichinopoly to assist the beleaguered garrison, and on 17 May 1753 he entered the town unmolested. At the same time Dupleix reinforced the French and Allied troops already on the nearby island of Srirangam and also persuaded large Mysore and Mahratta forces to join them there. The combined Allied army then left the island to take up a strong position about 3 miles south of the town in the mountainous outcrop known as the Five Rocks, thus cutting off Lawrence's supply route. He now had only one outpost left, a rocky eminence known as the Golden Rock about half a mile SW of his camp and manned by 200 sepoys. It seemed that Trichinopoly was at last within easy grasp of the French.

Battle: On 7 July Astruc started action with a mass attack on the Golden Rock which he succeeded in taking, killing or capturing all the defenders. Lawrence, observing what had happened, marched with a force of only 300 British infantry, 80 artillerymen and 500 sepoys towards the Golden Rock, now virtually surrounded by French troops with Mysorean and Mahratta cavalry in support. Lawrence ordered his grenadiers to fix bayonets and storm the Rock, and on their approach the enemy scrambled in panic down to the plain. Meanwhile Lawrence moved his men in column round the Rock, to fall on the left flank of the French battalion stationed there. Faced by this unexpected attack and surprised by enfilading fire from the British infantry now holding the Golden Rock, the French column broke and fled in disorder, leaving their guns behind. The Mahratta cavalry dashed forward to cover the retreat but strove in vain to pierce the phalanx of bayonets and retired with heavy losses. Then followed the critical operation of retreat across the plain back to camp amid swarms of enemy horse. Supported by field guns, the infantry formed two parallel lines of 800 men, against which not even the constant charges of 10,000 native cavalry could prevail, and Lawrence reached camp again safely after a most skilful action.

Result: The victory ensured the safe arrival of Lawrence's valuable convoy from the south, but Lawrence decided that he was too weak in numbers to hazard another engagement. As a result of his defeat M.

Astruc resigned his command, to be succeeded by M. Brennier, who continued the blockade of Trichinopoly. Astruc was, however, subsequently reinstated in time to suffer a further defeat at Stringer Lawrence's hands (see TRICHINOPOLY III).

TRICHINOPOLY (TIRUCHCHIRAPALLI) III (SUGAR LOAF ROCK) (Tamil Nadu, India)
Second Carnatic War   2 October 1753
Fought between the British under Major Stringer Lawrence and a French/Indian force under M. Astruc.
Strength: British 600 Europeans + 2,000 sepoys + 3,000 Tanjorine horse + 6 guns; French 600 Europeans + 3,000 sepoys + 30,000 Mysore and Mahratta horse and foot + 11 guns.
Aim: After his signal victory against the French/Indian army at Golden Rock on 7 July (TRICHINOPOLY II), Lawrence had marched with his army into Tanjore to meet reinforcements from Madras and persuade the Raja of Tanjore to provide him with some native horse. On returning to Trichinopoly with a large convoy he was obliged to fight his way back into the town against strong French opposition. Some reinforcements shortly afterwards reached both sides and Lawrence decided on action, taking up a position on an eminence known as Fakir's Tope in the plain south of the town. He now found that the French were deployed in strength around the Sugar Loaf Rock, some 2 miles distant, their line extending westwards to the Golden Rock which was held by a strong force with 2 field guns.
Battle: In bright moonlight in the early morning of 2 October 1753 Lawrence's force advanced in silence across the plain towards the Golden Rock, led by the British battalion with the grenadiers in the fore, supported by 6 field guns; in rear were the sepoys and the Tanjorine horse. Firing 1 volley the grenadiers swarmed up the Rock on three sides and the enemy fled down to the plain. Lawrence then ordered the battalion to advance through the Mysorean camp on to the left flank of the French battalion close to the Sugar Loaf Rock, followed by the sepoys making wild music on their native instruments. The Mysoreans fled before the din. As dawn broke the two opposing forces found themselves in close contact. Captain John Caillaud, commanding the grenadiers, now fell upon the left flank of the French, and a crushing volley followed by a bayonet-charge forced them back in confusion on their own centre. At the same time the British sepoys on the left had pushed on against the Sugar Loaf Rock and dispersed the French sepoys there. Now the whole of the French force broke and fled towards the island of Srirangam. French casualties were 100 killed and wounded, and 200 more—including M. Astruc and 10 of his officers—were taken prisoner. In addition, 11 guns were captured. British casualties amounted to no more than 40 killed and wounded.
Result: The reverses before Trichinopoly were a severe blow to the ambitions of the French Governor-General, the Marquis Joseph-François Dupleix. Although hostilities were to continue in a desultory fashion into 1754, French influence was on the decline and in August of that year Dupleix was recalled to France. His successor, M. Godeheu, agreed to a suspension of arms which, in January 1755, was expanded into a conditional treaty. This marked the end of the Second Carnatic War.

TRINOMALEE (TIRUVANNAMALAI) (Tamil Nadu, India)   First Mysore War   26 September 1767
Fought between the British under Colonel Joseph Smith and the Mysoreans under Haider Ali.
Strength: British 1,400 Europeans + 9,000 sepoys + 800 native cavalry + 24 guns; Mysoreans 42,000 infantry + 28,000 cavalry + 100 guns.
Aim: In 1767 the British position in S India was threatened by the emergence of Haider Ali, a Mohammedan soldier of fortune, who had become the powerful ruler of the state of Mysore. He was known to be conspiring with Nizam Ali, the Mogul Emperor's Viceroy of the Deccan, to supplant Mohammed Ali as Nawab of the Carnatic by his brother, and in August 1767 the two allies descended the E Ghats towards the Carnatic at the head of 70,000 men. To meet the threat, the main British force of some 6,000 infantry and 800 cavalry commanded by Colonel Smith, marching from Madras, engaged the Mysore forces at Changama and successfully repulsed them inflicting casualties of over 2,000 men. Owing to lack of food, however, Smith was obliged to retreat, falling back on Trinomalee (Tiruvannamalai), some 50 miles inland from Pondicherry, where he was reinforced by Colonel Wood's column.
Battle: At noon on 26 September Smith moved out of Trinomalee against the Mysorean position, a formidable line of redoubts, the approach to which lay over a treacherous morass, covered by Haider Ali's cannon. Smith accordingly directed his right column to proceed round a hill which he rightly divined

marked the extremity of the morass. This column came into headlong collision with the enemy's advance troops and dispersed them. As the British slowly advanced they were met by a vast body of horsemen which threatened to envelop them. Smith now turned 20 guns on the deep columns of cavalry facing them and before this tremendous fire they reeled and fled. Haider Ali then made a skilful withdrawal of the rest of his troops.

The next day the British renewed the attack on the retreating Mysore forces and captured 64 guns. Without sufficient cavalry support and supplies however Smith decided he was unable to continue the pursuit further, and retired once more to Trinomalee. Mysorean losses in this, the main action of the war, amounted to 4,000 killed and wounded, while Smith's casualties did not exceed 48 Europeans and 67 sepoys killed and wounded.

Result: There is no doubt that in this major engagement in an otherwise desultory and frustrating campaign, Smith completely outmanoeuvred and outfought his redoubtable opponent, who from thence onwards developed a marked respect for the military abilities of the British Commander, whom he avoided engaging in open combat wherever possible.

WANDIWASH (Tamil Nadu, India)   Third Carnatic War   22 January 1760
Fought between the British under Colonel Eyre Coote and the French under Comte Thomas-Arthur Lally de Tollendal.
Strength: British 1,980 Europeans + 2,100 sepoys + 1,250 Indian cavalry + 16 guns; French 2,100 European infantry + 150 European cavalry + 1,300 sepoys + 3,000 Mahratta horse + 30 guns.
Aim: During the course of the somewhat inconclusive campaign in the Carnatic during 1759, the British under Major Brereton had achieved a useful base by the capture of Conjeveram, 40 miles SW of Madras. In mid-November 1759 Eyre Coote arrived at the camp with 600 men of his own regiment with the intention of attacking Wandiwash, the most important French station between Madras and Pondicherry, which he duly captured on 29 November. Lally now collected his scattered forces from outlying garrisons and proceeded first to threaten Conjeveram, which drew Coote northwards from Wandiwash. Lally thereupon marched on Wandiwash which had been his main objective from the start and on 20 January 1759 commenced besieging the fort.
Battle: At sunrise on 22 January Coote's force had returned and advanced against the French positions before Wandiwash. At 7am that morning Coote was attacked by a force of 3,000 Mahratta cavalry which were dispersed with heavy loss by close-range gunfire and thereafter took no further part in the battle. Coote then drew up his main force in three lines, four European battalions in front with a battalion of sepoys on either flank, the grenadiers in the middle and the cavalry at the rear. Lally first attacked with his squadron of European hussars in a wide sweep on Coote's rear, but they were dispersed by artillery fire. Lally then ordered the Régiment Lorraine in column of twelve men abreast to charge with the bayonet, only to be met by a withering fire from the British line. The French nevertheless pressed on and fierce hand-to-hand fighting ensued, eventually resulting in the French collapse, and they fled in confusion. At the same time heavy fighting had developed near an entrenched tank (reservoir) which formed a pivot of the French position occupied by Lally's regiment under his second in command the Marquis de Bussy-Castelnau. A lucky shot from the British guns had blown up an ammunition wagon near the tank which caused a panic; however, the French fought with great gallantry until they were dispersed and de Bussy captured. The battalions in the centre on both sides had throughout kept up a continuous fire at long range, but when the French Régiment of India perceived both its flanks uncovered, it faced about and began to retreat, covered by the squadron of French horse which managed to save some of the guns. Coote's native horse refused to face the French cavalry, so Lally was able to set fire to his camp and retire in good order. French casualties were 200 Europeans killed and as many wounded, while 160 men and 24 guns were captured. British casualties numbered 63 men killed and 124 wounded.
Result: This defeat proved a mortal blow to French domination in India, and Lally now retired to Pondicherry, the main French base on the Coromandel coast.

WORGAOM (Maharashtra, India)   First Mahratta War   13 January 1779
Fought between the British under Colonel Charles Egerton and the Mahratta army under Mahadaji Scindia of Gwalior and Tookaji Holkar, Maharaja of Indore.
Strength: British 600 Europeans + 3,400 sepoys; Mahrattas 50,000 horse and foot.
Aim: At the end of 1777 a scheme for the restoration of Ragonath Rao (better known as Ragobah) as Peshwa, the official head of the Mahratta Confederacy, under British protection, was agreed by the

Bombay Presidency and approved by the Governor-General, Warren Hastings, who decided that Bengal should also assist Bombay with troops. Accordingly six battalions of sepoys and a corps of cavalry set out from Kalpi on the river Jumna commanded by Colonel Thomas Goddard to march across the subcontinent. At the same time a force of 4,000 men under Colonel Egerton accompanied by Ragobah and a small Indian cavalry contingent advanced from Bombay through the W Ghats towards Poona, the seat of the Peshwa.

Battle: On the approach of Egerton's force, the Mahratta leaders concentrated their army at Tullygaom, within 18 miles of Poona, whence they slowly retired before the British advance. However, Egerton, who was a sick man, suddenly fell into a state of deep despondency and decided to order his force to retire. After destroying a quantity of stores and sinking the heavy guns in a tank (reservoir), the force, now reduced to 2,600 men, began its retreat. By the following morning the Mahrattas had completely surrounded the retreating force, but nevertheless it continued its orderly withdrawal fighting a stubborn rearguard action. On the afternoon of 12 January the troops, now constantly harassed, entered the village of Worgaom, which was placed in a state of defence. Numerous attacks by Mahratta horse were repulsed, but the British had suffered casualties of 350 killed, wounded and missing in one day's fighting. Further retreat being deemed impracticable, it was then decided to negotiate with the enemy.

Result: A treaty, known as the Convention of Worgaom, was concluded on the spot with Mahadaji Scindia, restoring to the Mahrattas all the territories they had possessed in 1773. The humiliated troops were then permitted to return to Bombay. This convention, which Warren Hastings said 'almost made me sick with shame as I read it', was later repudiated by the Bombay government, Egerton being dismissed from the East India Company's service. Warren Hastings then gave instructions to Goddard to continue the campaign.

ZARGHAN (Iran) Persian Wars 15 January 1730
Fought between the Persians under Nadir Kuli Beg and the Afghans under Ashraf Shah.
Strength: Persians 25,000; Afghans 20,000.
Aim: After their defeat at Murchakhar (qv) the Afghans retreated to Shiraz, where they were allowed ample time to rally and reorganize, Nadir refusing to leave Isfahan until he had been granted the power of levying taxes which gave him almost sovereign authority. Reluctant to do so at first, Shah Tahmasp II realised he had no alternative but to yield and granted the authority to his indispensable Commander. Nadir then marched to give battle to the Afghans who made a last stand at Zarghan, 20 miles north of Shiraz.
Battle: On the approach of the Persian forces, the Ghilzai tribesmen mounted a fierce attack, but were repulsed by heavy musket-fire from the well-disciplined Persian infantry. Nadir ordered a general advance and the enemy broke and fled, reaching Shiraz some hours later in complete disorder.
Result: Ashraf, with some 200 of his bodyguard, escaped from the city, which was the signal for the remnants of the Afghan army to disperse in separate bands under their respective chiefs, hotly pursued by the Persian cavalry. Ashraf was finally killed by a Baluchi khan who found him wandering in the Lut Desert with only 2 followers and sent his head as a gift to Shah Tahmasp. Nadir was rewarded for his services with the provinces of Khorasan, Sistan, Kerman and Mazanderan and the title of Sultan.

SECTION THREE

AFRICA, ARABIA, PALESTINE, SYRIA

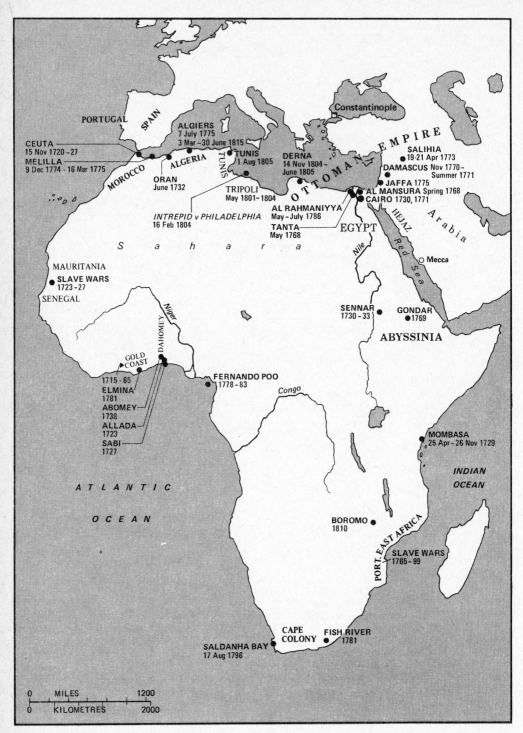

PORTUGAL
SPAIN
Constantinople

CEUTA
15 Nov 1720 – 27
MELILLA
9 Dec 1774 – 16 Mar 1775
MOROCCO

ALGIERS
7 July 1775
3 Mar – 30 June 1815
ALGERIA
TUNIS
TUNIS
1 Aug 1805
ORAN
June 1732
TRIPOLI
May 1801–1804

DERNA
14 Nov 1804 –
June 1805

SALIHIA
19-21 Apr 1773
DAMASCUS Nov 1770 –
Summer 1771
JAFFA 1775
AL MANSURA Spring 1768
CAIRO 1730, 1771

OTTOMAN EMPIRE

HEJAZ
Arabia

INTREPID v PHILADELPHIA
16 Feb 1804

AL RAHMANIYYA
May – July 1786
TANTA
May 1768
EGYPT

S a h a r a

Nile

Red Sea

Mecca

MAURITANIA
SLAVE WARS
1723 – 27
SENEGAL

Niger

SENNAR
1730 – 33
GONDAR
1769
ABYSSINIA

GOLD
COAST
DAHOMEY
1715 – 65
ELMINA
1781
ABOMEY
1738
ALLADA
1723
SABI
1727

FERNANDO POO
1778 – 83
Congo

ATLANTIC
OCEAN

MOMBASA
25 Apr – 26 Nov 1729

INDIAN
OCEAN

BOROMO
1810

PORT. EAST AFRICA
SLAVE WARS
1765 – 99

CAPE
COLONY
FISH RIVER
1781
SALDANHA BAY
17 Aug 1796

0   MILES   1200
0   KILOMETRES   2000

10   Africa, Arabia, Palestine and Syria

ABOMEY (S Dahomey, W Africa)   1738
The Eyoes (Oyos), a partially converted Moslem tribe from the northern part of the great southern migration as the Sahara extended its boundaries, invaded Dahomey and fought the Foys (Fons) of Dahomey at the gates of Abomey. Agaou, general of the Dahoman force, was defeated, Abomey fell and the Eyoes exacted tribute and took the towns of Caronina and Zassa.

ALGIERS I (Algeria)   Spanish-Algerian War   7 July 1775
Since the early sixteenth century Algiers had been the chief base of operations for the Barbary Corsairs. Following the failure of the Emperor Charles V's expedition of 1541, no major attack on the city was attempted until 1775, though a state of war between Spain and Algiers was virtually endemic. Command of the expedition was given to Alexander O'Reilly (1725–94), an Irishman in the Spanish service. After an initial naval bombardment on 7 July, O'Reilly began to disembark his 20,000 men. The Spanish artillery, however, got bogged down in the sand and the attackers were exposed to devastating fire from the enemy's positions in the hills.
   Bungled from the start, the abortive invasion was called off after it had cost the lives of 527 Spaniards, with about 2,000 wounded. Eight years later an equally fruitless attempt was made to subdue Algiers by bombardment from a fleet of 80 Spanish warships.

ALGIERS II (Algeria)   Algerian-American War   3 March–30 June 1815
During the War of 1812, American naval vessels had withdrawn from the Mediterranean, and the Dey of Algiers proceeded to prey on American shipping and commerce. The Dey declared war on the USA on 3 March 1815.
Strength: Algerians unknown; Americans naval squadron of 10 ships.
   Commodore Stephen Decatur with the US naval squadron moved into the Mediterranean, captured 2 Algerian ships of war, entered Algiers harbour, and informed the Dey of Algiers that he would bombard and attack Algiers unless the Dey agreed to his terms which were: (a) that all American prisoners must be released, (b) that all future tribute must be cancelled, and (c) that all piratical activity by the Algerians against American shipping must cease, to be underwritten by a guarantee to this effect from the Dey.
   Thus ended the actions of the Barbary pirates against the Americans as Decatur forced guarantees from other N African states.
   In August 1816 the British and Dutch took action against the Algerians, and the British were obliged to do so again in 1819 and 1824. Between 1827 and 1829 there were a number of incidents between the French and Algerians, which culminated in the French invasion and take-over of Algeria in the period 1830–47.

ALLADA (S Dahomey, W Africa)   1723
In one of the interminable tribal wars in W Africa a 'King' of the tribe in the Abomey area of S Dahomey, named Agadja, briefly showed above-average military skill and defeated his neighbouring rivals, including the kingdom of Allada. Only European annexation brought an end to these vicious internecine wars (see also SABI).

AL-MANSŪRA (outskirts of Cairo, Egypt)   Mameluke Wars   spring 1768
Khalīl Bey and Husayn Bey Kashkash combined their factions of Mamelukes and marched along the Nile to al-Mansūra, where they defeated the army of Alī Bey (see DAMASCUS).

AL-RAHMĀNIYYA (Egypt)   Mameluke-Ottoman Wars   May–July 1786
In May 1786, in order to suppress the Mameluke revolt, a Turkish fleet under Hasan Pasha landed an army at Alexandria in Egypt.
   The Turkish army then moved up the branch of the Nile to Rosetta, while the Mameluke army, under Murād Bey, moved down the Nile. The two armies met at al-Rahmāniyya. The Mamelukes were defeated and Hasan went on to occupy Cairo.

BOROMO (Upper Zambezi River, Portuguese E Africa)   1810
Fought between Portuguese, commanded by Governor Villas Boas Truâo, and native tribesmen. The Governor was killed and his entire force wiped out.

CAIRO I (Egypt)   Mameluke Wars   1730
Fought between the Qāsimiyya faction of the Mamelukes, led by Charkas, and Dhu'l-Faqār Bey of the
Faqāziyya party of the Mamelukes.
    Charkas and his troops entered Cairo and the followers of Qāsimiyya in the city joined him in battle
against the forces of the Faqāziyya. The Qāsimiyya faction won and Charkas was drowned in the Nile
while trying to escape. Dhu'l-Faqār Bey was assassinated during the engagement, unaware of his rival's
demise, but the Qāsimiyya retained their hold over Cairo.

CAIRO II (Egypt)   Mameluke Wars   April 1771
Abu'l-Dhahab, having deserted Alī Bey, formed his own army, including the remnants of Qāsimiyya,
marched against Alī Bey's forces and defeated them outside Cairo.

CEUTA (Morocco)   Spanish-Moroccan War   15 November 1720–27
Ceuta, conquered by the Portuguese in 1415, was retained by Spain after the ending of her sixty-year union
with Portugal (1580–1640). The sultans of Morocco constantly aimed to incorporate this foreign enclave
into their territory.
    In 1720 Philip V of Spain reinforced the Ceuta garrison with a 16,000-strong expeditionary force under
the Marquis of Lede which aimed at breaking through the investing Moroccan forces. On 15 November
the Spaniards made a sally in force, smashed through the enemy's lines, inflicted some 500 casualties and
took considerable booty. The Moroccans, however, regrouped in the hills, counter-attacked and forced
the Spaniards from their new positions.
    The following February the expedition re-embarked for Spain without achieving any permanent lifting
of the siege, which continued until the death of Sultan Muley Ismael in 1727.

DAMASCUS (Syria)   Mameluke-Ottoman Wars   November 1770–summer 1771
The old Mameluke Empire under the Turks consisted of Egypt, Syria and the vassal principality of the
Hejaz, of which Alī Bey controlled Egypt and the Hejaz (qv). In November 1770 Alī Bey sent an
expeditionary force led by Isma'-il Bey to Syria. There it combined with the troops of Shaykh Zāhir, and
then marched to Damascus, after which it withdrew to Jaffa. At Jaffa it joined with a second army sent by
Alī Bey and led by Abu'l-Dhahab.
    The combined Mameluke armies then met the Turkish forces, led by Uthman Pasha al-Sādiq, Governor
of Damascus, outside Damascus in the summer of 1771, and defeated them, capturing Damascus and
overthrowing Ottoman authority throughout Palestine.

DERNA (Libya)   Tripolitan-American War   14 November 1804–June 1805
Fought between a mixed force of Americans and mercenaries commanded by William Eaton, US Consul
at Tunis, a former American army officer, and the Bashaw of Tripoli, Yusuf Karamanli, and his Tripolitan
forces.
Strength: Americans 16, mercenaries 350 + 3 American naval vessels; Tripolitan unknown.
    Eaton, believing appeasement of the Barbary pirates was useless, persuaded the American naval
commander, Commodore Samuel Barron, to back the cause of Hamet Karamanli, the rightful but exiled
ruler of Tripoli. Eaton then collected 2 American naval officers and 14 sailors and marines, plus a
mercenary force of Greeks, Arab cavalry and other nationalities, which he equipped and paid out of his
own funds. Eaton then led this force across 600 miles of the Libyan desert and, aided by 3 American naval
brigs, stormed and took Derna on 26 April 1806, holding it against counter-attacks by the troops of the
Bashaw. The casualties on both sides are unknown.
    The capture of Derna led to a peace treaty with Tripoli which was handled by Captain William
Bainbridge, captured commander of USS *Philadelphia*, but Commodore Barron had negotiated another
treaty of peace with Yusuf Karamanli, the usurper, but reigning ruler of Tripoli. In exchange for $60,000,
the *Philadelphia* crew were released, and further payment of protection money ceased.
    Eaton's treaty with the rival ruler of Tripoli was not recognised by President Jefferson's administration,
and Eaton's expedition was withdrawn, leaving him an embittered man. However, his exploit has been
immortalised in the American marine hymn, 'From the Halls of Montezuma to the Shores of Tripoli'.

ELMINA (Ghana, W Africa)   1781
Fought between the British under Captain Shirley, RN, and the Dutch garrison of Fort Conraadsburg.
Strength: British 1 50-gun ship of the line + 1 sloop of war + 500 men (including 300 Africans); Dutch
1,500 men.
Aim: The British wished to eliminate the Dutch influence on the Gold Coast (Ghana).
Battle: The British force, under Captain Alexander Mackenzie, landed at Elmina and attacked Fort
Conraadsburg, but received no support from Captain Shirley's ships because of jealousy between the two
commanders. Mackenzie was repulsed. Shirley then bombarded the fort, but the navy was also forced to
withdraw, as the Dutch defences were too strong.
Result: The combined British forces withdrew, having failed in their objective.

FERNANDO POO (W Africa)   1778–83
By the Treaty of San Ildefonso (1777) Portugal agreed to cede to Spain the African islands of Fernando
Poo and Annobón, valuable as staging-posts in the African slave trade, in return for the colony of
Sacramento in S America. A Spanish expedition sent in 1778 from Montevideo under the Count of
Argelejo (1721–78) occupied the islands in the face of some resistance. Demoralisation and sickness led the
Spanish troops to mutiny. Under their ringleader, Sergeant Jerónimo Marín, the mutineers seized their
commander, Colonel Primo de Rivera, who had succeeded the Count of Argelejo on his death, and
returned to Montevideo (1783).

FISH RIVER (Cape Colony, S Africa)   1781
As the Dutch colonised Cape Colony, they came into conflict with the Xhosa tribes who had advanced
southwards, conquered the other native tribes, and occupied the territory north of the Fish River. There
had been a number of clashes between the Dutch and Xhosa during the period 1736 to 1781. In 1781 the
Boers accused the Xhosa of invading their territory. In the battle that followed the Boers defeated the
Xhosa at Fish River, and took control of the Xhosa territory beyond the river as far as the Kei River.
   The Boers held on to this area in spite of the Xhosas' attempts to regain their lost lands. The Dutch
finally decreed that no African without a special brass ticket could cross the Great Fish River. This may
have sowed the seeds of apartheid.

GOLD COAST (GHANA) (W Africa)   1715–65.
In an unbroken succession of wars the Ashanti tribesmen, whose capital was Kumasi, swept down over the
southern Gold Coast (Ghana) and conquered the tribes of the Denkera, Akims, Wassa, Seturi-Bekwai and
Sefuri-Awiasu. By 1765 they controlled all the territory between Kumasi, the Pra River, Takoradi, Accra
and the Volta Rivers. This control they were to exercise until the British took over complete sovereignity in
the nineteenth century after the Ashantis had fought a series of battles with the British, French and Dutch.

GONDAR (Ethiopia)   1769
The kings of Ethiopia had steadily been losing power and, in 1769, Yoas, the last Gondar king, was killed
along with thousands of his followers by Ras Mikael, Governor of Tigre, who took over the supreme
power in the land. From this date on the Ethiopian kings became puppets of the ras or governor who
controlled Gondar. New kings were appointed, dismissed, assassinated or reinstated from time to time,
the large number of royal princes imprisoned at Amba Weheni being used as a reserve to replenish
vacancies as they occurred.

HEJAZ (Saudi Arabia)   Turko-Wahabi War   1811–15
In 1811 Ahmad Tusun Pasha, commanding a Turko-Egyptian army, invaded the Hejaz, and captured the
port of Yanbo. Moving inland he captured Medina in 1812 and Mecca in 1813. The Hashemite dynasty
was restored, and the Hejaz remained under Turkish suzerainty until the Arab revolt of 1916.

INTREPID V PHILADELPHIA (Tripoli, Libya)   Tripolitan-American War   16 February 1804
Fought between the Americans commanded by Lieutenant Stephen Decatur, US Navy, and the
Tripolitans led by the Bashaw of Tripoli, Yusuf Karamanli.
Strength: Americans 74 officers and men + *Intrepid*; Tripolitans several thousands (including the
garrison of the Bashaw's palace beneath which *Philadelphia* was anchored).

Decatur and his crew entered the harbour of Tripoli at night aboard USS *Intrepid*, a captured Tripolitan vessel. They boarded, captured and destroyed USS *Philadelphia* by fire, and made good their escape, while Commodore Edward Preble and his American flotilla bombarded the harbour, although they could not enter through the dangerous channel. The Americans suffered only one casualty. Tripolitan casualties are not known, but a few hundred were killed and wounded, mostly in the bombardment.

This attack and other blockades and bombardments did not end the war, and little was achieved until the US Consul at Tunis, William Eaton, took action (see DERNA).

JAFFA (Israel)   Mameluke-Turkish Wars   1775
Abu'l-Dhahab and his Qāzdughliyya clan of Mameluke professed loyalty to the Ottoman sultanate, and in 1775 his forces invaded Palestine to suppress Shaykh Zāhir al-Umar and his army. The Mameluke army swept northwards up the Palestinian coast, capturing Jaffa, and besieged Zāhir's capital of Acre.

Abu'l-Dhahab died suddenly, whereupon the other Mameluke leaders lost their drive and enthusiasm and retreated with their armies to Egypt. Never again were the Mamelukes to show any ambition to conquer Syria.

MELILLA (Morocco)   Spanish-Moroccan War   9 December 1774–16 March 1775
Melilla, the N African *presidio* (enclave), was first captured by the Spaniards in 1497. In the winter of 1774 a Moroccan army under Sultan Sidi Mohammed ben Abdullah besieged the fortified town, which held out successfully under General Sherlock until 16 March 1775 when the Sultan was obliged to raise the siege.

MOMBASA (Kenya)   E African Slave Wars   25 April–26 November 1729
The Portuguese domination of the west coast of Africa had once been challenged by the Dutch, but their main rivals were the Arabs from the Oman in S Arabia, who raided down the coast to seize slaves and obtain elephant-tusks and spices.

Between 25 April and 26 November 1729 the Sultan of Oman, who considered all of the east coast north of Cape Delgado his own hunting ground, sent a fleet to besiege the Portuguese Fort Jesus at Mombasa. After a seven-month siege the Portuguese withdrew, allowing the Arabs to take over the lucrative slave trade to the Red Sea, Persian Gulf and India.

ORAN (OUAHRAN) (Algeria)   Spanish-Algerian Campaign   June 1732
Oran (Ouahran), an important *presidio* (enclave) on the N African coast, had been occupied by the Spaniards in 1509 and, after repulsing numerous attacks (in 1563, 1667, 1672, 1675, and 1688), it finally surrendered to the Algerians in 1708.

In June 1732 an expedition of more than 500 ships carrying 26,000 troops, commanded by General Carrillo de Albornoz (1671–1747), landed and threatened Mazalquivir, a key fortress guarding Oran. The latter was evacuated and the garrison at Mazalquivir capitulated, but the Spaniards suffered over 100 killed, including a number of senior officers, in an ambush.

Oran remained in Spanish hands until ceded to the Dey of Algiers in 1792.

PORTUGUESE EAST AFRICA SLAVE WARS (southern Africa)   1765–99
Fought between the Portuguese, commanded by Governor Balthasar Manuel Pereira do Lago, and native tribes in the Quiteve and Bandire districts in the southern part of Mozambique. The chief aim of the Portuguese was to enlarge trade in slaves and extend their territorial limits, in which they were successful.

SABI Dahomey (W Africa)   1727
Agadja, King of Abomey, after consolidating his conquests of his neighbouring tribes including Allada (qv), went on to attack and seize Sabi in 1727, which was the capital of the Whyelahs.

SALDANHA BAY (Cape of Good Hope, S Africa)   17 August 1796
Fought between the Dutch and the British under Admiral Sir George Elphinstone.

A Dutch relief force was dispatched to recover the Cape of Good Hope from the British. It consisted of 3 ships of the line, 4 frigates and 1 sloop. Sir George Elphinstone, with 7 ships of the line, 2 frigates and a number of sloops, captured the whole Dutch expedition.

As a result all Dutch possessions in the Cape fell into the hands of the British.

SALIHIA (AL-SĀLIHIYYA) (Syria)   Ottoman Wars   19–21 April 1773
Ali Bey, Governor of Egypt, supported in his revolt against the Turks by the Russians, marched into Syria to attempt to gain control of that country. He met a Turkish force at Salihia on 19 April 1773, against which he was initially successful. But Osman Pasha assisted by Abu Shal defeated the rebels and Ali Bey returned to Cairo. There he was betrayed by his adopted son, Mohammed Bey, to the acting Governor Abu Shal, who promptly sent his head to Constantinople in token of fidelity.

SENEGAL AND MAURITANIAN COAST SLAVE WARS West Africa Campaigns   1723–7
Ali Shandora, Emir of the Trarza Moors, renewed his allegiance to Maylāy Ismail, ruler of Morocco, following which, in the period 1723–7, a combined army of Trarza Moors and Moroccans known as 'Ormans' fought and defeated the Brakna tribesmen, thus gaining control of the Senegal and Mauritanian coast.

SENNAR (Sudan)   1730–3
The Coptic Christian Ethiopians under the Negus Yasu II attacked the Funj, who had been converted to Islam, and endeavoured to take over Sennar, a province of Sudan. The Funj were agriculturists, but also warriors with good weapons and personal armour who manned military frontier-posts. After many skirmishes the two armies met in battle and Yasu's force of 18,000 was annihilated.

TANTĀ (near Cairo, Egypt)   Mameluke Wars   May 1768
Fought between forces of Khalīl Bey and Husayn Bey Kashkash and the army commanded by Abu'l-Dhahab, chief lieutenant to Alī Bey. Abu'l-Dhahab laid siege to Tantā, where Khalīl Bey and Kashkash held out till their ammunition was exhausted. Then Kashkash went to Abu'l-Dhahab's camp to negotiate terms relying on a safe-conduct, but he was murdered. His ally, Khalil, surrendered under a promise of amnesty, but he was also put to death later.

TRIPOLI (Libya)   Tripolitan-American War   May 1801–4
Fought between Tripolitans led by the Bashaw of Tripoli, Yusuf Karamanli, and the Americans commanded by Commodore Edward Preble, Commodore Samuel Barron and Captain William Bainbridge.

The Americans had been paying almost $2 million, about one-fifth of the annual revenue of the United States, as protection money to the N African states of Morocco, Algiers, Tunis and Tripoli. The Bashaw, greedy for more money, declared war on the United States.

In 1801 and 1802, American navy ships endeavoured to blockade Tripoli, but were not effective. In 1803, Commodore Preble began to harass and attack Tripolitan ships. In 1804, Preble in *Constitution* began a series of bombardments on Tripoli ports, but on 31 October 1803 *Philadelphia*, commanded by Captain William Bainbridge, when pursuing a ship, ran aground off the harbour of Tripoli. The Tripolitans surrounded *Philadelphia* and Bainbridge and his crew, heavily outnumbered, were compelled to surrender.

The Bashaw refloated the American ship and took her into harbour as a prize.

TUNIS (Tunisia)   1 August 1805
Fought between the Americans, commanded by Commodore John Rodgers, and the Tunisians under the Bey of Tunis.

Commodore Rodgers in *Constitution* sailed into the harbour of Tunis, threatened the Bey with bombardment of his capital, and made him sign articles of peace, ending another N African protection racket.

SECTION FOUR

THE FAR EAST AND THE ANTIPODES

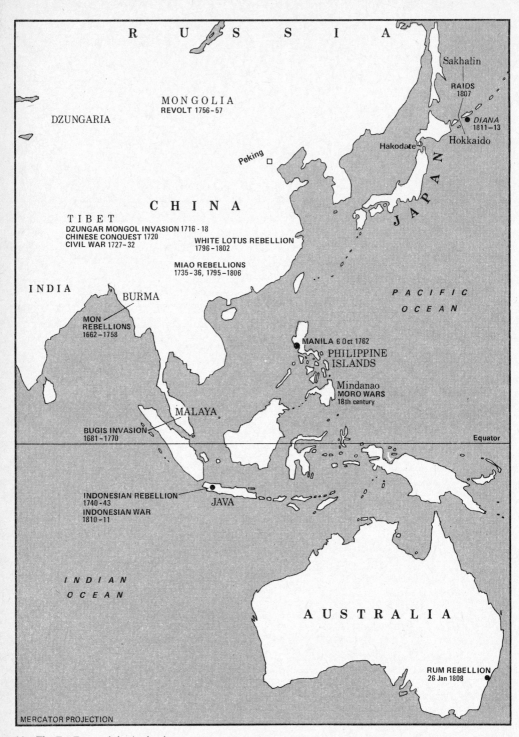

11　The Far East and the Antipodes

BURMA   see MON REBELLIONS

DIANA   1811–13
In the summer of 1811 a Russian cruiser, *Diana* (Captain Vasilii Golovnin), anchored off the coast at Etorofu on Hokkaido (Yezo), ostensibly to obtain supplies and fix her position. The Japanese, remembering the raids by Khostov and Danydov on Sakhalin and Yezo in 1807 (see SAKHALIN AND HOKKAIDO RAIDS), detained the cruiser and impressed the crew at Hakodote. After two years of negotiations *Diana* was brought around to Hakodote by a Japanese crew and handed over to Golovnin, who sailed back with his crew to Okhotsk.

INDONESIAN REBELLION   1740–3
The conflict was provoked by the massacre of Chinese merchants in Batavia, following persecution by the Dutch of Chinese traders in the major Javanese cities. The survivors of the massacre fled, joined Javanese dissidents and staged a major rebellion. The Dutch quelled the rising, annexing the north coast of Java and the rest of Madura.

INDONESIAN WAR   1810–11
Fought between the British under the 1st Earl of Minto (Gilbert Elliot), Governor-General of India, and the Javanese.
    Lord Minto took a large British expedition against Java. The fleet was commanded by Rear-Admiral the Hon R. Stopford and comprised 33 warships, 8 of which belonged to the East India Company. The land forces, 5,344 British and 5,770 native troops, under General Sir Samuel Auchmuty, consisted of two divisions from the Madras Army. Batavia was taken in August 1811 and in September the Dutch signed the Capitulation of Semarang, by which Java, Palembang, Timor and Macassar were ceded to the British. The casualties sustained by the expeditionary force amounted in all to 865 killed and wounded.
    In accordance with the treaties settling the Napoleonic Wars, Britain returned the rich and prosperous islands that had been ceded to her back to the Dutch. But the British intervention had unsettled the inhabitants and a long period of guerrilla warfare, known as the Great Java War, led by the guerrilla chief Dipo Negara, was fought until 1830, during which over 15,000 Dutch soldiers lost their lives. Similar insurrections occurred in the other islands.

MALAYA, BUGIS INVASION OF   1681–1770
In 1641 the Dutch East India Company, based at Batavia in the Sunda Straits in Java, laid siege to Malacca on the west coast of Malaya, capturing the port from the Portuguese who had been in occupation for over a hundred years. During the eighteenth century, however, the Dutch found that profits derived from the Malayan port did not compare with those obtainable from trade with Java and the Spice Islands. Malacca was consequently neglected and this situation permitted large-scale penetration of the whole peninsula by the Bugis rovers from Celebes, the 'Norsemen of the East'. Their particular areas of settlement were Selangor, where they established their ruler as Sultan as early as 1700, and also Johore. They proved excellent administrators, and there is hardly a member of the Johore civil service today who does not have Bugis blood in his veins. In 1770, the Bugis leader, Raja Haji, extended his sway northwards, seizing Perak and sacking Alor Star, the capital of Kedah. By that time, however, the Bugis had developed a new trading centre in the Rhio (Riau) archipelago to the south of Singapore, attracting European merchant traders.

MANILA (Philippine Islands)   Seven Years' War   6 October 1762
Fought between the British under Rear-Admiral Samuel Cornish and Colonel William Draper, and a Spanish garrison under Archbishop Manuel Rojo, plus some Pampanga levies.
    Towards the end of the Seven Years' War when France was facing defeat, a secret alliance–called a 'family compact'–was made between the Kings of Spain and France which resulted in an outbreak of war between Spain and Britain in 1762. Following successes in India and N America, Britain had sufficient forces available to mop up lucrative Spanish colonies around the world.
    A force of 1,000 Europeans, including British troops and 2,000 Indian sepoys (and impressed French soldiers captured in India) under Colonel William Draper, convoyed by 7 ships of the line and 4 frigates under Rear-Admiral Cornish, was sent from India, and sailed into Manila Bay on 22 September 1762. An

ultimatum from the British joint commanders having been rejected by Archbishop Rojo on the following day, the British landed. By 4 October the invading forces were ready.

Under cover of a naval bombardment Draper attacked the defended city on 5 October and, in spite of a counter-attack by 1,000 Spanish-led Pampango Indians, rapidly penetrated the defences. During a lull a further ultimatum was delivered that the city would be put to the sword unless the garrison surrendered at once, and also paid 2 million pesos in lieu of the customary sacking, with a follow-up of a further 2 million from Madrid. Rojo, surrendered and Manila, with part of the surrounding ill-administered territory and islands, was occupied by the British for twenty months until, on 31 May 1764, it was handed back to the Spanish under the terms of the Treaty of Paris.

Cornish had also captured the Acapulco galleon with $3 million on board. Thus, within less than a year after declaring war against Britain, Spain had been knocked out with considerable loss of treasury, and of some of her territories.

MIAO REBELLIONS (Hunan, Kwangsi, Kweichow, Yunnan, SW China)   1735–6; 1795–1806

The Miao tribes, original inhabitants of the mountainous districts of SW China, whose fate can be compared with that of the American Indians, revolted against the Imperial Manchu policy of turning them into Chinese citizens. The original purpose of the policy was to secure equal treatment of these colourful aborigines with the Chinese colonisers. But when the military seized arable land to settle retired soldiers, the Miao revolted at P'u-ssu in 1733 and T'ai-kung in 1735, both in Kweichow Province.

Owing to avaricious civil servants and grasping soldiers who did not follow the spirit of the Emperor's policy, further revolts occurred as the Miao were driven back into the mountain slopes where they could hardly make a living. This culminated in a long period of insurgency from 1795 to 1806 which covered the mountainous area of Hunan, Kwangsi, Kweichow and Yunnan. The rebels were eventually suppressed by the superior weapons of the Imperial Army.

Further revolts occurred at the time of the T'ai P'ing Rebellion (see *A Dictionary of Battles 1816–1976*). The Miaos, with other associated tribes, are recognised by the Communist government of China in a special autonomous region in Kweichow Province, and in the Kwangsi-Chuang autonomous region, with the Central government making much of their individual customs, art and dress.

MONGOLIAN REVOLT   1756–7

Fought between the Mongols led by Chingunjav, Prince of the Khotogoit, and the Manchus under General Chao Hui.

Aim: The Mongols were exasperated by the high-handed attitude of the Manchu Emperor and the commercial exploitation by the Chinese traders, and wished to drive them out.

Rebellion: Chingunjav and his deputy, Amursana, led the revolt, but the timing went wrong and Amursana started a revolt early in 1756 in Khalkka while Chingunjav raised the Mongols of Jungaria in the summer of the same year. The Manchu General, Chao Hui, separated these two insurrections and defeated them in turn. Chingunjav was captured and executed in Peking in March 1757. Amursana, repeatedly defeated and with his following split, suffered his last defeat in the autumn of 1757, after which he died of smallpox.

Result: The Manchu hold over Mongolia was intensified.

MON REBELLIONS (Burma)   1662–1758

The earliest civilised inhabitants of Lower Burma were the Mons, a people akin to the Khmers of Cambodia. Early in their history they developed relations with India, adopting a form of Buddhism and the Hindu ritual of coronation. In due course they became supreme in the whole of the Irrawaddy Delta, building the port of Bassein and founding the city of Pegu, their future capital. They were subsequently conquered by the Burmese from Upper Burma, who unified the whole country into the kingdom of Pagan. During the seventeenth century, however, the Mons partially re-established their independence, achieving a second golden age. The eighteenth century saw the development of a more aggressive spirit, and encouraged by French military assistance from India, the Mons, led by King Binnya Dala, revolted against the Toungoo dynasty in N Burma and in 1752 captured the capital city of Ava. The whole of Burma then passed for a time into Mon control. Their hegemony was not to last long as, before the end of the year, a popular Burmese leader, Alaungpaya, son of the headman of the town of Shewbo some 50 miles east of Ava, and subsequently the founder of the Konbaung dynasty, had driven the Mons out of Upper Burma and the Shan states. By 1758 he had regained the state of Manipur, defeating the Mons and their

French garrisons. Alaungpaya managed to provide his army with some artillery following the capture of 2 French ships with their gun crews. He then drove the Mons out of central Burma, destroying their capital of Pegu and massacring the garrison. Tenasserim in the SE was overrun and the Burman forces then carried the war into Siam (Thailand), annexing several districts. Whilst besieging Ayuthia, the Siamese capital, Alaungpaya was seriously wounded, and he died during the retreat.

During the late eighteenth century the Burmans under Alaungpaya's successors conquered Arakan (1784) and crushed successive Mon rebellions.

MORO WARS (Mindanao and Sulu archipelago, Philippine Islands)   18th century

During the 330 years of their occupation of the Philippines, the Spanish had never been able entirely to overcome the strong Moslem communities based on Mindanao and the Sulu archipelago. During the eighteenth century several revolts of these Moro Moslems occurred, centring on Jolo, Samboanga and Mandili. In the remoter areas of Mindanao the Muros were supported by non-Malay aborigine tribes, as well as by Chinese who had colonised part of the Philippines before the Spanish arrived, and had bitterly opposed their occupation and seizure of land from then on.

The most serious revolt took place after the British occupation of Manila (qv), in the period 1762–4, when Spanish prestige had plummeted. In spite of treaties with the Moros, revolts and piracy were endemic throughout the Spanish and American occupation.

PHILIPPINE ISLANDS   see MORO WARS

RUM REBELLION (Sydney, NSW, Australia)   26 January 1808

This was a conflict between the settlers, headed by the ex-naval officer and trader, John MacArthur, and the Governor of New South Wales, William Bligh, of *Mutiny on the Bounty* fame.

Bligh had been appointed in 1806 with orders to reassert the authority of the Governor, since the traders were taking the law into their own hands. He collided with MacArthur, who was equally obstinate and authoritarian and who had the backing of the military. The immediate cause of the trouble was the use of rum as a form of currency, as there was not enough coinage to go round. The conflict was mainly in the courts of justice, and was overshadowed by the exigencies of the Napoleonic Wars. Finally on 26 January 1808 MacArthur got the British army to arrest and depose Bligh, whereupon Lt-Colonel George Johnson took over the government.

This event occurred twenty years after the founding of the settlement in Botany Bay by the 1st Fleet as an alternative place to send convicts now that America, after the revolt of the thirteen states, was not available as a dumping-ground. Known as the Rum Rebellion, it had no immediate sequel, except that MacArthur, after a long, successful, quarrelsome career, died insane.

SAKHALIN AND HOKKAIDO (YEZO) RAIDS (Japan)   1807

In October 1804 a Russian Ambassador, Vasilii Rezanov, entered Nagasaki harbour in the *Nadezhda* but was told that instructions had come from Tokyo (Yedo) to leave at once, which he did, swearing vengeance for his humiliation.

Rezanov sailed on to Alaska and California where he began preparations for an attack on Sakhalin. He hired 2 Russian naval officers, Lieutenants Khostov and Danydov, who, in 1807, attacked settlements in Sakhalin and Hokkaido (Yezo), causing hundreds of casualties, and then sailed with their booty to Okhotsk. These officers, without authority, left messages to say that they would come back to avenge the insults to Rezanov unless Japan came to terms with Russia. The Japanese strengthened their defences and sent a note to the Russian Emperor saying that they would not submit to threats and would defend their territories. The incident led to the detention of the Russian cruiser *Diana* (qv) in 1811.

Vasilii Rezanov became so attracted to California that he tried to acquire it as a Russian possession, and since there was only feeble opposition from the Spanish colonists, had not his health failed he might well have done so. As it was, late in 1807 he died.

TIBETAN CIVIL WAR   1727–32

Civil war in Tibet broke out in 1727. The Manchu Emperor of China, Yung-cheng, the son of K'ang-hsi, sent in an army of 15,000 to restore order. The Dalai Lama, who was the source of the trouble, was exiled. The Chinese remained to garrison the country.

This resulted in further opposition supported by the Dzungar Mongols from central Asia, whom the Chinese armies fought with varying success until 1732 when the Dzungars were defeated and expelled.

TIBET, CHINESE CONQUEST OF   1720
The Manchus, who had conquered the whole of China during the latter half of the seventeenth century,
felt obliged to avenge the blow to their prestige inflicted by the Dzungars (see TIBET, DZUNGAR MONGOL
INVASION). So the Manchu Emperor K'ang-hsi sent two armies into Tibet, which defeated the Dzungars,
and appointed a more popular Dalai Lama supported by a Manchu garrison.

TIBET, DZUNGAR MONGOL INVASION   1716–18
In 1705 Chinese troops had occupied parts of Tibet and installed their own Dalai Lama. In 1716 a section
of the Oirat Mongols, the Eleuth or Dzungars, joined in the dispute about the accession of the Dalai Lama
and, with an invasion force of 6,000 men under Chewanlaputan, seized Lhasa. In 1718 a Chinese
Manchurian force, which was called in to save the Dalai Lama, was ambushed on the borders of E Tibet,
then dispersed and destroyed, suffering over 2,000 casualties.

WHITE LOTUS REBELLION (Honan, Hupeh, Shensi, Szechwan, central China)   1796–1802
In 1796 the White Lotus sect started a revolt in Honan, which spread to the provinces of Hupeh, Shensi
and Szechwan, in central W China. After a few years fighting the rebellion was suppressed by the forces of
the Manchu Emperor, Chia-ch'ing. Many of the rebels, now without homes or land but still strongly
imbued with the discipline of a revolutionary movement, joined the Nien-fei secret society which in the
1850s joined in with the T'ai P'ing Rebellion.

SECTION FIVE

NORTH AMERICA

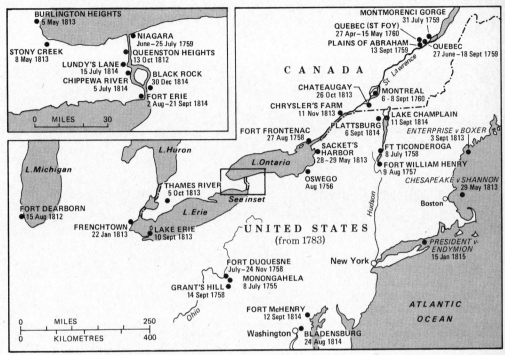

12 North America: The Seven Years' War and the War of 1812

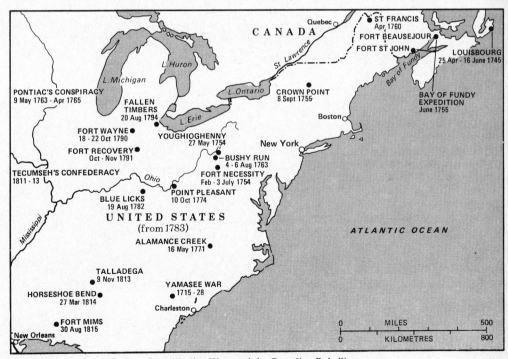

13 North America: The French and Indian Wars and the Canadian Rebellion

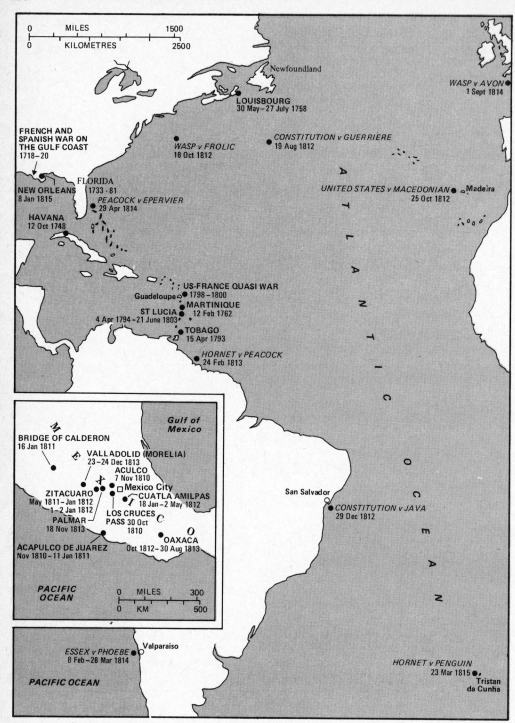

0 MILES 1500
0 KILOMETRES 2500

Newfoundland

WASP v AVON
1 Sept 1814

LOUISBOURG
30 May – 27 July 1758

CONSTITUTION v GUERRIERE
19 Aug 1812

FRENCH AND
SPANISH WAR ON
THE GULF COAST
1718–20

WASP v FROLIC
18 Oct 1812

FLORIDA
1733 · 81

NEW ORLEANS
8 Jan 1815

PEACOCK v EPERVIER
29 Apr 1814

UNITED STATES v MACEDONIAN
25 Oct 1812

Madeira

HAVANA
12 Oct 1748

A T L A N T I C

US-FRANCE QUASI WAR
1798 – 1800

Guadeloupe

MARTINIQUE
12 Feb 1762

ST LUCIA
4 Apr 1794 – 21 June 1803

TOBAGO
15 Apr 1793

HORNET v PEACOCK
24 Feb 1813

BRIDGE OF CALDERON
16 Jan 1811

Gulf of
Mexico

VALLADOLID (MORELIA)
23–24 Dec 1813

ACULCO
7 Nov 1810

ZITACUARO
May 1811 – Jan 1812
1 – 2 Jan 1812

Mexico City

CUATLA AMILPAS
18 Jan – 2 May 1812

LOS CRUCES
PASS 30 Oct
1810

PALMAR
18 Nov 1813

OAXACA
Oct 1812 – 30 Aug 1813

ACAPULCO DE JUAREZ
Nov 1810 – 11 Jan 1811

PACIFIC
OCEAN

San Salvador

CONSTITUTION v JAVA
29 Dec 1812

O C E A N

0 MILES 300
0 KM 500

ESSEX v PHOEBE
8 Feb – 28 Mar 1814

Valparaiso

PACIFIC OCEAN

HORNET v PENGUIN
23 Mar 1815

Tristan
da Cunha

14   Mexico (all naval actions refer to the War of 1812)

ACAPULCO DE JUAREZ (Guerrero, Mexico)   Mexican War of Independence   November 1810–11 January 1811
Fought between Mexican Insurgents, led by Father José María Morelos, José and Antonio Galeaño, and the Spanish and Loyalist force commanded by Francisco Paris, Governor of Acapulco province.
Strength: Mexicans 1,000; Spanish/Loyalists 3,000.
  Morelos and the Galeaños marched around the perimeter of Acapulco de Juárez, the leading port of Mexico and the haven of the Manila gold galleons. Paris gathered his forces and met the rebel force on the outskirts of Acapulco. Under cover of night, the Mexicans surprised and defeated the Loyalists on 11 January, capturing 800 muskets, 5 pieces of artillery, a large quantity of ammunition, and Paris's money chest. Mexican casualties were 200 killed and wounded. Spanish and Loyalist casualties numbered 400 killed and wounded, plus 700 taken prisoner.

ACULCO (Mexico)   1810 Peasant *(paisano)* Revolt   7 November 1810
Fought between the Mexican peasants led by Father Don Miguel Hidalgo y Costilla, and the Spanish Viceroy's troops commanded by Félix María Calleja del Rey, later Count de Calderón.
Strength: Mexicans 60,000; Spanish/Creole troops 15,000.
  The Spanish defenders of Mexico City advanced to meet the Mexicans at Aculco, a few miles from the capital. Calleja split his force into five columns and broke the Insurgent front. The Rebels fled in disorder and were killed in their thousands. Total Mexican casualties numbered 12,000 killed and wounded, while the Spanish and Loyalist Mexicans had 1,000 killed and wounded.
  Father Hidalgo managed to re-form his army from the fugitives of Aculco and, with most of his officers, retreated to Valladolid. His principal lieutenant, José Ignacio Allende, retreated with another group of Indians to Guanajuato, where he surprised and killed 250 Spanish civilians.

ALAMANCE CREEK (N Carolina, USA)   Colonial Wars of the United States   16 May 1771
Certain Irish/Scottish inhabitants of N Carolina in the west of the state, calling themselves Regulators, refused to have anything to do with the government of the state which was controlled largely by people from the east and south of the Carolinas. The Governor, William Tryon, raising a force of 1,018 Militia and 30 light cavalry, marched west to put down the rebellion. His chief tactic was the burning of homes and farms, but he encountered a force of 2,000 half-armed Regulators 20 miles west of Hillsboro on 16 May and, in a two-hour battle, killed 20, wounded 50 and captured 12, of whom 10 were later hanged. Tryon had 9 killed and 61 of his men wounded.
  The rebellion was crushed, but at the outbreak of the War of Independence most of the Regulators remained loyal to the British, while those in the east and south joined the Partisans. These Regulators were of great assistance to the British in the southern campaign and a number of them later opted to go to Canada and remain under the Union Jack.

BAY OF FUNDY EXPEDITION (Nova Scotia, Canada)   French and Indian Wars   June 1755
Fought between British-Colonial forces under Colonels Robert Monckton and John Winslow and the French and Canadians commanded by Captain Duchambon de Vergor.
Strength: British/Colonials 2,000; French/Canadians 1,600.
  This was a battle which none of those involved wanted or of which they appreciated the importance. The Militiamen from Massachusetts and the French-Canadian Arcadians (Nova Scotia was originally called Arcady by the French) had no appetite for the struggle. The side which could show some initiative would win, and that was how it turned out. The British Colonials made several feeble efforts to approach Fort St John (in New Brunswick) and Fort Beausejour (in Nova Scotia, across the Bay of Fundy). These half-hearted efforts, however, were sufficient to overcome the Arcadians, who had given themselves over to plundering their own garrisons and drinking themselves silly. Casualties were minor on both sides.
  This capture of the two ports of the Bay of Fundy, insignificant in itself, was the embryonic beginnings of the first British Empire and led to the conquest of Canada on the Plains of Abraham (qv) and the British defeat of the French throughout most areas of the world.

BLACK ROCK (Buffalo, New York, USA)   War of 1812   30 December 1814
Fought between the British under General Phineas Riall and a force of American Indians.
Strength: British 1,400; Indians 2,000.
Aim: The British sought to beat the Indians out of their position, to the west of Buffalo.

Battle: The British stormed the strong Indian position and beat them out of their entrenchments, dispersing the force.
Result: The British went on to capture Buffalo.

BLADENSBURG (Maryland, USA)   War of 1812   24 August 1814
Fought between the British under Major-General Robert Ross and the Americans under Major-General William H. Winder.
Strength: British 4,000; Americans 7,000.
Aim: The Americans attempted to stop the British invasion force.
Battle: The British launched a three-pronged invasion of the United States, the force under Ross to be the central prong which would also act as a diversion to support the attack on New York. A British fleet under Rear-Admiral Sir George Cockburn sailed into Chesapeake Bay to the mouth of the Patuxent River where, at Benedict, the British landed their troops. The lack of opposition enabled them to march northwards to Washington where Winder had organised an army composed chiefly of militia, but including a contingent of naval gunners under Commodore Joshua Barney. The Americans marched out to Bladensburg and occupied the only bridge over the Potomac River. A British force under Colonel Thornton attacked and carried the bridge, following which it assaulted the American army which broke and fled at the first attack. Only the naval gunners remained to fight a rearguard action. American casualties were 26 killed and 51 wounded, plus 100 captured. British casualties were 64 killed and 185 wounded.
Result: The British entered Washington unopposed the same day, the President, James Madison, being forced to flee into Virginia. Private houses and some public buildings, including the Capitol and White House, were fired in retaliation for the burning of York (now Toronto), Canada, on 24 April 1813, by Major-General Henry Dearborn. The following day the British returned to the Patuxent River and re-embarked.

BLUE LICKS (Kentucky, USA)   Indian Wars in America   19 August 1782
On 15 August a force of 240 Canadians and Indians under the Loyalist Simon Girty made an unsuccessful attack on the American fort of Bryan's Station, 5 miles north of Lexington. On the morning of the 18th they withdrew to the NE, pursued by 182 frontiersmen who had converged on Bryan's Station for this purpose. On the morning of the 19th the pursuers caught up with their quarry at Lower Blue Licks Springs on the Middle Fork of the Licking River. Colonel Daniel Boone, in command of the frontiersmen, advised waiting for reinforcements under Brigadier-General Benjamin Logan, but his second in command, Major Hugh McGary, led a disorganised charge across the ford, where his force was ambushed and routed in a few minutes with the loss of 70 killed and 20 wounded. Simon Girty, who lost 7 killed and 10 wounded, completed his withdrawal from this well-conceived raid.
  As the American War of Independence had concluded, this raid is considered as an Indian incursion.

BURLINGTON HEIGHTS (HAMILTON) (Ontario, Canada)   War of 1812   5 May 1813
Fought between the British under Major-General Henry Proctor and the Americans under General Clay.
Strength: British 1,000; Americans 1,300.
Aim: The British, having attacked an American position on Burlington Heights (now the city of Hamilton), were assailed by another American force which sought to enfilade them.
Battle: Clay attacked the British and broke through their line, seizing their guns. Proctor rallied his men and counter-attacked, routing the Americans with a loss to the latter of 1,000 killed, wounded or captured.
Result: The American objective was not achieved.

BUSHY RUN (BLOODY RUN) (Harrisburg, Pennsylvania, USA)   French and Indian Wars   4–6 August 1763
Fought between Ottawa Chief Pontiac and his confederation of tribes, and a British relief expedition commanded by Colonel Henri Bouquet.
Strength: Indians 1,000; British 500.
  Pontiac, an Ottowa Indian chief, had formed a conspiracy to rebel against the substitution of French for British control of Indian territory around the Great Lakes and in the Ohio valley after the French defeat in the Seven Years' War. By June 1763 Pontiac and his allies had overcome and destroyed every British fort

in the area west of Niagara except Fort Pitt (later Pittsburgh) and Detroit, which were besieged. Colonel Bouquet had been sent overland from Philadelphia to relieve Fort Pitt with a force of his own battalion of Royal Americans, a contingent of the Black Watch (42nd Foot) and some militia, totalling just over 500 men.

Pontiac laid an ambush at Bush Run (Bloody Run) (just west of Carlisle, Harrisburg), but Bouquet, adept at frontier warfare, anticipated this move. His well-drilled troops, as soon as fired upon, formed bivouac in a circle around his baggage train, leaving his light forces–which were in the rear of the column–some distance outside his perimeter as an external reserve. Next morning when the frustrated Indians attacked the camp, and were repulsed with heavy casualties, Bouquet's disciplined light forces awaited the right moment and attacked the Indians in the rear, routing them. Both sides suffered comparatively heavy casualties but Bouquet was able to march on the next 150 miles to relieve Fort Pitt.

(See also PONTIAC'S CONSPIRACY)

CALDERON BRIDGE (Jalisco, Mexico)   Mexican War of Independence   16 January 1811
Fought between the Mexican Insurgents, led by Father Don Miguel Hidalgo y Costilla and José Ignacio Allende, and the Spanish and Loyalist army, commanded by Félix María Calleja del Rey.
Strength: Mexicans 35,000 with artillery (but only 1,200 men had muskets); Spanish/Loyalists 14,000.

Father Hidalgo decided to risk battle with the Spanish army, although Allende endeavoured to dissuade him. Hidalgo chose to fortify the bridge of Calderon (20 miles from Guadalajara) and wait for the approach of the Spaniards. Calleja, after a delay in Guanajuato of six weeks, approached and attacked the rebel position at the bridge. The Mexicans repulsed these attacks, in one of which Count de Cadena, the leading Mexican Loyalist officer, was killed. The Spanish continued their assault and, when a rebel ammunition wagon exploded, the rebel Indians panicked. However, Hidalgo and Allende were able to retreat in good order. The rebel army dispersed over the provinces of northern Mexico with the Insurgent leaders, Hidalgo, Allende, Ignacia Rayon y Lopez, Juan Aldama and Mariano Abasolo retreating to Saltillo in the State of Coahuila with 4,000 troops. Mexican casualties were 3,000 killed and wounded; Spanish and Loyalist casualties , 400 killed and wounded.

Calleja was slow to pursue the Rebels and failed to occupy Guadalajara until 4 days after the victory for which he received the title of Count de Calderón bestowed by the Viceroy.

The Rebel commanders decided to leave Rayon in charge of the 4,000 men at Saltillo, while they themselves made up a deputation to the United States to purchase arms and recruit experienced officers. On the way to the American border they were met by a former Partisan, Ignacio Elizondo, who betrayed them to the Spanish for the high rewards offered for their capture. The leaders were taken to Chihuahua on 21 March 1811 and, after a long-drawn-out trial, Hidalgo, Allende, Aldama and Abasolo were shot in July 1811.

CALIBEE CREEK   see TALLADEGA

CHATEAUGAY RIVER (Quebec, Canada)   War of 1812   26 October 1813
Fought between the Americans under General Wade Hampton and the Canadian Militia.
Strength: Americans 4,000; Canadians 500.
Aim: The Americans invaded Canada with the intention of taking Montreal.
Battle: Two American forces left the United States, one under General James Wilkinson descending the St Lawrence. The other, under Hampton, went north from Plattsburg, NY. The two armies were to effect a junction 14 miles above Montreal and Hampton, arriving first, entrenched to await Wilkinson's arrival. On 26 October Hampton attacked an enemy position held by numbers much inferior to his own, but an assault failed to carry the Canadian lines and was repulsed with heavy loss. Then Hampton contrived to get himself and most of his force stuck in a swamp. He finally managed to withdraw into the United States without informing Wilkinson of his movements.
Result: The invasion did not succeed. Hampton was allowed to resign from the army the following year. It is not without significance that Hampton and Wilkinson entertained a mutual dislike for each other.

CHESAPEAKE v SHANNON (off Boston, Massachusetts, USA)   War of 1812   29 May 1813
In May 1813 the frigate *Chesapeake* (38) (Captain James Lawrence) was completing repairs in Boston harbour. Captain Philip Bowes Vere Broke, who had been commanding *Shannon* (38) since 1806 and had a remarkably well-trained crew, sent Lawrence a formal written challenge: 'As the *Chesapeake* appears now

ready for sea, I request you will do me the favour to meet the *Shannon* with her, ship to ship, to try the fortune of our respective flags.'

They fought about 20 miles east of Boston lighthouse. The action began when at 5.50pm William Mindham, gun-captain of *Shannon*'s aftermost starboard 18-pounder, hit *Chesapeake*'s second gun-port from forward with 2 round-shot and a keg of musket-balls. The 32-pounder carronades on *Shannon*'s quarter-deck swept her opponent's quarter-deck with grape- and round-shot. The men at *Chesapeake*'s wheel fell and she swung into the wind, so that *Shannon* could rake her unanswered.

The 2 frigates came together, until *Chesapeake* grappled on to *Shannon*'s bow-anchor. Broke ordered the ships to be lashed together, and the bosun, Mr Stevens, veteran of Rodney's victory of Les Saintes (1781), carried out the order–though his left arm was hacked off by cutlass blows as he did so. His task was no sooner complete than he fell shot down by musketry. Broke now boarded the forecastle and, after a fierce struggle lasting four minutes, the American ship was in British hands–only fifteen minutes after the first gun had been fired. Both ships then sailed to Halifax, where they were received with acclamation.

Casualties on *Chesapeake* were 61 killed and 85 wound; and on *Shannon* 24 killed and 59 wounded. Both captains were severely wounded, Lawrence mortally. His brave words 'Don't give up the ship!' remain an inspiration to the US navy.

CHIPPEWA RIVER (Ontario, Canada)   War of 1812   5 July 1814
Fought between the British under General Phineas Riall and the Americans under General Winfield Scott.
Strength: British 1,500; Americans 1,300.
Aim: The Americans, having seized Port Erie, forced the British back to the Chippewa River, near the Niagara Falls, where Riall ordered a stand.
Battle: General Jacob Brown, in overall command of the American invasion force, ordered an attack on the British who were under the orders of General Gordon Drummond, the overall commander of the British force. The Americans were bivouacked on the south bank of Street's Creek with a flat plain between them and the British. The following day the British crossed the river and attacked Brown's right, composed chiefly of Militia and Indians, driving it in. They then came up against American regulars–the first whom the British had met in the N American war–under Scott, who led a bayonet-charge. The British were driven back across the Chippewa to their entrenchments. British casualties were 137 killed and 375 wounded; American casualties, 48 killed and 227 wounded.
Result: The American offensive was successful.

CHRYSLER'S FARM (Quebec, Canada)   War of 1812   11 November 1813
Fought between the Americans under General John Parke Boyd and the British commanded by Colonel J. W. Morrison.
Strength: Americans 2,000; British 800.
Aim: The Americans, advancing on Montreal, sought to check a British force which was coming up behind them.
Battle: General James Wilkinson, who replaced General Henry Dearborn, commanded the water-borne prong of the American advance on Montreal. He left Sacket's Harbor, NY, (qv) with 8,000 men and began moving down the St Lawrence two weeks later. At Chrysler's Farm the flotilla halted and Boyd was sent back with a force to stop the British force which was in their rear. Boyd attacked piecemeal and was severely defeated, 102 of his men being killed, 237 wounded and 100 captured. British losses were 203.
Result: This defeat, coupled with the news that Hampton had retreated, prompted Wilkinson to go into winter quarters at French Mills on the Salmon River, where the Americans suffered great hardship. Both Wilkinson and Hampton were removed from command the following spring. Moreover, the American defeat encouraged the British to take the initiative in the war.

CONSTITUTION v GUERRIERE (south of Newfoundland)   War of 1812   19 August 1812
USS *Constitution* (56) (Captain Isaac Hull), broadside 736 pounds and 460 men, came up with the British ship *Guerrière* (38) (Captain James Durer), broadside 570 pounds and 244 men, about 500 miles south of Newfoundland. The action began at 5pm. After a severe fire-fight of more than an hour *Guerrière* was compelled to strike. The ship was such a shattered wreck that her captors set fire to her next morning and she blew up. British casualties were 78, including the captain, and the Americans' 14.

Captain Hull received a hero's welcome in Boston, the thanks of his government and a present of 50,000 dollars. He had fought warily as well as boldly. Durer was court-martialled.

CONSTITUTION v JAVA (off San Salvador, Brazil)   War of 1812   29 December 1812
USS Constitution (44) (Commodore William Bainbridge) together with *Hornet* and *Essex* were to form part of a raiding squadron in the South Seas. The first 2 ships sailed from Boston on 30 October and the other from Delaware on 27 October. On 29 December *Constitution* was lying 30 miles off San Salvador, (Brazil), waiting for *Hornet*, which had gone inshore to try and pick up *Essex*, which had not yet joined company. There she fell in with the British *Java* (38) (Captain Henry Lambert) towing the US merchant ship *William*, which she had recently captured.

Java had recently commissioned with a scratch crew, including many boys, and had sailed from Spithead on 12 November, bound for Bombay with the new Governor, Lt-General Sir Thomas Hislop and his retinue, baggage and stores aboard. These encumbered the ship and inhibited much training at the guns which was badly needed by this inexperienced ship's company.

On identifying *Constitution*, Lambert cast off the tow and gave chase. Bainbridge opened fire at long range, but the shooting was ineffective. Lambert continued to close, opening up a relatively effective fire when he was in range. Bainbridge managed to dodge behind the smoke and keep the action at *Constitution*'s superior range. Finally *Constitution* was able to close the by-now damaged *Java* and finish her off at close range. *Java* before this had attempted to board, but was unsuccessful, owing largely to the inexperience of her ship's company. *Java* suffered heavy casualties, including her captain who was mortally wounded. Lieutenant Henry Chads took over command, although himself badly wounded.

The aftermath of this action was marred by the cruel treatment inflicted on the British prisoners of war by Commodore Bainbridge.

CROWN POINT (Lake George, New York, USA)   French and Indian Wars   8 September 1755
Fought between British-Colonial troops and Indians, led by Brigadier-General Sir William Johnson, and a mixed force of French, Canadians and Indians, commanded by Baron Ludwig Dieskau.
Strength: British 3,500, Indians 300; French/Canadians/Indians 2,000.
Aim: The British were intent on defending Crown Point on Lake George from the threat of a French invasion from Canada.

Sir William Johnson was a civilian who had attained great influence over the Indians dwelling around Lake George and had therefore been appointed Brigadier-General to command a mixed force of Colonials and Indians against the French. The British Colonial troops advanced from Albany northwards towards Crown Point, while the French force marched along the Richelieu River to capture this settlement. The French were defeated and Dieskau, their commander, was among those taken prisoner.

Johnson, despite having to face constant insubordination and desertions, built Fort William Henry on Lake George and left a small garrison there. The majority of his force returned to their homes, while the French retreated to the fortifications at Fort Ticonderoga.

CUATLA AMILPAS (CUAUTLA) (Mexico)   Mexican War of Independence   18 January 1812–2 May 1812
Fought between Mexican Rebels led by Father José María Morelos, the Galeaño brothers and José María Fernandez and the Royalists commanded by General Félix María Calleja del Rey.
Strength: Mexicans 6,000; Spanish/Loyalists 7,000 (reinforced by Llano with 5,000).

On 18 February the two forces made contact in a skirmish in which Morelos was nearly captured but was extricated from danger by Ermengildo Galeaño. On 19 February Calleja made a strong attack on Cuatla Amilpas (Cuautla), 50 miles from Mexico City, with four columns of troops, but the Mexicans allowed them to approach within 100 yards of their lines before opening fire heavily, which broke up the assault and the Loyalists fled with heavy losses. Llano with his force was sent to aid Calleja and joined him on 1 March 1812 and they opened fire on Cuatla Amilpas on 4 March with their artillery. Part of the Mexican force endeavoured to attack Calleja's rear but were repulsed. Calleja then attempted to cut off the town's water supply, but the Mexicans thwarted this move. Morelos decided to evacuate Cuatla and on the night of 2 May the Mexican forces left the town and were attacked by the Loyalists. But there was much confusion, the Loyalists firing on each other, and the Mexicans dispersed and escaped, with instructions to rendezvous at Izucar. The Mexicans had casualties of 500 killed and wounded, the Spanish/Loyalists suffering 1,500 killed and wounded.

DUNMORE'S WAR, LORD   see POINT PLEASANT

EMUCKFAW   see TALLADEGA

ENOTACHOPCO   see TALLADEGA

ENTERPRISE v BOXER (off Portland, Maine, USA)   War of 1812   3 September 1813
The British brig-sloop *Boxer* (12) (Commander Samuel Blyth) when at anchor off Portland, Maine, sighted the US brig-sloop *Enterprise* (14) (Lieutenant William Burrows) in the offing. *Boxer* weighed and closed towards *Enterprise*, but the weather fell calm and, as *Enterprise* was a better sailer, she was able to dictate the action which was close fought and in which both commanders were killed. *Boxer* eventually became unmanageable because of damage to her masts and rigging. The ships were equally matched, but *Enterprise* had a superiority in her crew, both in numbers and training. Moreover, *Boxer* was short of officers.
    Enterprise captured the wrecked *Boxer* the same evening.

ESSEX v PHOEBE (off Valparaiso, Chile)   War of 1812   8 February–28 March 1814
The British ship *Phoebe* (36) (Captain James Hillyar) with the sloop *Cherub* (Commander Tudor Tucker) were off Valparaiso in search of *Essex* (32) (Captain David Porter) and her prizes, one of which had been renamed *Essex Junior* and armed. They were sighted at anchor on 8 February and *Phoebe* anchored in the near vicinity. Exchanges of signals, mostly of a propaganda type ('mottoes') continued over the next few days and several ruses were attempted by Porter in order to try and lure *Phoebe* off the scent, so that *Essex* could get clear and escape, as she was, in effect, blockaded. After *Phoebe* had opened fire and successfully destroyed *Essex*'s sails and rigging she was eventually beached and burned.

FALLEN TIMBERS (Toledo, Ohio, USA)   Old North-west Indian Wars   20 August 1794
Fought between the Indians and the US army under General Anthony Wayne.
Strength: Indians 1,300; Americans 1,000 volunteers + 2,000 regulars.
Aim: The subjugation of the Indian confederacy.
Battle: The Indians retreated to the Maumee River near what is today Toledo, Ohio, and there made a stand behind trees blown down in a heavy storm. The action took place within sight of a British garrison which was still–illegally–on American ground. It is possible that some British soldiers fought with the Indians. Wayne fixed the Indians with his infantry while the cavalry attacked the enemy's flanks. The Indians were routed, several hundred being killed or wounded. Wayne's casualties were 33 killed and 100 wounded.
Result: The Treaty of Greenville was signed the following year, ending hostilities in the area for seventeen years. The Indian stronghold and surrounding villages were also destroyed.

FLORIDA (USA) 1733–81
During the War of the Spanish Succession the possession of Florida had been disputed by Spain and England. In 1733 an English colony was established at Georgia by General James Oglethorpe, the Governor, but his attempts to take the Spanish seaport of St Augustine (1740 and 1743), with the help of Indian allies, failed. A Spanish attack on St Simon's Island (Georgia) was also repulsed at the Battle of Bloody Swamp (1742). Spain was obliged to cede Florida to England under the Treaty of Paris (1763) and many of the Spanish settlers emigrated to Cuba. Spain made a fresh attempt to win back Florida during the American War of Independence when she assisted the Colonists. Governor Gálvez of Louisiana invaded W Florida and occupied Manchac, Bâton Rouge and Natchez (1779), Mobile (1780) and Pensacola (1781). The ultimate beneficiary of this successful campaign was not Spain, however, but the newly independent United States, whose full sovereignty over the whole of Florida was finally recognised in 1821.

FORT DEARBORN (Chicago, Illinois, USA)   War of 1812   15 August 1812
Fought between the American garrison and a Pottawatomie force.
Aim: The garrison of Fort Dearborn was evacuating and making for Fort Wayne. The Pottawatomie party, British allies, attacked the garrison as it retreated.
Battle: War between Britain and the United States was declared on 18 June 1812 and an invasion of Canada was planned. General William Hull, in command of the western invasion force, was afraid that the garrison at Fort Dearborn (now Chicago) would not be able to hold out against the Indians, so he ordered

its evacuation. *En route* from Fort Dearborn to Fort Wayne, the garrison was attacked by a party of Pottawatomie Indians. Casualties were 12 soldiers, 12 Militiamen, 14 women and children killed and 29 soldiers and 13 women and children captured. The deserted Fort Dearborn was burnt.
Result: With the surrender of Detroit the following day, the British gained the upper hand in the area.

FORT DUQUESNE (Pittsburgh, Pennsylvania, USA)   Seven Years' War   July–24 November 1758
Fought between British-Colonial troops under Brigadier John Forbes and the French and Canadians led by Captain Ligneris.
Strength: British/Colonials 6,000–7,000; French/Canadians 500–600.
Aim: Fort Duquesne was the base for all threats to the British and Colonial settlers of the Ohio valley. In June 1758 Brigadier John Forbes was ordered to capture it.
Battle: Early in July 1758 the British advanced guard had reached Raystown (Bedford) in the Alleghany Mountains. Differences arose as to the route the force should follow to the Ohio valley. The Pennsylvanians desired to march through the forest to Fort Cumberland, while the Virginians wished to follow the trail taken by Braddock. In the end, Forbes chose the Pennsylvania route which was shorter and easier for supplies. The route had to be carved out of the wilderness, but Forbes was a cautious man who took great pains and a long time to build up his line of communications. When he finally came near to the French garrison in October 1758, they struck back at a British scouting party, killing, wounding and capturing 273 men (GRANT'S HILL). In early November reports were received that the French were in great difficulties through lack of supplies. On 18 November 1758 a force of 2,500 British and Colonials set out to capture Duquesne. When Forbes reached the French post on 24 November he found the fortifications destroyed, the barracks and storehouses burned to the ground, and the French garrison gone. Casualties sustained by the British and Colonials amounted to 350 killed, wounded and captured. The French and Canadians had 50 men killed and wounded.
Result: This withdrawal of the French lost them most of their Indian allies, and relieved the British colonies of the threat of war. It also opened the Ohio valley to British settlement. Forbes built a new fort, which he called Fort Pitt (later Pittsburgh) after the Prime Minister, at the Forks of the Ohio.

FORT ERIE (Ontario, Canada)   War of 1812   2 August–21 September 1814
Fought between the British under General Gordon Drummond and the Americans under General Edmund Gaines.
Strength: British 3,500 with 6 siege guns; Americans 2,000.
Aim: The British sought the reduction of the garrison at Fort Erie, on the Niagara River.
Battle: After the battle at Lundy's Lane (qv) the Americans withdrew to Fort Erie, which Drummond besieged. After a two-day bombardment, on 15 August the British assaulted the garrison, but were repulsed with heavy loss. The bombardment continued until 17 September, when a sortie led by General Peter Porter destroyed British batteries. On 21 September Drummond was forced to raise the siege. British casualties were 609 killed and wounded or missing. American losses were 511.
Result: The Americans withdrew from the Niagara River later in the year and Fort Erie was destroyed.

FORT FRONTENAC (KINGSTON) (Lake Ontario, Canada)   Seven Years' War   27 August 1758
Fought between a British-Colonial force commanded by Lt-Colonel John Bradstreet and the French and Canadians under Commandant de Noyan.
Strength: British/Colonials 3,000; French 150.
Aim: In case he could not take Fort Ticonderoga (qv) General James Abercrombie had detached part of his force under Bradstreet to surprise and seize Fort Frontenac at the junction of the St Lawrence and Lake Ontario.
Battle: Bradstreet made his way up the Mohawk valley to Oswego, where he collected a fleet of small boats in which he embarked his force on 22 August 1758. Three days later he landed on a point only some few hundred yards from Fort Frontenac. Taken completely by surprise de Noyan surrendered without a struggle, casualties being negligible on both sides. Bradstreet's force captured 9 armed vessels, carrying 8 to 18 guns, which was the entire French naval force on Lake Ontario. In addition, they took a large supply of provisions, naval stores and munitions. Bradstreet destroyed the fortifications and all the vessels except 2.
Result: This achievement by Bradstreet, one of the ablest of the provincial leaders, was a heavy blow to the already tenuous hold of the French on Lake Ontario. The loss of this stronghold, which supplied all the

forts of Upper Canada and the Ohio valley, cut the French line of communication between the St Lawrence and the Ohio, opened up a British line of advance into French Canada by way of Lake Ontario, and gave back the command of the Great Lakes to the British. The loss of Fort Frontenac was the greatest contributory factor to the French evacuation of the Ohio valley later in the year.

FORT McHENRY (Baltimore, Maryland, USA)   War of 1812   12–14 September 1814
Fought between the British under Rear-Admiral Sir George Cockburn and Major-General Robert Ross and the Americans under General Samuel Smith and General John Stricker.
Strength: British 10 ships of the line + 4,000; Americans 1,000 (garrison) + 3,200 (Militia).
Aim: After the burning of Washington (see BLADENSBURG), the British sought to reduce Baltimore.
Battle: At the mouth of the Patapsco Ross disembarked to march to Baltimore, 14 miles away, while the fleet moved up the river to where Fort McHenry guarded the town. The harbour was blocked by scuttled ships, so the British fleet opened a bombardment on the fort, which was stubbornly defended by the garrison under Smith. Ross's advance was harassed by the Militia under Stricker and it was not until the following day that the British reached the heights behind the fort, by which time Ross had been killed. The bombardment continued, but failed to cause a breach in Fort McHenry, so the assault was called off. The British troops re-embarked and the fleet sailed for Jamaica on 14 October. British casualties numbered 346 men. American casualties were 20 killed and 90 wounded.
Result: The British objective was not achieved.

FORT MIMS (Alabama, USA)   Creek War   30 August 1813
Fought between the Creek Indians under William Weatherford (Red Eagle) and the American garrison of Fort Mims.
Strength: Indians 800; Americans 550.
   The Shawnee Chief, Tecumseh, had approached the Creek Indians to persuade them to join the Indian confederacy, which they did not at once agree to do. During the following year, with the United States involved in the war against Britain, the Creek Indians went on the warpath. Attacking Fort Mims, on the east bank of the Alabama River (35 miles north of Mobile), they massacred more than 250 people, taking others prisoner. Many died when the fort was fired, and later in captivity. In consequence the frontiersmen in the area stood to arms.

FORT NECESSITY (near Uniontown, Pennsylvania, USA)   French and Indian Wars   February–3 July 1754
Fought between the French and Canadians under Colonel Coulon de Villiers and a British unit of American Colonial Militia led by Lt-Colonel George Washington.
Strength: French/Canadians 900; Colonial Militia 500.
   The Lieutenant Governor, Robert Dinwiddie, sent Washington, commanding a force of Virginian Militia, to build a fort at the conjunction of the Allighany and Monongahela Rivers (now Pittsburgh). The French had already built Fort Duquesne near this strategic junction. Washington therefore withdrew to Great Meadows, where he built Fort Necessity. The French and Canadians attacked Fort Necessity and, after a strong resistance, on 3 July 1754 Washington was compelled to surrender. The French allowed Washington and his garrison the honours of war. Casualties of the Colonial Militia were 20 killed and 50 wounded, while 20 French and Canadians were killed and wounded.
   The French had one aim: to hold open the line of communications between Canada and Louisiana, which at that time stretched from the Canadian border to the Gulf of Mexico. The British and Colonials had differing aims which were liable to change at short notice, depending on the vagaries of government policy in London.
   One result of this victory was that nearly all the Indian tribes of that area allied with the French.

FORT RECOVERY (Ohio, USA)   Old North-west Indian Wars   October–November 1791
Fought between the Indians under Little Turtle and the US army under General Arthur St Clair, Governor of North-west Territory (Indiana-Michigan).
Strength: Indians 2,200; Americans 2,000 approx (500–600 regulars + 1,500 Militia).
Battle: Leaving Fort Washington in October, St Clair marched north for 100 miles and camped on the site of what is now Fort Recovery on the banks of the Upper Wabash, 40 miles SW of Lima, arriving on 3 November. Weakened by desertions, the US army was attacked at dawn the following morning by a large

force of Indians commanded by Little Turtle. In this onslaught 900 men and women were massacred. As in the Fort Wayne (qv) expedition the previous year, most of the regulars were slaughtered while the ill-trained Militia ran away. The survivors escaped to Fort Jefferson, 22 miles away, and thence to Fort Washington.
Result: Continued marauding by the Indians in the Ohio valley.

General St Clair had been court-martialled and exonerated over his abandonment of Fort Ticonderoga during the revolutionary war. In the year following the Fort Recovery expedition he resigned his command, probably as a direct result of his failure in the campaign.

FORT TICONDEROGA (New York, USA)   Seven Years' War   8 July 1758
Fought between the British-Colonial forces commanded by General James Abercrombie and the French, Canadians and Indians under General the Marquis de Montcalm.
Strength: British/Colonials 12,000 (6,000 British regulars); French/Canadians/Indians 3,600.

Abercrombie's aim was to capture Fort Ticonderoga and so open a route from New York through to the St Lawrence. But the fort was stubbornly defended by Montcalm, and Governor Drucour's equally stubborn defence of Louisbourg (qv) prevented Abercrombie from receiving any reinforcements. Abercrombie's frontal attack was driven back for a loss of 1,600 men. He withdrew and was later replaced by General Lord Amherst. Casualties of the British and Colonials were 1,964 killed and wounded, while the French had 377 killed and wounded.

Abercrombie had failed but part of his force, an American contingent under Lt-Colonel John Bradstreet, was dispatched to surprise and seize Fort Frontenac (qv). The success of that attack achieved more than the capture of Fort Ticonderoga would have done.

FORT WAYNE (Indiana, USA)   Old North-west Indian Wars   18–22 October 1790
Fought between the Indian confederacy (Miami, Shawnee, Pottawatomie and Chippewa) under Little Turtle and the US army under General Josiah Harmer.
Strength: Indians 2,500; Americans 1,133.
Aim: The United States intended to crush dissident Indians who, encouraged by British border troops, blocked settlement of the war, although the North-west Territory had been established by Congress in 1787.
Battle: Harmer left Fort Washington (Cincinatti, Ohio) and on 18 October 1790 came upon an Indian town near the present site of Fort Wayne. In a sharply contested fight, the US forces were beaten. Four days later they suffered a second defeat in the same area and marched back to Fort Washington, having lost 200 men. In both engagements there were present only a small proportion of regular soldiers (320 left Fort Washington out of 1,133 men) and the rest of the Militia ran away when the Indians attacked, leaving the regulars to be slaughtered.
Result: Continued depredations by the Indians in the Ohio valley.

FORT WILLIAM HENRY (Lake George, New York, USA)   Seven Years' War   9 August 1757
Fought between the French, Canadians and Indians, commanded by General the Marquis de Montcalm and the British-Colonial garrison under Colonel Monro.
Strength: French/Canadians 5,000, Indians 1,600; British/Colonials 2,300.

Montcalm and his mixed force left Ticonderoga on 2 August 1757 and made their way by boat to the outskirts of Fort William Henry (at the southern end of Lake George) which, after putting up a fight, surrendered on 9 August. The casualties were minor. However, when the surrendered garrison marched out with honours of war they were treacherously attacked by Montcalm's Indians, who killed a number of them before the French could intervene. The French, Canadians and Indians had 20 killed and wounded. The British-Colonials had 50 killed and wounded, and 1,800 captured. The rest escaped singly or in groups.

Montcalm destroyed the fortification and withdrew northwards, leaving the colonists of Upper New York in a state of panic.

FRENCH AND INDIAN WARS (NE USA) 1754–63
The war was begun when the British, alarmed at the drift south of French settlers from Canada, took steps to stop the flow. The fighting soon escalated into a struggle for the control of border territory and was further complicated by the Seven Years' War in Europe where Britain supported Prussia, because the

French sided with Austria. By 1760 the English were victorious in Canada and their rule has been predominant ever since. The war ended with the Treaty of Paris, which also terminated the Seven Years' War.

FRENCH AND SPANISH WAR ON THE GULF COAST (USA)   1718–20
This N American conflict was an extension of the European War of the Quadruple Alliance. The main scenes of fighting were Florida and Texas. Much of the fighting was conducted by Indians acting as proxies for each side.

FRENCHTOWN (Detroit, Michigan, USA)   War of 1812   22 January 1813
Fought between the Americans (Kentuckians) under General James Winchester and a combined British and Canadian force under Major-General Henry Proctor.
Aim: General William Harrison had been assigned to the Detroit area in an effort to retake it from the British who, with the Canadian Militia and the Shawnee Indians under Tecumseh (commissioned a brigadier-general in the British army), had control of the area.
Battle: While Winchester, who had been sent by Harrison to launch the offensive in the area of Lake Erie, was still collecting and training his troops, he was attacked and defeated by the British at Frenchtown, one of the American outposts. In this action 500 American prisoners were taken and 400 were either killed in the battle or massacred by Indians.
Result: The British still had control of the Detroit region. They besieged Fort Meigs but, although they were driven off, the fact that they still controlled Lake Erie prevented Harrison from being able to take the offensive.

FUNDY   see BAY OF FUNDY EXPEDITION

GRANT'S HILL (Pittsburgh, Pennsylvania, USA)   Seven Years' War   14 September 1758
A British force of 800 Highlanders and Provincials under Major Grant attacked a body of Indians near the French post of Fort Duquesne. The British were repulsed and were in turn attacked by the garrison of Fort Duquesne, 3,000 strong, who defeated them at the expense to the British of 273 killed, wounded or captured. Grant himself was taken prisoner.

HAVANA (Cuba)   War of the Austrian Succession   12 October 1748
A British fleet of 7 sail under Admiral Charles Knowles met a Spanish fleet of similar size under Admiral Reggio. The engagement was not vigorously joined and the result was inconclusive, though the British took 1 ship. The Spaniards lost 298 men, the British having 179 men killed or wounded.

HORNET v PEACOCK (off Guyana, S America)   War of 1812   24 February 1813
USS *Hornet* (Captain James Lawrence), cruising off the Demarara River, sighted the British ship *Espiegle* at anchor refitting her rigging. *Hornet*, proceeding to work round into a favourable position for attack, sighted the brig-sloop *Peacock* (18) (Lieutenant William Peake). A close-fought action ensued, in which *Peacock* lost her commander. As *Peacock* was filling fast with water, owing to damage to her hull, she was forced to surrender and subsequently sank, after a combat lasting only eleven minutes.

HORNET v PENGUIN (off Tristan da Cunha, S Atlantic)   War of 1812   23 March 1815
On 20 March Captain Biddle of *Hornet*, who was waiting to make a rendezvous with the remainder of the US squadron off Tristan da Cunha, was informed by a neutral that peace had been negotiated. However, on 23 March she fell in with *Penguin*, a British 18-gun brig-sloop (Commander James Dickenson) and of a number of that class which had been hastily constructed to fulfil a wartime need and manned by a scratch crew, including a number of boys. *Penguin* attacked but suffered severe damage to her masts and rigging from the accurate fire with 'star and bar' shot from *Hornet*. Dickenson saw that his only hope was to board and, before being killed himself, he rammed *Hornet* with his bowsprit lodged by *Hornet*'s main chains. However, the bowsprit snapped and he was unable to work the guns on the engaged side. Having suffered heavy casualties from grape-shot, *Penguin* was obliged to surrender.

HORSESHOE BEND (Alabama, USA)   Creek War   27 March 1814
Fought between the Americans under General Andrew Jackson and General John Coffee and the Creek and Cherokee Indians.

Strength: Americans 2,000 Militia; Indians 900 warriors.
Aim: The Americans sought to crush the Indian uprising.
Battle: The Indians had taken up a strong position in the Horseshoe Bend (Tohopeka) of the Tallapoosa River. Jackson attacked the Indians and overwhelmed them, killing 700 warriors and capturing 500 women and children. American casualties were 51 killed and 48 wounded.
Result: Five months later most of the Indians signed the Treaty of Fort Jackson.

LAKE CHAMPLAIN (Vermont, USA)   War of 1812   11 September 1814
Fought between the British under Sir George Prevost and Captain George Downie, and the Americans under Captain Thomas Macdonough.
Strength: British 800 + 4 ships + 12 gunboats + 92 guns; Americans 850 + 4 ships + 10 gunboats + 86 guns.
Aim: The British had launched a three-pronged offensive on the United States, the northern one under Sir George Prevost, Governor-General of Canada, who had marched down west of Lake Champlain with 11,000 men. The Americans, having only 3,300 regulars, fell back. Prevost occupied Plattsburg (qv) and awaited naval support to continue the offensive.
Battle: As the British fleet rounded Cumberland Head, Prevost opened fire from the shore on the American squadron which was anchored across a narrow channel, the entry to the waterway from Plattsburg to New York. The British fleet engaged at a range of 500 yards, having greater fire-power at long range than the Americans. After a closely contested two-hour battle, the American flagship, *Saratoga*, which was being badly battered by the British flagship, *Confiance*, weighed anchor and, still on her stern anchor, swung round to engage *Confiance* with fresh and closer broadsides. The short-range guns splintered *Confiance*, Downie was killed and the flag was struck. British losses were 4 warships seized or destroyed, 57 men killed and 72 wounded. American casualties were 52 killed and 58 wounded.
Result: Prevost's feeble support was questioned and he was relieved. The battle proved to be decisive, the British being forced to retreat back to Canada. It was the last action fought in the war in the north.
   This is one of the few naval battles where ships at anchor have won the action.

LAKE ERIE (Ontario, Canada)   War of 1812   10 September 1813
Fought between a British flotilla under Commodore Robert Barclay and an American squadron under Captain Oliver Perry.
Strength: British 6 schooners with 65 guns; Americans 10 ships with 55 guns.
Aim: The British supremacy on the lake kept their hold on Detroit safe and the Americans on the defensive behind the Maumee River. Perry was sent to the north of the Sanduksy River to regain the initiative.
Battle: The British came towards the American anchorage at Put-in-Bay and Perry went out to meet them. The American flagship, the brig *Lawrence*, was engaged before the rest of the squadron could close and was sunk. Perry transferred to *Niagara* in a rowing-boat and then sailed through the British line, splitting it as Nelson had done to the French fleet at Trafalgar. *Niagara* put 3 British ships out of action, including Barclay's flagship. A detachment of soldiers under General William Harrison acted as marines and by 3pm the entire British fleet was crippled. This was the bloodiest naval engagement of the war. British casualties were 41 killed and 94 wounded; American casualties, 27 killed and 93 wounded.
Result: The defeat of the British forced them to retreat from Detroit. Consequently, the Americans gained naval supremacy in the Great Lakes for the duration of the war, forcing the British back to Niagara and the withdrawal of support of Tecumseh's Confederacy (qv), thus causing its downfall.
(See also THAMES RIVER)

LOS CRUCES PASS (Mexico)   1810 Peasant *(paisano)* Revolt   30 October 1810
Fought between the Mexican peasant Rebels, led by Father Don Miguel Hidalgo y Costilla and José Ignacio Allende, and the Spanish and Loyalist Mexicans commanded by Colonel Trujillo and Agostino (Augustín) Iturbide, an artillery officer.
Strength: Mexicans 60,000; Spanish/Loyalists 7,000.
   In a mountain pass between Mexico City and Toluca the Mexicans by sheer weight of numbers defeated the Spaniards and Loyalist Mexicans after the latter had put up a stiff resistance. The Mexicans suffered casualties of 5,000 killed and wounded, the Spanish/Loyalists 1,000 killed and wounded.

LOUISBOURG I (Nova Scotia, Canada)   War of the Austrian Succession/King George's War   25 April–16 June 1745

Louisbourg was the place of call for French ships homeward bound from the East Indies or the Pacific. It was besieged by Colonel William Pepperell of the Maine Militia and 4,000 men raised in the New England Colonies, supported by the English Commodore Peter Warren and a fleet of 100 vessels. The latter, except the men-of-war, were quite small. The British established a close blockade of the harbour on 25 April and, on 30 April, landed troops in Gabarus Bay. Supported by the guns from the fleet, Pepperell settled down in a somewhat casual fashion to a siege. The garrison of Louisbourg was in a state of mutiny. Warren's squadron was reinforced from England, and when he forced his way into the harbour right under the guns of the fortress, the Governor capitulated on 16 June. Military stores and a large number of merchant vessels whose cargo was of great value were taken.

At the Treaty of Aix-la-Chapelle (1748) Louisbourg was exchanged for Madras, a barter which intensely displeased the New England colonists by whose bold enterprise it had been taken.

LOUISBOURG II (Nova Scotia, Canada)   Seven Years' War   30 May–27 July 1758

Fought between British-Colonials under Admiral Edward Boscawen, General Lord Amherst and Colonel James Wolfe, and the French and Canadians commanded by Governor Drucour.

Strength: British/Colonials 11,600 + 23 ships of the line + 18 frigates and fire-ships; French/Canadians 4,300 with 234 guns + 5 ships of the line + 7 frigates with 540 guns and manned by 3,000.

Aim: The British sought to capture Louisbourg, which would enable them to sail up the St Lawrence River to Quebec and Montreal.

Battle: On 1 June 1758 the French at Louisbourg first sighted the British invading fleet. But storms delayed the attack until 7 June when the first of the troops, led by Colonel James Wolfe, landed through heavy surf at Gabarus Bay. By 25 June the British had developed their beachhead with their siege train in action, but the French sank 6 ships to make their defences more secure. Between 25 June and 25 July the French, commanded by the resolute and courageous Governor Drucour, held out against heavy pounding from the British navy and shore guns. On 25 July Boscawen sent a cutting-out expedition into the harbour which burnt one of the French ships of the line and drove another ashore alongside a British battery. On the following day, 26 July, Louisbourg surrendered, the French squadron was destroyed and the harbour defences were dismantled.

Result: Nova Scotia had fallen to the British, but Drucour's aim had been achieved. It had been the French commander's strategy to prolong the siege until it was too late for General James Abercromby's forces in their assault on Canada to be resupplied by Amherst.

LUNDY'S LANE (Ontario, Canada)   War of 1812   15 July 1814

Fought between the British under General Gordon Drummond and the Americans under General Jacob Brown.

Strength: British 3,000; Americans 2,600.

Aim: The British, retreating before the American pursuit after the victory at Chippewa River (qv), made a stand at Lundy's Lane.

Battle: Drummond deployed his men along the road on high ground and met the American attack led by General Winfield Scott. After a five-hour battle the Americans withdrew, neither side having gained a decisive advantage. It was the fiercest land action of the war. Casualties were 171 killed, 572 wounded and 110 missing of the Americans, and 84 killed, 559 wounded and 235 captured or missing of the British force.

Result: The Americans fell back to Fort Erie (qv) which the British besieged.

MARTINIQUE (West Indies)   Seven Years' War   12 February 1762

Following the British conquest of Canada, a naval force under Admiral George Rodney attacked the French island of Martinique in the West Indies. The islanders put up little resistance and the place surrendered on 12 February. The Windward Islands were also taken as a result of this conquest.

MONONGAHELA (W Virginia/Pennsylvania, USA)   Seven Years' War   8 July 1755

Fought between the British and American Colonial troops under Major-General Edward Braddock and the French and Indians under Captain Lienard de Beaujeu.

Strength: British/American Colonial troops 1,300; French 250, Indians 950.

Aim: The British aim was to cut the important lines of communication between the French bases at New Orleans in the territory of Louisiana and Quebec in Canada. The Ohio area led to all points on the great north-south river system of N America and the French had to hold it if they were to maintain their control.
Battle: The British, marching in a long column through the woods, were ambushed by the French and Indians who, after an initial panic, took cover and began to concentrate their musket-fire on the mounted British officers, and killed amongst others, General Braddock. The British, with the loss of their leader, in turn broke up into small groups, all trying to escape from the murderous fire as quickly as possible. After the British had been dispersed by the ambush the French and Indians became too busy robbing the dead and wounded to pursue their beaten foes. The British had 63 out of 86 officers killed or wounded, and 914 soldiers killed or wounded. The French Canadians and Indians had 44 killed and wounded.
Result: The British objective was not achieved.

MONTMORENCI (MONTMORENCY) GORGE (Quebec, Canada)   Seven Years' War   31 July 1759

During the siege of Quebec (QUEBEC I) a force of 5,000 men under General James Wolfe was dispatched to attack the left flank of the French position based on the rocky gorge of the Montmorenci (Montmorency) which was held by 12,000 men under Marshal Marquis de Montcalm. During the British landing, thirteen companies of Grenadiers under General George Townshend advanced to attack without any artillery support or awaiting the rest of the force to arrive. They were repulsed with such heavy loss that Wolfe was forced to retreat without pressing on with the assault. British losses were 443, in contrast to French losses which were negligible.

MONTREAL (Quebec, Canada)   Seven Years' War   6–8 September 1760

A three-pronged offensive was launched against Montreal in 1760. General Lord Amherst moved up from Oswego with 10,000 men, General William Haviland approached from Crown Point with 3,400 men up the Richelieu River and General James Murray came from Quebec up the St Lawrence with 2,500 men. The three columns arrived at Montreal on 6 September. Two days later the Governor-General, the Marquis de Vaudreuil-Cavagnal, surrendered. French outposts in the south soon followed suit and the colony of New France became the British Dominion of Canada under the Treaty of Paris (1763).

NEW ORLEANS (Louisiana, USA)   War of 1812   8 January 1815

Fought between the Americans under General Andrew Jackson and the British under General Sir Edward Pakenham.
Strength: Americans 5,000; British 7,500.
Aim: The southern prong of the offensive against the United States aimed to capture New Orleans, which was the chief port on the Gulf of Mexico and the entrance to the Mississippi valley.
Battle: A British fleet of 50 ships entered Lake Borgne and disembarked its troops who marched on New Orleans. Jackson marched to New Orleans from Baton Rouge and checked the British advance by a night attack. Falling back he constructed a breastwork of logs and cotton bales, positioned along a dry canal, the flanks of the Mississippi and on a cypress swamp. The British assaulted the American position but the Kentucky and Tennessee riflemen were able to pick the British troops off as they advanced in serried ranks. The British withdrew, reorganised and advanced again, but they were repulsed a second time, sustaining 2,036 killed and wounded in half an hour. Pakenham was killed during the assault. American casualties were 8 killed and 13 wounded.
Result: The British withdrew and re-embarked. At the time of the battle the Treaty of Ghent, concluding the war, had already been signed.

NIAGARA (Ontario, Canada)   Seven Years' War   June–25 July 1759

A force of 2,500 British and 900 Iroquois Indians under General John Prideaux advanced on Fort Niagara which lay at the confluence of the Niagara River with Lake Ontario. The fort was held by 600 French under Captain Pouchet. During the investment, Prideaux was killed by the premature explosion of a shell and was succeeded by Brigadier-General Sir William Johnson. On 24 July a relief force of 1,300 French and Indians under Colonel Ligneris approached the fort, but this was defeated with heavy loss at La Belle Famille by Johnson. Pouchet surrendered the following day.

OAXACA (S Mexico)   Mexican War of Independence   October 1812–30 August 1813
Fought between the Loyalists commanded by Brigadier Regules and the Mexicans led by Father José María Morelos and Miguel Mier y Terán.
    The Mexicans laid siege to Oaxaca and, after the Mexican artillery had silenced the Loyalist guard, they stormed the moat and took the drawbridge, giving them entry to the city.

OSWEGO (Lake Ontario, New York, USA)   Seven Years' War   August 1756
Fought between French and Canadians under General the Marquis de Montcalm and British-Colonial forces commanded by General John Campbell, Earl of Loudon.
Strength: French/Canadians 5,000; British/Colonials 10,000.
    Montcalm, who had brought reinforcements from France, was the first to take the offensive. After a few minor skirmishes, he laid siege to Oswego which surrendered without any struggle. French and Canadian casualties numbered 40 killed and wounded. British casualties were 50 killed and wounded, in addition to which 1,500 men and 100 guns were captured.
    The French burned the forts of Oswego, destroyed all the stores and artillery that they could not take away and left Oswego in ashes. In this victory, France had won the command of Lake Ontario and had safeguarded her communications between Louisiana and Quebec.

PALMAR (central Mexico)   Mexican War of Independence   18 November 1813
A force of Mexican Insurgents of the Morelos faction led by Mariano Matamoros defeated a large force of Spaniards at Palmar after a battle lasting eight hours.
    A few days later José María Morelos was surprised at night while encamped on a high rocky hill, supposedly impregnable, by a young mestizo colonel, Augustín de Iturbide, who had cut his way with his cavalry through the revolutionary army. The army was dispersed and Mariano Matamoros took refuge with some remnants at Puruarán. They were again decisively defeated, and Matamoros was captured and shot.
    Morelo's army, which had boasted a hundred victories, now disintegrated and Morelos, with a few followers, became a hunted fugitive.

PEACOCK v EPERVIER (off Florida, USA)   War of 1812   29 April 1814
The British 18-gun brig-sloop *Epervier* (Captain R. W. Wales) had earlier captured the American privateer-brig *Alfred* and it came to the ears of Captain Wales that the privateer's crew had disaffected a number of his ship's company. He reported this to his superiors in Halifax but was disregarded, and he then sailed with a convoy to the West Indies.
    On 25 April *Epervier* left Havana to return to Halifax, escorting the return convoy. On 29 April the convoy was chased by a strange ship flying English colours, which turned out to be *Peacock* (22) (Captain Lewis Warrington). The latter eventually hoisted her true colours and an engagement took place, *Epervier* having placed herself so as to protect the convoy. *Epervier* was at a disadvantage, not only in size, but also because of the half-heartedness of her crew and defective material in her armament. She was forced to strike her colours after a forty-five-minute gun-battle but the convoy escaped unharmed.

PLAINS OF ABRAHAM (Quebec, Canada)   Seven Years' War   13 September 1759
On the night of 12 September Rear-Admiral Charles Holmes's squadron lay anchored near the intended landing-place for the surprise attack on Quebec via the Plains of Abraham. On the night of 12–13 September 4,500 of General James Wolfe's men scaled the precipitous wooded cliffs in pitch darkness, reaching the Plains of Abraham by dawn. Ships' crews who had landed with the army silently hauled guns up to the top of the cliffs. These guns were to be a decisive factor in the action which followed.
    The French under General Marquis de Montcalm, came out of Quebec in equal strength and advanced on the British despite having no artillery to support them–as the Governor-General, the Marquis de Vaudreuil-Cavagnal, had refused to release any, having been taken in by a diversionary attack, a naval bombardment by Rear-Admiral Charles Saunders. From a range of 40 yards the British artillery and infantry opened fire and halted the unsupported French advance. Overwhelmed by the weight of fire Montcalm's men broke and the remnants of his force withdrew into Quebec, having sustained casualties of 1,400 killed or wounded. British casualties numbered 660 men. Montcalm and Wolfe were both mortally wounded.

PLATTSBURG (New York, USA)   War of 1812   6 September 1814
On 6 September 1814 the British under Sir George Prevost, Governor-General of Canada, occupied Plattsburg, on Lake Champlain, when it was evacuated by the Americans. Five days later, however, after they lost the Battle of Lake Champlain (qv), the British evacuated the town themselves.

POINT PLEASANT (Kentucky, USA)   Lord Dunmore's War   10 October 1774
John Murray, Earl of Dunmore, linked up with a force of 1,100 Virginians under Colonel Andrew Lewis at the confluence of the Kanawha River with the Ohio. On the night of 9 October the Shawnees under Chief Cornstalk crossed the Ohio and then attacked the Colonials at dawn. In a fierce fight, which lasted all day, the Colonials held their position and in the evening the Indians withdrew back across the Ohio, having suffered heavy casualties. The Virginians had 50 men killed and 100 wounded.
    This was one of the fiercest fights in the Indian wars east of the Mississippi and broke Indian power in the Ohio valley.

PONTIAC'S CONSPIRACY (Ohio valley and Great Lakes, USA)   French and Indian Wars   9 May 1763–April 1765
Fought between a coalition of N American Indian tribes settled around the Great Lakes and in the Ohio valley under Pontiac, Chief of the Ottawa tribe, and the British plus American Colonials under General Lord Amherst, and his successor, General Thomas Gage.
Strength: The Pontiac coalition consisted of 18 tribes, including the Ottawa Chippewa, Huron, Delaware, Mingoe, Kickapoo, Muscoatin, Seneca, Shawnee, totalling about 10,000 braves. The British were dispersed in a series of forts throughout the area manned by a few regulars, with Militia drawn from the local settlers as reinforcement.
    Although Amherst had enhanced his European reputation with victories over the French-Canadians at Crown Point, Fort Ticonderoga and Louisbourg II (qqv), he had shewn during the war nothing but contempt for the Indians whom he offended and alienated. When, therefore, after the French had been defeated, the Indian chiefs were asked to transfer their allegiance to the British, discontent grew. Throughout 1762 Pontiac schemed and conspired to organise a confederacy of eighteen powerful tribes to overthrow the British with, if possible, French help. The anti-British visions of a Delaware prophet gave divine inspiration to the cause.
    Colonel Henry Gladwyn, the Commanding Officer at Detroit, the headquarters of the area, was warned by an affectionate squaw that the Indians planned to enter the fort under the pretext of holding a conference and dance. So when, on 9 May 1763, Pontiac arrived with his Indian braves, Gladwin refused entrance. Pontiac promptly laid siege to Detroit and sent his allies against the outlying forts. Fort Sandusky (Ohio) fell on 16 May, Fort St Joseph (Michigan) on 25 May, and Fort Miami (Indiana) on 27 May. On 28 May Fort Ligonier (Pennsylvania) fell and Fort Pitt (now Pittsburgh) was besieged. On 28 May a British column bringing supplies from Niagara to Detroit was captured. Naval communication on Lakes Eyrie, Huron and Michigan remained open in spite of fanatical attacks by war canoes.
    The Indian successes continued. Fort Ouiatenon on the Wabash (Indiana) fell on 1 June, and Fort Michilimackinac (at the junction of Lakes Michigan and Huron) on 2 June. This latter fort was captured by a subterfuge, the Indians staging a lacrosse game against the garrison, then taking over the fort and slaughtering all those present, including families. Forts Venanga and Le Boeuf (north of Fort Pitt) and Présque Ile, on Lake Eyrie, were the next to fall. Fort Edward Augustus, the farthermost fort from the British base at Niagara, and west of Lake Michigan, was abandoned on 21 June, its garrison being picked up by the navy.
    Within two months' fighting the only forts to hold out in an area 500 miles by 800 miles overrun by the conspiracy, were Fort Pitt and Detroit. Niagara was suddenly the farthest effective western point of British hegemony in N America. Rumours that a Spanish-French force would march up from New Orleans sustained the Indians. But in July the navy reinforced Detroit. Then, on 4 August 1763, an expedition sent from SW Pennsylvania to relieve Fort Pitt was ambushed by Pontiac at Bushy Run (qv). Good generalship by its commander, the Swiss-born Colonel Henri Bouquet, averted disaster and Fort Pitt was relieved a week later. The news of the Treaty of Paris (10 February 1763), which the British disseminated amongst the Indian chiefs, and the more sympathetic actions of General Thomas Gage, Lord Amherst's successor (who was later made Governor of Massachusetts), won over a number of Indian tribes and caused dissension among the rest. This breaking up of the coalition, coupled with persuasion by a French officer, convinced Pontiac that he was wrong. He stopped the siege of Detroit. In

the spring of 1765 he accepted British rule, but his change of heart made enemies. He was murdered in 1769 by a Peoria Indian.

The ease with which the Indians temporarily ousted the British, and the prominent part that the Americans had played in the suppression of the insurgency, were remembered by the Colonists when it came to their turn to consider rebellion, nine years later.

PRESIDENT v ENDYMION (off Connecticut, USA)   War of 1812   15 January 1815
USS *President* (Captain Stephen Decatur) plus most of the crew from *United States* was blockaded in New York Bay, with the remainder of the squadron destined for the East Indies. Decatur decided to sail with *Macedonia*, leaving the remainder to rendezvous later. He finally got clear and was chased by 2 ships of the British squadron, *Majestic* and *Endymion* (Captain Henry Hope), a 49-gun frigate. The wind fell light and *Endymion*, leaving *Majestic* behind, managed to overhaul *President*. The latter tried, by quick manoeuvring, to escape from the running action which then followed. Eventually *President* was obliged to surrender as further British ships appeared–namely *Pomone* (Captain Lumley) and *Tenedos*. The British had 14 casualties to the American 75.

Stephen Decatur, one of America's foremost sailors, was later to lead an attack on the Barbary Coast pirates of Algiers, Tripoli and Tunis in 1815, after he had been captured and released on parole by the British with this object in view. He was killed in a duel at Bladensburg, Maryland, 22 March 1820.

QUEBEC I (Canada)   Seven Years' War   27 June–18 September 1759
The plan of the Prime Minister, William Pitt, to follow up the capture of Louisbourg (LOUISBURG II) with the swift seizure of Quebec, fell through when a small French squadron under Captain Bougainville managed to slip past the British navy with a copy of an intercepted letter disclosing the secret design of the campaign. At this time Quebec was undefended and General Marquis de Montcalm was way to the south preparing for General Lord Amherst's expected thrust northwards from Lake Champlain. Montcalm hurried back just in time to prepare the defences for the attack. The French aim was to hold their position covering Quebec until the sub-zero winter conditions forced the British to retire.

On 4 June a powerful British naval and military expedition sailed from Louisbourg and on 21 June entered the St Lawrence. General James Wolfe with 9,000 men had orders to capture Quebec. He was supported by 20 ships under Rear-Admiral Charles Saunders, which escorted the 200 transports carrying Wolfe's army. Wolfe had too few men for a complete investment so he sought to draw the French into battle. Montcalm had collected a force of 14,000 men to defend Quebec, but was hindered by the Governor-General, the Marquis de Vaudreuil-Cavagnal, who tried to interfere with Montcalm's plan. On 27 June British troops landed on the Ile d'Orléans, downstream from Quebec. Troops also occupied Pointe Levi, on the bank opposite the city. On 18 July the fleet carried men up-stream to threaten Quebec's communications. A force which had been landed down-stream of Quebec but on the same side of the river launched an attack on 31 July. This force, commanded by General George Townshend, was repulsed at the Montmorenci Gorge (qv) with the loss of 443 men. The British abandoned this position on 3 September. On 12 September Wolfe succeeded in slipping past the city at night and landing 4,500 men on the Plains of Abraham (qv). In the ensuing battle Montcalm was mortally wounded and Wolfe died on the field. The French retreated into Quebec, which was strongly fortified and, after the British navy had heavily bombarded the town, the Governor-General fled to Montreal and the garrison surrendered. The British army occupied the Upper Town while the navy marched into the Lower.

From beginning to end the British campaign had proved to be a perfect example of inter-service co-operation, loyalty and harmony. It was the turning point in the war.

QUEBEC II (ST FOY) (Canada)   Seven Years' War   27 April–15 May 1760
When the French lost Quebec in 1759 (QUEBEC I) they retreated up-river to Montreal. From here a force of 8,500 French, Indians and Canadians under General Duc de Lévis moved down-river to Quebec. On the way they encountered a British army of 4,000 under General James Murray. In a pitched battle at St Foy the British were defeated and forced to withdraw to Quebec, which was garrisoned by 2,500. The French at once besieged the town. Superior British artillery enabled Murray to hold the town until, on 15 May, a British squadron arrived and anchored by the city. The French supply ships arriving to the north of the St Lawrence and those sent down from Montreal were destroyed, forcing Lévis to raise the siege and retreat to Montreal, leaving behind 40 siege guns and all his sick and wounded. The last service the Royal Navy

performed in the successful offensive against Canada was to move the army up-stream and assist in the capture of Montreal (qv).

On 8 September the Governor-General, the Marquis de Vaudreuil-Cavagnal, capitulated and Canada became British.

QUEENSTON HEIGHTS (Ontario, Canada)   War of 1812   13 October 1812
Fought between the British (chiefly Canadians) under General Sir Isaac Brock and the Americans under General Stephen Van Rensselaer.
Strength: British/Canadians 4,000; Americans 5,000.
Aim: The Americans had undertaken a three-pronged invasion of Canada following the declaration of war between Britain and the United States. The western offensive had collapsed after the surrender of Detroit (qv). Van Rensselaer sought to regain the initiative for the Americans.
Battle: Van Rensselaer crossed the Niagara from New York State into Ontario and attacked Queenston Heights. The British were pushed back after severe fighting, during which Brock was killed and the Americans carried the Heights. The British rallied, however, and counter-attacked the Americans. Since the New York Militia refused to cross the state border, expected reinforcements did not arrive and the Americans were forced to surrender, 1,000 of them being taken prisoner.
Result: Van Rensselaer fell back across the border and resigned his command. His successor attempted to force the Niagara River before he was relieved. The eastern offensive was launched in November, but collapsed when the Militia reached the Canadian border and refused to go any farther.

SACKET'S HARBOR (Lake Ontario, New York, USA)   War of 1812   28–29 May 1813
Fought between the British under Sir George Prevost and the American garrison under General Jacob Brown.
Aim: Both the British and Americans sought control of Lake Ontario in New York State.
Battle: Sir George Prevost, Governor-General of Canada, led an amphibious assault on the garrison of 600 in Sacket's Harbor, but the determined resistance of the Americans forced the British to withdraw.
Result: The American resistance kept the issue alive at the eastern end of the lake while more decisive action took place on the western side.

ST FRANCIS (N Maine-New Brunswick border, USA/Canada)   French and Indian Wars   April 1760
Fought between pro-French Christian Indians who had been raiding New England from New France, and the New Hampshire volunteer unit, Rogers' Rangers, led by Major Robert Rogers.
Strength: Indians 350; Rangers 150.

In 1756 Captain Robert Rogers, with British acquiescence, converted his company of New Hampshire volunteers into a 'Ranger Force' for making raids and gaining intelligence. They served with distinction as a light scout force at Louisbourg II (qv), Beausejour, in the Lake Champlain valley campaign and with Wolfe at Quebec I (qv), where their co-operation and relationship with regular British forces were excellent. The Rangers' strength was increased to six companies in 1758 and Rogers was promoted Major. To a large extent his force helped cancel out the French advantage of having the support of the Indians. Scalps were taken by both sides.

St Francis was a Jesuit Christian village on the St John River to the east of the Notre Dame Mountains but was used as a base by pro-French Indians to carry out extensive terrorist raids against English settlers and Militia, 600 of whose scalps hung in their lodges. Rogers was ordered to eradicate this base. He took with him 200 men on this long 180-mile trek through the forests and on the waterways from Fort Henry on the Maine coast, but lost 50 *en route* from sickness, exhaustion and a gunpowder explosion. After reconnaissance, he timed his attack for the dawn following a celebration when most of the Indians were still drunk. One hundred of his Rangers attacked, set fire to all the lodges and killed most of the warriors. Those fleeing were caught in an ambush by the other 50 Rangers as they tried to cross the St John River. 200 corpses were counted. Rogers lost 1 man.

But, as so often happens in a raid, Rogers lost many more on his retreat through aroused hostile Indian territory. A relief expedition by the British forces, planned as part of the operation, failed to materialise and Rogers was forced to break up his command into small dispersal groups to make the long trek back, during which 49 rangers were killed.

St Francis as a raiding base was now finished. In recognition of his services General Lord Amherst instructed that certain French forts should surrender to him when the Marquis de Vaudreuil-Cavagnal,

Governor-General of Canada, capitulated. Rogers, who helped put down the Pontiac Conspiracy (qv), remained loyal to the British in the War of Independence. His memorable standing orders to his Rangers are still displayed on notice-boards of similar forces in Britain, the USA and France.

ST LUCIA (Windward Islands, West Indies)   French Revolutionary Wars   4 April 1794–21 June 1803
A mixed British naval and military force under Admiral Sir John Jervis and Lt-General Sir Charles Grey sought to capture the island of St Lucia from the French. This they succeeded in doing with the aid of a squadron under Sir John Jervis. However, the following year the British were less fortunate. French guerrilla leaders were landed and assisted a large French population and runaway slaves from Guadaloupe to dominate the mountainous and forested regions and prey upon the British garrison. By midsummer 1795 the small British garrison, greatly weakened by disease, could only cling on to the small port of Castries and its fortress Morne Fortuné in the NW of the island. On 19 June 1795 the British navy evacuated the garrison and St Lucia passed again into French hands.

But on the resumption of the war against the French, Commodore Samuel Hood and Lt-General William Grinfield landed at Choc Bay on 21 June 1803 and, after a successful storming of Morne Fortuné, the British once more took possession of St Lucia.

STONY CREEK (Lake Ontario, Canada)   War of 1812   8 May 1813
Fought between the British under General John Vincent and the Americans under Major-General Henry Dearborn and Captain (naval) Isaac Chauncey.
Strength: British 700; Americans 2,000.
Aim: The Americans sought to gain control of Lake Ontario by launching a joint military and naval expedition.
Battle: On 27 April 1,600 Americans raided York (Toronto) and burnt the public buildings. Falling back to Niagara on 8 May, the force obliged the British garrison in Fort George to withdraw. Pursued by the Americans Vincent fell back west. Ten miles from Hamilton, on the west end of Lake Ontario, the British stood at Stony Creek and, although heavily outnumbered, they repulsed the American army, capturing Generals William Winder and John Chandler.
Result: The Americans withdrew to Fort George.

TALLADEGA (Alabama, USA)   Creek War   9 November 1813
Fought between the Creek Indians and a force of Tennessee Militia under Generals Andrew Jackson and John Coffee.
After the massacre at Fort Mims (qv) Jackson sought to put down the Indian uprising by organising volunteer forces of sharpshooting riflemen. On 9 November 1813 at Talladega, north of Mobile, a group of Militia surrounded a Creek war party and killed more than 500 warriors with little loss to themselves. However, the Indians retaliated and the Tennessee Militia were repulsed at Emuckfaw (22 January 1814), Enotachopco Creek (24 January) and were disastrously beaten at Calibee Creek (27 January).

In the spring of 1814 General Jackson took a hand and, with Coffee, defeated the Creeks and their allies, the Cherokees, at Horseshoe Bend (qv) on the Tallapoosa River (27 March). The Creeks capitulated on 9 August 1814, ceded two-thirds of their lands to the United States, and agreed to withdraw to SW Alabama. At the Treaty of Greenville (22 July) the Creeks, with the Delaware, Miami, Seneca, Shawnee and Wyandot Indians made an alliance with the Americans and declared war on the British.

Jackson, when he became President, pursued a policy of extinguishing Indian land titles and moving west of the Mississippi. So the alliance of the Indians with the Americans against the British proved to be the death-knell to Indian freedom.

TECUMSEH'S CONFEDERACY (Great Lakes to Georgia, USA)   Indian Wars   1811–13
Fought between the Tecumseh Confederation of N American Indians led by Tecumseh (1768–1813), Chief of the Shawnees, supported in the latter stages by the British, and the Americans led by Brigadier-General William Harrison, Governor of Indiana Territory.
Aim: Tecumseh, with infinite patience wove together a great confederacy of Indian tribes stretching in an arc from the Great Lakes to Georgia including most of today's Middle West, with the idea of forming an Indian nation which would prevent the American colonies from expanding westward. By 1811 his confederacy was in being. But while Tecumseh was gathering adherents General Harrison advanced on Tecumseh's capital, 'Prophetstown' (50 miles south of Chicago), with 1,000 men to put a stop to his alleged conspiracy.

In an inconclusive battle at Tippecanoe Creek on 8 November 1811, against 450 Indians, Harrison lost 61 killed and 127 wounded against 36 Indians killed and about 70 wounded. The Indians, however, with Tecumseh away on a proselytising trip, lost their nerve and abandoned their base.

Early in 1812 Tecumseh returned to pick up the pieces of his movement, but the cohesion and determination had gone out of it. Nevertheless Tecumseh, now allied with the British, formed an army of 2,000 men in the Detroit area, destroyed a company of 200 Americans, and fought some other units to a standstill. With the British under General Sir Isaac Brock, Tecumseh surrounded Detroit, whose garrison under General William Hull numbered 2,500 to Brock's 730 Canadians and Tecumseh's 600 Indians. On 16 August Hull surrendered Detroit without a shot being fired.

By January 1813 the British under Major-General Thomas Proctor and Tecumseh, now a brigadier-general in the British army, held the initiative. The American General Harrison was ordered to recapture Detroit, but a part of his force of 850 Kentuckians were annihilated on the Raisin River and another unit of 800, trying to join Harrison, lost 650 men, which provided many scalps for the Indians.

But Tecumseh's good fortune was quickly reversed when Captain Oliver Perry defeated the British at the Battle of Lake Erie (qv) on 10 September 1813, and gained naval control of the lake. This British defeat and the subsequent advance and capture of Detroit (qv) by Harrison with the resultant total withdrawal of British support, caused the collapse of Tecumseh's confederacy. Tecumseh led his men to Canada. *En route*, at the Battle of the Thames River (qv) on 5 October 1813 in the face of 3,500 Americans under General Harrison, General Proctor fled the field (and was accused of cowardice), leaving Brigadier-General Tecumseh in command of 800 British regulars and 1,000 Indians, to fight on. After 12 of them were killed and 27 wounded the British morale collapsed and the remainder surrendered. Tecumseh's Indians fought bravely and held on until their chief was killed, when they too fled and dispersed, leaving 35 dead.

In spite of his success Harrison (who later was to become President) was ordered to disband his fine body of Militia, so he resigned. Brigadier-General Tecumseh was the only American Indian to command British troops in battle.

THAMES RIVER (Ontario, Canada)   War of 1812   5 October 1813
Fought between the Americans under General William Harrison and the British under Major-General Henry Proctor.
Strength: Americans 3,500; British 800 regulars + 1,000 Indians.
Aim: After the British defeat on Lake Erie (qv) Harrison sought to take the offensive on land against Upper Canada.
Battle: When Harrison crossed the west end of Lake Erie to Ontario, the British fell back, evacuating Detroit and Fort Malden, despite the protests of the Indians who were led by the Shawnee Chief Tecumseh. The Americans pursued the retreating forces, caught up with them at Chatham on the north bank of the Thames River and engaged them. American infantry attacked frontally while a mounted Kentucky regiment charged the British right which collapsed. The Indians held their ground until Tecumseh was killed, when they broke and fled. British casualties were 12 killed and 22 wounded, plus 477 captured. American casualties were 15 killed and 30 wounded.
Result: The British defeat left all the Old North-west Territory in American hands except for Fort Michilimackinac, which remained in British hands until the end of the war.

Colonel Richard Johnson, who led the Kentucky cavalry attack, was later to become Vice-President of the United States.

TIPPECANOE CREEK   see TECUMSEH'S CONFEDERACY

TOBAGO (Windward Islands, West Indies)   French Revolutionary Wars   15 April 1793
Tobago, which had been assigned to Britain by the Treaty of Paris (1763), had been taken by the French in 1781 during the American War of Independence. On hearing of the declaration of war (February 1793), the British mounted an amphibious operation from Bridgetown, Barbados. Vice-Admiral Sir John Laferey, Commander-in-Chief at the Leeward Islands, commanded the naval force, consisting of *Trusty* (50), *Nautilus* (18), the armed schooner *Hind* and the merchant ship *Hero*. The military force, under Major-General Cornelius Cuyler, consisted of 50 men of the Royal Artillery, 418 men of the 9th and 4/60th Regiments and 32 marines.

The troops landed in Great Courland Bay on 14 April and summoned the fort at Scarborough to surrender. Lt-General Monteil (32nd Regiment), the Commandant of the island, refused to do so. The fort mounted 21 guns, including 11 18-pounders. The British assaulted at 1 am the following day under a heavy fire of round-shot, grape and musketry, and succeeded, chiefly with their bayonets, in entering the works. Despite being compelled to storm, they admitted their captives to the privileges of prisoners of war. The British had 3 killed and 25 wounded. The French had 15 killed and wounded and about 200 prisoners taken.

By the Treaty of Amiens (27 March 1802) all the French, Dutch, Swedish and Danish colonies captured in the West Indies by the British were handed back to their previous owners. But when in 1803 war started again, a force under Commodore Samuel Hood and Lt-General William Grinfield, having captured St Lucia (qv) on 22 June 1803, moved on to Tobago, which fell on 1 July. The island was finally ceded officially to Britain in 1814.

UNITED STATES-FRANCE QUASI WAR   1798–1800
During the wars of the French Revolution, French interference with American shipping in the West Indies brought violence and, in its wake, almost brought war.

On 3 May 1798 a Navy Department was established and George Washington was recalled to command the army. An undeclared naval war started on 20 November when an American schooner *Retaliation* was captured off Guadeloupe and the US navy moved into the West Indies. On 9 February 1799 Captain Thomas Truxtun in USS *Constellation* (36) encountered the French frigate *L'Insurgente* (40) and captured her after an hour's fighting. *Insurgente* served as a vessel in the US Navy until she was lost at sea in 1800. On 1 February 1800 Truxtun met *Vengeance* (52) off Guadeloupe. In a five-hour battle during the night the French ship, which was much more powerful than the American one, was partly dismasted and her guns were silenced. She escaped under cover of darkness, however.

Eighty-five French vessels, mainly privateers, were taken before peace was concluded, the last engagement being between USS *Boston* (28) (Captain George Little) and the French privateer *Berceau*.

UNITED STATES v MACEDONIAN (Atlantic Ocean)   War of 1812   25 October 1812
United States (44) (Captain Stephen Decatur) parted company from Commodore Rodgers's squadron on 12 October in order to operate independently in the Atlantic. On 25 October she fell in with *Macedonian* (38) (Captain John Cardew). The latter bore down to attack with more valour than discretion, as *United States* was superior in size, weight of broadside as well as in the number and training of her crew–notably in gunnery. *Macedonian* was eventually completely disabled and, having suffered heavy casualties, was forced to surrender, and later became part of the US fleet.

VALLADOLID (MORELIA) (Michoacan, Mexico)   Mexican War of Independence   23–24 December 1813
Fought between the Mexican Insurgents led by Father José María Morelos and the Spanish and Loyalists commanded by Llano and Aqustín de Iturbide.

Morelos attacked the Loyalists on 23 December but was repulsed. On the following morning Iturbide and Llano counter-attacked the Rebel force, putting them to rout. The Insurgents retreated to Puruarán, near Tehaucan, SE of Veracruz (see PALMAR).

WASP v AVON (N Atlantic)   War of 1812   1 September 1814
USS *Wasp* (18) (Captain Jacob Jones) having been refitted since her action with *Reindeer* (WASP V REINDEER), sailed on 28 August and was cruising in the Atlantic when she encountered the British 18-gun brig-sloop *Avon* (Lieutenant the Hon James Arbuthnot). During the action *Avon* lost manoeuvrability, but was saved from capture by the arrival of the British ship *Castilian*, an 18-gun brig-sloop (Lieutenant David Braimer), at which point *Wasp* made off. *Avon* subsequently sank, but her crew were saved by *Castilian*.

WASP v FROLIC (off Baltimore, Maryland, USA)   War of 1812   18 October 1812
Frolic, a brig-sloop of 18 guns, (Captain Thomas Whinyates), was escorting a convoy from the West Indies to the United Kingdom. She had spent five years in the West Indies and many of her crew were sick. Off the US coast she ran into a severe gale, became separated from her convoy and suffered considerable damage to her masts and rigging. On 18 October, having rejoined some ships of the convoy, she was repairing her

rigging when a strange ship was sighted. This turned out to be the 18-gun American brig-sloop *Wasp* (Captain Jacob Jones), only five days out from Baltimore. Whinyates, fearful that *Wasp* would attack the ships of the convoy, closed to attack. A close and spirited action took place in a heavy swell which made it particularly difficult for *Frolic*, which was light and unmanoeuvrable because of storm damage to her masts. Soon *Frolic* was totally disabled. *Wasp* continued to fire and caused unnecessary loss of life, after all resistance had ended. *Wasp* had 10 killed or wounded and *Frolic* lost most of her crew.

WASP v REINDEER (English Channel)   War of 1812   28 June 1814
The US brig-sloop *Wasp* (Captain Johnston Blakely) and British 18-gun brig-sloop *Reindeer* (Commander William Manners) fought a hard and close action, during which *Reindeer* was badly damaged. Further resistance soon became impossible owing to the excellent marksmanship of the Americans who succeeded in picking off the British commander and most of his officers. *Reindeer* eventually surrendered.

YAMASSEE WAR (S Carolina, USA)   1715–28
The Yamassee and Lower Creek tribes in S Carolina drove settlers out of the region west of Savannah. Carolinians and Cherokees combined to drive the Yamassees south into Florida during 1716 and the colonists fortified the rivers Altamaha, Savannah and Santee to protect themselves from the French and Spanish. England had originally left to the proprietary companies, which had organised settlements in the area, the responsibility of providing for the defence of the settlers. But when the French and Spanish increased their pressure by supporting proxy Indian wars the British government gradually took over the responsibility for the defence of the S Carolina settlements. Forts were built at Columbia, Port Royal, and on the Altamaha, the Savannah and Santee as a defence against the French and Spanish, and the brief Anglo-Spanish War (February 1727–March 1728) gave a pretext for the colonists to march deep into Florida and destroy the Yamassee township of St Augustine on 9 March 1728.

YOUGHIOGHENNY (Pennsylvania, USA)   French and Indian Wars   27 May 1754
A minor skirmish took place at Youghioghenny at the outset of the French and Indian War, which became part of the Seven Years' War. Lt-Colonel George Washington, with 40 men, met a small French detachment under Captain Coleton de Jumouville which was sent on patrol by Colonel Coutrecoeur from nearby Fort Duquesne (Pittsburgh). The whole detachment, except for one, was killed or captured by the British-Colonials at Youghioghenny, near the Allegheny River.

Washington constructed Fort Necessity (qv) at Great Meadows, where he received reinforcements. He vigorously resisted an attack by a large French force under Colonel Coulon de Villiers, but finally surrendered on 3 July. He marched out of the fort with honours of war, and later commanded a Virginian regiment.

ZITÁCUARO (Michoacan, Mexico)   Mexican War of Independence   1–2 January 1812
Fought between the Mexicans led by Ignacio López Rayón and the Spanish and Loyalists under Colonel Felix Calleja del Ray.
Strength: Mexicans 20,000; Spaniards/Loyalists 5,000.
Calleja appeared before the fortified city of Zitácuaro and, after heavy fighting, took the city, killing most of the defenders and burning every building except the churches. The Mexicans suffered casualties of 7,000 killed and wounded, while the Spanish and Loyalists had 2,000 killed and wounded.
Calleja left the ruins of Zitácuaro and returned to Mexico City in truimph.

SECTION SIX

SOUTH AMERICA

NEW PROVIDENCE
3-4 Mar 1776
BAHAMAS
1703-83

HAVANA
20 June-
13 Aug 1762

CUBA

ATLANTIC OCEAN

BELIZE
1700-

HAITI

WAR OF
INDEPENDENCE
1794-1804

CARIBBEAN   SEA

Guadeloupe

LES SAINTES   Dominica
12 Apr 1782   MARTINIQUE
                 17 Apr 1780
St Lucia   CARENAGE BAY
           13 Dec 1778

GRENADA
6 July 1779

0   MILES   500
0   KILOMETRES   800

CARTAGENA
Apr - May 1741   CARACAS
                          1749-51
PORTOBELO
(PORTO BELLO)
20-21 Nov 1739   NIQUITAO
      SOCORRO   1 July 1813   HORNET v PEACOCK
      1780-82   24 Feb 1813
            Bogota
                          GUIANA

NEW GRANADA

Amazon

BRAZIL

PAITA
1741

PERU

Lima

REBELLION OF
TUPUC-AMARU
1780-81

CHARCAS
CATARIS REBELLION
1780-81
      GUARANI WAR
      1753-66

MINAS
GERAIS

TIRADENTES CONSPIRACY
1789

CONSTITUTION v JAVA
29 Dec 1812

RIO DE
ASUNCION
1721-32

LA PLATA

PACIFIC OCEAN

ESSEX v PHOEBE
8 Feb-28 Mar 1814   Santiago
      RANCAGUA   Buenos Aires
      1 Oct 1814

Paraguay

Parana

Uruguay

Rio de Janeiro

ATLANTIC OCEAN

SPANISH/PORTUGUESE WAR
1735-37
COLONIA DE SACRAMENTO
1680-1778

BOUNDARIES c.1800
0   MILES   1000
0   KILOMETRES   1600

WAR OF THE SEVEN REDUCTIONS
1752-56
SOUTH AMERICAN WAR OF
INDEPENDENCE 1806-24

Tristan de Cunha➤
350 miles
HORNET v.PENGUIN
23 Mar 1815

FALKLAND IS
1765-1833

15   South America

BAHAMAS (West Indies)   Anglo-Spanish Hostilities   1703–83
The islands, settled by the English in the seventeenth century, were invaded in 1703 by French and Spanish forces during the War of the Spanish Succession. New Providence was attacked and its inhabitants carried off. Resettled a few years later by the English, it became a place of asylum for Loyalists during the American War of Independence. New Providence was invaded in 1776 and again in 1782. In the latter invasion, launched by the Captain-General of Cuba, a prominent part was played by Francisco Miranda (1750–1816), subsequently a pioneer of the Spanish-American struggle for independence.

BELIZE (British Honduras)   British Dispute with Spain and Guatemala   1700 onwards
In the course of the seventeenth century English buccaneers and log-cutters established themselves in central America in the territory which later became the colony of British Honduras. Their presence (though not British sovereignty) was recognised by Spain in successive treaties, including that of Paris (1763). Attempts in the eighteenth century to dislodge the settlers failed, though they succeeded in confining them to the coastal zone. Following the repulse of an expeditionary force sent against them by the Governor of Yucatán (1798), the settlers claimed that the territory had become English by right of conquest. In 1832 it was declared a British colony, but the Republic of Guatemala (which inherited Spain's claims) has refused ever since to recognise British sovereignty or the independence of Belize.

CALDERON BRIDGE See N AMERICA (SECTION FIVE)

CARACAS REBELLION (Venezuela)   1749–51
Popular resentment at the commercial monopoly exercised by the Guipuzcoan Company led to a rising, headed by Juan Francisco de León. After two years of disturbances, during which the Governor was driven from the capital, Spanish reinforcements restored order in Venezuela.

CARTAGENA (New Granada, Colombia)   War of Jenkins' Ear   April–May 1741
After the sacking of Portobelo (qv) a British fleet under Admiral Edward Vernon sailed to Cartagena, entrepot for the merchandise and bullion of the Spanish treasure fleets, which he had bombarded the previous year. He had 51 warships and 135 transports, with a complement of over 2,000 cannon and 28,000 men. The Spaniards had 6 warships and 3,000 men, but their fortifications were reputed to be impregnable.
    Vernon attacked by the narrow Boca Chica channel leading into the Bay of Cartagena. 8,000 troops under the command of General John Wentworth reduced the St Luis fort on the north side of the channel and opened a passage for the ships. But the main fortress resisted all attacks. Under their resolute commander, the one-eyed, one-armed, lame Blas de Lezo, the Spaniards beat off the general assaults of 20–8 April, and the following month the remnants of the British land forces were re-embarked after the loss of more than half their strength through battle casualties and disease.
    Vernon sailed back to Jamaica and thence undertook equally abortive operations against Cuba.

CATARIS REBELLION (Charcas, Bolivia)   1780–1
The Andean Indians rebelled under the *cacique* (chief) Tomás Catari, shortly before the rebellion of Tupac Amaru (qv), with which the rising later became linked. Following Catari's death in 1781 at the hands of a white mine-owner, the rising assumed a violent racial character and spread throughout Upper Peru.
    After destroying Sorati and all its inhabitants by means of flooding, an army of 40,000 Indians under a chieftain calling himself Tupac Catari laid siege to La Paz. It was relieved by a Spanish force under Ignacio Flores after a siege of 109 days and the death of 10,000 whites. La Paz was besieged a second time by the Indians, but the dam they were building in order to flood it burst before completion. Troops sent from Buenos Aires and Lima finally suppressed the rising, which was also threatening Oruro and Chuquisaca, and its leaders were executed.
    The system of *corregidores*, forced labour, and other Indian grievances were subsequently abolished.

COMUNEROS OF ASUNCIÓN (Paraguay)   1721–32
A dispute over the nomination of a provincial governor developed into a challenge by the Creoles of Paraguay to the authority of the Spanish Crown.
    Asunción, capital of the Spanish province of Paraguay, had a tradition of unruly independence and of hostility to the Jesuits who controlled the 'Reductions', where the bulk of the Indian population lived. In

1717 the leading Asunción families refused to accept the governor nominated by the Crown. José de Antequera, an official sent to settle the dispute, sided with the Creoles, while the Jesuits' Indian militia supported the King's nominee. Civil war broke out. Antequera attacked the Reductions with the aim of enslaving the Indians. Troops from Buenos Aires entered Asunción in 1725 and re-established the royal authority. Antequera was seized, tried in Lima for treason, and executed.

The Creoles justified their defiance by claiming that authority was vested in the community (*común*–hence their name *comuneros*) and could be withdrawn from the Crown if the latter acted unjustly. Attempts to invoke this doctrine for the establishment of what was tantamount to a republican administration quickly degenerated into anarchy, and Spanish rule was reimposed on traditional lines. Though confused and abortive, the rebellion was a prelude to the Creoles' later struggle for independence.

COMUNEROS OF SOCORRO (New Granada, Colombia)   1780–2
A Creole and Indian protest movement, caused largely by excessive taxation, erupted in 1780 in the Spanish viceroyalty of New Granada. During the absence of the Viceroy in Cartagena, where an English attack was expected, his deputy imposed new taxes which provoked widespread popular discontent.

On 16 April 1780 a gathering or *común* of protesters (hence called *comuneros*) met at Socorro and then marched under their Creole leader Barbeo on the capital, Bogotá, where they had influential supporters in touch with the Indian rebel leader Tupac Amaru (qv). Similar movements of Creole and Indian unrest developed elsewhere in New Granada. The Archbishop of Bogotá negotiated a compromise with Berceo, after which most of his 20,000 armed followers melted away. The Viceroy, however, annulled the concessions made to the Rebels and sent troops against those still under arms. Some of the *comunero* leaders helped re-establish his authority, the taxes were reimposed, and the Creoles submitted and were pardoned.

Though little was achieved by the revolt, it heralded the Creoles' later struggle for independence.

FALKLAND ISLANDS (Islas Malvinas) (S Atlantic)   British Dispute with Spain and Argentina 1765–1833
The archipelago of the Falkland Islands consists of 2 large and about 200 small islands in the S Atlantic, 300 miles off Patagonia. E Falkland was colonised in the eighteenth century by seamen from St Malo (hence the Spanish designation of Las Islas Malvinas) to serve as a staging-post for French penetration of the Pacific. The colony was withdrawn as a result of protests from Spain, who claimed sole jurisdiction over S America, and a Spanish governor was appointed. W Falkland, meanwhile, had been claimed for Britain by Commodore John Byron in 1765.

In May 1770 a Spanish force of 1,400 soldiers arrived from Buenos Aires and ejected the British. This incident threatened to precipitate war between England and Spain, which the latter avoided by declaring that the Governor of Buenos Aires had acted without authority. On 16 September 1771 the settlement was formally restored to Britain, but since it proved too costly to maintain, the garrison was withdrawn three years later. In 1811 the Spaniards also evacuated E Falkland, and both islands remained uninhabited. In 1820 an American officer in the service of Argentina (which inherited Spain's claims) was sent to plant the Argentinian flag there in token of sovereignty, and the title of governor was granted to Louis Vernet (1792–1871), who maintained a precarious settlement between 1826 and 1831, in which year it was forcibly dismantled following a dispute over American fishing rights.

In January 1833 HM sloop *Clio* arrived to reassert British sovereignty, forcing the evacuation of the remnants of the Argentinian settlement and thus initiating the dispute with the Argentinian government which continues to this day.

GUARANÍ WAR (Paraguay)   1753–66
The Guaraní were an Indian tribe converted by the Jesuits and formed into flourishing 'Reductions' along the Paraguay River. Exposed to attacks by Brazilian slavers and warlike Indians, they were allowed to raise a militia which often assisted the Spanish authorities in their struggle against the Portuguese over Sacramento Colony (qv) and in other crises.

When, in 1750, Portugal agreed to cede Sacramento to Spain in return for territory inland which included seven Reductions, the incredulous Indians refused to pass under Portuguese rule or to evacuate their homeland, and even turned on the Jesuit Fathers. In 1753, still professing loyalty to the Spanish Crown which they had always served, they prepared to resist. The following year their militia clashed with a joint force of 2,000 Spaniards and 1,000 Portuguese advancing against the Reductions to enforce the

Treaty. In November 1754 the Portuguese commander, Gomes Freire, signed an armistice with the Guaraní *caciques* (chiefs), but a few months later a fresh Spanish-Portuguese force took the field against them. The Indians, under their leader Sepe and–after his death–Nicolás, had few firearms and possessed only 8 cannon made of bamboo canes reinforced with raw hide. On 10 February 1756 their army of 1,500 men was annihilated in the Battle of Caaibaté, most of the Indians being slaughtered, while only 3 Spaniards and 2 Portuguese were killed and about 30 wounded. By the end of May residual guerrilla resistance was at an end. The Portuguese and Spaniards, however, soon fell out among themselves, and in 1761 the seven Reductions reverted to the Spanish Crown.

In Europe, the war was misrepresented as being fomented by the Jesuits, and this was used as one of the pretexts for their expulsion from Paraguay in 1766.

HAITI (West Indies)   St Domingue War of Independence   1794–1804
Fought between the native islanders and the French.
Aim: The islanders sought to drive out the French officials and slave-owning landowners and gain independence.
In 1791, stimulated by the French Revolution and led by the ex-slave Toussaint L'Ouverture, the Negroes of St Domingue (later called Haiti) rose against their white masters. A dozen years of civil war left them in control of the colony and of much of the Spanish-owned part of Hispaniola (later called the Dominican Republic). A French expeditionary force commanded by General Victor Emmanuel Leclerc, Napoleon's brother-in-law, was defeated and decimated by yellow fever.
Result: Slavery was abolished and Haiti became the first country of Latin America to achieve independence.

HAVANA (Cuba)   Seven Years' War/English-Spanish Hostilities   20 June–13 August 1762
In March 1762 an expedition under General George Keppel, Earl of Albemarle sailed from England to attack Havana, Spain's chief military port in the Caribbean and the staging-post for her treasure fleets. The total British strength consisted of 26 ships of the line, 15 frigates and other vessels, and 150 transports and supply ships, with a complement of 27,000 soldiers and seamen.
On 6 June Albemarle began landing troops at Cojimar, 15 miles east of Havana, while Admiral Sir George Pocock proceeded with the main fleet to Havana. Juan de Prado (1716–70), Captain-General of Cuba, was taken by surprise and could muster only 3,000 to 4,000 regular troops, about the same number of armed militiamen, and the crews of 15 warships and the 100 merchantmen then in harbour. The Spaniards based their defence on the long ridge of La Cabaña, overlooking the city, and on the castle of El Morro, defending the narrow passage leading into the bay. While Albemarle advanced slowly from Cojimar and General Eliott (1717–90) captured Guanabacoa village farther inland, the Spaniards sank 2 ships to block the harbour entrance. Dysentery and malaria took toll of the British, but their ranks were reinforced by contingents from New York and Jamaica. The Spaniards were forced from La Cabaña and concentrated their resistance around El Morro.
After a month-long exchange of fire and of attack and counter-attack, El Morro was stormed with heavy losses and its gallant commander, Luis Vicente de Velasco (1711–62), mortally wounded. The city was surrounded by British batteries and forced to capitulate on 13 August after a forty-day siege. It remained in British hands until being restored to Spain under the Treaty of Paris the following year. Booty included 12 Spanish ships of the line and $15 million in cash and merchandise–which was a body-blow to the Spanish economy.

NIQUITAO (Venezuela)   Venezuelan War of Independence   1 July 1813
Fought between the Venezuelan Patriots under Simón Bolívar and the Spanish Royalists under General Ribas.
Aim: The Patriots sought to expel the Spanish from Venezuela.
Battle: Bolívar attacked the Spaniards and defeated them decisively.
Result: The battle was a step towards driving the Spaniards from Venezuela.

PAITA (PAYTA) (N Peru)   War of the Austrian Succession/Anglo-Spanish Hostilities   1741
In 1741 a British squadron under Admiral Lord Anson was sent to the Pacific with the aim of attacking Spanish ports and shipping and possibly co-ordinating operations with those against Portobelo and Cartagena (qqv) in the Caribbean.

Weakened by storm and disease, Anson's force could do little more than harass Spanish shipping and sack the port of Paita before sailing on across the Pacific to complete their circumnavigation of the globe. *En route* Anson intercepted and captured much rich booty including the famous 'Manila Galleon', which did much to compensate for the cost of his operations and the long time he was away.

PORTOBELO (PORTO BELLO)   War of Jenkins' Ear   20–1 November 1739
In July 1739, following the outbreak of the so-called War of Jenkins' Ear, a British squadron under Vice-Admiral Edward Vernon was sent to the West Indies with instructions to attack Spanish settlements and shipping.

On 20 November 6 ships of the line appeared before Portobelo (Porto Bello), the traditional point of departure for the Spanish treasure fleets. The city's formidable fortifications had been allowed to decay, many of its 200 cannon were unserviceable and the garrison was below strength. A landing party stormed San Felipe (the 'Iron Castle'), one of the forts guarding the entrance to the harbour, and the following day the remaining ports and the city capitulated. All the ships in the harbour were seized, the brass cannon carried off, and the forts blown up.

This action was hailed as a great victory in England, but its strategic consequences were slight, and it was followed by Vernon's setback at Cartagena (qv).

PORTUGUESE AMERICA (S America)   War of the Seven Reductions   1752–56
By the Treaty of Madrid the Spaniards ceded seven villages to Portugal. These were Spanish-Jesuit posts on the east bank of the Uruguay River. The Jesuits incited the Guaraní Indians to rise against Portugal over the question. The Portuguese subdued the rising and brought the seven villages under control but refused to cede Colonia, which had been agreed, so in 1761 the treaty was annulled.

RANCAGUA (Chile)   Chilean War of Independence   1 October 1814
Fought between the Chilean Patriots under Bernardo O'Higgins and the Spanish Loyalists under General Mariano Osorio.

The Patriot forces, split into two factions headed respectively by the Carrera brothers and Bernardo O'Higgins, were forced by the Spanish Loyalists to retreat northwards towards Santiago. One division, under Juan José Carrera, was cornered in the town of Rancagua. O'Higgins came to its assistance and held the centre against fierce Spanish attacks while expecting to be relieved by the 3rd Division under Miguel Carrera. The latter, however, turned back and the beleaguered Patriots were forced to fight their way out with very heavy losses.
Result: The defeat deepened the rift in the Patriots' ranks and forced the leaders to go into exile in Argentina, leaving Chile in the hands of the Spaniards until reconquered by the Army of the Andes.

SACRAMENTO COLONY (Uruguay)   Spanish-Portuguese Hostilities   1680–1778
The sparsely populated colony of Sacramento (also known as Colonia), covering roughly the territory of modern Uruguay and commanding access to the interior of S America, remained an apple of discord between Spain and Portugal for much of the eighteenth century. Occupied in 1680 by a force of 800 troops from Rio de Janeiro supported by Portuguese settlers, it was retaken by Spanish troops sent from Buenos Aires but restored by treaty to Portugal. Retaken by the Spaniards in 1704, the colony was briefly ceded again under the Peace of Utrecht, but was soon reoccupied by the Spaniards, who founded the city of Montevideo there in 1724.

A Portuguese-Spanish frontier agreement of 1750, ceding Sacramento to Spain in return for seven of the Jesuit-controlled 'Reductions' of the interior, provoked an armed rising of the Guaraní. The colony was retaken by the Spaniards in 1762 but restored the following year to Portugal under the Treaty of Paris, which ended the Seven Years' War. It remained in Portuguese hands until 1776, when it was finally reconquered by forces from Buenos Aires under Viceroy Cevallos. After the Spanish-American War of Independence it became an independent buffer state, the Republic of Uruguay.

SOUTH AMERICAN WAR OF INDEPENDENCE   1806–24
By the beginning of the nineteenth century, political and economic discontent had become widespread in Spain's overseas possessions. In 1806, Francisco Miranda led a short-lived rebellion in Venezuela. The Napoleonic Wars opened up new prospects. In 1808, after the French had invaded Spain and Portugal, Ferdinand VII was forced to surrender his throne to Napoleon's brother, Joseph Bonaparte. The Spanish

people revolted. The South American colonies turned against their Spanish masters, ostensibly in loyalty to Ferdinand, but in reality to gain national independence.

Their greatest leader was the Venezuelan Simón Bolívar. In 1813 he entered Venezuela with an army from Colombia (then New Granada) and liberated it. Forced into exile, he returned in 1817, reorganised his forces at Angostura and led them in a vast outflanking movement across the plains and over the Andes to defeat the Spaniards at Boyacá. Returning to Venezuela, he proclaimed its union with New Granada and Ecuador in the republic of Gran Colombia, and sealed its independence by the victory of Carabobo. Bolívar then worked in conjunction with the forces of José de San Martín, who had led his Army of the Andes from Argentina into Chile before striking at Peru. After the victories of Junín and Ayacucho Bolívar returned to Gran Colombia. Despite the leading part he had played in bringing about the independence of South America, political difficulties there caused his downfall and death in 1830.

British volunteers, including General O'Leary, Bolívar's trusted aide-de-camp, Admiral Lord Cochrane (Lord Dundonald), Commander of the Chilean navy, and General Miller, who became a Marshal of Peru, played a prominent part in the War of Independence.

TIRADENTES' CONSPIRACY (Brazil)   1789
Joaquim José da Silva Xavier (nicknamed 'Tiradentes', 'the tooth-puller') was a Brazilian dentist and militia officer. He hatched a conspiracy, in the rich mining state of Minas Gerais, whose purpose was to declare the independence of Brazil, abolish slavery, and effect other reforms. Though he had the support of some workers and a few intellectuals, the insurrection was easily crushed. Tiradentes, who was executed, is honoured today as the precursor of Brazilian national independence.

TUPAC AMARU, REBELLION OF (Peru)   4 November 1780–1
The rebellion of Tupac Amaru was the most serious of the periodic Indian risings and was provoked by administrative abuses, heavy taxes, forced labour and other grievances, against Spanish colonial rule in the Andean regions of Peru. Its leader was José Gabriel Condorcanqui, a respected *cacique* (chief) who claimed descent from, and took the name of, the Inca Tupac Amaru, who had been executed for rebellion against the Spaniards in 1572.

Condorcanqui started his rising on 4 November 1780 by ambushing the Spanish *corregidor* Arriaga, with whom he was at odds, and executing him. The first Spanish troops sent against the Rebels were defeated, and Condorcanqui marched on Curzco, the Andean capital. Fresh troops under Col Avilés, including the Pardos de Lima, a regiment of Negroes and mulattoes, dislodged Condorcanqui from his fortified camp near Tinta. Finally, a Spanish column from Cuzco, under Marshal del Valle, forced Condorcanqui from his positions at Combapata and pursued him to Langui, where he was betrayed and captured. He was then tortured and executed by quartering in the main square of Curzco.

The rebellion continued, however, for more than a year, with many atrocities on both sides, under the leadership of an uncle and nephew of Condorcanqui, and linked up with that of the Cataris. As many as 80,000 Indians may have perished in these troubles.

Although it failed, Condorcanqui's rebellion led to the correcting of several of the worst abuses against the Indians and prepared the ground for Spanish America's struggle for independence.

URUGUAY   Spanish-Portuguese War   1735–7
Spanish troops raided into Portuguese territory and captured Colonia in 1735 as well as other posts in Banda Oriental and S Brazil. Under the Treaty of San Ildefonso, Spain received Colonia and the Banda Oriental. Portugal kept the Upper Uruguay and Brazil.

SECTION SEVEN

AMERICAN WAR OF INDEPENDENCE 1775–1781

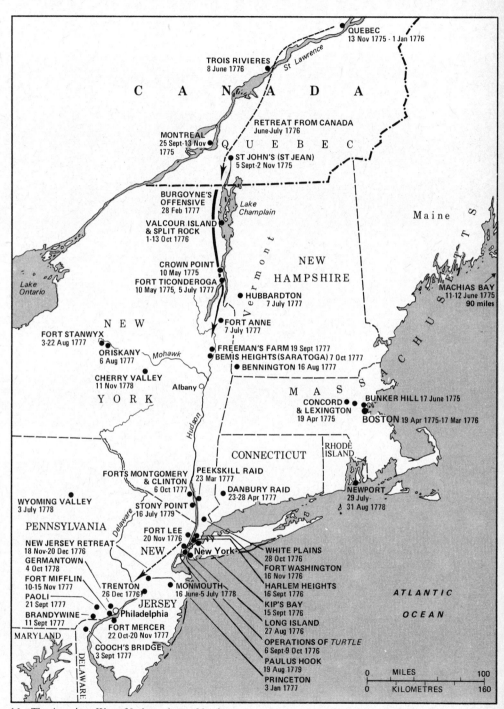

QUEBEC
13 Nov 1775 - 1 Jan 1776

TROIS RIVIERES
8 June 1776

St Lawrence

C A N A D A

RETREAT FROM CANADA
June-July 1776

MONTREAL
25 Sept-13 Nov
1775

Q U E B E C

ST JOHN'S (ST JEAN)
5 Sept-2 Nov 1775

BURGOYNE'S
OFFENSIVE
28 Feb 1777

Lake
Champlain

Maine

VALCOUR ISLAND
& SPLIT ROCK
1-13 Oct 1776

CROWN POINT
10 May 1775

NEW

FORT TICONDEROGA
10 May 1775, 5 July 1777

HUBBARDTON
7 July 1777

HAMPSHIRE

Lake
Ontario

Vermont

MACHIAS BAY
11-12 June 1775
90 miles

FORT ANNE
7 July 1777

N E W

FORT STANWYX
3-22 Aug 1777

ORISKANY
6 Aug 1777

Mohawk

FREEMAN'S FARM 19 Sept 1777
BEMIS HEIGHTS (SARATOGA) 7 Oct 1777
BENNINGTON 16 Aug 1777

CHERRY VALLEY
11 Nov 1778

Albany

Y O R K

M A S S

BUNKER HILL 17 June 1775

CONCORD
& LEXINGTON
19 Apr 1775

BOSTON 19 Apr 1775-17 Mar 1776

Hudson

CONNECTICUT

RHODE
ISLAND

FORTS MONTGOMERY
& CLINTON
6 Oct 1777

PEEKSKILL RAID
23 Mar 1777

WYOMING VALLEY
3 July 1778

STONY POINT
16 July 1779

DANBURY RAID
23-28 Apr 1777

NEWPORT
29 July-
31 Aug 1778

Delaware

PENNSYLVANIA

FORT LEE
20 Nov 1776

NEW JERSEY RETREAT
18 Nov-20 Dec 1776

NEW

New York

WHITE PLAINS
28 Oct 1776

GERMANTOWN
4 Oct 1778

FORT MIFFLIN
10-15 Nov 1777

TRENTON
26 Dec 1776

MONMOUTH
16 June-5 July 1778

FORT WASHINGTON
16 Nov 1776

HARLEM HEIGHTS
16 Sept 1776

ATLANTIC

PAOLI
21 Sept 1777

JERSEY

KIP'S BAY
15 Sept 1776

OCEAN

BRANDYWINE
11 Sept 1777

Philadelphia

LONG ISLAND
27 Aug 1776

MARYLAND

FORT MERCER
22 Oct-20 Nov 1777

OPERATIONS OF TURTLE
6 Sept-9 Oct 1776

DELAWARE

COOCH'S BRIDGE
3 Sept 1777

PAULUS HOOK
19 Aug 1779

PRINCETON
3 Jan 1777

MILES   0   100

KILOMETRES   0   160

16   The American War of Independence: North

154

FOR BATTLES IN
THIS AREA SEE
PREVIOUS MAP

N

PENNSYLVANIA

Philadelphia

NEW
JERSEY

L. Erie

Ohio

M A R Y L A N D

DELAWARE

VINCENNES
23-25 Feb 1779
150 miles

V I R G I N I A
UPRISING Mar 1775-July 1776
RICHMOND
5-7 Jan 1781
JAMESTOWN FORD
6 July 1781
YORKTOWN
Sept-Oct 1781

HAMPTON
24-25 Oct 1775
DELAWARE CAPES
16 Mar 1781   5-9 Sept 1781
GREAT BRIDGE
9 Dec 1775

Tennessee

GUILFORD COURT
HOUSE 15 Mar 1781
HAW RIVER
25 Feb 1781

NORTH CAROLINA

WILLIAMSON'S
PLANTATION
12 July 1780
KING'S MOUNTAIN
7 Oct 1780
COWPENS
17 Jan 1781
ROCKY MOUNT 1 Aug 1780
WAXHAWS 29 May 1780
BLACKSTOCKS
20 Nov 1780
FISHING CREEK 18 Aug 1780
HANGING ROCK 6 Aug 1780
FISHDAM FORD
9 Nov 1780
HOBKIRK'S HILL 25 Apr 1781
CAMDEN 16 Aug 1780
FORT NINETY-SIX
May-June 1781
SOUTH
LENUD'S FERRY (LANNEAU'S FERRY) 6 May 1780
WATEREE FERRY 15 Aug 1780
CAROLINA
KETTLE CREEK
14 Feb 1779
EUTAW SPRINGS 8 Sept 1781
MONCK'S CORNER 14 Apr 1780
CHARLESTON
(CHARLES TOWN)
Feb-May 1780
QUINBY BRIDGE 17 July 1781
SULLIVAN'S ISLAND 28 June 1776
STONO FERRY 20 June 1779
BRIAR CREEK
3 Mar 1779

MOORE'S CREEK BRIDGE
27 Feb 1776

Savannah

PORT ROYAL
3 Feb 1779

G E O R G I A
SAVANNAH
29 Dec 1778
Sept-Oct 1779

Chattahoochee

FLORIDA
(Span.)

ATLANTIC OCEAN

0   MILES   200
0   KILOMETRES   300

17   The American War of Independence: South

BEMIS HEIGHTS (New York)   American War of Independence/Burgoyne's Offensive   7 October 1777
This was the last battle of Major-General John Burgoyne's long march to Albany. He was opposed by the American army under Major-General Horatio Gates.
Strength: British/Hessians 5,000 regulars (of whom 1,500 were committed in this battle) + 600 auxiliaries; Americans 7,000 (available).
Aim: After the indecisive Battle of Freeman's Farm (qv) Burgoyne undertook another 'reconnaissance in force' to determine whether the American left was sufficiently vulnerable to warrant a full-scale attack the next day, or whether he should withdraw his army to the Batterskill.
Battle: The British force advanced from Freeman's Farm at 11am. Lt-Colonel the Earl of Balcarres with his Light Infantry was posted on the right flank, covered by Captain Edward Fraser with his Rangers and the auxiliaries in the woods on their right. Major-General Friedrich von Riedesel was in the centre, with Major John Ackland and his Grenadiers on the left. The main body formed a line 1,000 yards long, interspersed with their 10 cannon. General Gates ordered Brigadier-General Daniel Morgan to attack the British right flank, and Brigadier-General Enoch Poor the left. Poor's 800 men attacked first. The Grenadiers, firing downhill, tended to fire high, and their subsequent bayonet-charge was shattered by a volley from the enemy line. Major Ackland was mortally wounded in this attack. On the other side, Morgan routed Captain Fraser's covering force in the woods, and wheeled round to hit Balcarres in flank and rear. As the Light Infantry turned to meet this attack, they were routed by fire from Colonel Henry Dearborn's force which was now on their left. General Burgoyne then ordered a general retreat, but his ADC, Sir Francis Clerke, was mortally wounded and captured before delivering the order. This left the Hessians still fighting in the centre. However, with the enemy strength increasing, Riedesel took them back to the Balcarres redoubt. Major-General Simon Fraser led a delaying action with the surviving Light Infantry, but was killed, and the action collapsed. Reinforcements of New York Militia arriving on the scene were no longer needed. The battle had lasted fifty-two minutes.
    At this point Major-General Benedict Arnold, who had been relieved of his command after a row with General Gates, took charge of the action unofficially. He led two fierce attacks on the British entrenchments. Failing in his first attack on the Balcarres redoubt, he turned his attention to Lt-Colonel Heinrich Breymann's. Before the redoubt fell, Breymann was shot by one of his own men after killing four others with his sabre 'to keep them to their work'. British and Hessian casualties were 600 killed or wounded, and in addition they had 200 men and 10 guns captured. American casualties were 150 killed or wounded.
Result: With no more than three days' supply of food left to the British army, which was threatened by enemy forces in unmatchable strength, Burgoyne's officers unanimously agreed on 12 October that he should negotiate for surrender on honourable terms.

BENNINGTON (Vermont)   American War of Independence/Burgoyne's Offensive   16 August 1777
Fought between a mixed force of Hessians, Loyalists, Canadians, and Indians under Lt-Colonel Friedrich Baum and an American force commanded by Brigadier-General John Stark. A secondary battle was fought between supporting troops under Lt-Colonel Heinrich Breymann and Lt-Colonel Seth Warner.
Aim: Reaching Forts Edward and George on 29 July, Major-General John Burgoyne was faced with increasing supply difficulties over the 185 miles separating him from his Canadian base, and less Loyalist support than he had hoped for. A limited plan of Major-General Friedrich von Riedesel's for a raid on the Connecticut valley for horses was rejected in favour of a more ambitious programme devised by Burgoyne, that of taking a force of 800 men under Baum through Arlington, Manchester, and Rockingham. This was superseded at the last minute by a plan to raid the supply depot at Bennington. On 15 August Baum and his men camped at Cambridge.
    Meanwhile Stark had collected 1,500 men and marched towards Manchester, where Colonel Warner had reassembled his force after Hubbardton (qv). General Stark refused to serve under Major-General Benjamin Lincoln, also stationed at Manchester. Lincoln, however, agreed that Stark should remain independent and should 'cut in on Burgoyne's left rear'–a move which would bring him in direct opposition to Baum's raiding party.
Battle: As the two forces approached one another, both commanders sent for reinforcements, and on the morning of the 15th Colonel Breymann was sent by Burgoyne with 640 men and 2 six-pounders to assist Baum, and Colonel Warner set out from Manchester with 300 men to support Stark. Torrential rain slowed down the reinforcements, and also held up the battle.

Baum had drawn up his small force dangerously thinly. His main position was on a hill on the right bank of the Walloomsac River. There were, however, four other positions, one of which was as much as 4 miles from the main redoubt, at Sancoick's Mill. In the early afternoon of the 16th Stark made his attack, which took the form of a 'double envelopment'. Colonel Moses Nichols led 200 men on the right flank, and Colonel Samuel Herrick took 300 men to attack the rear. Colonels David Hobart and Thomas Stickney delivered a small pincer movement against the Loyalist redoubt on the left bank of the river. The Loyalists were routed after one volley, and two more Hessian positions were lost. Baum held out against the main force of the attack until, with little ammunition left, his reserve ammunition dump was blown up, and he himself was mortally wounded. At 4.30pm Breymann reached Sancoick's Mill, and, assuming that Baum was still holding out, continued his advance, to be met by Warner's force at Walloomsac. In the battle which followed the right flank of each force was hard pressed, but the lines held until, once again, the Hessians ran out of ammunition. Their retreat soon became a rout, though two-thirds of them were able to escape after dark. The Hessians and others suffered 205 killed or wounded, and 700 were captured. American casualties were 60 killed or wounded.

Result: The supply difficulties with which Burgoyne was faced were indicated both by the rashness of this raid, and its failure primarily from lack of ammunition. It was a pointer to the fate which was to overtake him, just two months later, at Saratoga (see BEMIS HEIGHTS).

BLACKSTOCKS (S Carolina)   American War of Independence   20 November 1780
Fought between Lt-Colonel Banastre Tarleton and the troops of his British Legion, and Brigadier-General Thomas (Gamecock) Sumter's Partisans.
Strength: British Legion 270 + 1 infantry troop; Partisans 1,000.
Aim: After the failure to check Sumter at Fishdam Ford Major-General Lord Cornwallis sent Tarleton to drive away these Partisans as they prepared to attack a Loyalist post commanded by Colonel James Kirkland on Little River, 15 miles from Fort Ninety-Six. On the 19th, hearing of Tarleton's approach, Sumter retreated followed by the British. By the 20th Tarleton decided that his movements were too slow, and he pushed forward with 190 dragoons and 80 mounted cavalry, leaving the infantry and 1 3-pounder to follow. As the Partisans reached the Tyger River Tarleton caught up with their rearguard, and Sumter turned to fight.
Battle: On Sumter's left there was a hill with 5 log-houses, to be held by Colonel Wade Hampton. Sumter also posted troops on a wooded hill on his right, and kept Colonel Richard Winn as reserve. Tarleton closed up to the enemy but, recognising that their position was too strong, he waited for his infantry. At the start of the battle, Sumter ordered Colonel Elijah Clarke to try to turn Tarleton's right, while he attacked the centre with 400 men. Both attacks were driven back, as was one by Colonel William Lacey on the left. Sumter himself was seriously wounded in the shoulder and spine. In the end Tarleton led a cavalry charge without appreciable effect, and then both sides withdrew. For two days Tarleton pursued the Partisans as far as the Pacolet River and Fishdam Ford, and Sumter's force was dispersed. Tarleton returned to Brierley's Ford on 1 December. British Legion casualties were 50 killed or wounded, while the Partisans had 3 killed and 5 wounded.
Result: On the face of it Tarleton did what was asked of him, and with a comparatively small force. In the event, the Carolina Gamecock rapidly recovered, collected a new force of Partisans, and was fighting again within three weeks. The quick resurgence of Partisans after defeat epitomises one of the problems with which Cornwallis was faced at this point of the war.

BOSTON (Massachusetts)   American War of Independence   19 April 1775–17 March 1776
With the return of the British force from Concord (LEXINGTON AND CONCORD), the pursuing armed Provincials laid siege to Boston.

By June, as a result of a decision of the Massachusetts Provincial Congress, some 15,000 men were encamped round the town, though they suffered an acute shortage of ammunition. On 25 May, Major-General Thomas Gage, Commander-in-Chief Boston, had been joined by Major-Generals John Burgoyne, William Howe, and Henry Clinton. By mid-June the British garrison consisted of 6,500 men. On 12 June Gage offered the King's pardon to all Insurgents except Samuel Adams and John Hancock. This had little effect except Insurgent derision, and was followed by the Battle of Bunker Hill (qv) on 17 June. On 2 July General George Washington took command of all the American troops at Cambridge. These numbered 17,000 though many of their engagements were due to expire in the New Year, necessitating the recruiting of a new army.

By mid-January, with Howe now in charge at Boston (Gage had been recalled in October 1775) and reinforcements due to arrive, Washington advised a surprise attack over the ice at Back Bay, but was overruled. In any event, by early March Howe had decided to evacuate Boston in order to pursue a campaign in New York. On the 17th Castle William was blown up, and the evacuation of 12,000 troops began. The Americans were subsequently able to retrieve from the town 69 usable cannon, all the British medical supplies, and 3,000 blankets.

Boston and Massachusetts were free from the British for the rest of the war.

BRANDYWINE (Pennsylvania)   American War of Independence/Philadelphia Campaign   11 September 1777
Fought between Major-General Sir William Howe's army advancing on Philadelphia, and General George Washington's army.
Strength: British 15,000; Americans 10,500.
Aim: General Howe's plan for an attack on Philadelphia had been approved by the British government earlier in the year (see BURGOYNE'S OFFENSIVE). His landing at the Head of Elk at the beginning of September opened this campaign, and produced an immediate decision by General Washington to oppose him at Brandywine Creek.
Battle: On Washington's side, the centre of the defence was at Chadd's Ford, and consisted of Major-General Nathanael Greene's Division, and Brigadier-General Anthony Wayne's Brigade. On their left Brigadier-General John Armstrong guarded Pyle's Ford, and Major-General John Sullivan on the right was responsible for all crossings north of Chadd's. Major-General William Alexander was held in readiness on the right to support either Greene or Sullivan, and Major-General Adam Stephen was in reserve to support the defence of Chadd's. Howe's plan of attack was similar to that at Long Island (qv). Major-General Baron Wilhelm von Knyphausen was to make what would be a diversionary attack with his 5,000 Hessians at Chadd's, while Howe and Lt-General Lord Cornwallis with 7,500 men made a wide flanking movement to turn the American right. By 10.30am Knyphausen was in position and exchanging artillery fire with the Americans. When this was not followed by an attempted crossing of the river, Washington realised that the main attack must come from elsewhere. By 11.30am reports of Lt-General Lord Cornwallis's movement north towards Taylor's and Jeffrey's Fords began to come in, and Washington directed Generals Alexander and Stephen to march to Birmingham Meeting House to cut off any turning movement. Washington himself proposed to attack across Chadd's Ford. However, this information was later contradicted in a message from General Sullivan, and both the march and the counter-attack were halted. By 2pm a report came in of two enemy divisions on Osborne's Hill, 2 miles north of Sullivan's flank. Sullivan was sent to meet this threat, while Alexander and Stephen resumed their march to Birmingham. At 4pm the British reached Birmingham, where Alexander and Stephen had drawn up their troops in a ploughed hill to the SW. Sullivan joined them, took over command, and was still drawing up his troops when the British attacked. By 5.30pm Washington arrived at the battlefield with the young Major-General Marquis de Lafayette, who was shot in the thigh during the engagement. By this time Sullivan's left was beginning to give way, though the right flank was shored up by support from Brigadier-General George Weedon's Brigade, which took over from Stephen's troops. Ultimately Sullivan's wing collapsed, and streamed back towards Chester. At the same time Knyphausen, after increasing his bombardment, made the crossing, driving back Wayne and Brigadier-General William Maxwell. With the American army in full retreat, Cornwallis and Knyphausen met at 7pm. British casualties were 580 killed or wounded. The Americans had 1,200 killed or wounded, 400 of the wounded being captured.
Result: After the battle Howe established his headquarters at Dilworth, while Washington reformed his army at Chester. Once more Howe had achieved a spectacular victory without clearing the way to his objective.

BRIAR CREEK (Georgia)   American War of Independence/Southern Campaign   3 March 1779
A large force of American Militia under Brigadier-General John Ashe was trapped by a British force under Lt-Colonel Mark Prevost and Major John Macpherson.
Strength: Americans 2,600 Militia + 100 regulars; British 900 troops (under Prevost) + 1 battalion and some Militia (under Macpherson).
Aim: Major-General Benjamin Lincoln, the American Commander in the South, ordered to break the British hold on Georgia, sent Brigadier-General Ashe with 1,400 Militia and 100 regulars under Colonel

Elbert, to join up with 1,200 troops lying across the river from Fort Augusta under the command of Brigadier-General Andrew Williamson. The two forces met on 13 February. They crossed into Georgia and moved down the Savannah River to Briar Creek. Brigadier-General Augustine Prevost, the British Commander-in-Chief Savannah, sent troops to check their advance.

Battle: On his arrival at Briar Creek on 27 February Ashe set about rebuilding the bridge and constructing a road to enable support to be given by troops under Brigadier-General Griffith Rutherford at Mathew's Bluff, 5 miles to the east. Meanwhile General Prevost had sent Colonel Prevost in a wide circuit to the west to attack the American position from the rear. Macpherson was to hold the south bank of the creek. The attack took Ashe completely by surprise, with a 3-mile-wide swamp behind him and the bridge unfinished. He formed his forces in three columns, but the first charge by the British broke through a gap in the ranks, the Halifax Regiment fled and the rest of the Militia panicked. Many were drowned in the swamp. American casualties were 200 killed or drowned, plus 170 captured, including Colonel Elbert. The British, in favourable contrast, had only 5 men killed and 11 wounded.

Result: The British maintained their hold on Georgia, General Ashe was court-martialled and censured for 'want of sufficient vigilance', while only 450 of the American Militia rejoined the army.

BUNKER HILL (Boston, Massachusetts)   American War of Independence   17 June 1775
Fought between part of the British garrison at Boston, under Major-General William Howe, and the American garrison on the Charleston peninsula, under Colonel William Prescott.

Strength: British 2,400 + 400 (reinforcements); Americans 1,600.

Aim: On 13 June the Americans besieging Boston learned that the British intended occupying the Dorchester peninsula on the 18th. This they countered by sending Colonel Prescott with a force to occupy the Charleston peninsula at 9pm on the 16th.

Battle: The American force arrived under cover of darkness, and industriously dug itself in throughout the night, though Prescott unhappily succumbed to advice to build his main fortifications on the lower Breed's Hill, rather than Bunker Hill. At dawn on the 17th the British ships *Glasgow, Lively, Somerset* and *Falcon* opened fire on the redoubt in preparation for the frontal assault upon which Major-General Thomas Gage had decided when the tide permitted. At noon Howe landed with his heavily burdened force of 2,400 men. The British troops were twice repulsed by close and accurate fire from the defenders. Joined by another 400 men under Major-General Henry Clinton, and with the Americans running out of ammunition, Howe's third attack succeeded in driving the defenders first from the redoubt, and then from both Breed's Hill and Bunker Hill. The Americans retired towards Cambridge, Howe halting the pursuit at the neck of the peninsula. The British suffered casualties of 1,050 killed and wounded, of which a high proportion were officers. The Americans had 100 killed and 270 wounded, 30 of the latter being captured.

Result: This was surely a Pyrrhic victory for the British. Their losses were prodigious, the destruction of Charleston during the bombardment much increased the hatred for them felt by the Americans, and the plan to march on Cambridge by way of Dorchester was abandoned.

BURGOYNE'S OFFENSIVE   American War of Independence
On 28 February 1777 a plan for a three-pronged attack with the purpose of isolating New England was submitted to Lord George Germain, Secretary of State for the Colonies, by Major-General John Burgoyne. (1) A main army of 8,000 regulars under Burgoyne was to push south from Canada down Lake Champlain and the Upper Hudson as far as Albany. (2) An auxiliary force was to operate from Oswego through the Mohawk valley. (3) A strong force under Major-General Sir William Howe was to move up the Hudson to meet Burgoyne at Albany.

This plan was approved, as was Howe's plan for an attack on Philadelphia, in the hope that this would be completed in time to meet Burgoyne.

In the event Burgoyne's army became more and more depleted as it made its way south, until the final collapse at Bemis Heights (qv). Howe was far too slow over his Philadelphia Campaign to be of assistance to Burgoyne. And General Henry Clinton became bogged down in New York City until it was too late. His attempt to relieve the pressure on Burgoyne by advancing on Forts Montgomery and Clinton (qv) came at the very moment when Burgoyne was negotiating terms for surrender.

CAMDEN (S Carolina)   American War of Independence/Camden Campaign   16 August 1780
Fought between Major-General Horatio Gates, Commander-in-Chief of the American Southern Department, and Lt-General Lord Cornwallis, Commander-in-Chief of the British army in S Carolina.

Camden Campaign: At the surrender of Charleston (qv) to the British in May, Major-General Johann Kalb was moving to the relief of the town with 2,000 men. When Gates was appointed C-in-C he joined Kalb at his headquarters at Coxe's Mill on 25 July to find a depleted and debilitated force of 1,200 men. Refusing support to Colonel William Washington and Colonel Anthony White, who were trying to build a force around the survivors of Lenud's Ferry and Monck's Corner (qqv) (Gates claiming that the South was not 'good cavalry country'), he ordered his troops immediately to march towards Camden.

At this stage Cornwallis's position was precarious. On paper he had 8,300 troops, but in fact many of these were sick, and there were twelve scattered posts to hold over a wide area. In anticipation of an offensive into N Carolina, Cornwallis had formed a forward post at Camden, with outposts at Hanging Rock, Rocky Mount (qqv) and Cheraw. He was not yet ready to face a major attack, but with 800 invalids in Camden he felt he had no choice.

The Partisan Brigadier-General Thomas Sumter (the Carolina Gamecock) had sent Kalb a report on the British dispositions, and Gates decided on attack. Starting out on 27 July, Gates rejected the longer route through the friendly country around Salisbury and Charlotte, and took a shorter course through barren country where there was no food available. On 3 August he was joined by 100 Militia under Lt-Colonel Charles Porterfield and Colonel Francis Marion (the Swamp Fox), and these ragged men, much despised by the regulars, were dispatched into the interior of S Carolina to watch and report on enemy movements. On 6 August Gates was joined by Major-General Richard Caswell with 2,100 Militia.

Lt-Colonel Lord Rawdon, in command at Camden, warned Cornwallis of the enemy's approach, and was instructed not to withdraw men from the outposts in case communications should be cut. Sumter in fact made two attempts to attack these outposts, at Rocky Mount and Hanging Rock, but without success. Rawdon moved his force forward to try to delay Gates at Lynches Creek, 15 miles NE of Camden, and Kalb suggested that they should try to bypass Rawdon, a move which Lt-Colonel Banastre Tarleton later claimed was a possibility, but Gates declined to take the risk. By the 13th the British had withdrawn their troops from the outposts, and on that day Lord Cornwallis arrived at Camden with 2,120 men.

At 10pm on the 15th Cornwallis and Gates both set out along the same road. By this time Gates had managed to gather some rations for his men, but had unhappily substituted molasses for rum, with disastrous effects to their bowels. At 2.30am on the following morning the antagonists met at Parker's Old Field, where there was some preliminary skirmishing between 40 British Legion troops and Colonel Armand's advanced guard. On the previous evening Gates had asked his officers' opinions at a conference. Only Brigadier-General Stevens ventured to reply–that it was now too late to do anything but fight.

Battle: The British, 2,100 strong, were drawn up with light infantry on the extreme right and with the whole right wing under the command of Lt-Colonel James Webster. The left wing was commanded by Lord Rawdon. Gates drew up his 4,000 men with the Militia on the left wing opposite the British regulars. The right wing was commanded by General Kalb. His 6 guns were in the centre, and Gates himself took up his position 600 yards back. When Webster attacked, the American Militia threw down their guns, still loaded, and fled. Tarleton went in pursuit of the Militia while Webster wheeled his troops against the American left flank. For a time the American line held on the right wing, but Kalb was wounded, led a counter-attack, and was wounded again–this time mortally. With Tarleton's return to attack from the rear, and Webster driving the American reserves from the field, the battle was over. The first wave of fugitives had in fact swept from the field Major-Generals Gates, Richard Caswell, and William Smallwood. Gates arrived at Hillsboro on the 19th, having covered the 200 miles in three days. American losses were 800 killed plus 1,000 captured to the British casualties of 324 killed or wounded.

Result: Coming on top of Savannah, Charleston, and Waxhaws (qqv), Camden and the subsequent Fishing Creek (qv) reduced the Americans to the nadir of despondency. General Washington made the admirable choice of Major-General Nathanael Greene to succeed Gates, and Cornwallis prepared for his invasion of N Carolina. The British enthusiasm was, however, soon to be dampened at King's Mountain and Cowpens (qqv).

CANADA, RETREAT FROM   American War of Independence   June–July 1776

With the final retreat from Quebec reduced to a rout by Major-General Sir Guy Carleton, the campaign in Canada was virtually over. Major-General John Sullivan attempted to organise a counter-attack at Trois Rivières (qv), but was then forced to fall back on St John's. From there, joined by Brigadier-General Benedict Arnold and the Montreal garrison, he withdrew his forces to Fort Ticonderoga in July. Carleton was later strongly criticised for his decision to postpone an attack on this stronghold.

At this stage of the war, both Carleton and Arnold recognised the importance of building fleets to control Lake Champlain, and both set about achieving this. In October of the same year their two fleets were to meet in the Battle of Valcour Island (qv).

CARENAGE BAY (St Lucia, Windward Islands, West Indies)   American War of Independence   13 December 1778
Fought between a combined British naval and military force under Admiral Sir Samuel Barrington and Major-General Sir William Meadows, and a French fleet under Admiral Comte d'Estaing with the garrison of St Lucia.
On the outbreak of the American war Admiral Barrington was one of the few commanders who acted with promptitude and energy. As soon as the awaited troop transports arrived from New York to support the West Indies fleet, Barrington promptly sailed for St Lucia and anchored in Carenage Bay and started to land his troops.
Aim: The seizure by the British of St Lucia, which would afford an excellent base for operations against the French in the West Indies. At this time, owing to the enormous amount of money being made from the sugar plantations, the British government and most influential merchants felt that the West Indies were of far greater importance than the small and unprofitable American colonies. The capture of St Lucia, although only 30 miles from France's principal naval station in the West Indies, Port Royal on Martinique, would deny the enemy its use and threaten the main base.
Battle: When half the British force had disembarked, d'Estaing appeared at the mouth of the bay with a squadron twice the size of Barrington's. The British Admiral that night brought his transports close inshore and anchored his warships in line across the mouth of the bay. This enabled the crew who normally manned the sails to assist manning the guns, all of which could be faced offshore thus doubling the fire-power. D'Estaing twice sailed along the British line, cannonading at long range but, realising that he had little hope of breaking the line, retired. Meadows, meanwhile, deployed his troops and attacked the garrison, which surrendered.
Result: The British acquired a fine base in the West Indies which they developed, compensating for the French capture of Dominica in the Leewards earlier in the same year. St Lucia was handed back to the French in 1782, but regained in 1794. The British garrisons installed on these islands mostly died, or were incapacitated for life, by yellow fever and other tropical diseases, which was a great drain on recruitment. As the historian Fortescue wrote: 'They poured these troops into these pestilential islands, in the expectation that thereby they would destroy the power of France, only to discover, when it was too late, that they had practically destroyed the British Army.'

CHARLESTON (CHARLES TOWN) (S Carolina)   American War of Independence/Charleston Campaign   February–May 1780
Fought between the American garrison, commanded by Major-General Benjamin Lincoln, and a British army under Lt-General Sir Henry Clinton.
Strength: Americans 5,600; British 11,200.
Aim: After the successful defence of Savannah (qv) in October 1779 Clinton felt strong enough to undertake a major offensive in S Carolina, leaving 10,000 troops under General Baron Wilhelm von Knyphausen at Sandy Hook to guard against a possible advance by General George Washington. A fleet of 90 transports and 10 warships, commanded by Admiral Marriot Arbuthnot, transported Clinton's army to Tybee, Georgia, setting out on 26 December 1779. So bad was the weather *en route* that the fleet did not reach its destination until the end of January 1780 with the horses and much of the artillery lost. Summoning reinforcements and fresh equipment from New York and Savannah, Clinton sailed once more for the Edisto River and St John's Island on 10 February. From here, keeping open his communications with the sea, he marched his army to the south bank of the Ashley River.
Battle: On 29 March Clinton's army crossed the Ashley 4 miles farther north than the Americans had expected, and by the next day had advanced to within 800 yards of the defences. Clinton then mounted a full investment of the town, demanding, but not getting, its surrender on 10 April. With Lt-Colonel Banastre Tarleton's defeat of the American forces under Brigadier-General Isaac Huger at Monck's Corner (qv) four days later, the American supply depot was destroyed, their line of communications cut,

and the town completely surrounded. Major James Moncrieff pushed forward the siege operations, using prefabricated mantelets, and by the 19th the British were within 250 yards of the American lines. Lincoln's offer of surrender with full honours of war was refused two days later, and at dawn on the 24th Lt-Colonel Henderson on the British right overran the first line of works. By 11 May, after an unusually heavy bombardment from both land and river, the Charleston Council, which had up to this point opposed surrender, gave way. The American defenders marched out of the town as prisoners on the following day. American casualties were 230 killed or wounded, plus 5,550–including 7 generals–taken prisoner. British casualties numbered 270 killed and wounded.
Result: Tarleton's victory at Waxhaws (qv) on 29 May brought the fighting in the Southern Provinces to an end. Clinton returned to New York with one-third of his army, leaving the remainder under the command of Lt-General Lord Cornwallis.

CHERRY VALLEY (New York)   American War of Independence/New York Border Warfare   11 November 1778
Fought between a Loyalist raiding party, led by Captain Walter Butler and Chief Joseph Brant, and the Patriots under Colonel Ichabod Alden.
Strength: Loyalists 700 + Brant's Indians; Patriots 250.
Aim: After the raid on Wyoming valley (qv) Major John Butler's son was given authority to lead another Loyalist force from Niagara, this time against the settlement at Cherry valley. The immediate intention of these raids was the harassment of the Patriot Border Settlements, though the broader purpose was to pave the way for Major Butler's Loyalists to join up with Lt-General Sir Henry Clinton's army.
Battle: In the spring of 1778 Colonel Samuel Campbell, whose fortified house in Cherry valley was a place of refuge for the inhabitants, had persuaded Major-General Marquis de Lafayette to have a new fort built in the valley, and this was now in use. The attacking Loyalists met Brant at Oquago (now Windsor), 60 miles SW of the valley. On 10 November this combined force had reached its objective, and captured one of a reconnaissance party from whom Butler learned that the officers were billeted outside the fort. On the night of the 10th there was deep snow, and at 11am on the 11th the Loyalists attacked under cover of haze and rain. Total surprise was prevented by their meeting with a Mr Hamble on his way to the fort, but they attacked Wells House, where Colonel Allan and other officers were killed. The fort itself held out, and the raiders withdrew at 3.30pm. There was then some carnage in the town (30 civilians were killed), though who was responsible for this is not clear–Butler's and Brant's supporters blamed each other. The raiders then withdrew with 71 prisoners, most of whom were released the next day. On the 12th Butler started on the return journey.
Result: Once again the Loyalists suffered the backlash of a 'massacre' complaint–this time, it would seem, with some justification. In retaliation Sullivan's expedition against the Iroquois was mounted, which lasted from May to November 1779.

CONCORD   see LEXINGTON AND CONCORD

COOCH'S BRIDGE (Delaware)   American War of Independence/Philadelphia Campaign   3 September 1777
Major-General Sir William Howe's army of 15,000 men had reached the Elk River, a few miles from Delaware Bay, by 24 August. Howe's advance on Philadelphia was in two columns, of which that under Lt-General Lord Cornwallis was met by Brigadier-General William Maxwell, sent by General George Washington to delay the British advance.
   At 9am on 3 September Maxwell's force fired on the advanced guard of Cornwallis's Grand Division at Cooch's Bridge over the Christiana River. Lt-Colonel Wurmb, the Jäger Commander on Cornwallis's left flank, enveloped Maxwell's right, and drove it back with a bayonet-attack. Maxwell withdrew his troops, but re-formed them to continue his delaying action. When the British Light Infantry came up in support, Maxwell retreated and rejoined Washington's main force at White Clay Creek. British casualties numbered 25 killed or wounded, while the Americans had 30 killed or wounded.
Result: This skirmish was on too small a scale to affect the advance of a substantial army, and eight days later Washington was forced to make his stand at Brandywine (qv).

COWPENS (S Carolina)   American War of Independence   17 January 1781
Fought between an American force under Brigadier-General Dan Morgan and a British force under Lt-Colonel Banastre Tarleton.
Strength: Americans 1,050; British 1,100.
Aim: Despite a number of setbacks, and in particular the defeat at King's Mountain (qv), Lt-General Lord Cornwallis still hoped for an offensive in N Carolina. However, by December of 1780 he recognised that the threat of Morgan's force in his rear must be eliminated. Since Major-General Nathanael Greene was 120 miles away, he thought that this task would not prove difficult.

It was Tarleton's proposal that he should take his British Legion and some supporting troops through rough country between Fort Ninety-Six and King's Mountain to attack Morgan, while Cornwallis moved his main body of troops from Winnsboro to cut off the 'Old Wagonner' from behind.
Battle: By 16 January Tarleton was 5 miles behind Morgan, who decided to make a stand on the high ground at Cowpens. He sent word to Colonel Andrew Pickens, who joined him with 70 men in the evening. Morgan's plan was to post a forward line of 150 Militia riflemen concealed in grass and trees, with instructions to fire–twice if possible–at 50 yards, then to withdraw firing at will. Pickens's men were drawn up on the first crest of high ground 150 yards behind them. As soon as the first Militia line had dropped back to reinforce them, they were to fire and withdraw similarly to the left flank of the third line. This line was drawn up farther up the hill, 150 yards from the second crest. It was commanded by Major John Howard, with Captains Triplett and Tate on the left and right, and Captain Beale on the extreme right. The reserve was half a mile in the rear.

At 3am Tarleton set out on the 4-mile march to Cowpens. As soon as a cavalry patrol made contact, Captain Ogilvie was sent out to reinforce them, and to feel out the enemy position. Tarleton drew up his troops 400 yards from Morgan's forward position. With orders to drive in the skirmishers, Ogilvie's line thinned out and advanced. Sporadic firing picked off 15 out of 50 dragoons, an ominous start to the operation. However, if Tarleton had any qualms at this juncture, he was by now committed to the battle, and at 7am gave the order to advance. By now the American forward line had moved back to support Pickens, and the second line delivered their fire, causing many more casualties among the advancing line. The second American retreat was rather chaotic, and some Militia made their escape. The British dragoons on the right charged, but met accurate fire from Triplett's riflemen and were counter-attacked by Captains George Washington and James McCall. The dragoons retired to reassemble behind the main line.

At 7.15am Tarleton re-formed his line and resumed the attack, which was checked but not halted by accurate fire from Howard's men. At 7.30am Tarleton rode back to order Major Archibald McArthur to envelop the American right. The Americans here, in refusing their flank, caused momentary disorder and a general retreat began, to be promptly halted by Morgan. The British followed them down the reverse slope but, at 50 yards, the fleeing Americans turned and fired, following up with a bayonet-attack. At the same time Washington and McCall hit the British flank and rear. Major Timothy Newmarsh's Regiment threw down their arms and surrendered.

The British right tried to escape to the rear but was rounded up by the American cavalry. On the left the Highlanders continued to engage Howard's entire line, but attacked by Pickens's Militia from the other flank, McArthur was forced to surrender. Tarleton, realising that despite the disaster the American forces were now well out of control, rode back to persuade his reserve Legionaries to undertake a final charge, at which proposal they turned and fled! Some 50 men rallied round Tarleton and rushed to save the guns, but they were just too late, and all the gunners were killed. Tarleton then retreated, pursued by Captain Washington, whom he turned to attack with sabre and pistol, wounding his horse. Tarleton then rode from the field, collected his 200 dragoons and recrossed the Broad river, returning to camp on the 18th. American casualties were 12 killed and 60 wounded. The British had 100 killed, 230 wounded (all captured), plus 600 captured unwounded.
Result: This defeat was a serious loss to the British, but a great boost for the Patriot cause. Before the battle, General Greene had written to Morgan: 'Colonel Tarleton is said to be on his way to pay you a visit. I doubt not but he will have a decent reception and a proper dismission.' The 'Old Wagonner' had surely complied with his General's requirements. Tarleton's reputation may have suffered from this defeat, but this can scarcely have comforted the Militia he routed two weeks later at Tarrant's Tavern (qv), or those he was soon to oppose at Guilford Courthouse (qv). Nevertheless, following the disaster at King's Mountain, this was a second link in Clinton's 'chain of evils'.

CROWN POINT   see FORT TICONDEROGA AND CROWN POINT

DANBURY RAID (Connecticut)   American War of Independence   23–8 April 1777
British troops under Brigadier-General William Tryon, after raiding an American supply base at
Danbury, were intercepted by an American force under Brigadier-General Benedict Arnold.
Strength: British 2,000; Americans 700.
Aim: This was one of a number of raids made by the British army (the first was at Concord–see LEXINGTON
AND CONCORD) to destroy American supplies.
Battle: After the success of the Peekskill Raid (qv) Major-General Sir William Howe sent Brigadier-
General William Tryon with a force of 2,000 men to destroy the supply depot at Danbury. On 23 April this
force left Long Island, landing near Fairfield on the evening of the 25th. Next day they marched the 23
miles to Danbury, arriving at 3pm. The 150 men stationed there had removed some stores, but the British
and Hessians burnt 19 houses, 22 barns and storehouses, great quantities of provisions and clothing, 1,700
tents, and 10 new wagons. The British then returned to the coast by a different route through Ridgefield, 15
miles to the south. Meanwhile General Arnold, scouring the countryside for troops, had collected 600 men
and 1 6-pound gun, with which he opposed the British and Hessian force on some high ground by the
Saugatuck River. Tryon sent out detachments to outflank the enemy, who withdrew. Joined by a force
under Brigadier-General David Wooster, Arnold pursued Tryon's force, but was driven back by a
counter-attack by Brigadier-General William Erskine with a force of 400 men, a victory which enabled
Tryon's troops to re-embark without further loss. The British had 150 men killed or wounded, including
10 officers. American casualties were 100 killed or wounded, including General Wooster and Colonel John
Lamb.
Result: The success of this raid was counterbalanced by stories of looting and wanton damage inflicted on
the inhabitants of Danbury, which tended to encourage recruitment to the local Militia.

DELAWARE CAPES I (Chesapeake Bay, Delaware)   American War of Independence   16 March 1781
Fought between a squadron of the British navy under Admiral Marriot Arbuthnot and a French squadron
under Commodore Sochet Destouches.
    Major-General Benedict Arnold who, on 23 September 1780, had defected from the Patriot forces and
joined the Loyalists, arrived in Hampton Roads in December 1780 with orders from Lt-General Sir Henry
Clinton to join with the Loyalists in Virginia and destroy American military depots, obstruct the passage
of reinforcements to Major-General Nathanael Greene in the Carolinas and generally encourage the
Loyalists throughout Virginia to take positive action against the American Patriots.
    To counter these operations General George Washington dispatched Major-General Marquis de
Lafayette (aged twenty-four) with his Prussian Director-General of training, Major-General Baron
Friedrich Wilhelm von Steuben, by sea from New York with 3,550 men to take command in Virginia.
    The British were now divided in two, their main force being under Clinton in New York, while their
Southern Army under Lt-General Lord Cornwallis was moving from the Carolinas to Virginia. Everything
now depended on the British navy maintaining naval superiority in the W Atlantic to keep open
communications for the two armies by sea and to prevent the movement by sea of American forces intent
on reinforcing fronts threatened by either British army. General George Washington, realising this, wrote
to Comte de Rochambeau: 'In all circumstances a decisive naval superiority is to be considered a
fundamental principle and the basis upon which every hope of success must depend.' But the British naval
commanders did not seem to appreciate this essential principle.
    Early in March Arbuthnot was sent with 8 ships of the line to intercept Lafayette and his men, who were
escorted by a French squadron also of 8 ships of the line under Destouches. An indeterminate action
developed off Cape Delaware wherein 3 British ships were badly damaged. But Destouches suffered
sufficient damage to force him to return to Newport. However, Lafayette, with the British fleet licking its
wounds and displaying little initiative, tried again and managed to reach Richmond on 29 April 1781 in
time to operate against Cornwallis, who arrived in Virginia from the Carolinas on 20 May.
    Cornwallis eventually moved to Yorktown (qv) in Chesapeake Bay in early August. Meanwhile the
French Admiral Comte François de Grasse had sailed from Brest via the West Indies and was heading for
Chesapeake Bay. Washington, realising that if de Grasse could keep command of the seas, Cornwallis
could not be reinforced and could be destroyed, gave the sedentary Clinton the slip and marched rapidly
with his continental army overland from New York to join Lafayette. Rear-Admiral Sir Samuel Hood
with a large naval force followed de Grasse north from the West Indies.
    The stage was all set for a second battle, Delaware Capes II (qv), to decide whether the French could
temporarily gain command of the seas in order to help an American victory on land.

DELAWARE CAPES II (Chesapeake Bay, Delaware) American War of Independence 5–9 September 1781

Fought between the French navy under Admiral Comte François de Grasse and the British navy under Rear-Admiral Thomas Graves.

The British effort to subjugate the Carolinas had caused a dangerous division of the British army in America. Sea communications became the vital link between their headquarters and main body in New York and the Southern Army under Lt-General Lord Cornwallis. In 1781 the Commander-in-Chief, Lt-General Sir Henry Clinton, decided, after pressure from his government, to strengthen the British position in the Carolinas by the conquest of Virginia. Consequently, but before plans had been co-ordinated, Cornwallis marched rather impetuously north into Virginia and formed a defended base at Yorktown (qv) where he waited, in vain, for reinforcements from New York.

Meanwhile General George Washington had sent Major-General Marquis de Lafayette and Major-General Baron Friedrich Wilhelm von Steuben with reinforcements to Virginia by sea, while he, with his well-trained Continental Army, gave Clinton the slip in New York and proceeded south overland by forced marches (see DELAWARE CAPES I). Clinton also moved south, but he arrived too late to affect the issue at Yorktown.

De Grasse with 28 ships of the line sailed from Haiti with its garrison of 3,500 men and arrived at Chesapeake Bay on 30 August. Admiral Sir Samuel Hood followed and actually reached the entrance of Chesapeake Bay two days before de Grasse had arrived. Seeing no signs of the French, however, Hood sailed on to New York to join Graves.

Now the Americans and their French allies closed in on Cornwallis's army. The British were penned in on the Yorktown peninsula by greatly superior land forces and were blocked from the sea by de Grasse with 24 ships of the line. A further squadron of 8 ships of the line under Commodore de Barras reinforced de Grasse when he brought transports carrying vital siege artillery for the reduction of the British fortifications.

Battle: On 5 September Graves, with 19 ships of the line and 7 frigates, arrived off Cape Henry at the mouth of Chesapeake Bay. De Grasse immediately gave orders to weigh anchor and attempted to come out and fight. But, owing to contrary winds, only 8 French ships made it out of the bay. Instead of seizing the opportunity while he had de Grasse's van completely at his mercy and attacking at once, Graves was overawed by the size of the French fleet he could see still in the bay, and fought cautiously. When he should have ordered a 'general chase', which admittedly would have lost him his control over his fleet but which surely would have obtained decisive results, Graves sailed on in line ahead so that half his ships never got into action at all. In the initial two hours of this indecisive engagement Graves lost 79 men killed and 230 wounded against the French 220 killed and wounded.

By this time de Grasse had moved all of his fleet out of the bay and was deployed in battle formation. For the next three days and nights Graves, now outnumbered, manoeuvred fruitlessly to seize an advantage, but de Grasse, with his highly mobile newly commissioned ships, was able to foil every intention of his opponent. Finally, on 9 September, Graves sailed back to New York. He might have changed the history of the world. Although severely criticised for his pusillanimity at Chesapeake, Graves was eventually promoted, did well in later battles and was made an Irish peer.

Result: Outnumbered, outfought and abandoned Cornwallis surrendered on 19 October 1781, and peace negotiations were opened on 12 April 1782. Britain regained mastery of the seas the following year at Les Saintes (qv), but too late to save America for the British.

EUTAW SPRINGS (S Carolina) American War of Independence/Southern Campaign 8 September 1781

Fought between a British army under Lt-Colonel Alexander Stewart and the American army under Major-General Nathanael Greene.

Strength: British 1,800; Americans 2,200.

Aim: With his army reinforced, Greene was again able to take the offensive in S Carolina, surprising and attacking Stewart's large British force. This was the first opportunity for American advance in the state since Major-General Horatio Gates's at Camden (qv) just a year before.

Battle: When a foraging party brought in two N Carolina deserters with news of Greene's approach, Stewart sent out a reconnoitring party under the Loyalist Captain John Coffin. Coffin was lured into an ambush 4 miles out of camp, losing 5 men killed and 40 captured. However, he returned to warn Stewart, who drew up his troops in front of the camp. Worried by American cavalry superiority he posted Major

John Marjoribanks on the right in a blackjack thicket where he would be invulnerable to a cavalry charge. With Coffin's foot and horse in reserve on the left, and Major Sheridan on the right rear to hold a brick house, Stewart drew up the remainder of his force facing south at right angles to the Santee River. At the beginning of the engagement Stewart was content to hold his ground, but inadvertently his left wing advanced, driving back the American Militia. Greene plugged the gap with Brigadier-General Jethro Sumner's troops, who drove the British back again, only to be driven back themselves by Stewart's reserves. Greene then committed his reserves and in fierce hand-to-hand fighting Stewart's left and centre were driven back to their tents. However, Marjoribanks's flank held, and first Colonel William Washington's cavalry and then Colonel Wade Hampton's were badly mauled.

Though Greene on the left was unaware of it, his centre disintegrated once they got amongst the drink in the British camp, while on the right Lt-Colonel Henry Lee sought to join with Major Joseph Egleston to defeat Coffin, only to find that Egleston had already been driven from the field. The battle finally centred on the brick house, where Marjoribanks led counter-attacks against the Americans, first capturing their guns, then driving them back to the woods, though he was mortally wounded in the action. The British casualties numbered 690 killed, wounded, or missing; while the Americans had 520 men killed, wounded, or missing.

Result: For the fourth time Greene had lost a battle but won a campaign. The British losses at Eutaw Springs were so great that the army had to withdraw to Charleston, and the South was once more virtually in the hands of the Patriots.

FISHDAM FORD (S Carolina)   American War of Independence   9 November 1780
Fought between Brigadier-General Thomas Sumter's Partisans and a British force under Major James Wemyss.
Aim: Hearing that Sumter was at Moore's Hill with 300 men, Lt-General Lord Cornwallis sent Wemyss with 100 mounted infantry and 40 cavalry from the British Legion to disperse this group.
Battle: At 1am on 9 November Wemyss's force met Sumter's outposts 5 miles south of Moore's Hill. In the skirmish which followed Wemyss was wounded in the arm and knee. Lieutenant John Stark then led a cavalry charge into Sumter's camp but his men, silhouetted against the camp-fires, suffered casualties. They were then supported by the infantry but, after some heavy fighting, both sides withdrew. Sumter escaped from the 5 Militia sent to take him, and went into hiding by the Broad River. After the battle Stark left Wemyss and others under a flag of truce, and returned to Winnsboro. There is some doubt about the number of casualties suffered, Sumter's seeming particularly low. They are given as: Partisans–5 killed or wounded; Loyalists–5 killed, 23 wounded.
Result: Sumter claimed the victory at Fishdam, and continued to gather recruits. Cornwallis sent for Lt-Colonel Banastre Tarleton as the one man likely to be able to catch the Carolina Gamecock. The next attempt was made on 20 November at Blackstocks (qv).

FISHING CREEK (N Carolina)   American War of Independence/Camden Campaign   18 August 1780.
Fought between Lt-Colonel Banastre Tarleton's British Legion and Brigadier-General Thomas Sumter's Partisans.
Aim: After the British victory at Camden (qv) Lt-General Lord Cornwallis decided to dispose of the Partisan forces which had continually harassed his army, and would otherwise continue to do so as he marched through N Carolina. Accordingly Tarleton, who caught up with Cornwallis's main body of troops at Rugeley's Mill, where they had moved after Camden, was dispatched to intercept the Carolina Gamecock (Sumter) on his retreat north.
Battle: On 17 August Tarleton started up the east side of the Wateree River with his force of 350 men and 1 cannon. By the evening he saw the Partisan camp-fires across the river, and bivouacked his men on the east side without fires in the hope that Sumter would cross during the night. In fact, Sumter moved north the next morning, whereupon Tarleton followed him to Fishing Creek. By this time his foot soldiers were exhausted, so he took 100 dragoons and 60 infantry to make a surprise attack. Seeing Sumter's men cooking, sleeping and bathing, with their arms stacked, he promptly deployed his men and charged. Sumter leapt coatless on to an unsaddled horse and fled, arriving at Major William Davie's camp two days later. Some of his men put up a defence from behind their wagons, and Captain Charles Campbell was killed. The British had 16 killed or wounded in the assault, which brought the release of 100 British prisoners together with 44 supply wagons. The Americans lost 150 killed and 300 captured.

Result: For the British, this was a highly successful mopping-up operation of the kind for which Tarleton was noted (see MONCK'S CORNER and WAXHAWS).

FORT ANNE (New York)   American War of Independence/Burgoyne's Offensive   7 July 1777
Fought between the British 9th Regiment, under the command of Lt-Colonel John Hill, and an attacking force of 150 men under Colonel Pierce Long and 400 New York Militia under Colonel Henry von Rensselaer.
Aim: After the taking of Fort Ticonderoga (qv) by the British and the capture of Skenesboro by Major-General John Burgoyne's pursuing troops, an American force under Colonel Long made its way to Fort Anne, where it was joined by 400 Militia sent by General Philip Schuyler. Here they attacked the British advanced guard sent to intercept them.
Battle: Assured by a spy that only a small British force had so far caught up with them, the Americans undertook a delaying action outside Fort Anne. Hill and his men scrambled up a 500-foot ridge, from where they fought off the attack for two hours. With ammunition running short on both sides, and an Indian war-whoop from the north apparently heralding the approach of General Burgoyne's main army, the Americans broke off the engagement, burned Fort Anne, and retreated to join General Schuyler at Fort Edward, 13 miles farther south. The force providing the war-whoop turned out to be a Captain John Money who, on the refusal of his Indians to advance, had given the appropriate signal and moved to the attack on his own.
Result: This incident was a part of the larger engagement in which once more the British failed to act swiftly enough after a victory (here the taking of Ticonderoga) to destroy the enemy forces.

FORT CLINTON   see FORTS MONTGOMERY AND CLINTON

FORT LEE (New Jersey)   American War of Independence/New York Campaign   20 November 1776
On the morning of 20 November 1776, after the capture of Fort Washington (qv), Major-General Lord Cornwallis crossed the Hudson with 4,500 troops 6 miles north of Fort Lee. For several days Washington had been evacuating his troops from the fort, and by this time, with Major-Generals Nathanael Greene and Israel Putnam, had left with 2,000 men. The British captured the fort, took 12 drunken American prisoners, and gathered in another 150 from the surrounding countryside. They also took 300 tents, 1,000 barrels of flour, 50 cannon, and a full complement of entrenching tools and baggage. What once again they failed to take was General Washington's army.

FORT MERCER (New Jersey)   American War of Independence/Philadelphia Campaign   22 October–20 November 1777
Fought between an American garrison force under Lt-Colonel Christopher Greene and a Hessian force under Colonel Carl von Donop.
Strength: Americans 400 with 14 guns; Hessians 2,000 with 2 guns.
Aim: After the fall of Philadelphia to the British, Major-General Sir William Howe was concerned to reduce the Delaware River forts which prevented supplies from being brought up-river. Fort Mercer, along with Fort Mifflin (qv), formed a part of the Delaware defence system.
Battle: Fort Mercer stood on Red Bank, on the New Jersey side of the river. It was a large earthwork of 14 cannon and an abatis on the land side. The French engineer du Plessis had strengthened the fort by building an interior wall cutting off the north wing.
  On 21 October Colonel Donop was detached from Howe's army with 2,000 men and 2 guns and instructions to take the fort. Camped overnight at Haddonfield, he set out at 3am on the 22nd, arrived at the fort at noon, and demanded its surrender, which was duly refused. By 4.30pm, as dusk fell, Donop was ready to attack. The attack was launched from the north by two Grenadier battalions and the von Mirbach Regiment, the rest going in from the west, leaving von Lengerke's battalion and a force of Jägers to protect their flank and rear. Observing the defenders retreating from the outer defences, the attackers charged confidently forward, to be mown down by withering fire from the inner defences as they cut their way through the branches of the abatis. Those on the north side fled first, the others quickly following their example. They re-formed and launched a second attack, this time to come under fire from the American galleys on the river. Twenty-two German officers were killed or wounded, including Colonel Donop who died three days later, and Lt-Colonel Minnigrode who died during the attack. Two British ships, *Augusta* and *Merlin*, which attempted to assist, were blown up. The Hessian soldiers, totally demoralised, turned

and ran. The Americans had 40 killed or wounded, while the Hessians had 400 killed or wounded, among whom were 120 prisoners. The 2 British ships were sunk.

Result: This expensive fiasco taught Howe to make more careful preparations for his attack on Fort Mifflin four weeks later. With the fall of Mifflin, Fort Mercer could no longer be held, and on 20 November Greene evacuated the garrison. The Delaware was now open to the British up to Philadelphia.

FORT MIFFLIN (Pennsylvania)   American War of Independence/Philadelphia Campaign   10–15 November 1777

This fort, which was part of the American Delaware River fort system, was commanded by Lt-Colonel Samuel Smith with 450 men. It was attacked by the British fleet led by *Eagle*, Admiral Lord Howe's flagship.

Aim: After the fall of Philadelphia to the British, Major-General Sir William Howe was concerned to reduce the Delaware River forts which prevented supplies from being brought up-river. The earlier Hessian/British disaster at Fort Mercer (qv) ensured that his preparations for this attack were more thorough.

Battle: Fort Mifflin stood on Mud Island, opposite Fort Mercer. Mifflin had a battery of 18 10-pounders, and 4 blockhouses of 4 guns each. Here Captain Hammond, in charge of a British naval force guarding the Delaware, had been driven back from a reconnaissance in May. However, by November the British were ready to force their way through the *chevaux de frise* which extended between the two forts, and on 10 November the attack began. A bombardment from 5 batteries on Province Island and a floating battery of 22 24-pounders up-stream of the island, supported by a fleet of 10 warships four days later, made the fort untenable. With Colonel Smith wounded, Major Simeon Thayer took command, but on the night of the 15th he had to abandon the fort and evacuate the survivors to Fort Mercer. The Americans had 250 killed or wounded, the British 7 killed and 5 wounded.

Result: The abandonment of Fort Mifflin made its sister fort, Mercer, untenable, and five days later this too had to be evacuated.

FORTS MONTGOMERY AND CLINTON (New York)   American War of Independence   6 October 1777

These two forts on the west bank of the Hudson River were commanded by Governor George Clinton. They were attacked by a strong force under Lt-General Sir Henry Clinton, at which point Governor Clinton took command of Fort Montgomery, leaving his brother, Brigadier James Clinton, in command of Fort Clinton.

Aim: Sir Henry Clinton, British Commander-in-Chief New York, began receiving urgent requests for help from Major-General John Burgoyne in September 1777 (see BURGOYNE'S OFFENSIVE). On 24 September, Clinton got reinforcements from England, bringing his strength up to 2,700 British and 4,200 Hessians. Feeling strong enough at this point to assist the hard-pressed General Burgoyne, he moved north on 3 October with 3,000 troops in three divisions. His immediate objective was the taking of the two forts, after which he could continue towards Albany in the hope of relieving the pressure on Burgoyne.

Battle: On the evening of the 5th Clinton landed troops on the east side across from Stony Point, where he routed an outpost. As he had hoped, Major-General Israel Putnam, in command of the American forces in the highlands of the Hudson River, withdrew 4 miles into the hills and demanded reinforcements from these two forts. Further to deceive Putnam, Clinton left 1,000 men at Verplancks Point, and landed the rest of his force at Stony Point in thick fog the next morning. He led his troops up a steep trail, through The Timp, an 850-feet pass, down to Doodletown, which lay 2½ miles from Fort Clinton. At 10am they drove back an American patrol, after which 900 men were sent around Bear Mountain to attack Montgomery from the west. The rest, after an encircling movement, were to attack Fort Clinton from the south. After several delaying actions, at 4.30pm the British were ready for simultaneous attacks. Fort Montgomery was taken without difficulty, though some of the garrison, including the Governor, escaped across the river. Fort Clinton presented greater problems. Its defences faced south, covering a 400-yards strip of flat ground between the Hessian Lake and the river. It was protected by an abatis and 10 cannon. The British had no artillery and little room for manoeuvre, and were forced to make a frontal attack, supported by one regiment which circled the lake to attack from the NW. However, Sir Henry's troops overcame both the abatis and heavy fire to take the fort. Casualties (all at Fort Clinton) were: Americans 250 killed or wounded, plus 67 guns and stores taken; British 300 killed or wounded.

Result: On 7 October the British broke through the boom and routed the garrison at Fort Constitution. Clinton's 'Nous y voici' dispatch to General Burgoyne, dated 8 October from Fort Mongomery, arrived at a point when Burgoyne was past caring. He was already negotiating terms of surrender.

FORT NINETY-SIX (S Carolina)   American War of Independence/Southern Campaign   May–June 1781
This Loyalist fort, under the command of Colonel John Cruger, was attacked by a Patriot force commanded by Major-General Nathanael Greene.
Strength: Loyalists 550; Patriots 1,000.
Aim: Once Colonel Lord Rawdon had abandoned Camden (qv) Fort Ninety-Six became a major target for the American forces, and in May 1781 Greene saw his way to attempting to reduce it.
Battle: Fort Ninety-Six was a fortified village protected by a star-shaped redoubt with stockade and abatis to the east, and Fort Holmes, for the protection of watering parties, to the west. Greene's adviser in this undertaking was Colonel Thaddeus Kosciuszko, who made two important initial mistakes. First, he directed his main effort against the Star Redoubt instead of the vital and more vulnerable Fort Holmes, and secondly he started the works within 70 yards of the Loyalist lines, where the working party was promptly wiped out. A fresh start was made at a distance of 400 yards and by 3 June, despite a number of raiding parties, work on the approaches had progressed far enough for Greene to demand the surrender of the fort. This was rejected. A Maham Tower was brought into action, but Cruger countered this by raising the height of the rampart. African arrows were fired into the fort, but Cruger stripped the roofs from the buildings.

On the 8th Colonel Harry Lee arrived with some prisoners from Fort Augusta, and opened siege operations to the west of the fort, but a successful counter-attack was launched against him. At this point Greene received a message from Brigadier-General Thomas Sumter that reinforcements were on the march from Charleston to raise the siege. Greene ordered Brigadier-General Andrew Pickens to join Sumter, and sent a warning to Brigadier-General Francis Marion, who was attempting to shadow Rawdon. He then ordered a co-ordinated attack upon Fort Holmes and the Star Redoubt by Lee and Colonel Richard Campbell respectively. Both attacks were repulsed and on the 19th Greene withdrew his troops towards Charlotte. Loyalist casualties were 85 killed or wounded, while the Patriots had 185 killed or wounded.
Result: Rawdon arrived with reinforcements on the morning of the 21st and pursued, but failed to catch, Greene on his retreat to Charlotte. Thus for the time being Ninety-Six remained in Loyalist hands.

FORT STANWYX (New York)   American War of Independence/Burgoyne's Offensive–St Leger's Expedition   3–22 August 1777
Fought between a force of Loyalists, Canadians, Indians and regulars under Lt-Colonel Barry St Leger, and an American garrison led by Colonel Peter Gansevoort.
Strength: Loyalists/Canadians 1,650 + 350 regulars; Americans 550 (garrison) + 2 relief forces, each of 800.
Aim: One line of Major-General John Burgoyne's advance towards Albany was blocked by Fort Stanwyx on the Mohawk River. Colonel St Leger was concerned to remove this obstacle.
Battle: St Leger left Fort Oswego with his mixed force on 25 July. Arriving at Fort Stanwyx on 2 August, he selected three main positions for his men: the regulars a quarter-mile to the NE of the fort, a force of Loyalists and Canadians on the west bank of the river, and a Loyalist post at Wood Creek. A cordon of Indians was deployed between these last two posts. On the 5th he learned that a relief force of 800 Militia under Major-General Nicholas Herkimer was 10 miles away, and he dispatched a force under the Mohawk Chief Joseph Brant to ambush them at Oriskany (qv). Herkimer, whose force was successfully prevented from reaching the fort, had sent a message to Gansevoort to ask for supporting action on his arrival. This message did not arrive until between 10 and 11am on 6 August, when the action at Oriskany was already under way. Gansevoort contented himself with a series of sorties into the depleted camps of the besiegers, taking some booty and sending Lt-Colonel Sir John Johnson flying in his shirt-sleeves. After the failure of Herkimer's force, a three-day truce was agreed between St Leger and Gansevoort, during which the American Commander took the opportunity of sending his second in command, Lt-Colonel Marinus Willett, and a Lieutenant Stockwell to advise General Philip Schuyler of the danger. The Commander-in-Chief dispatched another relief party of 800 men under Major-General Benedict Arnold on the 10th.

St Leger's Indians, already disenchanted by their losses at Oriskany and the attack on their camp, were further weakened in their resolve by the persuasive powers of their friend Hon Yost Schuyler, a mentally defective nephew of Herkimer's, who was sent by Arnold to undermine their support for St Leger. With the continued loss of his Indians, St Leger raised the siege on the 22nd, and retreated to Lake Oneida, which he was in the process of crossing when Arnold appeared.
Result: Arnold left 700 men at Fort Stanwyx, and rejoined the main army with 1,200 men. They were on their way to Saratoga.

FORT TICONDEROGA AND CROWN POINT (New York)   American War of Independence   10 May 1775

Ticonderoga was an isolated fort on Lake Champlain, containing a large supply of military stores under Captain William Delaplace, who had been warned of his vulnerability by Major-General Sir Thomas Gage, the British Commander-in-Chief Boston. An assault was made on the British garrison by a combined American force under Colonel Benedict Arnold and Major Ethan Allen.
Strength: British 50; Americans 83 (of 600 available).
Aim: The attack was suggested by Major Benedict Arnold (commissioned Colonel for the occasion) to get much needed supplies for the siege of Boston (qv). While he raised 400 men, Major Ethan Allen had another 200 men ready at Castleton (Vermont). Arnold met Allen on the 9th to claim the command, but Allen's men refused to serve under Arnold, and a joint command was agreed.
Battle: Before dawn on the 10th, 300 men were assembled at Hand's Cove, and with the decision not to wait for the rest, 83 of them were ferried across to the fort. Taken completely by surprise, Lieutenant Jocelyn Feltham emerged from his room, trousers in hand, to find the Americans in the passage outside. After questioning them he sent for Delaplace, and a surrender was agreed. There were no casualties, 2 British officers and 48 men, mostly invalids, being taken prisoner.

Crown Point, a fort some 10 miles north of Fort Ticonderoga, then fell without resistance to Major Seth Warner, 9 men and 10 women and children being taken.
Result: Material captured at these two forts amounted to 78 guns, 6 mortars, 3 howitzers, thousands of cannon balls, and 30,000 flints. The two posts were then held for the Americans by Colonel Benjamin Hinman with 1,400 men.

FORT TICONDEROGA II (New York)   American War of Independence/Burgoyne's Offensive   5 July 1777

This American fort, under the command of Major-General Arthur St Clair, was attacked by the British army under the command of Major-General John Burgoyne.
Strength: Americans 2,500; British 9,500.
Aim: This isolated fort on Lake Champlain had been taken by the Americans in 1775, and strongly held by them since that time. Burgoyne needed to reduce it on his march south towards Albany.
Battle: The Advance Corps under Brigadier-General Simon Fraser left Crown Point 26 June, capturing Mount Hope on 2 July. The rest of the British force arrived on the 3rd, and General Burgoyne occupied Mount Hope in force. Hessian troops under Major-General Friedrich Riedesel were posted on the east side of the lake to attack the American force holding Mount Independence. The 4th was spent constructing a road and moving artillery up to Mount Defiance on the west side of the lake. This move was fatal to the garrison of Fort Ticonderoga, for though at 2,200 yards the guns could not seriously damage the fort itself, they did command the lake and the bridge across it.

On 5 July St Clair decided to evacuate the fort. A heavy bombardment by the American defenders that evening might have warned Burgoyne of their intention, but failed to do so. Five hundred troops left soon after midnight, sailing south to Skenesboro. The rest left at 2am, crossed by the boat bridge, and made for Castleton. Despite a variety of mishaps the escape was successful.

At dawn Burgoyne acted promptly, organising pursuit both by land, under Fraser's command, and by water, under his personal command.
Result: On the 6th Burgoyne caught up with Colonel Pierce Long at Skenesboro, pursuing him to Fort Anne (qv). Fraser caught up with the rearguard of St Clair's column at Hubbardton (qv) where, supported by Riedesel, he won a costly victory.

FORT WASHINGTON (New York)   American War of Independence/New York Campaign   16 November 1776

Fought between the British army under the command of Major-General Sir William Howe, and the American garrison of Fort Washington under Colonel Robert Magaw. The concurrent defence of Harlem Heights (qv), 1½ miles south of the fort, was under Lt-Colonel John Cadwalader.

Strength: British/Hessians 7,000 men; Americans 2,850 (Magaw) + 800 (Cadwalader).

Aim: General George Washington hoped to delay the British advance from New York City by strengthening the defences of this fort and Fort Lee (qv) on the other side of the Hudson River.

Battle: Fort Washington was a crude earthwork on the top of Mount Washington (now Washington Heights). Its defence potential was greatly overrated by both the Americans and the British. After Magaw's refusal to surrender on the 15th, the British prepared a three-pronged attack overnight. Three thousand Hessians under General Baron Wilhelm von Knyphausen were to attack from King's Bridge; Brigadier-General Lord Hugh Percy was to lead 2,000 men up from the south to overcome the Harlem Heights defences; while Brigadier-General Edward Mathew's troops were to cross the Harlem River at midday, followed by Major-General Lord Cornwallis's reserves. An evening visit to the fort by Major-Generals Nathanael Greene and Israel Putnam had reassured General Washington that the men in the garrison were in fine spirits and would give a good account of themselves.

However, assisted by one William Demont, a spy in the American garrison, Howe had dispatched the Hessians up-river overnight, so that by morning, supported by heavy artillery fire, they were able to make their assault where the Washington fortifications were at their weakest. There was heavy hand-to-hand fighting before the defenders were driven back. Meanwhile Lord Percy, supported by Mathew and Cornwallis, and subsequently by Colonel Sterling with two more battalions, drove the defenders back from Harlem Heights in such confusion that 170 prisoners were taken before the remainder could reach the defences of the fort. In the early afternoon Magaw was once more challenged to surrender, and his request for a five-hour parley was refused. The surrender was made at 3pm. British and Hessian casualties were 460 killed or wounded (of whom 300 were Hessians). American casualties were 30 killed and 250 wounded, and in addition 2,820 were captured.

Result: The fall of Fort Washington forced the Americans to abandon Fort Lee on the other side of the river, and to continue their retreat. The advance into New Jersey was now open to General Howe.

FREEMAN'S FARM (New York)   American War of Independence/Burgoyne's Offensive   19 September 1777

Fought between the British army under Major-General John Burgoyne, marching south along the west bank of the Hudson River, and the Americans under Major-General Horatio Gates.

Strength: British/Hessians 2,600 (5,600 available); Americans 3,000 (7,000 available).

Aim: General Burgoyne, short of supplies and plagued by constant desertions, was in doubt whether to retreat or to push on in hope that he could meet up with Lt-General Sir Henry Clinton at Albany. He was inclining to the latter course when he found his way blocked at Bemis Heights (qv) by a large and increasing army under General Gates. He advanced cautiously in an attempt to probe the enemy's strength.

Battle: Burgoyne's army had crossed the Hudson on 13 September and had moved cautiously down the west bank. Six days later a 'reconnaissance in force' revealed General Gates's army strongly established on Bemis Heights. On the 19th Burgoyne moved his army forward in three columns: Brigadier-General Simon Fraser with 2,200 men on the right in a wide sweep to Freeman's Farm; a centre column under Burgoyne himself moving south then west to meet Fraser at the farm; and on the left Major-General Baron Friedrich von Riedesel and Major-General William Phillips, who were to move south along the river road. In broken, wooded terrain, this was a hazardous manoeuvre, with communication between the three columns difficult to maintain.

By 12.30pm Burgoyne had reached Freeman's Farm, where he waited to hear news of Fraser. By this time Riedesel was due east of him and 1½ miles distant. General Gates hesitated to commit his men, but was persuaded by Brigadier-General Benedict Arnold to send Brigadier-General Daniel Morgan and Colonel Henry Dearborn into the attack. At 12.45pm Morgan delivered a surprise volley that hit every officer in the advanced guard around Freeman's Cabin. Burgoyne fired a gun signal to tell the others that he was moving out, then formed up his men along the northern edge of the clearing. Morgan and Dearborn took up positions along the southern edge, supported by seven more regiments from Bemis Heights. For four hours the two sides drove each other back and forth across the clearing and into the woods beyond. Riedesel, hearing the firing, sent 4 guns and a liaison officer, who returned at 5pm with orders from Burgoyne to bring reinforcements and attack the American right, leaving a defensive force on the river road. Riedesel moved out with 500 infantry and 2 guns. Another regiment, that of Brigadier-General Ebenezer Learned, was sent to assist Morgan, but Learned inadvertantly led his men out to Fraser's flank and was lost to the battle. The British and Hessians completed a successful counter-attack as darkness fell. Casualties were British and Hessians 600 killed or wounded; Americans 300 killed or wounded.

Result: Burgoyne had been lucky to achieve a drawn battle. Had Gates been less dilatory he might have used some of the 4,000 men still at his disposal either to drive back Burgoyne or to attack the 800 troops left by Riedesel to guard supplies at the river. Though the position was still indecisive, the need for initiative still lay with Burgoyne, but his ability for effective action was fast declining.

FRENCH ALLIANCE WITH AMERICA   4 May 1778

In the early stages of the American War of Independence France, enraged by Britain's capture of Canada, gave unofficial backing to the Americans, ensuring that they could extricate themselves should the fight for independence fail. Without the supply of French arms, the American successes at Trenton, Princeton, and Bemis Heights (qqv) would have been impossible. However, the defeat of Burgoyne at Saratoga, and the staunch American attack at Germantown (qv) persuaded the French officially to recognise independence, and the American envoys at Paris were so informed on 17 December 1777. By 8 January 1778 the French were ready to ally themselves with the American cause.

In England, Lord North's ministry set itself to head off this disaster. During March and April a number of bills of reconciliation were passed: coercive acts were to be repealed, Parliament pledged not to impose revenue taxes on the colonies, and a Peace Commission under the Earl of Carlisle was appointed to negotiate with Congress and if necessary to suspend all acts since 1763. The Commission arrived in Philadelphia on 6 June, to find that Congress had already rejected its terms, demanding a withdrawal of British forces and recognition of independence. The Commission returned to England on 27 November.

Meanwhile on 4 May two treaties had been ratified between France and America. The first, of amity and commerce, recognised American independence; the second, a Treaty of Alliance in the event of war between France and England. Britain, already informed of this, had withdrawn her Ambassador in Paris. Spain made an offer of mediation, but war broke out on 17 June when Admiral Augustus Keppel, on manoeuvre with 20 ships in the Channel, fired on 2 French frigates.

In 1779 the Franco-Spanish Treaty underlined the importance of naval supremacy. However, in this same year France, with 50,000 troops ready to embark, hesitated to invade Britain, and Admiral Comte d'Estaing's many failures in America–in particular at New York, Newport and Savannah (qqv)–did no service to the cause of independence. It was the arrival of Lt-General Comte de Rochambeau in July 1780 and the support given by Rear-Admiral Comte de Grasse that led to the success of the Yorktown Campaign and the end of British military power in America.

GERMANTOWN (Philadelphia) American War of Independence/Philadelphia Campaign 4 October 1777

Fought between the American army under General George Washington and the British army under Major-General Sir William Howe.

Strength: Americans 11,000; British 9,000.

Aim: Though Washington had lost Philadelphia on 26 September, he still controlled the Delaware River forts (see FORT MERCER and FORT MIFFLIN). Howe had therefore to move supplies by land from Head of Elk and to provide substantial escorts for these movements. Furnished with the knowledge that Howe's army was split between the garrison under Lt-General Lord Cornwallis at Philadelphia and the main body 5 miles away at Germantown, and that at the beginning of October 3,000 of these were away on escort duty, Washington planned an attack of Germantown.

Battle: At 7pm on 3 October the Americans set out from Centre Point, which they had reached two days before, but did not reach Chestnut Hill, still NW of the British position, till dawn on the 4th. Washington's plan was for Major-General John Sullivan to advance along the Shippack Road with Brigadier-General William Alexander in reserve, while Major-General Nathanael Greene led a wide encircling movement against the British right. The Militia were to be deployed on both flanks. At 6am the American advanced guard was driven back on Airy Hill by Captain Allen McLane's Light Horse. At this stage Greene was not yet in position, so Sullivan ordered Brigadier-General Anthony Wayne to cover the left, and two regiments the right. The advance in the morning fog was delayed by Lt-Colonel Thomas Musgrave's 40th Regiment which had occupied Chad House on the British left, and here held up the American advance for a valuable thirty minutes. Greene pushed forward to encircle the British right, but this had now been strengthened, and he was forced to turn south to avoid being cut off himself. Major-General Stephen was now on Wayne's left, and Washington, assuming that all was well on this wing, was about to order a general advance when there was confused firing along Wayne's line. In the fog, Wayne's and Stephen's men had mistaken each other for the enemy, and panic ensued. Within minutes this was under control, but Washington felt it necessary to order a retreat. He was able to withdraw his army in good order without any vigorous pursuit by the British. Cornwallis, appearing with three fresh battalions from Philadelphia, followed Greene for 5 miles, but then returned to base. American casualties were 675 killed or wounded, plus 400 captured, as against British casualties of 540 killed or wounded, plus 14 captured.

Result: Though Washington's plan of attack had been over-ambitious, there was a general feeling on both sides that it had been a near miss. Indeed, this staunch attack of the Americans played some part in persuading the French to give them overt support in the war (see FRENCH ALLIANCE WITH AMERICA). After the battle the British remained in Philadelphia while the Americans withdrew NW to winter quarters in Valley Forge. General Stephen was duly court-martialled for the error which brought about the retreat, and was dismissed from the service.

GREAT BRIDGE (Virginia)   American War of Independence/Virginia Uprising   9 December 1775
Fought between a British force under the Governor of Virginia, John Murray, Earl of Dunmore, and an American force under Colonial William Woodford.

Strength: British 430; Americans 390.

Aim: The British force sought to prevent the Americans from marching on Norfolk.

Battle: Dunmore elected to oppose the advancing American force at Great Bridge, 9 miles from Norfolk, surrounded by swamps and crossing a defile. He fortified one end of the causeway in a virtually impregnable position. Colonel Woodford built a redoubt at the other end of the causeway, where he posted Lieutenant Travis with 90 men, taking the remainder of his force to a hill 400 yards in the rear. Dunmore ordered Captain Fordyce to make a frontal attack across the 40-yard bridge, supported by Captain Samuel Leslie with 230 men. In the first attack Fordyce was driven back, so brought up 2 cannon for the second. The Americans in the redoubt withheld their fire, deceiving Fordyce into thinking the redoubt abandoned. At 50 yards the Americans opened fire, killing Fordyce and driving back the attackers. The supporting force did not advance beyond the bridge. The whole action took 25 minutes, and in it the British had 62 men killed or wounded and lost 2 guns, while 1 American was wounded in the hand.

Result: The Americans continued on their way, and three weeks later Dunmore bombarded the town of Norfolk.

GRENADA   American War of Independence   6 July 1779
On 2 July 1779 a French fleet under Admiral Comte d'Estaing landed a force on the British-held West Indian island of Grenada, the most southerly of the Windward Islands. An English fleet of 21 ships under Admiral John Byron arrived to try to recapture the island. The force clashed with d'Estaing's 25 warships and 10 frigates off Georgetown. Byron was forced to withdraw after 7 of his ships were crippled, 4 of them dismasted, having sustained casualties of 183 men killed and 346 wounded. French casualties numbered 1,200 killed and 1,500 wounded.

   D'Estaing allowed the British to withdraw unmolested, while he himself sailed north to Savannah (qv) two months later.

GUILFORD COURTHOUSE (N Carolina)   American War of Independence/Southern Campaign   15 March 1781
Fought between an American army under Major-General Nathanael Greene and a British army under Lt-General Lord Cornwallis.

Strength: Americans 4,300; British 1,900.

Aim: Despite the British disaster at Cowpens (qv) Cornwallis persisted in his plan of advancing into N Carolina. Greene and Brigadier-General Daniel Morgan reunited their forces, and retreated in front of the British army as far as the river Dan, where Cornwallis was forced to turn back south, this time with Greene in pursuit. Despite his numerical inferiority Cornwallis was bent upon bringing Greene to battle, and when the Americans drew up at Guilford he readily seized the opportunity.

Battle: As at Cowpens the Americans drew up in three lines, though this time the lines were too far apart to permit the tactics which had served the 'Old Waggoner' so well at the earlier battle. The front line consisted of the weakest force, the Militia, under Brigadier-Generals John Butler and Pinketham Eaton. These stood behind a rail fence, their flanks strengthened by infantry troops and riflemen. Line two, drawn up in the woods, consisted of 1,200 more Militia under Brigadier-Generals Edward Stevens and Robert Lawson. The third line, 550 yards to the rear, was commanded by Brigadier-Generals Otho Williams and Isaac Huger. There was no reserve.

At 7.15am, after a 12-mile march, Cornwallis's advanced guard under Lt-Colonel Banastre Tarleton clashed with a force commanded by Brigadier-General William Campbell and Lt-Colonel Henry Lee, an engagement in which Tarleton distinguished himself with great courage despite a seriously injured right hand. Cornwallis then drew up his ten units to attack, leading on the right where the ground was more favourable, keeping in reserve Tarleton's dragoons, some Hessians, and Guards under Brigadier-General Charles O'Hara. At 2pm, after an ineffectual artillery exchange, the British advanced. The American front line delivered two volleys and fled. The second line held better, encouraged by a counter-attack by Colonel William Washington, but on the left Lawson was wounded and the line began to give. The first attack on the third line, led by Colonel James Webster, was driven back by accurate fire followed by a bayonet-charge. At this point Greene might have taken the initiative, but decided not to risk the loss of his army. On the British right Lt-Colonel Stuart then made a final attack, driving back the Americans under Washington and Captain Robert Kirkwood after some fierce fighting, and Greene ordered a general retreat. The time was 3.30pm. Greene retired for 3 miles to wait for stragglers, then moved his army to the Speedwell Iron Works at Troublesome Creek. Cornwallis stayed at Guilford until the 18th, then drew back to Wilmington. Casualties sustained by the Americans were 78 killed and 183 wounded; and by the British, 532 killed or wounded.

Result: In a war of attrition such an expensive victory was a luxury Cornwallis could not afford. The British army was now no more than seven months from final surrender. On being chided about his defeats Greene is supposed to have answered: 'As long as I keep losing battles we will win the war.'

HAMPTON (SE Virginia)   American War of Independence/Virginia Uprising   24–5 October 1775

The Governor of Virginia, John Murray, Earl of Dunmore, sent Captain John Squire with 6 tenders into Hampton Creek, from which he bombarded the town and landed a party to set fire to it. This party was driven back by riflemen. On 25 October Colonel William Woodford arrived with 100 Militiamen, and prepared to defend the town against a second attack. At sunrise the British opened fire and moved in, but accurate fire from Woodford's men forced a speedy withdrawal. Two sloops were beached and captured, 5 ships were sunk, and 1 captured with 7 sailors on board. There were no American casualties.

This was one of a number of follies for which the Governor was responsible, and which ensured the support of Virginia for the cause of independence.

HANGING ROCK (S Carolina)   American War of Independence/Camden Campaign   6 August 1780

Fought between a British/Loyalist force under Colonels Thomas Brown and Morgan Bryan and Major Carden, and a force of Partisans under Major William Davie.

Aim: The attack on this Camden outpost formed part of the pattern of harassment by the Partisans against the British forces in S Carolina. It followed immediately upon Brigadier-General Thomas Sumter's unsuccessful attack on Rocky Mount (qv).

Battle: Arriving on 5 August, Davie first attacked Bryan's Loyalists who were lodged in a farmhouse, capturing 60 horses and 100 rifles and muskets. The next day Bryan was joined by Sumter's Partisans from Rocky Mount. Sumter immediately attacked in three columns, driving Bryan's men back towards the centre. Carden attempted a counter-attack on the right, which was defeated by accurate fire from the Partisans. At this point Carden seems to have lost his nerve, and he resigned his command to Captain Rousselet. Forty mounted infantry of the British Legion joined in, to be driven back by Davie. While Sumter's men plundered the camp, Carden pulled himself together and formed his men into a square which, with the support of 2 guns, held out for the remainder of the engagement. The British had 190 killed or wounded, while Partisan casualties numbered 50 killed or wounded.

Result: Although tactically indecisive, this was another costly engagement for the British (see also WILLIAMSON'S PLANTATION and WATEREE FERRY).

HARLEM HEIGHTS (New York) American War of Independence/New York Campaign 16 September 1776
This was a heavy skirmish following immediately upon the successful British action at Kip's Bay (qv). After the British advance on New York, Washington had formed a three-line defence on the Harlem Heights. The British had established a line from Horn's Hook to Bloomingdale (now East 90th Street).
Strength: The American reconnaissance party under Lt-Colonel Thomas Knowlton contained 150 Rangers. These were later reinforced by 150 men under Lt-Colonel Archibald Crary. The British force consisted of 2 infantry battalions and some men of the Black Watch led by Brigadier-General Alexander Leslie.
Aim: The British concern was to drive Washington from the vicinity of New York. The American intention was to prevent for as long as possible any further advance by the British.
Battle: By the evening of 15 September the British outposts had reached three-quarters of a mile north of the established line (approx the present East 105th Street.) On the morning of 16 September an American reconnaissance party made contact with the British advanced troops. The British attacked Crary's force while 230 men led by Knowlton and Major Andrew Leitch attempted to encircle them from the right flank. The British withdrew, to re-form 200 yards back. Knowlton and Leitch were both killed, but by 2pm the British were back where they had started, this time reinforced to 5,000 men. Washington withdrew his force to avoid a general engagement. British casualties were 14 killed and 150 wounded. American casualties were 30 killed, and 100 wounded or missing.
Result: This engagement forced Major-General Sir William Howe to spend four weeks fortifying New York City against a possible attack from the north.

HAW RIVER (N Carolina) American War of Independence/Southern Campaign 25 February 1781
Fought between a Loyalist force under Colonel John Pyle and the Patriots under Brigadier-General Andrew Pickens and Colonel Henry Lee.
Aim: After the ineffectual pursuit of Major-General Nathanael Greene's army through N Carolina to the Dan River, Lt-General Lord Cornwallis was forced to retire once more to S Carolina, fighting a major battle at Guilford Courthouse (qv) on the way. On 18 February Greene sent Pickens and Lee across the Dan in advance of his army to break up a Loyalist uprising in the north.
Battle: Hearing that several hundred Loyalists were marching to join the British at Hillsboro, Lee waited for them at Haw River with Pickens's force hidden in nearby woods. On the arrival of Pyle with his 300 Loyalists Lee, whose men wore a uniform similar to that of the British Legion, posed successfully as Lt-Colonel Banastre Tarleton, asking Pyle to pull his troops to the side of the road to let his fatigued men through. Lee passed along the line of Loyalists at the head of his column, all of whom had their sabres drawn. He was in the act of shaking hands with Pyle when the Loyalist left observed Pickens's force and opened fire. In the mêlée that followed 90 Loyalists were killed and the rest wounded. Lee and Pickens suffered no losses.
Result: At the Battle of Guilford Courthouse three weeks later Cornwallis was without Loyalist support.

HOBKIRK'S HILL (Camden, S Carolina) American War of Independence/Southern Campaign 25 April 1781
An American army under Major-General Nathanael Greene, threatening Camden, was brought to battle by a British force under Lt-Colonel Lord Rawdon.
Strength: Americans 1,550; British 800.
Aim: During his excursion into N Carolina Lt-General Lord Cornwallis left the defence of S Carolina to Rawdon, who was based in Camden. With Cornwallis's retreat to Wilmington after Guilford Courthouse (qv), Greene was once more in a position to take the initiative and he moved on Camden.
Battle: After Guilford Courthouse Greene had sent Lt-Colonel Henry Lee (Light Horse Harry) and Brigadier-General Francis Marion (the Swamp Fox) to operate to the east, and Rawdon had despatched Colonel John Watson to intercept Marion. Reaching Camden at the end of his 140-mile march Greene learned, on 20 April, that Rawdon was prepared for him, and retired to Hobkirk's Hill to await reinforcements and supplies. After some desultory manoeuvring to prevent Watson from rejoining Rawdon (the job had already been done by Lee and Marion) Greene was back in position on the hill by the 24th, and Rawdon decided to attack.
    Greene drew up his main body on the hill with Captain Robert Kirkwood's crack regiment to the SE, covered by 2 outposts under Captains Perry Benson and Simon Morgan. He kept the dragoons and the N

Carolina Militia in reserve. Rawdon approached from the SE on the morning of the 25th. Observing that the British columns presented a relatively narrow front, Greene attempted a double-flanking movement. The British force was momentarily checked by the fire from 3 guns opening up at close range, but as soon as the American line advanced Rawdon moved up his second line to extend the first. Greene was now in danger himself of being outflanked. The American line was nevertheless making headway when Captain John Gunby's Regiment, on the left, collapsed. Their commander withdrew and tried to re-form them, but the British right seized their chance and broke the whole American left. Had the 5th Virginia Regiment not held in the right centre Greene's army might well have been annihilated. A general retreat was followed by a gallant, and successful, attempt to save the 3 guns. On the next day the American army moved back to Rugeley's Mill, taking with them their artillery and supply train. American casualties numbered 248 wounded and 18 killed. British casualties were 220 wounded and 38 killed.
Result: Despite his tactical victory, Rawdon was forced to evacuate Camden and to retreat towards Charleston.

HUBBARDTON (New York)   American War of Independence/Burgoyne's Offensive   7 July 1777
Fought between an American force under Colonel Seth Warner and a British force under Brigadier-General Simon Fraser.
Strength: Americans 1,000; British 750 (later supported by Riedesel's force).
Aim: After the fall of Fort Ticonderoga (qv), Major-General Arthur St Clair had led his troops on to Castleton, leaving Warner with 1,000 men (including Colonel Turbott Francis's and Colonel Nathan Hales's Regiments) to await the rearguard, then to rejoin the main body. Fraser had been sent on in advance of Major-General Friedrich von Riedesel's pursuing force of Hessians, and had halted 3 miles short of Colonel Warner's camp. Advised of this by his Indian scouts, Fraser decided to attack at dawn.
Battle: At 4.30am the attack was opened by a troop of Loyalists who routed Hales's Regiment. Fraser then attacked Warner and Francis. The first volley killed 21 British attackers, including Major Grant. The Americans then formed a 1,000-yard battle-line, with the left flank on what is now Zion Hill. Fraser strengthened his right, to attempt an outflanking movement, but the American left swivelled round as the British advanced. Meanwhile Francis pushed back the British left flank, which was saved by the arrival of Riedesel. He immediately attacked the American right, ordered his Grenadiers to try to outflank them, and sent an urgent message for his main troops to join him as quickly as possible. Colonel Francis was killed, and his regiment pulled back. At this moment Warner's Vermont Regiment was facing a fierce bayonet-attack. Warner's last order to his men was 'Scatter, and meet me at Manchester'.

This fierce two-hour action produced heavy casualties, in proportion to the forces involved. The Americans had 80 men killed or wounded, plus 320 captured. The British and Hessians sustained 35 killed and 150 wounded.
Result: Although this must be accounted a British victory, it was a costly one which did not bring nearer to fulfilment the larger purpose of cutting off St Clair's retreating troops. More immediately, the remainder of the Vermont Regiment did in fact meet Warner at Manchester.

JAMESTOWN FORD (Green Spring, Virginia)   American War of Independence/Virginia Campaign   6 July 1781
Fought between the British under Lt-General Lord Cornwallis and the Americans under Major-General Marquis de Lafayette.
Strength: British 7,000; Americans 900.
Aim: Cornwallis, under instructions to dispatch reinforcements to New York, decided against holding Williamsburg and prepared to cross the James River. Lafayette, following him cautiously, conceived a hope that he might destroy the British army as it crossed the river.
Battle: Cornwallis, aware that he was being shadowed by an American force, tricked Lafayette into believing that his main force had crossed the river by the afternoon of 6 July, leaving only the rearguard. In reality only Lt-Colonel John Simcoe's Rangers had crossed with the baggage, leaving the 7,000-strong British army concealed in woods 1 mile along the Williamsburg-Jamestown road. Towards these Brigadier-General Anthony Wayne's advanced guard of 500 men gradually drove Lt-Colonel Banastre Tarleton's outposts. By 5pm reinforcements arrived for the Americans, as Wayne closed in on the British position. Lafayette, by now suspicious of a trap, held back some reserve troops, leaving Wayne with 900 men and 3 guns. Making a personal reconnaissance from the river-bank, Lafayette suddenly realised the truth of the position and sent, too late, a warning to Wayne. Finding himself faced by the British army,

Wayne attacked, charged through grape-shot and musket-fire, and held the British for fifteen minutes before retreating in fair order to Green Spring. From here he was able to withdraw his force under cover of darkness. The British had 75 killed or wounded, and the Americans 130 killed or wounded.

Result: Cornwallis estimated that another half-hour of light would have enabled him to annihilate the whole American force. The failure of Lafayette's rash plan enabled the British army to pursue its way to its fatal stand at Yorktown (qv).

KETTLE CREEK (Georgia)   American War of Independence/Southern Campaign   14 February 1779
Fought between an American force under Colonel Andrew Pickens and a force of Loyalists under Colonel Boyd.

Strength: Patriots 300; Loyalists 700.

Aim: After the fall of Savannah (qv) Lt-Colonel Archibald Campbell dispatched Lt-Colonel John Hamilton with 200 mounted Loyalists to raise recruits from the back country of Georgia. Colonel Boyd, with a force of Loyalists from N Carolina, attempted to join Hamilton, raising his numbers to some 700 on the way. Patriot forces from Major-General Benjamin Lincoln's army were concerned to prevent this move.

Battle: The battle itself was preceded by much coming and going on either side of the Savannah River. Hamilton and Colonel McGirth drove back a Patriot force under Colonel John Dooley, then retired to Fort Carr. Dooley was joined by Colonel Pickens, who took command of the combined force of some 350 men, crossing the river at Cowen's Ferry on 10 February. As Colonel Boyd's force approached, Pickens set off in pursuit of this new target, recrossing the river near Fort Charlotte. Learning of this approach, Boyd tried to cross at Cherokee Ford, but was prevented by an outpost of 8 men and 2 guns. He moved 5 miles up-stream and crossed on rafts, continuing his march towards Fort Augusta. Pickens followed him on the Georgia side. On the morning of 13 February Boyd crossed the Broad River and camped near Kettle Creek. On the following morning, with their horses grazing and their men killing cattle, the Loyalists were taken by surprise by an attack by the Patriot force with Pickens commanding in the centre, Dooley on the right, and Colonel Elijah Clarke on the left. The Loyalists' pickets fired and fell back on their camp. Boyd managed to pull his troops together, and kept up the fight for 60 minutes, after which they were routed. Boyd himself was mortally wounded, and died on the same night. The Patriots had 30 men killed or wounded, the Loyalists 40 killed or wounded, plus 70 captured–of whom 5 were hanged.

Result: This put an end to Loyalist rallying in the South for some time, and gave encouragement to the Patriots. Some 300 of Boyd's force, however, succeeded in reaching Fort Augusta.

KING'S MOUNTAIN (S Carolina)   American War of Independence   7 October 1780
Fought between a Loyalist force under Major Patrick Ferguson and a mixed force of Partisans under the overall command of Colonel William Campbell.

Strength: Loyalists 1,100 (of whom 200 were on a foraging expedition); Partisans 900 (of 1,800 assembled at Cowpens).

Aim: After the fall of Charleston (qv) the British Commander, Lt-General Sir Henry Clinton, appointed Major Ferguson Inspector of Militia in the Southern Provinces, and he was successful in raising some 4,000 Loyalist Militia in the area around Fort Ninety-Six. On the other side Brigadier-General Thomas Sumter and others were beginning their Partisan operations, and between May and October a number of raids took place in the area (see WILLIAMSON'S PLANTATION, ROCKY MOUNT, HANGING ROCK and WATEREE FERRY). Major-General Horatio Gates's defeat at Camden (qv) prompted the Patriots to drop their plan of attacking Fort Ninety-Six and to retreat, pursued by Ferguson, who was then recalled to Camden where he was told of Lt-General Lord Cornwallis's projected campaign in N Carolina. Ferguson then undertook to push forward to Gilbert Town, while Cornwallis, on 7 September, took Charlotte, where he awaited Ferguson's return.

At the same moment that Ferguson was announcing optimistically that the rebellion was over in the area, Partisan forces were gathering under Colonels Isaac Shelby, John Sevier and William Campbell. One thousand men from both sides of the Blue Mountains and several hundred S Carolina Partisans met at the end of September and set out for Gilbert town. Major Ferguson, lying in their path, sent for support both to Fort Ninety-Six and to Cornwallis. Unhappily the Ninety-Six garrison was under-strength, and both Cornwallis and Lt-Colonel Banastre Tarleton were ill. On 6 October Ferguson halted at King's Mountain.

Battle: Ferguson took up his position on a rocky ridge with wooded and boulder-strewn slopes. It was a strong position, and his over-confidence led him to be careless over security measures, with the result that Colonel Shelby's force, one of eight advancing upon the ridge, was within a quarter of a mile before it was seen. After this unhappy start, Ferguson compounded his errors by ordering bayonet-attacks each time the enemy mounted the slopes. The Partisans would promptly drop back, thwarting the Loyalist attacks, and gradually wearing them down. In due course the Loyalists were pushed back, and finally surrounded in their camp at the east end of the ridge. Ferguson was killed, and Captain Abraham de Peyster, taking over command, surrendered. The Partisan leaders had difficulty in halting the firing, and another 'massacre' legend was born, this time directed against the Patriots. The Loyalists had 157 killed (163 too badly wounded to be moved) and 698 men captured. The Partisans had 90 men killed or wounded.

Result: The immediate result of this shattering defeat was to force Cornwallis to postpone his offensive for three months. It did much too, to encourage the Partisan forces. It was a remarkable example of the ability of highly individualist Partisan officers to work together when the need arose. Lt-General Sir Henry Clinton was later to claim this defeat as 'the first link in a chain of evils . . .' which 'at last ended in the loss of America'.

KIP'S BAY (New York)   American War of Independence/New York Campaign   15 September 1776
Fought between the Americans under General George Washington and the British under Major-General Sir William Howe.

Aim: Washington, under orders to defend New York City, had drawn up his forces in three groups under Major-Generals Israel Putnam, William Heath and Nathanael Greene. General Howe's aim was (a) to capture New York City, and (b) to destroy Washington's army.

Battle: On the morning of 15 September 5 British warships stood 200 yards off-shore. At 10am transports carrying 4,000 troops pulled out of Newton Creek, Long Island. At 11am the American defences were bombarded for over an hour by 70 cannon. At 1pm the troops landed on both sides of the bay. The defenders fled without firing a shot.

General Putnam, recognising that the British could not be contained in their bridgehead, galloped south to bring troops and artillery out of New York City. Leading them north along the Post road (now Lexington Avenue) he succeeded in evading the British and escaping with his men from the city. Meanwhile Major-General Henry Clinton had landed with 4,000 men and had occupied Onclenberg (now Murray) Hill, where he awaited reinforcements. He was joined by Howe at 2pm, and by 5pm all the troops had landed. They were deployed south and west to the Hudson River, and NW to Harlem Heights (qv).

Result: Howe had successfully occupied New York City without a fight, but for the second time had allowed Washington to withdraw his army more or less intact.

LENUD'S FERRY or LANNEAU'S FERRY (S Carolina)   American War of Independence/ Charleston Expedition   6 May 1780
Fought between Lt-Colonel Banastre Tarleton's British Legion and American forces under Colonel Anthony White and Colonel Abraham Buford.

Strength: British 150 (dragoons of the British Legion); Americans 350 (Buford) + mixed force (White).

Aim: After the defeat at Monck's Corner (qv) the American survivors, reinforced by more cavalry, made to join up with Colonel Buford's force at Lenud's Ferry. Tarleton was concerned to prevent this combination.

Battle: On 5 May Colonel White, crossing the Santee River at Dupuis' Ferry, captured an officer and 17 of Tarleton's men. In an effort to evade pursuit, Tarleton circled SE towards Colonel White's force at Lenud's Ferry. Then Tarleton, acting on information from a Loyalist, took the two forces completely by surprise as they met at the ferry. At 3pm on the 6th Tarleton attacked at the moment of White's arrival, with Buford's men standing around the ferry, and promptly dispersed the whole American force. The British sustained no casualties, while 40 Americans were killed or wounded, and 65 captured.

Result: Some of the American force, including Colonel White, escaped by swimming the river. Tarleton returned to the British army–which was besieging Charleston (qv)–with his prisoners, all the horses of White's cavalry, and an enhanced reputation.

LES SAINTES (BATTLE OF THE SAINTS) (between Guadeloupe and Dominica, West Indies) American War of Independence   12 April 1782
A combined Franco-Spanish expeditionary force of 150 vessels with a fleet commanded by Admiral Comte de Grasse was intercepted by a British fleet under Admiral George Rodney and brought to battle.

Strength: French 35 ships of the line; British 36 ships of the line + 5 frigates.

Aim: The Franco-Spanish allies planned an attack on Jamaica, but the British had been keeping a close watch on the French at Port Royal, Martinique.

Battle: The British frigates watching the French at Fort Royal, Martinique, reported that they had sailed on 8 April. Rodney gave chase immediately. Next morning the fleets met in action, in which de Grasse missed a chance of defeating Rear-Admiral Sir Samuel Hood's squadron which had become separated from the British main fleet. Following three days of pursuit the British at last caught up with the French on 12 April. The opposing fleets slowly passed by in different but parallel directions, firing at each other. De Grasse's flagship was becalmed and the French line of battle became ragged and gaps began to open. Rodney in his flagship *Formidable* seized his opportunity and, by a series of brilliant manoeuvres, led the 5 ships astern of him to pierce the enemy line in two places with Hood and his 12 ships following behind. The French line was cut in three places and was never to re-form. The immediate result was that the British could bring to bear superior concentrations on individual French ships in turn and their cannonades, which played a decisive part in the short-range actions, quickly dismasted and disabled 6 Frenchmen.

Twenty-five of the French got away, but De Grasse failed to re-form his fleet and was forced to surrender his flagship *Ville de Paris* to Hood. Rodney captured 5 more French ships. The remnants of the French fleet, many of them damaged, scattered and managed to find shelter in Haiti. This victory put paid to the French plan to invade Jamaica. De Grasse had suffered a devastating defeat at the hands of Rodney. The French had 6 ships captured plus 3 ships put out of action owing to collisions among the fleet. The British lost no ships.

Result: Rodney put into Jamaica, and the Battle of the Saints ended the fighting in the western hemisphere. The British command of the seas off America was restored, but too late to affect the outcome of the American Revolution. Rodney was later criticised in England for not pursuing the French and taking more ships.

LEXINGTON AND CONCORD (Massachusetts)   American War of Independence   19 April 1775

These were the opening engagements of the war between the British and the Americans.

Strength: The British force of 800 men was led by Lt-Colonel Francis Smith, though the skirmish at Lexington involved only the six companies of light infantry, some 200 men, in the van, led by Major John Pitcairn. At Concord, Colonel James Barrett lined up 150 men at the North Bridge. During the British withdrawal, Smith's force was augmented by another 1,400 at Lexington, while the American snipers numbered in all some 3,765 men.

Aim: Major-General Thomas Gage, British Commander-in-Chief Boston, under pressure to take decisive action against the rebellious Americans, decided on 14 April to seize and destroy the military supplies at the Concord depot, and to take prisoner any delegates to the Provincial Congress meeting there. The first engagement of the war took place at Lexington, 6 miles from the British objective. Here the American leaders Samuel Adams and John Hancock had been staying on their way from Concord to Philadelphia, where the Continental Congress was due to take place in May. Warned by Paul Revere, they had left precipitately on the night of the 18th.

Battle: Apprised of the British advance by Paul Revere and Will Dawes, Captain Parker had drawn up his 130 minutemen at midnight, dismissing them with the order to reassemble on the beat of a drum. At dawn Pitcairn reached Lexington and the minutemen were recalled. Such was the shortage of arms that only 70 men assembled on the Green, the rest running to the supply depot at the meeting-house. These 70 were faced by the 200 British regulars drawn up in three lines. Both sides were under clear instructions not to fire unless the order were given. As the British advanced to surround and disarm the Americans, Parker withdrew his men, and a shot was fired–by whom, no one knows. There was sporadic firing from both sides, and 8 Americans were killed and 10 wounded. One British soldier was wounded in the leg, and Pitcairn's horse suffered 2 wounds.

Result: On the arrival of the rest of the British force the march to Concord was resumed. But the Americans gained a psychological advantage by the spreading of the story of a wanton and brutal attack by the British on peaceful American citizens.

Concord: Neither Revere nor Dawes was successful in reaching Concord, but Dr Prescott arrived with the news of the British approach at 2am on 19 April. Colonel James Barrett, in command of the Militia, returned from the disposing of supplies on his farm to draw up his 150 men on a ridge behind the North Bridge against the British arrival at 7am. While Captain Walter Laurie advanced with three companies to the North Ridge, Barrett's farm and Concord were searched for hidden supplies. Here 'the embattled farmers fired the shot heard round the world'. Laurie's men were driven back with small losses, but reinforcements were brought up by Colonel Smith, and the engagement was broken off. At noon the British began the return march to Boston.

From Meriam's Corner, 1 mile out of Concord, the British were harassed by snipers' fire. They tried unsuccessfully to rally at Fiske's Hill, where Pitcairn lost his horse and pistols, and Smith was wounded. Reinforced at Lexington by Brigadier-General Lord Hugh Percy with 1,400 men and 2 6-pound cannon, the British made their way back to Boston, attacked relentlessly until they reached the protection of the naval guns at Charlestown Neck.

Of the total of 3,765 Americans involved in the whole engagement, 50 were killed and 40 wounded; 5 were missing. British casualties totalled 250 men killed or wounded (including 19 officers), plus 26 missing. *Result:* The British had gained their principal immediate objective, though narrowly missing Adams and Hancock. However, the engagement had proved the efficacy of irregular fighters with knowledge of the terrain. Within a week of Concord, the siege of Boston (qv) had begun.

LONG ISLAND (New York)   American War of Independence/New York Campaign   27 August 1776

This was the battle preliminary to the capture of New York City by the British under Major-General Sir William Howe. The Americans were commanded by Major-General Israel Putnam.
Strength: British 20,000, with another 2,000 joining during the battle. There were 5,000 under Colonel Grant on the left flank, 5,000 Hessians under General Philip von Heister in the centre, and 10,000 under Howe, Major-General Henry Clinton, and Major-General Lord Cornwallis on the right flank; Americans 10,000, of whom 3,500 were deployed behind the Heights of Guian, the remainder manning the Brooklyn Defences.
Aim: The British had collected a large army on Staten Island, supported by a fleet under the command of Admiral Lord Howe. This was the first engagement in the British advance upon New York.
Battle: On 22 August an American outpost on Long Island had reported British preparations to cross from Staten Island. During the next few days the crossing was effected, and the British moved north towards the Brooklyn Defences, to be held up by a ridge of high land, the Guian Heights, broken by four passes, but strongly held by the Americans. Howe's plan, which was to draw the American defenders by an attack on the left, enabling his main force to outflank them on the right, was fully successful. At 9am 2 signal cannon were fired, and the Hessians advanced in the centre, followed shortly afterwards by Grant on the left. Colonel Grant met stiff opposition (he himself was killed during the battle) but, reinforced by another 2,000 men from Staten Island, he was successful in drawing the American reserves to his flank. Howe was thus able to move his large force, supported by 28 guns, round behind the American left flank. In the centre the Americans were routed and Major-General John Sullivan was captured. Brigadier-General William Alexander fought a delaying action to protect the Americans' escape route before surrendering to General Heister. Some 2,000 Americans safely retreated to the Brooklyn Defences. British casualties were 380 killed or wounded, while the Americans had 1,400 men killed, wounded, or captured. *Result:* This success enabled General Howe to undertake the siege of the Brooklyn Heights, which were evacuated on 29/30 August.

MACHIAS BAY (Maine)   American War of Independence   11–12 June 1775

This was the first naval engagement of the war. The British schooner *Margaretta* (4), commanded by Midshipman James Moore, and 2 sloops, *Polly* and *Unity*, entered Machias Bay on 11 June to collect lumber for the garrison at Boston (qv). A plan to capture the crews in church on Sunday the 11th failed, Moore and his fellow-officers escaping and returning to their ships. They were pursued by Volunteers under Jeremiah O'Brien and Joseph Wheaton, and *Unity* was captured the same day, *Margaretta* on the following day. There were 7 casualties on each side, including Moore. O'Brien took command of *Unity*, to which he transferred the schooner's guns, renaming her *Machias Liberty*.

MARTINIQUE (West Indies)   American War of Independence   17 April 1780

Fought between a British fleet commanded by Admiral George Rodney and a French fleet by Admiral Comte de Guichen.
Strength: British 21 ships; French 23 ships + 5 frigates + 3,000 troop convoy.
Aim: Admiral de Guichen had sailed from Port Royal, Martinique, with the intention of attacking Barbados. On 16 April 1780 Rodney sighted the French fleet and, given the opportunity on the following day, planned to attack their rear and centre.

The fleets were almost equal in number, but the French were of superior design with better sailing qualities, all freshly out of their home base, thoroughly refitted and with clean bottoms. Furthermore, the French had a vastly better system of signalling, which was to have an important bearing on the result of the engagement.

Battle: Rodney signalled at 11.50am, 17 April 1780, for each of his ships to bear down on a vessel opposite it in the enemy line. Rodney's captains completely misinterpreted the signal. Instead of attacking the enemy ship directly opposite them, they carried on to reach station opposite their numerical opponents in order (i.e. the sixth ship in line sailing on until it reached the sixth ship in the French line), therefore committing the fleet to a disjointed attack instead of the concentration which Rodney had planned. After an indecisive action, during which Rodney's flagship *Sandwich*, after sailing practically unsupported through the French line, was severely damaged, both fleets withdrew. The British sustained casualties of 120 killed and 354 wounded, the French having 222 killed and 537 wounded.

Result: Both sides claimed victory, but de Guichen had to abandon his attack on Barbados and retreat to his base at Basselese in Guadeloupe Island. There was little doubt that the French Admiral had fought well and that his captains had given him admirable support. Rodney, on the other hand, had been badly let down. After penning a furious dispatch he spent the next few months teaching his naval captains 'what they had not been before, officers'.

MONCK'S CORNER (S Carolina)   American War of Independence/Charleston Expedition   14 April 1780

Fought between Lt-Colonel Banastre Tarleton and his British Legion and the garrison of an American supply depot commanded by Brigadier-General Isaac Huger.

Aim: During the siege of Charleston (qv) this important depot stood on the American lines of communication. Lt-General Sir Henry Clinton, investing Charleston, sent Tarleton's Legion to eradicate it.

Battle: Tarleton set out for Monck's Corner, 30 miles north of Charleston, on 13 April. After capturing a messenger, from whom he learned the details of Huger's dispositions, he attacked at 3am on the 14th, taking the Americans completely by surprise. He promptly routed the 300 cavalry in front of Biggins' Bridge and scattered the Militia guard. British casualties amounted to 3 men and 5 horses killed or wounded. The Americans had 20 killed or wounded, and 67 captured. In addition to their prisoners the British took 42 loaded wagons, 102 wagon horses and 83 dragoon horses.

Result: This raid, comparatively small in itself (the Charleston siege which it supported involved some 17,000 men) was of great importance to the British Commander-in-Chief, cutting off as it did valuable supplies, communications, and a possible line of retreat for the American garrison. Its speed and skill were typical of Bloody Ban's (Tarleton's) tactics, on which Lt-General Lord Cornwallis relied throughout his campaign (see LENUD'S FERRY and WAXHAWS).

MONMOUTH (New Jersey)   American War of Independence/Clinton's Retreat from Philadelphia   16 June–5 July 1778

Fought by a British force under the command of Lt-General Lord Cornwallis and the Americans under Major-General Charles Lee.

Aim: The British strategy in 1778 included the withdrawal of Lt-General Sir Henry Clinton's army of 10,000 men from Philadelphia to New York. By sea this would have necessitated a shuttle service which would be dangerously threatened by the French. Clinton therefore undertook the march through New Jersey as the less hazardous course. By the end of May, General George Washington was aware that preparations were being made in Philadelphia for some enterprise, and recognised that this might involve such a march. He decided to keep his army at Valley Forge until the British intentions became clearer.

Between 16 and 18 June Clinton moved his army out of Philadelphia and across the Delaware. The main body of troops marched to Haddonfield, while the heavy equipment, the invalids, and 3,000 Loyalists were shipped down-river. On 21 June Washington moved his 13,500-strong army to Coryell's Ferry. Here, correctly assuming that Clinton would move north, he sent orders to the Militia to hamper the march as far as possible. Major-General Philemon Dickinson was sent to watch the British right flank, and Major-General Benedict Arnold was instructed to send a force to harass the British rear. By 23 June Washington was at Hopewell, 7 miles NE of Princeton. At a council of war the following day Major-General Charles Lee was opposed to a major engagement with the British, on the grounds that this was an unnecessary hazard now that the French Alliance (qv) had assured the ultimate success of the American cause. Major-

Generals Nathanael Greene, Baron Friedrich Wilhelm von Steuben, and Marquis de Lafayette favoured more positive action. The decision was to avoid a full-scale battle, but to send 1,500 troops 'to act as occasion may serve, on the enemy's left flank and rear'. Colonel Charles Scott was in command of this force.

When Washington realised that Clinton was moving on Monmouth, he decided to increase this force to 5,000 with General Lafayette in command. Initially General Lee agreed to this plan, but later claimed his right as second in command to lead such a substantial force, and Washington sent him on to take over command from Lafayette, with orders to attack as soon as the British left Monmouth.

Battle: In the early morning of 28 June Washington was 8 miles to the west of Monmouth, with Lee's advanced guard 5 miles from the town. At 4am Major-General Baron Wilhelm von Knyphausen set out for Middletown with the baggage train. At 6am Lee belatedly sent out a force of 600 men and 4 guns under Colonel William Grayson to observe the enemy. Lee himself set out an hour later. Meanwhile Dickinson had been driven back in a skirmish, but the position was restored by the arrival of Grayson. By 8am Cornwallis had left Monmouth with the main body of the British army, leaving a rearguard of 1,500 men in the town. At 10am Lee launched an attack to isolate this detachment, but this foundered in part as a result of Lee's lack of planning and in part as a result of a misunderstood change of position by Lafayette which led to a retreat by the other officers. Clinton, hearing this engagement, covered his northern flank with some light dragoons from Knyphausen's Division, and turned back to face Lee. Lee's force, however, was in full retreat by this time, and angry words were exchanged between the two generals when Washington came to meet him. Washington then took over Lee's command and organised a line to hold the British while he established a defensive position behind the West Ravine. Here, under advice from Lt-Colonel David Rhea, who was familiar with the local topography, he made use of the high ground to his left with thick woods behind, and established an artillery post on Comb's Hill. Brigadier-General Anthony Wayne was placed in advance of the American centre, with Nathanael Greene on the right, and Major-General William Alexander on the left. For an hour the British attacked the American left, but then they were finally driven back. A massive attack on Greene's flank was repulsed, largely by flanking fire from Comb's Hill. Three British attacks in the centre were held by accurate fire. By 5pm only the artillery was firing, and a counter-attack ordered by Washington failed even to start, so exhausted were his men in the appalling heat. British casualties numbered 360 killed or wounded, of whom 60 died from sunstroke; by 6 July 600 deserters arrived back at Philadelphia. American casualties totalled 250 killed or wounded.

Result: Lee's deplorable handling of the engagement at Monmouth brought about his disgrace. He was found guilty by a court-martial on three counts: disobedience to an order in not attacking on 28 June; misbehaviour in the face of the enemy in that he ordered a 'shameful retreat'; and disrespect for his Commander-in-Chief in that he wrote two offensive letters to Washington after the battle. He was suspended from his command for twelve months. This failure enabled Clinton to continue his march to New York, where he arrived on 5 July.

MONTREAL (Quebec, Canada)   American War of Independence/Canadian Campaign   25 September–13 November 1775

During the American advance into Canada Brigadier-General Richard Montgomery invested St John's (qv), sending Colonel Ethan Allen on a recruiting expedition which was initially so successful that Allen decided to attempt an attack on Montreal. However, with his Canadian recruits steadily defecting, he was forced to return to St John's to link up with Colonel John Brown's force of 200 men.

The plan then was for Allen with his 110 men to cross the St Lawrence below the town, while Brown's 200 crossed above it. On the night of 24 September Allen made the crossing, but Brown was unsuccessful. At daybreak Allen's force was attacked by Major-General Guy Carleton with 35 soldiers and 200 Volunteers. Allen was captured with 40 of his men.

With the fall of St John's on 2 November, Montreal lay open to attack. On the 11th Montgomery landed above the town with a strong force. Carleton, with only 150 regulars and a few Militia, took to ships, but on the 19th his 11 ships surrendered, only Carleton and a few of his officers escaping capture. Carleton then joined the British garrison at Quebec.

Montreal surrendered on 13 November.

MOORE'S CREEK BRIDGE (N Carolina)   American War of Independence   27 February 1776

Fought between Militiamen and Rangers under Colonels Alexander Lillington, John Ashe, and Richard Caswell on the American side, and British regulars and Volunteers under Brigadier-General Donald McDonald and Colonel Donald McCleod.

Strength: Americans 1,000; British 1,780.

Aim: After the formation of the N Carolina Provincial Congress, the ex-Governor Josiah Martin had advised Major-General Sir Henry Clinton that support would be forthcoming if the British were to establish a base in the state. Major-General Sir Thomas Gage therefore sent a force under Brigadier-General Donald McDonald and Colonel McCleod, who raised the Royal Standard at Cross Creek (now Fayetteville) on 5 February 1776. Within a fortnight 1,000 Highland Scots and another 500 Loyalists had joined them. Meanwhile an American force under Colonel James Moore, reinforced by units under Colonels Lillington and Ashe, posed sufficient threat for the British to withdraw to the coast. At Moore's Creek Bridge, near Wilmington, the British found their way barred by Lillington and Ashe, who had been joined by 800 Rangers under Colonel Caswell.

Battle: Late on 26 February the British camped 6 miles to the west of the bridge. Scouts reported that the enemy occupied the west (*sic*) bank, though in fact Caswell had abandoned his earthworks on that bank to join Lillington and Ashe across the river, where between them they deployed 1,000 men to cover the crossing. The bridge had been partially demolished by the removal of planks.

At 1am on the 27th the British force set out, reaching the bridge at dawn. This force, commanded by Colonel McCleod, as the General was ill, consisted of an advanced guard of 80 picked Highlanders under Captain John Campbell, with the main body of 1,400 men commanded by McCleod, and 300 riflemen in the rear. The British advanced guard, deceived by the abandoned earthworks into the belief that the enemy had retired, charged over the bridge, to be shot down at close range. Campbell was killed, and 30 others were either shot or drowned in the river. The Americans then replaced the planks and advanced across the bridge to counter-attack, while a small force under Lieutenant Ezekiel Slocum forded the river to attack the British rear. During the retreat 30 more British were killed, including Colonel McCleod, and 850 including McDonald were taken prisoner. As to casualties, 2 Americans were hit, of whom 1 subsequently died; while 60 British were killed and 850 taken prisoner.

Result: General Clinton was forced to abandon plans for a base in N Carolina and, with the arrival of the fleet from Ireland, advanced on Charleston, S Carolina.

NEW JERSEY RETREAT   American War of Independence   18 November–20 December 1776
After the fall of Forts Washington and Lee (qqv), Major-General Nathanael Greene and General George Washington joined forces and retreated to the Delaware River, pursued by Major-General Lord Cornwallis. After repeated commands from Washington, Major-General Charles Lee crossed the Hudson into New Jersey, but on 13 December was captured by a British patrol. On 11 December Washington had crossed into Pennsylvania, to be followed by Major-General John Sullivan with Lee's troops on the 20th. Congress fled from Philadelphia to Baltimore, conferring almost dictatorial powers on General Washington.

NEWPORT (Rhode Island)   American War of Independence   29 July–31 August 1778
Fought between a British garrison at Newport, Rhode Island, under Major-General Robert Pigot, and a combined French-American force under Major-General John Sullivan and Admiral Comte d'Estaing.

Strength: British 3,000; French/Americans 10,000.

Aim: In December 1776 Newport had been taken by Lt-General Sir Henry Clinton, who had left a garrison under the command of Major-General Pigot. With the arrival of the French fleet under d'Estaing, Sullivan proposed a combined operation against the town. He himself had 1,000 regulars at Providence, and was joined by 6,000 Militia under Lt-Colonel John Hancock.

Battle: The plan was for Sullivan, with supporting columns under Major-General Nathanael Greene and Major-General Marquis de Lafayette, to land his troops at the NE of the island, preparatory to striking south against Newport. Early on 10 August the French were to land on the west and prepare to give supporting fire from off-shore. However, on the 9th Admiral Lord Howe's fleet appeared, and indulged in some light skirmishing with the French until both fleets were dispersed by a storm on the night of the 11th. Howe sailed back to New York and d'Estaing to Boston for repairs.

Lafayette made the return trip to Boston to persuade the French to renew their support. Sullivan continued the siege until the morning of 29 August when, pressed by a three-column British attack, the Americans retreated to Butt's Hill at the NW of the island. Here the British right under Major-General Richard Prescott was halted by Nathanael Greene, and three Hessian assaults under Brigadier-General von Lossberg were driven back to Newport for more artillery, but on the night of the 30th Sullivan retreated with his army to the mainland. He was just in time: on 1 September Sir Henry Clinton arrived

with reinforcements totalling 5,000. British casualties numbered 250 killed or wounded, and American casualties totalled 210 killed, wounded or missing.
Result: Sullivan took his army back to Providence. Lord Howe sailed with Clinton's troops to Boston, but then, deciding against an attack, he returned to New York.

On 11 October 1779 Clinton evacuated Rhode Island to concentrate on his Southern Campaign, sailing from New York on 26 December with 8,000 men to advance on Charleston (qv). On 10 July 1780 the island was taken over by the French army under Lt-General Comte de Rochambeau.

NEW PROVIDENCE (NASSAU) (Bahamas, West Indies)   American War of Independence   3–4 March 1776
Fought between the Americans under Commodore Ezek Hopkins, and the British under the command of the Governor of New Providence (now Nassau), Montfort Browne.
Aim: Commodore Hopkins, in command of a fleet of 14 ships, put to sea in February 1776 with orders to patrol the southern coast 'in such places as you think will most Annoy the Enemy'. New Providence, he rightly judged, was just such a place.
Battle: Arriving at the island on March, Hopkins put ashore 200 marines and 50 sailors under Captain Samuel Nicholas who, landing unopposed, seized first a fort outside the town and later, after collecting the keys from the Governor, Fort Nassau itself. Here they found *inter alia* 71 cannon, 15 brass mortars, and 24 large casks of gunpowder. After spending two weeks loading their haul, they returned to Rhode Island, capturing 8 small British ships on the way, but failing to take the British brigantine *Glasgow*, as (Hopkins subsequently explained) 'some that were on board had got too much Liquor out of the Prizes to be fit for Duty'.
Result: This highly successful raid, in which there were no casualties, earned Hopkins the prompt congratulations of Congress, though official enthusiasm cooled as the details of the engagement with *Glasgow* emerged. He was later censured for undertaking the raid without instructions, and for his failure to capture *Glasgow*.

ORISKANY (New York)   American War of Independence/Burgoyne's Offensive–St Leger's Expedition   6 August 1777
Fought between an American force under Major-General Nicholas Herkimer and a force of Indians, Loyalists and Canadians under the Mohawk Chief Joseph Brant and Lt-Colonel Sir John Johnson.
Strength: Americans 800; Indians/Loyalists/Canadians 400.
Aim: Lt-Colonel Barry St Leger, besieging Fort Stanwyx (qv), received information that a relief force under General Herkimer was 10 miles away. He therefore sent out a party to ambush and destroy them.
Battle: The locale of the ambush was a ravine 200 yards wide and heavily wooded on both sides. Sir John Johnson and Major John Butler with their Loyalists and Canadians were to hit the head of the column, while the Indians under Brant were to attack the flanks and rear. Herkimer's 60 Oneida scouts failed to spot the ambush, and the mile-long column marched straight into the trap. As soon as it was sprung, Lt-Colonel Richard Visscher's Regiment, bringing up the rear, fled, and Herkimer and a number of his officers were shot. (Herkimer later died after a botched leg amputation.) He continued to control the defence, however, and many of the Americans were able to reach high ground where they fought off their attackers in hand-to-hand combat. Three-quarters of an hour after the attack began at 10am a thunderstorm held up operations for an hour. St Leger sent in Major Stephen Watts with reinforcements, and these Butler ordered to turn their coats inside-out to deceive the enemy. The ruse was discovered at the last minute, and more hand-to-hand fighting ensued. After six hours the Indians retired, followed by Johnson and Butler with their troops. The Americans suffered casualties of 140 killed or wounded, after the defection of Visscher's 200 men. The Indians, Loyalists and Canadians had 70 of their number killed or wounded.
Result: This operation succeeded in its objective but at a considerable price. In the circumstances, the Indian losses were heavy and St Leger's promise of an easy ride if they supported him had scarcely been honoured. This certainly contributed to their defection over the next fortnight, and was responsible for the failure of the siege.

PAOLI (Pennsylvania)   American War of Independence/Philadelphia Campaign   21 September 1777
Fought between an American division under Brigadier-General Anthony Wayne and a British force commanded by Major-General Charles Grey.

Strength: Americans 1,500 with 4 guns; British 2 regiments + 1 light infantry battalion.

Aim: After the British victory at Brandywine (qv) General George Washington withdrew north, pursued by Major-General Sir William Howe. Brigadier-General Wayne was posted west of the Schuylkill River to harass the British advance. Wayne took up a secret position 2 miles SW of the Paoli Tavern, in the hope of striking at the enemy flank or baggage train. Learning of this plan, Howe sent General Grey to make a night attack on Wayne's Division.

Battle: Since surprise was to be the essence of this attack, General 'No-flint' Grey commanded his men not to load their weapons until the moment of attack–those who had already loaded them being ordered to remove their flints. The attack was made soon after midnight, producing chaos in the American camp. Those who ran in front of the camp-fires were shot, others were bayoneted. Wayne was successful in getting his cannon away, and collected survivors at daybreak. American casualties totalled 150 killed, wounded or captured. The British had 6 killed and 22 wounded. Of their 70 prisoners 40 wounded were left at houses on the way back.

Result: The way to Philadelphia was now clear for General Howe. The British cause was somewhat damaged by another massacre myth as a result of this engagement. Wayne was court-martialled for failing to heed 'timely notice of the attack' but was acquitted 'with the highest honours'.

PAULUS HOOK (New Jersey)   American War of Independence   19 August 1779

A British fort at Paulus Hook, under the command of Major William Sutherland, was attacked by an American force led by Major Henry Lee.

Strength: British/Hessians 200; Americans 300.

Aim: After the successful, but unprofitable, American attack on Stony Point (qv) Washington had still not solved his difficulties of communication. Accordingly he ordered Major Lee to prospect for an attack on Paulus Hook, a low point of land protruding into the Hudson, $1\frac{1}{2}$ miles from New York City across the river. The fort was protected on the land side by a salt marsh, a tidal moat and Harsimus Creek.

Battle: At 10.30am on 18 August Lee set out from Paramus with two companies and some wagons as if on a foraging expedition. At New Bridge, 4 miles away, he was joined by the rest of his force, and at 4.30 they started south to Bergen, 2 miles from their objective. Captain Allen McLane had reconnoitred the approaches, and the decision was to make the attack at 12.30am, allowing time to complete the engagement before high tide at 2am. Boats for their retreat were to be ready on the Hackensack River, west of Bergen.

However, a guide misdirected Lee, and a detour cost the attackers three hours. As they reached the marsh, Major Clark reported that half his Virginia troops were missing. By now the ditch was almost full; but Lee decided to press on with the attack, reorganising his force into two columns under Major Clark and Captain Forsyth, with a reserve force under Captain Levin Handy. They waded successfully through the marsh with their muskets unprimed, so that the enemy were alerted only when they entered the ditch. They crossed, found an opening in the main work, and captured a blockhouse and redoubt, with Handy dealing out men from his reserve as the firing indicated. A number of British and Hessians were captured, but Captain Schaller was able to hold out in the round redoubt. Since by this time dawn was approaching, and the alarm sounded in New York across the river, Lee, whose powder had been ruined in the crossing, ordered a retreat with 150 prisoners (one of whom claimed to be the Commanding Officer). The action had lasted thirty minutes.

On his retreat, Lee found that the boats on the Hackensack had been withdrawn on the assumption that the raid had been called off, and was faced with a long march back along the Bergen route. Fortunately for Lee, reinforcements arrived just before an attack was launched by Lt-Colonel van Buskirk and his Loyalists, who were then driven off.

The British and Hessians had 50 men killed or wounded, plus 150 captured. These did not, however, include Major Sutherland who had taken refuge in a blockhouse. The Americans had 2 men killed and 3 wounded.

Result: Young Henry Lee was duly thanked by Congress and given a gold medal to match that given to Anthony Wayne after Stony Point, and American morale received yet another boost.

PEEKSKILL RAID (New York)   American War of Independence   23 March 1777

Five hundred British troops with 4 light guns landed from a frigate and transports to destroy the magazine and storehouses at an American depot at Peekskill. The garrison under Brigadier-General Alexander McDougall was too small to do other than burn stores and withdraw. There were no casualties.

Though this was a comparatively small raid, it was not without its influence on the commanders-in-chief of both armies. Its success encouraged Major-General Sir William Howe to undertake the more substantial raid on Danbury (qv) one month later. It also alerted General George Washington to the vulnerability of his supply depots in the area, causing him to send eight regiments to Peekskill and seven to Ticonderoga.

PORT ROYAL (S Carolina)   American War of Independence/Southern Campaign   3 February 1779
Fought between a British force under Major Gardiner and an American force under Brigadier-General William Moultrie.
Strength: British 200 with 1 gun; Americans 320 with 3 guns.
Aim: After the British success at Savannah I (qv) and the taking of Fort Augusta Brigadier-General Augustine Prevost decided to take advantage of British naval supremacy to attack the island fortress of Port Royal.
Battle: The British attack lasted three-quarters of an hour. Their single gun was disabled early on, but they had the advantage of occupying woodland while the enemy fought in the open. After an indecisive encounter both sides ran out of ammunition and retreated simultaneously. Moultrie, however, sent his mounted troops in pursuit of the British, who had 50 men killed or wounded in the action. American casualties numbered 30 killed or wounded.
Result: The British survivors returned to Savannah by boat, while the Americans rejoined Major-General Benjamin Lincoln's army. The British were discouraged from further adventures until the fall of Charleston (qv) in May of the following year.

PRINCETON (New Jersey)   American War of Independence/New Jersey Campaign   3 January 1777
Fought between a British garrison force under Lt-Colonel Charles Mawhood, and an American force under the command of General George Washington.
Strength: British 1,200; Americans 1,600.
Aim: Encouraged by the success of his earlier attack on Trenton (qv), which had since been reoccupied by the British, General George Washington made a further sortie from his base in Pennsylvania. The resultant encounter at Princeton was really an improvised attack.
Battle: On 30 December 1776 Washington had recrossed the Delaware, moving again towards Trenton. He was met by British troops under Major-General Lord Cornwallis on the road from Princeton. Fighting a delaying action, Washington was able to maintain his force intact until night, at which point Cornwallis was confident of victory next day. Washington, however, leaving 400 men in camp with the camp-fires burning, slipped away and made for Princeton, which lay to the east.
At dawn on the same day (3 January) Colonel Mawhood had set out with two of his three garrison regiments to join Brigadier-General Alexander Leslie at Maidenhead on the Trenton-Princeton road. Mawhood's force was met by Brigadier-General Hugh Mercer with 350 men, and a skirmish took place in Clark's Orchard. The British drove the Americans back, and Mercer was killed. General Washington, Major-General Nathanael Greene and Brigadier-General John Cadwalader caught up with the British force, which they dispersed, some to Trenton and some back to Princeton. (The British suffered 65 killed or wounded, and had 35 men captured.) The Americans then marched on to Princeton, where the remaining garrison fortified the college building, to be rapidly flushed out by artillery fire. Two hundred prisoners were taken. Cornwallis's reinforcements arrived just after the Americans had left.
Result: Washington's troops were too exhausted to continue on to New Brunswick, where they might have been rewarded by a vast quantity of supplies and a £70,000 war chest. Instead, on 5 and 6 January they retreated to Morristown and into winter quarters.

QUEBEC (Canada)   American War of Independence/Canadian Campaign   13 November 1775–1 January 1776
Fought between the Americans under Colonel Benedict Arnold and Brigadier-General Richard Montgomery, and the British garrison under the command of Major-General Sir Guy Carleton.
Strength: Arnold reached Quebec with 650 men to be joined three weeks later by Mongomery with another 300. By the time Arnold and Montgomery were ready to attack the city, the garrison numbered some 1,700 men.
Aim: After the fall of St John's and Montreal (qqv) the fall of Quebec would have crowned the success of the American Expeditionary Force.

Battle: On 12 September 1775 Benedict Arnold had set out from Cambridge, Massachusetts, with 1,100 Volunteers on the 230-mile trek to Quebec–a journey through the most difficult terrain at the worst time of year. On 13 November the 650 men remaining with him crossed the St Lawrence and began a blockade of the city from the Plains of Abraham. However, it soon became clear that without artillery he could make little impression on so heavily fortified a town, and on the 19th he retired to Pointe aux Trembles (now Neuville) to await reinforcements under Brigadier-General Montgomery. Montgomery arrived from Montreal with 300 men on 2 December.

The attack planned for the night of 31 December involved a feint to the west while Arnold and Montgomery converged on the lower town from opposite sides. Sir Guy Carleton, foreseeing this plan of attack, planned accordingly. Approaching Point Diamond during the fiercest snowstorm, Montgomery was killed with 2 of his staff officers, following which Colonel Donald Campbell, taking charge, ordered a retreat. Arnold moved in with 600 men, entering the lower town by the Palace Gate. Arnold was wounded in the leg, and the command was taken over by Captain Daniel Morgan. After passing the first barrier, taking 50 prisoners, Morgan was persuaded to wait for Montgomery. At dawn, on 1 January, he attacked the second 12-foot barrier, but was driven back. Finding his retreat cut off by 200 men, at 9am he surrendered. The Americans had casualties of 60 killed or wounded, and 430 were taken prisoner. The British had 5 killed, 13 wounded.

Result: This failure was fatal to the American expedition into Canada. There was to be one unsuccessful attempt at a counter-offensive at Trois Rivières (qv), after which the campaign came to an end.

QUINBY BRIDGE (S Carolina)   American War of Independence/Southern Campaign   17 July 1781
Fought between the British 19th Regiment with some mounted Rangers, under Colonel John Crates, and a mixed American force commanded by the guerrilla leaders Brigadier-Generals Thomas Sumter and Francis Marion, and Colonel Henry Lee.

Threatened by Marion and Lee in his ouopst at Monck's Corner, Crates withdrew his force to Biggin Church on 14 July, and a further 18 miles to Quinby Bridge on the Cooper River on the 17th. Crates loosened the planks on the bridge across the river, but had to wait for his rearguard to cross before removing them. Meanwhile Lee arrived, and Captain Armstrong charged across the bridge with a cavalry force under Lieutenant Carrington. The British were driven back, but with the planks now dislodged Captain O'Neal was unable to join his compatriots who, in their turn were driven back. When Marion arrived he and Lee agreed that the British position was too strong to warrant further attack, but at 5pm Sumter appeared and overruled them.

The British then formed a square with their front covered by a howitzer and their flanks by buildings and fences on Captain Thomas Shubrick's plantation. The Americans drew up with Marion's infantry on the left, Colonel Thomas Taylor's Militia in the centre, and Colonel Horry's cavalry on the right. Taylor opened the attack across a field but was driven back by accurate fire. Marion attacked diagonally, but with 50 casualties and running out of ammunition he too was forced to withdraw. The attack finally foundered on Sumter's omission to bring up the artillery. Taylor was furious and refused to serve any more under Sumter, and Marion and Lee retreated 15 miles, taking their wounded and dead with them. With news of the approach of 700 British reinforcements Sumter himself retired, leaving Crates in possession of the field of battle.

RICHMOND (Virginia)   American War of Independence/Virginia Campaign   5–7 January 1781
Brigadier-General Benedict Arnold (who had defected from the American army in September 1780) attacked Richmond, which was under the command of Goveror Thomas Jefferson.

The township of Richmond (population 1,800) was a supply base for the American forces, and had been the seat of the Virginian legislature since May 1779. With the approach of Arnold, Jefferson was able to remove the military supplies, but with only 200 men could put up no more than token resistance. Lt-Colonel John Simcoe's Rangers drove the defenders back from Richmond Hill, and Arnold offered to spare the town if British ships could come up the James River to remove tobacco from the warehouses. Jefferson refused the offer, and Arnold entered the town at 1pm on the 7th, burned the warehouses and some private buildings, and left on the same day.

ROCKY MOUNT (S Carolina)   American War of Independence/Camden Campaign   1 August 1780
Fought between the Parisans under Brigadier-General Thomas Sumter and the British garrison of Rocky Mount commanded by Lt-Colonel George Turnbull.

Strength: Partisans 600; British 150.
Aim: After his success at Williamson's Plantation (qv) Sumter suggested to Major-General Johann Kalb that he might undertake an operation against the British Charleston-Camden line of communications at Rocky Mount.
Battle: On 30 July Sumter set out for Rocky Mount a few days before Major William Davie started on a similar operation to Hanging Rock (qv). Rocky Mount consisted of a small fort of three log-cabins protected by a ditch and abatis. Arriving on 1 August Sumter immediately demanded the surrender of the fort, which was refused. In the ensuing attack Lt-Colonel Thomas Neal broke through the abatis, but was killed with 5 of his men. Sumter then set fire to the buildings with burning wagons, and a white flag was hoisted, to be promptly withdrawn when a sharp shower extinguished the flames. After eight hours Sumter broke off the engagement and withdrew to the Catawba. Twelve men were killed or wounded on each side.
Result: Although this engagement did not realise Sumter's hopes, it was part of a pattern of harassment by the Partisan forces which constantly hampered the communications of the British army.

ST JOHN'S (ST JEAN) (Quebec, Canada)   American War of Independence/Canadian Campaign   5 September–2 November 1775
This stronghold, lying 20 miles south of Montreal and held by a British garrison under Major Charles Preston, came under a number of attacks by an American force led by Brigadier-General Richard Montgomery.
On 17 August Major-General Philip Schuyler had left Brigadier-General Richard Montgomery in charge of the Canadian Expeditionary Force of 1,200 men. Montgomery, hearing that 2 60-foot, 12-gun boats being built at St John's (now St Jean) were nearing completion, landed a force on the Ile-aux-Noix in the Richelieu River, to prevent these ships from reaching Lake Champlain. On his return on 4 September Schuyler not only approved Montgomery's action, but immediately advanced upon St John's–which consisted of a barracks fortified by 2 redoubts, and defended by 200 regulars, an Indian contingent, and several cannon. Landing half a mile from the barracks, Schuyler lost 16 men in an ambush by Indians under Captain Tice, and, advised by a spy that St John's was too strongly held, returned to the island. Here he was reinforced by 500 New Yorkers under Colonel Rudolph Ritzema. A further attack on 10 September also failed, despite three attempts by Ritzema.
Six days later Montgomery, once more in charge of the expedition, was further reinforced by 270 men. By this time Major-General Sir Guy Carleton had increased the garrison of St John's to 500 men, with another 90 at nearby Chambly. On 18 October Chambly surrendered, providing supplies with which the Americans were enabled finally to reduce St John's. On 30 Carleton tried unsuccessfully to relieve the fort by a crossing at Longueuil, but on 2 November, with three days' supplies left, Preston surrendered.
Though the capitulation of St John's made inevitable the fall of Montreal (qv), and though Carleton had by this time lost almost all his troops, he had bought precious time occupying the Americans in a winter campaign, and his stand was instrumental in saving Canada for Britain.

SAINTS, BATTLE OF THE   see LES SAINTES

SAVANNAH I (Georgia)   American War of Independence/Southern Campaign   29 December 1778
Fought between a British force under Lt-Colonel Archibald Campbell and an American force defending Savannah under Major-General Robert Howe.
Aim: Lt-General Sir Henry Clinton, who had relieved Major-General Sir William Howe as Commander-in-Chief of the British forces in May 1778, felt strong enough by the end of the year to embark on a campaign in the South. On 27 November, therefore, he detached a force of 3,500 men under Campbell, escorted by a naval squadron under Commodore Hyde Parker. This anchored off Tybee Island at the mouth of the Savannah River on 23 December. At the same time Brigadier-General Augustine Prevost, British Commander in E Florida, was ordered to march north to join Campbell. An American force of 1,050 men under Major-General Howe was at Sunbury, 30 miles south of Savannah. On Christmas Day General Howe arrived at Savannah with 850 of his men.
Battle: Finding the fortifications of the town in disrepair, Howe drew up his defending force half a mile SE of the town on the road from the British beachhead. Here there was a causeway with a bridge over a marshy stream with swamps on either side. Howe destroyed the bridge, dug a trench, and deployed his men under Colonel Samuel Elbert on the left, Colonel Isaac Huger on the right, with Colonel George Walton on the extreme right. He had 1 gun on each flank and 2 in the centre. On the 28 November Parker's

ships arrived at Giradeau's Plantation 2 miles below the town, and waited for the tide after driving off 2 enemy galleys. After a skirmish with a small force under Captain John Smith, a beachhead was secured, and the light infantry advanced guard was drawn up 800 yards from the defending line, with the main body of troops 200 yards behind these. Recognising that the Americans were expecting a frontal attack on the left, Campbell, 'desirous of cherishing this opinion', sent a battalion to join the light infantry on that flank. Meanwhile, learning from one Quamino Dolly of a path through the swamp on the American right, he sent Baird's light infantry and Turnbull's New York Volunteers to slip past and attack the enemy right flank (Walton) from the rear. Walton's unit was wiped out, and as this attack developed Campbell ran his guns forward and ordered his British infantry to charge. Howe ordered a general retreat across the Musgrove Swamp Causeway, but was intercepted by the advancing British forces. Some of the right and centre got through, but Elbert's Militia were either captured or drowned in the swamp. There was no pursuit, and Howe camped for the night at Cherokee Hill, 8 miles away, later retiring to join Major-General Benjamin Lincoln at Purysburg.

British casualties were 3 killed and 10 wounded. The Americans had 180 killed or drowned, plus 450 captured. In addition, the British took 3 ships, 3 brigs, 8 smaller craft, 48 cannon, 23 mortars, and supplies. This successful start, achieved before the arrival of General Prevost's troops, encouraged the British to take Fort Augusta and to carry the attack into S Carolina.

SAVANNAH II (Georgia) American War of Independence/Southern Campaign September–October 1779
A combined French/American force under Admiral-General Comte d'Estaing and Major-General Benjamin Lincoln attacked Savannah, the British headquarters of Brigadier-General Augustine Prevost.
Strength: French/Americans 6,000; British 3,200.
Aim: During the hot summer of 1779 operations had quietened down. On 20 July Sir James Wright had returned from England to take up once more the governorship of Savannah, and the French navy remained in the West Indies. On 3 September, however, d'Estaing appeared with his 39 ships off Charleston, producing consternation in the British high command, and irritation to General Washington who had hoped for his support in New York. Lt-General Lord Cornwallis was stopped from going to Jamaica, and the Rhode Island garrison was withdrawn to New York. On 6 September d'Estaing began disembarking troops on Tybee Island at the mouth of the Savannah, from which a British outpost hastily withdrew. Both sides gathered in what help was available. The British brought in Lt-Colonel John Cruger from Fort Sunbury, and Lt-Colonel John Maitland from Port Royal. On 11–12 September d'Estaing landed his troops at Beaulieu, 14 miles south of Savannah, where he was joined by American units under Brigadier-General Lachlan McIntosh and Brigadier-General Casimir Pulaski by the 15th. The next day d'Estaing demanded the surrender of the town 'to the arms of the King of France'. Prevost asked for twenty-four hours to consider this, during which time Lt-Colonel John Maitland arrived with another 800 men. The surrender was refused.
Battle: On 16 September Lincoln arrived and preparations for the siege began, against the advice of Brigadier-General William Moultrie who was in favour of an immediate assault. Bad weather prevented the arrival of the guns until 24 September, and the bombardment began on 3 October. Already d'Estaing was under pressure from his captains to withdraw, with the approach on the hurricane season and the need for repair to his ships, and a council of war on 8 October decided in favour of an assault at dawn the next day.

Captain James Moncrieff of the Royal Engineers had constructed a semicircular line of field fortifications from a redoubt (commanded by Lt-Colonel John Cruger) covering the road to the south to another redoubt at the NW, under command of Major James Wright. The 'Sailors' Battery' was to the west, and there was a strong redoubt in Spring Hill to the SW. In addition to these there were smaller redoubts and batteries. The Royal Navy armed brig *Germain* lay in the river to give supporting fire. The main French-American attack was planned against Spring Hill, with diversionary attacks on the flanks under General Théobald Dillon and Brigadier-General Isaac Huger. Both these flank attacks were driven back by heavy fire. The main attack was poorly co-ordinated, the French arriving at their positions late, then attacking early. D'Estaing's troops suffered severely while covering the 500 yards to the abatis. A brief success was scored by Lt-Colonel Francis Marion (the Swamp Fox), who broke through the SW abatis to take the Spring Hill redoubt. However, the pressure on this sector was too great, and Marion's withdrawal was followed by a counter-attack. Meanwhile Pulaski's cavalry had suffered heavily, and their commander was mortally wounded. McIntosh's force was misdirected into the swamp by d'Estaing, and was fired on from the river. After the withdrawal of the American/French forces, a heavy fog prevented pursuit. French/American casualties numbered 800 killed or wounded (of which 650 were French), plus 120 taken prisoner. The British had 60 men killed or wounded.

Result: By the end of the month Lincoln was back in Charleston and d'Estaing on the return journey to France. Lt-General Sir Henry Clinton, ever inclined to veer between the extremes of optimism and pessimism, claimed this to be 'the greatest event that has happened in the whole war'. At least he was now free to consider an assault upon Charleston (qv).

SPLIT ROCK   see VALCOUR ISLAND AND SPLIT ROCK

STONO FERRY (S Carolina)   American War of Independence/Southern Campaign   20 June 1779
Fought between the American garrison at Charleston, commanded by Brigadier-General William Moultrie, and the British and Hessian rearguard under the command of Lt-Colonel John Maitland.
Strength: Americans 1,200; British 900.
Aim: With Major-General Benjamin Lincoln advancing on Fort Augusta, Brigadier-General Augustine Prevost, British Commander-in-Chief Savannah, marched on Charleston, S Carolina, with the intention of driving the Americans out of Georgia. Hearing that Lincoln was pursuing him Prevost retreated, leaving a rearguard of 900 men at Stono Ferry on James Island under Lt-Colonel Maitland. Here there were 3 strong redoubts, an abatis, and a bridge of boats to Johns Island.
Battle: After crossing the Ashley River the American force, with Brigadier-General Jethro Sumner on the right, and Brigadier-General Isaac Huger on the left, after an 8-mile march, formed up in the woods 300 yards from the foremost defences of Stono Ferry. After an attack lasting one hour, the Highland Corps had suffered comparatively serious losses and the Hessians were in retreat. However, with the Americans already at the abatis, Maitland rallied the Hessians and threw in his reserves from Johns Island. The American force then withdrew, having suffered casualties of 150 killed or wounded, with an additional 150 missing. British and Hessian casualties totalled 130 killed or wounded, plus 1 missing.
Result: Maitland had already decided on 15 June to leave as soon as ships were available. He was able to leave on the 23rd, withdrawing his force to Beaufort on Port Royal Island.

STONY POINT (New York)   American War of Independence   16 July 1779
Fought between the British, under the command of Colonel Henry Johnson, and an American force under the command of Brigadier-General Anthony Wayne.
Strength: British 625; Americans 1,200.
Aim: On 1 June 1779 the British had taken the fort at Stony Point and Fort Lafayette at Verplanck's Point on the other side of the Hudson River. Guarding the nearest ferry to New York City, these two forts were of importance to the American east-west lines of communication. Washington therefore instructed Brigadier-General Wayne to study the possibility of retaking Stony Point, but decided against a simultaneous attack of Fort Lafayette.
Battle: By noon on 15 July the Americans, with 2 guns, began their 15-mile approach march from Sandy Beach, near Fort Montgomery, arriving within $1\frac{1}{2}$ miles of Stony Point at 8pm. The strictest security measures were taken to ensure surprise. There was to be a two-column attack, one from the north and one from the south. Each of these would be preceded by a party of 20 men to kill the sentries and to hack through the abatis, each of which was to be followed by an advance party of 150 men. In the centre Major Murfree, with a company of light horse, was to make a diversionary attack–and only these were permitted to fire. Soon after midnight the attacking columns forded the marsh around the fort, and the attack began. Colonel Johnson, deceived by Murfree's assault, led half the garrison down the hill where they were cut off and captured. After fifteen minutes of turmoil the British surrendered in isolated groups, having suffered casualties of 95 killed or wounded, plus 470 captured. The Americans had 100 killed or wounded. Twelve British guns were taken, but most of these were lost in the American galley carrying them to West Point.
Result: Washington's decision to leave Fort Lafayette proved a mistake. Lt-General Sir Henry Clinton promptly strengthened its defences and the later attack by Brigadier-General Robert Howe failed to capture it. On 18 July Stony Point had to be evacuated, and was reoccupied by the British the next day.

This attack proved something of a boost to American morale, and incited Major Henry Lee to make a similar attack on the fort at Paulus Hook (qv).

SULLIVAN'S ISLAND (S Carolina)   American War of Independence   28 June 1776
Fought between a British fleet of 55 ships under Commodore Peter Parker and the American garrison under the command of Colonel William Moultrie.
Aim: In N Carolina, soon after the disaster at Moore's Creek Bridge (qv), Major-General Henry Clinton waited for the expected British fleet from Ireland. It arrived in May 1776, commanded by Commodore Peter Parker. The Commodore persuaded Clinton to turn his attention from N to S Carolina, where Charles Town (Charleston) would prove a valuable prize.
Battle: The appearance of the fleet off Sullivan's Island at the beginning of June produced panic in the town, but bad weather held them up for three days. By the 8th the fleet had crossed the bar, and Clinton was able to consider his plan of attack. Meanwhile the American Major-General Charles Lee had arrived in Charles Town, which he set about fortifying. The fort on Sullivan's island guarded the entry to the bay, lying next to Long Island which Clinton occupied, endangering some 1,200 American troops. Lee was appalled by the lack of fortifications on Sullivan's Island where the Commander, Colonel Moultrie, appeared apathetic and on the whole uncooperative. However, Clinton's hesitation as a result of misinformation about the depth of water between the two islands enabled some work to be done on the half-finished fort.
    On the morning of 28 June the British fleet of 270 guns opened fire on the 25-gun fort, while Clinton launched a diversionary attack with 100 men from Long Island—an attack which was quickly repulsed. At sea *Thunder* attacked from 1½ miles out with mortar fire, and *Bristol* and *Experiment*, with 50 guns each, and the frigates *Active* and *Solebay*, formed a line 400 yards from the island, leaving room for *Syren*, *Actaeon*, and *Sphinx* to fire between them. It was soon clear that Colonel Moultrie's coolness was not unjustified. Cannon-balls thudded into the sand, and into the double line of palmetto logs, of which the fort was constructed, with very little effect. During the afternoon, in an ill-judged manoeuvre, *Actaeon* and *Sphinx* collided and both they and *Syren* ran aground. By late afternoon the island defenders, refreshed by a constant supply of rum in their fire-buckets, were beginning to produce havoc in the fleet with their slow-firing guns. At 9.30pm the fleet retreated. Forty-six men had been killed and 86 wounded on *Bristol*, 43 and 75 on *Experiment*, 170 men being killed or wounded in other ships. There had been 70 hits on *Bristol*.
Result: Clinton and Moultrie blamed each other for this unhappy engagement, while Lee received more than his share of congratulations from Congress. Charles Town was safe until the next year, when Clinton, as Commander-in-Chief of the British forces in America, returned to do the job properly

TARRANT'S TAVERN (N Carolina)   American War of Independence/Southern Campaign   1 February 1781
Fought between a force of British dragoons under Lt-Colonel Banastre Tarleton and a group of American militia.
    Immediately after the British army under Lt-General Lord Cornwallis had crossed the Catawba at Cowan's Ford, Tarleton was sent to attack the militia known to be assembling at Tarrant's Tavern. Tarleton tersely instructed his men to 'remember the Cowpens', which they duly did, charging and routing the opposing force. Tarleton claimed to have dispersed 500 militia, killed 50, and wounded many more in pursuit: Major-General Nathanael Greene himself narrowly avoided capture. The number of American casualties was disputed (it was felt that Tarleton may have been over-anxious to refurbish his reputation after Cowpens [qv]); however, there can be no doubt that this action severely limited militia activity as the British passed through North Carolina.

TRENTON (New Jersey)   American War of Independence/New Jersey Campaign   26 December 1776
This stronghold, defended by a Hessian garrison under Colonel Johann Rall, was attacked by an American force under Major-General Nathanael Greene.
Strength: Hessians 1,400; Americans 2,400 with 18 guns.
Aim: After the loss of New York City and his enforced retreat into New Jersey (qv), on 11 December General George Washington crossed the Delaware into Pennsylvania. The pursuing British army under Major-General Lord Cornwallis then went into winter quarters. Inaction and lack of enlistment were causing the gradual disintegration of Washington's army, and he determined on an offensive operation which would both weaken his enemy and boost the morale of his own men.
Battle: Washington's intention had been to launch the main attack under Greene, while Colonel John Cadwalader with 2,000 men made a diversionary attack on Bordenton, and Brigadier-General James

Ewing crossed at Trenton Ferry to the south with 1,000 men to cut off the Hessian retreat. In the event, Ewing failed to cross, and Cadwalader was too late to be of assistance at Trenton.

Colonel Rall, ignoring warnings of the intended attack, which he assumed would be on the usual small scale, had been carried to bed after a drunken Christmas party. Washington's men, held up by a fierce snowstorm, were unable to attack until 8am on 26 December, but still found the Hessians fully unprepared. General Greene from the north, and Major-General John Sullivan from the west, arrived simultaneously. They routed the outposts and were in the town before the garrison was aware of it. The Hessians tried desperately to improvise a street fight, but both the Rall and the Lossberg Regiments were driven east into the open fields, where Rall was killed. The Hessians surrendered at 9.30am, having suffered casualties of 105 men killed or wounded, and 920 of them taken prisoner. Two Americans were wounded but none killed, though 3 died from exposure during the subsequent retreat.

Result: This was an encouraging victory for the Americans during a somewhat bleak winter, though the failure of the supporting forces under Ewing and Cadwalader compelled Washington to withdraw his army once more.

TROIS RIVIERES (Quebec, Canada)   American War of Independence/Canadian Campaign   8 June 1776

Fought between the British, under Brigadier-General Simon Fraser, and an American force under the command of Brigadier-General William Thompson.

Strength: British 6,000; Americans 2,000.

Aim: With the colonial authorities demanding a further attempt on Quebec (qv) General Thompson, wrongly advised that the town of Trois Rivières, on the north bank of the St Lawrence, was held by no more than 800 British, made an attempt to renew the American offensive in Canada.

Battle: On 6 June General Thompson sailed up-river to within 10 miles of the town. At 3am on the 8th he landed within 3 miles of his objective, leaving 250 men to guard the boats. His main force contained the regiments of Colonels Arthur St Clair, William Irvine, William Maxwell, and Anthony Wayne. Misled by a guide, this force was lost for some hours in a swamp, and was unable to reach the river road till dawn. The attack was launched by 200 men under Colonel Wayne. This was initially successful, but they and the rest of Thompson's troops were driven back at the line of entrenchments. Unwilling to be burdened with a large number of prisoners, the British drove them back into the swamp. The survivors, together with the boat guard, reached Sorel on 11 June. British casualties amounted to 8 killed and 9 wounded. American casualties numbered 400 killed or wounded, and in addition 236 were taken prisoner.

Result: The failure of this expedition brought to an end the American invasion of Canada.

TURTLE, OPERATIONS OF   6 September–9 October 1776

Turtle was a 1-man submarine designed and developed by David Bushnell of Saybrook (now part of Westbrook) Connecticut, during the latter part of 1775. The hull was top-shaped, 7·5 by 6 feet, and consisted of 6-inch oak timbers bound together with iron bands and coated with tar. The vessel had a depth-gauge and compass, lighted by a phosphorescent plant, 'fox-fire'. It was stabilised by a 700-pound lead base, part of which was detachable, and bilge-tanks. A screw propeller was operated by a crank from inside. In December 1775 successful tests were carried out by David Bushnell's brother, Ezra, who was able to remain under water for half an hour. These were followed by others in Long Island Sound early in 1776.

The immediate purpose of *Turtle* was to blow up *Eagle*, Admiral Lord Howe's flagship, by attaching below the water-line a 'torpedo'–a cask containing 150 pounds of gunpowder activated by a timing device. An attempt to do so was made on 6 September, though Ezra Bushnell's illness had necessitated the training of another crewman, Sergeant Ezra Lee. *Turtle* was released into the bay by 2 whale-boats, but was carried past its objective by the tide. After two and a half hours of paddling and cranking, with the hatch open, Lee reached his target, but failed to attach the torpedo. As dawn was breaking he retreated past Governor's Island, narrowly escaping capture, and was rescued by a whale-boat after detaching the torpedo, which exploded in the water.

Early in October a second attempt was made, this time on a frigate in the Hudson River, but this too was unsuccessful. *Turtle* returned to its mother-ship, *Crane*, but both vessels, along with others, were sunk by the British on 9 October.

VALCOUR ISLAND AND SPLIT ROCK (Quebec, Canada)   American War of Independence/
Canadian Campaign   11–13 October 1776
Fought between American and British fleets, under Major-General Benedict Arnold and Major-General
Sir Guy Carleton respectively.
Strength: American fleet of 83 guns; British fleet of 87 guns (better manned).
Aim: After the raising of the siege of Quebec (qv) and the American failure at Trois Rivières (qv) both
Arnold and Carleton recognised the strategic importance of the control of Lake Champlain. Each of them
had built a fleet to enforce this control, and the Battle at Valcour Island was to decide the issue.
Battle: Arnold had left Crown Point with his fleet on 24 August, moving up to Windmill Point near the
border. On 19 September he withdrew to Cumberland Head, moving into the half-mile channel between
Valcour Island and the west shore of the lake on the 23rd.
   Carleton's fleet left St John's on 4 October sailing south, and overshooting the Americans by 2 miles.
Arnold ordered first *Revenge*, then 4 other ships, to draw the British into the southern end of the narrow
channel, recalling them once they had been sighted by the British fleet. During this manoeuvre *Royal
Savage* ran aground on the SW tip of the island.
   Carleton, a schooner of 12 6-pounders, led the attack, but a change of wind forced her to anchor. By
12.30pm there was a general engagement at a range of some 350 yards. At dusk, around 5.30pm, the
British gunboats withdrew, but continued firing till dark. Though many of the American ships had been
crippled (*Royal Savage* blew up after dark), Arnold evaded the British fleet during the night, escaping into
the lake. At dawn on 12 October the pursuit of Arnold's fleet began, continuing throughout the day, but by
the morning of the 13th Arnold was still 28 miles from Crown Point. With the turn of the wind, General
Carleton caught up with Arnold at 11am at Split Rock. Here *Washington*, with 110 men under Brigadier-
General Waterbury, surrendered, *Lee* ran ashore, while others Arnold took to the Vermont shore where
he beached them and set them on fire. Only *Trumbull, Enterprise, Revenge*, and *Liberty* survived to reach
Crown Point.
   The Americans lost 11 out of 15 vessels sunk or captured, and had 60 men killed or wounded. At Split
Rock, 20 Americans were killed or wounded and the crew of *Washington* was taken prisoner. The British
vessel *Carleton* was damaged at Valcour, but not sufficiently to prevent her from taking part in the pursuit.
Since not one of the British gunboats was hit, losses in personnel must have been few.
Result: For the present, the American attempt to control Lake Champlain had been thwarted, to the
advantage of the British.

VINCENNES (Indiana)   American War of Independence/Western Campaign   23–5 February 1779
Fought between the British, led by Lt-Colonel Henry Hamilton, and an American force under
Frontiersman George Rogers Clark.
Aim: The British held a number of scattered posts throughout the Mississippi valley under the Lt-
Governor, Henry Hamilton, based at Detroit. These settlements tended to be volatile in their allegiance,
and when Hamilton learned that Vincennes, on the Wabash River, had defected, he set out on 7 October to
try to recoup his losses. On 17 December he reached Vincennes with 500 men and took over. He then
released his Indians and half his Militia, and settled down to rebuilding Fort Sackville with the 80 men left
to him.
   George Clark's plan had been to persuade these settlements to accept American allegiance, and with a
force of 200 men he had taken Kaskaskia on the Mississippi on 4 July. By the beginning of February 1779
he had decided to reverse Governor Hamilton's enterprise at Vincennes, and on the 3rd set out to do so,
reaching the Little Wabash River on the 15th, to find the land flooded by an early thaw. By the afternoon
of 23 February they had reached high ground across the Wabash, where they rested and dried out.
Battle: Clark recognised that there would be no difficulty in taking the town, but that the fort would
present a problem. Speed was important, as Hamilton had sent a party up-river to hurry along supplies,
and this party could raise Indian reinforcements if the raid were not quickly over. Clark sent a note to the
townspeople, asking his supporters to keep indoors and his enemies to retire to the fort. He then spread out
his troops and displayed a large number of flags to persuade the enemy that they were to be attacked by a
large force. At 9am on 24 February Hamilton refused a call to surrender, but at 11am sent Captain
Leonard Helm to ask for honourable terms. These were rejected, and Clark underlined his determination
by killing 5 Indian prisoners in full view of the garrison. By evening Hamilton had agreed to surrender, and
the next morning he gave himself up with his 79 men. The British had 4 men killed. There were no
American casualties.

Result: Clark was able to hold all the Illinois country he had taken, but despite raids in 1779, 1780 and 1781, he failed to capture Detroit.

VIRGINIA UPRISING   March 1775–July 1776

Following a demand by the Provincial Convention for a 'posture of defence' on 23 March 1775, the Governor, John Murray, Earl of Dunmore, retaliated by seizing the powder supply at Williamsburg. On 2 May Patrick Henry led a force to retrieve this, and Lord Dunmore agreed to pay compensation of £330 for the powder, but by 8 June had outlawed Henry. On hearing of Major-General Thomas Gage's offer of the King's pardon to all Insurgents other than Samuel Adams and John Hancock (see BOSTON), Dunmore fled to a warship from which he bombarded Hampton (qv) on 24–5 October. He declared martial law on 7 November. On 9 December Colonel William Woodford led a force towards Norfolk, defeating Dunmore at Great Bridge (qv). On 1 January 1776 Dunmore bombarded and virtually destroyed the town of Norfolk. He tried to set up a base in Chesapeake Bay, but was driven out on 8–10 July. After the further failure of raids up the Potomac he returned to England via New York.

Virginia was now to be free from military action for three years.

WATEREE FERRY (S Carolina)   American War of Independence/Camden Campaign   15 August 1780

This was the last of the preliminary skirmishes before Camden (qv). fought between a part of Brigadier-General Thomas Sumter's Partisan force under Colonel Thomas Taylor and a British force under Colonel Isaac Carey.

Aim: Like the attack on Rocky Mount (qv) this was an attempt by the Americans to disrupt the British line of communications between Charleston and Camden.

Battle: From his Partisan force, reinforced by Major-General Horatio Gates to the extent of 400 men and 2 guns under Lt-Colonel Thomas Woolford, Sumter sent out one regiment under Colonel Taylor to surprise Fort Carey, a small fortification protected by one redoubt to the west of Wateree Ferry. Taylor was able to gain his objective without opposition, capturing Colonel Carey, 30 men, and 36 wagons of food, clothes and rum. Subsequently he took 50 supply wagons, 6 baggage wagons, and 700 head of cattle and sheep *en route* from Fort Ninety-Six (qv). Hearing of the approach of a British force to release the prisoners, he retreated up-river.

Result: This brief but highly successful raid kept up the pressure which Sumter was exerting on British outposts. The British prisoners were later released by Lt-Colonel Banastre Tarleton at Fishing Creek (qv).

WAXHAWS (S Carolina)   American War of Independence/Charleston Expedition   29 May 1780

Fought between an American force under Colonel Abraham Buford and a pursuing force of British under Lt-Colonel Banastre Tarleton.

Strength: Americans 350 (250 engaged); British 270 (200 engaged).

Aim: After the disaster at Lenud's Ferry (qv) Brigadier-General Isaac Huger ordered Colonel Abraham Buford to collect together what was left of his force and to withdraw to Hillsboro. On 18 May Lt-General Lord Cornwallis set off after them with 2,500 men. Recognising, however, that this large force moved too slowly to catch up with their quarry, he ordered Colonel Tarleton, with 40 dragoons, 130 cavalry and 100 infantry (mounted double with the cavalry), to complete the exercise. Tarleton covered 105 miles in fifty-four hours to catch up with Buford soon after noon on the 29th.

Battle: At 3pm on 29 May the British advanced guard met and mauled the American rearguard under Lieutenant Pearson. Buford, who had already rejected the surrender suggested by one of Tarleton's officers sent on ahead under a flag of truce, halted and drew up his men in a single line under cover of an open wood. Tarleton deployed his men in three columns: Major Cochrane with 50 infantry and 60 dragoons on the right; 30 dragoons and infantry under Tarleton himself on the left; and a third column in the centre. Behind the centre the remainder of his command were to form up as they arrived on a small hill, thus providing a rallying point. The British force formed up 300 yards from Buford's line. As they advanced the Americans were ordered to hold their fire, even at a distance of 50 yards. When it came it was ineffectual in breaking the charge, and the line collapsed, to be cut down first with sabres, then with bayonets. Tarleton's horse was killed, and as he fell his men thought that he was dead. As a result they gave way to a fearful carnage on the battlefield, and it was here that the bitterly ironic phrase 'Tarleton's quarter' was born. The Americans lost 113 men killed, and of the 203 captured 150 were too badly wounded to be moved. Buford and a few of his men escaped. The British lost 19 men and 31 horses killed or wounded.

Result: This was the last battle of the Charleston (qv) Campaign, and this final clearing of the communications before the British offensive allowed Cornwallis to advance on N Carolina, although two subsequent setbacks at King's Mountain and Cowpens (qqv) might reasonably have persuaded him to have second thoughts. Waxhaws increased the reputation of Tarleton among both the British and Loyalist ranks, and the fear of him in the American forces.

WHITE PLAINS (New York)   American War of Independence/New York Campaign   28 October 1776
Fought between the Americans, led by General George Washington, and the British, commanded by Major-General Sir William Howe.

Strength: Americans 6,000; British 13,000.

Aim: After taking New York City (see HARLEM HEIGHTS) Howe spent four weeks fortifying it against possible attack before moving his army to the mainland at Pell's Point on 13 October. General Washington withdrew to White Plains on the 23rd. Howe then sought to encircle the American army in an outflanking movement.

Battle: When Howe attacked the American army on 28 October, Washington was still preparing a defensive position. Only on that morning did he recognise the importance of the 180-feet Chatterton's Hill on his right, which he hastily fortified with 1,600 men and 2 guns under Brigadier-General Alexander McDougall. He sent out a delaying force under Major-General Joseph Spencer, which skirmished for an hour, then retreated to avoid being cut off, returning to the main army at 9.30am. Three Hessian regiments under Major-General Baron Wilhelm von Knyphausen built a bridge over the Hudson, which they crossed, as Brigadier-General Alexander Leslie forded the river farther south with two regiments. Leslie's men made a bayonet-charge, but were repulsed with some losses. The main attack took place when the whole army had crossed, at which point they were faced by heavy musket- and grape-shot fire from the Americans. The Massachusetts Militia, facing the dragoons on the American right, were the first to give way, then the centre retreated after withstanding two attacks and the hill was taken. Howe had ordered a full attack for the 31st, but a heavy storm forced a postponement of this. The Americans sustained casualties of 150 killed or wounded, and the British 310 killed or wounded.

Result: Howe's failure to follow up his initial success once more enabled Washington to withdraw his army, this time to Connecticut.

WILLIAMSON'S PLANTATION (BRATTONVILLE) (S Carolina)   American War of Independence/ Camden Campaign   12 July 1780
Fought between the Partisans under Brigadier-General Thomas Sumter and a British and Loyalist force under Captain Huck.

Strength: Partisans 90; British/Loyalists 400.

Aim: Learning that Sumter was gathering a force of Partisans, Lt-Colonel Lord Rawdon sent Captain Huck with a force of Loyalists and some of Lt-Colonel Banastre Tarleton's cavalry to thwart them. Arriving at Williamson's Plantation (now Brattonville) with 400 men Huck, after capturing two Patriots and looting some houses, set up camp half a mile away.

Battle: Sumter, at a distance of 30 miles, received warning of Huck's approach, and sent a force under Colonels Bratton and McClure to intercept him. The Partisans arrived on 12 July to find Huck's force camped between two wooden rail fences lining the road to the Plantation. They attacked immediately, pinning down Huck's force by firing at close range. The fences prevented the possibility of a bayonet-charge by the Loyalists and they were quickly routed. Huck himself was killed. The Partisans lost 1 man killed, to the British and Loyalists casualties of 90 killed or wounded.

Result: This encounter was one of many under Brigadier-Generals Sumter, Andrew Pickens and Francis Marion which caused constant concern to Lt-General Lord Cornwallis in his preparations for a northward push. As an immediate result it caused mistrust between Tarleton, who was furious at the profligate misuse of his cavalry, and his superiors, and materially assisted Sumter's recruiting, enabling him to make his attack on Rocky Mount (qv).

WYOMING VALLEY (Philadelphia)   American War of Independence/New York Border Warfare   3 July 1778
This settlement, in a 25-mile stretch of the Susquehanna River, had declared for the Patriots on the

outbreak of war, and was now attacked by a British raiding party under Major John Butler. Colonel Zebulon Butler was in overall charge of the settlement.

Strength: Patriots 360; Loyalists/Indians 900.

Aim: During the preceding year there had been some movement of Loyalists into this area, in particular the Wintermoot family. This had aroused much suspicion and arming of 'forts'–especially the Wintermoot Fort for the Loyalists and Forty Fort for the Patriots. During St Leger's Expedition in 1777 (see FORT STANWYX) there had been some Indian reconnaissance here, and early in 1778 a number of Loyalists had been arrested.

In June Major John Butler left Niagara with his Loyalists on the arduous 200-mile trek, to be joined by a party of Iroquois Indians under Chief Gi-en-gwatoh. By 28 June they were 20 miles from their objective, and were supplied with '14 head of fat cattle' by the Wintermoots. As soon as their approach was known, a company of 60 men under Captain Detrick Hewett assembled at Forty Fort, and Colonel Butler called up the Militia.

Battle: On 3 June the Loyalists entered the valley from the west and made their headquarters at Wintermoot Fort. On the same day the Patriots debated whether they should attack or await reinforcements for which they had sent, but whose arrival seemed unlikely (General Washington was in fact fully occupied with the Monmouth [qv] Campaign at the time). The decision was to attack, and they sent out a reconnaissance party, for which the Loyalists were unprepared, but were alerted when the party met 2 Indians and there was some firing. The main Patriot force then advanced. Colonel Butler drew up his men in a clearing, with himself on the right, Colonel Nathan Denison on the left, and Hewett's Regulars in the centre. On the other side Major John Butler commanded his Rangers on the left flank, the Indians were deployed on the right, with the Greens in the Centre. The Patriots on the left were soon surrounded, though Denison attempted a manoeuvre to avoid this, and those on the right were driven back to the river. The defence then collapsed.

Only 60 Patriots escaped–John Butler said that his Indians took 277 scalps. Loyalist and Indian casualties consisted of 2 Rangers and 1 Indian killed, and 8 Indians wounded.

Result: Colonel Butler escaped, but on the next day Colonel Denison surrendered, following which 1,000 houses were burned and 1,000 head of cattle, with some sheep and pigs, were taken. Another 'massacre' legend was born, the truth of which is hard to assess. John Butler later claimed that 'not a single person was hurt except such as were in arms, to these in truth the Indians gave no quarter'. Four days later John Butler withdrew his men, and by the 10th he was at Tioga on the way back to Niagara. In August Colonel Thomas Hartley brought a regiment to protect the valley, and the settlement was rebuilt.

YORKTOWN (Virginia)   American War of Independence/Virginia Campaign   September–October 1781

Fought between a combined American and French force under General George Washington and the British army under Lt-General Lord Cornwallis.

Strength: Americans/French 20,000; British/Hessians 9,750.

Aim: Lord Cornwallis's excursion into N Carolina at the beginning of the year, and his subsequent operations in Virginia, had not been in accordance with his Commander-in-Chief's plans. Lt-General Sir Henry Clinton, operating from New York, had instructed him to ensure that the British held S Carolina, and this operation he had left to Lt-Colonel Lord Rawdon, who had great difficulty in holding the widely scattered outposts there against persistent attacks by Major-General Nathanael Greene and the Partisan commanders. By the beginning of June, Clinton was for the second time offering his resignation to the British government and, as on the previous occasion, tended to leave Cornwallis to make his own decisions. On 15 June, however, he did advise Cornwallis 'to take a defensive station in any healthy situation you choose, be it at Williamsburg or Yorktown'. Cornwallis chose the latter.

Here, after sending Lt-Colonels Banastre Tarleton and Tom Dundas across the river to hold Gloucester, he concentrated his forces. The Yorktown defences were established close to the town, as the garrison was not large enough to man a perimeter longer than 1,000 yards. The inner line had 14 batteries, 65 guns and 10 redoubts. The principal strongpoint was the 'horn-work' to the south. Ahead of this there were outworks to defend the flat ground. To the west, covering the Williamsburg road, was the Fusilier Redoubt, with Redoubts 9 and 10 on the opposite flank. Cornwallis's immediate concern was to avoid the army of 4,500 men under Major-Generals Marquis de Lafayette and Anthony Wayne and Baron Friedrich Wilhelm von Steuben. The situation, however, was more critical than he had anticipated. In addition to this substantial force, General Washington and Lt-General Comte de Rochambeau, after making a show of attacking New York to ensure Clinton's inaction, marched south into Maryland and, via Chesapeake Bay, sailed to Yorktown by 26 September. This large combined force, supported by the fleets under Admiral Comte de Barras and Rear-Admiral Comte de Grasse, and with the British troops at Gloucester bottled up by General de Choisy, began the investment of the town on 6 October.

Battle: On 6 October the first 2,000-yard parallel was begun. By the 9th the bombardment had started, and work was already beginning on the second parallel. At this point it was necessary to reduce Redoubts 9 and 10. The former was attacked by a French force under Colonel Guillaume Deuxponts, the latter by a mixed force under Lt-Colonel Alexander Hamilton. At the same time diversionary attacks were mounted against the Fusilier Redoubt and Gloucester. Redoubt 9, under Lt-Colonel McPherson, inflicted heavy casualties as the French crossed the abatis, but surrendered after a bayonet-charge. Hamilton's attack was carried out successfully with few casualties. There was no counter-attack, but the defenders trained all available guns on these redoubts. The completion of the second parallel enabled batteries to be set up perilously close to the fortifications. A British attempt under Lt-Colonel Robert Abercrombie to combat this was made at 4am on 16 October, but was only partly successful. On the night of the 16th Cornwallis tried to ferry his men across the river to Gloucester, but was baulked by the combination of a sudden storm and a shortage of boats. On the morning of the 17th an even fiercer bombardment by 100 pieces was mounted, and at 10am Cornwallis asked for a truce to discuss terms. The surrender was signed by noon on 20 October. The Americans and French sustained casualties of 400 killed or wounded. British and Hessian casualties numbered 600 killed or wounded, plus 8,080 captured.

Result: Clinton arrived at Chesapeake with 7,000 reinforcements on 27 October, but *'il était trop tard. La Poule était mangée'*. Even had he arrived in time, de Grasse would have prevented him from getting his troops through to Yorktown. This second surrender of a British army was a bitter blow but not, on the face of it, a fatal one. Washington himself anticipated at least another year of fighting. However, when Lord North, the British Prime Minister, heard the news, he commented: 'Oh God! It is all over!' And for once he was right.

The temporary French naval superiority achieved by de Grasse in the western Atlantic had allowed Washington and Rochambeau to join Lafayette, Wayne and Steuben and prevented adequate reinforcements reaching Yorktown. Cornwallis's consequent capitulation and the resultant collapse of the morale of Lord North's ministry led to the final defeat of Britain by the Americans and the French, the independence of the thirteen colonies and the subsequent birth of the United States of America.

SECTION EIGHT

FRENCH REVOLUTIONARY WARS 1779–1800

198

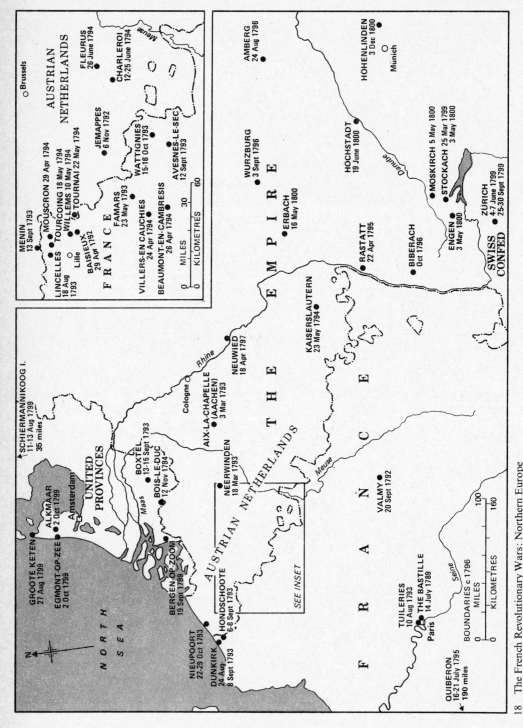

Inset (Austrian Netherlands / France)

AUSTRIAN NETHERLANDS

Brussels

FLEURUS
26 June 1794

CHARLEROI
12-25 June 1794

JEMAPPES
6 Nov 1792

MOUSCRON 29 Apr 1794

TOURCOING 18 May 1794

WILLEMS 10 May 1794

TOURNAI 22 May 1794

MENIN
13 Sept 1793

LINCELLES
18 Aug
1793

BAISIEUX
29 Apr 1792

Lille

FAMARS
23 May 1793

WATTIGNIES
15-16 Oct 1793

AVESNES-LE-SEC
12 Sept 1793

F R A N C E

VILLERS-EN-CAUCHIES
24 Apr 1794

BEAUMONT-EN-CAMBRESIS
26 Apr 1794

Meuse

MILES   30   60
KILOMETRES

Right inset (Empire / Swiss Confed.)

T H E   E M P I R E

AMBERG
24 Aug 1796

HOHENLINDEN
3 Dec 1800

Münich

Danube

WURZBURG
3 Sept 1796

HÖCHSTADT
19 June 1800

MOSKIRCH 5 May 1800

STOCKACH 25 Mar 1799
3 May 1800

ERBACH
16 May 1800

RASTATT
22 Apr 1795

BIBERACH
Oct 1796

ENGEN
3 May 1800

ZÜRICH
4-7 June 1799
25-30 Sept 1799

SWISS
CONFED.

Main map

SCHIERMANNIKOOG I.
11-13 Aug 1799
35 miles

UNITED
PROVINCES

Amsterdam

Rhine

NEUWIED
18 Apr 1797

KAISERSLAUTERN
23 May 1794

Cologne

AIX-LA-CHAPELLE
(AACHEN)
3 Mar 1793

GROOTE KETEN
27 Aug 1799

ALKMAAR
2 Oct 1799

EGMONT-OP-ZEE
2 Oct 1799

BOXTEL
13-15 Sept 1793

BOIS-LE-DUC
12 Nov 1794

Maas

NEERWINDEN
18 Mar 1793

BERGEN-OP-ZOOM
19 Sept 1799

HONDSCHOOTE
6-8 Sept 1793

AUSTRIAN NETHERLANDS

Meuse

T H E   E M P I R E

F R A N C E

VALMY
20 Sept 1792

NORTH
SEA

N

NIEUPOORT
22-29 Oct 1793

DUNKIRK
24 Aug.
8 Sept 1793

SEE INSET

TUILERIES
10 Aug 1792

THE BASTILLE
14 July 1789

Paris

Seine

BOUNDARIES c 1796

MILES   100   160
KILOMETRES

QUIBERON
16-21 July 1795
190 miles

18   The French Revolutionary Wars: Northern Europe

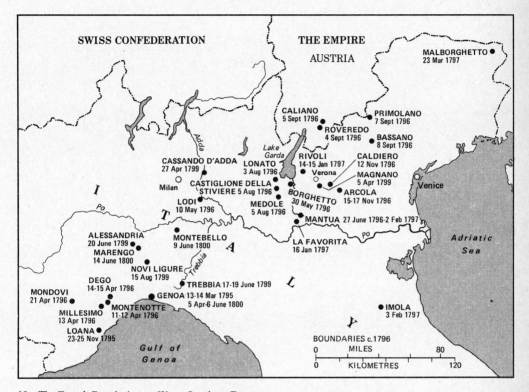

19   The French Revolutionary Wars: Southern Europe

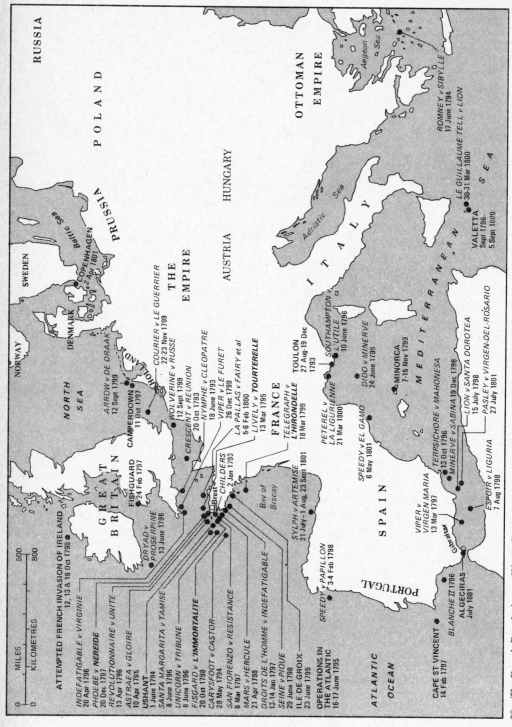

RUSSIA

POLAND

PRUSSIA

SWEDEN

NORWAY

DENMARK

COPENHAGEN
2 Apr 1801

Baltic Sea

HOLLAND

THE EMPIRE

AUSTRIA   HUNGARY

OTTOMAN EMPIRE

Aegean Sea

ROMNEY v SIBYLLE
17 June 1794

Adriatic Sea

I T A L Y

LE GUILLAUME TELL v LION
30-31 Mar 1800

VALETTA
Sept 1798-
5 Sept 1800

M E D I T E R R A N E A N   S E A

NORTH SEA

GREAT BRITAIN

A'ROW v DE DRAAK
12 Sept 1799

CAMPERDOWN
11 Oct 1797

COURIER v LE GUERRIER
22-22 Nov 1799

WOLVERINE v RUSSE
12 Sept 1799

CRESCENT v REUNION
20 Oct 1793

NYMPHE v CLEOPATRE
18 June 1793

VIPER v LE FURET
28 Dec 1799

LA PALLAS v FAIRY et al
5-6 Feb 1800

LIVELY v TOURTERELLE
13 Mar 1795

FRANCE

TELEGRAPH v L'HIRONDELLE
18 Mar 1799

TOULON
27 Aug-19 Dec 1793

SOUTHAMPTON v
L'UTILE
10 June 1796

DIDO v MINERVE
24 June 1795

MINORCA
7-15 Nov 1799

TERPSICHORE v MAHONESA
13 Oct 1796

LION v SANTA DOROTEA
15 July 1798

PASLEY v VIRGEN-DEL-ROSARIO
27 July 1801

MINERVE v SABINA 19 Dec 1796

SPAIN

VIPER v VIRGEN MARIA
13 Mar 1797

PETEREL v
LA LIGURIENNE
21 Mar 1800

SPEEDY v EL GAMO
6 May 1801

ESPOIR v LIGURIA
7 Aug 1798

Gibraltar

ALGECIRAS
July 1801

BLANCHE II 1796

PORTUGAL

SPEEDY v PAPILLON
3-4 Feb 1798

Bay of Biscay

Brest

CHILDERS
2 Jan 1793

SYLPH v ARTEMISE
31 July-1 Aug, 23 Sept 1801

USHANT

ATLANTIC OCEAN

CAPE ST VINCENT
14 Feb 1797

MILES   500
KILOMETRES   800

0

ATTEMPTED FRENCH INVASION OF IRELAND
12, 13 & 18 Oct 1798

INDEFATIGABLE v VIRGINIE
20 Apr 1796

PHOEBE v NEREIDE
20 Dec 1797

REVOLUTIONNAIRE v UNITE
13 Apr 1796

ASTRAEA v GLOIRE
10 Apr 1795

USHANT
1 June 1794

SANTA MARGARITA v TAMISE
8 June 1796

UNICORN v TRIBUNE
8 June 1796

FISGARD v L'IMMORTALITE
20 Oct 1798

CARYSFOOT v CASTOR
29 May 1794

SAN FIORENZO v RESISTANCE
8 Mar 1797

MARS v HERCULE
21 Apr 1798

DROITS DE L'HOMME v INDEFATIGABLE
13-14 Jan 1797

SEINE v PIQUE
29 June 1798

ILE-DE-GROIX
23 June 1795

OPERATIONS IN THE ATLANTIC
16-17 June 1795

FISHGUARD
24 Feb 1797

DRYAD v PROSERPINE
13 June 1796

20 The French Revolutionary Wars: General

'Man is born free, and everywhere he is in chains.'

Jean-Jacques Rousseau

From 1792 to 1815 there was a series of French wars, broken only by brief cessations of hostilities. The first part is known as the French Revolutionary Wars, and the second as the Napoleonic Wars.

On 20 April 1792 France declared war on Austria. Prussia and other powers allied themselves with the latter country, and at first the French army, weakened by the emigration of more than half the officers (in 1789 the French army had 9,500 officers; of these 6,600 were noblemen, and by the end of 1794 5,500 of them had gone), its discipline undermined by revolutionary fervour, and short of money and *matériel*, did not distinguish itself.

AIX-LA-CHAPELLE (AACHEN) (N Rhine-Westphalia, W Germany)   French Revolutionary Wars 3 March 1793
Fought between the French under General Francisco Miranda (who was born in Peru) and the Austrians under Friedrich Josias, Prince of Saxe-Coburg.
Aim: Continued offensive against the armies of the National Convention by the Allies.
Battle: In the fight the French were totally defeated and fled in disorder. Their losses were 3,500 killed and wounded and 1,500 prisoners.
Result: Check in the advance of the French, who had earlier that winter captured the Dutch fleet and acquired the Netherlands (known as the Batavian Republic) as an active military ally.

ALESSANDRIA (or MARENGO II)   French Revolutionary Wars   20 June 1799
Fought between the French under General Jean Moreau against the Austro-Russians under General Count Heinrich von Bellegarde.
Strength: French 14,000; Austrians/Russians 20,000.

Moreau was *en route* to join General Jacques Macdonald on the river Trebbia. Bellegarde, who was blockading Alessandria, had orders to prevent Moreau from linking with Macdonald who was engaged with the Russian general Count Suvorov. However, in a long and severe combat Moreau beat the Imperialists and drove Bellegarde back on Alessandria. The Austro-Russians lost 3,000 men and 4 guns, while 900 were taken prisoner. French losses were 900 men.

Macdonald was defeated by Suvorov on the Trebbia (TREBBIA II) the previous day. Before midnight on the 20th Moreau heard the news, decided that his position was untenable and prudently retreated. Curiously enough, articles blaming Macdonald, attributed to Moreau, appeared in the Paris newspapers. But had Moreau been more active he might have joined Macdonald on the Trebbia.

ALGECIRAS (Bay of Gibralter, Cádiz, Spain)   French Revolutionary Wars   July 1801
On 13 June Rear-Admiral Charles-Alexandre-Leon-Durand de Linois sailed from Toulon with 3 ships of the line, *Indomptable* (80), *Formidable* (80) and *Desaix* (74), with the frigate *Muiron* (38), having 1,600 soldiers aboard under General Pierre Devaux. His object was to proceed to Cádiz and effect a junction with Rear-Admiral Pierre-Etienne-Réné-Marie Dumanoir-le-Pelley, who was there with 6 newly built French ships of the line. In conjection with a Spanish squadron of 6 ships under Vice-Admiral Don Juan Joaquîn de Moreno they were then to carry reinforcements to Bonaparte's army in Egypt.

There was a British squadron off Cádiz consisting of 7 ships of the line under Rear-Admiral Sir James Saumarez: *Caesar* (80), flagship, the 74s *Pompée, Spencer, Vénérable, Superb*, (detached on 1 July to watch the mouth of the Guadalquivir), and *Hannibal* and *Audacious*. In addition, Saumarez had the frigate *Thames* and the brig *Pasley*.

Linois's squadron was sighted from Gibraltar on 1 July, but the only British warship there was the polacre-sloop *Calpé* (14). Beating through the Straits against a strong WNW wind Linois, after a lively chase, took the brig-sloop *Speedy* (14) (Captain Lord Cochrane), on the 3rd.

Learning that Cádiz was blockaded by a superior force Linois bore up for Algeciras, where he anchored at 5pm on 4 July in full view of the Rock. At 2am on the 5th Saumarez received news of his appearance.

At daylight on the 5th, after sending *Thames* to recall *Superb*, Saumarez bore away from the Gut with a moderate NW breeze. Later in the day the squadron was for a time becalmed, but at 7am on the 6th the ships, sailing in line ahead, sighted the French, who had moored in line completely under the protection of the Spanish batteries and forts, and had the support of 14 Spanish heavy gunboats. The signal was made by *Caesar* to engage the enemy on arriving up with her in succession. The battery on Cabrita Point opened fire at 7.50am. A furious cannonade followed as the British ships, baffled by the want of wind, struggled to get into action. Hot shot as well as shells were fired by the Spanish batteries. *Hannibal* tacking for *Formidable* ran aground at about 11am. Soon after, a light breeze sprang up from the NE, and Linois, hoping to get farther out of reach of the British ships, gave his ships the signal to cut their cables and run themselves on shore, which they did, though it took a long time as the wind fell while they were wearing ship.

Frustrated by the unfavourable weather as well as the serious opposition of the enemy's batteries and shipping, Saumarez discontinued the action at 1.35pm, leaving the dismasted and shattered *Hannibal* in the hands of the French. The British squadron had sustained a great deal of damage and lost many of its boats.

| | CASUALTIES | | |
	British	French	Spanish
Killed	121	306	11
Wounded	240	280	13
Missing	14	—	—
TOTAL	375	586	24

Two of the French captains, Moncousu *(Indomptable)* and Lalonde *(Formidable)*, were killed. The Spaniards had 5 gunboats sunk and 2 badly damaged.

As soon as he had refloated his ships and his prize, Linois sent an express to Cádiz for assistance before the British could repair the damage and renew their attack.

On the afternoon of the 8th *Superb*, cruising with *Thames* and *Pasley* off Cádiz, saw 6 sail of the line, 3 frigates and a lugger come out. At daylight on the 9th the Franco-Spanish squadron, except for *Saint-Antoine* (74), put to sea. Early in the afternoon *Pasley* 'came crowding into Gibraltar with the signal for an enemy flying', and soon after the squadron cast anchor in the road of Algeciras *Superb* and *Thames* anchored in Gibraltar Bay. Next morning the *Saint-Antoine* joined the enemy.

Meanwhile the British were sparing no exertion to prevent the escape of Linois to Cádiz. *Pompée* was too shattered to be got ready in time, and *Caesar* was not much better. But it was not until noon on the 12th that the enemy began to move, forming their line off Cabrita Point. *Hannibal*, towed by the frigate *Indienne*, could not keep up and returned to Algeciras.

The chase began about 8pm, *Superb* (Captain Richard Goodwin Keats) being sent ahead to attack the sternmost of the enemy squadron. She sighted 3 ships at 11.20pm and set the *Real-Carlos* (112) on fire with her third broadside. At 11.50 she brought the *Saint-Antoine* to action and, after thirty minutes, compelled her to surrender. About fifteen minutes after midnight the *Real-Carlos* blew up, but meanwhile she had fallen foul of another Spaniard and set her ablaze. This was *San-Hermenegildo* (112) which, taking her for a foe, had engaged her. She too blew up about a quarter of an hour later.

It started to blow very hard during the early hours of the 13th. *Vénérable* engaged *Formidable*, they mauled each other and *Vénérable* went aground. With *Caesar*, *Superb* and *Audacious* in sight the Spanish admiral took what remained of his squadron into Cádiz. The weather continuing calm *Vénérable* was hove into deep water and made her way back to Gibraltar.

Of the crews of *Real-Carlos* and *San-Hermenegildo*, some 2,000 men, only about 300 survived. The sole prize was *Saint-Antoine*, an old 74 of 1,700 tons, which ended her days in Portsmouth.

ALKMAAR II (N Holland)   French Revolutionary Wars   2 October 1799
Fought between the French under General Guillaume Brune and the Russo-British army under Frederick Augustus, Duke of York and Lt-General Ivan Ivanovich Hermann.
Strength: French 30,000; Russians/British 30,000.
Aim: The Allies sought to drive the French from the Netherlands.
Battle: The Russians drove in the French advanced posts while the Duke of York outflanked them. When the Duke was in position, a simultaneous attack by the Allies on the French left and centre forced the French to give ground, enabling the Allies to occupy Alkmaar.
Result: Although their immediate objective was gained, once the Allies were inside the town they were besieged by the French, who forced the Duke of York to treat sixteen days later. The Treaty of Alkmaar was then signed.

Of all the offensives launched by the Second Coalition against France, this was the only one to make no headway. Later in the year Czar Paul I, annoyed by the lack of co-operation shown by Britain and Austria, took Russia out of the Coalition (ZURICH II).

AMBERG (Upper Palatinate, W Germany)   French Revolutionary Wars   24 August 1796
Fought between the French under General Jean-Baptiste Jourdan and the Austrians under Archduke Charles.
Strength: French 45,000; Austrians 48,000.
Aim: The Austrians sought to halt the French invasion of Germany.
Battle: The French launched an offensive against the German states of the Holy Roman Emperor, the Army of the Sambre-et-Meuse under Jourdan marched into Franconia and the Army of the Rhine-et-Moselle under General Jean-Charles Pichegru went into Swabia and Bavaria. By the summer of 1796 most of S Germany was in French hands. On 24 August Archduke Charles, brother of the Holy Roman Emperor, mounted a counter-attack against the French right flank while General von Wartensleben, who had been pressed by Jourdan before Charles's arrival, attacked from the front. The French were decisively beaten and fell back to the NW.
Result: Archduke Charles tried to widen the gap between the two French armies and, on hearing of Moreau's success at Friedburg on the same day as Amberg, shadowed Jourdan, who regrouped his men near Würzburg (qv).

ARCOLA (Nerona, Italy)   French Revolutionary Wars   15–17 November 1796
Fought between the French under Bonaparte and the main Austrian army under General Josef Alvinzi (Baron von Borberek).
Strength: French 20,000; Austrians 17,000. (Note: Both sides gradually increased their strength during the three-day engagement. Figures shown are their maximum strength on the third day.)
Aim: Bonaparte sought to prevent the junction of the Austrians with General Baron Davidovich who was descending from the Tyrol.
Battle: Bonaparte swung round the back of Alvinzi, crossing the Adige and moving through a marshy area in order to cut the Austrian communications. On 15 November he occupied the village of Arcola, but despite French attempts to storm a bridge over the Alpone in which Bonaparte personally led the attack, they were repulsed. The village was evacuated overnight and attacked again by the French on the second day, when the Austrians again held their ground. On the third day an assault was made by General André Masséna on the main bridge once more, while General Pierre Augereau crossed the Alpone by a trestle bridge below the village. At the same time a detachment of French cavalry went to the rear of the Austrian lines, blowing bugles. The Austrians, thinking they were encircled, broke and retreated.
Austrian losses have been estimated as being from 6,000 to 10,000. French losses were also heavy, amounting to 4,600.
Result: A French victory. Bonaparte left the pursuit of Alvinzi on hearing the Vaubois had been driven back from Verona by Davidovich the same day, and chased Davidovich into Trento.

ARROW v DE DRAAK (Vlie, Texel, Holland)   French Revolutionary Wars   12 September 1799
The British warships *Arrow* (28) (Captain Nathaniel Portlock) and *Wolverine* (13) (Captain William Bolton) took the Dutch ship *De Draak* (24) (Lieutenant Van Esch) and the brig *De Gier* (14). Since she was very old and considered unserviceable, the former Dutch vessel was burnt. However, the brig was taken into the British service.
On 15 September another Dutch ship, *Dolfyn* (24), surrendered. She was taken into the British navy as *Dolphin*.

ASTRAEA v GLOIRE (off Ushant)   French Revolutionary Wars   10 April 1795
Astraea (32) (Captain Lord Henry Paulet) was part of a British squadron of 5 ships of the line and 3 frigates under Captain John Monckton (HMS *Colossus* [74]) on patrol. On 10 April 1795 3 French sail were sighted, and they promptly scattered. *Astraea* pursued *Gloire* (36). The action which followed lasted from 6pm to 11.30 pm, the last hour being fought in close combat, after which *Gloire* struck her colours.
British casualties were 1 killed and 7 wounded; French, 40 killed and wounded.

ATLANTIC I   SEE OPERATIONS IN THE ATLANTIC I

AVESNES-LE-SEC (Nord, France)   French Revolutionary Wars   12 September 1793
Nine Austrian cavalry squadrons (about 2,000 horse, including the émigré regiment Royal-Allemand from the French service), with no guns, attacked and totally dispersed 4,663 French, mostly infantry, under General Nicolas Declaye. In this engagement 2,000 French were killed, 2,000 captured and 18 guns taken. Austrian losses were 69 killed.

This cavalry action, taken on the spur of the moment, is one of the most brilliant in cavalry history. The French cavalry were routed at the outset, and though their infantry formed a square, the Austrians rode right over them. Declaye was arrested but escaped the guillotine: proof that the Convention knew its troops were not very steady!

BAISIEUX (Nord France)   French Revolutionary Wars   29 April 1792
General Theobald, Chevalier de Dillon, with 2,300 men advanced from Lille on Tournai but, on sighting the Austrian outposts, raised the cry of *'Nous sommes trahis'* (We are betrayed) and fled in confusion.

At Lille the French murdered their general, mutilating his corpse which they hung up by the heels. This gives an idea of the misconduct and poor morale of the revolutionary forces during the early stage of the war.

BASSANO (Vicenza, italy)   French Revolutionary Wars   8 September 1796
Fought between the French under General Bonaparte and the Austrians under Field-Marshal Count Dagobert von Würmser.
Aim: The repulse of the Austrians by the French.
Battle: Having taken the Austrian guard at Primolano (qv) on 7 September, Bonaparte reached the Austrians who were trying to concentrate their forces at Bassano after an unsuccessful offensive against Mantua (qv). General Pierre Augereau attacked along the left bank of the Brenta (the east side) and General André Masséna down the right bank. Surrounded, an entire Austrian division surrendered with only a few units escaping to the east. Würmser led 12,000 survivors to Mantua. Austrians losses were 3,000 prisoners, 35 cannon and more than 200 wagons.
Result: The French victory further weakened Austrian forces in Italy. The distance the French marched during this campaign was prodigious, even by Napoleonic standards.

BASTILLE, THE (Paris, France)   French Revolutionary Wars   14 July 1789
The Bastille was a grey stone medieval fortress with eight pointed towers, a dry moat and two drawbridges. It had an evil reputation as a state prison, but since 1776 few people had been imprisoned there. The Governor, De Launay, irresolute and anxious, was very ill-prepared to defend the place, though he had at least 18 guns as well as a small garrison of Swiss and veterans.

On 14 July, in the midst of a heat-wave, a ferocious mob, already excited by the Affaire Reveillon (17 April) and the charge of the Prince de Lambesc and the Royal Allemand Regiment near the Tuileries (12 July), assembled in great numbers in the Faubourg St Antoine. After a parley they broke into the Cour du Gouvernement without resistance, by cutting down the drawbridge. Only now did the garrison open fire, but with musketry; they only fired 1 cannon and that but once.

Against the insurgents led by Pierre Hulin, a laundry manager, and reinforced by 5 cannon and some of the Gardes Françaises under their sergeants, the Bastille could easily have held out, but the invalids sympathised with the mob and, when he had sustained no more than three casualties, the unfortunate Governor surrendered. Despite the protection of Hulin he was murdered and his head paraded on a pike. Many of the wretched invalids were massacred without pity.

The 7 prisoners found included 4 forgers, 2 lunatics and de Sade confined at the request of his family for 'monstrous crimes'. On hearing of this exploit, Charles James Fox, the Whig statesman, wrote: 'How much the greatest event it is that ever happened in the world! and how much the best!'

'The fall of the Bastille was the signal for the collapse of the old order. Authority was gone. All over France the peasants rose and destroyed the records which embodied the conditions of their dependence. It seemed as though chaos were come again, and everywhere the peaceable citizens armed themselves for the maintenance of Order.' (Spencer Wilkinson, *The French Army before Napoleon*, p. 105) Thus the National Guards came into existence. By June 1790 no less than 2½ million had been enrolled.

BEAUMONT-EN-CAMBRESIS (Nord, France)   French Revolutionary Wars   26 April 1794
Major-General Otto, commanding a division of Austrian and British cavalry (18 squadrons), cheerfully atacked 20,000 French infantry and routed them, taking 41 guns.

Aim: General Charles Pichegru, as part of a general advance, planned to raise the Allied siege of Landrecies.

Battle: Beaumont-en-Cambrésis is really only part of a larger battle, but is by far the most striking episode in it. The French plan was, using their two-to-one numerical superiority, to attack the Allied army covering the siege of Landrecies. Through the courage and skill of Archduke Charles of Austria, two of the French attacks were beaten off, but on the western edge of the battle a far more remarkable success was achieved.

General Renée-Bernard Chapuy (Chapuis) led one French column along the road from Cambrai to Le Cateau, while a second column of 4,000 advanced through the villages of Ligny and Bertry, a little farther to the south. Favoured by a dense fog they managed to drive the Allied advanced posts from the village of Inchy and Beaumont-en-Cambrésis on the high-road, and Troisvilles, Bertry and Maurois to the south. They then began to form up along the ridge on which these villages stand, but before the formation was complete, the fog lifted, and the Duke of York was able to see that the French left flank was unsupported. He staged a noisy demonstration with his artillery against the French centre, sent some light troops to engage their right, and formed up all his cavalry against the French left between the villages of Inchy and Béthencourt. The cavalry was drawn up in three lines under General Otto, the first line being Austrian cuirassiers, the second and third British, the whole being nineteen squadrons.

Otto advanced skilfully and cautiously, some French cavalry first being overthrown, and General Chapuy wounded and captured. They then charged into the flank of the French infantry which was still serenely facing east. Major-General John Mansel, who was determined to clear himself of the stain of supposed cowardice at Villers-en-Cauchies (qv) two days before, attacked far ahead of his men, followed by his two sons. Mansel and one son were killed at once, but the attack went home and in a few minutes the whole mass of the French was broken and flying to the south under merciless pursuit. Mansel's second son was wounded. Meanwhile Chapuys's second column, farther to the south, was also broken up by a mixed Austro-British light cavalry force.

The allied casualties numbered 15 officers and 384 men. French losses have been put as high as 7,000, of whom 3,200 are said to have been sabred. The prisoners numbered at least 350 including their general, Chapuis.

Result: This was one of the greatest days ever for British cavalry, but the victory was not followed up.

BELLE-ILE-EN-MER   see ILE-DE-GROIX

BERGEN-OP-ZOOM (N Brabant, Holland)   French Revolutionary Wars   19 September 1799
Fought between the French under General Dominique-Joseph-René Vandamme and the Russo-British army under Frederick Augustus, Duke of York, and Lt-General Ivan Ivanovich Hermann.
Strength: French 35,000; Russians/British 35,000.
Aim: The French sought to repel the invasion of the Allies in the Netherlands.
Battle: Vandamme attacked the Allies at Bergen on 19 September. Because the Allies could not co-ordinate their operations, the battle went very unevenly. On the right wing the Russians were overwhelmed and nearly all Hermann's division were taken prisoner, though the British repulsed the French attack with heavy loss. Despite the success of the British, the Allies were forced to continue the retreat towards Zijpe. French losses were 3,000 men killed and wounded. British losses were 500, but the Russian casualties amounted to 3,500 men and in addition they lost 26 guns.
Result: Although the Allies were forced to retreat immediately after the battle, they advanced again two weeks later.

BIBERACH (S Baden, W Germany)   French Revolutionary Wars   October 1796
Fought between the French under General Jean Moreau and the Austrians under Archduke Charles.
Aim: Consolidation of the Austrian victory at Würzburg (qv).
Battle: Moreau, retreating through the Black Forest, was attacked by the Austrians whom he defeated, thereafter continuing his withdrawal unmolested.
Result: A setback for the Austrians.

BLANCHE II (off Spain)   French Revolutionary Wars   19 December 1796
On 10 December 1796 *Blanche* (32) (Captain D'Arcy Preston), in company with *Minerve* (38) (Commodore Horatio Nelson) on passage from Gibraltar to Porto Ferraro, came up with 2 Spanish

frigates. *Blanche* was instructed to engage the smaller of the frigates, which surrendered after a short action. However, 2 other ships of a Spanish squadron, followed shortly by a 3-decker–*Principe D'Asturies*–appeared. Preston decided to close on his Commodore, who had been in action with the larger of the 2 original frigates and was then engaged with *Matilda* (34), and took on *Ceres*. The presence of a very much superior force, however, decided Preston, although his ship had suffered neither damage nor casualties, to content himself with a trophyless triumph.

BOIS-LE-DUC (N Brabant, Holland)   French Revolutionary Wars   12 November 1794
Fought between the Dutch and Austrians under Frederick Augustus, Duke of York, and the French under General Jean Moreau.
Aim: Moreau wished to enter Holland at a time when the dykes would be no obstacle to his advance. His enemy sought to prevent this.
Battle: Moreau attempted to cross the Meuse at Fort Crèvecoeur, Bois-le-Duc, near s'Hertogenbosch, but the Allied army contested his passage so hotly that Moreau was obliged to withdraw and abandon his project.
Result: The French advance was temporarily halted.

BORGHETTO (Mantua, Italy)   French Revolutionary Wars   30 May 1796
Fought between the Austrians under General Baron de Beaulieu and the French under Bonaparte.
Strength: Austrians 19,000; French 28,000.
Aim: The French aim was to force the passage of the Mincio.
Battle: Beaulieu had his forces strung out along the river Mincio from Lake Garda to Mantua. Arriving on 29 May Bonaparte repaired the bridge at Borghetto under heavy fire and crossed it on 30 May, forcing the Austrians to evacuate Peschiera. Beaulieu narrowly escaped with his life. The battle is also known as the Passage of the Mincio. The French took 500 prisoners.
    This French success marked the conclusion of the second phase of the Italian campaign. The whole of the Lombardy Plain and the area of the Quadrilateral, with the notable exception of Mantua (qv), were now under French control.

BOXTEL (N Brabant, Holland)   French Revolutionary Wars   13–15 September 1793
Fought between the French under General Jean-Charles Pichegru and the Dutch/British/Hanoverians under Frederick Augustus, Duke of York.
Aim: The French made an attack on the Allied forces as a feint to distract attention from their attempt to encircle the Allied left wing.
Battle: On 13 September the French advanced and on the 14th took an Allied outpost, capturing two Darmstadt battalions at Boxtel. In response on 15 September the Duke of York ordered Major-General Ralph Abercromby to counter-attack with ten battalions and ten squadrons. This move nearly ended in disaster, as Abercromby found himself entangling with the main body of the French army. Abercromby quickly retreated but in good order, covered by the 33rd Regiment which was commanded by the young Lt-Colonel Arthur Wellesley, later Duke of Wellington. It was at this engagement that Wellesley came under fire for the first time.
Result: The French objective was not achieved.

CALDIERO I (Verona, Italy)   French Revolutionary Wars   12 November 1796
Fought between two Austrians armies under General Baron Paul Davidovich and General Josef Alvinzi (Baron von Borberek) and the French under Bonaparte.
Strength: Austrians 18,000 (Davidovich) + 29,000 (Alvinzi); French 30,000.
Aim: The Austrians intended to relieve Mantua.
Battle: In early November Davidovich pushed the French back down the Adige to Rivoli (qv) while Alvinzi overran French outposts in his path. When Davidovich encamped, however, the French concentrated on Alvinzi. From Verona Bonaparte sent two divisions to attack the Austrians. General Pierre Augereau on the right and General André Masséna on the left. Their objective was the Austrian advanced guard of 8,000 men. But a sleet-storm prevented them from reaching the enemy at Caldiero and, while the Austrians held their ground, the main body arrived and Alvinzi attacked the French, repulsing them. The French lost 2,000 men, and 5 general officers were wounded.
Result: The French withdrew to Verona, their defeat being avenged within a week by the Battle of Arcola (qv).

CALIANO (Trento, Italy)   French Revolutionary Wars   5 September 1796
Fought between the French under Bonaparte and the Austrians under General Baron Paul Davidovich.
Strength: French 34,000; Austrians 20,000.
Aim: The Austrian army had divided, Würmser and Davidovich commanding the two halves. Field-Marshal Count Dagobert von Würmser with 26,000 men was to march on Mantua (qv) while Davidovich was to defend the Tyrol. Bonaparte sent General André Masséna after Davidovich and stayed with Würmser. When Davidovich's intention became apparent, Bonaparte sought to prevent the design being effected.
Battle: Before a forced march by Bonaparte to Caliano, the French beat Davidovich's advance guard out of Marco. At Caliano the battle began with a barrage of artillery. A furious charge followed which drove the Austrians out of Caliano. Austrian losses were 6,000 men and 20 cannon.
Result: Davidovich abandoned Trento and retreated into the Alps. Bonaparte turned against Würmser and beat him at the Battle of Bassano (qv).

CAMPERDOWN (Holland)   French Revolutionary Wars   11 October 1797
Fought 7 miles off the Dutch coast (opposite the area between the villages of Egremont and Camperdown) between the Dutch fleet under Admiral Jan Willem de Winter and the British fleet under Admiral Adam Duncan.
Strength: Dutch 18 ships of the line with 1,108 guns; British 16 ships of the line with 1,066 guns.
Aim: The British sought to prevent the Dutch from aiding the French, who were planning a landing in Ireland.
Battle: Duncan intercepted and promptly attacked the Dutch as they sailed out of the Texel. The British fleet in two groups under Duncan and Vice-Admiral Richard Onslow broke the Dutch fleet into three groups. The British captured 9 vessels, including the flagship, *Vrijheid*, but opposition was so obstinate that the British suffered severe damage and none of the prizes could be used. British losses were 1,040 killed and wounded and Dutch 1,160 killed and wounded plus 6,000 prisoners.
Result: The Dutch fleet was prevented from joining the French. Duncan's victory, coming so soon after the great mutinies at the Nore and Spithead, was received with enthusiasm.

CAPE ST VINCENT I (Spain)   French Revolutionary Wars   14 February 1797
Fought between the Spanish fleet under Admiral Don José de Cordova and the British fleet under Admiral Sir John Jervis.
Strength: Spanish 27 ships of the line with 2,308 guns; British 15 ships of the line with 1,232 guns.
Aim: The Spaniards sought to join the French fleet for a proposed invasion of England. The British sought to prevent their junction.
Battle: Jervis, with the former Mediterranean fleet, was cruising off Cape St Vincent when he encountered the Spanish fleet which was divided into two groups of 9 and 18 ships. Jervis sailed into the midst of them in line, and turned on the larger group which, though officers and men were inexperienced, might have got away had not Commodore Horatio Nelson, acting without orders, broken away from the line. Taking his ship *Captain* (74) in a wide sweep, he placed it in the path of the group of 9 Spanish ships, engaging them until Jervis was able to come up. In the ensuing mêlée 4 Spanish ships were taken, two of them–*San Nicolas* (84) and *San Josef* (112)–by Nelson. The remains of the Spanish fleet managed to escape to Cadiz the next day.
    Spanish casualties were at least 200 killed and 1,284 wounded, and in addition 2,300 were taken prisoner. The Spanish flagship, *Santissima Trinidad* (136), had some 200 casualties. British losses were 75 killed and 227 wounded. The expenditure of ammunition was prodigious, yet not a single gun burst on the British side–most unusual by eighteenth-century standards.
Result: The victory marked the end of the Spanish threat to England.
    Nelson's action in the battle contributed largely to the British success. It proved the effectiveness of attacking in a mêlée as opposed to attacking in line, given a superior standard of seamanship.

CARYSFOOT v CASTOR (Bay of Biscay)   French Revolutionary Wars   29 May 1794
Fought between HMS *Carysfoot*, a 28-gun frigate (Captain Francis Laforey) and the French 32-gun Frigate *Castor* (Captain L'Huillier).
    Castor had previously been captured by the French on 19 May 1794 while under the command of Captain Thomas Troubridge. In this engagement, ten days later, it was recaptured by *Carysfoot* SW of Ushant in the Bay of Biscay, and 20 British seamen were recovered.

CASSANO D'ADDA II (Milan, Italy)   French Revolutionary Wars   27 April 1799
Fought between an Austro-Russian army, under General Michael von Melas and Field-Marshal Count Suvorov, and the French under General Jean Moreau.
Strength: Austrians/Russians 65,000; French 30,000.
Aim: The Allied army sought to drive the French out of Italy.
Battle: Moreau had dug in along the Adda River line. The Allies stormed the French defences and overran them. Their losses were 6,000 killed and wounded. The French suffered many casualties and 7,000 of them were taken prisoner.
Result: The rout of the French army enabled Suvorov to enter Milan and Turin in triumph while the French fell back towards Genoa. Because of differences with the Austrian government Suvorov did not continue his pursuit of the defeated French and his campaign deteriorated into the besieging of small French garrisons in N Italy, which dissipated his forces.

CASTIGLIONE DELLE STIVIERE (Mantua, Italy)   French Revolutionary Wars   5 August 1796
Fought between the French under Bonaparte and the Austrians under Field-Marshal Count Dagobert von Würmser.
Strength: French 30,000; Austrians 24,000.
Aim: The destruction of the opposing forces.
Battle: On 3 August the Battle of Lonato (qv) took place, and two days later the victorious French massed at Castiglione, General Pierre Augereau having held the Austrians south of the lake during Lonato. Bonaparte, concentrating all his forces, attacked Würmser on both flanks and, turning the Austrian left, attacked their rear in the same continued movement. The Austrian army was not sufficiently drilled to change front to a flank in the midst of battle, and fell into disorder. Würmser was forced back across the Mincio. Total Austrian losses from both battles were 16,000 men and all their artillery.
Result: Bonaparte, by putting himself between two enemy forces and concentrating all his own forces on each one in turn at Lonato and Castiglione, had decisively defeated them both. The French victory caused a general Austrian retreat towards the Tyrol.

CHARLEROI (Hainaut, Belgium)   French Revolutionary Wars   12–25 June 1794
The French under General Jean-Baptiste Jourdan laid siege to Charleroi, in Allied hands. Jourdan had moved up from the Moselle and formed the Army of the Sambre-et-Meuse totalling 75,000–80,000 men, a mixture of a few veterans and many conscripts raised in the Levée en Masse.
    On 12 June Jourdan invested Charleroi, and on 25 June the town fell before Friedrich Josias, Prince of Saxe-Coburg, commanding an Allied force of 52,000 men, had time to relieve it.

CHILDERS (off Brest, Finistère, France)   French Revolutionary Wars   2 January 1793
French shore batteries guarding the harbour of Brest fired on the British brig-sloop *Childers* (16) (Captain Robert Barlow), destroying one of her guns with a 48-pound shot.
    France did not in fact declare war on Great Britain until 1 February. Nevertheless, this incident appears to have been the first hostile act presaging the wars which lasted, on and off, from 1793 to 1815.

COPENHAGEN I (Denmark)   French Revolutionary Wars   2 April 1801
Fought between the British fleet under Admiral Sir Hyde Parker and Vice-Admiral Lord Nelson and the Danish fleet, which consisted of armed hulks and floating batteries as well as warships.
Strength: British 20 ships of the line + frigates; Danish 10 ships of the line + shore batteries.
Aim: The British sought to deliver an ultimatum to Crown Prince Frederick, Regent for Christian VII (who was insane), King of Denmark and Norway. Three northern powers, with Russia, had formed the Second Armed Neutrality in defence of what they considered were their shipping rights against the continental blockade of Europe imposed by the British navy and aimed at the French. Britain, after the collapse of the Second Coalition, had only this powerful blockade weapon available to foil Napoleon's ambitious plans. Under pressure from the French, the Danes sought to prevent the entry of the British into the Baltic. After diplomatic approaches had failed Nelson sailed in.
Battle: The Danish position was of difficult access, and seemed vulnerable to an attack from the north. The greater draught of the bigger British ships would make them difficult to use in the narrow shoal waters. Nelson managed to persuade the far less energetic Admiral Hyde Parker that an attack by the smaller British ships of the line from the south would be possible. Very careful surveys of the area over

which the ships would have to sail were made by the British, principally by Captain Edward Rion and Captain Thomas Hardy. On 1 April Admiral Nelson sailed his squadron, consisting of 12 of the smaller British line ships and 5 frigates, with various smaller ships, to a position at the southern end of the middle ground via the Hollander Deep. On the morning of 2 April they sailed, led by *Edgar*, towards the Danish fleet, whereupon 3 of the largest British ships ran aground–1 in such a position as to be totally out of action, 2 where they could only fire at long range. Nonetheless, the British attack went on. The British frigates, gallantly led by Captain Rion, did their best to fill in for the grounded ships. The shore batteries having been silenced, the British turned on the Danish fleet.

The main action began at 10am and the fighting raged with extraordinary ferocity, the Danes proving much tougher opponents than expected. At about 2pm the Danish flagship was seen to be on fire and drifting. She blew up at 3.30pm. Although most of their guns had by now been dismounted, the Danes still fought on. Nelson, to prevent further bloodshed and to prevent the Danish firing on their own ships which had been taken as prizes, sent one of his officers (Captain Thesiger, who spoke Danish) to propose a truce, which was, after some negotiation, accepted. By now the leading ships of Hyde Parker's division had got close enough to intervene and Nelson took the opportunity to get the most damaged ships clear. It was at the height of this battle that the famous blind-eye episode occurred, Hyde Parker signalling 'Discontinue action' and Nelson (and Rear-Admiral Thomas Graves, his senior subordinate) ignoring the order. The Danish casualties were 1,035 killed and wounded. They lost 1 ship destroyed, the remainder of their flotilla being disabled and captured. The British casualties were 944 officers and men killed and wounded including Captain Rion.

Result: The Danes accepted a truce, and as the Czar Paul I had been assassinated some days previously, the Armed Neutrality collapsed. The new Czar, Alexander I, remained friendly to Britain thereafter. The immediate naval result was that Hyde Parker was removed and Nelson, who had disobeyed his superior officer's orders, was appointed Commander-in-Chief.

CORNWALLIS'S RETREAT   see OPERATIONS IN THE ATLANTIC I

COURIER v LE GUERRIER (North Sea)   French Revolutionary Wars   22–23 November 1799
Cruising off Flushing, the hired cutter *Courier* (12) (Lieutenant Thomas Searle) saw a suspicious sail bring-to a brig, and, learning that the other vessel was a French privateer cutter, crowded sail in pursuit. At 9am on 23 November *Courier* overtook the French vessel, *Le Guérrier* (14) (Captain Félix L. Lallemand), 10 or 12 leagues SE of Lowestoft and, after a warm and close action of fifty minutes, compelled her to surrender. *Courier* had 1 killed and 2 wounded, while *Guérrier* had 4 killed and 6 wounded.

CRESCENT v REUNION (English Channel)   French Revolutionary Wars   20 October 1793
The British frigate *Crescent* (36) (Captain James Saumarez) sailed from Spithead on a cruise. Two French frigates, based on Cherbourg, had made valuable prizes. One usually quitted that port in the evening, stood across the Channel during the night, and returned next morning with whatever prizes she had picked up. On the night of 19 October Saumarez ran close off Cap Barfleur and there, at dawn on the 20th, sighted *Réunion* (36) (Captain François Dénian) and a large cutter, *Espérance* (14). After a close and brave action of two hours and ten minutes *Réunion* struck, *Espérance* escaping into Cherbourg.

Crescent's crew of 257 suffered 1 casualty: a seaman whose leg was broken by the recoil of his gun. *Réunion*, with a crew of 300, suffered casualties of at least 33 killed and 48 severely wounded. Saumarez took his prize into Portsmouth.

DEGO (Savona, Italy)   French Revolutionary Wars   15–15 April 1796
Fought between the French under Bonaparte and the Austro-Sardinian army.
Strength: French 17,000; Austrians/Sardinians 5,000.
Aim: After the French victory at Montenotte (qv), Bonaparte sought to drive the Allied armies away from each other.
Battle: On 14 April Bonaparte attacked the Austro-Sardinian garrison at Dego and drove the defenders out. General André Masséna, however, left the town weakly guarded and on 15 April the Austrians retook it. On the same day, Bonaparte attacked once more and drove the enemy out of Dego to the north.
Result: The Allies retreated, General Baron de Beaulieu to the north and the Sardinians towards Turin, their capital, which they wanted to protect. Bonaparte followed the latter, under General Baron Colli.

DIDO v MINERVE (between Minorca and Toulon)   French Revolutionary Wars   24 June 1795
The British frigates *Dido* (28) (Captain George Henry Towry) and *Lowestoffe* (32) (Captain Robert Gambier Middleton) attacked the French frigates *Minerve* (40) (Captain Perrée) and *Artémise* (36) (Captain Charbonnier).

The French were sighted at 4am and pursued, but at 8am they turned to fight. *Dido* got under *Minerve*'s stern and cannonaded her steadily, but eventually the *Minerve* became locked in *Dido*'s mizzen rigging, and her crew attampted to board. By the time they broke clear *Dido* was almost a wreck.

Lowestoffe now (9am) engaged *Minerve* and in six or eight minutes so damaged her masts that she could not escape. *Artémise* fired an ineffectual broadside into each British frigate and then made sail for Toulon, pursued by *Lowestoffe* until a shot disabled her mizzenmast.

Recalled by Captain Towry *Lowestoffe* raked *Minerve*, which surrendered at 11.45, being by that time in an utterly unmanageable state. Of *Lowestoffe*'s crew of 212, 3 were wounded. *Dido*, with a complement of 193, had 6 killed and 15 wounded, while *Minerve*, with a crew of 318, suffered casualties of 20 killed and wounded, Captain Perrée being among the latter.

Had *Artémise* supported *Minerve* as well as *Lowestoffe* seconded *Dido* the outcome would have been very different. Captain Towry's noble conduct in singling out an opponent of nearly double his size and force was handsomely rewarded. *Minerve* was taken into the British navy as a 38-gun frigate, and Towry became her captain.

DROITS DE L'HOMME v INDEFATIGABLE (off Ushant/Bay of Audierne, France)   French Revolutionary Wars   13–14 January 1797
In December 1796 the French attempted a descent upon Ireland, but foiled by foul weather and lack of provisions, despaired of success. Their warships made their separate ways back to France.

Droits de l'Homme (74), under Commodore Jean-Raymond Lacrosse, a very able and experienced officer, with General Jean-Joseph-Amable Humbert and a battalion of soldiers aboard, made for Belle-Ile-en-Mer. But in a rising storm she was pursued–initially, 150 miles off Ushant–by the British frigates *Indefatigable* (44) (Captain Sir Edward Pellew) and *Amazon* (36) (Captain Robert Carthew Reynolds) and, in a long hard action, was driven on to the rocks 200 yards off-shore in the Bay of Audierne, 30 miles south of Brest. *Amazon* also ran ashore.

Droits de l'Homme had three times Pellew's fire-power, outnumbered him five to one in manpower, and fired at least 4,000 rounds. She had 103 killed and 150 wounded and, of the survivors, only about one-third struggled ashore during the next five days. The rest died of starvation and exposure, though both Lacrosse and Humbert were saved. The survivors of *Amazon* rafted themselves ashore and became prisoners of war.

DRYAD v PROSERPINE (off S Ireland)   French Revolutionary Wars   13 June 1796
About 36 miles SE of Cape Clear, *Dryad* (44) (Captain Lord Amelius Beauclerk) sighted and gave chase to the French *Proserpine* (42) (Captain Etienne Pevrieux), which had become detached in fog from Commodore Moulston's squadron (UNICORN V TRIBUNE). Although her sails and rigging were badly shot up by *Proserpine*'s stern chasers, *Dryad* got into close action and forced *Proserpine* to surrender. Had the French ship not fled, she could have brought more guns to bear. *Dryad*, with a complement of 251, had 2 killed and 7 wounded. *Proserpine*'s casualties were 30 killed and 45 wounded out of a crew numbering 348.

Proserpine, a valuable acquisition, was taken into the British navy as the frigate *Amelia*.

DUNKIRK (DUNKERQUE) (Nord, France)   French Revolutionary Wars   24 August–8 September 1793
Fought between Anglo-Hanoverian forces under Frederick Augustus, Duke of York, and the French under General Jean-Nicolas Houchard.
Aim: The British wanted to occupy the port of Dunkirk as a springboard on the continent for further operations against the French Revolutionaries and in support of the French Monarchist forces. Dunkirk was garrisoned by about 8,000 French supported by a well-organised artillery defence.
Battle: Prince Frederick Augustus advanced with 13,000 disciplined and well-trained British and Hanoverian troops and started the investment of Dunkirk on 24 August after an engagement at Lincelles (qv) on 18 August *en route*. Meanwhile the Prince of Orange's Netherland forces linked York to the Austrians farther east.

On the French side Lazare Carnot, a stern uncompromising soldier of the old régime, had combined regular veterans with enthusiastic raw recruits and conscripts raised in the Levée en Masse on 23 August. (In his two-year tenure of office the great effort made by Carnot in reorganising the French army and defeating the attempts at the invasion of France by the Allies earned him the soubriquet 'Organiser of Victories'.)

On 6 September 42,000 French under General Houchard attacked the Duke of York's regulars at Hondschoote (qv). By sheer weight of numbers and with appalling casualties the French forced back the British and Hanoverian troops and overran their siege guns. Houchard then turned on the Prince of Orange and routed him at the Battle of Menin (qv) on 13 September, but failed to push the Austrians out of E France, with the result that Houchard was guillotined and General Jean-Baptiste Jourdan took his place. On 8 September the Duke of York raised the siege of Dunkirk.

Result: Although the siege was unsuccessful, partly owing to lack of preparation in England, the disciplined British/Hanoverians played an important part in creating a diversion for the main operation of the Austrians under Friedrich Josias, Prince of Saxe-Coburg (WATTIGNIES).

EGMONT-OP-ZEE (Noord, Holland)   French Revolutionary Wars   2 October 1799
Fought between the Russo-British under Frederick Augustus, Duke of York, and the French under General Guillaume Brune.

The Duke of York inflicted a defeat upon the French, the British casualties sustained being 1,348 killed and wounded. Despite a further success on 9 October, the French managed to pen the Duke and his Russian Allies in their narrow bridgehead, and on 17 October he signed the Treaty of Alkmaar (qv). By this he agreed to quit Holland and to arrange the release of 8,000 French prisoners of war. The Duke was severely criticised at the time, especially by anti-Royalist factions. But later judgement, in the light of further research, takes the view that the Duke was the first general to inflict a major strategic defeat on Bonaparte–which he did without fighting–between 1803 and 1805. However, after the present battle he never again commanded in the field.

ENGEN (S Baden, W Germany)   French Revolutionary Wars   3 May 1800
Fought between the French under General Jean Moreau and the Austrians under General Baron Paul Kray von Krajowa.

Strength: French 56,000; Austrians 110,000.

Aim: The Austrians sought to prevent the French advance into Baden by blocking their path through the Black Forest.

Battle: The action took place between half the French army and the main Austrian army at the same time as Stockach II (qv), when the right wing of the French army engaged the Austrian rearguard. Moreau was attacked by 40,000 Austrians, whom he repulsed. Both sides lost about 2,000 men killed and wounded, and 5,000 Austrians were taken prisoner.

Result: The defeat of both parts of the Austrian army forced von Krajowa to retire towards Ulm, closely pursued by the French army under Moreau.

ERBACH (S Hesse, W Germany)   French Revolutionary Wars   16 May 1800
Fought between the French under General Gilles-Joseph de St-Suzanne and the Austrians under General Baron Paul Kray von Krajowa.

Strength: French 15,000; Austrians 36,000 (12,000 cavalry).

Aim: The Austrians, retiring before the French advance, sought to halt their progress.

Battle: The Austrians attacked vigorously with superior numbers; but the French, though forced back at some points, were not routed, and when after twelve hours fighting General Larent Gouvion-St-Cyr's Corps approached, the Austrians were forced to retire.

Result: The Austrian defeat gave France a strategic advantage.

ESPOIR v LIGURIA (W Mediterranean)   French Revolutionary Wars   7 August 1798
The brig-sloop *Espoir* (14) (Captain Loftus Otway Bland), while escorting part of a convoy from Oran to Gibraltar, sighted a strange ship–*Liguria*–bearing down with the evident intention of cutting off some ships from the convoy. On closing, *Liguria* invited *Espoir* to surrender. This invitation was ignored and an exchange of fire ensued. *Liguria* eventually surrendered. Although a much superior warship, *Liguria* was Genoese with a cosmopolitan crew who were not well trained. Nevertheless, credit is due to Captain Bland for engaging her.

FAMARS (Nord, France)   French Revolutionary Wars   23 May 1793
Frederick Josias, Prince of Saxe-Coburg, reinforced by the Duke of York's 13,000 well-disciplined British and Hanoverian veterans, decided (prior to investing Valenciennes) to attack the French under General Adam Custine encamped at Famars.

Saxe-Coburg chose to attack in six columns abreast making maximum use of the flat terrain. The attack, although delayed by fog, was sufficient to cause the French to evacuate their untenable position overnight, and the way was open for the siege of Valenciennes. Valenciennes fell soon afterwards, on 29 July.

For this defeat and lack of fighting spirit Custine was guillotined on orders of the Committee of Public Safety, establishing a pattern which perhaps put backbone into all the French revolutionary commanders from thereon and helped account for the turn of the tide and their victories thereafter.

FISGARD v L'IMMORTALITE (off Brest, France)   French Revolutionary Wars   20 October 1798
After a long and well-fought action the ex-French frigate Fisgard (38) (Captain Thomas Byam Martin) took L'Immortalité (42) (Captain Jean-François Legrand) on her way home after the 12 October action (IRELAND, ATTEMPTED FRENCH INVASION OF). She had 240 soldiers aboard, and consequently her loss was proportionately very great. French casualties were 64 killed and 61 wounded; British, 10 killed and 26 wounded.

The 2 ships were nearly of equal force, and on the British side this is considered one of the most brilliant frigate actions of the period.

FISHGUARD (Dyfed, Wales)   French Revolutionary Wars   24 February 1797
During the night of 22 February a French squadron of 4 warships under Captain Jean-Baptiste Laroque, after appearing off Ilfracombe (20 February) landed 1,200 French soldiers in Fishguard Bay. They were under General Tate, an Irish-American adventurer.

Colonel Lord Cawdor called out the Yeomanry, Militia and Volunteers and marched to oppose them, accompanied by multitudes of peasantry with pikes and scythes, and numbers of Welsh women in national costume, high black hats and red shawls. It seems the French took them for redcoats, for Tate promptly surrendered.

This strange expedition, which had been intended to sack Bristol and Liverpool, caused a run on the banks, and the Bank of England was authorised to issue £1 and £2 notes as legal tender. Since this paper money was freely accepted the country's gold was freed to pay the foreign subsidies which kept the Allies in the war.

FLEURUS (Hainaut, Belgium)   French Revolutionary Wars   26 June 1794
Fought between the Allied army (chiefly Austrian) under Friedrich Josias, Prince of Saxe-Coburg, and the armies of the National Convention under General Jean-Baptiste Jourdan.
Strength: Allies 52,000; French 73,000.
Aim: The Austrians had advanced to Charleroi (qv) to relieve it, unaware that it had fallen the previous day. They met the French army.
Battle: The Allies attacked the French, who were lying in five columns in a 20-mile radius round the town, and they were at first successful all along the line. Then French counter-attacks, despite heavy losses sustained by them and poor co-ordination between the columns, halted the Allied army. General Jean Kléber drove the Prince of Orange from the field and General Jourdan led a counter-attack in the centre. Although the Allied left wing was gaining on the over-extended French right wing, Saxe-Coburg broke the engagement off after six hours of fighting. The following day he retreated across the Meuse, thus conceding victory to Jourdan. The Prince made for Brussels in order to cover that city. His losses in the battle were only half those of Jourdan's men. In this battle the French employed an observation balloon.
Result: Following the Allies' failure to stop the French advance at Fleurus, Austria evacuated her troops from the Netherlands, which was annexed by France. Holland capitulated during the winter. Prussia and Spain dropped out of the war the following year. England withdrew her expeditionary force but, with Austria and Piedmont, remained in alliance against the National Convention. Because of its repercussions this battle may be categorised as one of the decisive conflicts of European history.

GENOA II (Italy)   French Revolutionary Wars   13–14 March 1795
Fought between the British under Vice-Admiral William Hotham and the French under Admiral Pierre Martin.

Strength: British 13 sail of the line + 6 frigates; French 15 sail of the line + 6 frigates.
Battle: On 13 March the French, with the refurbished Toulon fleet, clashed with the British all day. On the following day the French retired, leaving 2 line-of-battle ships in British hands. The British lost 74 killed and 284 wounded in the action.
Result: A tactical victory for the British, though indecisive.

GENOA III (Italy)   French Revolutionary Wars   5 April–6 June 1800
Fought between the French garrison under General André Masséna and the Austrians under General Baron Michael von Melas, then under Major-General Otto.
Strength: French 36,000; Austrians 95,000.
Aim: The Austrians sought to reduce the garrison and to capture an excellent harbour and naval base for co-operation with the British fleet under Admiral Lord Keith. On the French side, General Masséna was appointed Commander-in-Chief of the Army of Italy in November 1799 with the job of pulling together the shattered remnants of the French army, which was clinging to positions along the crest of the Maritime Alps after their numerous defeats. Bonaparte, now First Consul, wanted Masséna to maintain pressure on the Austrians, and thus to divert their attentions from his activities with the Army of Reserve. Bonaparte thought that the best way to achieve this would be to defend Genoa. This was a land commander's viewpoint, but the British possession of Genoa materially helped their eventual domination of the Mediterranean.
Battle: With the British army covering the seaward approaches, General Melas attacked on 5 April, and rapidly cut the French communications along the coast. Masséna ordered a counter-attack but, despite heroic efforts, he was forced back. Day by day the noose tightened. Masséna rejected a request by Lord Keith to surrender. The British naval blockade of Genoa was so tight that it inflicted serious hardships on the garrison and citizens as food and supplies ran down. At the end of April Masséna reported that he had rations for only thirty days.
   During a sortie made on 13 May General Nicolas-Jean de Dieu Soult, Masséna's senior subordinate commander, was wounded. Masséna had learned that Bonaparte was on the move, and decided he must at all costs hold out until 30 May. But sickness and deaths were increasing rapidly.
   On 1 June Masséna sent his acting chief of staff, Andrieux, to negotiate an exchange of prisoners, but General Otto quite rightly demanded surrender. Immediately after this Otto received orders from Melas to abandon the siege and turn to face Bonaparte. Otto disobeyed this order. After three more days of negotiation a capitulation was signed on the 4th and the 7,000 survivors of the French garrison marched out on the 6th with honours of war.
Result: Masséna had fulfilled his assignment. As Melas's chief of staff said to General Louis-Alexandre Berthier, on the morrow of Marengo (MARENGO III), 'You won this battle, not in front of Alessandria, but in front of Genoa.'

'GLORIOUS FIRST OF JUNE, THE'   see USHANT II

GROOTE KETEN (Den Helder, N Holland)   French Revolutionary Wars   27 August 1799
The object of the 'Secret Expedition' of June 1799 was to attempt to free Holland from the French. At first it was expected that Prussia might play the leading role, and that the British would co-operate by seizing Walcheren. In the event the invading force consisted of 30,000 British and 18,000 subsidised Russian troops.
   Lt-General Sir Ralph Abercromby made an opposed landing in N Holland in the teeth of a Dutch brigade. The British numbered 6,000 men to the Dutch 6,500. The first brigade put ashore was that of Major-General John Moore. British casualties were 27 officers and 440 men killed and wounded. Abercromby and Admiral Sir Charles Mitchell followed up this success by capturing the Dutch ships in Den Helder.
   On 13 September Frederick Augustus, Duke of York, arrived with reinforcements, and took the offensive against the French under Generals Guillaume Brune and Hermann-Wilhelm Daendels, whom he defeated at Bergen-op-Zoom (qv) on 19 September and then on 2 October at Egmont-op-Zee (qv).

GUT OF GIBRALTAR   see ALGECIRAS

HÖCHSTÄDT II (Swabia, W Germany)   French Revolutionary Wars   19 June 1800
Fought between the French under General Jean Moreau and the Austrians under General Baron Paul Kray von Krajowa.
Strength: French 60,000; Austrians 70,000.
Aim: The Austrians, falling back before the French advance, sought to defend their position on the left bank of the Danube.
Battle: Kray von Krajowa retired to Ulm. Moreau, swinging east, crossed the river below Ulm and attacked the Austrians 30 miles down-stream. The Austrians were not prepared for the battle and, after eighteen hours of fighting, the French captured Ulm. Many prisoners were taken, but casualties on both sides were relatively light.
Result: The French gained a secure hold on the east bank of the Danube. The Austrians were forced to retreat eastwards beyond the Inn River. Though Moreau occupied Munich, his original objective, in July, hostilities were suspended while Bonaparte held truce talks with the Austrians after his victory at Marengo (MARENGO III).

HÖHENLINDEN (Upper Bavaria, W Germany)   French Revolutionary Wars   3 December 1800
Fought between the French under Jean Moreau and the Austrians under Archduke John.
Strength: French 90,000 (rising to 119,000); Austrians 83,000 (rising to 130,000).
Aim: Austrian forces, having been reinforced, were sent to prevent the French advance towards Vienna.
Battle: Twenty miles east of Munich the armies clashed in a disorganised action. The Austrians fought piecemeal, without committing a large enough force for a concerted attack against the French whose speed and energy and better trained subordinate field officers gave them the advantage. They drove the Austrians back with a loss of 20,000 casualties, at the same time managing to surround large portions of the Austrian army.
Result: Moreau proceeded towards Vienna, driving the Austrians before him. At the same time, General Jacques Macdonald marched into the Tyrol from Switzerland and General Guillaume Brune advanced north from Italy. The three-pronged attack precipitated peace negotiations.

HONDSCHOOTE (Nord, France)   French Revolutionary Wars   6–8 September 1793
Fought between an Anglo-Hanoverian army under Frederick Augustus, Duke of York, and the French under General Jean-Nicolas Houchard.
Strength: Allies 13,000; French 42,000.
Aim: The French sought to raise the siege of Dunkirk (qv), threatened by the Allies.
Battle: The Allies, who were covering the siege of Dunkirk, were attacked by the French. The conflict lasted three days, by which time the French, though poorly organised, gained the upper hand through sheer weight of numbers, their chief tactic being to shoot at the enemy from behind hedges and dykes. The Allies managed to withdraw, losing their siege artillery.
Result: The French objective was achieved, in that the siege of Dunkirk was raised, but Houchard failed to pursue the enemy hard enough and was defeated a week later at Courtrai (Kortrijk). Houchard was then arrested and on 16 November guillotined.
   Had the Allied army chosen to march on Paris, at this time almost undefended due to the chaotic state of the armies of the National Convention, the outcome might have been the fall of the French capital, particularly as the Austrians were at the same time beginning an advance via Maubeuge (see WATTIGNIES).

ILE-DE-GROIX (Morbihan, France)   French Revolutionary Wars   23 June 1795
Fought between the British under Admiral Lord Bridport and a French squadron under Vice-Admiral Louis Villaret de Joyeuse, off Ile-de-Groix, near Belle Ile-en-Mer, on the NW coast of France.
Strength: British 14 sail of the line including 8 3-deckers + 5 frigates; French 12 sail of the line + 11 frigates.
Aim: The British Channel fleet, commanded by Admiral Lord Bridport, sailed from Spithead on 12 June 1795 with the object of protecting an expedition to Quiberon Bay (QUIBERON) destined to aid the Royalist guerrillas operating in the Vendée, south of the Loire. The French fleet, under Villaret de Joyeuse, was surprised by the British, and being outnumbered, tried to avoid action.
Battle: At 6.25pm on 22 June Lord Bridport ordered his fleet to close the French but, owing to lack of wind, it was not until 2am the next morning that it was possible to get close enough to attack. The first shot was fired by *Queen Charlotte* at 6.15pm on the 23rd. Soon afterwards 8 British ships were engaging 7

French. *Queen Charlotte* compelled the French *Alexandre* to surrender but was herself so badly damaged that when Lord Bridport came up he ordered the action to be discontinued. The remainder of the French took refuge between the de Groix and the entrance to Lorient.
Result: The Quiberon Bay convoy escaped attack, and the way was cleared for the Quiberon expedition. Lord Bridport captured 3 French ships having had 3 of his own damaged. British casualties were 31 killed and 113 wounded; French 670 killed and wounded.

IMOLA (Bologna, Italy)   French Revolutionary Wars   3 February 1797
Fought between 8,000 French and Italians, under General Claude Victor, and some 4,000 indifferent Papal troops under the nominal command of the Austrian general, Baron Colli, who had remained in Rome.
   The French advanced from Imola and found the Papal levies entrenched on the river Senio, half-way to Faenza. They had cut the bridge, but General Jean Lannes forded the river and took them in the rear when their front was already under attack. Victor's column lost some 40 killed or wounded, the Papal forces 400 or 500 killed.
   This was the only serious fighting in a comic opera campaign, which led to the fall of Rome.

INDEFATIGABLE v VIRGINIE (English Channel)   French Revolutionary Wars   20 April 1796
Having despatched *Révolutionnaire* (qv) with the prizes, *Indefatigable* (64) (Captain Sir Edward Pellew) was lying to off the Lizard with the remainder of the squadron–*Argo, Amazon* and *Concorde*–in company. The French *Virginie* (40) was sighted. Having detached *Argo* for Plymouth, Pellew gave chase for fiteen hours over 168 miles. *Indefatigable*, being a faster ship, eventually caught up with *Virginie* (Captain Jacques Bergeret), which had been prevented by the direction of the wind from escaping towards Ushant. A close action which lasted for two hours ensued, in which both ships were badly damaged. *Indefatigable* was unable to back her sails and had difficulty in avoiding being raked. Her two consorts arrived on the scene in due course and *Virginie* was forced to surrender. There were 14 killed and 27 wounded on *Virginie*, while the British sustained no casualties. (See also DROITS DE L'HOMME V INDEFATIGABLE)

IRELAND, ATTEMPTED INVASION OF (off Tory Island, NW Ireland)   French Revolutionary Wars   12, 13 and 18 October 1798
At noon on 11 October a British squadron under Commodore Sir John Borlase Warren sighted a far less powerful French squadron under Commodore Jean-Baptiste-François Bompart, which carried 3,000 troops intended for the invasion of Ireland and the British commodore made signal for a general chase. At 5am on 12 October, in moderate weather, the French were sighted about half a league to windward, and cleared for action. The British squadron consisted of *Canada* (74), flagship, *Robust* (74), *Foudroyant* (80), *Magnanime* (44), *Anson* (44), *Ethalion* (38), *Melampus* (36) and *Amelia* (44).
   By nightfall *Le Hoche* (80), *L'Ambuscade* (40), *La Coquille* (40) and *La Bellone* (40), had been taken, but then the remaining 5 French ships were lost sight of. Next day, however *Melampus* (36), boarded *La Résolue* (36), *L'Immortalité* (42), which was in company, rendering her no assistance. *Mermaid* (32) fell in with and crippled *La Loire* (46), but was herself too much disabled to pursue. But on the 18th *Anson* (44) and the brig *Kangaroo* (18) took *La Loire* off Cape Clear, after a gallant action of an hour and a quarter in which the French casualties were 48 killed and 75 wounded. *Le Hoche* and *Le Bellone* were taken into the British navy as *Donegal* and *Proserpine*. Of the French squadron only *La Romaine* (40), *La Sémillante* (36) and the schooner *La Biche* (8) escaped, for *L'Immortalité* was taken later (see FISGARD V L'IMMORTALITE).
   This success came at a time of great public tension and Commodore Sir John Borlase Warren, his officers and seamen received the thanks of both English and Irish Parliaments, and the captains a gold medal each.

ISLAND OF SCHIERMANNIKOOG (Friesland, Holland)   French Revolutionary Wars   11–13 August 1799
On 11 August the boats of the sloop *Pylades* (16) (Captain Adam M'Kenzie), the brig *L'Espiègle* (16) (Captain James Boorder) and the cutter *Courier* (10) (Lieutenant Thomas Searle), which formed part of a light squadron under Captain Frank Sotheron in *Latona* (38), cut out the gunboat *Crash* (12) which was armed with carronades. *Crash* had previously been taken from the British (26 August 1798). At the same time a schooner and a rowboat were burnt. The operation demanded tricky navigation in narrow and shallow waters.

On 13 August the boats of *Pylades* and *Crash*, commanded by Lieutenant James Slade, 1st Lieutenant of *Latona*, took the gunboat *Undaunted* (2), and *Vengeance* was burnt to prevent capture. *Courier* should have covered the operation, but ran aground and was only saved with difficulty. The British then landed and either spiked or brought off the shore guns. The British suffered no casualties.

JEMAPPES (Hainaut, Belgium)   French Revolutionary Wars   6 November 1792
Fought between the Austrians under Archduke Albert of Saxe-Teschen and the French under General Charles-François Dumouriez.
Strength: Austrians 13,000 with 30 guns; French 40,000 with 100 guns.
Aim: The French intended to 'unlock' the Austrian position which they had taken up as winter quarters after the raising of the siege of Lille.
Battle: When Dumouriez approached Flanders, the Austrians retreated, taking up a strong position on the heights above Jemappes, just across the Belgian (Austrian Netherlands) border. The French followed them and succeeded in chasing them off the heights.
Result: The French took Brussels (16 November) and sent a squadron of ships up the Scheldt to besiege Antwerp. Saxe-Teschen resigned his command.

KAISERSLAUTERN (Rhenish Palatinate, W Germany)   French Revolutionary Wars   23 May 1794
The Prussian general, Wichard von Mollendorff, inflicted a defeat on the French newly formed Army of the Rhine-et-Moselle commanded by General Jean Moreau. But this setback did not deter Moreau from crossing the Upper Rhine and investing Mainz.

LA FAVORITA (Turin, Italy)   French Revolutionary Wars   16 January 1797
Fought between the French under Bonaparte and the Austrians under General Provera, who sought to relieve the beleaguered garrison in Mantua (qv). The French made a forced march from the battlefield of Rivoli (qv) and attacked Provera, totally routing his force. A sortie made by the Austrian garrison was also repulsed at bayonet-point. Provera surrendered with 5,000 men.

LAHN, THE   see NEUWIED

LA PALLAS v FAIRY et al (Sept Isles, France)   French Revolutionary Wars   5–6 February 1800
The French warship *La Pallas* (38) (Captain Jacques Epron) was crippled during the night of 5–6 February by 2 British ships, *Fairy* (16) (Captain Joshua Sydney Horton) and *Harpy* (18) (Captain Henry Bazely). She was taken next day by a British squadron including, in addition to the other 2 ships, *La Loire* (46) (Captain James Newman Newman), *Danaë* (20) (Captain Lord Proby) and *Raileur* (20) (Captain William James Turquand).
   La Pallas was taken into the British navy as *La Pique*.

LE GUILLAUME TELL v LION et al (Mediterranean Sea off Valetta)   French Revolutionary Wars   30–31 March 1800
Fought between the French ship *Le Guillaume Tell* (84) (Captain Saulnier) and The British ships *Lion* (64) (Captain Manley Dixon), *Foudroyant* (80) (Captain Sir Edward Berry) and *Penelope* (36) (Captain Henry Blackwood).
   Le Guillaume Tell, the largest of the French ships which survived the Battle of the Nile, bearing the flag of Rear-Admiral Denis Decrès, came out of the harbour of Valetta at 11pm on 30 March during a strong southerly gale. *Penelope*, having discovered her and warned *Lion*, then raked *Le Guillaume Tell* and by dawn had done her a great deal of damage. *Lion* came up about 5am and cannonaded steadily until so damaged that she dropped astern. *Foudroyant* arrived at 6am and renewed the fight, with much damage to the masts and rigging on both sides. At 8.20am, with *Foudroyant* to starboard, *Lion* to larboard and *Penelope* close ahead, *Le Guillaume Tell*, rolling an unmanageable hulk on the water, struck. The other British ships being crippled, *Penelope* towed the prize to Syracuse. The French losses were some 200 out of 919. *Foudroyant*, with a crew of 719, had 8 killed and 69 injured. *Lion*, with only 300 aboard, had 8 killed and 38 wounded. *Penelope* had 2 killed and 2 wounded.
   Without Blackwood's promptitude, gallantry and perseverance the French ship would probably have escaped. As it was, her heroic defence won the admiration of her enemies. She was taken into the Royal Navy as the *Malta*.

LINCELLES (Nord, France)   French Revolutionary Wars   18 August 1793
During the siege of Dunkirk (qv) a Guards brigade (3 battalions) 1,122 strong, under Major-General Gerard Lake, was sent to support the Prince of Orange who had met with a reverse near Lille.

   Lake, unable to rally the Dutch, stormed the French positions with his brigade, driving out the enemy at the point of the bayonet. The guardsmen hustled and cuffed the raw French troops 'Like a London mob'. The French, who admitted that they had twelve battalions present, lost 12 guns besides another 6 they had taken from the Prince of Orange. British casualties were 38 killed and 143 wounded.

   This action was considered the most brilliant affair of the year.

LION v SANTA DOROTEA (W Mediterranean, off Spain)   French Revolutionary Wars   15 July 1798
The 64-gun ship *Lion* (Captain Manley Dixon), about 90 miles SW of Cartagena, sighted 4 Spanish frigates–*Pomona* (F. Villamil with broad pendant of Commodore Felix O'Neill), *Proserpine* (Q. Bial), *Santa Cazilda* (D Errara) and *Santa Dorotea* (M. Gerrard). Dixon bore down on the frigates which were in close order in a line of bearing with *Dorotea*, which had been damaged a bit astern. Dixon decided to cut off *Dorotea* and attack her. Meanwhile the three others tacked and attempted, ineffectively, to draw off *Lion*, which continued to chase *Dorotea*, suffering some damage or inconvenience from *Dorotea*'s stern chasers in the process. The other 3 frigates made two subsequent but equally ineffective attempts to help their consort before making off. *Dorotea* kept up a stubborn resistance before finally surrendering.

   Spanish casualties were 20 killed and 32 wounded. British losses were trifling.

LIVELY v TOURTERELLE (English Channel)   French Revolutionary Wars   13 March 1795
Forty miles NE of Ushant, *Lively* (32) (Lieutenant George Burlton, acting for Captain Lord Garlies who was sick on shore), which was standing down-Channel, sighted 3 strange sail and gave chase. The largest of the 3 ships–*Tourterelle* (Captain Guillaume Montalan)–tacked and stood towards *Lively*. The ensuing action lasted three hours before *Tourterelle*, which had been badly damaged and dismasted, surrendered. *Lively* had some damage to her masts and rigging from red-hot shot. *Tourterelle*, in spite of being outgunned put up a gallant resistance. Montalan may have mistaken *Lively* for something less formidable before attacking her. The 2 other ships, both prizes, were also taken by *Lively*.

LOANO (Savona, Italy)   French Revolutionary Wars   23–25 November 1795
Fought between the French, under the overall command of General Barthelemy Scherer and individual command of General André Masséna, and the Allies (chiefly Austrians).
Aim: After defeats in the north, the Holy Roman Emperor Francis II concentrated his army in N Italy in order to attempt to drive the French out.
Battle: In a battle lasting three days Masséna dislodged the Allies from their positions in the mountains behind the Italian Riviera, forcing their withdrawal.
Result: In the first battle in Italy the French were victorious, prompting Napoleon Bonaparte, head of the Army of the Interior, to launch a full-scale offensive in Italy which he led himself as Scherer was unwilling to do so. Bonaparte, who commanded the artillery during this battle, had been the author of the plan of action for the operations carried out by Scherer.

LODI (Milan, Italy)   10 May 1796
Fought between the Austrians under General Baron de Beaulieu and the French under Bonaparte.
Strength: Austrians 10,000; French 30,000.
Aim: The Austrian rearguard sought to defend the bridge at Lodi against the French who were pursuing the retiring Austrian army.
Battle: Beaulieu retired north of the Adda before Bonaparte, leaving the road secure to Milan for the French. Wishing to safeguard his right flank, Bonaparte turned eastward and entered Lodi. Setting up a battery of 30 guns, Bonaparte began to batter the Austrian defences on the far bank. A detachment of cavalry was sent to the Austrian rear while 6,000 infantry rushed the 600-feet wooden bridge in a bayonet charge led by Bonaparte, and Generals Louis-Alexandre Berthier and André Masséna. The Austrians were able to inflict heavy casualties on the advancing French–400 French fell in the charge alone–but this failed to check them. When other French columns forded the Adda above and below Lodi, Beaulieu retired towards Mantua (qv). Total losses were about 2,00 killed and wounded on both sides, while the Austrians lost 20 guns and had 2,000 prisoners taken.

Result: Bonaparte's part in the charge across the bridge earned him the nickname of 'Little Corporal' among his men. It may be that it was this remarkable success that really made Bonaparte believe in himself as the Man of Destiny.

LONATO (Brescia, italy)   French Revolutionary Wars   3 August 1796
Fought between the French under Bonaparte and the Austrians under General Quasdanovich.
Strength: French 47,000; Austrians 18,000.
Aim: After Bonaparte had invested Mantua (qv), Field-Marshal Count Dagobert von Würmser marched from Austria with a new army of 50,000 men. This he divided into three columns: one under himself which marched down the Adige valley; another, 5,000 strong, was to come down the Brenta valley; and the third, under Quasdanovich, came down the west side of Lake Garda towards Brescia with the aim of cutting off Bonaparte's communications. Bonaparte raised the siege of Mantua and concentrated his troops on Quasdanovich's position on the west end of Lake Garda, leaving Würmser to join the garrison at Mantua, harassed by General Pierre Augereau's division.
Battle: Quasdanovich divided his army into three columns, cutting the Milan-Mantua road, and advanced, expecting to reunite with Würmser, thus enveloping the French army. On 3 August Bonaparte attacked and routed Quasdanovich, one entire column surrendering while the survivors of the remainder fled northward to the head of Lake Garda.
Result: The total defeat of Quasdanovich left Bonaparte free to concentrate on Würmser (see CASTIGLIONE DELLE STIVIERE).

MAGNANO (Verona, Italy)   French Revolutionary Wars   5 April 1799
Fought between the Austrians under General Baron Paul Kray von Krajowa and the French under General Barthelemy Scherer.
Strength: Austrians 52,000; French 53,000.
Aim: Each army sought to repulse the advance of the other into Italy.
Battle: After sighting each other in the area of Verona, the two armies moved south to attack each other. Scherer attacked the Austrians and was at first successful until von Krajowa sent his reserves against the French right wing, which broke. The French army retired in disorder.
Result: The French fell back towards the Adda, where General Jean Moreau took command. General Count Suvorov joined von Krajowa soon after the battle and the two armies pursued the French, leading finally to the Battle of Cassano (CASSANO D'ADDA II).

MALBORGHETTO (Udine, Italy)   French Revolutionary Wars   23 March 1797
Fought between the French under General André Masséna and the Austrians under Archduke Charles.
Strength: French 41,000; Austrians 33,000.
Aim: After completing his conquest of Italy, Bonaparte moved northwards in the direction of Austria itself. Archduke Charles sought to prevent the French advance by blocking the passes in the Alps.
Battle: The French reached the Carnic Alps and routed the Austrian detachment at Malborghetto which was defending the Friuli Pass.
Result: The Archduke was compelled to fall back to avoid being surrounded and Bonaparte crossed the Alps with his army in three columns. Barthélemy-Catherine Joubert, in the Tyrol, pushed the Austrians back and joined Bonaparte. They advanced to Leoben where, on 18 April, a truce was signed.

MANTUA (Italy)   French Revolutionary Wars   27 June 1796–2 February 1797
Fought between the Austrians under General Campo d'Irles and the French under Bonaparte and General Jean Sérurier.
Strength: Austrians 13,000 (rising to 27,000) with 500 cannon; French 9,000, but constantly reinforced after casualties.
Aim: The French sought the reduction of the garrison of Mantua, held by the Austrians.
Battle: The siege took place in two halves. After the battle at Borghetto (qv), the Austrian army under General Baron de Beaulieu, which Bonaparte had been pursuing, was divided into two, one half retreating northward up the Adige River, the other joining General d'Irles in Mantua. On 4 June Bonaparte was aready investing this fortress with 9,000 men commanded by General Sérurier. When the Milan citadel capitulated on 29 June the French heavy guns were moved to Mantua to aid the siege there. On 31 July the approach of Field-Marshal Count Dagobert von Würmser and a large Austrian army forced Bonaparte to

raise the siege and Mantua was victualled. The defeats Würmser suffered at Lonato and Castiglione delle Stiviere (qqv) drove him back, and on 24 August Bonaparte resumed the siege. The garrion was now 15,000 strong. On 13 September Würmser, who had been defeated at Caliano and Bassano (qqv), fought his way into Mantua with 12,000 men and, on 15 September, he made a sortie to the east to try and increase the Austrian-held ground. He was beaten back with the loss of 4,000 men and 24 cannon by Generals André Masséna and Charles Kilmaine. In January General Josef Alviniz Baron von Borberek made the fourth attempt to relieve the siege and an Austrian column, 9,000 strong, got as far as the edge of Mantua, when Würmser tried to make a sortie. The attack was foiled and on 2 February the garrison surrendered, 16,000 men and 1,500 guns being taken as well as 24 colours. During the siege 18,000 Austrians and 7,000 French were lost chiefly, it is thought, from disease.
Result: The surrender of Mantua after a 7 months' siege virtually completed Bonaparte's conquest of Italy. He then marched against Austria itself.

MARENGO II   see ALESSANDRIA

MARENGO III (Alessandria, Italy)   French Revolutionary Wars   14 June 1800
Fought between the French under Bonaparte and the Austrians under General Baron Michael von Melas.
Strength: French 18,000 (rising to 32,000) with 15 guns; Austrians 31,000 with 100 guns.
Aim: Bonaparte's first objective was to prevent an Austrian invasion of France. Finding that he could obtain no replacements from General Jean Moreau's Army of the Rhine, he had to attack with whatever forces he had available.
Battle: The French advanced on the fortress of Alessandria (qv) where the Austrians were concentrating their forces. Thinking that Melas himself was still in Turni, Bonaparte had his army widely scattered so that when Melas attacked on the day after his arrival he was unprepared for battle, having only 18,000 men at his disposal. The Austrians surrounded the French right wing under General Jean Lannes and, by the end of five hours' fighting, the front line was beginning to give way. Despite committing all available reserves, the French continued to be driven back and by 3pm they had retreated 4 miles. The Austrians, thinking they had won, pursued the French in march formation and old Melas turned over command to his subordinates, retiring to rest in Alessandria.
    Bonaparte sent for and received reinforcements under General Louis Desaix and in the late afternoon launched a counter-attack under which his divisions were able to re-form. Desaix was killed early on, but the French beat back the Austrians towards Marengo, the repeated cavalry charges led by General François Kellermann (son of the hero of Valmy [qv]) turned the Austrian retreat into rout. Half the Austrian army was scattered, cut down or taken prisoner. The battle had ended by nightfall.
    Austrian losses were 9,402 killed and wounded, and 8,000 prisoners. French losses were 8,835 killed and wounded.
Result: The French victory, though a narrow one, enabled Bonaparte to complete his dominance of Italy. The Austrians retired east of the Mincio River and north of the Po.

MARS v HERCULE (off Brest, Finistère, France)   French Revolutionary Wars   21 April 1798
At 2pm on 21 April 1798 *Mars* (74) (Captain Alexander Hood), part of the Channel squadron under Lord Bridport, whilst chasing 2 smaller vessels, sighted *Hercule* (74) (Captain L'Heritier) on the horizon, on its first commission. After her sister ship *Ramillies* (74) (Captain Henry Inman), had damaged *Hercule*, Hood took up the chase. At about 9pm he caught *Hercule* at anchor in the Passage du Raz. After an hour's exchange of broadsides at close quarters L'Heritier surrendered.
    British casualties were 29 killed and 42 wounded. French casualties were 315 killed and wounded, and 390 were captured. Both captains were mortally wounded.

MEDOLE (Mantua, Italy)   French Revolutionary Wars   5 August 1796
Fought between the French under Bonaparte and the Austrians under Field-Marshal Count Dagobert von Würmser.
Strength: French 23,000; Austrians 25,000.
Aim: The French sought to defeat the Austrians.
Battle: Würmser had revitualled Mantua (qv) in the days leading up to the battle (3–5 August) at great cost to his men. His losses amounted to 20,000 men and 60 guns. Bonaparte beat the Austrians back to Roveredo (qv); they lost 2,000 killed and wounded, as well as 1,000 prisoners and 20 guns.
Result: Bonaparte's position was consolidated. By 24 August he had reinvested Mantua.

MENIN (W Flanders, Belgium)   French Revolutionary Wars   13 September 1793
Fought between the French under General Jean-Nicolas Houchard and the Dutch under the Prince of Orange.
Strength: French 40,000 (mainly untrained but eager young recruits); Dutch 20,000.
Battle: On 6 September Houchard had attacked the Duke of York's regulars with his mass of untrained young recruits (who had been the outcome of the Levée en Masse only a fortnight before) at Hondschoote (qv). Houchard then went on to attack on 13 September the Prince of Orange's army which linked the British to the Austrians farther to the east. Houchard drove back the Dutch troops but was unable to maintain his momentum and initiative against the well-trained Austrian veterans farther down the line, and manoeuvre them out of E France. He decided to retreat and it turned into a rout.
Result: Houchard was arrested (23 September) and guillotined, General Jean-Baptiste Jourdan taking his place.

MILLESIMO (Savona, Italy)   French Revolutionary Wars   13 April 1796
Fought between the Piedmontese under General Baron Colli and the French under Generals Pierre Augereau, André Masséna and Amédée-Emmannel-François Laharpe.
Aim: The dislodgement of the Austrians from their entrenchments by the French.
Battle: The divisions of Generals Augereau, Masséna and Laharpe attacked the Austrians, driving them back and cutting Colli's line of communication with General Baron de Beaulieu, the Austrian Commander-in-Chief. The Piedmontese lost 6,000 men and 30 guns.
    The Battles of Dego (qv) with the Austrians on 14–15 April and Mondovi (qv) with the Piedmontese on 21 April, when Bonaparte defeated each in turn, followed.

MINCIO, PASSAGE OF THE   see BORGHETTO

MINERVE v SABINA (W Mediterranean)   French Revolutionary Wars   19 December 1796
Minerve (38) (Captain George Cockburn, wearing the broad pennant of Commodore Horatio Nelson) with *Blanche* (32) (Captain D'Arcy Preston) in company on passage from Gibraltar to Port Ferraro, fell in with 2 Spanish frigates. *Blanche* was instructed to engage the lee frigate. *Minerve* closed and engaged the larger *Sabina* (Jacobo Stuart). After a gallant action *Sabina* surrendered. The firing of the Spanish was very accurate, whereas the British may have been hampered by the unaccustoméd French equipment. Cockburn put a prize crew (Lieutenants Culverhouse and Hardy–later Admiral Sir Thomas Hardy) aboard *Sabina* and took her in tow.
    Later that afternoon another Spanish frigate, *Matilda* (34), was sighted. Cockburn cast off the tow and went into action. *Matilda* soon hauled off to rejoin the remainder of the squadron–*Principe de Asturias* (112) and the frigates *Ceres* (40) and *Perla* (34) which had appeared on the scene. Cockburn was faced with an action with a considerably superior force and, as *Minerve* was damaged, decided to seek safety. The Spanish squadron gave up the chase at nightfall.
    Meanwhile Culverhouse in the prize had done his best to draw the fire of the Spanish squadron and did not surrender until completely dismasted.

MINORCA (Balearic Islands, Spain)   French Revolutionary Wars   7–15 November 1799
Fought between the British under General Sir Charles Stuart and Commodore John Thomas Duckworth and the Spanish.
Aim: The British navy, having regained the command of the Mediterranean at the Battle of the Nile (1798), decided to capture the Island of Minorca to obtain the facilities of the fine harbour of Port Mahon as a base in the W Mediterranean. The Spanish, at that time allied to the French, sought to prevent this.
Battle: General Stuart and Commodore Duckworth had secretly planned the capture, but a spy alerted the Spaniards five weeks before the projected date of the invasion. However, on 7 November 800 men successfully made an opposed landing on the north of the island and clung on until the main body under General Stuart came to their support. On 8 November Stuart sent Colonel Thomas Graham (later Lord Lynedoch) to cut the main road across the island. Port Mahon was occupied by *coup de main* soon after, without resistance. Stuart then decided to attack the Spanish army (which outnumbered his) now based at Ciudella whilst Duckworth sailed to intercept a Spanish squadron bringing reinforcements. Stuart deceived the Spaniards that his army was much larger than theirs and bluffed them into surrender, although he was outgunned by at least five to one.

Result: The capture at minimal loss of one of the finest harbours and a secure base in the W Mediterranean. The historian Fortescue wrote to the effect that 'This feat, though bloodless and absolutely forgotten, forms one of the most striking examples in history of the powers of impudence in War.'

MONDOVI (Cuneo, Italy)   French Revolutionary Wars   21 April 1796
Fought between the French under Bonaparte and the Piedmontese forces under General Baron Colli.
Aim: Bonaparte's aim was to divide the Austrians and Piedmontese armies and defeat them in detail.
Strength: French 45,000; Piedmontese 25,000.
Battle: After the Battle of Dego (qv) on 14–15 April the Austrians and Piedmontese retired in different directions, the Austrians under General Baron de Beaulieu NE to Acqui and the Piedmontese under Baron Colli to the west. Bonaparte, seeing this, hastily pursued Colli, brought him to battle and defeated him.
Result: Colli sued for an armistice, and on 28 April 1796 the Piedmontese were put out of the war.

MONTEBELLO I (Pavia, Italy)   French Revolutionary Wars   9 June 1800
Fought between the French under General Jean Lannes and the Austrians under General Karl Ott.
Strength: French 8,000; Austrians 17,000 with 35 guns.
Aim: After the fall of Milan, Ott was marching northwards in order to effect a junction between his army and General Baron Michael von Melas. The French were on their way to the relief of Milan, unaware that the garrison had already surrendered.
Battle: The advanced guard of the French army met Ott 15 miles south of Pavia, which they had been sent ahead to occupy. The French were attacked by Ott and, severely outnumbered, held their ground until General Claude Victor's corps of 6,000 men came up, when Lannes assumed the offensive. The French proceeded to drive the Austrians from the field with heavy loss. The Austrians retired before the French towards Alessandria. French casualties were 500 killed and wounded. Austrian casualties were 4,000 killed and wounded, and 5,000 were taken prisoner.
Result: The Austrians continued to amass troops at Alessandria and Bonaparte, advancing from the Alpine passes, converged his troops to the same place.

MONTENOTTE (Savona, Italy)   French Revolutionary Wars   11–12 April 1796
Fought between the French under Bonaparte and the Austro-Sardinians under General Baron de Beaulieu.
Strength: French 40,000 with 60 guns; Austrians/Sardinians 55,000 with 150 guns.
Aim: The Allies sought to expel the French from Italy.
Strength: On 10–11 April General d'Argenteau with the central division of the Austro-Sardinian army attacked the French at Montenotte under General Jean-Baptiste Cervoni. The French were driven back, but Tampon managed to hold the position with 1,500 men. On 12 April Bonaparte launched an attack against the Austrian right wing and carried Montenotte. Finding himself outflanked, d'Argenteau was compelled to withdraw with the loss of 2,500 killed and wounded, 2,000 prisoners and some guns.
Result: The French victory effectively cut communications between the Allied armies of Beaulieu and Vittorio Amedeo II.

MÖSKIRCH (Bavaria, W Germany)   French Revolutionary Wars   5 May 1800
Fought between the French under General Jean Moreau and the Austrians under General Baron Paul Kray von Krajowa..
Strength: French 50,000; Austrians 60,000.
Aim: The French sought to take the heights around Möskirch, strongly held by the Austrians.
Battle: The French advance guard under General Claude-Jacques Lecourbe attacked the Austrian position on the heights but without success. However, when the main body of the French army came up under Moreau, the scales were turned in France's favour and the heights were carried, the Austrians having to abandon all their positions. Austrian casualties were about 5,000 killed and wounded, and French casualties about 3,500.
Result: Kray von Krajowa was forced to retreat farther into Bavaria.

MOUSCRON (W Flanders, Belgium)   French Revolutionary Wars   29 April 1794
Fought between the French under General Joseph Souham and the Austrians under General Count von Clerfayt.
Aim: The Austrians sought to prevent the French from advancing into their territory.
Battle: This battle was really the other half of the French advance, which had got off to such a bad start at Beaumont-en-Cambrésis (qv) on 26 April. Friedrich Josias, Prince of Saxe-Coburg, had learnt of the French plans from papers captured there with General René-Bernard Chapuy (Chapuis). He had ordered General von Clerfayt to move to the relief of Menin, but General Jean-Charles Pichegru was too quick, and on 29 April Generals Souham and Nicolas Bertin struck Clerfayt's column at Mouscron in front and flank, with a superiority of three to one, and forced him into an increasingly disorderly retreat. He lost 2,000 men and 23 guns.
Result: This defeat sealed the fate of Menin. The garrison, however, succeeded in cutting their way out on 30 April. The loss of Menin and also Courtrai (Kortrijk) breached the Allied front.

NEERWINDEN II (Liège, Belgium)   French Revolutionary Wars   18 March 1793
Fought between the Austrians under Friedrich Josias, Prince of Saxe-Coburg (actual command being exercised by Archduke Charles) and the Chief of Staff, Baron Karl Mack von Leiberich), and the French under General Charles-François Dumouriez.
Strength: Austrians 40,000; French 45,000.
Aim: The Austrians sought to prevent an offensive by the French in Holland.
Battle: Dumouriez attacked the Austrians with the intention of turning their left. Advancing in eight columns, the French were repulsed in disorder.
Result: The French were forced to retreat. The Austrians retook Brussels and drove the French out of the Austrian Netherlands. Accused of treason, Dumouriez went over to the Allies.

NEUWIED (Rhineland-Palatinate, W Germany)   French Revolutionary Wars   18 April 1797
Fought between the Austrians under General Werneck and the French under General Lazare Hoche.
Strength: Austrians 30,000; French 80,000.
Aim: Hoche, who had replaced General Jean-Baptiste Jourdan as Commander of the Sambre-et-Meuse Army, planned a crossing of the Kehl in conjunction with General Jean Moreau's army. Werneck held the Lower Rhine. Hoche therefore sought to beat him.
Battle: Crossing the Rhine between Düsseldorf and Koblenz (Coblenz), Hoche attacked Werneck at Neuwied, 7 miles NW of Koblenz, and routed him, driving the Austrians eastward across the Lahn River. The action is also known as the Battle of the Lahn. Austrian casualties were 8,000 men killed and wounded and they lost 80 cannon.
Result: Hoche and Moreau were able to join forces to drive the Austrians back to Rastatt (qv). On the same day Archduke Charles signed a truce with Bonaparte which led to peace between Austria and the French Directory.

NIEUPORT (NIEUPOORT) (W Flanders, Belgium)   French Revolutionary Wars   22–29 October 1793
General Dominique-Joseph-René Vandamme, the French Commandant of Dunkirk, with 1,200 men, took Furnes on 22 October and then besieged and bombarded Nieuport, but, having only field artillery, was foiled. The garrison also flooded the country and the French retreated in some disorder. Vandamme was placed under arrest, but later, on 11 November, released.
    The garrison, which had consisted of the 53rd (or the Shropshire) Regiment of Foot, had casualties of 13 killed and 33 wounded. The garrison also contained two Hessian companies and a company of the Black Watch as well as some artillery.

NOVI LIGURE (Alessandria, Italy)   French Revolutionary Wars   15 August 1799
Fought between the French under General Barthélemy-Catherine Joubert and the Russians under Field-Marshal Count Suvorov and the Austrians under General Baron Melas.
Strength: French 35,000; Allies 50,000.
Aim: The French sought to retrieve the position in Italy which the shattered forces of Generals Jean Moreau and Jacques Macdonald could no longer do. The Allies were reconquering the country.

Battle: The French deployed in the hills north of Genoa and the Allies under Suvorov attacked their position there at Novi Ligure. After sixteen hours of heavy fighting they carried the heights, driving the French across the Apennines. The French suffered casualties of 11,000, including killed, wounded and those taken prisoner, and lost 18 guns. The Allied casualties were 8,750 killed and wounded, of whom about 2,700 were Russian. The French Commander, Houbert, was killed in action. The action is also known as the Battle of Novi.

Result: Generals Moreau and Laurent Gouvion-St-Cyr collected the remnants of the French army and retreated into the hills. Suvorov pursued them until he heard that the French Army of the Alps had crossed into Italy under Jean-Etienne Championnet.

NYMPHE v CLEOPATRE (off Start Point, S Devon, England)   French Revolutionary Wars   18 June 1793
Fought between the British and the French.
Nymphe (40) (Captain Edward Pellew) fought *Cléopatre* (40) (Captain Jean Mullon) about 6 leagues from Start Point and, after a severe action, 'dished her up in 50 minutes'. (This phrase occurs in a letter written by Edward Pellew to his elder brother Samuel.) British casualties were 23 killed and 27 wounded; French 63 killed and wounded. The heroic Captain Mullon, who was mortally wounded, attempted to bite to pieces the list of French coast-signals, as he lay dying. (He actually expired whilst devouring his commission, which he had taken from his pocket by mistake.)

On 21 June Pellew brought his prize into Portsmouth. For this, the first successful single ship action of the war, he was knighted. *Cléopatre* was purchased by the British government and became *L'Oiseau* (36).

OPERATIONS IN THE ATLANTIC I (NW French coast)   French Revolutionary Wars ·   16–17 June 1795
Fought between the British fleet under Vice-Admiral William Cornwallis and the French fleet under Vice-Admiral Louis Villaret de Joyeuse off the NW French coast, near Belle-Ile-en-Mer.
Strength: British 5 ships of the line + 2 frigates + 1 sloop; French 12 ships of the line + 11 frigates + 5 corvettes + 2 cutters.
Aim: Cornwallis's fleet was covering the move of a fleet of troop transports under Admiral John Warren to Quiberon Bay (QUIBERON).
Battle: Cornwallis's force was not strong enough to face the French. However, his ships included some very slow sailers, and thus he could not avoid action. The French opened fire at 9am on the 17th. By noon all the British were engaged. To save the damaged *Mars*, Cornwallis with *Royal Sovereign* (100) attacked the nearest French ships. This caused the other French ships to retreat, and at 6.40pm the French abandoned the pursuit. Cornwallis had 2 ships damaged and about 12 of his men were wounded.

Cornwallis's success can be ascribed to excellent discipline, faultless behaviour and bold but sound tactics. It has been suggested that one reason why the French gave up their pursuit was the deception tactics of the British frigate *Phaëton*, which was on the horizon signalling to an imaginary fleet.
Result: Admiral Warren's troop convoy to Quiberon Bay escaped unscathed.

PASLEY v VIRGEN-DEL-ROSARIO (Mediterranean Sea)   French Revolutionary Wars   27 July 1801
The British hired brig *Pasley* (16), with a crew of 54 men and boys under Lieutenant William Wooldrige, was chased by the Spanish privateer polacre-ship *Virgen-del-Rosario* (10), with a crew of 94, which caught up with her. After about an hour's animated engagement Wooldridge found the Spaniards' guns too heavy for him. He ran the *Pasley* athwart *Rosario*'s hawse and lashed her bowsprit to his own capstan. The British boarded and after fifteen minutes sanguinary hand-to-hand fighting carried the *Rosario*. The British had 3 killed and 8 wounded, including the Commander. The Spaniards had 21 killed and 13 wounded.

Pasley had previously, on 19 June, taken the privateer felucca *El Golondrina* (2) off Cape St Vincent.

PETEREL v LA LIGURIENNE (Bay of Marseilles, France)   French Revolutionary Wars   21 March 1800
The British sloop *Peterel* (16) (Captain Francis William Austen) drove off a French corvette of equal force and a xebec and, after a well-contested action lasting more than an hour and a half, took the brig *La Ligurienne* (16) (Lieutenant François-Auguste Pelabend) within point-blank range of 2 shore batteries. *Mermaid* (32) (Captain Robert Dudley Oliver) was in sight to leeward, but so situated as to be unable to give material assistance.

PHOEBE v NEREIDE (English Channel)   French Revolutionary Wars   20 December 1797
Off Ushant, *Phoebe* (36) (Captain Robert Barlow) gave chase to a French frigate, *Néréide* (36) (Captain Antoine Canon). After a long chase, much manoeuvring in the dark and a running fight, *Néréide* surrendered at 10.45pm. Both ships suffered considerable damage to masts and rigging, and *Néréide* to her hull. *Phebe*, with a crew of only 261, had 3 killed and 10 wounded. *Néréide*, whose crew numbered 330, had 20 killed and 55 wounded.

PONT-A-CHIN   see TOURNAI

PRIMOLANO (Vicenza, Italy)   French Revolutionary Wars   7 September 1796
Fought between the French under Bonaparte and the Austrians under Field-Marshal Count Dagobert von Würmser.
Aim: The French sought to advance on the defiles of the Brenta and cut Würmser's communications.
Battle: At dawn the French marched from Borgo di Val Sugana. General Charles-Pierre-François Augereau dislodged the Austrians from their position behind Primolano and took the fort de Covolo. Bonaparte bivouacked that night at the village of Cismona, having covered nearly 60 miles in two days.
Result: The French caught up with the Austrians at Bassano (qv) the following day and beat them.

QUIBERON (Morbihan, France)   French Revolutionary Wars   16–21 July 1795
Fought between French Royalists and a Revolutionary army under General Lazare Hoche.
Battle: On 27 June, the British landed 3,600 French émigrés on the Quiberon peninsula in S Brittany where they were immediately joined by thousands of Royalists. Hoche marched into the area and managed, in a series of engagements, to capture 6,000 rebels who were poorly led, thus causing part of the uprising.
Result: Of the 6,000 prisoners, 700 were identified as émigrés and executed. About 1,800 re-embarked for England. The uprising continued off and on in a guerrilla form of resistance under the Marquis de La Rochejacquelin and others, in spite of General Jean Kléber's 'infernal columns' *(colonnes infernales)*, until such time as the Napoleonic administration acceded to the Vendéeans' demands–freedom from conscription and liberty of worship–and granted an amnesty. The final revolt occurred in 1823 when the restoration government tried to go back on this arrangement.
   Owing to lack of understanding of guerrilla warfare, the émigrés, urged on by stereotyped British advisors, tried to fight pitched battles and were hopelessly defeated. This defeat fragmented the rebels and they resorted to successful guerrilla warfare tactics, remaining a thorn in the side of the French administration for many years, by tying down large forces required elsewhere.

RASTATT (S Baden, W Germany)   French Revolutionary Wars   22 April 1795
Fought between the French under General Jean Moreau and the Austrians under Archduke Charles.
Aim: The French sought to capture the Austrian position.
Battle: After a series of sharp encounters, Moreau seized the heights which the Austrians had held.
Result: Archduke Charles was forced to retreat to the Danube and the Peace of Leoben was signed, which brought operations to an end.

REVOLUTIONNAIRE v UNITE (off Ushant, France)   French Revolutionary Wars   13 April 1796
Révolutionnaire (38) (Captain Francis Cole) was one of a squadron of frigates under Captain Sir Edward Pellew cruising off Ushant which gave chase to a strange frigate. *Révolutionnaire*, being the nearest, was detached to cut her off. She was lost in the darkness and haze, but sighted again at 9pm. At about 11.30pm Cole hailed the frigate, which was *Unité* (36) (Captain Charles-Alexandre Durand), and warned her of the proximity of superior forces. Durand refused to surrender and an action ensued. *Unité* was close to the land, and she surrendered after the second broadside.
   Révolutionnaire suffered no casualties, whereas *Unité* had 9 killed and 11 wounded.

RIVOLI (Verona, Italy)   French Revolutionary Wars   14–15 January 1797
Fought between the French under Bonaparte and the Austrians under General Josef Alvinzi (Baron von Borberek).
Strength: French (14 January) 10,000–20,000 with 20 guns, (15 January) 14,000 with 14 guns; Austrians (14 January) 12,000–28,000 with 35 guns, (15 January) 20,000 with 30 guns.

Aim: The Austrians sought to dislodge the French from their position on the heights of Rivoli, as part of the campaign for the relief of Mantua (qv).
Battle: Alvinzi attacked in six columns. Three were to attack Bonaparte frontally, two were to flank each wing and the other was to advance round the back of his army. At first the Austrians forced the French back with their frontal attack, and the right flank was threatened by the arrival of one of the Austrian columns. General André Masséna arrived and, under a flag of truce, Bonaparte gained an hour's respite wherein he redeployed his army. The French then held the Austrians on their right flank and, after advancing on the right of the Austrian centre, repulsed the frontal attack. The Austrian column on the French left wing was surrounded. Alvinzi was driven from the field. The column which had been marching on Bonaparte's rear arrived too late after the end of the battle. They laid down their arms. French losses were 2,000 men. Austrian losses were 3,300 men, as well as 7,000 prisoners at the battle and a further 6,000 taken during the pursuit.
Result: Bonaparte pursued the Austrian army, sending General Gabriel-Venance Rey's Division to strike at the flank and rear of the Austrians; the van of the division under Colonel Joachim Murat, which had been ferried across Lake Garda, smashed Alvinzi's efforts to reorganise. Masséna caught and surrounded an Austrian column outside Mantua. The defeat of the Austrians ended the plan to relieve Mantua.

ROMNEY v SIBYLLE (Aegean Sea)   French Revolutionary Wars   17 June 1794
Romney (50) (Captain the Hon William Paget), escorting 1 British and 7 Dutch merchant vessels from Naples to Smyrna, discovered at anchor in the roads of the small island of Miconi the French frigate *Sibylle* (44) (broad pennant of Commodore Jacques-Mélanie Rondeau) and 3 merchant ships. Paget ordered his convoy to join the frigates *Inconstant, Leda* and *Tartar*, from which he had parted company the day before but which were still in sight. He entered the roads and anchored within about a cable's length of *Sibylle* and, wishing to avoid unnecessary bloodshed, called to Rondeau to surrender. This Rondeau refused to do and Paget, having warped *Romney* into a favourable position opened fire. The action continued for over an hour before *Sibylle* surrendered with the merchant ships. *Romney* was at the time very short-handed and it is possible that the knowledge of this may have influenced Rondeau's defiant decision. *Romney*, which had but 266 men and boys aboard, had 8 killed and 30 wounded; while *Sibylle* had 46 killed and 112 wounded of a total crew of 380.

ROVEREDO (ROVERETO) (S Tyrol, Italy)   French Revolutionary Wars   4 September 1796
Fought between the French under Bonaparte and the Austrians under General Baron Paul Davidovich.
Strength: French 30,000; Austrians 25,000.
Aim: The French sought to defeat the Austrians.
Battle: Bonaparte attacked the Austrian entrenchments and despite heavy resistance carried them, driving the Austrians out of Roveredo and Caliano (qv). The Austrians had 7,000 prisoners taken and 15 guns.
Result: The remnants of the Austrian army fled to the Tyrol and General André Masséna was able to occupy Trent the next day.

SAN FIORENZO v RESISTANCE (off Brest, Finistère, France)   French Revolutionary Wars   8 March 1797
San Fiorenzo (36) (Captain Sir Harry Neale) with *Nymphe* (36) (Captain John Cooke), having reconnoitred Brest, were about 10 miles off when they sighted 2 ships standing in towards the port. These were *Résistance* (40) (Captain Jean-Baptiste Laroque) and the corvette *Constance* (22) (Captain Desauney). The British frigates tacked to windward of the French and Neale, in view of the fact that the wind was from the direction of Brest and the French fleet was in sight from *San Fiorenzo*'s top, decided to concentrate on *Résistance*. After a short action *Résistance* surrendered. *Constance* had by then come up and, being attacked by both British frigates, in turn also gave up. The British ships suffered neither damage nor casualties. *Résistance* and *Constance* suffered 19 and 14 casualties respectively.
  Résistance was taken into the Royal navy and renamed *Fisgard*.

SANTA MARGARITA v TAMISE (off Ushant, France)   French Revolutionary Wars   8 June 1796
Santa Margarita (36) (Captain Thomas Byam Martin), in company with *Unicorn* (Captain Thomas Williams), was about 50 miles west of Ushant when, at 2am, together they sighted and closed 3 strange ships on their lee beam. These were 2 French frigates and a corvette, which formed close quarter line for mutual support and impeded the progress of the British frigates with accurate fire from their stern chasers.

Eventually *Santa Margarita* managed to lay herself alongside the smaller frigate–*Tamise* (Captain J.-B.-A. Fradin), which surrendered. (She was orginally the British *Thames* captured in 1793.) British casualties were very light, but the French lost 32 killed and 19 wounded. (See also UNICORN V TRIBUNE)

SEINE v PIQUE (Bay of Biscay)   French Revolutionary Wars   29 June 1798

Jason (38) (Captain Charles Stirling), in company with *Pique* (36) (Lieutenant David Milne) and *Mermaid* (32) (Captain James Newman), sighted off Pointe des Penmarches the French frigate *Seine* (46) (Lieutenant Julien-Gabriel Bigot), and gave chase. *Mermaid* stood to the north in order to cut her off from the land, but as *Seine* tacked to the south, *Mermaid* got left out of the main action. *Pique* and *Jason* continued the chase. By evening *Pique* had come up and at about 9pm engaged the enemy in close action for two and a half hours, but, having her main topmast shot away, she was forced to drop astern. *Jason* then came up and Stirling desired *Pique* to anchor; Milne did not hear and she grounded soon after. Pointe de la Trenche was by now close at hand and soon after both *Jason* and *Seine* also took the ground. The latter was completely dismasted, but, with daylight, the action continued, *Seine* firing broadsides into *Jason*'s stern. However, finally, seeing *Mermaid* returning, *Seine* surrendered.

   Jason was hauled off by *Mermaid* and *Seine* was eventually refloated, but *Pique* became a total loss.

   Seine, which had 610 men aboard including 280 refractory soldiers, suffered casualties of 170 killed and about 100 wounded. While *Jason* had 7 killed and 12 wounded, *Pique* had only 2 killed and 6 wounded although she had borne the brunt of the fighting.

SOUTHAMPTON v L'UTILE (Hyères Islands, Côte d'Azure, Mediterranean)   French Revolutionary Wars   10 June 1796

Fought between the British frigate *Southampton* (32) (Captain James Macnamara) and the French corvette *L'Utile* (24) (Lieutenant François Vega).

   The operation, to take *Utile*, positioned under the heavy guns on the NE side of Porquerolles, was odered by Admiral Sir John Jervis himself. Initially, *Utile* took *Southampton* for a French or neutral frigate, and Macnamara was able to get within pistol-shot and summon the Frenchman to surrender, whereupon *Utile* fired a broadside. After three broadsides Lieutenant Charles Lydiard boarded, Vega fell at his post and in ten minutes his ship was taken. *Southampton* had 1 marine killed, while *Utile* had 8 killed and 17 wounded.

   Macnamara succeeded in towing his prize out of range of the batteries with little damage. It was then commissioned as a British sloop of war with Lydiard as her commander.

SPEEDY v EL GAMO (off Barcelona, Spain)   French Revolutionary Wars   6 May 1801

The sloop *Speedy* (14) (Lieutenant Lord Cochrane) had been operating against coastal shipping during April. The Spanish xebec *El Gamo* (32) (Captain Don Francisco de Torris) enticed her close to by masking her gunports. When within hailing distance *El Gamo* opened fire. *Speedy*, realising that she had no escape as the xebec was a better sailer, masqueraded as a Danish vessel, and, after a conversation, the ships parted. On 6 May the ships met again and after a one-sided action during which *Speedy* succeeded in frustrating *El Gamo*'s attempts to board, *Speedy* boarded in turn and *El Gamo* struck.

   Of her crew of 54 *Speedy* lost 4 killed and 11 wounded. The Spanish crew of 319, including 45 marines, lost their commander and 14 others killed, with 41 wounded.

SPEEDY v PAPILLON (off coast of Portugal)   French Revolutionary Wars   3–4 February 1798

Speedy, a brig-sloop of 14 guns (Captain Hugh Downman), when 25 miles west of Vigo sighted the large brig *Papillon* (14), which bore down on her and then at 3pm opened fire. Action continued with varying fortune and little damage owing to the heavy swell. The wind fell light at dusk and with that and *Papillon*'s superior sailing ability the contestants drifted apart. During the night *Papillon* fired on and recaptured a Spanish brig which *Speedy* had captured the day before. The prize crew managed to escape in a boat and rejoin, though *Speedy* was 4 leagues to windward! However, at daylight the breeze freshened, which enabled *Speedy* to fetch up to her adversary. A cat-and-mouse action continued all that day and *Speedy* retook her prize on the 5th. Credit is due to Downman for his persistence in seeking to continue the action in spite of heavy damage which necessitated a refit in Lisbon. It may be presumed that *Papillon* broke off the action because of severe losses. *Speedy* had 5 killed and 4 severely wounded.

STOCKACH I (S Baden, W Germany)   French Revolutionary Wars · 25 March 1799
Fought between the Austrians under Archduke Charles and the French under General Jean-Baptiste Jourdan.
Strength: Austrians 60,000; French 35,000.
Aim: The Austrians sought to drive the French out of Germany.
Battle: The Archduke marched his men to Baden, where the French lay, and Jourdan determined to attack the Austrians at Stockach, where he met the Archduke with a reconnaisance force. Attacking the Austrians, he at first gained ground, but when the rest of the Archduke's army came up and counter-attacked the French centre, Jourdan's loosely linked divisions were smashed. Forced to withdraw, Jourdan made good his retreat over the Rhine and handed over his command to General André Masséna. French losses were 5,000 to the Austrian casualties of 6,000.
Result: The French offensive into Germany was repulsed.

STOCKACH II (S Baden, W Germany)   French Revolutionary Wars   3 May 1800
Fought between the French under Generals Jean Moreau and Claude-Jacques Lecourbe, and the Austrians under General Baron Paul Kray von Krajowa.
Strength: French 56,000; Austrians 110,000.
Aim: The French were advancing into Baden. The Austrians sought to prevent the French advance by blocking their path in in the Black Forest.
Battle: The action at Stockach was one half of a two-part engagement. The right wing of Moreau's army under General Lecourbe, 25,000 men strong, overtook the Austrian rearguard, driving them into and through Stockach and capturing 4,000 men as well as a depot of munitions and stores. The action is associated with that at Engen (qv) which took place at the same time between the main Austrian army and the rest of the French army.
Result: Both halves of the battle were victories for the French who forced the Austrians to retire towards Ulm, all the while closely pursuing them.

SYLPH v ARTEMISE (off Santander, Spain)   French Revolutionary Wars   31 July–1 August; 28 September 1801
The sloop *Sylph* (18) (Captain Charles Dashwood) chasing an armed schooner, sighted a large frigate, fought her during the night and, being much damaged, edged away to effect repairs. Seeing that the frigate did not pursue she hove to. At about 7am on 1 August *Sylph* discovered her opponent to the NW apparently disabled, but still too formidable for the battered sloop to tackle.
   After a refit in Plymouth *Sylph* rejoined the fleet. On 28 September she chased a ship in the NW, which appeared to be a French frigate of the same force as the one she had engaged on 31 July. *Sylph* caught her up and in a severe conflict of two hours and five minutes *Sylph* put her opponent to flight. Though her rigging was cut to pieces she had only one casualty. Dashwood thought his opponent was *Artémise* (44).

TELEGRAPH v L'HIRONDELLE (Ile de Bas, France)   French Revolutionary Wars   18 March 1799
After a close action of three and a half hours the hired brig *Telegraph* (16) (Lieutenant James Andrew Worth) took the French privateer brig *L'Hirondelle* (16). Both sides tried several times to board, but at length *L'Hirondelle*, her rigging shot away, became unmanageable and struck her colours. *Telegraph* had 5 wounded out of her crew of 60. *L'Hirondelle*'s casualties numbered 5 killed and 14 men wounded out of a complement of 89.

TENERIFE (21–24 July 1797)   see page 232.

   TERPSICHORE v MAHONESA (Cartagena, Spain)   French Revolutionary Wars   13 October 1796
Fought between the British 32-gun frigate *Terpsichore* (Captain Richard Bowen) and the Spanish 34-gun frigate *Mahonesa* (Captain Don Tomas Ayaldi).
   On 13 October 1796 *Terpsichore* was cruising off Cartagena, where she sighted a frigate to windward. *Terpsichore* had left 30 sick at Gibraltar and she had more sick and convalescents aboard. At 9.30am, the Spaniard having closed up, action commenced. After a while the Spanish fire slackened and at 11am *Mahonesa* tried to make off. Although her rigging and spars had been damaged, *Terpsichore* was still able

to pursue. *Mahonesa* surrendered. British casualties in a crew of 182 were 4 wounded. Spanish casualties in a crew of 273 were 30 killed and 30 wounded.

Captain Bowen brought his prize to Lisbon, but *Mahonesa* was too badly damaged to repair.

TOULON III (Var, S France)   French Revolutionary Wars   27 August–19 December 1793
Fought between the Allied garrison and the French under General Jacques Dugommier.
Strength: Allies 2,000 marines; French 11,500.
Aim: Reduction by the French of the garrison at Toulon.
Battle: Vice-Admiral Lord Hood, with 21 ships of the line, entered the port of Toulon, which at once declared for the monarchy. The naval arsenal was seized together with more than 70 vessels, 30 of them ships of the line–nearly half the French navy. A Spanish squadron under Admiral Juan de Langara accompanied the British force. A small garrison under Lord Mulgrave (Sir Henry Phipps) was put into the town. On 7 September the garrison was invested by the Republicans. General Dugommier adopted the plan of an artillery *chef de bataillon*, Napoleon Bonaparte, which contributed largely to his successful attack. By 18 December most of the landward defences had been carried and the town had become untenable. On 19 December the British evacuated by sea, taking with them or destroying most of the French fleet.
Result: The French regained the town, but lost part of their navy. Fifteen of their ships remained unscathed, however, owing to the neglect of the Spaniards. It was the last engagement of the war in which Spain acted as an ally of Britain. As a result of this action, Napoleon Bonaparte was promoted General de Brigade.

TOURCOING (TURCOING) (Nord, France)   French Revolutionary Wars   18 May 1794
Fought between the Allied army under Friedrich Josias, Prince of Saxe-Coburg, and the French under General Charles Pichegru.
Strength: Allies 72,000; French 82,000.
Aim: Both sides had launched spring offensives. One wing of the French offensive had been blunted at Beaumont-en-Cambrésis (qv), and now the Allies aimed to blunt the other.
Battle: The fighting was spread over a large area between Menin, Courtrai (Kortrijk), Lille and Tournai. Tourcoing is a village in the centre of this area. Although Saxe-Coburg was nominally in command the plan of attack was devised by the Austrian Chief of Staff, General Baron Mack. On 16 May Mack divided the army into six columns and attempted a double envelopment of the French; but owing to the close nature of the country, this complicated plan was very difficult to put into effect. A thick fog made co-ordination of column movement much more difficult.

The fighting started on 17 May. General Count von Clerfayt's column failed to reach his rendezvous, but Major-General Otto's and Frederick Augustus, the Duke of York's columns fared better. In a second attack in the evening the Duke of York was left in an exposed position. The two southern columns under General Kinsky and Archduke Charles both had long approach marches and advanced too cautiously so that they failed to reach the battlefield on 17 May.

The two centre columns were thus isolated. The French Command, which at that time consisted of a sort of committee of senior generals including Jean-Charles Pichegru, Joseph Souham, Jean Moreau, Jacques Macdonald and Jean Reynier decided to mask the laggardly columns to the north and south and attack in the centre. On 18 May they concentrated 60,000 men against General Otto and the Duke of York. The result was a rout. General von Clerfayt attacked the flank of the French thrust, but neither of the other two columns to the south achieved anything. Allied casualties were 5,000, and French 3,000.
Result: The French, with undefeated armies on their flanks, were not in a position to pursue, but General Pichegru went on to capture Charleroi (qv).

TOURNAI (or PONT-A-CHIN) (Hainaut, Belgium)   French Revolutionary Wars   22 May 1794
Fought between the French under General Jean-Charles Pichegru and the Allies.

The battle began about 5am when the French, some 62,000 strong, attacked the Allies, who lay before Tournai, their position resting on the Escaut above and below the town. Heavy fighting went on until 9pm, and the village of Pont-à-Chin had changed hands four times and was in the hands of General Jacques Macdonald, when Major-General Henry Edward Fox's 'Little Brigade' (14th, 37th and 53rd Foot) stormed the village with colours flying and music playing. The French fled and were unable to rally, and at 10pm the last shot was fired. Pichegru had apparently been dining near Pont-à-Chin in supposed security when the cry *'Les Anglais, les habits rouges!'* (The English, the Redcoats!) caused a panic, he and his officers scrambling out of the windows. The French lost 7 guns and at least 6,000 men, of whom 280 were beheaded by an Austrian battery which caught them wedged in an orchard. The Allies sustained 4,000 casualties, among whom the regiments of Fox's Brigade had 196 killed and wounded. This was not surprising, for they had repulsed the whole French army, a fine feat of arms, especially in view of what the brigade had suffered already–particularly at Tourcoing (qv) on 18 May.

TREBBIA II (Ligurian Appenines, N Italy)   French Revolutionary Wars   17–19 June 1799
Fought between the French under General Jacques Macdonald and the Allies under Field-Marshal Count Suvorov, and General Karl Ott.
Strength: French 25,000; Russians/Austrians 30,000.
Aim: The Russians sought to end the French offensive in Italy.
Battle: Suvorov found himself between two French armies, one under General Jean Moreau and the other under Macdonald, who had been wounded on the 12th. In order to prevent them from uniting, Suvorov turned on Macdonald by the Trebbia River. The action, which took place in a disorganised fashion along the banks and on the islands of the river, lasted for two days. On the night of 18–19 June Macdonald pulled out and retreated, pursued by Suvorov. French casualties were 4,000 killed and 12,000 wounded, missing or captured. They lost another 5,000 men on the retreat. Russian casualties were 6,000 men.
Result: Macdonald finally joined with Moreau, but the French evacuated Italy shortly afterwards.

TUILERIES (Paris, France)   French Revolutionary Wars   10 August 1793
When at 5.30am King Louis XVI emerged from his apartments to inspect his troops it became apparent that his nerve had gone. Reluctant to shed the blood of his subjects–however rebellious, however criminal–he delivered himself and his family to the National Assembly.

   The heroic Maréchal de Mailly (Joseph-Augustin, Comte de Mailly, Marquis d'Ancourt; Marshal 1783)–he was then eighty-six–rallied the few defenders of the château, 750 Swiss Guards, a handful of National Guards, and 200 nobles, who behaved extremely well, until the King sent a written message to command the Swiss to cease fire. In consequence they were, for the most part, massacred. Lieutenant Napoleon Bonaparte, who was present, intervened to save the life of one of the Swiss.

   De Mailly survived only to be guillotined on 25 March 1794. His last words were *'Vive le Roi!* I say it as did my ancestors!'

UNICORN v TRIBUNE (off Ushant, France)   French Revolutionary Wars   8 June 1796
After the capture of *Tamise* by *Santa Margarita* (SANTA MARGARITA V TAMISE) about 50 miles west of Ushant, *Tamise*'s consort, *Tribune* (44) (broad pendant of Commodore Jean Moulston), endeavoured to escape and was chased by *Unicorn* (40) (Captain Thomas Williams). Equality of sailing ability and clever manoeuvring by Moulston kept the 2 ships in a running action for ten hours, during which time *Unicorn* suffered damage to her masts and rigging. After dark the wind dropped which enabled *Unicorn* to close windward of *Tribune*, take her wind and engage in close combat.

   Tribune, practically dismasted, eventually surrendered. The action was marked by clever seamanship, manoeuvrability and sail drill on both sides. *Unicorn* suffered no casualties, but *Tribune*, which had a larger complement (330 to 240), had 37 killed and 14 wounded, including her commander. As a result of this action Captain Williams was knighted.

USHANT III ('THE GLORIOUS FIRST OF JUNE') (off Finistère, France)   French Revolutionary Wars   1 June 1794
Fought between the French under Rear-Admiral Louis Villaret de Joyeuse and the British under Lord Howe.
Strength: French 26 ships; British 26 ships.
Aim: The French were escorting a convoy of grain ships across the Atlantic. It was the British intention to intercept them and prevent them reaching port.
Battle: After four days of skirmishing the fleets took part in a decisive action on 1 June, by which time 4 more ships had joined Villaret. Howe sailed his ships into the centre of the French and in the ensuing fight 6 French ships were captured while a seventh was sunk. Villaret withdrew to Brest. This battle is also known as 'The Glorious First of June'.

Result: A tactical victory for Howe, but the 130 ships carrying grain had reached port safely during the battle, so it may be said that Villaret accomplished his mission.

This was the first major naval engagement between the British and the French in the war. During the battle a son was born to a Mrs McKenzie aboard *Tremendous* (74). Fifty-four years later Daniel Tremendous McKenzie received the Naval General Service Medal, with clasp '1st June 1794'. It seems highly unlikely that anyone else has ever been decorated for an action which took place on the day of his birth.

VALETTA (Malta)   French Revolutionary Wars   September 1798–5 September 1800
Fought between the French garrison under General Vaubois and the Maltese and British under Captain Sir Alexander Ball, RN.
Strength: French 3,500; Maltese/British 10,000, including insurgents in final attack+civilians.
Aim: The reduction by the French of Valetta.
Battle: Bonaparte had occupied Malta on his way to Egypt (10 June 1798). After the Battle of the Nile, the British once again controlled the Mediterranean. Local Maltese guerrillas staged an uprising against the French occupation. Rear-Admiral Lord Nelson sent some of his frigates to blockade Malta and to land troops on the island to support the insurgents. Sir Alexander Ball commanded an attack which reconquered all of Malta except Valetta, where Vaubois had retired. The British and Maltese laid siege to Valetta. Two years later Vaubois surrendered because of starvation. Maltese losses were 20,000 men.
Result: Malta was taken out of French hands, though, by the time Valetta capitulated, the importance of the island and Valetta harbour had decreased, as the war had moved away from that theatre.

VALMY (Marne, France)   French Revolutionary Wars   20 September 1792
Fought between part of the Allied army (Prussians, Austrians, Hessians and French émigrés) under Karl Wilhelm Ferdinand, Duke of Brunswick, and two French armies under General François Kellermann and General Charles-François Dumouriez.
Strength: Allies 34,000 with 48 guns; French 36,000 with 54 guns.
Aim: The French sought to halt the invading force of the Allied army.
Battle: Brunswick had advanced slowly towards Paris, leaving his army strung out along the line of communication. Kellermann was joined by Dumouriez and part of his army in an effort to halt the Allies. The Allies, though superior in numbers, were not of as high a calibre as the French who were veteran regulars of the old Royal Army. The Allies circled behind the French who were guarding the frontier between France and the Netherlands. The French turned and made a stand north of the Châlons road. After an artillery exchange in heavy fog at a range of 1,300 yards, the Prussian infantry advanced, but fell back before the accuracy of the expert French gunners, without coming into musket range. On the French lines, Kellermann's men bore the brunt of the enemy cannonade. At nightfall the Allies retired without any major engagement of the two armies. Casualties on both sides were slight.
Result: Brunswick withdrew into Germany across the Rhine ten days later.

Brunswick's whole campaign had been somewhat half-hearted owing to his own doubts about the wisdom of an invasion of France. Although there was little fighting at this battle, the repulse of the Prussian Allied army served as an inspiration to the French which was to set off a series of events with repercussions lasting for the next twenty-three years, culminating with the Battle of Waterloo. It may therefore be described as one of the decisive battles of history.

VILLERS-EN-CAUCHIES (France)   French Revolutionary Wars   24 April 1794
Fought between the French and Allied forces.
Strength: French 10,000; Allies 300 (with a further 1,000 in the neighbourhood).
Battle: The 15th Light Dragoons and two squadrons of the Leopold Hussars, under Major-General Otto, in a desperate but successful action against superior numbers, prevented the forces of the Emperor of Austria from being surprised. This was a most daring and dashing cavalry action. The Dragoons and Hussars, besides wrecking the enemy's squares and overrunning the guns on their first assault, pursued them for a mile and then turned back and charged through a French column of 50 guns and ammunition wagons. Then, finding themselves cut off, they had again to charge through a French line before reaching safety.

The French sustained 1,200 casualties–all said to have been sabred–of which 800 were killed and 400 wounded. They also had 3 guns taken. Allied casualties were 79 killed and wounded, plus 94 horses. As a reward for this action, all the officers of the Light Dragoons were made Knights of the Order of Maria Theresa.

VIPER v LE FURET (English Channel)   French Revolutionary Wars   26 December 1799
The British cutter *Viper* (14) (Lieutenant John Pengelly) sighted the French lugger privateer *Le Furet* (14) (Citizen Louis Bouvet) with her crew of 57 at 10.15am, some 7 or 8 leagues south of the Dodman, and brought her to close action. After a running fight, two well-directed broadsides compelled Bouvet to strike. Pengelly was slightly wounded as well as 1 seaman. The French lost 4 killed and 8 wounded, including their captain.

VIPER v VIRGEN MARIA (W Mediterranean)   French Revolutionary Wars   13 March 1797
The British cutter *Viper* (14) (Lieutenant John Pengelly) fought a creditable action with the Spanish 10-gun brig privateer *Virgen Maria* 20 miles NW of Alboran Island while in passage from Gibraltar to Algiers, in which *Virgen Maria* was taken. *Viper* lost none of her crew of 48. The Spaniards had 2 killed and 6 wounded out of a complement of 42.

WATTIGNIES (Nord, France)   French Revolutionary Wars   15–16 October 1793
Fought between the Allies (chiefly Austrians) under Friedrich Josias, Prince of Saxe-Coburg, and the French under General Jean-Baptiste Jourdan.
Strength: Allies 26,000; French 50,000.
Aim: The French sought to relieve the siege of Maubeuge.
Battle: On 15 October the French attacked the Allied position on the plateau of Wattignies but were beaten back in disorder because of their poor organisation. During the night, French commanders moved 8,000 men from their left wing to the right, overlapping the Austrian left wing so that the Allied army was rolled back on itself when the French attacked the following day. As a result the Prince of Saxe-Coburg was forced to withdraw and the Allies went into winter quarters.
Result: The fortress of Maubeuge was the last block to the Allied advance to Paris. The French victory meant that the threat to Paris was lifted.

WILLEMS (Hainaut, Belgium)   French Revolutionary Wars   10 May 1794
A French division, 23,000 strong, under General Jacques Philippe Bonnaud, attacked Frederick Augustus, Duke of York, at Marquain, before Tournai (qv). Most of the fighting was at Baisieux and Camphin on the Lille-Tournai road. The Duke turned the French right with his heavy cavalry, whereupon the French cavalry fled in confusion. The French infantry were advancing in fair order when Major-General David Dundas's heavy cavalry brigade got among them, sabring some 2,000 of them. The French, who went off in disorder lost 14 guns and had 450 prisoners taken, and admitted a loss of 5 guns and 500 men. The British cavalry suffered 121 casualties–40 killed and 81 wounded.

The importance of this action is that it was the first time that the infantry of the French Revolutionary Army managed for a time to resist cavalry charges penetrating their squares. It was to be eighteen years before British cavalry managed to break French squares again.

WOLVERINE v RUSSE (off Boulogne, France)   French Revolutionary Wars   12 September 1799
In foggy weather off Boulogne *Wolverine* (Captain Lewis Mortlock) a barque-rigged sloop of 12 guns sighted 2 French luggers–the privateers *Russe* (16) (Captain Pierre Audibert) and *Furet* (14) (Captain Denis Fourmentin). *Wolverine* hoisted Danish colours. On closing she hoisted her true colours and opened fire. Both luggers closed alongside and attempted to board. After a furious hand-to-hand struggle, in which Mortlock was mortally wounded, *Wolverine* was set on fire.

The British were outnumbered in the mêlée and *Wolverine* was captured and towed into Boulogne.

WÜRZBURG (NW Bavaria, W Germany)   French Revolutionary Wars   3 September 1796
Fought between the Austrians, under the Archduke Charles and the Holy Roman Emperor Francis II, and the French under General Jean-Baptiste Jourdan.
Strength: Austrians 45,000; French 40,000.
Aim: After returning from repulsing the French invasion at Amberg (qv), Archduke Charles sought to prevent the junction of two French armies under Jourdan and Jean Moreau.
Battle: The Archduke enveloped both French flanks with his cavalry, forcing Jourdan to retreat towards

the Rhine and extricating himself in a series of running fights. At the Rhine an armistice was concluded. The French lost 2,000 men and 7 cannon.

Result: Jourdan retreated across the Rhine and Charles turned his attention to Moreau who, seeing Jourdan's defeat, retired. The German campaign was at an end.

ZÜRICH I (Switzerland)   French Revolutionary Wars   4-7 June 1799

Fought between the Austrians under the Archduke Charles and the French under General André Masséna.

Strength: Austrians 40,000; French 25,000.

Aim: The Second Coalition sought to remove the French from Switzerland.

Battle: Charles attacked along a 5-mile front and, after a four-day battle which was costly to both sides, Masséna withdrew due to continued Austrian pressure and the doubtful loyalty of the Swiss.

Result: The Allies occupied Zürich. Soon after, the Archduke Charles Louis fell ill and was replaced by the Russian General Rimsky-Korsakov with 30,000 troops. At the same time, Field-Marshal Count Suvorov, having defeated the French in Italy, began moving across the Alps. Masséna began to prepare a counter-offensive.

ZÜRICH II (Switzerland)   French Revolutionary Wars   25-30 September 1799

Fought between a French army under General André Masséna and an Austro-Russian army under the Russian General Rimsky-Korsakov.

Strength: French 50,000; Austrians/Russians 45,000.

Aim: Field-Marshal Count Suvorov had driven the French out of the N Italian plain but could not advance farther because of Masséna's army in W Switzerland. So Suvorov planned an ambitious converging attack on Masséna by Rimsky-Korsakov's army in Switzerland and his own from Italy.

Battle: Masséna took the initiative. He first attacked Korsakov, drove him out of Zürich and, then, continuing his attack, turned Korsakov's retreat into a rout. Rimsky-Korsakov lost 8,000 men and 100 guns, and was forced to leave Switzerland.

To his south, with the future Marshal Nicolas-Jean de Dieu Soult in command, Masséna threw back the Austrians in two days of hard fighting. Suvorov, meanwhile, had made a crossing of the St Gothard Pass, but, by 30 September, the other columns of the pincer movement having failed, he found himself isolated. Only by stupendous efforts, harassed all the way by French mountain troops under General Claude-Joseph Lecourbe, and by Masséna's army, did he manage to escape to the Rhine on 10 October with 14,000 survivors.

Result: Suvorov blamed the Austrians for his defeat at the hands of the brilliant Masséna. The Czar Paul I was so disgusted at the lack of Allied support that he withdrew from the Coalition and joined the Second Armed Neutrality directed against Britain. Suvorov's career was over and he was recalled in disgrace early in 1800 and died the following year. France had been saved at a most critical moment.

TENERIFE (Santa Cruz, Canary Islands)   French Revolutionary Wars   21-24 July 1797

Fought between Rear-Admiral Sir Horatio Nelson and Don Juan Antonio Gutierrez, Governor of Tenerife.

Strength: British 4 ships of the line + 3 frigates + 960 sailors and marines; Spanish 8,000 regulars and local militia.

Aim: To capture Santa Cruz in order to seize the Viceroy of Mexico's treasure ship and to capture or destroy any other enemy vessels.

Battle: Two landings took place, one by night on 21 July under Captain Thomas Troubridge, which failed to achieve surprise and the landing parties were withdrawn. The second attempt by a force led by Nelson was directed at the mole and harbour of Santa Cruz on 24 July. Owing to a severe gale at night only 500 sailors and marines got ashore and were stuck there. After negotiations with the Governor the British withdrew under a flag of truce.

Of the British, 7 officers and 139 men were killed or drowned and 5 officers (including Nelson who lost an arm) and about 100 men were wounded. Spanish casualties were under 100.

Result: Complete failure.

SECTION NINE

PENINSULAR WAR 1808–1814

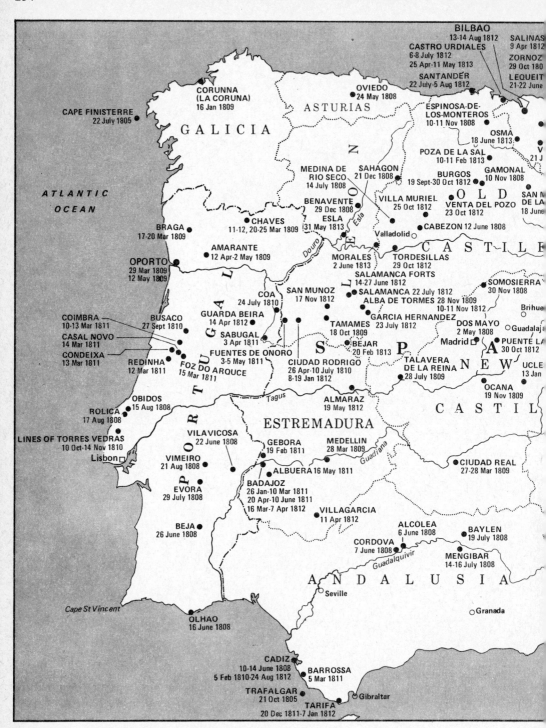

BILBAO
13-14 Aug 1812
CASTRO URDIALES
6-8 July 1812
25 Apr-11 May 1813
SANTANDER
22 July-5 Aug 1812

SALINAS
9 Apr 1812
ZORNOZ
29 Oct 180
LEQUEIT
21-22 June

CORUNNA
(LA CORUNA)
16 Jan 1809

OVIEDO
24 May 1808

ASTURIAS

CAPE FINISTERRE
22 July 1805

GALICIA

ESPINOSA-DE-
LOS-MONTEROS
10-11 Nov 1808

OSMA
18 June 1813

V
21 J

POZA DE LA SAL
10-11 Feb 1813

MEDINA DE
RIO SECO
14 July 1808

SAHAGON
21 Dec 1808

BURGOS
19 Sept-30 Oct 1812

GAMONAL
10 Nov 1808

ATLANTIC
OCEAN

BENAVENTE
29 Dec 1808

VILLA MURIEL
25 Oct 1812

VENTA DEL POZO
23 Oct 1812

SAN M
DE LA
18 June

ESLA
31 May 1813

CABEZON 12 June 1808

BRAGA
17-20 Mar 1809

CHAVES
11-12, 20-25 Mar 1809

Valladolid

CASTIL

AMARANTE
12 Apr-2 May 1809

MORALES
2 June 1813

TORDESILLAS
29 Oct 1812

OPORTO
29 Mar 1809
12 May 1809

SALAMANCA FORTS
14-27 June 1812

SOMOSIERRA
30 Nov 1808

COA
24 July 1810

SAN MUNOZ
17 Nov 1812

SALAMANCA 22 July 1812
ALBA DE TORMES 28 Nov 1809
10-11 Nov 1812

GUARDA BEIRA
14 Apr 1812

GARCIA HERNANDEZ
23 July 1812

DOS MAYO
2 May 1808

Guadalaj

Brihue

COIMBRA
10-13 Mar 1811

BUSACO
27 Sept 1810

SABUGAL
3 Apr 1811

TAMAMES
18 Oct 1809

CASAL NOVO
14 Mar 1811

FUENTES DE ONORO
3-5 May 1811

BEJAR
20 Feb 1813

Madrid

PUENTE L
30 Oct 1812

NEW

CONDEIXA
13 Mar 1811

REDINHA
12 Mar 1811

FOZ DO ARQUCE
15 Mar 1811

CIUDAD RODRIGO
26 Apr-10 July 1810
8-19 Jan 1812

TALAVERA
DE LA REINA
28 July 1809

UCLE
13 Jan

OBIDOS
15 Aug 1808

Tagus

ALMARAZ
19 May 1812

OCANA
19 Nov 1809

ROLICA
17 Aug 1808

ESTREMADURA

CASTIL

LINES OF TORRES VEDRAS
10 Oct-14 Nov 1810

VILAVICOSA
22 June 1808

GEBORA
19 Feb 1811

MEDELLIN
28 Mar 1809

CIUDAD REAL
27-28 Mar 1809

Lisbon

VIMEIRO
21 Aug 1808

ALBUERA 16 May 1811

EVORA
29 July 1808

BADAJOZ
26 Jan-10 Mar 1811
20 Apr-10 June 1811
16 Mar-7 Apr 1812

VILLAGARCIA
11 Apr 1812

ALCOLEA
6 June 1808

BAYLEN
19 July 1808

BEJA
26 June 1808

CORDOVA
7 June 1808

MENGIBAR
14-16 July 1808

Guadalquivir

ANDALUSIA

Cape St Vincent

Seville

Granada

OLHAO
16 June 1808

CADIZ
10-14 June 1808
5 Feb 1810-24 Aug 1812

BARROSSA
5 Mar 1811

Gibraltar

TRAFALGAR
21 Oct 1805

TARIFA
20 Dec 1811-7 Jan 1812

21 The Peninsular War, 1806–14; also Trafalgar and St Vincent

235

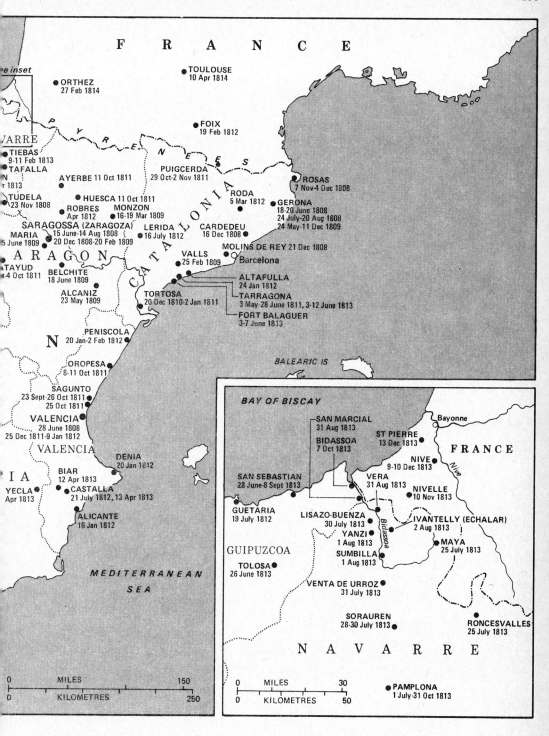

F R A N C E

ORTHEZ
27 Feb 1814

TOULOUSE
10 Apr 1814

P Y R E N E E S

re inset

VARRE

FOIX
19 Feb 1812

TIEBAS
9-11 Feb 1813
TAFALLA
r 1813

PUIGCERDA
29 Oct-2 Nov 1811

AYERBE 11 Oct 1811

ROSAS
7 Nov-4 Dec 1808

TUDELA
23 Nov 1808

HUESCA 11 Oct 1811
ROBRES   MONZON
Apr 1812   16-19 Mar 1809

RODA
5 Mar 1812

GERONA
18-20 June 1808
24 July-20 Aug 1808
24 May-11 Dec 1809

SARAGOSSA (ZARAGOZA)
MARIA   15 June-14 Aug 1808
5 June 1809   20 Dec 1808-20 Feb 1809

LERIDA   CARDEDEU
16 July 1812   16 Dec 1808

A R A G O N

CATALONIA

MOLINS DE REY 21 Dec 1808

TAYUD
4 Oct 1811

BELCHITE
18 June 1809

VALLS
25 Feb 1809

Barcelona

N

ALCANIZ
23 May 1809

TORTOSA
20 Dec 1810-2 Jan 1811

ALTAFULLA
24 Jan 1812

TARRAGONA
3 May-28 June 1811, 3-12 June 1813

FORT BALAGUER
3-7 June 1813

PENISCOLA
20 Jan-2 Feb 1812

OROPESA
8-11 Oct 1811

BALEARIC IS

SAGUNTO
23 Sept-26 Oct 1811
25 Oct 1811

VALENCIA
28 June 1808
25 Dec 1811-9 Jan 1812

VALENCIA

DENIA
20 Jan 1812

BAY OF BISCAY

Bayonne

SAN MARCIAL
31 Aug 1813

ST PIERRE
13 Dec 1813

F R A N C E

BIDASSOA
7 Oct 1813

NIVE
9-10 Dec 1813

IA

BIAR
12 Apr 1813

SAN SEBASTIAN
28 June-8 Sept 1813

VERA
31 Aug 1813

NIVELLE
10 Nov 1813

YECLA
Apr 1813

CASTALLA
21 July 1812, 13 Apr 1813

GUETARIA
19 July 1812

LISAZO-BUENZA
30 July 1813

IVANTELLY (ECHALAR)
2 Aug 1813

ALICANTE
16 Jan 1812

YANZI
1 Aug 1813

MAYA
25 July 1813

GUIPUZCOA

SUMBILLA
1 Aug 1813

M E D I T E R R A N E A N
S E A

TOLOSA
26 June 1813

VENTA DE URROZ
31 July 1813

SORAUREN
28-30 July 1813

RONCESVALLES
25 July 1813

N A V A R R E

0   MILES   150
0   KILOMETRES   250

0   MILES   30
0   KILOMETRES   50

PAMPLONA
1 July-31 Oct 1813

In 1808 the Spaniards rose against the French invaders, and received extensive support from the British, who landed an army in Portugal. The Emperor Napoleon made a brief personal appearance, but more concerned with affairs at home, in central Europe and in Russia, he made an unsuccessful attempt at running the war by remote control through his lieutenants: *'On ne dirige pas la guerre à trois ou quatre cents lievres de distance.'* (General Paul Thiebault)

In an effort to settle the war, Napoleon ordered Marshal André Masséna to attempt the conquest of Portugal, only to find himself confronted by Wellington's lines of Torres Vedras. This was the high-water mark of French military success in the Napoleonic Wars. Later the Allies got the upper hand, and when Napoleon became involved in Russia a counter-attack could be attempted. Wellington won his great victories at Salamanca (1812) and Vitoria (1813). The news of the latter persuaded the Austrians to throw in their lot once more against Napoleon. When the war ended Wellington had invaded S France and defeated Marshal Nicolas-Jean de Dieu Soult at Toulouse.

Napoleon recognised that 'the Spanish ulcer' drained away his strength. To him the Peninsula was a fated 'Second Front'. It gave the British government a theatre of war where its relative small military forces could be deployed to advantage. The Spaniards, especially their irregular forces, the *guerrilleros*, made Wellington's victories possible by tying up thousands of French troops in the vain attempt to police the occupied provinces. Portuguese units, reorganised by Marshal Beresford and a number of British officers, fought with distinction as an integral part of Wellington's army.

ALBA DE TORMES I (León, Spain)   Napoleonic Wars/Peninsular War   28 November 1809
Fought between a Spanish army under the Duque del Parque and a French army under General François Christophe Kellermann.
Strength: Spanish 1,500 cavalry + 30,000 infantry; French 3,000 cavalry + 13,000 infantry.
Aim: The French sought to complete the defeat of the Spanish offensive and to take advantage of the division of the Spanish army.
Battle: After his victory at Tamames (qv) Del Parque advanced to Salamanca, but on 5 November fell back to the passes. Receiving news of French forces withdrawing to Madrid, he advanced and occupied Salamanca again on 18 November. The French fell back, and Del Parque pushed on towards Medina Del Campo.

By 24 November the overall French commander in the area, General Kellermann (son of the victor of Valmy), had regrouped about Puente de Duero. Del Parque had now heard of Ocaña and decided to withdraw on the passes via Alba de Tormes. He gained a day's start, but Kellermann, though outnumbered, went in pursuit. On the 28th Kellermann's cavalry reported that the Spanish army was encamped about Alba de Tormes. Del Parque, believing he had shed his pursuers, had allowed his army to be divided by the Tormes River. Kellermann decided to attack without waiting for his infantry. The French cavalry broke the division of General Losada, and the right of the Conde de Belveder's, capturing 2,000 men and a battery of guns. The remnants fell back on Alba jamming the bridge. Kellerman then attacked the rest of Belveder's and La Carrera's divisions, which managed to beat him off. But they were cut off from the bridge, and when the French infantry arrived, they had to make off as best they could. Kellerman drove the Spanish rearguard out of Alba, but there the fighting ended.

The Spanish lost 5 flags, 9 guns, most of their baggage, but only 3,000 killed or captured. French casualties were less than 300.
Result: The Spanish army broke up as it retreated, and it was a month before Del Parque could collect it.

ALBA DE TORMES II (León, Spain)   Napoleonic Wars/Peninsular War   10–11 November 1812
Fought between elements of the French army under King Joseph Bonaparte and Marshals Nicolas-Jean de Dieu Soult and Jean-Baptiste Jourdan, and the Allied army under the Marquess of Wellington.
Aim: Soult wished to find out whether Wellington was prepared to make a stand, or was willing to continue his retreat to Portugal.
Battle: The Allies retained Alba de Tormes as a bridgehead across the Tormes River. Its defences had been hastily repaired and it was garrisoned by Major-General Kenneth Alexander Howard's Brigade of the 2nd Division, supported by Lt-General Sir John Hamilton's Portuguese Division and 12 Portuguese guns.

On 10 November operations began by the driving in of General Long's cavalry piquets, and then Soult deployed 18 guns and 12 voltigeur companies. A lengthy bombardment followed, which caused little damage, and the voltigeur companies came forward three times without success. Hamilton reinforced the garrison with Brigadier Antonio Da Costa's Brigade. At dawn on 11 November the cannonade recommenced, but with no more effect and the bombardment was called off after a few hours.

Casualties among the British were 79 men, and among the Portuguese 44. French casualties were 158 men.

Result: The Allies held on until 14 November when, the river having fallen, the French crossed higher up, and the Allies pulled back.

The castle of Alba was retained under garrison by a Spanish battalion commanded by Major José Miranda. After a gallant defence, the garrison cut their way out and escaped.

ALBUERA (Extremadura, Spain)   Napoleonic Wars/Peninsular War   16 May 1811
Fought between an Anglo-Portuguese and Spanish army under Marshal Sir William Beresford and a French army under Marshal Nicolas-Jean de Dieu Soult.
Strength: Allies 35,000 (British 10,000, Portuguese 10,000, Spanish: under General Blake 12,000; under Captain General Castaños 2,500), including 3,700 cavalry; French 24,200, including 4,000 cavalry.
Aim: Marshal Beresford had been detached by Wellington for a counter-offensive on the southern Spanish-Portuguese border. Beresford was besieging Badajoz (BADAJOZ II). Soult sought to relieve Badajoz and Beresford fought to prevent him.
Battle: Wellington had given Beresford instructions to fight to cover the siege or not as he thought best, and had pointed out Albuera as the best position available. Beresford was not keen to fight, but when he met Captain-General Don Joachim Blake on 13 May (Blake had agreed to place himself under Beresford's orders for this action only) he found him determined on a battle. 'For Beresford the battle of Albuera was a succession of disastrous misfortunes caused by the incompetence and worse of his subordinates. He overcame every one of them with pertinacity and courage, but has been pilloried by historians ever since.' (Michael Glover, *The Peninsular War 1809–1814*)

Blake's men, coming from the SE, only arrived at 3am on the morning of the 16th. Beresford had to allocate to them the vulnerable right or southern wing of the Allied positions. Immediately to their north were the British 2nd Division on the ridge and Major-General Count von Alten's Brigade of the King's German Legion holding the village of Albuera to the front. Behind the 2nd Division was the 4th Anglo-Portuguese Division, reduced to two brigades. On the left was Lt-General John Hamilton's Portuguese Division. Soult launched a feint attack by Godinot's Brigade at Albuera, while moving the bulk of his army to its left to attack the Allies in the flank. Beresford ordered Blake to wheel his line to the right into a strong position across the ridge behind a dip. Blake still thought the French would launch a frontal attack. He did not pass this order on, nor did he tell Beresford that he had not done so. However, General José Zayas on his own initiative wheeled his weak division. When Beresford became aware of Blake's failure, he went over to superintend the change of front. The Spanish, many of them raw recruits, could only manoeuvre very slowly. Thus, Zayas's 2,000 men had to face 8,000 French alone.

Beresford had ordered Major-General the Hon William Stewart, commanding the 2nd Division, to support Zayas. As soon as his three leading battalions came up Stewart ordered them to deploy and attack the French flank. This manoeuvre ended in disaster. The British gunfire shattered the French, but two regiments of cavalry, one of the Polish lancers, struck the rear of the brigade in a rain-squall which rendered the muskets unworkable. The three battalions were wrecked in seconds: they had started 1,650 strong, but lost 1,250 men, almost half of them as prisoners.

The remaining Spanish infantry would not advance to support Zayas whose men, running out of ammunition, began to fall back. The French attack now fell upon General Daniel Houghton's Brigade. They stood their ground, and it was here that the 57th Foot acquired their nickname 'The Diehards'. Soult, realising that Beresford's army was stronger than he expected, failed to push home his advantage. Beresford ordered Major-General Count von Alten to leave the village and come to Houghton's aid. Alten refused to move until Hamilton replaced him. But Major-General Lowry Cole, commanding the 4th Division, on his own responsibility, at the suggestion of Lt-Colonel Henry Hardinge, one of Beresford's staff, counter-attacked. He avoided Stewart's mistake, formed his Portuguese Brigade so as to protect the flank of his British fusiliers, and, after a dreadful fire fight in which more than half the fusiliers became casualties, the French columns broke up and fled. British casualties were 4,159, Portuguese 389, Spanish 1,308, and French 5,936.
Result: Beresford had won his battle, without much help from his subordinate generals. Soult held his ground on 17 May, then, when the convoy of wounded had got a start, withdrew towards Seville. The siege of Badajoz was restarted.

ALCANIZ (Aragón, Spain)   Napoleonic Wars/Peninsular War   23 May 1809
Fought between part of the French 3rd Army Corps under General Louis-Gabriel Suchet and a Spanish army under Captain-General Don Joachim Blake.
Strength: French 7,200 infantry + 550 cavalry + 320 artillery + 18 guns; Spanish 8,000 infantry + 450 cavalry + 245 artillery + 19 guns.
Aim: Suchet sought to reassert the French hold on Aragón.
Battle: When Suchet arrived in Saragossa to replace General Andoche Junot on 15 May he found French affairs in Aragón to be in a deplorable state. 3 Corps had only about 10,000 of its nominal 20,000 fit for duty, and morale, particularly in the new units, was very low. Suchet thought that the only way to secure his position was to attack. On 17 May he left Saragossa and on 23 May he came up against General Blake's troops drawn up on a line of hills east of Alcañiz, covering the town and its bridge. Tactically it was a good position, but the bottleneck of a single bridge would have made defeat into disaster. The Aragónese forming the Spanish north flank were on the highest hill, the Cerro de los Pueyos. The central hill, Las Horcas, was held by three Valencian battalions and all the Spanish guns, and lay immediately in front of the bridge. The south flank on the lowest of the hills, La Perdiguera, was held by the remaining Valencians and the cavalry.

In the afternoon Suchet launched two attacks against the Cerro de los Pueyos, which caused Blake to move his two reserve battalions there, but the French were repelled by General Juan Carlos Areizaga without difficulty. When the fighting on the northern flank died down, Suchet launched his main attack against Las Horcas. This attack by two regiments of Musnier's Division failed to make the usual progress, for, when they reached the crest, they were halted by the Spanish artillery on the line of a ditch. Eventually they were driven back down the hill. Suchet, who was wounded in the foot, was unable to get his men to attack again.
Result: Suchet's unhappy début as Commander of 3 Corps did his men's morale no good. A new panic broke out in the French troops during the night, and they poured into San Per and Hijar in disorder the following day. Suchet had the initiator of the panic shot.

Blake followed up his victory slowly. He waited until the reinforcements he was expecting from Valencia joined him. Within three weeks he had gathered 25,000 men and felt himself strong enought to march on Saragossa.

ALCOLEA (Córdova, Spain)   Napoleonic Wars/Peninsular War   6 June 1808
Fought between a portion of General Comte Dupont de L'Etang's French Army Corps and some Spanish levies under Colonel Don Pedro de Echávarri.
Strength: French 13,000; Spanish 1,400 (regulars and militia) with 8 guns + approx 12,000 peasant levies.
Aim: Napoleon saw where the two most dangerous foci of the Spanish insurrection lay, but had not yet realised how difficult the subjugation of Spain would be. Thinking in terms of police actions, he sent General Dupont with a portion of his army corps to deal with the Andalusians. Dupont pushed south from Madrid and decided to make Córdova his objective. Don Pedro de Echávarri, a retired colonel whom the local Junta had appointed to command its levies, decided, probably for political rather than for military reasons, to make a stand in defence of Córdova, and thus brought on the first engagement of the Peninsular War.
Battle: Echávarri barricaded the bridge of Alcolea covering it with his regulars, militia and guns. On each flank he placed a few thousand levies. The rest, including all his mounted troops, were sent across the river into some hills to threaten the French flank. Dupont bombarded the Spanish position and then set his vanguard to storm the bridge. The leading battalion succeeded and began to cross the river. At this moment the levies across the river appeared. Dupont sent his cavalry to deal with them, which they swiftly did. Dupont's infantry rapidly overpowered the Spanish regulars, whereupon the rest of the levies fled.

The Spanish suffered 200 casualties. The French had 30 killed and 80 wounded.
Result: The road to Córdova was now open.

ALICANTE (Alicante, Spain)   Napoleonic Wars/Peninsular War   16 January 1812
Fought between a French force under General Louis Pierre Montbrun and a Spanish garrison under General Nicolas Mahy.
Strength: French 4,000 infantry + 1,500 cavalry + 6 guns; Spanish 6,000.
Aim: Montbrun, wishing to distinguish himself in an independent operation, sought to take Alicante by *coup de main.*

Battle: Montbrun appeared before the city, whose fortifications had been greatly improved, advanced into the suburbs and was halted by the new defences. He threw a few useless shells into the city, was met with a very heavy fire, and retreated.

Result: This repulse heartened the Spaniards, downcast after the fall of Valencia (VALENCIA II). Montbrun's misguided manoeuvres delayed his return to Marmont for ten days at a time when the Marshal needed him to interfere with Wellington who was besieging Ciudad Rodrigo (CIUDAD RODRIGO II).

ALMARAZ (Extremadura, Spain)   Napoleonic Wars/Peninsular War   19 May 1812
Fought between an Allied force from Wellington's army under Lt-General Sir Rowland Hill and the French garrisons of the forts covering the bridge of Almaraz over the Tagus.

Strength: Allies 7,000 (British 4,500 with 6 guns, Portuguese 2,500 with 6 guns); French 1,000.

Aim: The bridge of Almaraz was a key link between Marshal Auguste Marmont's Army of Portugal and General Comte Drouet d'Erlon's force facing Hill in Spanish Estremadura. Wellington wished to have it destroyed to facilitate his planned advance against Marmont.

Battle: Hill marched north from his headquarters at Almendralejo on 8 May and, moving as rapidly as possible, neared Almaraz on the 17th.

The plan was for Colonel Charles Ashworth's Portuguese Brigade and the artillery to keep to the main road, and demonstrate frontally against the outlying fortress of Miravute, while Lt-General Christopher Tilson-Chowne was to attempt to storm it from the rear. Meanwhile Major-General Kenneth Alexander Howard was to assault the forts by the river. But after a thorough inspection Hill decided Miravete was too strong to be rushed, especially as surprise had been lost. Instead he turned his attentions to the forts by the river. On the south bank was the strong fort Napoleon, while to the north was the weaker Fort Ragusa. The new plan was to mask the Castle of Miravete while rushing Fort Napoleon with Howard's Brigade. At 6am on 19 May the lead company came upon Fort Napoleon. After a short delay, owing to the brigade being strung out along the narrow paths, Hill attacked with the 50th and half the 71st Foot, in three columns. Despite heavy fire all the columns succeeded, and the fort was captured.

Many of the garrison fled towards the bridge, with the British in close pursuit, and the latter captured the bridgehead. The garrison of Fort Ragusa, thoroughly panicked, fled. Allied casualties were 189; French 400, as well as the loss of 18 guns and 20 pontoons.

Result: The bridge was destroyed, and the French lacked the means to replace it. The forts were blown up.

ALTAFULLA (Catalonia, Spain)   Napoleonic Wars/Peninsular War   24 January 1812
Fought between a French force from the garrison of Barcelona under General Maurice Mathieu, and a Spanish force under General Baron Eroles.

Strength: French 8,000; Spanish 4,000.

Aim: The French sought to relieve Tarragona (qv), which was being blockaded by Spanish troops.

Battle: Eroles decided to make a stand at Altafulla, unaware of how strong the French force was. The French, who marched all night, came on under cover of fog. His resistance was creditable, but eventually his men were routed. However, his troops breaking up and fleeing across the hills managed to escape, although 2 guns and the rearguard he left behind were lost. The Spanish suffered 600 casualties.

Result: The French relieved Tarragona. Eroles blamed Captain-General Luis Lacy, claiming that promised support had not materialised.

AMARANTE (N Portugal)   Napoleonic Wars/Peninsular War   12 April–2 May 1809
Fought between a Portuguese force under Brigadier Francisco da Silveira and a French force under General Louis Henri Loison.

Strength: Portuguese 10,000 troops (of very mixed quality); French gradually rising as April passed to 9,000.

Aim: The Portuguese sought to prevent the French crossing the river Tamega and pushing back into Tras-os-Montes.

Battle: After recapturing Chaves (qv), the Military Governor of the Portuguese province of Tras-os-Montes, Brigadier Francisco da Silveira, marched down the Tamega and took up a position at the bridge of Amarante. When General Loison arrived he found the Portuguese in strength and halted. Silveira crossed the river to attack, but Loison beat him off and Silveira retired across the river again (12 April). Marshal Nicolas-Jean de Dieu Soult reinforced Loison, who attacked Silveira (17 April), but failed to cross the bridge. Soult reinforced Loison still further, but Silveira hung on against repeated French attacks until 2 May when the French forced a crossing and dispersed his men.

Result: Silveira had occupied many of Soult's men for most of April and prevented a further French advance until Sir Arthur Wellesley, who landed in Lisbon on 22 April, could begin his counter-offensive. Silveira was promoted Marechal de Campo (Major-General), as a reward, and in 1811 was made Conde de Amarante.

AYERBE-HUESCA (Aragón, Spain)   Napoleonic Wars/Peninsular War   11 October 1811
Fought between a Spanish guerrilla band under Francisco Espoz y Mina and a French (Italian) force under Colonel Ceccopieri.
Strength: Spanish 4,000; French 800.
Aim: The Spanish sought to make a diversion in favour of Captain-General Don Joachim Blake's defence of Valencia (VALENCIA II).
Battle: Mina attacked the French garrison of Exea, who cut their way out and united with a battalion of Italian infantry under Colonel Ceccopieri. Ceccopieri, underrating his opponent's strength, marched to relieve Ayerbe. He was surprised by Mina's whole force, and in a running fight the column was surrounded and exterminated.

French (Italian) casualties were 200 killed and wounded, as well as 600 prisoners. Spanish casualties are not known.
Result: This disaster failed to break the French grip on Aragón, owing to General Honoré Reille's move from Navarre, or to distract Suchet from Valencia.

Mina demonstrated the illusory nature of French control in N Spain, for he marched 200 miles across Navarre, Alava and Biscay to the sea at Motrico, where he delivered his prisoners to a British frigate, and then marched back, without being intercepted.

BADAJOZ I (Extremadura, Spain)   Napoleonic Wars/Peninsular War   26 January–10 March 1811
Fought between the Spanish garrison under General Rafael Menacho and Brigadier José Imaz and a French army under Marshal Nicolas-Jean de Dieu Soult.
Strength: Spanish 5,000 (initially, rising to 10,000); French 6,000 infantry (initially + 6,000 from 3 February) + 10 companies of artillery + 7 companies of sappers + 6 regiments of cavalry.
Aim: The French sought to capture Badajoz as the first stage in a diversion in favour of Marshal André Masséna.
Battle: The city of Badajoz was one of the strongest fortresses in the Peninsula. It lies on the river Guadiana, with the town on one side, and a strong outwork on the other, the dominating Fort San Cristóbal. The city slopes down from the castle at the NE of the place, to the river which is crossed by a long bridge. Running round the eastern wall is the Rivillas Brook; the front of the place has eight regular bastions, and a solid wall towards the river. The bastions reach to a height of about 30 feet from the bottom of the ditch. There were two strong outworks, the Picurina lunette lying beyond the Rivillas, and the larger Pardaleras fort opposite the south point of the city.

Soult moved forward from Olivença on 26 January, his cavalry blockading the north of the city, and the infantry the south. Soult's engineers decided that the best point of attack was the southern front, and that first the Paradaleras fort had to be taken. Trenches were opened on the night 28–29 January, and the first parallel commenced on the night of 30–31 January. On the following day General Menacho sent out a sortie, which captured the French trenches momentarily. But so little damage was done that the first battery could be armed next day.

On 3 February Menacho launched another sortie, which stormed the first parallel, but was driven back by the newly arrived infantry of General Gazán's Division. On the 5th all was changed by the arrival of Lt-General Gabriel Mendizabal's army (GEBORA). With this battle won, Soult went on with the siege. On 4 March Menacho sent out his last sortie. This did considerable damage, but Menacho was killed, and he was replaced by Brigadier Imaz. The defence now became passive. On 4 March the besiegers had lodged themselves in the Demi-Lunes of the bastion of San Juan, and began to build a battery. On the 8th it began to fire at a range of 60 yards: by the 10th there was a breach 70 yards wide.

Soult was in a hurry, for he knew relief was on the way, and sent in a message to ask for surrender. Imaz called a council. Most of the speakers gave very depressing opinions, Imaz made heroic noises, voted for continued resistance, and opened negotiations. He surrendered at 3pm on the 10th although he knew help was on the way, and on the following day his men marched out.

Spanish casualties were 1,850 killed and wounded, 7,900 surrendered and in addition 1,000 were sick in hospitals. French casualties numbered 2,000.

Result: Badajoz was found to contain rations for 8,000 men for more than a month, 150 serviceable cannon, 80,000 pounds of powder, 300,000 infantry cartridges, and 2 bridge equipages. There is no doubt that had Menacho lived the garrison would have held out until it was relieved by Marshal Sir William Beresford. Instead, it was to take Wellington 13 months and three attempts to recover the city.

BADAJOZ II (Extremadura, Spain)   Napoleonic Wars/Peninsular War   20 April–10 June 1811
Fought between an Allied (British/Portuguese/Spanish) army under Marshal Sir William Beresford, later superseded by Viscount Wellington, and a French garrison under General Armand Phillipon.
Strength: Allies 22,000; French 5,000.
Aim: Wellington needed to recover this fortress, which had surrendered when help was on the way, to secure the defence of the southern Portuguese frontier.
Battle: Before Badajoz fell on 11 March 1811 Wellington detached Marshal Beresford to relieve the place. Marshal Nicolas-Jean de Dieu Soult, shaken by the news of Barrossa (qv) fell back on Seville, leaving Marshal Edouard Mortier with 11,000 men to occupy Spanish Extremadura. By 22 March Beresford had a force of 22,000 Anglo-Portuguese concentrated 40 miles from Badajoz, while on 21 March Mortier captured Campo Mayor. On 26 March Beresford recovered Campo Mayor and then moved against Badajoz. On 20 April the siege of Badajoz started under the immediate direction of Wellington, who had ridden south to join Beresford. Then Wellington returned north, leaving Beresford with detailed instructions.

On 5 May, the proper siege works were begun, trenches were opened on the 8th, for all three attacks, but the stony ground opposite San Cristóbal proved unsuitable for digging. On 10 May Phillipon launched an unsuccessful sortie, but on 12 May news came that Marshal Soult was approaching, and the siege had to be lifted until he was driven off (ALBUERA).

The siege was restarted by Lt-General John Hamilton's Portuguese Division on 18 May. Wellington was now in a position after Fuentes de Oñoro (qv) and the fall of Almeida to bring reinforcements to Beresford. He arrived on 19 May and took charge, adding the 3rd and 7th Divisions from the north to the besieging force. However, the siege went on no better. The inadequate guns, and the ill-judged direction of attack being the major causes. On 6 June an attack was launched against an inadequate breach in San Cristóbal. This failed and there were 92 casualties out of the 180 who assaulted. The battering went on, and another assault was delivered on 9 June. This time, 500 men were used but again the assault failed, suffering 139 casualties. On 10 June Wellington decided to abandon the siege, as he had heard that Marmont was soon to join Soult.

Wellington, it should be noted, had never been very good at sieges. It seemed that he did not take them–and all the paraphernalia required–seriously enough, in comparison with his European counterparts.

BADAJOZ III (Extremadura, Spain)   Napoleonic Wars/Peninsular War   16 March–7 April 1812
Fought between an Allied (Anglo-Hispano-Portuguese) army under Lord Wellington and a French garrison under General Armand Phillipon.
Strength: Allies 22,000 with 58 guns (besieging force) + 33,000 (covering force, Generals Graham and Hill); French 4,700.
Aim: Wellington needed to capture this fortress to prepare the way for his offensive into Spain.
Battle: On 19 February Wellington began to move his divisions south from the Almeida-Ciudad Rodrigo area. Already his artillery commander Alexander Dickson had gone to supervise the movement of the siege train. On 5 March Wellington himself left Freneda, and on 12 March reached Elvas, the major Portuguese frontier fortress opposite Badajoz.

Preparations were far more thorough than at the previous siege of Badajoz (BADAJOZ II), and the artillery was a good modern train. On 16 March the army moved forward, Lt-General Sir Thomas Graham with three divisions and two cavalry brigades advancing to the SE, Lt-General Sir Rowland Hill going east with two divisions and two brigades of cavalry to cover the siege. Meanwhile the investing force moved up, and this time the British engineers decided to abandon the idea of attacking San Cristóbal. Instead the attack was to be made on the bastions of Santa Maria and La Trinidad on the SE side of the town. This choice had apparently been made following the arrival of a French sergeant-major who had deserted his own ranks and brought with him a plan of the defences.

By 6 April the three breaches had been formed, and an assault was planned for that night. The 3rd Division was to attempt to attack the castle, while the 5th Division was to try to attack the bastion of San Vicente. But Phillipon had prepared very careful and strong defences at the breaches, and when the stormers went forward at 10pm they were thrown back with terrible losses. They persisted in their assault, reinforced by reserve battalions, for more than two hours, and sustained severe casualties. The Light Division lost 929 out of 3,000 men, the 4th Division 925 out of 3,500 and the 2,200 Portuguese with them more than 400.

But while these attacks failed, the 3rd Division succeeded in entering the castle at the third attempt from a different direction and, by midnight, it was secured. San Roque was also stormed, and Brigadier George Walker's Brigade gained San Vicente at about 11pm. They gradually spread through the town and took the breaches in the rear. At dawn Phillipon surrendered. British casualties number 3,940 men, and Portuguese 730.

Result: The discipline of the triumphant stormers broke down completely and there followed some of the most appalling scenes of sacking, rape, pillage and murder that have ever disgraced the British army. Order was not re-established until the morning of 8 April. Now that Badajoz was captured, the way was open for Wellington's summer offensive.

BARROSSA (Andalucia, Spain)   Napoleonic Wars/Peninsular War   5 March 1811
Fought between an Anglo-Portuguese force under Lt-General Thomas Graham together with a Spanish force under General Manuel la Peña, and a French army under Marshal Claude Victor.
Strength: British 4,900 with 10 guns, Portuguese 330, Spanish 9,600 with 14 guns; French 7,440 with 12 guns.
Aim: Originally the Allies had sought to raise the siege of Cádiz, but now they were trying to make good their retreat into the city.
Battle: Marshal Nicolas-Jean de Dieu Soult had withdrawn nearly all the cavalry and one regiment of infantry from Marshal Victor's 1 Corps which was blockading Cádiz. This left Victor with 19,000 men. The garrison of Cádiz consisted of 20,000 Spanish plus 6,000 Anglo-Portuguese under General Graham. The Allies decided to take advantage of this opportunity by attacking the French siege lines from the rear, in conjunction with a sortie by the remainder of the garrison. A force of 10,000 Spaniards and 5,000 Anglo-Portuguese (partly from Gibraltar, but mainly from Cádiz) were gathered at Tarifa, the southernmost point of Spain, and on 28 February began to march north towards Cádiz. They met only light resistance, but on 5 March as the Allied force approached Cádiz, Manuel la Peña, the Spanish overall commander, changed his plans, and attempted only to re-enter the city. He asked General Graham to cover the retreat, but the Spanish component of the rearguard failed to appear and Lt-Colonel John Frederick Brown, commanding a mixed battalion from the Gibraltar garrison, found himself alone. Brown saw the two French divisions Victor had collected converging upon him from the north, sent a message to Graham, and began to withdraw.

Graham turned his column round and rode back to Brown, whom he ordered to attack the Cerro del Puerco to gain time for the army to deploy. Graham sent one of his brigades under Brigadier William Thomas Dilkes to support Brown and storm the summit. Twice they were attacked by French columns, but drove them off, reaching and, with the remnants of Brown's men, holding the summit. The other brigade, Wheatley's, supported by all the guns, struck at a French division which was trying to cut in between the British and the Spaniards. The fighting here was also savage, and equally successful for the Allies. At no time during the two and a half hours of fighting did Graham receive any Spanish support. British casualties were 1,182 men, Portuguese 56 and French 2,062, Spanish casualties are not known.
Result: A tactical triumph for Graham, who had attacked uphill against odds of nearly two to one, though futile strategically. The blockade of Cádiz was resumed on 8 March after the Allied withdrawal was completed.

BAYLEN (BAILEN) (Andalucia, Spain)   Napoleonic Wars/Peninsular War   19 July 1808
Fought between the French under General Comte Dupont de l'Etang and the Spanish under General Xavier de Castaños.
Strength: French 23,000 (including 3,500 cavalry); Spanish 33,000 (including 2,600 cavalry).
Aim: As part of the plan for establishing his brother Joseph on the throne of Spain, Napoleon sent an army under Dupont into the south, but this advance was stalled by mounting Spanish opposition, and Dupont now sought to escape from a Spanish encircling movement.

Battle: Twenty miles north of Jaén, which he had recently sacked, Dupont was beginning a withdrawal along the Seville-Madrid road, encumbered by much loot. He had allowed his army to become divided, and part of the Spanish army under General Teodoro Reding had occupied Baylen, while the main Spanish force under Castaños, the overall commander, followed him up the road.

Dupont tried four times to break through the roadblock without success. His inexperienced men were tired, hot and thirsty, and the looting had lowered morale. When Castaños began to threaten his rear, Dupont entered into negotiation for surrender. On 23 July he finally surrendered on condition he should be repatriated by sea. The capitulation included the French troops which were on the Madrid side of Baylen. He had sustained 2,000 casualties.

Result: This was the first surrender of a French army since 1801, and gave great confidence to the Spanish and all the Allies. The French army was not repatriated, in part because the British admiral off Cádiz, who was not party to the surrender, refused to allow French soldiers to go home to fight again.

BEJA (Alentejo, Portugal)   Napoleonic Wars/Peninsular War   26 June 1808
When news of the Spanish insurrection reached Lisbon, General Andoche Junot decided to concentrate his men, and so he ordered outlying garrisons to withdraw.

Some units anticipated this order, among them 1,200 men under Colonel Jean-Pierre Maransin at Mertola. He fell back via Beja, whose citizens tried to defend its ancient walls against him. He stormed the place without difficulty, sacked it, and went on safely to Lisbon.

BEJAR (Extremadura, Spain)   Napoleonic Wars/Peninsular War   20 February 1813
The only break in the tranquillity of the winter quarters of the Allied army at this time came when General Maximilien Foy, commanding the French division at Avila, heard, incorrectly as it transpired, that the most outlying of Lt-General Sir Rowland Hill's detachments, the 50th Foot at Béjar, kept a poor look-out. Setting out on 19 February with 1,500 men, he attempted to rush the town. But Lt-Colonel John Bacon Harrison was a cautious officer who had barricaded the town, and Hill had recently reinforced him with the 6th Caçadores (Portuguese light infantry). Foy was met with hot fire and driven off. He made a hasty retreat. He admitted to casualties of 2 killed and 5 wounded.

BELCHITE (Aragón, Spain)   Napoleonic Wars/Peninsular War   18 June 1809
Fought between part of the French 3rd Army Corps under General Louis-Gabriel Suchet and a Spanish army under Captain-General Don Joachim Blake.

Strength: French 13,000; Spanish 12,000 with 9 guns.

Aim: Suchet sought to complete the defeat of the Spanish army which he had worsted on 15 June 1809 at María (qv).

Battle: The Spanish troops who had won at Alcañiz (qv), had suffered severely in their morale despite their creditable performance at María. Blake's army had lost something like 3,000 men from desertion when it halted at Belchite, while Suchet had drawn in Laval's and Robert's troops and was thus stronger than at María. Blake's position in front of Belchite was poor, the centre was in low ground much cut up by olive groves, while the wings were on two low hills. The left was the weaker flank. Suchet feinted with Habert's Brigade against the Spanish right while using all of Musnier's Division and a regiment of cavalry against the left. When this attack was well developed the Spanish left fell back into Belchite. But before the attack could be renewed the Spanish right collapsed. A chance shell exploded an ammunition caisson behind the Spanish right centre. The fire spread to other wagons and the whole group exploded. The entire Spanish right wing panicked; whole battalions threw down their arms and bolted. Only a delay in forcing a gate of Belchite prevented wholesale slaughter. As it was, the Spanish army was scattered to the winds, and all its artillery, though few men, was captured.

Result: Only 10,000 of the original Spanish 25,000 who had invaded Aragón could be gathered on 1 July. Suchet could now continue at his leisure to reassert French control on the plain of Aragón.

BENAVENTE (Leon, Spain)   Napoleonic Wars/Peninsular War   29 December 1808
Fought between the British, the rearguard of Sir John Moore's army under Lt-General Lord Paget (later Marquess of Anglesey), and French cavalry under General Comte Charles Lefèbvre-Desnouettes.

Strength: British 1,000 cavalry; French 500–600 cavalry (chasseurs of the Imperial Guard).

Aim: The British wished to gain time for their infantry to get away on the road to Corunna (La Coruña) (qv).

Battle: As the French chasseurs crossed the river Esla, General Slade's Brigade counter-attacked twice, but in insufficient strength. A further charge by more troops under Lord Paget pushed the French across the river, leaving 55 killed and wounded. Most of the chasseurs managed to get across, but Lefèbvre-Desnouettes, who was slightly wounded, was captured.

Result: The British gained the time they needed, and Napoleon, realising he had failed to catch Moore, turned over the pursuit to Marshal Nicolas-Jean de Dieu Soult and went back to France.

BIAR (Valencia, Spain)   Napoleonic Wars/Peninsular War   12 April 1813
Fought between Colonel Frederick Adam's Brigade of the Allied Army of Eastern Spain and elements of Marshal Louis-Gabriel Suchet's French army.

Strength: Allies 2,200 (1 British and 2 Italian battalions, 2 German rifle companies) with 4 guns; French 6,500 infantry and cavalry.

Aim: Suchet sought to break up the Allied retreat after his success at Yecla (qv).

Battle: This neat example of rearguard fighting took place in and about the village and pass of Biar. Adam had occupied Biar village with an Italian battalion, flanked by the 2/27th British and the rifle companies of the 3rd Battalion King's German Legion. The rest of the brigade was on the hills above the pass, with the guns on the road.

The leading French battalion assaulted the village, and was beaten off with heavy loss. Then, as the French outflanked the village, the garrison retired unharmed, and the troops on the hills halted the flanking columns. Suchet then deployed a battalion to sweep Adam away. Adam retired, steadily, making the French pay for each furlong gained, using his guns to great effect, although 2 that had each lost a wheel had to be abandoned. When the crest was reached Suchet sent in his cavalry, but Adam ambushed them with three companies of the 2/27th and beat them off. After five hours fighting, Adam's Brigade marched into its allotted place in Castalla (CASTALLA II) with his formation intact. The Allies had 300 casualties and the French 320.

Result: The Allied occupation of Castalla could proceed quietly.

BIDASSOA (BIDASOA) (Franco-Spanish border)   Napoleonic Wars/Peninsular War   7 October 1813
Fought between a British, Portuguese and Spanish army under the Marquess of Wellington and a French army under Marshal Nicolas-Jean de Dieu Soult.

Strength: British 39,000, Portuguese 25,000, Spanish 25,000; French 61,000.

Aim: Wellington sought to cross the river Bidassoa as the first phase of his invasion of S France.

Battle: Marshal Soult's solution to the problem of defending the Pyrenean chain was radically different from Wellington's. His line was 30 miles long, and he was aware that it was too long. He set to work to strengthen it with field fortifications. Wellington did everything to confirm Soult's belief that he would attack the inland flank. Soult divided his line into three sectors, the left under General Jean-Baptiste Drouet, Comte d'Erlon with four divisions, the centre under General Bertrand Clausel with three divisions and the right, the Bidassoa front, under General Honoré Reille with two divisions. The reserve was positioned at St Jean de Luz behind the right. Soult considered the Bidassoa estuary uncrossable; he failed to discover that at low tide there were fords. Wellington attacked on the morning 7 October. Soult was detained at his left by a feint attack. One hour after dawn, at low tide, the 5th Allied Division crossed. Hendaye was cleared, one brigade pushed ahead, while the rest of the division wheeled right to assist the 1st Division and the Spaniards who attacked a little higher up. The French, hopelessly outnumbered, retreated. Once the bridgehead was secure, Wellington halted his troops. The crossing cost less than 400 casualties.

Farther inland the Light Divison and Colonel Francisco Longa's Spaniards assaulted the outer defences of Mont Larroun. To their right two Andalusian divisions attacked Mont Larroun itself. The Light Division attacked up two spurs with Longa's men linking across the re-entrant. The fighting here was stiffer as a series of field works had to be stormed, but both the spurs and the main ridge were cleared. The Spaniards farther east were heavily engaged against the Great Rhune, as Mont Larroun was known to the Allies, and were unable to capture it. It fell next day because it had been outflanked. The Allied casualties in this sector were about 800, including the feint attack. The French lost 1,250.

Result: The French had been turned out of their position and the Allies had made a shallow penetration into France. The French defence had been shown to be too inflexible. However, Soult's army was intact and would have to be defeated again.

BILBAO (Viscaya, Spain)   Napoleonic Wars/Peninsular War   13–14 August and 27–29 August 1812
Fought between a British amphibious force under Commodore Sir Home Popham, Spanish forces under
General Gabriel Mendizabal, Colonel Francisco Longa and Colonel Renovales, against French forces
under Generals Rouget and Louis-Gabriel Caffarelli.
Strength: British 3 74-gun ships of the line + 4 or 5 frigates + 2 sloops + some smaller vessels + 1,000
marines, Spanish 6,000; French 7,000.
Aim: This complex of engagements was the climax of Commodore Popham's campaign to distract French
forces from Wellington, with the aid of local Spanish forces.
Battle: After the fall of Santander (qv) Popham planned further measures with General Mendizabal.
Eventually a general attack on Bilbao was planned. Mendizabal marched on Bilbao with two of Porlier's
battalions, and one from Alava. Popham carried three battalions under Colonel Renovales to Lequeitio,
whence they marched overland. Popham then made for Portugalete at the mouth of the Bilbao River. The
triple attack was successful. The French came out to meet the land attacks, stripping Portugalete for the
purpose, and Popham was able to take it easily. The French then pulled towards Durango, abandoning
Bilbao on 13 August.
     The next day the French launched a counter-attack but were beaten off by all Mendizabal's men at
Ollargán. General Rouget then pulled back, and called for help from Caffarelli.
     The 7,000 men the two French generals were able to gather counter-attacked from 27 to 29 August, and
after continued fighting against Mendizabal, who had now been joined by 3,000 more under Longa,
recaptured Bilbao. The defeated Spaniards dispersed in all directions, but Renovales's men were caught
and cut up at Dima.
Result: Despite the French recovery of Bilbao, their position in this area was still very insecure.
Commodore Sir Home Popham's Division was still operating very successfully in Wellington's favour.

BRAGA (Minho, Portugal)   Napoleonic Wars/Peninsular War   17–20 March 1809
Fought between Marshal Nicolas-Jean de Dieu Soult's French Army Corps and the levies of northern
Portugal.
Strength: French 18,000; Portuguese 24,000 (with only 5,000 firearms).
Aim: Soult sought to open the way to Oporto and to complete the first stage of his conquest of Portugal.
Battle: After his capture of Chaves (qv) Soult moved on Oporto through Braga. This brought him into
contact with the large but poor quality forces of Lt-General Bernardim Freire de Andrade e Castro. Freire
failed to support the local peasantry who occupied the mountain defiles. Soult brushed them aside and on
17 March his advance guard closed up to the village of Carvalho d'Este, a few miles east of Braga, which
Freire's men were occupying. Freire planned to retreat towards Oporto, but when the survivors from the
mountain defiles surged into his lines in an ugly mood, his men's suspicions of him began to rise. He
decided to flee secretly on the 17th, but he was recognised and captured a few miles on the road to Oporto
and brought back as a prisoner. In Braga the army acclaimed Colonel Frederick, Baron Eben, a Prussian
officer in the British service, as their new General. Eben consigned Friere to Braga city gaol, to 'protect his
life'. Eben left for the army, after which some peasantry came back and murdered Freire and some of his
staff. Eben was now trapped, committed to a battle which could only end in disaster. On 20 March Soult
launched a simple frontal assault which succeeded easily. The cavalry following up cut savagely into the
enemy.
     French casualties amounted to 400 men, while the Portuguese had 4,000 killed and 400 captured with 17
guns and all Eben's stores.
Result: The road to Oporto was now open.

BURGOS (Castile, Spain)   Napoleonic Wars/Peninsular War   19 September–30 October 1812
Fought between a portion of Wellington's Allied army and a French garrison under General Dubreton.
Strength: Allies 14,000 with only 3 heavy guns and 5 heavy howitzers; French 2,000 with 26 guns.
Aim: Wellington's reason for besieging Burgos, except for political purposes, remains obscure.
Battle: Burgos city was not fortified but its castle is set on an isolated hill to the NW of the city. In 1808
Napoleon had ordered it to be fortified. His scheme was not fully carried out; instead in 1812 there was a
series of partial works, only strong enough to resist the Spanish guerrillas.
     Wellington had come ill-prepared for a siege, and went about it in a haphazard way. On 19 September
he invested Burgos, and decided to storm the outer defences, which was done with Brigadier Denis Pack's
Portuguese Brigade and various British detachments. This attack succeeded with heavy casualties, largely

owing to the courage and leadership of Major John Somers Cocks. The garrison now brought tremendous fire to bear on the areas captured, but by 23 September a battery, with 2 of the Allied guns, was ready to begin the bombardment. On the same day Wellington decided to try another assault. This failed disastrously and more regular siege methods had to be employed. Both bombardment and mining were tried, the mines being given priority. On the night of 29–30 September the mine was exploded, but did little damage. Another assault was tried, but that too failed. Wellington then tried to bring his guns into action as well. Two of his guns were quickly damaged, although they could still be used at a slow rate. On 4 October a breach was made and at 7pm the second mine was fired, another breach formed, both breaches were stormed, and the French were forced back into their inner defences. On the 5th the French counter-attacked, and captured many of the Allies' entrenching tools, but were driven back. The Allies now began to sap forward, but the shortage of tools delayed them. On 8 October the 2 guns were damaged, Dubreton launched another successful sortie, and at the same time the Allied ammunition supply ran out.

The siege thereafter made little progress, despite all manner of ingenious expedients. Nevertheless, by 18 October another storm appeared to be possible. On that day at 4.30pm another mine was fired, and an assault force attempted to go through this breach, while two other detachments tried elsewhere. The result was total disaster, and on 20 October news came that General Joseph Souham, now commanding the French Army of Portugal, was approaching. On 21 October Wellington ignominiously pulled out, having failed to capture Burgos. Allied casualties were 2,000 men; French, 626.

Result: Dubreton's admirable defence deserves much praise. Wellington's siege technique was seen at its worst in this rather pointless and expensive attack.

BUSACO (BUÇACO/BUSSACO) (Portugal) Napoleonic Wars/Peninsular War 27 September 1810 Fought between an Anglo-Portuguese army under Viscount Wellington and a French army under Marshal André Masséna.

Strength: Allies 61,500 (British 30,000, Portuguese 31,500) with 78 guns; French 65,000.

Aim: The French sought to drive the Allies from their position astride the road to Coimbra and Lisbon.

Battle: On 15 September the French under Masséna, after the capture of Almeida (qv), moved forward into central Portugal. Wellington chose to make a stand at Busaco, one of the first defensive positions in Europe. The Anglo-Portuguese army was spread along a 10-mile long, 1,000-feet high ridge, crossed by only two roads. Wellington manned the key points and kept strong reserves in hand.

The French advanced guard arrived at the foot of the ridge on the evening 25 September. On the following morning Marshal Michel Ney made a swift reconnaissance, and formed the opinion that the Allies were in some strength across the main road, while the bulk of the Allied army was in retreat. He sent back a message to this effect to the Commander-in-Chief, Marshal Masséna, who was too busy with his mistress to pay much attention. After a two-hour delay while Ney's messenger shouted through the bedroom door, Masséna rode forward, glanced at the Allied position, and ordered an attack for the following morning. Ney was to move up the northern (main) road, while General Jean Reynier had to reach the crest up the other road. Masséna assumed that Reynier's attack would be beyond the Allied right flank. Actually it was nearer the centre.

Reynier's two divisions began to climb the mountain at 6.30am on the 27th, one division climbing the road, the other aiming at a point about a mile north. The southern French column managed to reach the summit, but Allied reinforcements from the south drove it off again. The northern column made more serious inroads, and before it too was driven down the slope the fighting was much fiercer. Reynier's force was spent.

Ney also attacked in two columns. The northern one was opposed by Major-General Robert Craufurd's Light Division. Pushing up the main road, and clearing the Allied skirmish line from the village of Sula, General Louis Henri Loison's men came up to the first crest of the hill. Craufurd had positioned two battalions (1/43rd and 1/52nd) just behind the crest, and as the French approached, he ordered them to advance, fire and charge. The French column collapsed and fled down the hill. Another battalion of this column was repulsed by Brigadier Francis Colman's Portuguese Brigade, while Ney's second column, Marchand's Division, advanced against Brigadier Denis Pack's Portuguese Brigade, but did not press its attack home, and was recalled when Loison's attack failed.

Thus the battle ended, since Wellington would not counter-attack. Next day the French found a route round Wellington's left, and he began to withdraw to the Lines of Torres Vedras (qv) again.

The British sustained 626 casualties, the Portuguese 626, and the French 4,487.

Result: A marked tactical victory for the Allies, which did much to consolidate their self-confidence, and the training of the new Portuguese army.

CABEZON (Old Castile, Spain)   Napoleonic Wars/Peninsular War   12 June 1808
Fought between a French cavalry unit under General Comte Lasalle and a Spanish army under Captain-General Don Gregorio de la Cuesta.
Strength: French 9,000; Spanish 5,000 (mostly raw recruits).
Aim: Cuesta was threatening the French communications and Marshal Bessières ordered Generals Lasalle and Pierre Merle to clear his flank.
Battle: Cuesta drew up his men in a single line with the river Cabezón at their backs. Lasalle, commanding the French cavalry, fell upon the Spanish infantry and dashed their line to pieces at the first shock. The Spanish cavalry fled, hundreds of raw infantry were cut down and many more were drowned. Cuesta fled towards Medina de Rio Seco (qv), and Valladolid fell undefended into French hands.
Result: Bessières' right flank was secured for the time being at the cost of 12 killed and 30 wounded.

CADIZ I (SW Spain)   Napoleonic Wars/Peninsular War   10–14 June 1808
The remains of the French fleet defeated by Admiral Lord Nelson at Trafalgar in 1805 took refuge in Cádiz. The Spanish Revolution of 1808 destroyed their safe refuge. Unable to escape owing to the British blockade, Admiral François Rosily could only await his fate. On 10 June the Spanish, after refusing British help, sank blockships to prevent the French escape, and erected batteries with furnaces for heating shot, with which to bombard the French. The Spanish were unwilling to wreck the French ships. Rosily was twice summoned to surrender before, eventually, the batteries opened fire. On 14 June Rosily, knowing his position was hopeless, surrendered.

CADIZ II (SW Spain)   Napoleonic Wars/Peninsular War   5 February 1810–21 August 1812
Between the Spanish and Anglo-Portuguese garrison of the city of Cádiz and of the Isla de León, and a French besieging force commanded, directly or indirectly, by Marshal Nicolas-Jean de Dieu Soult, Duc de Dalmatie.
Aim: The French sought to capture the city of Cádiz to secure their hold on Andalusia.
Battle: After the crushing defeat at Ocaña (qv), Andalusia, the last remaining large area of Spain not occupied by the French, was left virtually unprotected. The Spanish could only scrape together about 30,000 troops to defend the many passes in the 150-mile mountain chain separating La Mancha from Andalusia. The French, however, were not strong enough to put together a major offensive southwards as well as another into Portugal against Wellington.

By the middle of December, King Joseph Bonaparte had decided to attack Andalusia as soon as possible. The plan eventually chosen was for about 23,000 troops under Marshal Claude Victor to march on Córdova via Almadén and Villanueva de la Jara, while the French main body, 40,000, under King Joseph and Marshal Soult were to force the passes in front of La Carolina, and thrust the Spanish main body into Victor's arms.

On 19 January 1810 this operation was put into effect, and on the 20th the French main body launched a simultaneous attack on all points. The attack succeeded against the hopelessly outnumbered Spaniards, with little real fighting. The Spanish, abandoning any hope of covering Seville, fell back on Jaén, and the road south was open to the French. Victor also found little opposition, though his road was more difficult.

José and Soult decided to send General Comte Sébastiani to conquer Granada, while the bulk of the army marched on Seville, the capital of the Spanish Central Junta. This concentration allowed the Duke of Alburquerque, who commanded the extreme west of the Spanish forces, to beat the French to Cádiz, and put the city into a state of defence. He arrived there on 3 February with about 10,000 men. Seville fell to the French on 1 February. The Junta had to flee, but they found a secure new refuge.

Cádiz was almost impregnable to an army which did not control the water. The city lies on the end of a long sand-spit, running out from the Isla de León, which is itself separated from the mainland by the salt-water channel of the Rio San Petri, 300–400 yards wide. The Isla, protected by this enormous wet ditch, presents a front of about 7 miles to the mainland. General Francisco Venegas, the Military Governor of Cádiz, had gathered in all the boats of the district, thus making a crossing more difficult.

The French appeared before the city on 5 February, but their summons to surrender was angrily rejected. Anglo-Portuguese reinforcements arrived on 15 February. Thereafter the siege settled down to a stalemate, largely uneventful, though the French built some enormous mortars which could fire across the harbour into the city. The major event was the campaign of Barrossa (qv).

The siege was eventually lifted on 24 August 1812, when Soult was forced to abandon Andalusia, in order to concentrate French forces against Wellington after his victory at Salamanca (qv).

Result: The tying down of large French forces in a hopeless siege prevented their being able to complete the conquest of Andalusia.

CALATAYUD (Aragón, Spain)   Napoleonic Wars/Peninsular War   26 September–4 October 1811
Fought between Spanish guerrilla bands under El Empecinado (Juan Martin Díaz) and José Durán, and French garrisons of the area.

Strength: Spanish 5,500; French 800 (Calatayud garrison) + 1,000 (relieving force from Saragossa garrison).

Aim: The Spanish sought to capture the town of Calatayud as a diversion in favour of Captain-General Don Joachim Blake's defence of Valencia (VALENCIA II).

Battle: On 26 September the Empecinado and Durán appeared in front of Calatayud, rushed the town and drove the French into the fortified convent of La Merced. While Durán besieged the convent, the Empecinado went to the defile of El Frasno, where he blocked the Saragossa road, and beat off a French relieving column from Saragossa, under Colonel Gillot, who was killed. Durán lacking heavy guns, had to attack by mining. The first mine blew in a corner of the chapel, killing many of the defenders, his second on 3 October created an enormous breach. The following day the garrison, still 500 strong, surrendered.

Result: This enterprise did much to shake the French hold on W Aragón, but failed to divert Marshal Louis-Gabriel Suchet from Valencia. General Honoré Reille, who moved down from Navarre, sent General Bourke with 3,500 men to relieve Calatayud. He arrived on 5 October, but the convent had been blown up, and the Spanish had gone with their prisoners.

CARDEDEU (Catalonia, Spain)   Napoleonic Wars/Peninsular War   16 December 1808
Fought between a Spanish army under Captain-General Vives, and a French army under General (later Marshal) Laurent Gouvion-St-Cyr.

Strength: Spanish 8,400 infantry + 600 cavalry + 7 guns; French 16,000.

Aim: St-Cyr sought to relieve Barcelona before the food supply ran out.

Battle: St-Cyr had been delayed for a month by the defence of Rosas (qv). This cut into his schedule for reaching Barcelona. In front of him was an intricate series of obstacles. The greatest problem was Gerona, which he could not hope to capture in time. It had to be bypassed. St-Cyr would have to abandon all his wheeled transport, march by rough tracks, and stake everything on success, while trying to mislead the Spanish commander as to his objective. St-Cyr left General Honoré Reille with 5,000 troops to protect his bases, and set off on 9 December with three divisions. Feinting towards Gerona, he worked round the Spanish forces opposite him. On 11 December he sent back all his guns and transports and, carrying so little that if he did not reach Barcelona in six days, or had to fight more than one action, he would be helpless, he set off into the hills.

General Vives detached a small portion of his army, which failed to halt St-Cyr. It was not until 15 December that Vives himself marched out and, moving all night, he joined his detached force at Cardedeu. Failing to concentrate all his available troops, he occupied a position just in front of the town.

St-Cyr could make out little of the Spanish position, but he decided to attack at once. The methods he chose were crude: leaving three battalions to cover his rear against the 9,000 Spanish who were behind him, he formed 13,000 men into a single strong column, which was to charge straight forward and punch a way through the Spanish line. General Pino, commanding the leading division, pushed forward but, finding himself exposed to flanking fire, he deployed seven battalions, and attacked on a wide instead of a narrow front. His left-flank attack failed. St-Cyr was horrified to see what his subordinate's disobedience had done. He formed up his second division, General Joseph Souham's, and sent it forward. It punched through the Spanish right wing. St-Cyr's cavalry followed up and the Spanish army collapsed. The Spanish sustained casualties of 1,000 killed and wounded, the French taking 1,500 prisoners and 5 guns. Vives escaped by being rescued by HMS *Cambrian*. St-Cyr admitted to 600 casualties.

Result: The road to Barcelona was open and St-Cyr reached the city on 17 December.

CASAL NOVO (central Portugal)   Napoleonic Wars/Peninsular War   14 March 1811
Fought between the rearguard of the French army of Portugal under Marshal Michel Ney and the vanguard of the Allied army under Wellington.

Strength: French 11,000; Allies 12,000.
Aim: The French sought to gain time for their withdrawal.
Battle: After his withdrawal from Condeixa (qv) Ney had placed General Jean-Gabriel Marchand's Division in a strong position at Casal Novo. Sir William Erskine, the temporary commander of the Light Division, thought fit, despite a heavy fog, to march straight at the French. His leading units ran into French pickets, and when the fog lifted, the Light Division clubbed together under the guns of Marchand's Division, while the 3rd Division and Brigadier Denis Pack's Brigade were some way off. The Light Division had to deploy under fire and fight to hold on. When the 3rd Division began to work round Marchand's left flank the French pulled out. Later in the day the French were manoeuvred out of two more strong positions, without heavy fighting. British casualties were 130 men, Portuguese 25, and French 55.
Result: The rather unnecessary casualties in the Light Division included William Napier, later the great historian of the Peninsular War, and his brother George. For the first time in Marshal André Masséna's retreat prisoners began to be taken in substantial numbers, 100 being taken on this day.

CASTALLA I (Valencia, Spain)   Napoleonic Wars/Peninsular War   21 July 1812
Fought between a Spanish army under General Joseph O'Donnell and a French force under Colonel Delort.
Battle: General O'Donnell, whose mission was to contain the French to his front and risk nothing, decided to try to surprise General Jean-Isidore Harispe's Division by a concentric movement. He had 10,000 infantry and 1,000 cavalry and he marched them throughout the night, in three separate columns, so that they arrived, very fatigued, at 4am in presence of a French force under Colonel Delort.

O'Donnell occupied Castalla and then attacked in a leisurely fashion. A brilliant charge by the French 24th Dragoons, 400 strong, broke up the three battalions of Mijares' brigade. The dragoons then charged again, two abreast, across a narrow bridge commanded by O'Donnell's 2 guns, which fired one round each before they were ridden over. The brigade supporting the guns gave way.

Delort now attacked with two battalions and the 13th Cuirassiers, and drove Montijo's Brigade from the field. The 6,000 infantry of O'Donnell's centre broke up, except for the Cuença Battalion (Montijo's Brigade) which went off in good order. The French cavalry cut up the rest in droves.

General Philip Keating Roche managed to get his division away to Alicante without loss, as did General Santesteban with the cavalry. O'Donnell lost 3,000 men, including 2,135 unwounded prisoners, 3 colours, and the only 2 guns which had got to the front. Marshal Louis-Gabriel Suchet admitted 200 casualties.
Result: This disaster put the Murcian army out of action for many months.

CASTALLA II (Valencia, Spain)   Napoleonic Wars/Peninsular War   13 April 1813
Fought between an Allied Army under Lt-General Sir John Murray and a French army under Marshal Louis-Gabriel Suchet, Duc d'Albufera.
Strength: Allies 13,429 infantry (8,274 British, Germans, Anglo-Italians, Calabrese + 1,136 Sicilians + 4,109 Spanish–2 divisions under British generals) + 886 cavalry (British, Sicilian, Spanish) + 500 artillery (British, German and Portuguese) with 30 guns; French 11,912 infantry + 1,424 cavalry + 232 artillery with 24 guns.
Aim: General Murray's force was to contain Suchet in the east, to prevent him interfering with Wellington's projected spring offensive. Suchet sought to defeat Murray and to confirm his control of NE Spain.
Battle: Murray had placed his army, an unusually heterogeneous one even by Peninsular War standards, near and on a ridge to the west of Castalla. On the Guerra ridge on the left was General Samuel Ford (Samford) Whittingham's Spanish Division, with Colonel Frederick Adam's 'British' Brigade next, and General John Mackenzie's Division linking the right of the ridge to the Castalla castle hill. The castle was occupied by the 1/58th of General William Clinton's Division, and two batteries of guns. To the right a stream which had been dammed protected the flank, with Clinton's Division and part of General Philip Keating Roche's Spanish Division behind it. The remaining two battalions of Roche's Division and the cavalry were out in front. This was a strong position, but the incompetent Murray thrice thought of abandoning it.

Suchet was slow to attack, apparently disliking the prospect. At noon he sent all his cavalry to his left and deployed his infantry on the Cerro del Doncel, a low hill facing Murray's left and centre. He planned to leave Castalla alone, and concentrate on the Allied left. Habert's Division contained Mackenzie, while five light companies were sent to turn Whittingham's left, and six battalions of Robert's Division were to assault frontally when they were well forward. This was the moment of danger, for Whittingham had received an order, which Murray later denied giving, to turn the French right. This could have been disastrous, but Whittingham left three battalions in his original position, and only took three with him. As it was he was able to throw one of the latter against the French light companies, and use the others, after a swift counter-march to support his fighting line as they were needed.

The left of the French main assault failed disastrously against the British 2/27th of Adam's Brigade; and as these troops collapsed into the valley below, Whittingham was able to complete the eviction of the French from his position. Suchet promptly pulled back to the pass of Biar, where he was able to stand overnight owing to the feebleness of Murray's pursuit.

The French sustained 1,300 casualties, the Spanish 233, and other Allied forces 170 men.

Result: This battle did much credit to the fighting qualities of the infantry and to Whittingham's training of his division, but none whatever to Murray. His troops won despite him.

CASTRO URDIALES I (Biscay, Spain)   Napoleonic Wars/Peninsular War   6–8 July 1812
(For *Strength* etc see LEQUEITIO)
Commodore Sir Home Popham, after his success at Lequeitio (qv) and a failure at Guetaria (qv) attacked Castro Urdiales. Here on 6 July he was joined by Colonel Francisco Longa's men. The united force drove off a French relieving force on 7 July, and on 8 July the French Governor with 150 men and 20 guns surrendered.

Popham garrisoned Castro Urdiales with some of his men as a temporary base. On 11 July he bombarded Portugalete at the mouth of the Bilbao River, but he and Longa were driven off. However, he was very successfully keeping the north coast of Spain in uproar.

CASTRO URDIALES II (Biscay, Spain)   Napoleonic Wars/Peninsular War   25 April–11 May 1813
Fought between a Spanish garrison under Colonel Pedro Alvarez, and a British naval squadron against a French force under General Maximilien Foy.
Strength: Spanish 1,000 (assisted by some British sloops); French 11,000.
Aim: Napoleon had ordered General Bertrand Clausel to begin his efforts to pacify the north by taking Castro Urdiales and cutting the guerrillas' easiest communication with the Royal Navy.
Battle: After an abortive attempt at the end of March 1813, which showed him he could not hope to rush Castro Urdiales, Clausel turned the job over to General Foy.

Foy marched from Bilbao, and reached Castro Urdiales on 25 April. Leaving General Palombini to block the place up, he went to drive off General Gabriel Mendizabal, which he did on 29 April. He returned to the siege, leaving Sarrut to cover it. The Governor of Santoña managed to run siege guns across to Bilbao when the British blockading squadron was away, on 4 May. They were then brought on by road.

Three batteries were built, and despite interference from the ships and strong fire from the town, the wall began to crumble and a large breach was made by 11 May. At 7.20pm the French attacked in three columns, all attacks succeeded, and the garrison was driven through the town into the castle, where they maintained themselves. An evacuation was organised by the boats of the British squadron; the last rearguard threw the guns into the sea and fired the magazine. Just before dawn the bulk of them escaped, apparently because the French had turned to looting and were drunk.

The Spanish had 180 casualties, the French 180.

Result: The French had recovered Castro-Urdiales, but the extraordinary thing is that 11,000 French were tied up for three weeks before this insignificant place just when Wellington was about to launch his great 1813 offensive.

CHAVES (Tras-os-Montes, N Portugal)   Napoleonic Wars/Peninsular War   11–12 and 20–5 March 1809
Fought between parts of Marshal Nicolas-Jean de Dieu Soult's French Army Corps and Portuguese forces under Brigadier Francisco da Silveira.
Strength: French 2nd Army Corps 18,000 infantry + 1,300 cavalry + 54 guns; Portuguese 12,000 (mostly irregulars).
Aim: The French needed to capture this town to clear the road to Oporto (qv).
Battle: After the withdrawal of the British from Corunna (La Coruña) (qv) Soult was ordered to invade Portugal. He began to move his army towards the frontier in February 1809, and reached the river Minho

on the 8th. On 16 February he attempted a crossing which failed. He now decided to attack through the inland portion of the northern Portuguese frontier. However, it was not until 7 March that he crossed the frontier on the road from Monterrey to Chaves.

The duty of defending this frontier fell on the Military Governor of Tras-os-Montes, Brigadier Francisco da Silveira. He had gathered at Chaves two line regiments of infantry, four regiments of militia, parts of two cavalry regiments and a mass of local peasantry. The whole, 12,000 men, had 6,000 firearms. Silveira realised he could not defend Chaves, whose walls had never been repaired since a Spanish siege in 1762. He retreated on 11 March but many of his troops stayed behind. Chaves was thus defended by a motley garrison including some regulars of the 12th or Chaves Infantry Regiment, perhaps 4,000 strong. On the 12th, Soult drove Silveira farther away and the defenders of the garrison, who had fired off most of their ammunition, surrendered. Soult sent the peasantry home and incorporated the regulars into a Portuguese Legion. When he marched on, he left behind one infantry company, the Portuguese Legion and 1,200 convalescents and sick to garrison it.

When Silveira heard that Soult had left he returned to the town with 6,000 men. Colonel Messager, the French Commander of the Chaves garrison, retired into the citadel and surrendered after a siege of five days, largely because his legionaries threatened to open the gates. Twelve hundred were captured, of whom only one-third were fit Frenchmen.

Result: Silveira's recovery of Chaves greatly encouraged the local population, who now flocked to his standard.

CIUDAD REAL (New Castile, Spain)   Napoleonic Wars/Peninsular War   27–8 May 1809
Fought between a French army under General Comte Sébastiani and a Spanish army under General Cartaojal.
Strength: French 10,500 infantry + 2,000 cavalry; Spanish 10,000 infantry + 2,500 cavalry.
Aim: General Cartaojal's manoeuvres in La Mancha had provoked General Sébastiani to punish him.
Battle: On 27 March Sébastiani, having seized the bridge of Peralvillo near Ciudad Real, launched his force against Cartaojal, who decided on retreat, leaving his cavalry as a rearguard. The Spanish cavalry was charged and broken, and Sébastiani then dispersed several units of retreating Spanish infantry. The pursuit continued the following day until halted by rain.

The Spanish had 2,000 prisoners and 3 guns taken, but had few killed and wounded. French casualties were less than 100.
Result: The Spanish were cleared out of La Mancha and fell back into the mountains.

CIUDAD RODRIGO I (Léon, Spain)   Napoleonic Wars/Peninsular War   26 April–10 July 1810
Fought between the Spanish garrison under General Don Andreas Herrasti (Andrej Errasti) and the French Army of Portugal under Marshal André Masséna, the besieging force being commanded by Marshal Michel Ney.
Strength: Spanish 5,510 (706 regular infantry + 1,174 militia infantry + 2,243 volunteer infantry + 750 Urban Guard + 398 artillery plus assigned infantry + some additional details; also present initially 200 Guerrilla Lancers under Don Julian Sánchez); French 30,000 (siege force) + 50 heavy guns (siege train) + 17,000 (covering force under General Junot).
Aim: The French sought to take the fortress which blocked their approach to Portugal.
Battle: Ciudad Rodrigo was a city of 8,000 souls on a knoll, with medieval walls, and a modern wall which served as an outer protection. The river Agueda ran close under the southern walls. Outside the eastern gate lay the suburb of San Francisco which had been included in the defences. A small suburb across the river, and the strong convent of Santa Cruz, 200 yards outside the NW angle of the town, were also fortified. A short distance outside the northern angle were two hills, the Great and Little Tesons, which were too large to be included in the defence plan, but which dominated the walls.

The French appeared before the walls on 20 April, but it was not until 30 May that Marshal Ney came up to complete the investment. On 8 June the siege train began to arrive.

On 15 June the French opened their first parallel on the Great Teson, only 500 yards from the town. Herrasti launched two ineffectual sorties. Six batteries were started on the 19th, while the French dug towards Santa Cruz and the northern angle of the town. Julian Sánchez broke out on the night of 21–2 June.

On the night of 23–4 June Ney tried to storm Santa Cruz, but his grenadiers were driven off. On the 25th the French batteries began to fire with 40 guns. The town's counter-fire was very effective and 2 French magazines exploded. After nightfall Santa Cruz was captured. The French could not get much closer, and four days' battering burnt half the town, and also did much damage to the walls. Ney sent a summons to surrender, which Herrasti rejected.

On 1 July a new parallel, 250 yards from the town, was opened on the Little Teson and a lodgement was made in the suburb of San Francisco. A new battery was built on the Little Teson. Herrasti sent messages to Wellington asking for aid, which Wellington had to refuse.

By 9 July Ney's engineers told him the breach was 'practicable', and preparations for a storm were made, while a summons to surrender was sent in. Herrasti agreed, and on 10 July the garrison marched out.

Spanish casualties were 61 killed and 994 wounded, and 4,000 surrendered. French casualties were 180 killed and 1,000 wounded.

Result: The first of the two fortresses blocking the French invasion of Portugal had fallen, and 118 guns were captured. Herrasti's food supply was nearly spent. Herrasti had made a gallant defence, especially as he was aware Wellington would not help him.

CIUDAD RODRIGO II (Léon, Spain)   Napoleonic Wars/Peninsular War   8–19 January 1812
Fought between the Allied army (made up of British, German, Portuguese and Spanish forces) under Lt-General Viscount Wellington, and a French garrison under General Barrié.
Strength: Allies 20,000 (besieging force); French garrison 1,600 infantry + 370 artillery and sappers + siege train of the Army of Portugal, 153 heavy guns and huge quantities of ammunition.
Aim: Wellington sought to capture Ciudad Rodrigo in order to clear the way for an advance into Spain.
Battle: Wellington had been looking for an opportunity to attack Ciudad Rodrigo for some months, and, while holding the fortress under a loose blockade, had been gradually building up siege stores and guns in Almeida and other centres. At the end of December 1811 news came that French troops were moving east to support Marshal Louis-Gabriel Suchet's assault on Valencia (qv) and also being withdrawn for the Russian campaign. Wellington knew that there would not be much time in which to capture the city, whose fortifications the French had recently repaired. On 6 January the British units, which had previously been concentrated for this purpose, moved forward to invest Ciudad Rodrigo.

On the night of 8–9 January Lt-Colonel John Colborne (later Field-Marshal Lord Seaton) stormed and captured the redoubt Teson, suffering only 25 casualties. A parallel was at once opened. By 14 January the batteries were ready, and work was begun on a flying sap towards the inner fortifications. On 15 January Barrié launched a sortie, which was successfully repulsed. At 7pm on 19 January the 3rd and Light Division assaulted the two breaches made in the defences and captured the town. Major-Generals Robert Craufurd and Henry Mackinnon were both killed. As was the custom, the town was sacked. Wellington's greatest prize was the capture of the French siege train. French casualties were 600 killed and wounded, and 1,300 surrendered. Allied casualties were 1,100 killed and wounded.
Result: Wellington achieved his objective.

COA (Portuguese-Spanish frontier)   Napoleonic Wars/Peninsular War   24 July 1810
Fought between the Anglo-Portuguese Light Division under Brigadier Robert Craufurd and Marshal Michel Ney's Corps of Marshal André Masséna's French Army of Portugal.
Strength: Allies 4,500 (2,500 British infantry + 1,100 Portuguese infantry + 900 British cavalry) + 6 guns; French 21,000 infantry + 3,000 cavalry.
Aim: The French sought to destroy Craufurd's force and to invest the fortress of Almeida.
Battle: On 21 July, eleven days after the capture of Ciudad Rodrigo (CIUDAD RODRIGO I), the French advanced. Craufurd pulled back to a position about Junca, where he chose to stand. On 24 July Ney advanced again, with two cavalry brigades in front and three infantry divisions behind. The Allied pickets were driven in, and the Light Division got hastily under arms, on a line starting 800 yards south of Almeida. Craufurd decided to hang on until he was forced back. His position against reasonable odds was good, but his five battalions were attacked by thirteen of Louis Henri Loison's Division. The initial rush was halted, but a French cavalry regiment cut in between Almeida and Craufurd's left, overran a rifle company, and began to roll the Allied line up. They were halted by a stone wall, and Craufurd decided to retreat. The cavalry, guns and Portuguese were sent back to cross the single narrow bridge across the river Coa, while the British battalions covered the withdrawal. There was a delay at the bridge, and the covering troops had to fight to allow the block to be cleared. After a most perilous retreat they eventually made good their escape. Ney ordered the bridge to be stormed, but three times his troops were driven back with

heavy casualties. Craufurd pulled out after midnight. The British had 248 casualties, the Portuguese 45 and the French 527.
Result: Almeida was invested, but Craufurd, because of the courage and skill of his men, had got away, and Ney had sustained many unnecessary casualties.

COIMBRA (central Portugal)   Napoleonic Wars/Peninsular War   10–13 March 1811
Fought between Portuguese militia under Colonel Nicholas Trant and part of General Louis Pierre Montbrun's Cavalry Corps of Marshal André Masséna's French Army of Portugal.
Strength: Portuguese 3,000 militiamen with 6 guns; French 4,000 (part of Montbrun's Cavalry Corps + 1 infantry battalion).
Aim: The French sought to force a crossing of the Mondego River.
Battle: Masséna's original intention when he fell back from Río Maíor was apparently to cross the river Mondego and take up a position north of the river. Colonel Trant, the Governor of Oporto, was occupying Coimbra, which stands on the north bank of the river and, with the river at a high level, the only crossing available was the main road bridge of which two arches had been destroyed.

   Montbrun appeared before the city on 10 March, failed to find a ford on the 11th, engaged in an ineffective artillery duel on the 12th while the infantry tried and failed to capture the bridge. On the 13th Montbrun asked for the town's surrender, but the artillery commander, Sergeant José Correia Leal, managed to delay giving an answer until Montbrun received news of Marshal Michel Ney's precipitate retreat from Condeixa (qv). Then, with the position untenable, he withdrew eastward.
Result: This nearly bloodless affair was one of the decisive episodes of the Peninsular War. It was now impossible for the French to hold a position in central Portugal, and a retreat to Spain was inevitable.

CONDEIXA (central Portugal)   Napoleonic Wars/Peninsular War   13 March 1811
Fought between the rearguard of Marshal André Masséna's French Army of Portugal under Marshal Michel Ney, and the vanguard of Wellington's Anglo-Portuguese army.
Strength: 12,000 British + 6,000 Portuguese; French 5,500 (25,000 in support).
Aim: Wellington sought to force Ney from his exposed position and force a French withdrawal towards Spain.
Battle: Condeixa stands on the crossroad where the last road running east on the south bank of the Mondego meets the highroad from Lisbon to Coimbra. With a French movement across the Mondego blocked by Colonel Nicholas Trant (COIMBRA), a change in direction of the French retreat was inevitable, and this made Marshal Ney's job more vulnerable, for he could no longer retreat to his rear, but would have to march to his left. When Wellington repeated the manoeuvre of the previous day (REDINHA), Ney saw the 3rd Allied Division threatening his line of retreat, and fell back swiftly to Casal Novo (qv). Very few casualties were sustained.
Result: The skill of Wellington's manoeuvre, and the speed of Ney's retreat, caused some confusion in the French army and Marshal Masséna was nearly captured by a British cavalry patrol. With the hope of a Mondego crossing gone, the French army was condemned to a retreat back to the frontier.

CORDOVA (Andalusia, Spain)   Napoleonic Wars/Peninsular War   7 June 1808
The sack of Córdova by the forces of General Comte Dupont de l'Etang was one of the earliest of the many atrocities in the Peninsular War. After his success at Alcolea (qv) Dupont pushed on towards the city, which he expected to find unguarded. He found the gates closed and was met by a few scattered shots. He took this as an excuse to storm the place, which was done very easily, with only 2 killed and 7 wounded.
   There followed an orgy of looting until the following day.

CORUNNA (LA CORUÑA) (NW Spain)   Napoleonic Wars/Peninsular War   16 January 1809
Fought between a French army under Marshal Nicolas-Jean de Dieu Soult and a British army under Lt-General Sir John Moore.
Strength: French 16,000 infantry + 4,000 cavalry + 40 guns; British 15,000 infantry with 9 guns.
Battle: The British army, after its long retreat, marched into Corunna on 11 January. It was not until the 13th that the French followed up. However, the transport ships had not arrived, and the British had now to fight with the sea at their backs. On the night of the 14th the transports arrived and embarkation began. Moore positioned his four infantry divisions to protect the harbour. Two divisions (Lt-General John Hope and Lt-General Sir David Baird) were placed in line on the Mero ridge, with the left (Hope) meeting

on the estuary of the Mero. The other two divisions were kept in reserve. Soult decided to attack the right of the Mero ridge while trying to work round it towards Major-General Edward Paget's Division. He ordered the divisions of Delaborde and Merle to engage Hope and Baird in front, while Mermet and the bulk of the cavalry were to attack Baird's right and to try to cut in between Baird and Paget. This attack was delayed, and did not start until 2pm, by which time Moore had decided Soult would not attack, and had ordered Paget to march for the ships. Paget was ordered to counter-march, while Moore joined Baird.

The main attack fell on the brigade of Major-General Lord William Bentinck. Moore brought up two Guards battalions to support Bentinck, and it was while he was directing them that Moore was mortally wounded by a cannon-ball. Paget drove back the French flanking attack and by dusk he had reached the French station. A second advance by Bentinck and the Guards pushed the French back as well, and the battle petered out. Lt-General Sir John Hope (later Earl of Hopetoun), now Commander-in-Chief, halted the army. British casualties were between 700 and 800 men, while the French sustained casualties of between 800 and 1,000.

Result: By 18 January the British made their escape.

Moore was buried on the ramparts of Corunna. Soult erected a monument to his opponent, with the inscription, *'Hic Cecidit Iohannes Moore dux exercitus Britannici, in pugna Ianuarii XVI, 1809, Contra gallos a duce Dalmatiae doctos'.*

The Spanish Governor of Corunna surrendered when the British had evacuated. The British had apparently received a decisive defeat and been chased from Spain, but actually Moore had dislocated Napoleon's plans, and prevented the conquest of Portugal and S Spain in 1808.

DENIA (Valencia, Spain)   Napoleonic Wars/Peninsular War   20 January 1812
Denia, with a small fortified fort south of Valencia, had been abandoned by General Nicolas Mahy in the general panic after Captain-General Don Joachim Blake's surrender of Valencia. General Harispe seized the town, finding 60 guns mounted on the walls, and 40 small merchant vessels, some fully laden. The French garrisoned the place and fitted out some of the ships as privateers.

Mahy should certainly have destroyed the guns and sent the ships to Alicante (qv). His neglect contributed to his removal by the Cádiz Regency from command of the Army of Murcia.

DOS MAYO (DOS DE MAYO) (Madrid, Spain)   Napoleonic Wars/Peninsular War   2 May 1808
This event is generally taken as the signal for the outbreak of the Spanish insurrection against the French. On 10 April King Fernando VII of Spain had left Madrid for Bayonne under French escort, leaving Marshal Joachim Murat, Grand Duke of Berg, later King of Naples, occupying Madrid with 35,000 men. The people of Madrid were restless, and were further offended by a number of gratuitous insults by Murat, such as the removal of Francis I's sword from the Royal Arsenal where this trophy of the Battle of Pavia (1525) was kept.

As news of Napoleon's treachery at Bayonne reached Madrid on 29 April, the tension rose. On 2 May an excited mob attacked the Royal Palace, the enforced departure of Infante (Prince) Don Francisco being the signal. One of Murat's ADCs was stoned. Murat turned out the battalion on guard at his palace, and dispersed the unarmed crowd with a dozen volleys. At the sound of firing the Spaniards flew to arms, and using knife, fowling-piece and blunderbuss cut up any French soldiers they found. They also attacked Murat's guard, but his 1,000 men easily held their own. Swiftly French reinforcements came pouring into the city and the fight became a massacre. Cavalry charges, led by the Mamelukes of the guard, slaughtered many hundreds. The Spanish troops in the city (3,000) did not intervene, except at the artillery park where two captains, Daoiz and Velarde, issued arms to the people. With 40 soldiers and 500 civilians they beat off two French assaults, but were destroyed by the third attack.

The whole eruption lasted for four hours, Murat taking revenge by executing 100 citizens. About 1,000 people in all were killed, of which 200 were French. Francisco Goya the painter immortalised this uprising of the citizens of Madrid against the French oppressors.

Result: The Spanish insurrection flared into a most effective guerrilla warfare which for the next four years tied down three-quarters of all the French troops in the Peninsula, leaving never more than a quarter of the total garrison available to fight the regular forces of Britain and her Allies.

ESLA (León, Spain)   Napoleonic Wars/Peninsular War   31 May 1813
Wellington's plan for the great offensive of 1813 was for the left wing of the Allied army to cross the Douro (Duero) inside Portugal, and to swing round the northern flank of the French army. The right wing

meanwhile was to march NE, and arrive at the Douro by Toro and Zamora in Spain. The right wing, whose main job was to attract the attention of the French, moved off on 22 May; while the left, under Lt-General Sir Thomas Graham, moved across the Portuguese frontier on 26 May.

The first major obstacle in front of Graham was the river Esla, a tributary of the Douro, running from the north. Fortunately the attention of the French had been drawn away from this area, so that when Graham was ready to force a crossing, there were almost no troops to face him. On 31 May, Graham (now joined by Wellington) sent his cavalry to lead the army across three fords.

Colonel Colquhoun Grant's Hussar Brigade had a difficult crossing at Almendra, each man of the leading squadron having an infantryman hanging on to his stirrup. But, although some infantrymen were swept away and drowned, the crossing in the main was successful, and a French cavalry picket of 33 men was captured complete. Four miles to the north Major-General Baron von Bock's German and Brigadier Benjamin d'Urban's Portuguese cavalry had an even more difficult crossing at Palomilla, some men and horses being drowned, but they too made good their crossing. Major-General George Anson's cavalry leading the third column failed to find a ford, and they had to use that at Almendra. A pontoon bridge was swiftly laid at Almendra and the rest of the army crossed.

Result: The French position was turned, and Wellington began the great march which ended at Vitoria (qv).

ESPINOSA DE LOS MONTEROS (Old Castile, Spain)   Napoleonic Wars/Peninsular War   10–11 November 1808
Fought between a Spanish army under Captain-General Don Joachim Blake and a French army under Marshal Claude Victor.
Strength: Spanish 22,500 with 6 guns; French 21,000; guns unknown.
Aim: After his defeat of Zornoza (qv), General Blake stood his ground again at Espinosa.
Battle: Blake had a strong position in front of Espinosa. General Villatte's Division, the French-led division, went straight at the Spanish. Six battalions contained the Spanish centre, while six more attacked the Spanish right. The Conde de San Román's Division, the next unit in the Spanish army, made a fine defence. Victor, coming up with two more divisions, continued the attack, but Blake held out all day.

On the 11th the Marshal went about things more scientifically. Assuming, correctly, Blake would have reinforced his right, Victor switched his attack to the other flank, where the Spanish were of lower quality. Their troops swiftly broke up, 3 Spanish generals being killed as they tried to rally their men. The French now wheeled inwards, combining this manoeuvre with a renewed frontal attack. The Spanish army collapsed, abandoned their guns and fled.

The Spanish had 3,000 casualties, the French 1,000.
Result: His flank now being cleared, Napoleon, who had reached Vitoria (qv), could strike south.

EVORA (Alemtijo, Portugal)   Napoleonic Wars/Peninsular War   29 July 1808
After his concentration around Lisbon was complete, General Andoche Junot decided to attempt to reopen his communications with Elvas and thus to Spain. He sent General Louis Henri Loison with 7,000 men to do this.

Loison marched via Evora, where on 29 July he came upon a mixed force of Portuguese and Spanish, about 3,000, under General Francisco de Paula Leite (later Visconde de Veiros), and the Spaniard Colonel Moretti. These determined upon a stand, although many of their men were poorly armed peasants, and they drew up their line in the open outside the town.

Loison's first attack broke their line, and he then stormed his way into Evora, which he sacked with great brutality. The conflict cost the Portuguese 2,000 men, beside the French casualties of 290.
Result: Loison reached Elvas, but had to withdraw when news of Wellington's landing arrived. This sort of atrocity could only stimulate the insurgents.

FOIX (Ariège, France)   Napoleonic Wars/Peninsular War   19 February 1812
While General Baron Eroles paralysed General Honoré Reille's force (RODA), General Pedro Sarsfield raided from Catalonia, ravaged the French valleys beyond Andorra and, seizing Foix, the chief town of the department of Ariège, levied a ransom of 70,000 dollars. The Emperor Napoleon, not unnaturally, was enraged.
Result: This action was the best possible reply to Napoleon's claim that he had incorporated Catalonia into France.

FORT BALAGUER (Catalonia, Spain)   Napoleonic Wars/Peninsular War   3–7 June 1813
Fought between a British force under Colonel William Prevost and a French garrison.
Strength: British 1,000 with 3 guns and the assistance of HMS *Invincible*; French 150 with 12 guns.
Aim: Lt-General Sir John Murray sent Prevost to capture Fort Balaguer, as it was desirable to use it to block the road Marshal Louis-Gabriel Suchet must use to come to the aid of Tarragona (TARRAGONA II).
Battle: After reconnoitring the place on 3 June, Prevost discovered that Fort San Felipe de Balaguer was a small work, 60 yards square, perched in an inaccessible spot. He managed with the aid of *Invincible*'s marines to get 2 guns and a howitzer to within 700 yards, but their fire proved ineffective. They were moved to within 300 yards. On 7 June a lucky shell from the howitzer exploded one of the French magazines. With one-third of the garrison injured, the French surrendered.
Result: The only road Suchet could use was blocked, and this persuaded the pusillanimous Murray to keep the siege of Tarragona going for two more days.

FOZ DO AROUCE (central Portugal)   Napoleonic Wars/Peninsular War   15 March 1811
Fought between the rearguard of Marshal André Masséna's French Army of Portugal under Marshal Ney and the vanguard of the Anglo-Portuguese army under Wellington.
Strength: French 9,000; British/Portuguese 10,000.
Aim: Ney committed himself to an unnecessary rearguard action, apparently against Masséna's orders, and Wellington chose to take advantage of this error.
Battle: Masséna, having destroyed most of his remaining transport at Miranda de Corvo on 14 March, fell back to a position behind the river Ceira. Ney halted half of his corps and a cavalry brigade on the east bank of the Ceira, in a strong position on a ridge, but with a single damaged bridge behind him.
  Wellington's pursuit started late, because of fog. As the 3rd and Light Divisions moved forward, they picked up many stragglers and then came upon Ney's men. Generals Sir William Erskine and Sir Thomas Picton halted their men, but Wellington resolved to attack at once. Picton was ordered to attack the French left, the Light Division their right. While the frontal attacks went on, some companies of the 95th Rifles penetrated down a hollow road, and arrived close to the bridge almost unopposed. The sound of firing in their rear seems to have panicked the French right centre, the 39th Regiment fled down to the bridge, and joined against some cavalry. Some tried to ford the river, and were drowned. The regimental eagle was abandoned in the river and later recovered by the Allies, and the French colonel was captured. Ney saved the situation by charging in person at the head of another battalion. The French troops then made their escape in some disorder, under shellfire from the British and their own guns in the gathering dusk.
  Allied casualties were 71 men, French 250.
Result: Ney had made a mistake, a rare thing for this expert in rearguard fighting.
  After this action Wellington broke off his close pursuit, because he had outmarched his supplies. He had in any event achieved his main aim of driving the French army away from the main road and towards Spain.

FUENTES DE ONORO (Spanish-Portuguese border)   Napoleonic Wars/Peninsular War   3–5 May 1811
Fought between the Allied army under Viscount Wellington and the French Army of Portugal under Marshal André Masséna.
Strength: Allies 37,000 (British 25,250 [1,500 cavalry], Portuguese 11,750 [300 cavalry]) with 48 guns; French 43,000 infantry + 4,500 cavalry + 40 guns.
Aim: Masséna sought to relieve the garrison of Almeida which Wellington was blockading.
Battle: After being thrown out of Portugal, Masséna regrouped his army and, receiving a small reinforcement from Marshal Bessières, he moved forward. Wellington had taken up a strong but extended position behind the Das Casas stream. On 3 May Masséna attacked the village of Fuentes de Oñoro frontally. The fighting between the fourteen French battalions and the 2,500 defenders was fierce but the French were repelled.
  The next day was quiet, but on the 5th Masséna attempted a winding, sweeping movement against the 7th Division which was Wellington's right flank unit, 2 miles south of Fuentes de Oñoro. This cavalry movement was repulsed by the 7th, but the supporting infantry was too strong to be resisted. Wellington ordered a withdrawal, sending out the Light Division to help. The withdrawal was successfully completed, and Wellington re-formed his right at right angles behind Fuentes de Oñoro. Masséna then assaulted

Fuentes de Oñoro again from the east with three divisions, and here there was very savage fighting, but eventually the French were beaten off and the battle ended.

The British sustained 1,500 casualties, the Portuguese 300, and the French 3,300.

Result: A narrow victory for Wellington, but the Almeida garrison made good its escape on the night of 10–11 May. Masséna was replaced by Marshal Auguste Marmont, although orders for this change of command had been given before the battle.

GAMONAL (Burgos, Spain)   Napoleonic Wars/Peninsular War   10 November 1808

Fought between a portion of the Spanish Army of Extremadura under the Conde de Belveder, and the French 2nd Army Corps under Marshal Nicolas-Jean de Dieu Soult.

Strength: Spanish 11,000; French 9,000.

Aim: The French advance southwards, aimed initially at Burgos, was being headed by Soult's Corps.

Battle: On 6 November, the day he reached Vitoria, Napoleon ordered a general advance. The Conde de Belveder, facing an enemy of unknown strength, ignored the defences of Burgos, and marched forwards to a very weak position in front of the village of Gamonal. This force was not fully formed up when the French struck. Soult advanced with his cavalry to the right, and infantry on the left. The French cavalry drove the Spanish cavalry away, and then destroyed the Spanish left-flank infantry battalions, which did not even know how to form a square. Part of the French cavalry rode on to Burgos, while the rest joined the infantry in attacking the Spanish right. Only one Spanish battalion got away in reasonable order, and 16 guns were lost. Spanish casualties were 2,500 killed and wounded, and 900 prisoners were taken. The French had a total of 65 casualties.

Result: The French sacked Burgos. Napoleon could now carry on with his great offensive.

GARCIA HERNANDEZ (Salamanca, Spain)   Napoleonic Wars/Peninsular War   23 July 1812

Fought between the advanced guard of Wellington's Allied army and the rearguard of the French Army of Portugal.

Strength: Allies 1,500 cavalry; French 4,000 infantry + 1,000 cavalry + 6 guns.

Aim: The Allies sought to beat up the French rearguard.

Battle: Wellington, after his victory at Salamanca (qv), sent the cavalry brigades of Generals George Anson and Baron von Bock in pursuit. Seven miles beyond Alba De Tormes, they came upon the French rearguard. Wellington, apparently only able to see the French cavalry, ordered Anson to attack them, while Bock was to turn their flank. The French cavalry, much mauled the previous day, did not stand. But as Bock's 1st Heavy Dragoons, King's German Legion, went in pursuit, they received a volley into their flank from a French infantry square they had not noticed before. This came from the 1st Battalion 76th Ligne. Promptly the 3rd Squadron, under Captain von der Decken, undamaged by the volley, wheeled and charged the square. The next volley from the square, delivered at 80 yards, killed several men, including von der Decken. But even though another volley was received, the charge went home, and the square broke up–a very rare event on the part of good infantry in a properly formed square, and a still more extraordinary feat for a single squadron of cavalry.

Some way away two battalions of the 6th Léger, seeing this disaster and the rest of the Germans sweeping towards them, began to retreat rapidly uphill. There two units in column, the remainder of the 1st Heavy Dragoons, now accompanied by the 2nd, fell upon them and the French units were smashed. The dragoons, however, pushed on and were beaten off by further French squares.

Allied losses were 127 men, and French 1,100–only 50 of the 1/76th escaped.

Result: In one of the finest feats of cavalry in the Peninsular War the Allied army achieved its objective.

GEBORA (Badajoz, Spain)   Napoleonic Wars/Peninsular War   19 February 1811

Fought between a Spanish (and Portuguese) army under Lt-General Gabriel Mendizabal and a French army under Marshal Nicolas-Jean de Dieu Soult.

Strength: Allies 12,400 (9,000 Spanish infantry + 2,100 Spanish and 900 Portuguese cavalry + 400 artillerymen); French 4,500 infantry + 2,500 cavalry + 12 guns.

Aim: The Spanish sought to disrupt the French siege of Badajoz (BADAJOZ I).

Battle: Soult's invasion of Spanish Extremadura was delayed by the campaign of General Ballasteros in the Condado da Niebla, and the consequent detachment of General Gazán to deal with him. Initially he had to confine himself to besieging Olivenca, which fell on 22 January 1811. After this, under pressure from the Emperor, he decided to attempt the siege of Badajoz. Meanwhile Wellington and General the

Marquis de la Romana had decided to reinforce the frontier in an attempt to check Soult. La Romana died suddenly on 23 January, and the command fell to General Mendizabal. On 28 January Soult sent a reconnaissance towards Portugal, and he was not surprised when a week later a substantial force began to press his outposts. On the night of 5–6 February General Fay De La Tour-Maubourg withdrew the French cavalry up the north bank of the river Guadiana to Montijo, and Mendizabal camped on the heights of San Cristóbal where he was in communication with Badajoz.

Wellington and La Romana had agreed upon a cautious strategy, but Mendizabal planned to launch a major sortie against the French siege lines on the south side of the River. This was made on 7 February and failed. Mendizabal now withdrew his army from the city, and encamped on the heights with his cavalry to his rear in the plains of the river Caya.

Soult kept up the siege, and waited for a chance to attack Mendizabal. On the 18th he moved. It was a foggy morning and Soult was able to surprise Mendizabal. Some French cavalry which had been sent round the Spanish northern (left) flank rode into the camp of one Spanish regiment, and, although the Spanish flew to arms, they were never able to form up properly. Marshal Edouard Mortier, to whom Soult had committed the conduct of the battle, poured all his troops across the river Gébora, with the cavalry on the right and the infantry on the left. The cavalry was to turn the Spanish flank, one brigade assaulting the infantry, and the other riding down upon the Allied cavalry, while the infantry was to attack frontally. The Allied cavalry broke and fled towards Portugal. The infantry battle was only just beginning when the flanking French cavalry charged and Mendizabal ordered his men to form squares. These were penetrated easily and the disaster was complete.

The Allies had 850 killed and wounded, and 4,000 prisoners taken, with 17 guns. French casualties were 400 men.

Result: The Spanish Army of Extremadura was destroyed and Soult could continue the siege.

GERONA I AND II (Catalonia, Spain)   Napoleonic Wars/Peninsular War   18–20 June and 24 July–20 August 1808
Fought between French forces under General Duhesme, the Spanish garrison of Gerona, nominally commanded by Bolivar, actually commanded by Colonels O'Donovan and La Valeta, and a relieving force under Brigadier the Conde de Caldagues.
Strength: French (I) 5,900, (II) 14,000; Spanish (I) 350 regulars + 2,000 armed citizens, (II) 1,700 regulars + 2,000 armed citizens + 7,000 relieving force (mostly irregulars).
Battles: Needing to clear the communications between France and his base, Barcelona, General Duhesme reached the city of Gerona on 18 June 1808. He assumed that the town could be rushed; he had no choice as he had no battering train. He attempted to storm the place twice on 20 June, and under cover of a faked third assault he pulled back to Barcelona.

When Duhesme learnt that General Honoré Reille was moving south from France, he moved north, and on 24 July the two units linked up outside the city. Duhesme had brought an ample siege train with him. He opened two attacks, one against the lower part of the place, the main one against the citadel. The approaches were prepared very slowly, and it was not until 12 August that battering commenced. This delay had two important consequences: news of Baylen (qv) arrived to encourage the defenders; and time was allowed for reinforcements from Menorca to be landed.

The Captain-General Del Palacio sent Brigadier Caldagues with 2,500 men to harass Duhesme. He was joined by local levies, 'Sonatenes'. Colonels O'Donovan and La Valeta were able to get out and attend a conference with Caldagues. They decided to attempt a relief. On 16 August the Spanish struck. Fourteen hundred of the garrison sallied out and swept away the trench guards. At which moment Caldagues's force appeared and Duhesme promptly abandoned the siege, sending Reille north, and pulling back to Barcelona himself.
Result: Duhesme's generalship was surprisingly incapable. The road to France remained blocked.

GERONA III (Catalonia, Spain)   Napoleonic Wars/Peninsular War   24 May–11 December 1809
Fought between the Spanish garrison of Gerona under General Mariano Alvarez de Castro, and French forces under General Laurent Gouvion-St-Cyr, later replaced by Marshal Pierre Augereau, Duc de Castiglione.
Strength: Spanish 5,700 (7 battalions regulars + 3 battalions Miqueletes + 3 local corps + 1 squadron of cavalry + 278 artillerymen + 370 volunteers and 1,000 of the Citizens' Crusade); French 16,000.

Aim: After Molins de Rey (qv), St-Cyr's offensive in Catalonia stalled owing to lack of supplies. St-Cyr had to capture Gerona in order to reopen his communications with France.

Battle: Napoleon ordered General Honoré Reille in N Catalonia to carry out the siege, but he was too weak. Reinforcements were sent and preparations begun, but Napoleon decided to replace St-Cyr with Augereau, and Reille with General Jean-Antoine Verdier. Augereau, however, was detained at Perpignan with gout. St-Cyr reinforced Verdier with up to 14,000 infantry and 2,000 cavalry plus artillery, and he commenced operations against Gerona on 24 May by a loose investment.

The French started their traditional bombardment and sapping on 6 June and the first assault on 19 June was repulsed. They attacked again, this time on 7 July, but again without penetrating the defences. Bombardment continued from 9 July to 4 August and mines were exploded under the glacis on the night of 8–9 August. A prepared attack was foiled by a Spanish sortie and from that date some reinforcements infiltrated into the town to assist the garrison. Food was now running low but Verdier had lost 5,000 men from sickness besides quite heavy battle casualties.

On 31 August a relieving Spanish army under Captain-General Don Joachim Blake made its presence felt on the besiegers. Blake sent Dr F. Rovira and Claros to make a demonstration while one division under Garcia marched around St-Cyr's flank and drove into the starving garrison 1,000 mules and cattle plus sufficient reinforcements to bring Alvarez's garrison up to strength.

St-Cyr, who was now in charge of the siege, suspended further assaults and decided to rely on starvation. A further attempt by Blake on 26 September to relieve Gerona was repulsed. Among the many who died or were taken ill was Alvarez, and he had to hand over to General Juliano Bolivar. Bolivar capitulated on 11 December and marched out with the 3,000 survivors.

Casualties sustained by the Spanish army were 7,000 killed or died of sickness and starvation, while 6,000 out of 14,000 citizens died. French casualties were 13,000 killed and wounded plus 6,000 sick.

The defence of Gerona for seven months was one of Spain's greatest achievements in the whole war and gave tremendous heart to all the guerrillas fighting the French throughout the Peninsula.

GUARDA-BEIRA (Portugal)   Napoleonic Wars/Peninsular War   14 April 1812
While the main Allied army was besieging Badajoz (BADAJOZ III), the defence of N Portugal was left to the frontier fortresses, and the Militia of northern Portugal under General Manoel Pinto Bacelar, Visconde de Montealegre. He covered the supply routes up the Douro (Duero) River, while other groups under Brigadiers Frederico Lecor, Sir Nicholas Trant, and John Wilson were farther south.

Marshal Auguste Marmont decided that he would invade the Beira, to try to distract Wellington from Badajoz. Pushing General Carlos D'España away from Ciudad Rodrigo (30 March) and reconnoitring Almeida, he turned south towards Sabugal, and sent out parties to ravage the countryside.

Trant, who was at Guarda, heard that Marmont was dispersed and planned to attack Sabugal with his Militia. But on the day he planned to move, 14 April, he was surprised. Trant and his colleague Wilson had barely enough time to get their men into order and on to the march, as the rain started. But they had only gone 2 or 3 miles when the French cavalry struck, wrecking the 40 cavalry the Portuguese had, and then cutting their way through the Oporto Militia brigade, whose muskets would not fire in the wet. Fifteen hundred prisoners were taken, although the French contemptuously let many go.

The French, however, did not push their pursuit, as on 15 April Marmont learnt Badajoz had fallen, and Wellington was free to come north again.

GUETARIA (N coast of Spain)   Napoleonic Wars/Peninsular War   19 July 1812
(For *Strength, Aim,* see LEQUEITIO)
Commodore Sir Home Popham, after an abortive attempt on this strong position–it lay close to the main road from France to Spain–in the first week of July, returned to it. He was joined by a band of Jauregui's guerrillas. Although he landed some guns and marines, he failed to take the place. This activity drew the attention of the Bayonne garrison, and General D'Aussenac with 3,000 men came out and drove Jauregui away. Popham lost 30 men and 2 guns in a hasty embarkation.

Popham now switched his attention to the west. He made a third attempt in August, but failed again.

IVANTELLY (ECHALAR) (W Pyrenees, Franco-Spanish border)   Napoleonic Wars/Peninsular War   2 August 1813
As Marshal Nicolas-Jean de Dieu Soult completed his retreat to France after Sorauren (qv) he gathered

his men (25,000) on the ridge north of Echalar. Wellington had only 12,000 exhausted men to attack this formidable position. Yet, aware of the state of French morale, he determined upon an attack.

The 4th and 7th Divisions were directed to attack the French centre on either side of Echalar while the Light Division assaulted the western flank. The 7th Division under Lt-General Lord Dalhousie attacked frontally. French resistance crumpled. The 4th Division then attacked in support of the 7th, while the Light Division smashed the French right wing, losing only 27 casualties in taking the formidable peak of Ivantelly from forces that outnumbered it.

Result: Soult, with his centre smashed and his right dispersed, had to retreat.

LA HUEBRA   see SAN MUNOZ

LEQUEITIO (N coast of Spain)   Napoleonic Wars/Peninsular War   21–2 June 1812
Fought between a British amphibious force under Commodore Sir Home Popham the Guerrilla band of Don Gaspar, El Pastor, and a French garrison under Chef de Bataillon Gillort.
Strength: British HMS *Venerable* and *Magnificent* (74s) (the latter replaced by *Abercrombie* for part of the campaign) + *Medusa, Diadem, Surveillante, Rhin* and (for a brief while) *Bellepoule* (frigates) + *Sparrow* and *Lyra* (sloops) + some smaller vessels and 1,000 marines, Spanish guerrillas; French 350.
Aim: Popham sought to aid the guerrillas on the north coast of Spain in breaking up French control of the area, and thus diverting French forces from opposing Wellington. Lequeitio was the opening move in this campaign.
Battle: On 21 June Popham appeared before Lequeitio, landed a heavy gun and some marines, and linked up with the guerrilla band of El Pastor. The defences consisted of a fort and a fortified convent. The 24-pounders battered the fort, which was stormed by the Spanish, the garrison being killed or captured. On 22 July the gun was then turned on the convent, and Gillort promptly surrendered. 290 French surrendered.
Result: Popham moved off to Bermeo and Plencia, which were hastily evacuated by the French. The effect of this on General Louis-Gabriel Caffarelli, French GOC Army of the North, was great. He broke off his efforts to reinforce Marshal Auguste Marmont.

LERIDA (Catalonia, Spain)   Napoleonic Wars/Peninsular War   16 July 1812
General Luis Lacy planned, despite the protests of General Pedro Sarsfield and General Baron Eroles, for Spanish employees in the French powder magazine to blow it up. In the ensuing confusion he would storm the fortress. In the explosion 100 of the garrison and many citizens perished, whilst many houses and a bastion fell. The Governor, the heavy-handed General Henriod, got his men under arms and manned the breach. Lacy, who had arrived late, made no attempt to storm but departed as quickly as he had advanced. He had killed hundreds of his compatriots to no purpose. This the Catalans, who already detested him, never forgave him.

LERIN (Navarre, Spain)   Napoleonic Wars/Peninsular War   31 March 1813
As a result of Francisco Espoz y Mina's success at Tafalla (qv), General Bertrand Clausel sent Barbot's Division to assist General Abbé in Navarre. Having reached Tolosa on 30 March, Barbot sent out two battalions to requisition provisions at nearby Lerín. On 31 March, they had just broken up to find food, when two of Mina's battalions attacked, while two more with 200 lancers cut the French retreat. Surprised, the French rallied and began to fight the 8 miles back to their division. In a running battle they were much mauled, and had to form a square to resist the lancers. In this unsuitable formation they faced a long fire fight, and eventually the square collapsed when the cavalry charged. Barbot made no effort to help.

The French battalions were nearly annihilated and 28 officers and 635 men were captured.
Result: Clausel had to detach more men to deal with Mina, a task which was not completed in June, and thus Clausel's men missed the Battle of Vitoria (qv). Barbot's failure caused Mina considerable surprise.

LIZASO-BEUNZA (Franco-Spanish frontier)   Napoleonic Wars/Peninsular War   30 July 1813
After his success at Maya on 25 July General Comte Drouet d'Erlon only advanced very slowly, though he outnumbered the forces opposing him under Lt-General Sir Rowland Hill by 18,000 to 14,000. Wellington sought to prevent D'Erlon joining Marshal Nicolas-Jean de Dieu Soult before Sorauren (qv). Soult's new

plan on 30 July called for D'Erlon to hold open the Pamplona-San Sebastian road. To carry this out, he attacked Hill's men, who had been drawn up along a wooded ridge half a mile south of Lizaso.

Brigadier Charles Ashworth's Portuguese formed his centre, with one regiment of Da Costa's Portuguese on the right and the other, with Colonel John Cameron's British, on the left. Pringle's Brigade was in reserve. D'Erlon ordered the 8,000 men of General Abbé's Division, supported by General Jean-Pierre Maransin, to attack the Allies' left flank, while Darmagnac was to demonstrate frontally. This ruse succeeded, but only after heavy fighting. Hill retreated to a new position in front of the village of Yguaras, where another attack was repulsed.

D'Erlon was re-forming his men when the leading elements of the British force following up their victory of Sorauren approached, and D'Erlon contented himself with having held the road open. British casualties were 156 men, Portuguese 900, and French 800.

Result: A technical success for D'Erlon, but the French offensive was really over.

MARIA (Aragón, Spain)   Napoleonic Wars/Peninsular War   15 June 1809
Fought between a Spanish army under Captain-General Don Joachim Blake and the French 3rd Army Corps under General Louis-Gabriel Suchet.
Strength: Spanish 12,000 infantry + 600 cavalry with 16 guns; French 7,500 infantry + 800 cavalry with 12 guns (approaching reinforcements 3,000 infantry).
Aim: Suchet sought to regain the hold on central Aragón against Blake's offensive.
Battle: After the Battle of Alcañiz (qv) Suchet concentrated his whole available force at Saragossa (Zaragoza), save two battalions, and called upon King Joseph Bonaparte for help. All José could send were six battalions. Blake's delay in following up his victory allowed Suchet to reorganise his army, and his efforts caused a great improvement in morale. He sent all his sick and heavy baggage to Tudela and Pampeluna (Pamplona) before leaving Saragossa on 14 June. Suchet saw that the Spanish, now in the valley of the Huerba 10 to 12 miles away, were so close that he was under threat of immediate attack. So he moved, although he would have preferred to wait for the 6th Battalion. Blake had only 20,000 of his 25,000 men available and, with two of his three divisions, marched to the village of Maria 12 miles from Saragossa. General Carlos Areizaga's Division was at Botroita 6 miles away.

The two armies came into contact on 14 June. Musnier's Division came up against Blake's vanguard and pushed it back, but had to give way before the Spanish main body. Suchet discovered that Areizaga led the weaker of the Spanish groups. He left only five battalions to contain Areizaga, but he delayed his assault on Blake until the 3,000 men of Colonel Robert's Brigade, due at noon on 15 June, arrived. Blake had taken up a position on rolling hills, with the river Huerba on his right and the village of Maria some way behind his right. His infantry was drawn up in two lines, Roca's Division on the northern ridge and Marquis of Lazán's behind it on the second. The Spanish cavalry filled the gap between the hills and the river. Two battalions and half a battery were in reserve and the remaining artillery was in the spaces of the first line. Suchet put his troops on a lower line of heights facing Blake, Habert's Brigade on the left by the river with the two cavalry regiments. Musnier's Division was on the right with one squadron of Polish cavalry beyond, and two battalions in reserve.

After a peaceful morning Blake pushed his right forward, more to induce Suchet to counter-attack than with offensive intentions of his own. He was driven off. Still Suchet stood his ground. Blake decided to attack, but failed to involve Areizaga. Instead he used his extreme left. Suchet ordered the Poles to charge the Spanish flank while one battalion took them in front. Suchet now ordered a general attack with Musnier's Division, as Robert had arrived. This attack made some progress but failed to break through. Suchet had to draw from his tiny reserve and from Habert's Brigade to maintain the assault. Then a violent hailstorm swept down on the armies, separating them for half an hour. After it Suchet decided to attack all along his line, using Robert to support Habert. As the infantry closed in on the low ground, the French cavalry charged and the Spanish cavalry fled without crossing swords. The French cavalry then destroyed the right wing of the Spanish infantry. Habert attacked the flank, now exposed, of the Spanish centre. Blake faced disaster, for the only road by which he might retreat was cut. However, he drew his right wing back, called the remaining battalions of Lazán's Division into line and made a fighting withdrawal southwards across country. Robert's men were not actually engaged.

The Spanish sustained casualties of 1,000 killed and 3,000 to 4,000 wounded, losing several hundred prisoners and all but 2 of their guns. French casualties numbered 800.

Result: Blake got his army away intact and joined Areizaga at Botorita where he made a stand. Suchet, aware of the exhaustion of his troops, began to manoeuvre the Spanish from their position.

MAYA (Franco-Spanish frontier)   Napoleonic Wars/Peninsular War   25 July 1813
Fought between elements of Wellington's Allied army under Lt-General the Hon William Stewart, and a
French army corps under General Comte Drouet d'Erlon.
Strength: Allies 6,000 (3 brigades–all British); French 26,000 (3 divisions).
Aim: Marshal Nicolas-Jean de Dieu Soult sought to thrust through the Maya Pass to cut Wellington's
army in half as part of his attempt to relieve Pamplona (qv).
Battle: D'Erlon's troops attacked up the carriage road from Bayonne to Pamplona through Maya, and up
a secondary road 1½ miles farther east. As D'Erlon attacked, the outnumbered British, after a stiff
resistance, fell back. Reserves counter-attacked the tired French troops in the flank. This allowed Stewart
to fall back on Elizondo which still effectively blocked this route. The British sustained 1,500 casualties,
the French 2,000.
Result: The French did not achieve their objective.

MEDELLIN (Estremadura, Spain)   Napoleonic Wars/Peninsular War   28 March 1809
Fought between a Spanish army under Captain-General Don Gregorio de la Cuesta and a French army
under Marshal Claude Victor.
Strength: Spanish 20,000 infantry + 3,000 cavalry + 30 guns; French 13,000 infantry + 4,500 cavalry.
Aim: The French sought to destroy the Spanish army in order to open the way for the southern prong of
their invasion of Portugal.
Battle: Cuesta positioned his army in a wide semicircle with its right on the south bank of the Guadiana
River, and the Hortiga River on its left. Victor's army was drawn up on a shorter line, 1½ miles to the SE of
Medellín. Victor advanced with General Fay de La Tour-Maubourg's cavalry on his right, General
Antoine Lasalle's on his left, and his centre somewhat refused. As the French closed in, Cuesta advanced.
Victor gave orders for his cavalry to charge if they saw a good chance. However, La Tour-Maubourg's
charge was turned back by the Duque del Parque. Victor ordered a fighting retreat, until his chosen
fighting line was reached. The French then faced about. The Spanish infantry came on steadily, and
attacked the French guns. They were actually among them when La Tour-Maubourg charged again.
Cuesta ordered his own cavalry to attack, but they only came forward a few paces, before they bolted,
riding their own Commander-in-Chief down.
    The result was disaster for the Spanish right wing. La Tour-Maubourg sent one of his brigades after the
Spanish cavalry, while the other attacked the infantry. Lasalle at the other end of the French line followed
his colleague's example, driving the Spanish cavalry away and then, with the aid of infantry, assaulted the
Spanish infantry. The Spanish infantry put up a show of resistance, but when two of La Tour-Maubourg's
cavalry regiments returned from pursuing the Spanish cavalry, the Spanish infantry, attacked from the
front, rear and flanks, collapsed.
    The French pursuit was ferocious, and it was only a thunderstorm, and the gallantry of two Spanish
cavalry regiments from the centre, which saved any of their infantry. Spanish casualties were over 10,000,
they had 1,850 prisoners taken and lost 20 out of 30 guns. French casualties numbered 1,000.
Result: Most of the Spanish cavalry (3,000) got away, but only 7,000 infantry could be rallied by 8 April.

MEDINA DE RIO SECO (León, Spain)   Napoleonic Wars/Peninsular War   14 July 1808
Fought between the Spanish Army of Castile under Captain-General Don Gregorio de la Cuesta, the
Spanish Army of Galicia under Captain-General Don Joaquim Blake, and a French army under Marshal
Bessières.
Strength: Spanish (Army of Castile) 6,000 infantry + 550 cavalry, no guns, (Army of Galicia) 15,300
infantry + 50 cavalry + 20 guns; French 11,800 infantry + 1,150 cavalry + 30 guns.
Aim: The French sought to protect their communications with Madrid, and open the way for another
advance southwards.
Battle: General Blake commanded the best of the Spanish armies, but, against his advice, the Junta of
Galicia insisted he should push forward into Castile. On 10 July he linked up with the Army of Castile
which was being reorganised under Cuesta after their defeat at Cabezón (qv), at Villalpando. Blake, who
was junior to Cuesta, seeing their weakness in cavalry, asserted it would be lunacy to risk battle in the
plains of Castile. Cuesta insisted on an advance towards Valladolid.
    On 13 July General Antoine Lasalle's light cavalry contacted Cuesta's forces near Medina de Rio Seco.
Cuesta positioned his army on the forward slope of a gentle hill, exposed to artillery fire and suitable for
cavalry, with the town and the dry river Sequillo behind. This right was protected, but his left was in the

air. But the way he occupied this bad position was worse. Blake was on the right with the bulk of the Galician army. The rest was half a mile to Blake's left rear. Bessières decided to contain Cuesta, while he threw the main weight against Blake. The attack on Blake, after an artillery duel, went forward cautiously. Meanwhile, five battalions contained Cuesta, and the gap between the two portions of the Spanish army was not filled. Then the French cavalry attacked Blake's left. The Spanish battalions were unready for this, and most of the left collapsed. The Spanish guns were captured, and only one Navarrese battalion, which formed one square, and at the cost of one-third of its strength, gained enough time for the rest to get away.

Bessières then turned on Cuesta, who ordered the 4th Galician Division to attack uphill. It made remarkable progress but, heavily overweighted, it was broken up. Cuesta now withdrew, and the French were too tired to pursue. Casualties sustained by the Spanish Army of Castile were 155, and by the Army of Galicia 400 dead and 500 wounded, which also had 1,200 prisoners taken and lost 10 guns. French casualties were 105 killed and 300 wounded.

Result: The Galicians returned to their mountains, Cuesta went into León. King Joseph Bonaparte was able to return to Madrid.

MENGIBAR (Near Baylen, Spain)   Napoleonic Wars/Peninsular War   14–16 July 1808
Fought between a portion of General Xavier Castaños's Spanish Army of Andalusia under General Teodoro Reding, and a portion of General Comte Dupont de l'Etang's French army corps under Generals Gervais Vedel and Liger-Bellair.
Strength: Spanish 10,000; French varying numbers up to 10,000.
Aim: The Spanish sought to force a crossing of the river Guadalquivir as the first stage of their plan to cut the main road through Baylen (qv), and attack General Dupont in the rear.
Battle: On 14 July Reding appeared before General Liger-Bellair's force at Mengíbar, and pushed his outpost back. On the following day Reding tried a more serious attack, but finding the whole of Vedel's Division drawn up opposite, he desisted. Vedel pulled back, leaving Liger-Bellair. On the 16th Reding attacked again. Liger-Bellair called for help from Gobert, who had replaced Vedel at Baylen. He was unable to prevent defeat, and was killed. In the evening Dufour, who replaced Gobert, withdrew to Baylen and then to the passes.

The way to Baylen was open, but Reding rested his men all the following day.
Result: Owing to the inefficiency of the French, the Spanish had scored a substantial success, and divided the French army.

MOLINS DE REY (Barcelona, Spain)   Napoleonic Wars/Peninsular War   21 December 1808
Fought between a French army under General Laurent Gouvion-St-Cyr and a Spanish army under Captain-General Vives.
Strength: French 18,000; Spanish 14,000 with 25 guns.
Aim: St-Cyr sought to complete the siege of Barcelona.
Battle: Barcelona had been relieved after Cardedeu (qv), but parts of the Spanish force were still in the vicinity. Brigadier the Conde de Caldagues with 11,000 men who had not been involved in the Battle of the Cardedeu, and General Teodoro Reding with 4,000 survivors of that battle were lining the river Llobregat, a few miles from the city. Reding and Caldagues wished to withdraw, but could get no guidance from Vives.

On 21 December St-Cyr moved and, ordering Chabran with 4,000 men to demonstrate against the bridge of Molins de Rey, he attacked across the fords of the Lower Llobegrat with 14,000 men. Chabran's demonstration drew Reding's attention and the French attacks across the fords succeeded, especially at the extreme right of the Spanish flank. Chabran did not convert his threat into a proper attack. Most of the Spaniards got away, losing 1,500 prisoners, including the Conde de Caldagues, and all their 25 guns.
Result: The blockade of Barcelona was ended, and the French divisions occupied the whole of the Llobegrat.

MONZON (Aragón, Spain)   Napoleonic Wars/Peninsular War   16–19 March 1809
Fought between a French brigade under General Habert and a force of Spanish irregulars under Colonel Perema.
Strength: French approx 3,000 (6 battalions + 1 regiment of cavalry); Spanish approx 4,000.
Aim: The French sought to recover Monzón from the Spanish.

Battle: With the threat of war with Austria growing, Napoleon moved Marshal Edouard Mortier's 5 Corps from Aragón nearer to France and replaced General Andoche Junot with General Louis-Gabriel Suchet in command of 3 Corps. This reduced the French garrison of Aragón to 15,000, a force much too weak for its task.

In the interregnum before Suchet's arrival, affairs went badly for the French. Colonel Perema from Lérida attacked Colonel Solnicki's detachment of Grandjean's Division holding Monzón. Solnicki fell back to Barbastro, the HQ of General Habert's Brigade. Habert decided to try to recover Monzón, and on 16 May he attempted to ford the river Cinca below Monzón at the Pomar ferry. Just as his vanguard had crossed, a sudden storm caused the river to rise, cutting off the vanguard. Habert moved north to Monzón to force a passage, but failed, and the 1,000 men who had crossed were eventually forced to surrender on 19 May when their ammunition was exhausted. Only the cavalry escaped.

Result: The French lost their grip on the Cinca valley, and Habert fell back to Villafranca on the Ebro.

MORALES (near Toro, Spain)   Napoleonic Wars/Peninsular War   2 June 1813
Fought between Colonel Colquhoun Grant's British Cavalry Brigade of Wellington's Allied army and part of General Alexandre Digeon's Cavalry Division of the French Army of the South.
Strength: British 1,000; French 900.
Aim: The British seeking information, took a chance to damage a French rearguard.
Battle: Wellington had sent cavalry units to reconnoitre all the roads leading east and north from Toro, his HQ. On 2 June Colonel Grant's Brigade went east towards Tordesillas, and came up with Digeon's rear at Morales, 6 miles from Toro. The two French regiments were drawn up with a swamp in front and bridge behind. Grant charged furiously with the 10th Hussars, supported by the 18th on one flank, and broke the first French regiment, whereupon the next went to the rear and was chased for 2 miles. Eventually the men took shelter behind Daricau's Infantry Division drawn up across the road, and Grant halted.

British casualties were 10 to the French 200.
Result: The British achieved their objective. This proved to be a good first days' work for the 10th Hussars, newly arrived in the Peninsula.

NIVE (SW France)   Napoleonic Wars/Peninsular War   9–10 December 1813
Fought between the Allied army under Field-Marshal the Marquess of Wellington and a French army under Marshal Jean-Nicolas de Dieu Soult, Duc de Dalmatie.
Strength: Allies 63,000 (British 36,000, Portuguese 23,000, Spanish 4,000); French 54,500 in field army + 8,000 in Bayonne garrison.
Aim: Wellington sought to expand his area of occupation in S France, and close up to Bayonne. Soult sought to take advantage of Wellington's manoeuvres to inflict a sharp reverse on the Allies.
Battle: After the Battle of Nivelle (qv) Bayonne was exposed but difficult to attack because of its position. The Adour flows west into the Atlantic and the Nive flows north into the Adour. The city straddles the Nive, mainly on the south of the river, with strong fortifications on both banks of the Adour. It had a powerful garrison. The river Nive was the key.

On 16 November Wellington pushed the French back from their bridgehead at Cambo, but then made no further advance, delayed in part by the unsatisfactory news from N Europe. He was also unable to use his full strength for fear that the underfed and vengeful Spaniards might commit atrocities. He could not afford to antagonise the French civilian population. Wellington chose to risk an advance down both banks of the Nive, but first he had to cross it. On 9 December Lt-General Sir Rowland Hill's Corps crossed near Cambo, and while General Pablo Morillo's Spaniards formed a flank guard, the rest turned north and made for the Adour. Marshal Sir William Beresford crossed with two divisions farther north on pontoon bridges. Soult offered little resistance, retreating into Bayonne.

Meanwhile Lt-General Sir John Hope advanced north between the Nive and the sea, and again little resistance was met. After a reconnaissance in force, Hope left an outpost line, and pulled most of his men back to their cantonments.

Soult now sought to take advantage of the division of Wellington's forces and his own interior lines. At 9am on 10 December he struck at Hope's outposts on the two roads leading from Bayonne west of the Nive. These two roads, with other byroads, were to form the central feature of the confused day's fighting that followed, as the ground was wooded, marshy and waterlogged; thus movement on them was difficult.

The Light Division on the Ustaritz road was attacked first and pushed back 2 miles. It took position on the hill of Arcangues, hastily fortifying the château and the church. The French attack against this position lacked thrust, and the Light Division held on. A French attack between Arcangues and the Nive ran into the 7th Division positioned to protect the bridge of Urdains. The attack was halted and fighting here died away by early afternoon. Meanwhile the French advance down the main road farther west drove the Allied picket line back 3 miles to where two Portuguese independent brigades (Brigadier Archibald Campbell and Major-General Thomas Bradford) stood at a point where the road passes between a lake and a wood near the home of the Mayor of Biarritz. A full French division attacked but was halted by the Portuguese; a second French division attacking farther east was halted by the 5th Division coming up in support. A third French attack nearly took the Mayor's house by turning the Allied right flank, but Major-General Baron Aylmer's independent British brigade came up just in time. This day's fighting, unsatisfactory to both sides, then died away.

The French sustained 2,000 casualties, the Allies 1,800.

Result: Soult suffered a more serious loss when three German battalions deserted, under orders from their ruler who had changed sides. The French failed to achieve their aim, and the Allied position held by a narrow margin.

NIVELLE (Franco-Spanish frontier)   Napoleonic Wars/Peninsular War   10 November 1813
Fought between the Allied army under Field-Marshal the Marquess of Wellington and a French army under Marshal Nicolas-Jean de Dieu Soult, Duc de Dalmatie.
Strength: Allies 80,000 (British 35,000, Portuguese 20,000, Spanish 25,000); French approx 60,000.
Aim: Wellington sought to expand his foothold in SW France.
Battle: When Pamplona (qv) finally surrendered, Wellington was in a position to exploit his initial crossing of the Bidassoa (qv) into France. He considered an attack by his right through Roncesvalles, but this pass was often choked with snow in winter. The first third of the front from the sea to the village of Ascain was heavily fortified and was defended by three full divisions and a reserve equivalent of another. The remainder, twice as long, was held by only five divisions. The key position was the Lesser Rhune, only 700 yards from the Great Rhune, but separated from it by a ravine. The French position was strong, and further strengthened by earthworks.

Wellington's plan was the opposite of his plan of 7 October, and again he deceived Soult. A fake attack by Lt-General Sir John Hope on the coastal sector, with 25,000 against 23,000 French, was to hold French attention. Meanwhile Marshal Sir William Beresford and Lt-General Sir Rowland Hill were to attack between Ascain and Mondarain, astride the river Nivelle, with 55,000 against 40,000.

The Allied attack went in on 10 November. As a result of careful reconnaissance, Wellington had found a route by which the Light Division could approach the Lesser Rhune, working round the head of the position, and assaulting it from the flank. The plan worked successfully and by 8am the Lesser Rhune was in Allied hands. The way was now open for the rest of the Allied advance.

West of the Nivelle, of Beresford's units, the 4th Division captured the fortified village of Sare before 9am; the 7th, commanded by Major-General Frederico Lecor, a Portuguese General, captured the Grenade redoubt; and the 3rd Division captured the bridge of Amots, cutting the best lateral communication the French had. Hill's troops to the right caught up with Beresford's men on the other side of the river, General Sir John Hamilton's Portuguese capturing Ainhoa village before noon. The French had condemned themselves to static defence in their fortifications and lacked reserves to use against Allied concentrations.

After waiting for the other units to catch up, the Light Division pushed on up the St Ignace valley, and captured two more lines of redoubts. Meanwhile all day long Hope appeared to be about to launch an attack, and there was enough fighting to convince the French that the threat was real. With all Allied units having reached the objective, they halted. There was not enough daylight left for a further move.

The French sustained 4,300 casualties and lost 59 guns. The Allies had 2,700 casualties.

Result: Soult retired to Bayonne, west of the Nive, but held on east as far as Cambo, with a bridgehead on the west bank there.

OBIDOS (central Portugal)   Napoleonic Wars/Peninsular War   15 August 1808
A minor skirmish, involving four companies of British riflemen (60th and 95th Rifles) who, while endeavouring to drive the rearguard of General Delabordes's Division back, managed to get themselves into difficulties for a moment, through inexperience and over-enthusiasm. They were brought off by Major-General Sir Brent Spencer.

This engagement is notable only as the first action fought by the British army in the Peninsular War.

OCANA (Castile, Spain)   Napoleonic Wars/Peninsular War   17 November 1809
Fought between a Spanish army under General Areizaga, and the French led by King Joseph Bonaparte of Naples and Spain and Marshal Nicolas-Jean de Dieu Soult.
Strength: Spanish 53,000; French 30,000.
Aim: General Areizaga was ordered by the Spanish Central Junta (which was on the verge of breakdown) to 'free Madrid' before French reinforcements set at liberty by the end of the Austrian war could reach Spain.
Battle: Areizaga had hoped to obtain some co-operation from the British but Wellington's forces, exhausted and depleted by their victory at Talavera (qv) and now starving in Portugal, remained in their cantonments. Areizaga bravely tried to carry out orders and advance north on Madrid but was overwhelmingly defeated at Ocaña on 17 November 1809 by the experienced French forces, sustaining casualties of 5,000 killed and wounded plus 20,000 prisoners, against French losses of only 1,700.
Result: This victory gave the French the whole of Andalucia and, as they were now masters of all Spain except for Galicia, Valencia and Catalonia, allowed them to menace Portugal. The Spanish Central Junta abdicated on 29 January 1810 before handing over to an elected Cortes. Wellington, with 27,000 British and 30,000 untried Portuguese troops, retired behind the lines of Torres Vedras. But the Spanish guerrillas, led by such legendary heroes as Juan Martin Diaz (The Empecinado), Julian Sanchez, Juan Diaz Porlier, Don Mariano de Renovalos Longa, and the two Minas (uncle and nephew), followed the example of the Catalans and played havoc with the French garrisons and communications throughout Spain.
   Spain became a nation of guerrillas who did as much at that time, if not more–as Wellington was quiescent–than the British to defeat Napoleon's immediate designs in Spain. The French had to expend three-quarters of their strength in Spain fighting or defending themselves against these Spanish guerrillas which allowed them only a quarter of their forces to form a field army to operate against Wellington. Wellington fully understood their value and sent his best staff and commissariat officers to support the guerrillas which the Royal Navy, operating around the coast, also ably assisted whenever an opportunity occurred.

OLHAO REVOLT (Algarve, Portugal)   Napoleonic Wars/Peninsular War   16 June 1808
The revolt of the small fishing town of Olhão on 16 June gave the signal to the rest of the province. The capital, Faro, rose on the 18th. General Maurin, the French Governor of Algarve, who was sick, was taken with 70 men, and sent aboard an English warship. His second in command, Colonel Jean-Pierre Maransin (1st Légion du Midi), with 1,200 men retreated to Mertola in the Alemtejo. From the Algarve, the revolt spread north, and soon French control in Portugal was limited to the area round Lisbon. A similar rising took place in the North.

OPORTO (PORTO) I (N Portugal)   Napoleonic Wars/Peninsular War   29 March 1809
Fought between the garrison and populace of Oporto and a French army corps under Marshal Nicolas-Jean de Dieu Soult.
Strength: Portuguese 24,000 (2,000 regulars + 3,000 militia + 15,000 ordenanças [armed peasantry]) with 200 guns (but only 1,000 gunners). French 21,400 with 54 guns.
Aim: Soult sought to capture Oporto to complete the first stage in Napoleon's planned conquest of Portugal.
Battle: The citizens of Oporto had been engaged for the previous three weeks in the construction of an enormous set of field works 6 miles long, to cover the northern side of the city and the entrance to the Douro river, armed with 197 guns. But the city was in a state of 'anarchy tempered by assassination', under the leadership of its Bishop. Soult, on approaching the city on 28 March, sent in a captured Portuguese officer to ask for its surrender. The Bishop and his council refused. Soult then preparted a general assault. He committed almost all his troops to the first attack, in three columns. He had but 16,000 men available, 3,000 of whom were cavalry. But he knew now the quality of the Portuguese and did not doubt of success. His plan was for his two-flank columns to attack first, trying to draw in all the Portuguese reserves. This would be followed by a heavy assault in the centre.
   At 7am the two-flank columns attacked. Brigadier José Vaz Parreiras, the Portuguese centre commander, did as Soult hoped and denuded his sector to support the flanks. Then the centre column attacked, and broke in easily. With their centre smashed, the Portuguese flanks gave way. Brigadier Antonio Marcellino Victoria, on the right (east) flank, pulled his troops out eastward intact, along the

Vallongo road. On the left the commander, Brigadier Antonio de Lima Barretto, also ordered his men to retreat. They refused, he insisted and was shot down as a traitor. The French then got in among them, and penning them in the angle between the Douro and the sea, slaughtered or drove into the water some thousands. In the centre Parreiras escaped across a bridge of boats, and he was followed by many thousands of terrified fugitives, military and civilian. Then someone ordered the removal of the central pontoons, and enormous numbers of fugitives, not realising there was now a gap, rushed in to it, and were forced by those behind them into the river, where many drowned.

It is impossible to assess the Portuguese casualties accurately, estimates vary between 4,000 and 20,000. The French had 430 killed and wounded.

Result: Soult had completed the first stage of his advance. But he was too weak to push on.

OPORTO (PORTO) II (N Portugal)   Napoleonic Wars/Peninsular War   12 May 1809
Fought between an Anglo-Portuguese army under Lieutenant (Marshal)-General Sir Arthur Wellesley and a French corps under Marshal Nicolas-Jean de Dieu Soult.
Strength: Allies 29,300 (Anglo-Portuguese 23,800 [Wellesley 18,000, Beresford 5,800] + 4,000 various elements [Silveira] + 1 brigade 1,500 [Wilson]); French 20,000 (10,000 in Oporto, 6,000 on the Tamega, 4,000 to the north).
Aim: The Allies sought to expel the French invaders from N Portugal.
Battle: After Soult had captured Oporto, his offensive halted. Meanwhile the British and Portuguese were beginning to organise themselves for a counter-offensive. On 22 April the one British general who really believed in the possibility of defending Portugal had arrived in Lisbon. Pausing only long enough to consult the Portuguese government and to be appointed Marshal-General, and therefore Allied Commander-in-Chief, on 29 April, Sir Arthur Wellesley began a forward concentration to attack Soult. His plan was to go north himself on the main road with the bulk of the army, while sending Marshal William Carr Beresford with a flanking column to cross the Douro higher up, at Lamego, link up with Brigadier Francisco da Silveira and cut Soult's network eastward. On 3 May news was received that Silveira had been driven from Amarante (qv) and was lying at Lamego with about 4,000 men. This caused no alteration in the plan although Beresford might be delayed. By 11 May Wellesley had driven the French outposts back into Oporto and was facing Soult across the Douro. Soult had about 10,000 men in Oporto, and, aware that he could not hope to hold this position for long, had decided to pull out to Spain.

On the morning of 12 May Lt-Colonel John Waters found, with the aid of a Portuguese barber, a small boat on the south bank of the river and saw 4 wine barges moored on the north side, at a point a short way above the town and out of sight of the French. Waters and a few Portuguese brought these over to the south bank. Wellesley ordered them to be used for a crossing, and a company of the Buffs (3rd Foot) was sent across the river to occupy a stoutly built seminary. The barges had crossed four times, and Major-General the Hon Edward Paget had almost a whole battalion across, before the French spotted them. The French launched a series of uncoordinated attacks upon the seminary, which were beaten off by the garrison supported by artillery from the south bank, Paget losing an arm. Soult sent the troops garrisoning Oporto waterfront into the attack, at which the townspeople brought everything which would float, and the 29th Foot was sent over into the town. Oporto was no longer tenable, and Soult ordered an immediate retreat eastwards towards Amarante.

Wellesley had sent his strongest infantry brigade and two cavalry squadrons to cross at a ferry a few miles upstream. But the Commander, Major-General John Murray, just sat down and watched the French stream past. Wellesley's Adjutant-General, Brigadier the Hon Charles Stewart did what he could with the cavalry, taking 300 prisoners, at the cost of 35 out of 110 cavalrymen present. There the pursuit ended.

The Allies sustained 125 casualties. The French had 300 killed and wounded, and 1,800 were taken prisoner.

Result: As the Amarante was now blocked again, Soult abandoned his guns and baggage and struck north into the mountains. He hoped to reach Vigo but was cut off by Wellesley. He could not go NE because of Beresford, but did find a small gap, and got his men out to Spain abandoning all they could not carry. Portugal was cleared for a second time. When later in the year Wellesley was made Viscount Wellington, he took as a second title Baron Douro, and was always known by that name to his Portuguese soldiers.

OROPESA (E coast of Spain)   Napoleonic Wars/Peninsular War   8–11 October 1811
Fought between a Spanish garrison and a portion of Marshal Louis-Gabriel Suchet's French army.
Strength: Spanish 400; French 1,500 (actually Neapolitans).

Aim: Suchet sought to clear the way for his siege artillery to move down the road towards Sagunto (qv).
Battle: As part of his plan for the defence of Valencia Captain-General Don Joachim Blake had committed a small garrison to the defence of two medieval towers at Ordopesa, which blocked the main coast road. On 6 October Suchet linked up with his siege train which was coming south from Tortosa (qv). On the 8th he appeared before Oropesa. First he attacked the tower nearer the road, which was easily breached, and on 10 October its 215 men garrison surrendered. The next day HMS *Magnificent* (74) sent her boats in with a squadron of Spanish gunboats, and rescued the 150 garrison of the other tower.
Result: The French had opened the way to Sagunto for their guns.

ORTHEZ (Pyrénées-Atlantique, SW France)   Napoleonic Wars/Peninsular War   27 February 1814
Fought between the Allied (British/Portuguese) army under the Marquess of Wellington and a French army under Marshal Nicolas-Jean de Dieu Soult.
Strength: British/Portuguese 39,000 infantry + 3,400 cavalry + 1,500 artillery with 42 guns; French 29,000 infantry + 3,500 cavalry + 3,500 artillery.
Aim: Wellington sought to drive the French army away from Bayonne in order to facilitate the siege of that city and to consolidate his position in SW France.
Battle: After the Battles of the Nive and St Pierre (qqv) there was a pause while the weather deteriorated and Wellington waited for news of the Allies. Wellington planned a crossing of the Adour River below Bayonne, and thus he needed to drive Soult away to the east. On 14 February he was ready, and by manoeuvring against Soult's left he was able to achieve his aim.

On the morning of 16 February Soult ordered a retreat to the line Peyrehorade-Sauveterre-Navarreux, and began to concentrate his forces, but on the 18th the weather broke and the advance halted for four days. When the advance recommenced Soult's new line was easily penetrated, and he fell back to the town of Orthez on the east bank of the Gava de Pau. On 27 February Wellington was ready to attack. Lt-General Sir Rowland Hill was to demonstrate against the town, and the French left, while preparing to cross the river. Marshal Sir William Beresford, who was already across the river, was to attack the French right, with two divisions going up one spur, and two up another. The left of these two attacks was originally intended if the main one failed, but Wellington changed his plan: the right attack was to be pruned, while the 1/52nd was to attack diagonally up the re-entrant. These attacks succeeded, Hill forced the crossings, and Soult retreated. The Allied pursuit lacked penetration, possibly because Wellington was slightly wounded–for the only time in the war.

The Allied army sustained 2,160 casualties. The French had 4,000 casualties, this number including 1,350 prisoners. Many new recruits deserted.
Result: All connection between the French field army and Bayonne was broken and Soult fell back on Toulouse. Wellington for his part was able to detach Beresford to take Bordeaux.

OSMA (Old Castile, Spain)   Napoleonic Wars/Peninsular War   18 June 1813
Fought between elements of Wellington's Allied army and elements of General Honoré Reille's French Army of Portugal.
Strength: Allies 20,000; French 10,000.
Aim: The French were on a misconceived foray to cover Bilbao as Wellington closed in on their main position at Vitoria (qv).
Battle: Reille was marching from Espejo towards Osma when he discovered that Lt-General Sir Thomas Graham's forces were debouching on Osma from Berberena and the NW. Expecting the arrival of Maucune's Division (see SAN MILLÁN) Reille at first stood his ground. But later, when Lt-General Sir Lowry Cole's 4th Allied Division appeared on Graham's right, he decided to pull out. He threw out his light troops to skirmish and fell back on Espejo. He got away, but his rearguard suffered some loss. The Allies had 60 casualties, the French 120.
Result: The British concentration on Vitoria could continue.

OVIEDO (Asturias, Spain)   Napoleonic Wars/Peninsular War   24 May 1808
When news of the Dos de Mayo (qv) arrived on 9 May, there were riots. Then on the 24th the Asturians, after days of secret preparation, rose. Stirred up by the Marquis of Santa Cruz, President of the Junta General, the principality formally declared war on Napoleon Bonaparte, and ordered a levy of 18,000 men to defend their rugged mountains from French invasion. On 30 May the Junta sent two emissaries (one was the historian Toreño, author of *Guerra de la Independencia*), sailing in a Jersey privateer, to interest

Great Britain in their rising. They reached London on 7 June and were interviewed by George Canning, the Tory Foreign Secretary, who acted with commendable speed. Five days later the emissaries were told that the Asturias might draw upon England for whatever was required in arms, munitions and money.

The importance in the other provinces of the example of the Asturias can scarcely be exaggerated. The province's own resources were but meagre, yet the Asturias had a creditable record throughout the war.

PAMPLONA (Navarre, Spain)   Napoleonic Wars/Peninsular War   1 July–31 October 1813
In the aftermath of the Battle of Vitoria (qv) Wellington took up a position along the western Pyrenees, but two fortresses remained under French control–Pamplona and San Sebastian (qv). Wellington decided to besiege the latter formally, while merely blockading and attempting to starve out the garrison of Pamplona.

Initially the blockade was entrusted to the Army Corps of Lt-General Sir Rowland Hill, but this was to be replaced by other units as they returned from the pursuit of General Bertrand Clausel in eastern Navarre. On 2 July the Spanish troops under General Enrique O'Donnell, Conde de Abispal, became available, and were ordered to replace Hill. It took eleven days for the Army of the Reserve of Andalusia to arrive, and finally on 12 July its 11,000 men replaced Hill.

To cover the blockade Allied troops were placed along the passes of the Pyrenees, and it was these troops who were to repel the French efforts to relieve the fortresses at the Battles of the Pyrenees (qv), which brought fighting close to Pamplona, at Sorauren (qv), and later battles.

There had always been a shortage of supplies in Pamplona, and steadily starvation gripped the garrison. Early in October a letter from General Cassan to Marshal Nicolas-Jean de Dieu Soult was captured, which announced that he could hardly last beyond 25 October. As that date approached, Cassan tried to obtain honourable terms by threatening to blow up the fortifications. But General Carlos d'España, now commanding the blockading force, was ordered by Wellington to reply by threatening to shoot all officers, NCOs and 10 per cent of the garrison. On the 25th Cassan sent out a flag of truce, but negotiations broke down angrily, and Cassan charged his mines. On 27 October Wellington ordered preparations for an attack. On the 30th Cassan agreed to surrender and go to England, if his men could march out with the honours of war. On the 31st his famished men staggered out, and Wellington was free to plan his invasion of France.

PENISCOLA (Valencia, Spain)   Napoleonic Wars/Peninsular War   20 January–2 February 1812
Fought between a French army under Marshal Louis-Gabriel Suchet and a Spanish garrison under General García Navarro.
Strength: French 2,000 (under immediate orders of Severoli); Spanish 1,000.
Aim: Suchet sought to complete his conquest of the Province of Valencia.
Battle: Peñiscola, often called 'Little Gibraltar', a towering rock connected to the mainland by a spit of sand 250 yards long, was one of the most strategically secure places in Spain. On 20 January Suchet ordered General Severoli with four battalions and some siege guns to attack the place. Trenches were opened on 28 January. Although the place was evidently inaccessible and was in easy communication with the sea, when Severoli sent in a summons on 2 February, General Navarro surrendered on very favourable terms. This was simple treachery.
Result: This was Suchet's last success.

POZA DE LA SAL (Old Castile, Spain)   Napoleonic Wars/Peninsular War   10–11 February 1813
Fought between a part of General Palombini's Division of the Army of the North and Spanish guerrillas under Colonel Francisco Longa.
Aim: The 'French' were trying to clear the communications between Vitoria and Burgos.
Battle: On the night of 10 February Palombini fixed his headquarters at Poza de la Sal while sending most of his battalions to look for food. He found himself attacked after dark by three columns. Longa had achieved complete surprise, but Palombini managed to gather his 500 men together till daylight, when his outlying battalions relieved him, and the Spanish disappeared with some baggage and prisoners.
Result: Palombini had had a lucky escape. He returned to Vitoria.

PUENTE LARGA (Madrid, Spain)   Napoleonic Wars/Peninsular War   30 October 1812
Fought between the rearguard of the Allied (Anglo-Portuguese) Army Corps under Lt-General Sir Rowland Hill and the advance of the French army under Marshals Nicolas-Jean de Dieu Soult and Jean-Baptiste Jourdan, and King Joseph Bonaparte.

Strength: British/Portuguese 4,000 with 6 guns; French 5,000 with 6 guns.

Aim: The Allied rearguard was fighting to secure the retreat of Hill's Corps.

Battle: The Jarama River is crossed by the Puente Larga–an immense structure of 16 arches. An attempt had been made to destroy one of the arches, but the 2 mines set off on the morning of 30 October had left a portion of the bridge intact. Therefore a breastwork had been built. Behind this Colonel John Skerrett, the rearguard commander, had placed two companies, the 95th Rifles and part of the 2/47th Infantry, while the rest of the 2/47th and the 2/87th were in support. Three Portuguese guns were also there, while the other 3 guns of the battery, the 3/1st Footguards and the 20th Portuguese Infantry, were half a mile to the rear.

The morning was misty, and from 9am rain fell steadily. Soult sent Reymond's Division forward and an artillery duel ensued for some hours, until the Portuguese ran out of ammunition. Then the French twice attempted to storm the bridge, but were repulsed both times. After dark Skerrett withdrew quietly.

The Allies had 63 casualties, the French 100.

Result: A successful rearguard action. The Allies got a good start in their retreat.

PUIGCERDA (Cerdagne, France)   Napoleonic Wars/Peninsular War   29 October–2 November 1811
General Luis Lacy, commanding the Spaniards in Catalonia, finding that the passes of the Pyrenees were thinly manned, sent General Baron Eroles with 3,000 men to raid the valleys of the Cerdagne. He defeated two battalions of the French National Guard and got away with thousands of sheep and cattle, having levied large money contributions from the villages. Napoleon, incensed by this raid, which he called an 'insult', was compelled to send more National Guards to guard the Pyrenees.

PYRENEES (Franco-Spanish frontier)   Napoleonic Wars/Peninsular War   25 July–2 August 1813
Fought between the Anglo/Spanish/Portuguese army under Wellington and the French under Marshal Nicolas-Jean de Dieu Soult.

Battle: After the Battle of Vitoria (qv) King Joseph Bonaparte's armies were expelled from Spain, leaving behind the fortresses of San Sebastian and Pamplona (qqv). Wellington could not move forward until these two places had been captured and he had heard that the war in Germany had been resumed. He took up a position along the line of the frontier. The sector from the sea along the Bidassoa River was occupied by Lt-General Sir Thomas Graham's Corps (1st British and 5th Anglo-Portuguese Division, Major-General Thomas Bradford's Portuguese Brigade and 15,000 Spaniards), with the job of carrying out the siege of San Sebastian.

To their right the Light and 7th Anglo-Portuguese Divisions held the pass of Echalar and the heights of Santa Bárbara opposite Vera. The centre, the Val de Baztán, was Lt-General Sir Rowland Hill's responsibility, the 2nd Anglo-Portuguese Division, less one brigade holding the Maya Pass, while three Portuguese brigades held the lesser passes farther east as far as Les Aldudes. The right flank was held by Lt-General Sir Lowry Cole, with his own 4th Division, Byng's Brigade of the 2nd Division holding the pass of Roncesvalles (qv) and Morillo's 4,000 Spaniards slightly farther east. In reserve were the 6th Anglo-Portuguese Division at Santesteban and the 3rd at Olague. The bulk of the cavalry, less two brigades on army communication duty, was useless in the mountains and was left at Vitoria. General Enrique O'Donnell's Spanish of the Army of the Reserve blockaded Pamplona, and Francisco Espoz y Mina was near Saragossa (qv) covering the right rear.

This line was obviously overlong, it was always open to the French to throw the bulk of their forces at a few points, and the roads on the French side of the frontier were much better for lateral movements than on the Spanish side. Wellington hoped the forward brigades would be able to hold on long enough in the passes to allow reinforcements to concentrate.

Napoleon heard the news of Vitoria on 4 July, and instantly he sent Marshal Nicolas-Jean de Dieu Soult, Duc de Damatie, to replace, and if necessary arrest, King Joseph and reorganise the army. Soult took command of the army on 12 July, by a mixture of bombastic proclamation and fine administration. He swiftly reorganised it into three corps under Generals Bertrand Clausel, Honoré Reille, and Comte Drouet d'Erlon, with a very strong reserve under General Villatte. Soult planned to throw two of the three corps, Reille's and Clausel's against Cole, while D'Erlon was to storm the Maya. Clausel was to use the old Roman main road, while Reille used a goat-track a little to the west aimed at Linduz. These assaults went in on 25 July. There then followed a week of complicated fighting (see MAYA, RONCESVALLES, SORAUREN, LIZASO-BEUNZA, SUMBILLA, YANZI and IVANTELLY) before Soult was again evicted from Spain, and the Allied position was secured.

French casualties were 13,500 out of 60,000 men, and Allied casualties 7,100 out of 40,000 men actually engaged.
Result: The French attempt to stop Wellington's advance into France had failed.

REDINHA (central Portugal)   Napoleonic Wars/Peninsular War   12 March 1811
Fought between the rearguard of Marshal André Masséna's French Army of Portugal and the advanced guard of Wellington's Anglo-Portuguese army.
Strength: French 5,500 infantry (with another 25,000 within supporting distance but not engaged); Allies 19,250 (British 12,650, Portuguese 6,600).
Aim: The French sought to delay the Allied pursuit.
Battle: On 4 March 1811 Masséna retreated from the Rio Maior position. Wellington went in pursuit but it was not until 10th that the Allied vanguard closed up behind Marshal Michel Ney's Corps at Pombal. After a minor skirmish there on the 11th, Wellington attempted an extensive operation against Ney's rearguard on the 12th. At 5am he moved to attack Venta da Cruz, but Ney had already retired to Redinha, where there is a bridge over the river Soure, with a ridge in front. Wellington did not attack this position until the afternoon, when he attempted to encircle General Julia Augustin Mermet's Division on the ridge. As the flanking attack closed in, Ney fell back across the bridge, losing some men in a traffic jam from the fire of the Light Division's skirmishers. When the Allies crossed and moved forward again, Ney retired without resistance. The Allies sustained 205 casualties, the French 227.
Result: A fine rearguard action. Ney twice got away at the right moment to prevent himself becoming seriously engaged while preventing Wellington from advancing more than 10 miles in twenty-four hours.

ROBRES (Navarre, France)   Napoleonic Wars/Peninsular War   April 1812
As a result of his successes, from 23 to 28 April 1812 the French launched a campaign against Francisco Epoz y Mina.
    Thanks to the treachery of a subordinate guerrillero chief, General Pannetier surprised Mina at dawn, and the latter had a narrow escape. Those of his men who were not killed or captured made a hazardous retreat to the Rioja. Mina afterwards had the pleasure of hanging his treacherous Lieutenant and three local alcaldes, who had failed to warn him of the approach of the French. Even on the run Mina was keeping thousands of French troops away from their field armies facing Wellington.

RODA (Catalonia, Spain)   Napoleonic Wars/Peninsular War   5 March 1812
As part of General Honoré Reille's campaign to consolidate French control of Catalonia General Bourke was sent to destroy General Baron Eroles' men.
    Baron Eroles with 3,000 Catalans took up a strong position, with a torrent bed covering his front, and offered battle. General Bourke, who greatly outnumbered him, made a frontal attack and was repulsed with a loss of 600 men. The French were compelled to turn more troops against the Baron, whose trifling force paralysed half General Reille's army during much of the spring of 1812.

ROLICA (central Portugal)   Napoleonic Wars/Peninsular War   17 August 1808
Fought between a French division under General Henri François Delaborde and an Anglo-Portuguese army under Lt-General Sir Arthur Wellesley.
Strength: French 5,000; Allies 14,500 (British 13,000, Portuguese 1,500).
Aim: Delaborde sought to delay Wellesley's advance on Lisbon long enough to allow General Andoche Junot, Duc d'Abrantes, to concentrate his army.
Battle: Delaborde positioned his troops about the village of Roliça. At 7am the Allied army moved forward with the Portuguese as the right-flank column, four British brigades in the centre, and Brigadier Roland Fergusson with two brigades and some riflemen on the left. As soon as the flanking columns began to press, Delaborde pulled back to a position about Columbeira on a sharp ridge broken by dry watercourses. The Allied deployment was repeated. Wellesley, trying to prevent another French breakaway, decided to press them harder with his centre. He planned to attack up four watercourses, each attack by one battalion supported by another. Fergusson was delayed, the Portuguese never came into action, and one battalion commander, Lt-Colonel the Hon George Lake of the 29th, misunderstood his orders and attacked alone. The result was a minor disaster, Lake was killed, the Commanding Officer of the 9th, the supporting battalion, was mortally wounded, and the two units lost heavily. Wellesley was

forced to order the other attacks to go in at once, Fergusson appeared, and the French withdrew skilfully. However, Delaborde was delayed at the defile of Zambugeira and lost 3 guns.

The British had 474 casualties–the 29th 190 and the 9th 72–and the French 600, Delaborde being wounded, plus the loss of 3 guns.

Result: Wellesley could continue his advance.

RONCESVALLES (Franco-Spanish frontier)   Napoleonic Wars/Peninsular War   25 July 1813
Fought between two 'corps' of the French Army of Spain under Generals Honoré Reille and Bertrand Clausel, and an Allied force under Lt-General Sir Lowry Cole.
Strength: French 35,000; Allies 13,000 (British 5,500, Portuguese 3,500, Spanish 4,000).
Aim: Marshal Nicolas-Jean de Dieu Soult planned to use this pass as the route for his main thrust towards Pamplona (qv).

The French advanced up mountain tracks on a broad front. The Allies, from strong positions, inflicted heavy casualties on the separate French columns which outnumbered them, and then carried out an orderly retreat in the evening covered by mountain mists, to an alternative position at Pamplona. The Allies sustained 600 casualties, the French 1,200.

ROSAS (Catalonia, Spain)   Napoleonic Wars/Peninsular War   7 November–4 December 1808
Fought between the Spanish garrison of the town, and British naval forces in support, and French troops under General Laurent Gouvion-St-Cyr.
Strength: Spanish 1,000 regulars and 2,000 irregulars (Miquelettes), later reinforced by one weak regular battalion+HMS *Excellent, Fame* and *Impérieuse* and 2 bomb vessels; French 11,000 (Reille).
Aim: General St-Cyr was trying to relieve Barcelona, where General Duhesme was being blockaded. However, the main road was blocked by Gerona (qv), so St-Cyr decided to use the coast road. Rosas had to be captured to clear this road.
Battle: Rosas town was protected by a ditch and earthworks; the main strength of the fortress was the citadel, a pentagonal stone work. But it was weakened, for the breach made by the French siege of 1794 had not been repaired. It was hastily patched up by the garrison. A mile to the north Fort Trinity had been built to protect ships lying in the roadstead. It was a curious structure, as it was dominated from 100 yards on the inland side by a ridge. To protect it against this, a broad tower 100 feet high covered the whole inland face of the fort.

The investment of Rosas began on 7 November, with General Honoré Reille's own division opposite the town and Pino's opposite the fort. That day a battalion of Pino's Italians was badly mauled by some local irregulars (Somatenes) while the 2,000 of the garrison sallied out to beat up his camp. Some success was achieved, but part of the raiding party had to be rescued by Captain West and the boats of HMS *Excellent* (74).

Several days' rain then held up the French attack on the town, whose low-lying ground was flooded, but an attempt was made to storm Fort Trinity, which failed.

Reille received his siege guns on 16 November, whereupon he built 2 batteries to force into Trinity, and 1 more, which *Excellent* silenced to bombard the town. On 21 November *Excellent* was replaced by *Fame* (74), and Captain Bennett withdrew his marines from Trinity on 23 November thinking it untenable. At that moment *Impérieuse* (38) (Captain Lord Cochrane) appeared, and Cochrane persuaded Bennett to allow him to reoccupy Trinity. His men had barely got in when another storm was attempted which also failed. Cochrane tried to destroy the battery against Rosas, but his sally failed disastrously.

On 26 November the town was assaulted, and the garrison withdrew into the citadel. Reille built a battery which isolated the town from the ships. Trinity had now been battered for ten days and a breach formed in the tower. However, the French guns were unable to hit the base of the tower, so the breach was 60 feet up the wall. Cochrane built internal fortifications, and a sort of man-trap, which defeated the next assault on 30 November.

The French now turned against the citadel. On 3 December Governor O'Daly launched another sortie, which only achieved limited success, and on 4 December negotiations were opened for surrender. It was impossible to rescue O'Daly, who surrendered with 2,336 men, leaving 400 more in hospital. Cochrane pulled his men out. The Spanish had 700 killed and wounded as well, while the French had 1,000 casualties.

Result: At the cost of one month in his tight two-month schedule to reach Barcelona, St-Cyr's road was open.

SABUGAL (Portuguese-Spanish frontier)   Napoleonic Wars/Peninsular War   3 April 1811
Between portions of the Allied (Anglo-Portuguese) army under Wellington and General Jean Reynier's
Corps of Marshal André Masséna's French Army of Portugal.
Strength: British/Portuguese 30,000; French 10,000.
Aim: Wellington sought to destroy Reynier's Corps, which was isolated from the bulk of the French army.
Battle: Wellington planned to turn the left flank of Reynier's position with the Light Division, while
assaulting frontally with four other divisions. However, 3 April dawned foggy and, while the other
divisions halted and waited for orders, the incompetent Major-General Sir William Erskine, temporary
commander of the Light Division, ordered his men to push on. Lt-Colonel Sydney Beckwith's Brigade,
leading, lost its way and crossed half a mile to the left, but now Erskine halted its support, Colonel George
Drummond's Brigade. Beckwith found himself opposed by two French divisions, which counter-
attacked, but were beaten off. The brigade must have been driven back into the river Coa had not
Drummond ignored Erskine and come to its support. The Light Division now counter-attacked. At this
moment the fog lifted, the main British attack went forward, and Reynier, who had overcommitted
himself against the Light Division, had to withdraw hastily under cover of a heroic rearguard action. The
Allied army sustained 161 casualties, the French 760.
Result: The last French holding in Portugal, save Almeida, was now removed.

SAGUNTO I (Valencia, Spain)   Napoleonic Wars/Peninsular War   23 September–26 October 1811
Fought between a French army under Marshal Louis-Gabriel Suchet and the Spanish garrison under
Colonel Luis Andriani.
Strength: French 18,000; Spanish 2,666 (officers and men, including 150 artillerymen and sappers) with 17
guns.
Aim: Suchet had to take the fortress of Sagunto before he could advance on his main objective, Valencia.
Battle: Sagunto was a fortress of great importance, newly restored by Captain-General Don Joaquim
Blake, the enceinte had been repaired, and new batteries built, but by September 1811 this construction
work was not complete, and very few guns had arrived. Suchet reached Sagunto on 23 September and on
the 27th he decided to attack some of the weakest points. At midnight three columns of 300 volunteers
each pushed towards two gaps in the walls above the town of Murviedro, while a diversion was due to be
delivered against a distant part of the defences. The assault columns did not wait for the diversion and the
Spanish were not surprised. Suchet ordered a withdrawal.
    This failure convinced Suchet he had to wait for his siege train, which was a slow progress because
Oropesa had to be taken first. Oropesa (qv) having been taken, the siege train arrived on the evening of 12
October. By 16th October 5 batteries were set up. By the 18th the French thought they had made a
practicable break. Suchet attacked that evening but failed. Suchet now reverted to systematic battering,
but there was no need for a third assault, for on 25 October a major battle was fought just outside
(SAGUNTO II) and the Spanish relieving army was defeated. The disheartened garrison surrendered on 26
October. The French had 700 casualties; the Spanish of whom 2,300 surrendered, had 100 plus 200 left in
hospital.
Result: The road to Valencia (VALENCIA II) was now open.

SAGUNTO II (Valencia, Spain)   Napoleonic Wars/Peninsular War   25 October 1811
Fought between a French army under Marshal Louis-Gabriel Suchet and a Spanish army under Captain-
General Don Joachim Blake.
Strength: French 12,500 infantry + 1,400 cavalry and artillerymen; Spanish (right wing) 9,000 infantry
+ 1,100 cavalry + 18 guns, (left wing) 16,000 infantry + 1,800 cavalry + 18 guns.
Aim: The Spanish sought to break the French siege of Sagunto.
Battle: Suchet placed his army on the narrow coastal plain and the foothills of the Sancti Espiritus range
just south of Sagunto. He placed the bulk of his men (10,000) in the low ground, putting 4,000 to the right.
Blake's plan was to push his right up the coast road, while his left destroyed the weak French right. On the
morning of 25 October Blake advanced. Blake's best divisions, veterans of Albuera (qv), fighting against
odds, made progress on the right; but on the left, the large force with great superiority of numbers fought
disgracefully. Seven thousand Valencian infantry, with 1,700 cavalry in support, were routed by half their
numbers in ten minutes. The Spanish left had 2,000 prisoners taken and several guns, yet only 400 were
killed and wounded.

On the right the battle hung in the balance for a while, and it was the success of Suchet's last reserve, the 13th Cuirassiers, in breaking the Spanish cavalry which turned the day. The two Spanish infantry divisions began to make a fighting withdrawal, but in the end they were broken and destroyed. In all, Spanish casualties were 1,000 killed and wounded, and in addition they had 4,461 prisoners and several guns taken. The French sustained 1,000 casualties.

Result: The garrison of Sagunto, who could see the battle, were much disheartened, and on 26 October surrendered (SAGUNTO I).

SAHAGON (Castile, Spain)   Napoleonic Wars/Peninsular War   21 December 1808
Fought between a British cavalry force under Lt-General Lord Paget (later Marquess of Anglesey) and a French cavalry force under General Debelle.
Strength: British 1,200 cavalry + 4 guns; French 800 cavalry.
Aim: This action was the extreme northern extension of Lt-General Sir John Moore's advance. Paget aimed at the destruction of Debelle's force.
Battle: This small engagement, fought in appalling wintry conditions, saw the surprise and near destruction of the French force. Indeed, if General Paget's plan had been properly executed, the whole French force might well have been destroyed. As it was they had 120 killed and 167 prisoners taken, in contrast to British casualties of 2 killed and 23 wounded.
Result: There was no lasting result to this skirmish, as on 23 December Moore learnt that Napoleon was moving to attack him, and began to withdraw to Corunna (La Coruña) (qv).

ST PIERRE (Gascony, France)   Napoleonic Wars/Peninsular War   13 December 1813
Fought between a French army under Marshal Nicolas-Jean de Dieu Soult, Duc de Dalmatie, and part of the Allied (Anglo-Portuguese) army under the Marquess of Wellington, under the direct command of Lt-General Sir Rowland Hill.
Strength: French 40,000; British/Portuguese 14,000 with 12 guns.
Aim: Soult, having failed at the Nive (qv), tried again to exploit the division of Wellington's army.
Battle: Soult used the bridges inside the fortress of Bayonne to switch his men to the west side of the Nive, where General Hill was unsupported, as Marshal Sir William Beresford's men had not been brought back after the battle.

On the night of 12 December Hill's men could hear the rumbling of French transport through Bayonne. However, late that afternoon the Nive had risen suddenly and the bridge of Villafranque had collapsed. Thus the only link between Hill and the bulk of the Allied army was the bridge of Ustarite, which would entail a long march. Hill's position ran from the Nive to the Adour, along a line of low hills beyond two narrow millponds which divided the front into three sectors. The main Bayonne–St Jean-Pied-De-Port road ran through the centre, and this was the most open sector. On the right was open high ground. On the left the area open to attack was limited to a narrow sector, because of the sodden ground and woods. The three sectors were from left to right 400, 900 and 500 yards respectively. Major-General William Pringle's British Brigade, 2nd Division, held the left; on the right was Major-General John Byng's Brigade of the 2nd Division; and the remainder of the 2nd Division, Major-General Edward Barnes's British and Brigadier Charles Ashworth's Portuguese, were in the centre. Major-General Frederico Lecor's Portuguese Division was in reserve. A full French division of 5,000 men attacked Pringle's 1,800, but accomplished little.

On the right the leading British battalion, 3rd Foot (Buffs–East Kents), was 800 yards from its nearest support, and its Commanding Officer, Lt-Colonel William Bunbury, pulled out with unnecessary haste. Soon Byng was heavily engaged. The French attack lacked thrust, but Byng's defence was not clever either, and gradually the British were pushed back.

In the centre the initial French attack by one and a half divisions led to heavy fighting. The two French columns came on steadily. But Ashworth's four Portuguese line battalions halted them. Lt-General the Hon William Stewart, the local commander, fed in his reserves gradually, and for three hours the French were held below the crest. He sent forward the 1/71st, but Lt-Colonel Nathaniel Peacocke the new Commanding Officer panicked, ordered a withdrawal and fled to the rear. Stewart had to re-form them and lead his men forward personally. Stewart had used his last reserve when Hill ordered up Lecor and borrowed two battalions from Byng to launch a counter-attack in the centre. This attack, using every man Hill could find, proved decisive, and the French flanking forces, disheartened by the failure in the centre, also fell back.

Wellington had by now appeared, but refused to take the command, and left Hill to finish his own victory. This he did easily, hardly drawing on the reinforcements who were just arriving. Soult withdrew into Bayonne. Allied casualties numbered 1,773 and French 3,300.

Result: A great triumph for the steadiest and most reliable of Wellington's subordinates. Bunbury was allowed to sell out, and Peacocke was cashiered.

SALAMANCA (León, Spain)   Napoleonic Wars/Peninsular War   22 July 1812

Fought between a British, Portuguese and Spanish army under General the Marquess of Wellington and a French army under Marshal Auguste Marmont, Duc de Raguse.

Strength: Allies 51,939 (incl. staff) with 60 guns (British 25,577 infantry + 3,553 cavalry + 1,186 artillery + 54 guns, Portuguese 17,421 infantry + 482 cavalry + 110 artillery + 6 guns, Spanish 3,360 infantry and cavalry); French 49,000 (incl. staff) with 78 guns (43,000 infantry + 3,500 cavalry).

Aim: Wellington was looking for an opportunity to inflict an inexpensive defeat on the French before the French could be reinforced. Marmont for his part was looking for a mistake by Wellington, while pushing him back towards Portugal.

Battle: After the capture of the Salamanca forts (qv) Wellington drove the French army northwards across the Douro River, but Marmont managed to complete his concentration when, on 4 July, General Jean-Pierre-François Bonet's Division joined him. Marmont took the offensive on 15 July and caught Wellington off balance by his brilliant manoeuvres. Wellington ordered a retreat on Salamanca.

On 16 July Wellington received a captured letter King Joseph Bonaparte had written to Marmont promising to come to his aid with 13,000 men. He now knew that there was only limited time in which he could hope to deal with Marmont, before he would be outnumbered and forced back to the Portuguese frontier. During the next few days the armies marched parallel, often only a few hundred yards apart, both generals looking for an opportunity to attack. On the 21st the Allies neared Salamanca and the lead divisions crossed the ford of the Tormes at Santa Marta. The French crossed a few miles up-stream at Huerta.

On the 22nd Wellington placed his army in an L-shaped position a few miles south of Salamanca with his left facing east and the right and centre bending around the key point of the Lesser Arapil to face south. Marmont was not seeking a decisive engagement but was trying to manoeuvre Wellington out of his position by threatening his communications to Ciudad Rodrigo, which ran SW. Marmont had seen the dust of Wellington's baggage train as it moved off, and assumed that he was in the presence of only a strong rearguard. Marmont began to extend his left, led by General Jean-Guillaume-Barthelémy Thomière's Division and General Jean-Baptiste Curto's cavalry brigade. Early in the day Wellington, who knew that this might well be his last chance, attempted to take the Greater Arapil, but he was dissuaded by Marshal Sir William Beresford from making a stronger attempt.

While Wellington was eating his lunch, news came of a gap developing between the extending French left and their centre. He galloped over to his brother-in-law, Major-General Edward Pakenham, who was commanding the 3rd Allied Division, and ordered him to attack. Pakenham's attack began with a 2-mile approach march, mostly out of sight of the French and, while this was being made, Wellington set in motion his main attack. Pakenham was to attack the exposed French left flank, while the 4th and 5th Divisions, flanked by two Portuguese brigades, and supported by the 6th and 7th Divisions, were to strike the French left in front.

The battle began when Brigadier Benjamin D'Urban's Portuguese Dragoons charged the flank of Thomière's Division, followed swiftly by Pakenham. Thomière's Division swiftly broke up. The 5th Division followed up by breaking the squares of Maucune's Division, at which point General John Le Marchant's British Heavy Dragoons, striking between the 3rd and 5th, smashed Maucune's Division and broke up a brigade of General Antoine-François Brenier's before Le Marchant himself was killed, and his cavalry went out of control.

Meanwhile Marmont had been wounded, as had his deputy Bonet, and it was some time before General Bertrand Clausel could re-establish control. He made a valiant attempt to salvage the situation. Brigadier Denis Pack's Portuguese Brigade had been beaten off from the Greater Arapil, and this left the 4th Division's flank exposed. Clausel sent Bonet's Division to attack this flank, but Beresford staved off this attack with Brigadier William Spry's Portuguese Brigade of the 5th Division, although he was wounded in the process.

Then the second wave of the Allied attack went in, the French defence buckled, the Greater Arapil was captured by the 1st Division and the French made off into the night covered by their only intact division,

General Maximilien Foy's. The French were retreating to the angle of the river Tormes, and Wellington, thinking that the castle of Alba De Tormes was held by Spanish troops, ordered the pursuit to go by Huerta. But General Don Carlos D'España had withdrawn his men against orders, so the pursuit missed the target.

British casualties were 3,129 killed, wounded and missing, Portuguese 1,627 killed, wounded and missing, Spanish 6 killed and wounded. The French had 7,000 killed or wounded, as well as having 7,000 men, 20 guns and 2 eagles captured.

Result: The French power in Spain was severely shaken, and Andalusia had to be abandoned in order to drive Wellington back. Meanwhile Madrid was occupied by the Allies.

As a consequence of this battle Wellington was made a marquess. His comment was, 'What the devil's the use of making me a Marquess?' Salamanca was undoubtedly one of his tactical masterpieces, and showed the French that he was more than a defensive general. Foy commented: *'Elle* [Salamanca] *classe Lord Wellington presque à la hauteur du duc de Marlborough'* (It classes Wellington nearly on the level of the Duke of Marlborough).

SALAMANCA FORTS (León, Spain)   Napoleonic Wars/Peninsular War   14–27 June 1812

Fought between portions of Wellington's Allied (British/Portuguese/Spanish) army and French garrisons under Chef de Bataillon Duchemin.

Strength: British/Portuguese/Spanish 5,600; French 800 men with 36 guns.

Aim: Wellington needed to capture these forts before he could continue his offensive, and he hoped to attract Marshal Auguste Marmont into attacking him.

Battle: Salamanca possessed no formal fortifications. However, the French had converted three convents which stood on the high ground in the SW corner of the city into fortresses. To do so they had demolished a large part of the old university quarter of the city. The largest, San Vincente (Vicente), occupied a height overlooking the river; the two smaller, San Cayetano and La Merced, were on another rise separated from San Vincente by a steep ravine, and also overlooked the river.

Wellington had come ill-prepared to besiege convents and was surprised by their strength. The very small battering train he had brought, 4 18-pounder guns with only 100 rounds of ammunition–6 24-pounder howitzers were also on their way–proved inadequate. The 4 guns were positioned 250 yards from San Vincente, together with field guns which were borrowed from the navy. The 6th Division had been allocated to do the digging, but they lacked experience in this kind of work, and by daylight on 18 June the battery was only knee-high. King's German Legion marksmen had to be used to keep the French garrison's counter-fire down. On the night of 18–19 June the battery was completed and on the 19th the 4 guns opened fire. On the 23rd fire had to be discontinued because ammunition ran out, and replacements could not arrive until the 26th.

Meanwhile Marmont began to make demonstrations against the Allied covering army at San Cristóbal. However, no heavy fighting ensued, and Wellington would not attack himself.

On 23 June firing continued against the fortifications, in which the remaining 60 rounds of ammunition were used, supplemented by field-gun fire. Attention was now turned on San Cayetano, but when a storm was attempted at 10pm on the 23rd it failed, with 120 casualties out of 400 men.

On 26 June another 1,000 rounds arrived, and battering recommenced, still concentrated on San Cayetano. Many fires were started, but all were put out. However, heavy damage was done. By the morning of 27 June a practicable breach was formed, while a new fire broke out in San Vincente. San Cayetano was about to be stormed, when a white flag was hung out. The French commander attempted to haggle, so the storming party attacked and French resistance collapsed.

Meanwhile as a result of the fire, Duchemin hung out a white flag. But he also attempted to haggle, so the attack went in there too, and the 9th Portuguese Cacavires captured the convent. La Merced was not untenable.

The French sustained 200 casualties and had 600 prisoners taken. Allied casualties numbered 430.

Result: Although this was typical of the rather unsatisfactory nature of his sieges, Wellington was now able to pursue his offensive.

SALINAS PASS (PUERTO DE ARLABAN) (Navarre, Spain)   Napoleonic Wars/Peninsular War   9 April 1812

After eluding a very determined French effort to destroy him in March 1812, Francisco Espoz y Mina, the greatest of the guerrilla leaders, returned to his old haunts in Navarre. On 9 April he surprised an immense convoy escorted by 2,000 French, on the march from Vitoria to Mondragón, in the Salinas Pass. The 7th Polish Regiment, on its way to Russia, lost 500 killed. In addition 150 prisoners were taken, 450 Spanish prisoners were rescued, and enormous booty fell into Mina's hands.

This was one of Mina's most remarkable exploits.

SAN MARCIAL (Franco-Spanish frontier)   Napoleonic Wars/Peninsular War   31 August 1813
Fought between a portion of the French army under Marshal Nicolas-Jean de Dieu Soult and Spanish troops under the command of Wellington.
Strength: French 18,000; Spanish 15,000.
Aim: The French were making a last effort to relieve San Sebastian (qv).
Battle: Soult, well aware of the state of the fortress of San Sebastian, launched another attack on the Allied line. His policy was a simple attack on the Bidassoa River line. This position, which was less than one day's march from San Sebastian, was held by Spanish troops of the Army of Galicia under General Manuel Freire, and Colonel Francisco Longa's Cantabrians. The Spanish were occupying the ridge of San Marcial, which runs parallel to and a mile to the south of the Bidassoa.

In the early morning of 31 August Soult sent two divisions to ford the river, under cover of a fog. The first attack did not wait for a third division which was intended to cross lower down the river, or for its guns. General Freire's troops were well placed on the ridge, and the French units broke formation as they advanced. The Spaniards met the French half-way up the hill, fired a volley and charged. After a brief fight the French were driven back.

By this time the tide had fallen further, so that the 3rd French Division could now cross the river and went forward to the attack, managing to reach the crest and capture a portion of it. Freire sent for help to Wellington, who refused, judging that this local French success could not be sustained, and leaving the Spanish to win the battle by themselves. This they duly did, the French retiring across the Bidassoa. The French suffered 2,500 casualties, the Spanish 1,700.
Result: Soult had failed. San Marcial was an undoubted Spanish victory, as no other troops were engaged.

SAN MILLAN DE LA COGOLLA (Logroño, Spain)   Napoleonic Wars/Peninsular War   18 June 1813
Fought between elements of Wellington's Allied army and General Antoine-Louis Maucune's French Division.
Strength: Allies 5,500 infantry + 1,000 cavalry; French 5,000 infantry.
Aim: Maucune was marching to join General Honoré Reille in his manoeuvre to cover Bilbao, while Wellington was concentrating his army for the Battle of Vitoria (qv).
Battle: Maucune had been ordered to march from Frias to join General Reille, and he went by a short cut, sending his cavalry and guns by the main road through Puente Lara. His two brigades were a considerable distance apart. The first had just reached San Millán de la Cogolla when the King's German Legion cavalry scouts came upon them. The four French battalions swiftly deployed while the leading Allied brigade–Major-General John Vandeleur's of the Light Division–attacked. Maucune began to pull back, and he was being hotly pursued when his second brigade appeared unexpectedly. This brigade started to make off, but its route took it past where Vandeleur was pursuing its counterpart, and thus they came in upon the rear of the 52nd Light Infantry, which wheeled about at the run and charged. The French, seeing themselves between the two lines of the 52nd and Major-General James Kempt's Brigade, scattered in disorder eastwards, joining Reille at Espejo. The Allies sustained 110 casualties, the French 300, and they lost all their baggage.
Result: Maucune's Division was too shaken to take part in the Battle of Vitoria and had to be sent off as the Convoy Guard.

SAN MUNOZ (or LA HUEBRA) (central Spain)   Napoleonic Wars/Peninsular War   17 November 1812
Fought between elements of Wellington's Allied army and elements of the French army under King Joseph Bonaparte, and Marshals Nicolas-Jean de Dieu Soult and Jean-Baptiste Jourdan.
Aim: Soult thought that he had an opportunity to damage the Allies' rearguard as they crossed the Huebra.
Battle: As the Light Division, the Allied rearguard, was about to cross the Huebra, it was attacked by French infantry and had to throw out skirmishers, who held the French while the main column crossed,

when the skirmishers rushed down and crossed under fire. Soult showed signs of seeking to force a crossing, and brought up 4 batteries to shell the Light and 7th Divisions of the Allied army. However, the effect of the bombardment was lessened by the sodden ground and he desisted. The French sustained 220 casualties. British losses were 365–including 178 stragglers picked up individually by the French who were not involved in the fight.

Result: The French failed to inflict serious damage on the Allied rearguard, and had not accepted Wellington's challenge to fight a battle.

SAN SEBASTIAN (Guipúzcoa, Spain)   Napoleonic Wars/Peninsular War   28 June–8 September 1813
Fought between elements of Field-Marshal the Marquess of Wellington's Allied army and a French garrison under General Emmanuel Rey.

Strength: Allies (initially) 4 Spanish battalions + (later) 5th Anglo-Portuguese Division + Major-General Thomas Bradford's Independent Portuguese Brigade + artillerymen and a siege train of 70 guns + (on 31 August) 700 volunteers from other Anglo-Portuguese brigades; French (initially) 3,185 (by 15 August) 2,996, despite 850 casualties, following replacements by sea.

Aim: The capture of this fortress was essential to the preparations for Wellington's projected invasion into S France.

Battle: After Vitoria (qv) Wellington had expelled all French forces from W Spain except the garrisons of Pamplona (qv) and San Sebastian. Wellington halted on the line of the Pyrenees, while he took these fortresses.

The town of San Sebastian stands on a long promontory, with a large rocky hill at the seaward end. An approach along a sandy isthmus would be immensely costly, and the nearest thing to a weak point was on the eastern side of the town, where the walls, washed on this face by the river Urumea, joined the wall facing the isthmus. The breaching batteries were placed to the east to bombard this point.

The town was blockaded on 28 June by Spanish troops under General Gabriel Mendizabal. Lt-General Sir Thomas Graham visited them on 6 July and recommended that they be replaced by better troops. The siege train began to land at Pasajes, 2 miles to the east, on 7 July. First it was necessary to clear the convent of San Bartolomé. After two days' bombardment General Oswald ordered an attack. This failed and after two more days' battering was repeated, successfully, on 17 July. On 20 July the bombardment of the town itself began. On 24 July General Graham ordered an assault to be attempted, but it had to be put off until 25 July. General Emmanuel Rey was thoroughly prepared. The assault was disastrous, 571 casualties being sustained. Owing to Marshal Nicolas-Jean de Dieu Soult's offensive (PYRENEES) the artillery had to be removed to sea again. General Rey, taking advantage of this, launched a sortie on the night of 26–7 July. The French did substantial damage to the siege works and took 198 prisoners.

After the battles of the Pyrenees, the siege was recommenced. The siege train was relaid and battering restarted on 25 August with a salvo of 57 guns, and continued for five days. A storm was ordered for 31 August at 11am, for the foot of the breach was only accessible for two hours on either side of low tide. General Rey had prepared defences behind the breach with great care and, as a result, when the 1,000 men of the storming party moved forward, they reached the top of the breach but could get no farther. General Graham now ordered forward the 700 volunteers from the 1st, 4th, and Light Divisions, whom Wellington had called for after the failure of 25 July, to attack. At the same time a brigade of Portuguese waded across the whole bay and attacked a lesser breach farther to the right. Again no progress was made, but General Graham and Colonel Alexander Dickson, the artillery commander, set the breaching batteries to fire again, against the inner defences, and this remarkable feat of gunnery (the balls had to pass a few feet above the heads of the men at the breaches) cleared a way for the stormers, who forced an entry. The French garrison made good their retreat into the citadel hill. Discipline among the storming troops broke down and the town of San Sebastian was comprehensively sacked, a large part being burnt down.

Rey held out on the citadel hill with his remaining 1,300 men. Bombardments were made on 1, 2, and 3 September, and then Graham sent in a flag of truce. Rey refused to surrender. Further breaching batteries were set up, and on 8 September, after two hours' bombardment, Rey held out the white flag. He and his men deserve much credit for their stubborn defence.

The whole siege cost the Allies 3,700 men. Among the British casualties was Colonel Sir Richard Fletcher, the Commanding Engineer, who was killed. Among the 2,371 casualties on 31 August were two GOCs 5th Division, Generals James Leith and John Oswald, wounded. The French lost 2,000 men, not counting unwounded prisoners.

Result: Wellington now had a secure base, and port.

SANTANDER (Old Castile, Spain)   Napoleonic Wars/Peninsular War   22 July–3 August 1812
Fought between a British amphibious force under Commodore Sir Home Popham, a portion of Juan Diaz Porlier's guerrilla band under Campillo, later joined by General Gabriel Mendizabal against a French garrison under General Dubreton.
Strength: (For the British force see LEQUEITIO)
Battle: On 22 July Popham appeared off the harbour, and Campillo's men invested the landward side. Landing guns, the Commodore entered the harbour after the fire of the castle had been subdued. The French evacuated the castle which was occupied by marines. On 27 July the town was unsuccessfully assaulted, 2 British naval captains being wounded. But Popham and Campillo held on, and on 2 August they were reinforced by Mendizabal, who knew from a captured dispatch that the French planned to evacuate the place. On the night of 2–3 August Dubreton broke out with 1,600 men and successfully joined General Gabriel Caffarelli, who was marching from Vitoria to bring him off. He left behind 18 spiked guns.
Result: Popham now held the only really good harbour between Ferrol and the French frontier, thus providing Mendizabal and the guerrillas with a good base, and communications with the sea.

SARAGOSSA (ZARAGOZA) I (Aragón, Spain)   Napoleonic Wars/Peninsular War   15 June–14 August 1808
Fought between the Spanish garrison and citizenry of Saragossa (Zaragoza) under Captain-General José Palafox, later Duke of Saragossa, and a French force under General Charles Lefèbvre-Desnouettes, later superseded by General Jean-Antoine Verdier.
Strength: Spanish 7,400 (rising to 13,500); French approx 15,000 (6,000 [Lefèbvre-Desnoutte] + 3,500 [Verdier] + siege train and reinforcements).
Aim: The French sought to capture Saragossa, capital of Aragón, focus of resistance in that province and the major block to their progress down the Ebro valley.
Battle: When the insurrection broke out in Aragón, the Patriots found themselves with little but their enthusiasm to use against the French. They sacked their elderly and ineffective Captain-General Guillelmi and replaced him, on 26 May 1808, with a twenty-eight-year-old nobleman, José Palafox, who had no real military experience but was an organiser and a leader.
   Starting with the 1,300 regulars available, by 8 June Palafox organised seven new regiments, 7,400 men, and started a powder factory and small-arms workshops. Eventually he managed to raise 30,000 men. He sent forward a small force under his elder brother Luis Palafox, Marquis of Lazán, but they were routed by the French and driven back towards Saragossa. José Palafox made a stand at Alagon, but again his raw troops were beaten and on 8 June he fell back to the city.
   Saragossa lies in an extensive plain, with the great river Ebro on the north side, and on the east the shallow river Huerba. The city's south and west faces are exposed to attack. It was surrounded by a wall 10–12 feet high, interrupted by convents and barracks, whose outer walls continued the enceinte. The city, with a population of 60,000 in 1808, was a complicated mass of narrow streets and lofty, stoutly built houses, each a small fortress. Outside the city were a number of minor defences, including the Aljafería, a medieval castle 200 yards from the western gate, the Puerto Del Portillo, and, across the Ebro, the suburb of Arrabál. But most important was the 180 feet high Monte Torrero which overlooked the southern part of the city, at a range of 1,800 yards. There had been no time to organise its defence properly.
   When Lefèbvre-Desnouettes appeared before the city on 15 June, he resolved to try to storm the place out of hand. Palafox, disheartened by his defeat at Alagón, and aware of the weakness of the defences, had left the city to raise the province, and thus the French were met by an extemporised defence. The first attack was delivered in the most daring style. A squadron of Polish lancers charged over the defences covering the Santa Engracia gate and rushed into the city, where they were trapped and nearly annihilated. The supporting infantry attack stalled in front of the Santa Engracia Convent. Another attack on the gates of Portillo and Carmen was also beaten back. Lefèbvre-Desnouettes ordered another attack, but that also failed, and the Spaniards, counter-attacking, decimated Lefèbvre's battalions. The French had 700 casualties plus some guns, to the Spanish 300.
   Palafox was surprised by this success and sent Lazán to take charge of the defence, while Lefèbvre pulled back some way and demanded reinforcements. Palafox gathered insurgents from SW Aragón, including a company of 80 Capuchin friars and a troop of mounted smugglers, and marched to cut the French communications. Lefèbvre sent Colonel Chlopiski against Palafox with 3,000 men, while he maintained the siege. Chlopiski defeated Palafox at Epila on 24 June and returned to the siege.

On 27 June General Verdier assumed command of the siege after arriving with reinforcements. He began by attacking Monte Torrero, on which the Spanish had put 2 small batteries, some trenches and 500 men, only half of them regulars. He attacked in three columns aided by a careless workman who exploded the main powder magazine in the seminary of Saragossa, wrecking many houses and starting a big fire. The garrison of the hill fought badly and fled. The Colonel was later court-martialled and shot for cowardice. On 28 June Verdier began to build breaching batteries on Monte Torrero and other places. On 30 June 30 guns, 4 mortars and 12 howitzers began to fire. On 2 July, just as Palafox returned to the city, Verdier attacked along the south and west fronts. But the bombardment had done more damage to buildings than to men and the garrison had gained confidence from the repulse of the first assault. None of the six French columns made a lodgement. The hardest fighting was at the Portillo gate, and it was here that the incident of the Maid of Saragossa, celebrated by Byron, occurred. The artillerymen of the battery were being picked off by French marksmen and, as the French storming column approached, the last was disabled before the loaded guns could be fired. Agustina Zaragoza, whose lover, an artillery sergeant, had just been killed, grabbed his linstock and fired the guns into the head of the advancing French column at 10 yards range. This encouraged the citizenry and the French were beaten off. Palafox gave Agustina a pension for life, and commissioned her sub-lieutenant of artillery, which duties she carried out. The French sustained 500 casualties, the Spanish 400.

Verdier now resolved to try more formal methods, and on 3 July began to construct parallels. He sent troops to blockade the Arrabál suburb. By 15 July his trenches were close to the walls, and the next days were spent fighting over the convents of San José, the Capuchins and the Trinitarians which stood outside the walls between the Carmen and Quemada gates. By 24 July the French had captured them and began to establish batteries. Heavy guns began to fire on 4 August. Within five hours breaches were made and many buildings wrecked, including the hospital. At 2pm Verdier sent three columns (thirteen battalions) forward to attack three breaches. They forced an entry and took 1,000 yards of the walls. Verdier sent in a laconic note, 'Headquarters–Santa Engracia–peace and capitulation', to which Palafox replied, 'War to the knife'. Steadily the French pushed forward towards the centre of the city, suffering and inflicting terrible casualties. But on 5 August news came of General Comte Dupont de l'Etang's surrender at Baylen (qv). Also a reinforcement for Palafox reached Villa Mayor, 7 miles away on the north bank of the Ebro. Palafox joined them; he knew a Valencian division was approaching. Verdier, however, was ordered to hang on for a while, and so he resumed his bombardment with greater intensity so as to fire away as much as possible of the ammunition he would otherwise have to abandon.

On 8 August Palafox attacked the French covering force on the north bank, which was far inferior to him in numbers, and broke through, carrying in an enormous convoy of supplies. Verdier decided to pull out, falling back on 14 August.

Total French casualties were 3,500 men, and Spanish 4,500 men.

Result: The Spanish had held out for two months, and continued to do so even after their city was entered. The French force was not strong enough for its task. The lifting of the siege was one of the most important consequences of Baylen.

SARAGOSSA (ZARAGOZA) II (Aragón, Spain)   Napoleonic Wars/Peninsular War   20 December 1808–20 February 1809
Fought between the citizenry of Saragossa and a Spanish garrison under Captain-General José Palafox, later Duke of Saragossa, and French forces under, successively, Marshal Moncey, Duc de Cornegliano; Marshal Edouard Mortier, Duc de Trevise; General Andoche Junot, Duc d'Abrantes; and Marshal Jean Lannes, Duc de Montebello.
Stength: Spanish 32,000 infantry + 2,000 cavalry (in regular units, many of them newly raised) + 10,000 irregular citizen volunteers with 160 guns; French (initially) 30,000 (3rd Army Corps) + 22,500 (5 Army Corps) + 3,500 sappers and artillerymen with 60 siege guns and 84 field pieces (Commanding Engineer, General Lacoste).
Aim: As in Saragossa I (qv), the French sought to capture the city.
Battle: The Saragossans, after their great victory (SARAGOSSA I), were euphoric, and, for a while, reluctant to devote much energy to the defences of the city. Work was put in hand, but when the renewed French offensive began in November 1808, it was far from complete. After the Battle of Tudela (qv) refugees rapidly reached the city, but Palafox was able to galvanise the citizens into new efforts on the defence works, although the planned defences on Monte Torrero were never finished. On 30 November French forces, advancing from Tudela, appeared before the city. However, Lannes had returned to France and

Marshal Michel Ney was ordered to march into New Castile, which left Marshal Moncey with just 15,000 men of 3 Corps, far too few to undertake a siege. So he fell back to Alagón and waited until Marshal Mortier arrived with 20,000 men of 5 Corps. The French reappeared before the city on 20 December.

The temporary withdrawal of the French and the three weeks' respite improved the citizens' morale and provided a chance to make much more extensive preparations. The defences were reinforced considerably and barricades prepared. A field of fire 800 yards wide round the city was cleared of every obstruction. Palafox carefully accumulated food supplies, ammunition was prepared and, to avoid the explosion which had been so devastating in the first siege, the powder workshops were dispersed. Perhaps the only criticism that can be made of Palafox was that he had put too many of his troops into the city, and there were no forces, except a small division under Lazán, outside the city.

During his halt at Alagón, Moncey had devoted himself to the preparation of siege stores and gathering in heavy guns and ammunition from Pamplona. On 20 December the two marshals moved forward, leaving four battalions as depot guard at Alagón and three more at Tudela to guard their communications. Gazán's Division moved down the north bank while the remainder moved on the city.

The siege falls into three phases: first, 20 December to 15 January, the attack and capture of the two great bridgeheads across the Huerba, the forts of San José and Our Lady of the Pillar; second, 16 January to 27 January, when the French broke through the enceinte; third, 28 January to 20 February, devoted to street fighting. The two marshals decided that their first task was to capture Monte Torrero by storming it. At 8am on 21 December 3 French batteries began to bombard the hill and an hour later the infantry moved forward. Moncey committed twenty battalions to the attack. St March's Valencian Division, which formed the garrison, wavered, abandoned 7 guns, and retreated into the city. Meanwhile, across the river Ebro, Gazán tried to storm the Arrabál suburb but failed after severe fighting and a well-timed counter-attack led by Palafox. Lacoste now decided to attack San José and Our Lady of the Pillar, to the east, with a spoiling attack on the Aljaferia to the west. But before the first parallel could be opened, on 29 December Moncey was recalled to Madrid, and replaced by Junot. 5 Corps was suffering appalling losses from sickness, and by the beginning of January it was down to under 13,000 fit men.

The attack on San José moved faster than that on the Pillar and on 1 January a second parallel was opened. Batteries were ready by 9 January. On 2 January Mortier was ordered by Napoleon to move with one division to Cala Tayud (Calatayud), leaving Junot in charge of the siege. Mortier took with him General Louis-Gabriel Suchet's Division, the strongest in the army, 10,000 men, leaving Junot with only 24,000 for the siege. However, Palafox failed to take advantage of this, sending out only small and ineffectual sallies.

On 10 January the French batteries opened fire on San José and the Pillar. At 4pm on 11 January General Grandjean sent forward seven companies to occupy San José, which they did easily, but the Pillar was not stormed until the night of 15–16 January. Lacoste now connected these two works by a third parallel. It was now necessary to cross the Huerba. On 17 January French batteries in the third parallel opened up on the city wall, doing severe damage. Palafox realised he needed help and sent his younger brother Francisco to Catalonia. More seriously, however, fever had broken out in the city and by 20 January there were 8,000 sick among the 30,000 regular troops. On 22 January Marshal Lannes returned and took over command from Junot. He faced a critical situation, for Francisco Palafox had begun to raise the country and, moreover, sickness was thinning the French ranks rapidly. Lannes decided to draw Mortier's men back, and they were used to attack the levies, and these they smashed at Alcaniz on 26 January, capturing 20,000 sheep and 1,500 sacks of flour. On 24 January the French managed to cross the Huerba. On 27 January the crisis came. The three breaches were practicable and two were stormed at noon that day. At the third the French reached the crest but could get no farther.

Lannes planned to take each block of houses one by one, breaching them formally before sending in the infantry to clear them. The fighting was of a fierceness unparalleled in the Peninsular War, progress only being made by mining through the rubble. Every little block took a day to break up and another to entrench. Conditions in the city were terrible with the population jammed in damp cellars under constant shelling, and sickness increasing. Eventually Palafox fell ill, yet he continued to command from his bed, issuing proclamations whose increasing hysteria is perhaps explained by his fever.

Meanwhile the attack on the suburb of Arrabál was formalised. On 8 February Gazán's men stormed the outlying Jesu Convent. But Lazán and Francisco Palafox had gathered their men. Lannes went out to attack them, but they withdrew. Eventually, on 10 February, the French reached the Coso, Saragossa's main street, and a huge mine was exploded under the San Francisco Convent causing the capture of that key point. By 11–12 February it was clear that the defence was weakening. On 18 February the Arrabál suburb was cleared. The spirit of the defenders collapsed and Palafox, very ill, resigned, handing over to St March. He also sent an aide-de-camp to Lannes to open negotiations. Lannes demanded unconditional surrender. St March was ill-received as Commander after the loss of Monte Torrero and a junta of thirty-three took over. They asked for twenty-four hours to surrender. Lannes gave them two to capitulate. This they did.

On 21 February the 8,000 survivors of the garrison marched out. On the Spanish side 54,000 people died in the siege–6,000 in action, the rest of disease. French casualties numbered about 10,000.

Result: Fanatical courage had delayed the French for three months; equal skill might have delayed them much longer. Palafox was taken as a prisoner to France.

SOMOSIERRA (Castile, Spain)   Napoleonic Wars/Peninsular War   30 November 1808
Fought between French forces under Napoleon and Spanish forces under General San Juan.
Strength: French 6,000 infantry + (initially) 87 Polish cavalry + (later) 1,000 cavalry; Spanish 9,000 with 16 guns.
Aim: Napoleon sought to clear the road to Madrid.
Battle: General San Juan had deployed his guns with a shallow earthwork in front across the head of the Somosierra Pass, with his infantry in support. Napoleon sent forward Ruffin's Division of Marshal Claude Victor's Corps, which, deploying on a wide front in the pass and up the flanking heights, began to work forward. Napoleon, however, disdained such systematic methods, turned to his escort squadron, and ordered them to charge the Spanish guns frontally. This was a suicidal order, as they could only charge 4 abreast, and would, for 400 yards, be exposed to the fire of 16 guns. The Poles, led by Napoleon's aide-de-camp Philippe de Ségur, charged. The result was disaster: of 8 officers (including Ségur) and 80 men, 4 officers and 40 men were killed, and 4 officers and 12 men wounded (the latter including Ségur). The leading riders got to within 30 yards of the guns.

Napoleon now had to await the development of Ruffin's attack, and when this had taken place, General Louis-Pierre Montbrun with 1,000 cavalry cleared the Spanish position.
Result: The road to Madrid was now open.

SORAUREN (Navarre, Spain)   Napoleonic Wars/Peninsular War   28–30 July 1813
Fought between a part of the Allied (British/Portuguese/Spanish) army under the Marquess of Wellington and a French army under Marshal Nicolas-Jean de Dieu Soult.
Strength: Allies (first day) 25,000 (British 12,000, Portuguese 6,000, Spanish 7,000), (second day) 31,000 (British 16,000, Portuguese 8,000, Spanish 7,000); French 35,000.
Aim: Soult sought to capitalise on his success at Roncesvalles (qv), while Wellington tried to prevent the relief of Pamplona (qv) while gathering forces for a counter-attack.
Battle: (first day, 28 July 1813): After falling back from Roncesvalles (qv) Lt-General Sir Lowry Cole took up a position on a ridge in front of Pamplona. Wellington, having made hasty preparations to reinforce this position, himself rode up on to the left front of the Allied position. He was instantly recognised by his Portuguese and then his British troops, who began to cheer. It is said Soult called off an attack, thinking that the cheering meant Allied reinforcements were arriving, not Wellington completely alone.

On the 28th Soult attacked, sending one division to fend off Major-General Denis Pack's 6th Anglo-Portuguese Division, which was arriving in the Ulzana valley, while directing five divisions against the Allies on the ridge. These attacks failed completely, after heavy fighting by the Allies who were outnumbered two to one.

Of the Allied casualties the British numbered 1,358 men, the Portuguese 1,102, and the Spanish 192. French casualties numbered 4,000 men.
Battle (second day, 30 July 1813): On 29 July the two armies remained passive, while Wellington waited for further reinforcements and Soult missed his last chance. On the 30th Wellington, now joined by the 7th Anglo-Portuguese Division, planned an attack. Soult meanwhile made up his mind to retreat, but instead of going back towards Roncesvalles, he decided to go up the Ulzana valley towards the Maya, picking up General Comte Drouet d'Erlon on the way. This movement began before dawn on 30 July, so Wellington flung his men into the assault. Lt-General Sir Thomas Picton's Division stormed up the Agra valley, Cole launched his men down from the ridge, while three columns under Major-General Edward Pakenham (who had replaced Pack, wounded on the 28th) struck at Sorauren. Farther north Lt-General Lord Dalhousie with the 7th Division also went on to the offensive to support this attack. The Allies were still outnumbered, but French resistance did not maintain its old quality. Maucune's Division in Sorauren was

practically wiped out, and the French army was divided. Picton cut the Pamplona-Roncesvalles road, and General Maximilien Foy's Division was forced to pull out to the NE, abandoning all its transport, and shepherding a motley crew of disbanded units. The French divisions in or near the Maya road got away more or less intact. The British sustained 583 casualties, the Portuguese 300, and the Spanish 200. The French suffered 4,000 casualties.

Result: Soult's offensive was smashed, and now he could only make his way back to France as best he could.

SUMBILLA (W Pyrenees)   Napoleonic Wars/Peninsular War   1 August 1813
The Allied pursuit after the Battle of Sorauren (qv) lacked real thrust. But on 1 August Lt-General Sir Lowry Cole's 4th Division caught up with General Bertrand Clausel's men as they tried to escape along the north bank of the Bidassoa River. An hour's confused fighting ensued on the heights above Sumbilla, and involving Taupin's men in the valley below. The French made no serious attempt to stand and managed to get off with 150 casualties, inflicting only 48 on Cole's twelve battalions.

TAFALLA/TIEBAS (Navarre, Spain)   Napoleonic Wars/Peninsular War   9–11 February 1813
Francisco Espoz y Mina, the great guerrilla leader, had received 2 siege guns landed at Deba. He set out to besiege Tafalla, only 30 miles from Pamplona. General Abbé, French Governor of Navarre, set out to relieve Tafalla with 3,000 men. He was met 10 miles from Tafalla at Tiebas, where Mina had four battalions drawn up across the road. Abbé tried all day but failed to break through and had to fall back to Pamplona. The disheartened garrison of Tafalla surrendered on the next day, 11 February. Eleven officers and 317 men surrendered and many had already been killed.

Result: Mina's success set the whole of Navarre alight. On 11 March one of Mina's subordinates, Leguia, stormed and captured the castle of Fuenterrabia within sight of France.

TALAVERA DE LA REINA (Toledo, Spain)   Napoleonic Wars/Peninsular War   28 July 1809
Fought between the British and Spanish Allied armies under Lt-General Sir Arthur Wellesley and Captain-General Don Gregorio de La Cuesta, and a French army under the nominal command of King Joseph Bonaparte and actual command of Marshals Jean-Baptiste Jourdan and Claude Victor.

Strength: Allies 54,000 (British 20,000, Spanish 34,000) with 60 guns; French 40,000 with 80 guns.

Aim: When Wellesley drove the French army out of Portugal, he obtained permission from London to assist the Spanish Patriots to drive the French from the Peninsula. He agreed a plan with General Cuesta and advanced into Spain along the Tagus to join battle with the French. The French aim was to halt the Hispano-British offensive.

Battle: Wellesley had obtained a promise from the Spanish to supply food. When this failed to appear, he halted at Talavera de la Reina. Cuesta, who had advanced too far in front of this position, retired in some confusion to the line indicated by Wellesley, where he fell in on the British right.

Victor, under-estimating the British whom he had only seen in retreat, gambled with a night attack on the left of the British line on the dominating Cerro de Medellín. After some confused fighting, Major-General Rowland Hill, commanding in this sector, gathered reserves and drove the French back. Victor then decided to attack the Cerro again at dawn, with Ruffin's Division, supported by 54 guns. King Joseph and Jourdan disliked the idea but were not strong enough to prevent it. The British infantry, lying concealed behind the crest, stood up as the French approached, fired, charged, and the French fled. After a pause the French launched a co-ordinated frontal attack: 3,000 cavalry watched the Spanish while 34,000 infantry were committed against the British. General Comte Sébastiani, on the left, came nearest to breaking the British line, but was beaten off by Wellesley bringing up the 1/48th infantry, which allowed the Guards Brigade to rally. The third French attack on the Cerro de Medellín was a fiasco, for the French troops were not keen on a project which had failed twice. Only on the very left did the French have any success, for there a British cavalry squadron was ordered to charge the flank of Victor's attack, but got into trouble by trying to gallop across a large ditch. Thereafter the battle petered out and in the night the French withdrew. The British had 5,363 casualties, the French 7,208 as well as the loss of 7 guns. The Spanish casualties are not known.

Result: King Joseph's retreat was not followed up by the Allies. Wellesley's army was exhausted and, on 30 July, Wellesley learnt that Marshal Nicolas-Jean de Dieu Soult with three army corps was coming down on his rear from the north. Cuesta and Wellesley sent Brigadier Robert Craufurd, whose Light Brigade joined him the day after the battle, to siege the bridge of Almaraz. Once there Wellesley could halt, but

Cuesta abandoned Talavera, and all the British wounded. Eventually Wellesley fell back to Portugal. He refused to become involved in any further Spanish plans. He was created Viscount Wellington and Baron Douro after the battle.

TAMAMES (León, Spain)   Napoleonic Wars/Peninsular War   18 October 1809
Fought between a Spanish army under the Duque del Parque and 6 Corps of the French Army of Spain under General Jean-Gabriel Marchand.
Strength: Spanish 20,000 infantry + 1,500 cavalry + 18 guns; French 12,000 infantry + 1,200 cavalry + 14 guns.
Aim: After the Talavera (qv) campaign, the Spanish Central Junta demanded new offensives, based on political rather than on rational military motives. The plan was for a convergent attack by three armies. The Duque del Parque was to command one of them, that of the north.
Battle: On 5 October Del Parque moved from the hills above Ciudad Rodrigo towards Salamanca by the highroad. He reached Tamames the same night, and halted. General Marchand, the temporary commander of 6 Corps at Salamanca, decided to attack. On 17 October he left Salamanca, and on the following afternoon he came up with the Spanish army.

Marchand saw that the Spanish left would be easier to attack. He ordered General Antoine-Louis Maucune's Brigade, six battalions, supported by three cavalry regiments, to attack it. When this assault was well developed, Marcognet's Brigade, six battalions, was to attack the Spanish centre to the east of the village of Tamames, while two battalions of the 25th Léger were to demonstrate against the Spanish right. Maucune forced the Spanish left back, the French cavalry charged and broke the Spanish infantry. The Spanish cavalry attempted a counter-attack but were beaten off. Maucune continued to advance but, coming up against fresh Spanish infantry at the crest of the ridge, his men were halted. Meanwhile the French attack on the Spanish centre stalled, the Spanish counter-attacked and the French only rallied behind their reserves. Maucune then retreated, the demonstration by the 25th was not pressed and the battle ended, the French sustaining 1,400 casualties to the Spanish 713.
Result: The Spanish had achieved their first victory since Baylen (qv). They had superiority in numbers and a good position, but it should be noted that Del Parque's generalship was in glowing contrast to that of some of his colleagues. On 25 October he occupied Salamanca.

TARIFA (Andalusia, Spain)   Napoleonic Wars/Peninsular War   20 December 1811–7 January 1812
Fought between an Anglo-Spanish garrison under Lt-Colonel John Skerrett and Captain-General Francisco Copons and a French force under Marshal Claude Victor.
Strength: Allies 3,400 (British 1,750, Spanish 1,650); French 10,000.
Aim: Marshal Nicolas-Jean de Soult, Viceroy of Andalusia, wished to prevent the spread of insurgency in the province, by destroying General Ballasteros's potential care of Tarifa.
Battle: Tarifa is commanded on all sides by hills, but when the French appeared before the walls on 20 December 1811, their approach march having been delayed by appalling weather, they decided to attack the northern side of the town, where the ground was least exposed to the counter-fire of the defenders. Despite a gale and heavy rain, the French attacked on 29 December and created a breach in the defences. Skerrett prepared to withdraw but he was dissuaded by the Spaniards and his subordinates who thought the defence could be maintained, and then he was delayed by an order from General Colin Campbell at Gibraltar. On 30 December the French had made a breach 60 feet long, but the attack was stopped by a torrential downpour and the garrison was able to make some repairs. Next day the attack recommenced but the French were beaten back by musket-fire. By 3/4 January the French had consumed most of their supplies, and in the barren countryside could get no more. Victor began to withdraw on 4/5 January, and when he reached Béjer the siege was over.
Result: The French lost about 500 men, and much prestige. The battalions were so weak and exhausted as to be incapable of further activity.

TARRAGONA I (Catalonia, Spain)   Napoleonic Wars/Peninsular War   3 May–28 June 1811
Fought between a French army under General Louis-Gabriel Suchet and a Spanish garrison under General Juan Senen Contreras.
Strength: French 15,000 (including 1,400 cavalry + 2,000 artillery + 750 engineers); Spanish (initially) 7,000 (10,000 by 10 May).
Aim: Suchet saw that Tarragona was the key to his approach to the province of Valencia and the conquest of the east coast of Spain.

Battle: Suchet arrived before the walls of Tarragona on the night of 3–4 May 1811 and decided to attack the west front as it was the weakest. But it was first necessary for him to take Fort Olivo which overlooked the area, and to drive away the British fleet from the north side of the harbour, as it might be able to fire into the trenches from there.

On 13 May the French set up a 24-pounder battery which drove the British fleet to the south side of the harbour where it would do little damage. On 29 May Fort Olivo was taken by a determined assault, and direct approaches to the town could begin. On 1 June the final attack on the city, and on Fort Francoli, began. By 16 June the batteries were in position, the French could bombard the city, and damage to the enceinte was done. Meanwhile a diversion staged by General the Marquis of Campoverde and some Spanish Partisans in favour of the city failed in its effect because it was staged too far from Suchet's lines to bother him.

On 21 June Suchet took the lower part of the town by another assault, and thus he closed the harbour to the British. On the 27th a British force under Lt-Colonel Skerrett arrived to help, but judging the situation hopeless they promptly left again. This obviously had a bad effect on the morale of the defenders. On 28 June Suchet attacked the upper town through a breach, and after heavy street fighting resistance collapsed, the French taking the most vicious reprisals against the citizens. The Spanish lost 2,000 killed and had 8,000 taken prisoner. Contreras was captured. French casualties were 924 killed plus 3,372 wounded which, coupled with the sick, made a total of 6,000.

Result: The Spanish lost control of their last major port in NE Spain. Suchet was promoted Marshal for his achievement, and the way was now open for his invasion of Valencia (qv).

TARRAGONA II (Catalonia, Spain)   Napoleonic War/Peninsular War   3–12 June 1813
Fought between an Allied force under Lt-General Sir John Murray and Captain-General Francisco Copons and a French garrison under General Bertoletti.
Strength: Allies 23,000 (Murray's force: [infantry] British, Germans, Italians etc 8,400, Sicilians 1,100, Spanish 4,852 + 740 cavalry + 820 artillery + 24 guns; Copon's force: 7,000 Spanish); French 1,600.
Aim: As part of the diversion plan for his great 1813 offensive, Wellington ordered Murray, commanding at Alicante, to besiege Tarragona, and thus prevent Marshal Louis-Gabriel Suchet from detaching troops to help King José.
Battle: Murray sailed from Alicante under convoy, in a fleet commanded by Rear-Admiral Sir Benjamin Hallowell, on 31 May. His forces arrived off Tarragona on 2 June, disembarking 8 miles from their objective, after detaching a force to capture Fort Balaguer (qv). Murray was then joined by General Copons with 7,000 men of the Army of Catalonia.

The garrison of Tarragona was too weak to interfere with the disembarkation, but maintained itself quietly in the Upper City and 2 outworks, the Fuerte Real, and the bastion of San Carlos, which were intended to prevent the British ships using the roadstead. Murray surveyed the situation as it confronted him on 3 June, and instead of storming the defences out of hand, decided, despite their obvious weakness, to besiege them formally. On 4 June batteries were built under cover of a naval bombardment, and on 6 June these began to fire. Bertoletti expected Murray to try to attack them, but Murray forbade an assault, contenting himself with moving the batteries closer in. Then on the fourth day of the bombardment, Murray, on the advice of his Chief Engineer, Major Thackeray, changed his direction of attack, which could only mean delaying the assault until 21 June. Between 7 and 10 June new batteries were constructed to attack the Upper City.

Meanwhile Murray was working himself into an absurd panic, for both Marshal Louis-Gabriel Suchet and General Charles Decaen, Commander of the French forces in Catalonia, delayed over their preparations, and only General Maurice Mathieu made any aggressive move. Mathieu scraped together 6,300 men from Barcelona and set off to impede Murray. This force was not strong enough, however, and on the night of 12/13 June he withdrew. Murray, despite Wellington's instructions which explained to him, quite correctly, that the French could not gather more than 14,000 men to oppose him, saw overwhelming forces everywhere. On 11 June he rode over to see Copons and, on his return, he read some reports which drained his will to fight. He decided to flee by sea, but even this he could not carry out properly, for he calculated, absurdly, that he had only eighteen hours to complete his evacuation. He filled 12 June with so many orders and counter-orders that guns which had been used by Wellington against Badajoz (qv) had to be spiked and abandoned.
Result: This fantastic tragicomedy was followed by a well-deserved court-martial, in which Murray got off very lightly. However, Suchet did not detach any troops to help King José.

TOLOSA (Guipúzcoa, Spain)   Napoleonic Wars/Peninsular War   26 June 1813
Fought between part of Wellington's Allied (British/Portuguese/Spanish) army under Lt-General Sir Thomas Graham and a French force under General Maximilien Foy.
Strength: (British/Portuguese/Spanish) 30,000; French 12,000.
Aim: Foy, who was unaware of the full results of the Battle of Vitoria (qv), thought King José Bonaparte was marching to join him and decided to make a stand.
Battle: Tolosa is an important road junction. Foy having sent the 'great convoy' on with four battalions under General Berlier, placed de Conchy's Brigade in the fortified town; Bonté's Brigade and St Pol's Italians on a ridge to the SE; his own second brigade on the hill of Jagoz on the same flank nearer the town; Rouget's Brigade on a ridge on the other flank; and General Antoine-Louis Maucune's Division in reserve on the high road behind the town. This was a strong position against a frontal attack.
   Graham recognised this and planned to outflank the position. In the centre the 1st Division, Major-General Denis Pack's Portuguese Brigade, and General Pedro Giron's Spaniards marched up the main road and halted some way off. Colonel Francisco Longa's Cantabrians and General Juan Diaz Porlier's Asturians were sent on a long detour to the right to cut the main road some miles north of the town. A narrower sweep on the same flank was made by Major-General Thomas Bradford's Portuguese Brigade and three battalions of the King's German Legion. One Portuguese battalion and some of Giron's light Companies were to operate round the French right, while General Gabriel Mendizabal was also to demonstrate against the road farther north.
   An indecisive fight took place in the morning between Bradford and Bonté and St Pol. At 6pm firing was heard to the north as Longa and Mendizabal came into action. Graham ordered a general attack which brought on heavy fighting. The Allied attack along the road failed, but Bradford and the KGL made greater progress, forcing the French back against the walls of Tolosa, whence they counter-attacked and escaped. The longer sweeps were now succeeding and Foy ordered a hasty retreat just as the German battalions broke into Tolosa. There was some street fighting, but Foy got away and Graham did not push the pursuit. British and Portuguese casualties numbered 400, and Spanish 200. The French had 600 casualties.
Result: Foy, leaving a garrison in San Sebastian (qv), retreated into France.

TORDESILLAS (Castile, Spain)   Napoleonic Wars/Peninsular War   29 October 1812
Wellington, on his retreat from Burgos (qv), had taken up a position behind the Pisuerga and Douro Rivers. General Joseph Souham sought for a way to force a crossing.
   On 29 October Captain Guingret (6th Léger) with 10 officers and 44 men swam across the Douro, their muskets on a raft. Meanwhile the artillery of Foy's Division covered them by shelling the tower that covered the bridge end. When the swimmers landed they drove away the picket of the Brunswick Oëls occupying the tower, taking 9 prisoners, and the battalion failed to counter-attack.
   This exploit secured the crossing of the Douro for the French, and Wellington was forced to retreat.

TORRES VEDRAS, LINES OF (central Portugal)   Napoleonic Wars/Peninsular War   10 October–14 November 1810
The idea of a line of defence covering the port of Lisbon and the Tagus estuary was not new in 1809, when serious thought was turned by various people to the best way to defend Portugal. In the autumn of 1809 Wellington decided to prepare defences. On 20 October 1809, after a thorough examination of the peninsula of Portuguese Estremadura, and aided by Portuguese surveys, he issued instructions to his Chief Engineer, Lt-Colonel Richard Fletcher, RE, to begin the construction of a line of works to cover Lisbon and the British embarkation point at São Julião da Barra, west of Lisbon. This plan underwent a number of substantial modifications in succeeding months, so that the initial limited number of strong entrenched camps which could aid the fighting of delaying actions became a scheme for a pair of defensible lines stretching from the Tagus to the sea, with a third line around São Julião, and a fourth on the heights south of the river. They were not continuous lines, but instead a series of closed works, 128 by October 1810, and eventually 152. The ground over which they were built was very broken, and there were few routes, only four major ones, by which Lisbon could be approached. The works were designed to block these routes, using the interdependent fields of fire of the cannon they mounted. There forts were accompanied by extensive defence works of other types. Miles of hillside were blasted away to form steeper slopes; streams were damned and inundations created.

But Wellington was not planning a static defence. Instead he allocated only second-line troops, Portuguese Militia and Ordenança, and some Spanish units to hold the forts, with many hundred guns. Meanwhile the engineers improved the lateral communications behind the lines, and elaborate signalling systems, using naval personnel, were prepared, to allow Wellington to switch his field army rapidly in face of any French threat.

In addition the fortresses of Peniche and Abrantes were put in a state of defence, the latter with no guns bigger than 12-pounders, so that if it fell the French would not be provided with a siege train, and the navy provided gunboats to control the Tagus. Thus the French would find themselves in a box, which Wellington planned to have swept clean of supplies. If they attacked, they would find themselves drawn into a battle on very unfavourable terms.

After Busaco (qv) Wellington fell back into his positions, occupying them on October 10. The French arrived on the 11th. Marshal André Masséna realised at once they were too formidable to attack, and although there was some skirmishing, particularly in the sector around Sobral De Monte Agraço, he made no serious attempt to break in. After a month before the lines, on 14 November 1810 Masséna pulled back to a position near Santarem on the Rio Maior. He hung on here while his troops starved and died until 5 March 1811.

Result: The high-water mark of French success in the Iberian Peninsula had been reached. Wellington was secure in Lisbon as long as the British retained command of the sea. While his army was active, the French could not hope to complete their conquest of Spain and Portugal.

TORTOSA (Tarragona, Spain)   Napoleonic Wars/Peninsular War   20 December 1810–2 January 1811
Fought between a Spanish garrison under the Conde de Alacha and a French army under Marshal Louis-Gabriel Suchet.
Strength: Spanish 7,179 (including 600 artillery); French 7,000.
Aim: Tortosa commanded the one land route by which Catalonia communicated with Valencia, and covered a major bridge over the river Ebro. It was necessary for the French to capture it before the siege of Tarragona and the invasion of Valencia could be undertaken.
Battle: The French arrived before the city on 15 December 1810. The weak points of Tortosa were the bastion of San Pedro and the demi-line of El Temple, where the ground was soft and suitable for digging, and not overlooked.

On the night of 20/1 December the French opened their attack on San Pedro and began to dig their parallels. Despite unsuccessful sorties by the Spanish on the night of 28/9 December, French batteries were opened on the 29th, and rapidly silenced the Spanish gunfire. On 2 January a 4-gun battery opened up opposite San Pedro, swiftly making a 15-yard-wide breach, and the French miners reported they were ready to explode their mines. Suchet began to collect his storming columns; but Alacha, who was thoroughly frightened, hoisted the white flag, and Suchet was able to browbeat him into surrender. Nevertheless, firing was still going on at Yriarte, as the Spanish second in command was not informed. It did not cease until Alacha came in person to tell him to withdraw. The town was then sacked by the French. The French sustained 400 casualties. The Spanish had 1,400 killed and wounded, the remaining surrendering.
Result: The way was now open for the siege of Tarragona (TARRAGONA II).

TOULOUSE (Haute-Garonne, S France)   Napoleonic Wars/Peninsular War   10 April 1814
Fought between an Allied (British/Spanish/Portuguese) army under Wellington and a French army under Marshal Nicolas-Jean de Dieu Soult.
Strength: Allies 46,573 (Anglo-Portuguese 30,789 infantry [6 divisions] + 3,617 cavalry + 2,250 artillery, staff etc with 46 guns; Spanish 9,917 [1½ infantry divisions]); French 42,000 (33,500 infantry + 3,000 cavalry + 5,500 artillery, staff, engineers etc).
Aim: Wellington sought to destroy Soult's army before Marshal Louis-Gabriel Suchet could bring help to his fellow marshal, while Soult used the defence of Toulouse to make a stand.
Battle: After the failure to trap Soult at Tarbes Wellington followed the Marshal's retreat to Toulouse.

The city of Toulouse stands largely on the east bank of the Garonne, with only the fortified suburb of St Cyprien on the west. Two miles below the town the river Ers joins the Garonne, and a similar distance above is the entry of the Ariège. Curving round the north and west of the city is the Canal de Languedoc, from its point of junction with the Garonne. Thus three-quarters of the city is protected by water barriers. The obvious direction of attack was from the unprotected south, but two attempts at bridging from this direction failed, and it was not until 4 April that a bridge was made to the north of the town above the confluence of the Ers and the Garonne. A crossing was made by 19,000 men under Marshal Sir William Beresford, but then the river rose, the bridge broke, and Beresford was isolated for four days, although Soult did not attack.

The key to the defences was the Calvinet ridge between the river Ers and the Canal de Languedoc to the east of the city. Soult built redoubts here, and allocated four divisions to defend the ridge. Another was put into the St Cyprien suburb, to defend the fortifications of the city proper, and a cavalry division under the Marshal's brother Pierre to cover the southern approaches.

Wellington fixed his attack for 10 April, Easter Sunday. Lt-General Sir Rowland Hill was to launch a holding attack against St Cyprien with two divisions. The 3rd and Light Divisions were to threaten the Canal de Languedoc, and, with two heavy cavalry brigades, to act as reserve. The main attack was to be made on the heights of Calvinet, by the 4th and 6th Divisions under Beresford, which had to march down a narrow corridor between the ridge and the river Ers before wheeling to their right to attack. When they charged, the Spaniards under Freire were to attack the northern end of the ridge.

Hill began his assault at dawn, and, without becoming heavily involved, made some progress in street fighting. Lt-General Sir Thomas Picton, with the 3rd Division, had a rush of blood to the head and turned a feint attack into an all-out assault, sustaining 400 unnecessary casualties. Meanwhile, Beresford's approach march, across sodden ploughed fields, took longer than expected. His guns were difficult to move, so he ordered them to unlimber and bombard the northern end of the ridge. Freire mistook this for the beginning of Beresford's attack and sent his men forward. They got up the hill as far as a sunken road, where they stopped. The French sent forward a body of skirmishers who fired down into the milling mass and, despite the gallantry of their officers, the Spanish recoiled, rallying however in the rear of the Light Division.

Eventually Beresford was ready and began his attack. The Spanish also moved forward again, with great gallantry, but they were repulsed. However, Beresford's men reached the crest, and after a pause while the guns were dragged up, began to clear the redoubts, moving northward. After some stiff fighting, only the great redoubt at the northern end remained to be cleared when Soult withdrew his men into the city. The Allied casualties number 4,500, of which Freire lost 2,000 and the 6th Division 1,500. As to the French, Soult admitted casualties of 3,236, including 1,650 wounded men left in Toulouse when he withdrew.

Result: Toulouse would now become untenable as soon as Wellington got his heavy guns on to the crest. At 9pm on 11 April Soult withdrew southwards on the Carcassone road. Wellington was promptly invited into the city by the municipal authorities, and was dining there at 5pm on 12 April when news came of Napoleon's abdication.

TUDELA (Navarre, Spain)   Napoleonic Wars/Peninsular War   23 November 1808
Fought between a French army under Marshal Jean Lannes, Duc de Montebello, and a Spanish army under Captain-General Xavier Castaños.
Strength: French 30,000; Spanish 45,000.
Aim: Napoleon planned the destruction of the Spanish armies and, as part of this plan, Marshal Lannes was instructed to attack Castaños frontally while Marshal Michel Ney was to cut in behind him.
Battle: The Spanish had withdrawn down the Ebro, halting at Tudela. The Spanish position was fairly strong, with its right flank resting on the river Ebro, and most of its front protected by the river Quieles. But the position, stretching $10\frac{1}{2}$ miles, was over-extended. Castaños placed two divisions of the Army of Andalusia on the left in and to the south of the villages of Cascante and Urzante. There was then a gap of about 3 miles to the position intended for the divisions which had camped on the previous night to the north of the Ebro. This was partly on the ridge running south from Tudela, with another division on another ridge west of the town. But these divisions were only crossing the Ebro, and coming into the line as the French approached.

Castaños had no cavalry picquets out. His first warning of impending attack was the arrival of a regiment of General Wathier's cavalry in front of Tudela. Lannes approached in two columns: one, Marshal Bon Andrien Moncey's Corps, along the high road was directed on Tudela; the other, of two cavalry brigades and Lagrange's infantry division, directed on Cascante. The Spanish troops engaged in crossing the Ebro had to occupy their intended positions against the opposition of French skirmishers. But the Spanish left wing did not move to close the 3-mile gap. Castaños rode off to move them, leaving the right wing without an overall commander, as Captain-General José Palafox had ridden off that morning towards Saragossa. Castaños was crossing the gap when he was attacked by French cavalry, and was driven far to the rear. He was unable to reach Cascante, and when he returned to Tudela he found the right wing broken.

Lannes, leaving Lagrange and the cavalry to watch the Spanish left, committed Morlot's Division against Roca's Division forming the Spanish extreme right in front of Tudela, and pushed General Maurice Mathieu's larger division against Generals O'Neille and St March on the ridge south of the town. Both these attacks succeeded. Roca's troops collapsed back into Tudela, and fled down the road to Saragossa. Matthieu succeeded in pushing O'Neille from the ridge. General Comte Charles Lefèbvre-Desnouettes, the overall French cavalry commander, launched Wathier's three cavalry regiments at the junction between St March's and O'Neille's Divisions. Bursting through, these regiments wheeled outwards, and then attacked the Spanish divisions in the flank. The latter broke and fled, some reaching Saragossa, 150 miles away, next day. Meanwhile La Peña, commanding the Spanish troops at Cascante, did nothing. He escaped southwards in the evening.

Casualties sustained by the Spanish right were 3,000 killed and wounded, and in addition 1,000 prisoners and 26 guns were taken. The Spanish left had 200 killed and wounded. The French had 600 casualties.

Result: Ney had been set to march too far and was unable to cut the Spanish line of retreat. The way was now open for the second siege of Saragossa (SARAGOSSA II).

UCLES (Madrid, Spain)   Napoleonic Wars/Peninsular War   13 January 1809
Fought between a Spanish army under General Francisco Venegas and the French 1st Army Corps under Marshal Claude Victor.
Strength: Spanish 9,500 infantry + 1,800 cavalry + 4 guns; French 16,000.
Aim: The French sought to destroy Venegas's army and its threat to the French hold on central Spain.
Battle: General Venegas had taken up a position on a long ridge with the town of Uclés in the centre. Four battalions occupied the town, with eight to the right and six to the left, all in a single line, with only one battalion in reserve. The cavalry and guns were placed in front of the town. This position was absurdly over-extended. The units were in poor shape and had not recovered from their sufferings at Tudela (qv).

Victor ordered one of his divisions (General Ruffin's) to make a detour and attack the Spanish right in the flank. Most of his other division (General Villatte's), was drawn up in front of the town, with the dragoons in the centre and a battery in front. This was only a demonstration, for Villatte's second brigade (General Puthod's) was sent out to take the Spanish line in the flank from its left. This brigade fell on the Spanish flank and rolled it up. Venegas tried to switch troops from his right, then Villatte attacked the Spanish right, his assault having easy success. Venegas's army fled, at which moment they came on Ruffin's Division.

Most of the Spanish cavalry and a few infantry units got away, but of Venegas's 11,000 men, 1,000 had been killed or wounded. Four generals, 17 colonels, 306 other officers and 5,560 rank and file surrendered. Victor lost about 150 men.

Result: Despite their easy victory, the French acted with great savagery. They looted Uclés and shot 69 of its notables. The escort of the prisoners sent to Madrid had orders to shoot all who could not keep up. The orders seem to have been obeyed. This savagery was partly caused by the increasing effect of the Spanish guerrillas against the French lines of communication.

VALENCIA I (E Spain)   Napoleonic Wars/Peninsular War   28 June 1808
The French, still believing in the summer of 1808 that all that was necessary to quell the Spanish was local police actions, sent Marshal Bon Adrien Moncey to subdue the city and province of Valencia. Moncey left Madrid on 4 June. The route he took, which was the more difficult of the two possibilities, surprised the Spanish Captain-General of Valencia, the Conde de Cervellón, who had blocked the other road. Brushing aside weak Spanish forces, Moncey appeared before Valencia and demanded its surrender.

The Junta of Valencia had scraped together three regular battalions and 7,000 Valencian levies, and these made a stand outside the city. It took Moncey a day to push them aside. On the next day, 28 June, Moncey delivered a general assault, but the Valencians determined on a stand. Thereupon Moncey launched two assaults, both of which failed, thus demonstrating, as was frequently to be done, that, while the Spanish were not much use in the open, behind fortifications they were very tough.

Moncey, lacking heavy artillery, could make no progress and, having lost about 1,200 men, realised that he could not stay where he was. He was now in a dangerous position but, owing to the miscalculations of the Conde de Cervellón, he made good his retreat, reaching Madrid on 15 July.

Result: This French failure, coupled with the decisive Spanish victory at Baylen (qv) and the rapidly developing activity of the guerrillas, convinced Napoleon and his generals that more was required than mere police action and indeed that some heavy fighting had to be done.

VALENCIA II (E Spain)   Napoleonic Wars/Peninsular War   25 December 1811–9 January 1812
Fought between the French Army of Aragón under Marshal Louis-Gabriel Suchet and the Spanish Army of Valencia under Captain-General Don Joaquim Blake.
Strength: French 30,000; Spanish 22,000.
Aim: Suchet sought to complete the conquest of the three eastern provinces of Spain by capturing the capital of the third, Valencia.
Battle: After the Battle and fall of Sagunto (SAGUNTO II) Blake pulled his men back to Valencia. Suchet considered himself too weak to strike at once. He decided to summon General Severoli's Division as well as General Honoré Reille's Division from Aragón. The movement of the latter would require permission from Paris, which meant a long delay.

Blake, finding himself unassailed, spent his time strengthening his defensive works around Valencia city, and sent out one brigade under the Conde de Montijo, to support the guerrillas under the 'Empecinado', Juan Martin, and others. They, however, were able to achieve nothing decisive in favour of Valencia.

The eventual French plan for the capture of Valencia involved a large concentration of troops, drawing in not only Reille's and Severoli's troops, but also ordering King José to send troops from the Army of the Centre to Cuenca, and Marshal Auguste Marmont to send troops from the Army of Portugal to replace them. For this latter, two divisions were detached, just at the moment when Wellington was planning to attack Ciudad Rodrigo (qv). Caffarelli also sent some battalions from the Army of the North to replace Reille and Severoli in Aragón. Thus the whole French position in W, N and central Spain was jeopardised in favour of Suchet.

On the night of 25 December Suchet's men moved forward from their start-line north of the city. The city of Valencia stands on the south bank of the river Guadalaviar, a few miles inland from the Mediterranean. The lines Suchet planned to attack were long rather than strong. There was a line of earthworks from the sea to Monte Oliveto which covered the flank of a great entrenched camp south of the city. Thence the line continued up-stream to Manises, a total of 8 miles. Three of the bridges across the Guadalaviar had been left intact, with good defended bridgeheads so that Blake could easily attack northwards.

Habert's Division was ordered by Suchet to march along the coast, Palombini's just west of Valencia, while Generals Harispe and Musnier and the cavalry moved farther up-stream. Reille and Severoli were to extend the French right still farther. Suchet planned the main blow to be struck to the west of the main Spanish position. This plan was carried out, though some Spanish units got away to the south. The only serious fighting was where Palombini tackled one of the defended bridgeheads. The encirclement was successfully completed on the night of 26 December, at the expense of only 521 casualties.

Blake's position was now very difficult, for he knew that 100,000 citizens of Valencia had food for only ten to twenty days. He called a council of war, which voted Valencia untenable, and recommended a break-out. This might have succeeded on the 27 December when Suchet had not completed his blockade arrangements. But when attempted at 6pm on 28 December it failed. Suchet's line was now properly formed. The sortie was directed northwards, but only 600 men escaped. After this Spanish morale began to crack, for next day many deserters appeared in the French camp.

On 4 January the French bombardment began, causing Blake to abandon his entrenched camp the next day. Suchet moved his guns in closer, and on 6 January, after 1,000 shells had been dropped into the city, he sent in a message demanding surrender. Blake refused. The bombardment continued, and on 8 January another Spanish council of war voted for negotiation. On 9 January the city surrendered, and Blake, at his own request–perhaps to save himself from the vengeance of the Valencians–was sent straight to France, where he was imprisoned in Vincennes until April 1814.

Of the Spanish forces, 16,270 regular troops, including 1,500 sick, surrendered with 374 guns.
Result: Suchet was surprisingly favourably received when he entered the city. He imposed a fine of 53,000,000 francs. Nevertheless, although this success marked the high-water mark of the French in E Spain, and Suchet was made Duc d'Albufera for his victory, the diversion of troops from Marmont had allowed Wellington to capture Ciudad Rodrigo (CIUDAD RODRIGO II).

VALLS (Catalonia, Spain)   Napoleonic Wars/Peninsular War   25 February 1809
Fought between French forces under General Laurent Gouvion-St-Cyr and Spanish forces under General Teodoro Reding.
Strength: French 23,000 (13,800 in the battle); Spanish 30,000 (11,000 in the battle).
Aim: The Spanish sought to destroy St-Cyr's forces gathered round Barcelona.
Battle: In the month after Molins de Rey (qv), while there was only outpost fighting in Catalonia, General Reding reorganised his forces. He gradually extended a screen round St-Cyr's forces along a line of 60 miles. He planned a complicated concentric offensive.

Both sides moved on 15 February, St-Cyr striking first at the Spanish left at Igualada on the Upper Llobregat River. On 18 February he defeated these troops, capturing their magazines. Using internal lines he now switched to the Spanish right. Reding gathered his left-wing troops together but, worried about Tarragona, he left General Louis Wimpffen to watch Igualada while he marched back by the high road through Valls. This meant he had to attack General Joseph Souham's Division which was blocking that route. After a night march Reding's advanced guard struck Souham at 6am on 25 February. Souham hastily marched to support his outposts, but his 6,000 men were hopelessly outnumbered and Reding forced open the road to Tarragona. But then he ordered his men to rest.

St-Cyr came rushing over from Pla, where he was blocking the other road. He regrouped Souham's forces, and Reding, realising St-Cyr must have big reinforcements coming up, changed his plan and fell back to the heights of Francoli. When Pino's Division came up, St-Cyr formed his infantry into four brigade columns, with his Italian cavalry betweeen two of them, and his French cavalry on the right wing. The Spanish, as the French came on, fired one tremendous volley and then retreated, sweeping away their second line. Only on the extreme left, where Reding and his staff charged the French cavalry, was there a collision. Reding got away, but with three wounds which eventually proved fatal. The Spanish lost 3,000 men, half of them as prisoners, and the French suffered 1,000 casualties.
Result: The Spanish objective was not achieved.

VENTA DEL POZO (Castile, Spain)   Napoleonic Wars/Peninsular War   23 October 1812
Fought between elements of the French Army of Portugal under General Joseph Souham and Wellington's Allied army.
Aim: The French sought to mop up the Allied rearguard. .
Battle: The advanced guard of the French Army of Portugal, consisting of General Jean-Baptiste Curto's light cavalry division supported by General Antoine-Louis Maucune's infantry division, came upon the British cavalry vedettes at Villa Buniel. The latter retired on their supports–Brigadier George Anson's cavalry brigade, Julian Sánchez's and Marquinez's guerrillas into Anson's flank, causing confusion. Eventually the Venta del Pozo was reached, and Anson was joined by Major-General Baron von Bock's heavy German cavalry in defending a new line behind a watercourse.

At that moment two more French cavalry brigades came up, and Souham ordered them to charge. What followed was not planned by either side. One brigade was unable to find a crossing, while Bock was unable to take advantage of the moment when the French cavalry was jammed in a bridge, because of a mistake which masked his supporting artillery. There followed a very confused mêlée, which was settled in favour of the French, who had more reserves. The Allied cavalry fell back behind Halkett's battalions at Villadrigo, which formed a square and beat the French off. Anson and Bock had by now re-formed their men and covered the further Allied withdrawal.

The Allies had 230 casualties, the French 300.
Result: The Allied army was able to complete its withdrawal behind the Pisuerga.

VENTA DE URROZ (W Pyrenees)   Napoleonic Wars/Peninsular War   31 July 1813
As the French retreated after their defeat at Sorauren (qv) Lt-General Sir Rowland Hill attacked their rearguard under General Comte Drouet d'Erlon. He extended the attack to include Lt-General William Stewart, who unfortunately detailed Fitzgerald's Brigade of the 2nd Division for the attack as this brigade had suffered particularly heavily at Maya (qv), and was only 1,000 strong. They were beaten off with some loss by the 7,000 French rearguard. Stewart then added another exhausted brigade, Pringle's, but they also failed to make any impression. A third attack by Lt-General Lord Dalhousie's fresher 7th Division succeeded in inflicting more casualties than they received.

VERA (Franco-Spanish frontier)   Napoleonic Wars/Peninsular War   31 August 1813
Fought between elements of the French Army of Spain under Marshal Nicolas-Jean de Dieu Soult and elements of the Allied army under Lord Wellington.
Strength: French 24,000; Allies 12,000.
Aim: In co-operation with Soult's attack at San Marcial (qv) the French sought to relieve San Sebastian (qv).
Battle: Wellington guessed what Soult's strategy would be, as it was initially a copy of that used by the French in 1794. He ordered Lord Dalhousie, GOC 7th Division, to make demonstrations beyond and behind the French left flank to slow it up, while opposing it directly with the Light Division, a Portuguese brigade, and Major-General William Inglis's brigade. General Bertrand Clausel, commanding the French in this sector, advanced cautiously. The other two divisions allowed themselves to be involved in an inconclusive fire fight with Miller's Portuguese and Inglis's brigade.
   At dusk, under drenching rain, Clausel withdrew. The only crossing available to the French was the bridge of Vera. Brigadier John Skerrett, despite the pleadings of his staff, refused to reinforce the single company of 95th Rifles (80 men) who held it unsupported for two hours. Eventually the French main force, 10,000 in all, burst through after suffering 200 casualties. The Allies had a total of 850 casualties, the French 1,300.
Result: Soult had failed to relieve San Sebastian, which was stormed the same day.

VILA VICOSA (Alentejo, Portugal)   Napoleonic Wars/Peninsular War   22 June 1808
As the insurrection against the French spread through Portugal, the citizens of Vila Vicosa besieged the French garrison, one company of the 80th line. General Jean-Jacques Avril marched from Estremoz, drove off the insurgents, and brought away the garrison.

VILLAGARCIA (LAS ROSAS) (Spanish Extremadura)   Napoleonic Wars/Peninsular War   11 April 1812
Fought between the rearguard of General Comte Drouet d'Erlon's Corps of the French Army of the South, and British cavalry under Lt-General Stapleton-Cotton.
Strength: French 3,480 (2 brigades); British 4,000 (1 light and 2 heavy cavalry brigades).
Aim: Stapleton-Cotton, following up Drouet's retreat, sought to destroy his rearguard.
Battle: Stapleton-Cotton came upon Drouet's rearguard under General Lallemand on 11 April 1812. The latter seems to have thought that he faced only Ponsonby's light cavalry brigade, and so he took up a position with his own brigade in front. In fact Stapleton-Cotton's heavy dragoons were working round his left flank. The 5th Dragoon Guards, rapidly deploying, struck the French flank and rolled up the French line just at the moment when Ponsonby attacked. The French retreated in some confusion, rallying on their reserve behind a broad ditch. Stapleton-Cotton, regrouping his men, charged again and drove the French cavalry back to where Drouet's 12,000 infantry were drawn up in front of the town of Llerena.
   The British had 51 casualties, the French 53 killed and wounded, and in addition had 136 prisoners taken.
   This was a fine vigorous action by British cavalry.

VILLA MURIEL (Old Castile, Spain)   Napoleonic Wars/Peninsular War   25 October 1812
Fought between part of Wellington's Allied army and the French Army of the North under General Joseph Souham.
Aim: General Souham sought to force a crossing of the river Carrión, and then to force Wellington to retreat.
Battle: Wellington was occupying the line of the river Carrión. Souham decided to attack the bridges of Palencia, Villa Muriel and San Isidro. The attack on Palencia by two divisions under General Fox succeeded easily. The Galician units in the town were bustled out so quickly that the mine under the bridge was not exploded. The Allies fell back towards Villa Muriel, protected by cavalry.
   Souham took his own division towards Villa Muriel and sent Gauthier's to San Isidro. The mine under the Bridge of San Isidro failed to destroy the bridge properly and the French managed to rush it, but failed to break out of their bridgehead. The bridge of Villa Muriel was effectively destroyed. Souham lined the river-bank and looked for fords. At 3pm a squadron of cavalry crossed undetected at one of the fords, capturing 34 men of the 1/9th (British) Foot. Eight light companies followed. A crossing in force was then made, but the French contented themselves with occupying Villa Muriel.

Wellington decided he had to recapture the village to secure the retreat of the troops from Palencia. He sent forward Losada's Spanish Brigade and Pringle's British Brigade. The Spanish failed and had to be replaced by Barnes's British Brigade with Spry's Portuguese Brigade in support. Villa Muriel was recaptured and the French retreated across the river. They sustained 350 casualties to the Allies' 650.
Result: The line of the Carrión had collapsed. Wellington retreated.

VIMEIRO (central Portugal)   Napoleonic Wars/Peninsular War   21 August 1808
Fought between an Anglo-Portuguese army under the immediate command of Lt-General Sir Arthur Wellesley (later Duke of Wellington) and a French army under General Andoche Junot, Duc d'Abrantes.
Strength: Allies 18,000 (British 16,322 infantry + 240 cavalry + 226 artillery with 16 guns; Portuguese 2,000); French 13,056 (10,405 infantry + 1,951 cavalry + 700 artillery)with 23 guns.
Aim: The British and Portuguese were trying to liberate Portugal, while the French sought to hang on to their few isolated positions in Portugal.
Battle: Wellesley's position covered the bay of Maceira where the brigades of Brigadiers Robert Anstruther and Wroth Palmer Acland landed just in time for the battle. Six of Wellesley's brigades were on the Valongo ridge, which runs at right angles to the sea, SW of Vimeiro village. Two more were on Vimeiro hill, east of the village, facing SE, while one battalion was placed on the ridge to the north.
General Junot decided there was no way over the Valongo ridge, but that his main attack should be through Vimeiro village, to which he allocated two brigades, with a further brigade in support. Another brigade was ordered to make a wide turning movement to the north to come in on Wellesley's flank. Wellesley, seeing the columns of dust raised by the French troops, shifted five brigades from the Valongo ridge to his left flank. Junot attacked Vimeiro before its northern brigade was ready. They eventually drove the British riflemen back, and came upon Lt-Colonel William Robe's artillery, which used the new shrapnel shells with great effect. Both brigades were beaten off by the British infantry. Junot threw in his remaining reserve, 2,000 picked grenadiers. This attack also failed. The Allied cavalry counter-attacked, and, although the 20th Light Dragoons had some initial success, they went out of control and were cut up by the French cavalry.
Junot had realised that Wellesley was shifting forces to his left, and sent a second brigade, the one originally intended to support the first attack at Vimeiro, to attack the British left. No attempt was made to co-ordinate its movements with the other brigade. This second brigade, that of General Solignac, attacked first, and its assault was smashed by Major-General Ronald Ferguson's brigade supported by one battalion of Brigadier Miles Nightingall's. At this point the first French brigade (Brennier) intervened. It attacked two battalions, 71st of Ferguson's and 85th of Nightingall's which were resting in a hollow and guarding captured French guns. They were driven back, but rallied at the top of the slope and, with the 29th as yet unengaged, charged downhill and drove the French back in confusion, wounding and capturing Brennier.
By now every French battalion had been engaged and defeated, while three British brigades had not fired a shot. But Lt-Generals Sir Harry Burrard and Sir Hew Dalrymple, who were senior to Wellesley, had arrived and forbade any pursuit. The Allied army suffered 720 casualties. The French had 1,500 killed and wounded, had 300 prisoners taken, including 3 generals, and lost 14 guns.
Result: The French opened negotiations for the convention later called the Convention of Cintra (Sintra), by which they were evacuated to France in British ships. Portugal was liberated.

VITORIA (Alava, Spain)   Napoleonic Wars/Peninsular War   21 June 1813
Fought between the Allied army under the Marquess of Wellington, Duke of Victoria (Portugal), and of Ciudad Rodrigo (Spain), and the French Army of Spain under King Joseph Bonaparte and Marshal Jean-Baptiste Jourdan.
Strength: Allies 79,062 (British/German infantry 27,372 + 7,424 cavalry + 3,000 artillery with 78 guns; Portuguese 27,569 infantry + 893 cavalry + 300 artillery with 12 guns; Spanish 6,800 infantry + 200 artillery); French 68,024 (52,114 infantry + 10,002 cavalry + 5,868 artillery) with 138 guns.
Aim: Wellington sought to clear the French out of Spain, while the French wanted to gain time for their large convoys to retreat to France.
Battle: Vitoria lies in an oval plain, 7 miles across and 12 long. The Zadorra River runs 2 miles to the north of the city, flowing east to west, to Tres Puentes, where it makes a hairpin bend 6 miles west of the city and then wanders SW to the defile of La Puebla. The hills around the valley are not impassable. The valley was not a good defensive position. The French army deployed with the Army of the South blocking the crest of

the Puebla defile. The Army of the Centre was in the second line, and the Army of Portugal was at the east end of the valley, protecting the exit of the main road, with one division on either side of the river. There was a 6-mile gap between the two wings of the army, and the only reserve was the Royal Guard.

Wellington divided his army into four columns. The left wing under Lt-General Sir Thomas Graham (20,000) was to attack down the Bilbao road, aiming at cutting the French retreat on the main road. On the right Lt-General Sir Rowland Hill's column (20,000) was to force the Puebla defile, and attract French attention. In the centre two columns under Wellington himself and Lord Dalhousie were to cross the Zadorra and attack the bulk of the French army. Hill's attack made slow progress but convinced the French that Wellington intended to work around their left. Jourdan switched troops to the south, away from Wellington's actual assault. The two centre columns found crossings near the hairpin bend of the river and a line of Allied troops formed south of the Zadorra. There was now a pause while Wellington awaited the development of Graham's attack. In this sector fighting was heavy and only one small lodgement was made on the south bank by Colonel Francisco Longa's Spaniards, but this sufficed to cut the main road. When Wellington's main attack went in, the French did not make a proper stand and their retreat rapidly became a rout as they fled up the Salvatierra road, the only one open. However, in and around Vitoria an orgy of looting developed. Among the captures secreted by the Allied troops was all but $100,000 of the $2 million in the French military chest. The Allied pursuit never really got going.

Of the Allies the British sustained 3,675 casualties, the Portuguese 921, and the Spanish 552. The French had 7,999 casualties and lost all but 2 of their guns.

Result: The French kingdom of Spain was at an end, and the French retained only San Sebastian and Pamplona (qqv). They withdrew beyond the Pyrenees and began to reorganise. The Allied victory had most extensive effects. In Germany the war had been halted by the armistice of Pleischwitz (4 June) and the news of Vitoria encouraged the Allies, joined by Austria, to restart the fighting, which led to the decisive Battle of Leipzig (see Section Ten). Vitoria was the first non-Russian victory to be celebrated by an official Russian *Te Deum.*

Among the impedimenta found on the battlefield was Marshal Jourdan's baton. Wellington sent it to the Prince Regent (later George IV), who ordered that he be sent the baton of a British field-marshal in return. This caused some embarrassment at the Horse Guards as there was no such thing. One was hastily designed and Wellington was duly promoted.

YANZI (W Pyrenees)   Napoleonic Wars/Peninsular War   1 August 1813
The advanced guard of the French army endeavouring to escape after the Battle of Sorauren (qv) had to pass the defile of Yanzi. Here General Honoré Reille's men came across Spanish troops from Barcena's Brigade of the Army of Galicia under the temporary command of the one-time guerrilla Colonel Francisco Longa. The French prepared to burst through the small Spanish force, when gunfire began to pour into the flanks of the long French column. The French cavalry panicked and bolted to the rear, where they ran on to the leading infantry causing great confusion.

An infantry battalion attacked, cleared the road, but then pushed on, not leaving anyone to secure the defile. The Spanish returned and resumed their ambush. The clearing operation had to be repeated, but the Spanish had been reinforced and closed the defile again. They held on for two further hours, while all was confusion on the road. At last General Abbé managed to disentangle four or five battalions, and cleared the road block.

The Spanish inflicted 300 casualties on the French, suffering but one themselves. It was a fine guerrilla action by Longa's troops, causing the maximum amount of casualties and delay for the minimum effort.

YECLA (Murcia, Spain)   Napoleonic Wars/Peninsular War   11 April 1813
Fought between the French, consisting of General Harispe's Divison of Marshal Louis-Gabriel Suchet's army, and the Spanish, Genral Mijares's Murcians.
Strength: French 4,500 (1,000 cavalry + 3,500 infantry); Spanish 3,000 (including 1 squadron of cavalry).
Aim: Suchet, puzzled by the inactivity of the Allies, decided to take the offensive and break up Allied detachments.
Battle: General Harispe was sent to attack the isolated Murcian division of General Mijares at Yecla. Mijares was surprised and hopelessly outnumbered. He tried to make off towards Jumilla, but the French cavalry wrecked his two rear battalions, cutting down or capturing nearly all of them. The Spanish had 400 men killed and 1,000 çaptured. French casualties numbered 79 men.
Result: This disaster caused an Allied retreat.

ZORNOZA (Biscay, Spain)   Napoleonic Wars/Peninsular War   29 October 1808
Fought between part of the Spanish Army of Galicia under Captain-Genral Don Joaquim Blake, and the
4th French Army Corps under Marshal François Lefèbvre, Duc de Dantzig.
Strength: Spanish 18,000; French 21,000.
Aim: Marshal Lefèbvre, burning to distinguish himself, determined to attack, despite the French policy of
standing on the defensive while waiting for reinforcements.
Battle: Under cover of a dense fog Lefèbvre's men moved forward in a simple frontal attack. As soon as
Blake realised what was happening, he sent his guns away and, when the ten battalions of General Comte
Sébastiani's division cut through his centre, began to retreat in good order. The Spanish had 300 killed and
wounded and 300 prisoners taken. French casualties numbered 200 men.
Result: Blake got clean away, abandoning Bilbao on 1 November.

SECTION TEN

NAPOLEONIC WARS/EUROPE

BOUNDARIES AS AT 1 APR 1812

| 0 | MILES | 200 |
| 0 | KILOMETRES | 300 |

NORTH
SEA

BALTIC
SEA

DENMARK

SWEDEN

PRUSSIA

COPENHAGEN
16 Aug - 7 Sept 1807

DANZIG
1 Apr - 26 May 1807
Jan - 19 Nov 1813

HELIGOLAND
31 Aug 1807

LÜBECK
5 Nov 1806

Hamburg

STETTIN
30 Oct 1806

Amsterdam

Berlin

GRAND DUCHY
OF WARSAW

GROSSBEEREN
23 Aug 1813

KATZBACH
22 Aug 1813
26 Aug 1813

LEITSKAU (LÜBNITZ)
27 Aug 1813

DENNEWITZ
6 Sept 1813

WARTENBURG 3 Oct 1813
LEIPZIG 12 Oct 1806, 16, 18 - 19 Oct 1813
LÜTZEN 2 May 1813
RIPPACH 1 May 1813
JENA-AUERSTADT
14 Oct 1806
SAALFELD 10 Oct 1806

KOENIGSWÄRTHA
19 May 1813

LOWENBERG
21 Aug 1813

BAUTZEN
20 - 21 May 1813

Breslau

DRESDEN
26 - 27 Aug 1813

KULM
30 Aug 1813

Brussels

Cologne

WATERLOO
18 June 1815

WAVRE
18 - 19 June 1815

QUATRE BRAS
16 June 1815

LIGNY
16 June 1815

F R E N C H

CONFEDERATION
OF THE
RHINE

HANAU 30 - 31 Oct 1813

Prague

AUSTRIA

LAON 9 - 10 Mar 1814
CRAONNE 7 Mar 1814

PARIS
30 - 31 Mar
1814

REIMS 13 Mar 1814
CHAMPAUBERT-MONTMIRAIL
10 - 14 Feb 1814
ARCIS-SUR-AUBE 20 Mar 1814
BRIENNE-LE-CHATEAU 29 Jan 1814
LA ROTHIERE 1 Feb 1814
BAR-SUR-AUBE
27 Feb 1814

MONTEREAU
17 Feb 1814

MORTMANT 17 Feb 1814

E M P I R E

RATISBON (REGENSBERG)
23 Apr 1809

ABENSBERG
20 Apr 1809

ECKMÜHL
22 Apr 1809

ULM
17 Oct 1805

GUNZBURG
9 Oct 1805

LANDSHUT
21 Apr 1809

Münich

HASLACH
11 Oct 1805

ELCHINGEN
14 Oct 1805

EBERSBERG
3 May 1809

AUSTERLITZ
2 Dec 1805

ZNAIM 14 July 1809

HOLLABRUNN
16 Nov 1805

MICHELBERG
16 Oct 1805

WAGRAM
6 July 1809

AMSTETTEN
5 Nov 1805

Vienna

RAAB
14 June 1809

DURRENSTEIN
1 Nov 1805

MARIA ZELL
8 Nov 1805

ASPERN-ESSLING
21 - 22 May 1809

HUNGARY

HELVETIAN
REPUBLIC

SACILE
16 Apr 1809

KM OF ITALY
CALDIERO
30 Oct 1805

Venice

ILLYRIAN
PROVINCES
(Fr)

OTT.
EMP.

Po

FERRARA
12 Apr 1815

ADRIATIC SEA

Marseilles

GOLFE JUAN
1 Mar 1815

(Fr)

Elba

TOLENTINO
2 - 3 May 1815

MEDITERRANEAN SEA

MAIDA 4 July 1806
350 miles

22 The Napoleonic Wars: Western Europe

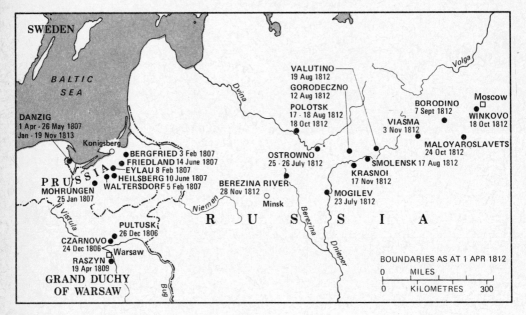

23   The Napoleonic Wars: Eastern Europe and Russia

ABENSBERG (Bavaria, W Germany)   Napoleonic Wars/Europe   20 April 1809
Fought between the French under Napoleon and the Austrians under Archduke Charles.
Strength: French 90,000; Austrians 80,000.
Aim: The Austrians sought to trap Marshal Louis Davout at Ratisbon (qv) (Regensburg).
Battle: Davout, realising Archduke Charles's intention, fought his way SW to join up with Marshal
François-Joseph Lefèbvre's 7 Corps (Bavarian) at Abensberg. Napoleon, on his way from Paris to take
direct command, sent Marshal Jean Lannes ahead with 25,000 men to attack the over-extended Austrian
centre. This Lannes did, cutting the Austrian army of 200,000 in half, one part retreating to Eckmühl (qv),
the other part to Landshut (qv), forced back when their right flank, exposed by the defeat of the other half
of the army, was turned by Napoleon. French casualties were 3,000 killed and wounded. Austrian losses
were 7,000.
Result: The Austrian army was now in two vulnerable halves.

AMSTETTEN (Lower Austria)   Napoleonic Wars/Europe   5 November 1805
Fought between the French, under Marshals Joachim Murat and Jean Lannes, and the Austrians.
Aim: A rearguard action fought by the Austrians who were falling back on Vienna.
Battle: The French, consisting of Murat's cavalry and a portion of Marshal Lannes's Corps, defeated the
Austrians, who had 1,000 casualties–including killed, wounded and those taken prisoner.
Result: Further harassment of the Austrians.

ARCIS-SUR-AUBE (Marne, France)   Napoleonic Wars/Europe   20 March 1814
Fought between the French under Napoleon and the Austrians under Field-Marshal Prince von
Schwarzenberg.
Strength: French 23,000; Austrians 60,000.
Aim: The French sought to halt the Allied advance into France.
Battle: The Austrian army, concentrated between the Aube and Seine Rivers, was attacked by a French
force which struck its northern flank. The Austrians barely managed to hold their ground, despite their
superior numbers; but when Napoleon drew off the Allies pressed forward, having lost 2,500 men. French
losses were 1,700.
Result: The French objective was not achieved, though Napoleon did not lose the battle itself.
   The indestructible Marshal Nicolas-Charles Oudinot was struck full in the chest by a musket-ball, but
the plaque of the Grand Cross of the Legion of Honour deadened the blow and he survived the battle. By
the time he died in his bed aged eighty, he had survived at least twenty-two wounds.

ASPERN-ESSLING (Suburb of Vienna, Austria)   Napoleonic Wars/Europe   21–2 May 1809
Fought between the French under Napoleon and the Austrians under Archduke Charles.
Strength: French 48,000 with 144 guns; Austrians 95,000 with 264 guns.
Aim: When Napoleon occupied Vienna the Austrians did not sue for peace, but instead rebuilt their army
and placed it on the NE side of the city, on the far side of the Danube. Four miles down-stream from
Vienna Napoleon constructed a pontoon bridge into the island of Löbau, on the farther side of the river,
and began to send troops across. By 21 May 23,000 men were across the river, and Marshal André
Masséna's Corps had occupied the village of Aspern, while Marshal Jean Lannes's Corps held Essling.
The Austrians sought to drive them back.
Battle: Archduke Charles attacked the bridgehead, held by the French who were outnumbered by the
Austrians. Nightfall ended this conflict with nothing gained by either side. Under cover of darkness
Marshal Bessières's troops crossed the river and, by the next morning, there were 48,000 men to defend the
bridge and attempt to smash the Austrian army. Lannes assaulted the Austrian centre, but gained no
ground. At the same time all the other forces engaged, neither side succeeding in forcing the other to
withdraw. The early destruction of the bridge stopped French reinforcements and ammunition from being
brought up. The Austrians fell back after a while and began to bombard the bridgehead with most of their
artillery. The French suffered very heavy casualties, but held on until nightfall when they retired to Löbau
Island. The village of Aspern was taken and retaken ten times during the battle. French casualties were
20,000 men, including Marshal Lannes who was mortally wounded (he died on 31 May). Other French
casualties were Generals Comte d'Espagne, killed; Le Blong, Comte de St-Hilaire, mortally wounded, and
Nicolas-Charles Oudinot wounded.

Result: The Austrians contained the French advance. Napoleon lay low for six weeks, building up his forces for another attack.

In 1810 Marshal Masséna was created Prince of Essling.

AUERSTADT   see JENA-AUERSTADT

AUSTERLITZ (Czechoslovakia)   Napoleonic Wars/Europe   2 December 1805
Fought between the French under Napoleon and an Allied army under Czar Alexander I, the Holy Roman Emperor Francis II and General Mikhail Kutuzov.
Strength: French 70,000 with 139 guns; Allies 85,000 (Russians 60,000, Austrians 25,000) with 278 guns.
Aim: Napoleon sought to trap the Allies into battle.
Battle: Having left 20,000 troops in Vienna, Napoleon marched northward and, reaching Brno (Brünn), halted to rest his men. At Olmutz the Allies planned a counter-offensive and began to advance towards Napoleon in late November with the object of attacking his right wing and cutting him off from Vienna. Napoleon, who had occupied a position on the Pratzen plateau 2 miles west of the village of Austerlitz, withdrew his army to low ground and, deliberately deploying his right wing over 2 miles, concealed the rest of his army. The Allies occupied the plateau and, thinking Napoleon's right wing was over-extended, decided to attack at that weak point.

At dawn on 2 December the Russian general Count Friedrich Wilhelm von Buxhöwden advanced with 40,000 men on the 10,500 men of Marshal Louis Davout's 3 Corps, which was placed behind the Goldbach brook. A third of the Allied army was engaged in this assault, with further men marching across the front of the main French body when Napoleon launched his attack. Although the French right wing had been forced back, it had not broken. Marshal Nicolas-Jean de Dieu Soult stormed and took the plateau despite the efforts of Grand Duke Konstantin Pavlovich to bring up the reserve. By 10am the Allied centre had broken. Soult then surrounded the Allied left, which had faced Davout, and rolled it up, driving it back in confused retreat. On the French left wing Marshals Jean Lannes and Jean-Baptiste-Jules Bernadotte (later King Charles XIV John of Sweden and Norway), aided by Marshal Joachim Murat's cavalry, succeeded in breaking the Allied right, despite Kutuzov's efforts to rally his men. During their retreat the men of the Allied army had to cross a frozen lake. French artillery broke the ice in many places, causing many Russians to drown. Allied casualties were 15,000 killed and wounded, and in addition they had 11,000 prisoners taken and lost 185 guns. French casualties were 2,000 killed and 7,000 wounded.
Result: The Allied army was widely scattered and almost completely destroyed.

This battle, also known as the Battle of the Three Emperors, is regarded as a tactical masterpiece. Napoleon regarded the great French victory as a personal triumph, and did not give any of his marshals the title of Duc d'Austerlitz–though Marshal Soult certainly coveted it.

BAR-SUR-AUBE (Aube, France)   Napoleonic Wars/Europe   27 February 1814
Fought between the Russians and Bavarians under the Prince of Sayn-Wittgenstein-Ludwigsburg and General Prince Karl von Wrede, and the French under Marshal Nicolas-Charles Oudinot.
Aim: After Napoleon had defeated the Allies, forcing them to retreat from Troyes beyond the Aube, he went northwards to the Marne valley where Field-Marshal Gebhard von Blücher was threatening Paris. Field-Marshal Prince von Schwarzenberg prepared to take the offensive in the Troyes area.
Battle: Oudinot, occupying a weak position astride the Aube, was attacked by Wittgenstein and Wrede who, with superior numbers, defeated the French. Oudinot fell back to Troyes, pursued by the Allies.
Result: The Allied army once again had the initiative in the area.

BAUTZEN (Saxony, E Germany)   Napoleonic Wars/Europe   20–1 May 1813
Fought between the French under Napoleon and the Prussians and Russians under General Gebhard von Blücher and the Prince of Sayn-Wittgenstein-Ludwigsburg.
Strength: French 115,000; Prussians/Russians 100,000.
Aim: In January 1813 the Prussians defected from the French to join the Russians in order to end Napoleon's domination of Europe. The French had therefore to raise a new army and beat the Allies out of Germany.
Battle: When Napoleon occupied Dresden the Allies fell back east between the Elbe and Oder Rivers, making a stand at Bautzen on the Spree River. Napoleon sent Marshal Michel Ney with nearly half the army on a wide sweep north of Dresden with the intention of surprising the Allies by attacking their flank.

Napoleon himself forced a crossing of the Spree by attacking frontally, beating the Allied front line back and taking the town of Bautzen. The following day Napoleon assaulted the Allied second line, while Ney drove in the Allied flank. Ney, however, did not grasp the full tactical significance of the manoeuvre, and he made no attempt to block the Allies' retreat or to cut off their lines of communication. Wittgenstein was therefore able to draw off in good order and the French did not pursue because they lacked the cavalry to do so. Allied casualties were 15,000 killed and wounded. French losses were 13,000.
Result: The Allies fell back into Silesia where a two-month truce came into effect. At the end of that time, Austria declared war on France.

BEREZINA (BERESINA) RIVER (USSR)   Napoleonic Wars/Europe   26–8 November 1812
Fought between the French under Napoleon and the Russians under Admiral Tchitchakov and the Prince of Sayn-Wittgenstein-Ludwigsburg.
Aim: The Russians sought to annihilate the French army as it retreated.
Battle: During the retreat from Moscow, Russian harassment by Cossacks and guerrillas forced the French north, where the weather conditions and more well-organised guerrillas under General Denis Davidov caused a multitude of casualties. By the time he reached Orsha, 80 miles east of Borisov, Napoleon had only 25,000 men fit for action. At Borisov the French found the Russians holding the bridge over the Berezina (Beresina) River. On 26 November Marshal Nicolas-Jean de Dieu Oudinot's 2 Corps forced a crossing at Studenka, 8 miles north of Borisov. Napoleon contrived to bluff the Russians on the west bank until the last moment, and then the French managed to fight off attacks made by Admiral Tchitchakov. Most of the army was across, with Marshal Claude Victor's 9 Corps holding the bridgehead on the east bank for stragglers, when they were attacked by 40,000 Russians under the Prince of Wittgenstein. On the west bank Oudinot, who was wounded, and Marshal Michel Ney fought desperately to keep the bridgehead open, and by daybreak some of those left on the east bank had managed to cross. The panic of those waiting to go over contributed to the difficulty of the manoeuvre. At dawn, the bridge of boats was blown up and those French left on the east bank abandoned. Most of them were massacred by Cossacks and local Russian guerrillas. Russian sources say 36,000 French bodies were recovered after the thaw.
Result: The French retreat continued and on 13 December the Niemen River was crossed. Ney was said to be the last French soldier to leave Russian soil.
   Russian losses during the campaign were 250,000 men. French losses were 400,000 men, 1,000 cannon and 175,000 horses. France received little help from her allies during this disastrous retreat.

BERGFRIED (N Poland)   Napoleonic Wars/Europe   3 February 1807
Fought between the French under Marshal Nicolas-Jean de Dieu Soult and the Russians.
Aim: The French sought to drive the Russians out of the village of Bergfried, 100 miles NE of Gdansk (Danzig).
Battle: General Jean-François Leval's Division of Soult's Corps attacked the bridge at Bergfried, carrying both it and the village after a short encounter. Russian losses were about 1,000 men.
Result: The French objective was achieved.

BORODINO (USSR)   Napoleonic Wars/Europe   7 September 1812
Fought between the Russians under Field-Marshal Prince Kutuzov and the French under Napoleon.
Strength: Russians 72,000 infantry + 17,500 cavalry + 7,000 Cossacks + 10,000 Militia + 14,300 artillery with 640 guns and howitzers; French 86,000 infantry + 28,000 cavalry + 16,000 artillery with 587 guns and howitzers.
Aim: The Russians sought to block the French advance on Moscow.
Battle: After the French capture of Smolensk (SMOLENSK II), the Russians retreated as far as Borodino, where Field-Marshal Prince Kutuzov ordered a line to be fortified behind the town. On 5 September Marshal Joachim Murat's cavalry found the Russians occupying a strong position on high ground running east to west astride the Moscow road and along the Koltza River to a redoubt on higher ground 1 mile south of Borodino, thence to the village of Ulitza, 1 mile farther south, on the Russian left. Napoleon deployed his troops on 6 September. At 6am on 7 September the French opened an artillery bombardment and Marshal Louis Davout led the assault on the French right. Prince Eugène de Beauharnais, the Viceroy of Italy, led an attack on Borodino. On the right, Davout took Ulitza and some Russian field works, the latter being retaken during the fighting. Having reached Ulitza, however, the French did not progress any

farther. Fighting in the field was hard and evenly matched until Napoleon sent reinforcements to the Semanovsky sector in the Russian centre which drove the Russians back. At 3pm the French carried the field work called the Great Redoubt, but Russian Guards retook it. A French artillery bombardment with 200 guns supported by a cavalry attack enabled them to take it again. Despite repeated Russian counter-attacks the French held the Redoubt until, late in the afternoon, the Russians retreated to a ridge to the rear of the position they had occupied before the battle. The French also retreated to the ground they had held before the battle. Losses on both sides were enormous. French casualties were 30,000, including 14 generals of division. Marshal Davout was among the wounded and Generals Comte Montbrun and Comte de Caulaincourt were killed. Russian casualties were 15,000 killed and 25,000 wounded. Prince Petr Bagration was mortally wounded during the battle.
Result: Napoleon's technical victory enabled him to march on Moscow, which he entered on 14 September. The French pursuit of the Russians after Borodino had not been vigorous because Napoleon was ill.

BRIENNE (BRIENNE-LE-CHATEAU) (Aube, France)   Napoleonic Wars/Europe   29 January 1814
Fought between the French under Napoleon and the Russians and Prussians under Field-Marshal Gebhard von Blücher.
Strength: French 18,000; Russians/Prussians 30,000.
Aim: The French sought to halt the Allied advance into France.
Battle: Taking advantage of Blücher's scattered troops after they had bridged the Rhine to cross into France, Napoleon attacked the Allies and drove them from their positions, taking the Château de Brienne. After nightfall, the Russians attacked the château under General Sacken, but they were beaten back, failing to dislodge the French. Allied casualties were 4,000, French casualties were 3,000 killed and wounded. Marshals Louis Alexandre Berthier and Nicolas-Charles Oudinot were among the wounded. The latter had both thighs grazed by a cannon-ball, but was in action again three days later.
Result: The Allied armies of Blücher and Field-Marshal Prince von Schwarzenberg fell back while a joint offensive was planned. The French occupied La Rothière (qv).

CALDIERO II (Verona, Italy)   Napoleonic Wars/Europe   30 October 1805
Fought between the French under Marshal André Masséna and the Austrians under Archduke Charles.
Strength: French 37,000; Austrians 50,000.
Aim: It was Napoleon's objective to force the retreat of the three Austrian armies of the Holy Roman Emperor, Francis II, each of which was commanded by one of his brothers–Ferdinand, John and Charles. Napoleon himself concentrated on Ferdinand in Germany, Marshal Michel Ney was sent into the Tyrol after John and Masséna was to deal with Charles in Italy.
Battle: Archduke Charles, realising the French intention, attacked the French at Caldiero, 5 miles east of Verona. Masséna beat the Austrians back, but the assault had given the Austrians time to send their baggage train eastward. Charles retired from Caldiero, pursued by Masséna, and fighting only rearguard actions.
Result: The gambit gave Charles time enough to make good his retreat. When he reached the Tagliamento River he halted long enough to cover the Archduke John's retreat from the Tyrol, both armies then continuing their withdrawal into what is now Hungary.

CAPE FINISTERRE III (NW Spain)   Napoleonic Wars/Europe   22 July 1805
Fought between a British fleet under Rear-Admiral Sir Robert Calder and a combined fleet of French and Spanish vessels under Admiral Pierre de Villeneuve.
Strength: British 15 ships of the line; French/Spanish 20 ships of the line.
Aim: The British sought to intercept the fleet returning from the West Indies.
Battle: The British attacked and took 2 enemy ships. Villeneuve made for port, pursued by the British, but Calder lost him the next day owing to fog and light winds. British casualties were 183 killed and wounded; French casualties, 149 killed and 327 wounded.
Result: Villeneuve sailed for Cádiz, where he was reinforced. Calder was censured for his failure to win a bigger victory and court martialled, though he was later cleared and promoted to Admiral.

CHAMPAUBERT/MONTMIRAIL (Marne, France)   Napoleonic Wars/ Europe   10–14 February 1814
Fought between the French under Napoleon and the Russians and Prussians under Field-Marshal Gebhard von Blücher and General Count Hans Yorck von Wartenburg.

Strength: French 35,000 with 120 guns; Allies 110,000 (Russians 35,000, Prussians 75,000).
Aim: Napoleon sought to halt the Allied advance on Paris.
Battle: As Blücher's army advanced in three divisions they became too widely separated to be mutually supporting. Napoleon took the opportunity offered to launch an offensive. He marched rapidly despite difficult conditions and fell on the second of Blücher's corps under General Alsusieff at Champaubert, destroying it. Marching west, he interposed his army between the two corps near Montmirail the following day and attacked General Sacken who, with 20,000 men, formed the van of Blücher's army. Sacken was defeated and forced to retire towards Château-Thierry, abandoning the main road. The other corps was driven west of Montmirail. On the next day Napoleon encountered Yorck von Wartenburg at Château-Thierry with 30,000 Russians and Prussians. This force he attacked and drove out of the town with heavy loss, forcing them back across the Marne. Meanwhile Blücher had come up with the rest of his army, intending to strike the French rear. Marshal Auguste Marmont fought a rearguard action as the French moved from Château-Thierry to Vauchamps, east of Montmirail, while Napoleon marched to Marmont's assistance. Blücher retired, but east of Champaubert he came upon General Emmanuel de Grouchy's Corps. The Allies fought their way through and began to head for Chalons-sur-Marne, Blücher leaving a Russian division at Etoges on the way. The French pursued and almost annihilated the Russians that night. Allied losses were: Alsusieff, 2,000 captured and all guns; Sacken, 6,000 casualties; Yorck, 7,000 men and 20 guns; Blücher, 7,000 men, 16 guns and most of the supply trains. French losses were 2,500.
Result: The offensive was brilliantly deflected by Napoleon who had then to march against Field-Marshal Prince von Schwarzenberg.

COPENHAGEN II (Denmark)   16 August–7 September 1807
Fought between the British under Admiral Sir James Gambier and General Lord Cathcart, and the Danes under General Peiman.
Strength: British 37,000 + 26 ships of the line; Danes 18 ships of the line + 15 frigates.
Aim: The seizure by the British of the Danish navy, of which, under a secret clause in the French-Russian Treaty of Tilsit, Napoleon was entitled to gain possession, thus giving him control of the entrance to the Baltic Sea.
Battle: An expeditionary force of British and Hanoverian troops was landed in Köge (Kjöge) Bight, south of Copenhagen, and began to invest the Danish capital. On 29 August Major-General Sir Arthur Wellesley (later Duke of Wellington) beat off a Danish relief force, following which the British fleet drew in close and bombarded the city for four days. The Danish Crown Prince, Frederick, Regent for the mad King, surrendered two days later, giving the British 18 Danish ships of the line and 15 frigates which would otherwise have fallen into the hands of Napoleon. The British then withdrew. The prize money of the two commanders-in-chief amounted to £300,000.
Result: The British objective was achieved and Napoleon was prevented from using the Danish fleet to control the Baltic. (For COPENHAGEN I see Section 8.)

CRAONNE (Aisne, France)   Napoleonic Wars/Europe   7 March 1814
Fought between the French under Napoleon and the Allies under Field-Marshal Gebhard von Blücher.
Strength: French 40,000; Allies 90,000.
Aim: The Allies intended to make a stand on the Craonne plateau in an effort to stop the French pursuit. Napoleon pre-empted the plan.
Battle: Blücher's attempt to march on Paris had been harassed by repeated attacks on his left flank. Forced to retreat north Blücher decided to make a stand at Craonne while his rearguard, a Russian corps under Field-Marshal Baron Ferdinand von Wintzingerode, enveloped the right rear of the French army. Before this offensive got under way, however, Napoleon sent the corps of Marshals Michel Ney and Claude Victor to attack Blücher's position on the heights. The French carried the position with a bayonet-charge, forcing the Allies back on Laon. Allied losses were 5,000. French casualties were 5,400, and included Marshal Victor, who was wounded.
Result: Napoleon had successfully taken the initiative out of Blücher's hands, but it was an expensive victory, as the French at the time could not easily obtain replacements. Blücher prepared a stand at Laon; the French had failed to trap him at Craonne and his army was still more or less intact.

CZARNOVO (Poland)   Napoleonic Wars/Europe   24 December 1806
Fought between the French under Napoleon and the Russians under General Count Ostermann-Tolstoy.
Strength: French 40,000; Russians 15,000.

Aim: The French sought to drive the Russians out of the town of Czarnovo, 25 miles north of Warsaw.
Battle: With Marshal Louis Davout's Corps, Napoleon crossed the Ukra and made a night attack on the Russians. The French drove Tolstoy out of Czarnovo with a loss of 1,600 and some guns. French losses were 700.
Result: The French gained their objective, and owing to the bitter cold and exhaustion, Napoleon went into winter quarters. His forces were now spread across N Poland and Prussia from the Bug to the Baltic.

DANZIG (GDANSK) II (Poland) Napoleonic Wars/Europe 1 April–26 May 1807
Fought between the French under Marshal François-Joseph Lefèbvre and the Russians and Prussians under General Count von Kalckreuth.
Strength: French 18,000; Russians/Prussians 15,000.
Aim: Though Napoleon had bypassed Danzig (Gdansk) the previous year during his push against the Russians under General Count Bennigsen, the garrison now threatened his left rear. Lefèbvre was sent to reduce the town.
Battle: Lefèbvre cleared the area round Danzig of enemy troops and began to invest the town on 1 April, encompassing a circuit of about 17 leagues. On 12 April an outwork was carried while Bennigsen launched a two-pronged amphibious attack on the French to relieve the city. On 15 May the Russian attack was repulsed and a day later the Prussian offensive collapsed. No further relief was possible and Lefèbvre prepared for an assault on 21 May. Before this date, however, Kalckreuth requested a truce, his garrison having been reduced to only 7,000. On the relief attack, the Russians lost 2,000 men out of 8,000, the French losing only 400.
Result: The garrison surrendered five days later and the way was clear for Napoleon to launch a spring offensive against the Russians at Königsberg (Kaliningrad).
   For his part in the siege, Marshal Lefèbvre was created Duc de Dantzic.

DANZIG (GDANSK) III Napoleonic Wars/Europe January–November 1813
Fought between the French garrison under General Comte Jean Rapp and the Allies under the Duke of Württemberg.
Strength: French 30,000; (10th Corps) Allies 30,000.
Aim: The reduction of the garrison of Danzig (Gdansk) by the Allies. The French were trying to hold the outposts of the Napoleonic Empire.
Battle: After the retreat from Moscow, Rapp returned to Danzig where he was besieged by the Duke of Württemberg. The garrison put up a strong defence, but the siege works were gradually carried by the Allies and the garrison was reduced in strength by exposure and starvation. By the time Rapp surrendered, he had only 18,000 men left.
Result: The Allied objective was attained, and Napoleon's field army was deprived of a valuable corps of veteran troops.

DENNEWITZ (Neubrandenburg, E Germany) Napoleonic Wars/Europe 6 September 1813
Fought between the French under Marshal Michel Ney and the Allies under the former French marshal, Bernadotte.
Aim: The French sought to divert the Allies' attention with a small force while the main army marched on Berlin.
Battle: Ney, in command of the northern French army, had detached a division under General Bertrand to mask Dennewitz while the rest of the men marched round the position and on to Berlin. The screen, however, delayed so long that it was forced into an engagement which compelled Ney to bring up the rest of the army. Bernadotte attacked and routed the French, inflicting upon them 10,000 casualties and a loss of 43 guns.
Result: The Allies prevented the march on Berlin.

DRESDEN (E Germany) Napoleonic Wars/Europe 26–7 August 1813
Fought between the French under Napoleon and the Russians, Prussians and Austrians under the Prince of Sayn-Wittgenstein-Ludwigsburg, General Friedrich von Kleist and Field-Marshal Prince von Schwarzenberg.
Strength: French 70,000; Russians/Prussians/Austrians 150,000.
Aim: The Allies sought to drive the French out of Germany.

Battle: Although lesser French commanders were being beaten back in the north and east, Napoleon concentrated on the defence of Dresden where Marshal Marquis Laurent Gouvion-St-Cyr's 14 Corps was alone facing the 158,000 men of the Allied army. As the Allies approached Dresden from the Bohemian Mountains in the south, Napoleon marched three corps up to the city very quickly. On 26 August, and with three monarchs (Czar Alexander I, Francis I and Frederick William III) watching, Schwarzenberg launched his attack in a great semicircle, both his flanks on the Elbe, north and south of Dresden. Despite the skill of St-Cyr's defence, the French were forced back by sheer weight of numbers, though the Allies lost heavily in the assault. At 5.30pm Napoleon launched a three-pronged counter-attack with the corps he had brought up and by nightfall the weary Allies were driven back to their point of departure. On the following day, Napoleon took the offensive. On the Allied left, Marshal Joachim Murat assaulted and turned the flank which was separated from the rest of the army by the Planen ravine. On the Austrian right, Marshal Edouard Mortier achieved equal success; in the centre, Marshal Jean Moreau also beat the Allies back, though he himself was mortally wounded. The allies retreated back into Bohemia having lost 38,000 men. French losses were under 10,000.
Result: After the battle, Napoleon fell ill and his troops were too exhausted to pursue with any vigour. Only Dominique-Joseph-René Vandamme realised the opportunity and moved rapidly to block the retreating army's line of communication by marching around Schwarzenberg's east flank.

DURRENSTEIN (Lower Austria)   Napoleonic Wars/Europe   1 November 1805
Fought between a French corps under Marshal Edouard Mortier and the Russians under General Mikhail Kutuzov.
Strength: French 12,000 (approx); Russians 40,000.
   During Napoleon's advance on Vienna, a French division under General Honoré-Théodore-Maxime Gazan encountered a large force of Russians and after desperate fighting was in danger of being overwhelmed when the timely arrival of another French division under General Pierre Dupont de l'Etang prevented complete defeat. The Russians lost 4,000 men, and Gazan's Division 3,000.

EBERSBERG (W Germany)   Napoleonic Wars/Europe   3 May 1809
Fought between the French under Marshal André Masséna and the Austrians under Archduke Charles.
Strength: French 50,000; Austrians 30,000.
Aim: The French sought to take the bridge and castle at Ebersberg, 20 miles SE of Munich.
Battle: Masséna's Corps stormed the bridge and carried it. In the ensuing slaughter in the streets of Ebersberg the Austrians lost 3,000 killed and wounded and had 4,000 prisoners and many guns taken before being driven out of the town and castle. The French admitted losses of not more than 1,700 men.
Result: The French objective was achieved.

ECKMÜHL (EGGMÜHL) (Bavaria, W Germany)   Napoleonic Wars/Europe   22 April 1809
Fought between the French under Napoleon and the Austrians under Archduke Charles.
Strength: French 50,000; Austrians 35,000.
Aim: After the Battle of Abensberg (qv), Napoleon sent the bulk of his army after the Austrians at Landshut (qv), thus leaving Marshal Louis Davout with 20,000 men exposed to the main Austrian army. Archduke Charles sought to beat the French.
Battle: Occupying a strong position on high ground above Eckmühl (Eggmühl), Charles Louis attacked rather lethargically, planning to turn the French left flank along the Danube SW of Ratisbon (qv) (Regensburg). By 1pm the French were beginning to waver, but the arrival from Landshut of Marshal Jean Lannes, who counter-attacked the Austrian left, reversed the situation. The Austrian left collapsed and Lannes captured Eckmühl. Marshal François-Joseph Lefèbvre also counter-attacked from the west, so that by nightfall the Austrians had lost the battle. Charles Louis drew his troops off towards Ratisbon in fairly good order, leaving 5,000 prisoners and 7,000 killed and wounded. French casualties were 6,000.
Result: The Archduke Charles was forced to withdraw north of the Danube leaving only a small garrison at Ratisbon, which the French stormed the following day. Both armies now raced towards Vienna.

ELCHINGEN (OBER-ELCHINGEN) (W Germany)   Napoleonic Wars/Europe   14 October 1805
Fought between the Austrians and the French under Marshal Michel Ney.
Aim: The French sought to cut off the Austrians in Ulm (qv).

Battle: Ney's troops repaired the bridge at Elchingen under fire from Austrians in the village. They then stormed and captured the place, including a convent, driving out 20,000 Austrians and taking 3,000 prisoners and a number of guns.
Result: This minor success contributed to Napoleon's overall strategic plan.

EYLAU (NE Poland)   Napoleonic Wars/Europe   8 February 1807
Fought between the French under Napoleon and the Russians and Prussians under General Count Bennigsen.
Strength: French 45,000 with 200 guns; Allies 77,000 (Russians 67,000, Prussians 10,000) with 400 guns.
Aim: The French were making for the Russian position at Königsberg (Kaliningrad), but the Russian commander had launched an offensive, attacking and beating back Marshal Michel Ney's contingents south of the town. Napoleon ordered a counter-offensive from Warsaw.
Battle: Napoleon moved north in order to strike the Russian left flank, cutting them off from Königsberg and their communication line. Alarmed by the rapid concentration of Napoleon's troops at Preussisch-Eylau (Bagrationowsky), Bennigsen retreated northwards towards Königsberg. At Preussisch-Eylau Napoleon deployed his men through the town facing the Russians who held low hills to the east. Napoleon attacked rapidly without awaiting the arrival of the corps of Marshals Ney and Louis Davout, which were expected by noon that day. The Prussian force of 10,000 was also expected by the Russians, but it was held up at Waltersdorf (qv). The battle began with a heavy artillery duel, following which Marshal Pierre Augereau's Corps attacked the Russian centre in a blinding snowstorm. The attack made no impression on the Russian infantry which held its ground, beating the French back with heavy loss. Meanwhile, Davout had arrived and began a manoeuvre to roll up the Russian left. His progress was checked by the arrival of the Prussians under General Anton Wilhelm Lestocq and, even when Ney came up, the French did not succeed in breaking through the Allied front. The engagement continued until nightfall. Fearing encirclement by the French, Bennigsen withdrew under cover of darkness. Both sides lost heavily. French casualties were 20,000 killed and wounded and 10,000 captured. Russian and Prussian casualties were 25,000 killed and wounded (11,000 killed), plus 3,000 men and 23 guns captured.

The 14th of the Line (Augereau's Corps) greatly distinguished itself by its last stand in which 28 officers and 590 soldiers were killed. Augereau's Corps was never reconstituted. The French casualties included 2 marshals wounded–Augereau and Davout–besides 21 generals hit, of whom 8 died. General Comte d'Hautpoul, the celebrated heavy cavalryman, was terribly wounded and died on the 14th.
Result: This indecisive engagement was a check to the Grande Armée. Napoleon drove the Russians out of Ostrolenka a week after the battle, after which both armies retired to winter quarters to refit and bring up reinforcements.

FERRARA (Italy)   Napoleonic Wars/Europe   12 April 1815
Fought between the Italians under Marshal Joachim Murat and the Austrians under General Baron de Bianchi.
Strength: Italians 50,000; Austrians 60,000.
Murat endeavoured to force a passage across the river Po while facing an Austrian army. He was repulsed with heavy loss and forced to retreat south.

FRIEDLAND (Lithuania, USSR)   Napoleonic Wars/Europe   14 June 1807
Fought between the French under Napoleon and the Russians under General Count Bennigsen.
Strength: French 26,000 (initially, increasing to 80,000); Russians 60,000.
Aim: The French sought to prevent the junction of Bennigsen with General Anton Wilhelm Lestocq as the former retreated north.
Battle: Napoleon pushed northwards as part of his spring offensive, forcing Bennigsen before him. As the Russians crossed the Alle River and Friedland, Napoleon sent Marshal Jean Lannes to hold Bennigsen while he concentrated the rest of the French army to the west. Bennigsen attacked Lannes, opening battle at 3am with an artillery duel which lasted until 7am when he assaulted the French with 46,000 men, the rest of his army being in reserve across the river. For nine hours the French withstood the attacks of the Russians under General Prince Petr Bagration. At 5pm Napoleon's main army launched its attack, Marshal Michel Ney's 7 Corps opening the action by assaulting and rolling up the Russian left. When the troops reached Friedland, Ney was halted until the arrival of Marshal Claude Victor's 1 Corps, which reinforced Ney's left flank. Victor's chief gunner then positioned 30 guns at a point-blank range of 120

yards from the village. The village was crammed with Russian troops who suffered great slaughter under the canister and grapeshot thrown at them by the French. Within two hours all the troops in Friedland had been killed, captured or drowned. Darkness ended the fighting at about 10pm. The Russians had been driven back across the river in great disorder, their army shattered.

Russian casualties were enormous; they lost 25,000 killed or wounded, had 10,000 prisoners taken, and an unknown number were drowned when Ney beat the left flank back to the Alle. French casualties were 1,372 killed and 9,108 wounded, plus 55 captured.
Result: Soult occupied Königsberg (Kaliningrad) on 16 June and Czar Alexander I negotiated a truce a week later.

GOLFE-JUAN (Alpes-Maritimes, S France)   Napoleonic Wars/Europe   1 March 1815
At 1pm the brig *l'Inconstant* from Elba entered the gulf, and by 5pm Napoleon and his Guard had landed and were marching on Cannes. This was the beginning of the extraordinary progress which was to bring back the Emperor in triumph to the Tuileries (20 March). His 'Reign of a Hundred Days' followed (21 March–22 June) (see HUNDRED DAYS).

GORODECZNO (USSR)   Napoleonic Wars/Europe   12 August 1812
Fought between the French under General Comte Reynier and their Austrian allies under Field-Marshal Prince von Schwarzenberg, and the Russians under General Alexander Tormazov.
Strength: French/Austrians 36,000; Russians 36,000.
Aim: The Russians sought to block the Allied advance.
Battle: The French attacked the Russians' position and drove them out with a loss of 4,000 men. Allied losses amounted to 2,000.
Result: The French advance was able to proceed.

GROSSBEEREN (E Germany)   Napoleonic Wars/Europe   23 August 1813
Fought between the French under Marshal Nicolas-Charles Oudinot and the Swedes and Prussians under the Crown Prince of Sweden (Bernadotte) and General Baron von Bülow.
Strength: French 66,000; Swedes/Prussians 80,000.
Aim: When Austria declared war on France Napoleon sent Oudinot to take Berlin. The Swedes and Prussians sought to prevent the occupation.
Battle: The Swedes, covering the road through Grossbeeren to Berlin, were beaten back by the French who stormed Grossbeeren, General Comte Reynier's centre corps being the main force behind the move. The Prussians rallied, however, and recaptured the town. Although the divisions of Generals Baron Fournier-Sarlovèse and Baron Guilleminot recovered Grossbeeren, the French were not strong enough to pursue the Allies and they retired with a loss of 1,500 men and 8 guns.
Result: This small Allied victory saved Berlin from occupation, Oudinot withdrawing to Wittenberg, his momentum gone.

GUNZBURG (Upper Danube, W Germany)   Napoleonic Wars/Europe   9 October 1805
Fought between the Austrians and the French under Marshal Michel Ney.
Aim: The French sought to drive the Austrians from three bridges they were holding over the Danube.
Battle: Ney's Corps attacked and carried the three bridges at or near Gunzburg, near Ulm, on the Danube. The Austrians were driven off with a loss of 300 killed and wounded and 1,000 taken prisoner.

HANAU (Hesse, W Germany)   Napoleonic Wars/Europe   30–1 October 1813
Fought between the French under Napoleon and the Bavarians under General Prince Karl von Werde.
Strength: French 95,000; Bavarians 43,500.
Battle: After the Battle of Leipzig (LEIPZIG II) the Allies pursued the French somewhat lethargically, knowing that the Bavarians under Prince von Werde were now on their side and blocking the French lines of withdrawal. At Hanau the French met the Bavarians. Napoleon, concentrating on his left wing, attacked and, by skilful use of his artillery, drove the Bavarians back. The French main body was able to occupy and pass through Hanau, leaving three divisions as a rearguard. On the second day Marshal Edouard Mortier attacked Werde at Hanau, and when Werde himself was wounded, his successor, General Fresnel, drew off, leaving the road completely clear. The French sustained 6,000 casualties, the Bavarians 10,000.

Result: Napoleon was able to continue his retreat and prepare for the defence of France. Meanwhile, isolated garrisons still in French hands in Germany began to surrender.

HASLACH (W Germany)   Napoleonic Wars/Europe   11 October 1805
Fought between the French under General Pierre Dupont de l'Etang and the Austrians.
Strength: French 6,000; Austrians 60,000.
Aim: The French, who were marching on Ulm (qv), found themselves confronted by a force ten times their own size and sought to hold it off.
Battle: Dupont entrenched his force in the village of Haslach, south of Frankfurt, while the Austrians were posted on the Michelberg. The French were attacked by 25,000 Austrians under the Archduke Ferdinand, but they held their position until after dark when Dupont retired, taking with him 4,000 enemy prisoners.
Result: The French objective was achieved.

HEILSBERG (LIDZBARK WARMINSKI) (USSR)   Napoleonic Wars/Europe   10 June 1807
Fought between the French under Marshals Joachim Murat and Nicolas-Jean de Dieu Soult and the Russians under General Count Bennigsen.
Strength: French 30,000; Russians 80,000.
Aim: The French sought to drive the Russians farther north.
Battle: Bennigsen had endeavoured to forestall Napoleon's spring offensive by attacking him, but his assault was repulsed after two days. Napoleon now resumed the initiative by advancing up the Alle. Bennigsen fell back to his fortified camp at Heilsberg (Lidzbark Warminski), near Königsberg. Here, Murat's advanced guard of cavalry and Soult's 4 Corps attacked the main Russian army, driving them back into their entrenchments. But against savage Russian resistance no further progress was made, and had it not been for the arrival of Lannes the French might have been defeated. As it was, the action was inconclusive. French casualties were 8,000 killed and wounded, Russian casualties 10,000 men.
Result: After the battle Bennigsen continued his retreat along the right bank of the Alle.

HELIGOLAND (North Sea)   Napoleonic Wars/Europe   31 August 1807
The British North Sea squadron under Vice-Admiral Thomas Russell captured the island of Heligoland which had been held by the Danes and, during the rest of the war, it was used as a depot for English trade with Germany. The British mustered it as a man-o'-war, HMS *Heligoland.*
   Heligoland remained a British possession until 1890, when it was ceded to Germany and became part of the Prussian province of Schleswig-Holstein.

HOLLABRUN (OBERHOLLABRUNN) (Austria)   Napoleonic Wars/Europe   16 November 1805
Fought between the French under Napoleon and the Russians under General Prince Petr Bagration.
Strength: French 120,000; Russians 6,000.
Aim: The Russians sought to delay the French advance so as to allow General Mikhail Kutuzov time to withdraw.
Battle: After his success at Ulm (qv) Napoleon wheeled about to march down the Danube valley, the only resistance coming from the Russians under Kutuzov, who had come to the aid of the demoralised Austrian Emperor, Francis I. Having seized Vienna, Napoleon turned north, wanting to trap Kutuzov's army of 40,000 in Lower Austria. However, 25 miles north of Vienna Bagration set up a strong roadblock with 7,000 men. On 16 November Marshal Joachim Murat's cavalry, Marshal Jean Lannes's 5 Corps and part of Marshal Nicolas-Jean de Dieu Soult's 4 Corps engaged the Russians all day without succeeding in breaking through. At nightfall Bagration retired under cover of darkness, having lost 3,000 men. Hollabrunn (Oberhollabrunn) was reduced to ashes.
Result: This magnificent delaying action enabled Kutuzov to retire safely to the east of Brunn, and it saved the main Russian army.

HUNDRED DAYS, THE   27 February–18 June 1815
On 27 February 1815 the Emperor Napoleon, with 1,000 followers, sailed from Elba, where he had been exiled by the victorious Allies after his first abdication in 1814. Napoleon sought to take advantage of the

discontent he believed was growing in France against the restored Bourbons. On 1 March 1815 he landed in the Gulf of Juan near Cannes, and marched on Paris via Grenoble and Lyons. The troops sent against him changed sides, especially at Auxerre where those of Marshal Michel Ney, Prince de la Moskowa, who had promised to bring Napoleon to Paris in an 'iron cage', was persuaded to join him. On 20 March Napoleon entered Paris as the Bourbons fled to Belgium.

On 13 March 1815 the representatives of the Allies, gathered for the Congress of Vienna, declared Napoleon 'the enemy and disturber of the peace of the world'. Russia, Prussia, Austria and the United Kingdom pledged themselves to keep 150,000 men in the field against Napoleon until he should be rendered incapable of making further trouble. Britain promised subsidies of £5 million to her allies and paid out a further £2 million for failing to maintain her full quota of troops.

Napoleon faced enormous problems, for much of the old army had been disbanded, stocks of arms and equipment had been run down and the abolition of conscription was one of the genuinely popular actions Louis XVIII had taken. He faced threats from many directions: from the Low Countries, where the Anglo-Dutch-Belgian-German army commanded by the Duke of Wellington and the Prussian army under Field-Marshal Prince Blücher von Wahlstadt were gathering; the Upper Rhine, where Austrian and Russian armies were moving; from Italy, from Spain, and also from internal revolt, particularly in the Vendée. His only ally, Marshal Joachim Murat, who had retained his position as King Joachim I of Naples, had attacked prematurely and was swiftly defeated by the Austrians under General Baron de Bianchi at Tolentino (qv) on 2–3 May 1815. Napoleon and his new Minister of War, Marshal Nicolas Davout, Prince d'Eckmühl, by heroic administrative efforts, were able to put 200,000 men in the field by the beginning of June, 125,000 of them forming the Armée du Nord under Napoleon himself. With this army Napoleon planned to attack Wellington and Blücher. The two Allied field-marshals were awaiting the arrival of the Russians and Austrians before starting a co-ordinated offensive.

The army that Napoleon had gathered was possibly the finest, but also the most brittle, that he ever commanded. The junior officers and other ranks were mostly veterans, but there was much distrust between the lower ranks and the senior officers, and most of the old marshals and generals were unavailable. Marshal Louis Alexandre Berthier died during the Hundred Days by falling from a window at Bamberg and was, inadequately, replaced as Chief of Staff by Marshal Nicolas-Jean de Dieu Soult, Duc de Dalmatia. The cavalry was given to the newly promoted Marshal Emmanuel de Grouchy, because Murat was in disgrace. Marshals Guillaume Brune and Louis-Gabriel Suchet were needed on other fronts. Marshal Edouard Mortier, the Guard Commander, fell ill just as the campaign opened, while other marshals had gone to Belgium with Louis XVIII. One wing of the army had to be entrusted to Marshal Ney, who only arrived as the offensive began.

Napoleon planned to divide the two Allied armies, and to destroy them separately. This strategy required surprise, which was attained by well-organised security measures.

The two Allied armies were quartered over a wide area of S Belgium, and their concentration would take time. Blücher commanded an army of 124,000 men, organised in four army corps. They were all Prussian troops under experienced generals, but they included a high proportion of new recruits. Wellington commanded a motley assortment of British, Dutch, Belgian, Hanoverian, Nassauer and Brunswick troops:

Nationality	Infantry	Cavalry	Artillery	
British	23,543	5,913	5,030 +	102 guns
King's German Legion	3,301	2,560	526 +	18 guns
Hanoverian	22,788	1,682	465 +	12 guns
Brunswick	5,376	922	510 +	16 guns
Nassau	2,880	—	—	
Dutch and Belgian	24,174	3,405	1,635 +	56 guns
TOTAL	82,062	14,482	8,166	204 guns

GRAND TOTAL 105,710 men with 204 guns

Far too many of Wellington's men were inexperienced, even among the British forces, and many of the Dutch/Belgians had been fighting for Napoleon in 1814. Wellington was, therefore, committed to defensive battles. (See LIGNY, QUATRE BRAS, TOLENTINO, WATERLOO, WAVRE.)

JENA-AUERSTADT (E Germany)   Napoleonic Wars/Europe   14 October 1806
Fought between the French under Napoleon and the Prussians under King Frederick William III.
Strength: French 27,000 with 114 guns; Prussians 130,000 with 350 guns.
Aim: The Prussians sought to prevent the French invasion of Prussia.
Battle: Advancing rapidly, Napoleon succeeded in marching his army around the Prussian left flank, thus placing himself nearer Berlin than the Prussian army. Marshals Louis Davout and Prince Bernadotte were ordered to move west to cut the Prussian line of communication, while the bulk of the French army went on towards Jena. The Prussians faced about to meet the French and the King divided his army into two parts, sending Karl Wilhelm Ferdinand, Duke of Brunswick, with 63,000 men to Auerstadt, 15 miles north of Jena, and deploying the rest of his troops under Prince Friedrich Ludwig Hohenlohe-Ingelfingen between Weimar and Jena. The Prussians now faced their line of communications to the east. At Jena, Napoleon attacked at daybreak with the bulk of his army. The Prussians counter-attacked in parade-ground formation, firing volleys on command. They were severely depleted by heavy French musket- and artillery fire, chiefly from Marshal Jean Lannes's 5 Corps. When the Prussian line began to waver, Napoleon sent in the corps of Marshals Nicolas-Jean de Dieu Soult and Pierre Augereau (4 and 7) which, together with that of Lannes, launched an assault on Hohenlohe's troops, pushing their lines back. Simultaneous cavalry attacks served to break the lines further. By the evening, Napoleon had reached Weimar with the loss of 5,000 men. Prussian casualties were 11,000 killed and wounded as well as 15,000 captured.
    At Auerstadt, Davout encountered the bulk of the Prussian army under Brunswick. Bernadotte, who had misunderstood his orders, was not with Davout. The French held their ground, though they had only a third of the Prussian numbers, and when the Duke of Brunswick was mortally wounded, the King himself took command. Thereafter the Prussians dissipated their strength in a series of piecemeal attacks which the French withstood for more than six hours. As rumours of the Prussians' defeat at Jena reached the Duke's troops, they began to become disheartened. They fell back on both flanks far enough for the French to move their artillery forward to enfilade the entire Prussian line. The French fire had a devastating effect and the Prussians began to break. Bernadotte, miles away from the fighting, realised that he must have mistaken Napoleon's command and marched towards the sound of gunfire. He came upon Hohenlohe's broken troops and went on until at 4pm his corps, nearly 20,000 strong and completely fresh, fell on the rear of the King's army, which then disintegrated. French casualties at Auerstadt were 8,000 killed and wounded. The Prussians sustained casualties of 12,000 killed and wounded, had 3,000 prisoners taken and lost 115 guns.
Result: The Prussians retired, the remnants of their army converging upon the Weimar road, whence they proceeded south. The French, with no one between them and Berlin, proceeded north.
    By the rapidity and skill of his manoeuvre, Napoleon had gained the strategic advantage before the tactical campaign against Prussia had really begun. Marshal Davout was created Duc d'Auerstadt.

KATZBACH I (Poland)   Napoleonic Wars/Europe   22 August 1813
Fought between the Prussians under General Gebhard von Blücher and the French under Napoleon.
Strength: Prussians 95,000; French 150,000.
Aim: The French sought to stop the Prussians from advancing.
Battle: Blücher broke the Allied-French truce by marching from Breslau on 14 August. Napoleon concentrated his men against the Prussians, stopped their advance and counter-attacked. Blücher withdrew first behind the Haynau and, under continual pressure from the French, was forced back across the Katzbach with considerable loss.
Result: The immediate French objective was achieved.
    After checking the Prussians, Napoleon saw the threat of an Austrian attack from the south, so turned command over to Marshal Jacques MacDonald.

KATZBACH II (Poland)   Napoleonic Wars/Europe   26 August 1813
Fought between the French under Marshal Jacques Macdonald and the Prussians under General Gebhard von Blücher.
Strength: French 90,000; Prussians 195,000.
Aim: The French sought to cross the river Katzbach in order to force an engagement.
Battle: In defiance of Napoleon's orders, Macdonald began crossing the Katzbach in three widely separated columns. Macdonald himself and the right wing got to the other side, but while he was waiting

for his left wing and cavalry under General Comte Souham, Blücher wheeled about and, in a blinding rainstorm, attacked Macdonald and drove him back. As Macdonald retired, however, Souham arrived; but before the latter was able to deploy and attack, Blücher, with superior cavalry and artillery, assaulted and routed him, inflicting considerable casualties. General Comte Lauriston, who commanded the centre, also suffered heavy casualties in recrossing the river. Macdonald lost 15,000 men and 100 guns.
Result: Napoleon was forced to go on the defensive and Blücher's army from Silesia was infused with new confidence.

KOENIGSWARTHA (E Germany)   Napoleonic Wars/Europe   19 May 1813
Fought between an Italian division of the French army under General Peyri and the Russians under General Mikhail Barclay de Tolly.
Strength: Italians 8,000; Russians 15,000.
Aim: The Russians sought to inflict a defeat on the French and their allies.
Battle: Barclay de Tolly attacked Peyri's Division near Dresden and defeated it, inflicting casualties of 2,000 killed and wounded. Only the arrival of Marshal Michel Ney's cavalry corps prevented the complete destruction of Peyri's men.
Result: The immediate Russian objective was achieved.

KRASNOI (KRASNOYE) (USSR)   Napoleonic Wars/Europe   17 November 1812
Fought between the French, under Marshals Louis Davout and Michel Ney, and the Russians under Field-Marshal Prince Kutuzov.
Strength: French 25,000; Russians 50,000.
Aim: The Russians sought to harass the French during their retreat, whereupon the French turned to fight.
Battle: After skirmishes during the two days prior to the engagement when the Russians had inflicted heavy losses on the French, Napoleon deployed the few fit men he had left to attack the enemy, who had encircled him in order to bar the road, some 30 miles west of Smolensk. The French, chiefly Davout's Corps and the Young Guard, drove the Russians off. Ney's Corps fought a rearguard action to save the rest of the army, and by nightfall only 800 of his men were left. French casualties were about 5,000 killed and wounded and 8,000 missing.
Result: The French continued their retreat relatively unmolested, except by guerrillas who continued to cut off stragglers and generally harass the retreating army.

KULM (Bohemia, Czechoslovakia)   Napoleonic Wars/Europe   30 August 1813
Fought between the French under General Dominique-Joseph-René Vandamme and the Russians, Prussians and Austrians under Field-Marshal Prince von Schwarzenberg, Count Ostermann-Tolstoy and General Friedrich von Kleist.
Strength: French 32,000; Russians/Prussians/Austrians 44,000.
Aim: The French sought to block the Allied line of retreat by cutting their line of communication. The Allies sought to halt the pursuit.
Battle: On 29 August the Allies occupied Kulm, from which they were driven by Vandamme who unexpectedly found Allied troops in Priesten while attempting an encircling movement of the Allies' left wing. The Allies counter-attacked, but Vandamme held his ground. On the following day Vandamme did not receive the expected reinforcements–in fact no other French division had followed him into the mountains–and he was compelled to remain on the defensive. The unexpected arrival of a Prussian force under Kleist von Nollendorf in the French rear meant that Vandamme was completely surrounded. Only half his men escaped the trap and Vandamme himself was wounded and captured. The French losses were 6,000 killed, plus 7,000 men and 48 guns captured.
Result: Vandamme's Division was virtually destroyed and Allied morale affected by the defeat at Dresden (qv) was restored.

LANDSHUT (Bavaria, W Germany)   Napoleonic Wars/Europe   21 April 1809
Fought between the French under Marshal Jean Lannes and the Austrians under General Baron Hiller.
Strength: French 35,000; Austrians 30,000.
Aim: The French sought to smash the divided army of the Archduke Charles of Austria after the Battle of Abensberg (qv).

Battle: Napoleon, not realising that the Austrian left wing under Hiller, which retreated to Landshut–30 miles NE of Munich–after Abensberg (qv), represented only a small part of the Austrian army, sent the bulk of his army after it under Lannes. The Austrians were in danger of being cut off completely because of the approach of Marshal André Masséna from the SW. The French overtook and crushed the Austrian rearguard on the outskirts of Landshut; then, charging across the burning bridge, they stormed the city on the far side of the Isar River. Austrian resistance was desperate, but they were forced to retreat hurriedly by the imminence of Masséna's arrival. Austrian losses were 9,000 men and most of their baggage and artillery.
Result: The French captured Landshut, but the success was on the point of being nullified by a battle at Eckmühl (qv).

LAON (Aisne, France)   Napoleonic Wars/Europe   9–10 March 1814
Fought between the French under Napoleon and the Allies under Marshal Gebhard von Blücher.
Strength: French 47,000; Allies 85,000.
Aim: The French intended a turning movement from the east by Marshal Auguste Marmont's 6 Corps, but Blücher made a stand.
Battle: Napoleon placed 6 Corps east of Laon and 3 Corps south of it, across the Soissons road, with the Guard south of them. Blücher attacked 3 Corps and drove it back in disorder, rout being saved only by the arrival of the Guard. 6 Corps arrived late in the afternoon and Napoleon attacked and took the village of Arden. Nightfall brought a pause in the fighting, the French camping on the ground they had gained, but Blücher made a night attack which drove 6 Corps from the field towards Reims. In order to avoid total rout, Napoleon ordered the advance of the forces to the south, a move which could result in destruction. The gambit paid off, for Blücher, who was sick, called off the pursuit of 6 Corps and his left wing returned to the field. Retreating, Napoleon engaged the Allies throughout the following day, retiring along the Soissons road at 4pm. He was not pursued. French losses were 6,000 to the Allies 4,000.
Result: Blücher once again had the advantage on the march to Paris. Napoleon's scheme had ended in complete failure.

LA ROTHIERE (Lorraine, France)   Napoleonic Wars/Europe   1 February 1814
Fought between the French under Napoleon and the Allies under Marshal Gebhard von Blücher.
Strength: French 40,000; Allies 53,000.
Aim: The Allies sought to regain La Rothière, which had been taken by the French three days earlier.
Battle: Blücher advanced with the Allied army and Napoleon, deciding that his army was too inexperienced, ordered a withdrawal. The order came too late, however, and Blücher attacked frontally on 1 February. The French, holding a strong position, kept the Allies at bay until nightfall, when Blücher captured the village. Napoleon retook it with the Young Guard, but Russian Guards drove them out and the French did not attempt to take it again. French losses were 5,000. Allied casualties were 8,000.
Result: The French were beaten back and though Field-Marshal Prince von Schwarzenberg was advancing on Paris from the SE, Napoleon decided to continue his offensive against Blücher.

LE FERE CHAMPENOISE (Aube, France)   Napoleonic Wars/Europe   25 March 1814
Fought between the French under Marshals Auguste Marmont and Edouard Mortier and the Allies under Field-Marshal Prince von Schwarzenberg.
Strength: French 30,000; Allies 110,000.
   The corps of the 2 French marshals met the Allied army which was marching on Paris at the village of Le Fère Champenoise. The French were beaten and forced to retire, with the loss of about 5,000 men and many guns.
   This, apart from some French resistance around Paris, was the last battle fought in the north of France before Napoleon's abdication.

LEIPZIG I (E Germany)   Napoleonic Wars/Europe   12 October 1806
Captain (later General) Hippolyte-Marie-Guillaume Piré, profiting by the panic among the Prussians that followed their defeat at Jena (qv), seized the city with 50 men of the 10th Hussars.

LEIPZIG II (E Germany)   Napoleonic Wars/Europe   16 and 18–19 October 1813
Fought between the French under Napoleon and the Allied army (Austrians/Russians/Prussians/Swedes) under Field-Marshal Prince von Schwarzenberg.

Strength: French 185,000 with 600 guns; Allies 220,000 (Austrians/Russians 160,000, Prussians/Swedes 60,000) with 1,400 guns.

Aim: After failing to take Berlin, Napoleon fell back to Leipzig, intending to use that town on the Elster River as a major forward base. When General Gebhard von Blücher and the Crown Prince of Sweden (Bernadotte) forced a crossing of the Elbe to the north (Blücher at Wartenburg [qv], the Crown Prince farther down-stream), and Schwarzenberg, masking Dresden, marched on Leipzig from the south, Napoleon was forced to go on the defensive.

Battle: Napoleon massed as many of his men as he could in Leipzig while the Allies converged in an ever-tightening arc. On 16 October the Russians under General Mikhail Barclay de Tolly assaulted Napoleon's southern defences, but the attack was disorganised and, when the French counter-attacked, the Russians were driven back. Blücher attacked Marshal Auguste Marmont simultaneously but, although his numbers were superior, he failed to dislodge the French so that by nightfall the French held the advantage, though they had actually gained no ground. During the night, both sides were reinforced so that Napoleon had 150,000 men and the Allies 300,000. Casualties sustained on 16 October were 27,000 on the French side and 35,000 by the Allies. Little fighting was done on 17 October, but Napoleon withdrew all his troops within the perimeter of Leipzig. On 18 October the Allies launched a series of simultaneous attacks on the French–Blücher, Bernadotte, General Count Bennigsen, Schwarzenberg and Mikhail Barclay de Tolly leading the various assaults. The French were forced to drive the Allies back and leave a road of retreat open. Little actual ground was gained by the Allies' continual assault, but Napoleon knew he could not hold his position indefinitely. By nightfall he had been pushed back into Leipzig, and under cover of darkness he withdrew his army over the only serviceable bridge across the Elster towards Erfurt. By the early hours of 19 October, only Prince Josef Poniatowski's Corps was left in the town fighting a rearguard action. The premature explosion of the bridge left these 20,000 men stranded. Poniatowski, who had been wounded, and Marshal Jacques Macdonald were forced to cross the river by swimming their horses across. Poniatowski drowned, but Macdonald gained the far bank. Total French casualties were 38,000 killed and wounded–plus 15,000 wounded who were in the city's hospitals before the battle began and who were captured with Leipzig, as well as 15,000 taken prisoner, among whom were Generals Comte Lauriston and Comte Reynier. Marshals Michel Ney and Marmont were among the wounded, the latter having two fingers of his right hand blown off. Eighteen generals of division were hit, 5 dying; General Fay de La Tour-Maubourg lost a leg, and General Baron Pajol was injured when his horse was hit by a shell. Comte Belliard, Comte Campans, Baron Gérard, Baron Maison, Comte Souham and Comte Sébastiani were among the distinguished French generals wounded in the severe fighting. The Allied army sustained 52,000 casualties.

Result: This resounding French defeat forced Napoleon to retreat towards France with the remnants of his Grande Armée; but the Allies should not have let the French escape so easily after the battle.

LEITSKAU (LÜBNITZ) (E Germany)   Napoleonic Wars/Europe   27 August 1813
Fought between the French under General Baron Girard and the Prussians under General Hirschberg, aided by some Cossacks under General Czernitchev.
Strength: French 5,000; Prussians/Cossacks 20,000.
Aim: The Allies sought to push the French back out of Germany.
Battle: The Allies attacked the French at Leitskau, near Dresden, heavily defeating them. Besides many killed and wounded, including Girard, the French had 1,500 men taken prisoner and 6 guns captured.
Result: The immediate Allied objective was achieved, and Girard was blockaded in Magdeburg.
   To the French this battle is known as Lübnitz.

LIGNY (Belgium)   Napoleonic Wars/Europe   16 June 1815
Fought between a part of the French Armée du Nord under the Emperor Napoleon and a Prussian army under Field-Marshal Prince Blücher von Wahlstadt.
Strength: French 68,000 (initially, incl 12,500 cavalry + 210 guns, with an additional 10,000 men + 32 guns after Lobau arrived [7pm]); Prussians 84,000 (incl 8,000 cavalry) with 224 guns.
Aim: Napoleon, as a first stage in his planned Belgian campaign, sought to destroy the Prussian army whose forward concentration had left it exposed.
Battle: Blücher was committed to a defensive battle because the largest of his army corps, General Baron Friedrich von Bülow's, had not arrived. He took up a position, astride the Ligny stream, in a convex semicircle. The Prussian 1 Corps under Lt-General Graf von Zieten occupied the villages of St Amand and

Ligny, with reserves on the ridge of Bry behind. Major-General George von Pirch's 2 Corps was in general reserve farther north. 3 Corps (Lt-General Freiherr von Thielemann) formed the Prussian left at Sombreffe, Tongrines and Point du Jour. Blücher thus held a position 7 miles long with only 84,000 men. Also the Prussian reserves, largely on the front slopes of the ridges, were exposed and well within range of the French artillery.

Napoleon positioned the bulk of his infantry opposite General Zieten at Ligny and St Amand, containing Thielemann with Comte Exelmans's and Comte Pajol's cavalry corps. Napoleon intended to thrust General Comte Drouet d'Erlon's Corps, and possibly Marshal Michel Ney's men, if Ney succeeded in clearing the Allies from Quatre Bras (qv) quickly, against the Prussian right wing along the Bavai-Liège road. To achieve this it was necessary to fix the Prussians and complete the concentration of his own army, for 6 Corps under General Georges Mouton, Comte de Lobau, had not yet arrived. Once Napoleon knew Ney's advance had begun at 2.30pm he ordered General Dominique-Joseph-René Vandamme (2 Corps) to send General Baron Lefol's Division against St Amand. After heavy fighting the Prussians were driven from their position. However, Major-General Karl von Steinmetz called in four more battalions and recovered the village. Vandamme now ordered General Baron Berthèzene's Division to attack and also sent General Baron Girard's Division against St Amand La Haye and Hameau de St Amand on the (French) left. Again the Prussians were driven back, but Steinmetz again counter-attacked and recaptured most of St Amand. But Girard's attack succeeded, and more Prussian reserves were drawn in. Girard was mortally wounded, but his troops hung on to St Amand La Haye, putting Blücher's left in danger. General Baron Habert's Division, positioned by Vandamme to cover his left, drove off a Prussian cavalry counter-attack. Blücher threw in more reserves, but still Girard's men hung on though both brigadiers of the division were killed.

A little while after Vandamme's attack General Etienne Gérard (4 Corps) launched General Baron Pécheux's Division against Ligny. He failed to take the village in spite of renewed assaults. Gérard then reinforced Pécheux with one of General Baron Vichery's brigades. After a furious mêlée, in which more Prussian reserves were involved, the battle lapsed into a fire-fight across the Ligny stream. Blücher's army was being gradually worn down. Soon after 5pm Blücher brought his 2 Corps into the fight and Napoleon committed his Young Guard and part of his Middle Guard to support Vandamme and Gérard.

At this point a mysterious column was observed approaching the French left. It was d'Erlon's Corps, which, for reasons which have never been adequately explained, wandered all day between the battlefields of Ligny and Quatre Bras but never intervened in either. However, as soon as they were identified, Napoleon could commit himself to his final stroke. After further heavy fighting the Prussian 2 Corps was beaten off. Blücher decided to make one more effort, using almost his last reserves to break the French left, but this too failed.

Napoleon now sent the Old Guard and the remainder of the Middle Guard, with cavalry support, against Ligny. At 7.45pm, after a heavy artillery preparation, they attacked. The Ligny defences collapsed, the cavalry stormed through, and the Prussian centre was pierced. Blücher gathered his last remaining squadrons and charged. In the ensuing confusion Blücher's horse was killed, rolled over the seventy-two-year-old Marshal, who was for a while *hors de combat*. This charge gained time for the Prussian army to pull out, but it fell to Lt-General Count Graf von Gneisenau to make the crucial decision to withdraw on Wavre (qv) rather than Namur. This decision was of vital importance, for it made Prussian intervention at Waterloo (qv) possible. The French sustained 12,000 casualties to the Prussian 16,000 and 21 guns. The Prussians lost something like 9,000 deserters during the night after the battle.

Result: The French had 'damnably mauled' the Prussians, as Wellington had prophesied. But the Prussian army was intact, Thielemann's Corps had hardly been engaged, and Bülow's men had not been present. After a short period they would be fit to fight again.

Napoleon failed to follow up the Prussians effectively, and when the pursuit began on the following afternoon, it was misdirected.

(See HUNDRED DAYS)

LOWENBERG (Poland)   Napoleonic Wars/Europe   21 August 1813
Fought between the French under Napoleon and the Prussians under General Gebhard von Blücher.
Strength: French 130,000; Prussians 80,000.
Aim: The French sought to beat the Prussians back as they were trying to halt their advance.
Battle: Napoleon attacked the Prussians strongly. Blücher fell back behind Hanau without offering any very great counter-offensive. Prussian casualties were 2,000 killed and wounded.

Result: Napoleon turned command over to Marshal Jacques Macdonald, who precipitated the battle of the Katzbach (KATZBACH II) where Blücher decisively beat the French.

LÜBECK (Schleswig-Holstein, W Germany)   Napoleonic Wars/Europe   5 November 1806
Fought between the Prussians under General Gebhard von Blücher and the French under Marshals Nicolas-Jean de Dieu Soult and Jean Bernadotte.
Strength: Prussians 22,000; French 2 corps, perhaps 40,000.
Aim: The French sought the surrender and capture of Blücher and his men.
Battle: After the French success at Jena-Auerstadt (qv), Marshal Louis Davout occupied Berlin and another French column captured 10,000 Prussians under Prince Friedrich of Hohenlohe-Ingelfingen at Prenzlau. Stettin (qv) fell. The ablest commander left in the field was Blücher who fell back on the Danish port of Lubeck, hotly pursued by Bernadotte and Soult. The day after Blücher's arrival, the city was stormed and taken by the French. Blücher escaped to Ratkow with 10,000 of his army, but General Gerhard von Scharnhorst with another 10,000 surrendered.
Result: On 7 November Blücher decided to surrender. All Prussia was now in French hands. Napoleon turned his attention to the Russians who were mobilising troops in support of the Prussian King.

LÜBNITZ   see LEITSKAU

LÜTZEN (E Germany)   Napoleonic Wars/Europe   2 May 1813
Fought between the French under Napoleon and the Russians and Prussians under the Prince of Sayn-Wittgenstein-Ludwigsburg and General Gebhard von Blücher.
Strength: French 120,000; Russians/Prussians 75,000.
Aim: The French sought to break up the Allied offensive which was being mounted against them.
Battle: On the same day that General Comte Lauriston captured Leipzig, the Allies attacked the French right rear at Grossgorschen and neighbouring villages. Napoleon concentrated his men against Wittgenstein's army and attacked it. The battle centred upon villages SE of Lützen, near Leipzig, which were taken and retaken several times. The French infantry bivouacked in squares and were charged by Allied cavalry and fired on by their artillery. Having no cavalry themselves, they were unable to counter-attack. The divisions of Marshal Michel Ney, who was wounded, and of Marshals Nicolas-Charles Oudinot and Auguste Marmont withstood the attacks, and at nightfall the Allied monarchs ordered their armies to withdraw to the east. The French sustained 22,000 casualties, the Allies 20,000.
Result: The advantage remained with the French, but the considerable losses inflicted by the Allies prevented pursuit.

MAIDA (Calabria, Italy)   Napoleonic Wars/Europe   4 July 1806
Fought between the British under Major-General Sir John Stuart and the French under General Comte Reynier.
Strength: British 5,200; French 6,500.
Aim: The French sought to expel the British expeditionary force, which had landed in Calabria, from Sicily.
Battle: Napoleon had deposed the King of Naples and put his elder brother, Joseph, on the throne. This action prompted Britain to send an invading force to Italy. The French attacked the British at Maida on 4 July, but were received with steady volleys followed up by fierce bayonet-charges which the French, though veteran soldiers, could not withstand. French losses were heavy both in the action and subsequent pursuit.
Result: The British won this action, but Stuart proved quite incapable of exploiting it. In September Marshal André Masséna began to concentrate forces against him and he was compelled to re-embark. Naples came completely under the control of Bonaparte.
    This battle was a clear illustration of the tactical superiority of the British line over the French column.

MALOYAROSLAVETS (USSR)   Napoleonic Wars/Europe   24 October 1812
Fought between the French under the Viceroy of Italy, Eugène de Beauharnais, and the Russians under Field-Marshal Prince Kutuzov.
Strength: French 15,000; Russians 20,000.

Aim: The Russians sought to intercept the French column retreating SW towards Kaluga. The French sought to retreat by a road they had *not* used during their advance on Moscow.

Battle: After the evacuation of Moscow, Napoleon sent a force SW under Eugène de Beauharnais to spearhead the retreat towards Smolensk. At Maloyaroslavets, Kutuzov intercepted the French by occupying the village and holding the bridge over the steep-banked river Luzha. Unable to manoeuvre, de Beauharnais was forced to make a head-on attack. The two armies fought bitterly for control of the bridge, and the village changed hands seven times during the day. Finally, the French drove off Kutuzov's troops with a loss to the latter of 6,000. French casualties totalled 5,000.

Result: The French managed to gain control of the road, but an important strategic decision resulted from this engagement. This was to take the French army out of Russia by the northern route instead of the southern one for fear of too much opposition on the latter road by well-armed and well-organised Cossacks and local guerrillas. However, General Denis Davidov organised a formidable network of guerrillas across Napoleon's new route and wrought havoc on his tired veterans, ably helped by contingents of marauding Cossacks from the Kuban and elsewhere from the southern boundaries of Russia. The Cossacks were given a free hand to take what booty they could capture from the remains of the Grande Armée. The guerrillas and the Cossacks were more feared by the French than the comparatively slow-moving regular Russian forces, but the latter took most of the kudos for the casualties caused, although often they were many miles from the scene of action.

The Czar felt it impolitic to give much acclaim to the Partisans in case they got big ideas and started a revolt. So the general policy was to write down the effects of the Partisan war and allot all the glory of the victory to the duller, slow-moving Russian regular forces and their generals.

MARIA ZELL (Austria)   Napoleonic Wars/Europe   8 November 1805

A minor action fought between the corps of Marshal Louis Davout and the Austrians, 10,000 strong, under General Count von Merfeldt, in which the Austrians were driven from the field in disorder, ceding 2,000 prisoners.

The French resumed their advance on Vienna, which Davout entered on 15 November.

MICHELBERG (Bavaria, W Germany)   Napoleonic Wars/Europe   16 October 1805

Fought between the French under Marshal Michel Ney and the Austrians.

Aim: The French sought to drive the Austrians back into Ulm (qv).

Battle: A two-pronged attack on the Austrians, by Marshal Jean Lannes who carried the Frauenberg and Ney who beat the Austrians off the Michelberg, drove them back into Ulm.

Result: The French objective was achieved. On 17 October General Baron Karl Mack von Leiberich capitulated with 30,000 men.

MOGILEV (USSR)   Napoleonic Wars/Europe   23 July 1812

Fought between the French under Marshal Louis Davout and the Russians under General Prince Petr Bagration.

Strength: French 26,000; Russians 49,000.

Aim: The French sought to prevent the junction of the two Russian armies under Bagration and General Mikhail Barclay de Tolly.

Battle: Prince Jérôme Bonaparte, commanding one of the three columns which were advancing almost unchecked into Russia, failed to carry out Napoleon's instructions which were designed to lead to the crushing of both Russian armies in turn. Davout replaced Prince Jérôme and took Minsk, in spite of unusual heat which drained the French of much of their vitality and caused an attack of colic among the horses. The Russians continued to fall back, playing for time. Bagration realised the French intention and, when Davout occupied Mogilev on the Dnieper, the Russians attacked. Despite their superior numbers, the Russians were repulsed by the French whose strong position gave them the advantage. The French sustained 1,000 casualties, while Russian caualties totalled 4,000 men.

Result: Bagration was forced to retreat eastwards across the Dnieper. He joined Barclay de Tolly at Smolensk (qv). Therefore, although the French won the engagement, they did not prevent the Russian armies from linking.

MOHRUNGEN (USSR)   Napoleonic Wars/Europe   25 January 1807

Fought between the French under Marshal Jean Bernadotte and the Russian advanced guard under General Marhof.

Strength: French 10,000; Russians 14,000 (with many more in support).
Battle: Near Königsberg (Kaliningrad) Bernadotte held the Russians for a time. Finally, both sides lost about 1,000 men, and the French withdrew southward.
Result: The long-term success of the French campaign was not affected by Bernadotte's withdrawal.

MONTEREAU (Aube, France)   Napoleonic Wars/Europe   17 February 1814
Fought between the French under Napoleon and the Allies under the Duke of Württemberg.
Aim: The French intended to reach Troyes ahead of the Austrians. The Allies, by holding the key village of Montereau, hoped to cover their retreat.
Battle: General Comte Gérard was commanding 2 Corps under Marshal Claude Victor, whose idleness had given Prince Eugène de Beauharnais time to adopt a strong position. A heavy bombardment developed and when the Guard artillery came up the French got the upper hand. Soon after 3pm the French stormed the ridge which was the key of the Allied position. Württemberg then ordered a withdrawal. Napoleon in person led his guns on to the captured ridge, and General Comte Pajol, though wounded, led his cavalry corps–mostly recruits–in a brilliant, if improbable, cavalry charge, which flooded down through Montereau to the river Yonne. Before the Allies could blow up the bridges Marshal François-Joseph Lefèbvre, aged fifty-nine, led the Emperor's staff and escort in a dashing charge down the main road to Bray, and the Allied retreat became a rout. But heavy frosts enabled Württemberg's men to move across the fields, and so much of his artillery and transport got away. The Allies lost 6,000 men and 15 guns. The French casualties numbered about 2,500.
Result: Field-Marshal Prince von Schwarzenberg was compelled to continue his retreat eastward.

MORTMANT (Aube, France)   Napoleonic Wars/Europe   17 February 1814
Fought between the Russians under General Count Pahlen and the French under Marshal Claude Victor.
Aim: The French sought to beat off an attack on their rearguard by the Russian van.
Battle: The Russians attacked the French rear and were beaten back with casualties of 3,000 killed and wounded and the loss of 11 guns.
Result: The French were able to disengage safely and continued their retreat.

OSTROWNO (USSR)   Napoleonic Wars/Europe   25–6 July 1812
Fought between the corps of Marshal Michel Ney and Prince Eugène de Beauharnais, and Marshal Joachim Murat's cavalry, and the Russian corps of Count Ostermann-Tolstoy and Lt-General P. P. Konovnitzyn.
Aim: The French sought to advance into Russia.
Battle: At Ostrowno on both 25 and 26 July the Russians were driven back by the French. Russian casualties were 3,000 killed and wounded, and in addition they had 800 prisoners and 8 guns taken. French casualties were about 3,000.
Result: The French advance continued.

PARIS I (France)   Napoleonic Wars/Europe   30–1 March 1814
Fought between the French, under Marshals Edouard Mortier and Auguste Marmont, and the Allies under Field-Marshal Prince von Schwarzenberg.
Strength: French 20,000; Allies 110,000.
Aim: The Allies sought to capture the French capital.
Battle: Although Napoleon tried to disrupt the Allied line of communications, four columns advanced in order to converge on Paris. Napoleon began to mass troops at Fontainebleau. In Paris Joseph, ex-King of Spain, failed to strengthen the city. The Allies attacked at Vincennes, Belleville and Montmartre, sending their fourth column against the extreme left of the French line at Montmartre. At 2am on 21 March the Allies turned the French left, capturing Montmartre, and the city surrendered. Joseph fled. Napoleon, racing to the aid of the capital, heard of the surrender when he was 11 miles outside the city and was unable to rally his men for an assault. French casualties were 4,000 men; Allied casualties, 8,000.
Result: The Allies demanded the abdication of Napoleon and his exile to the island of Elba. On 11 April Napoleon agreed to the terms.

POLOTSK I (USSR)   Napoleonic Wars/Europe   17/18 August 1812
Fought between the French and Bavarians under Marshal Nicolas-Charles Oudinot, until wounded, and then General Laurent Gouvion-St-Cyr and the Russians under the Prince of Sayn-Wittgenstein-Ludwigsburg.

Strength: French/Bavarians 33,000; Russians 30,000.
Aim: Oudinot's Corps, the left wing, was advancing so as to protect the Grand Army from the north.
Battle: The French crossed the river Dvina, surprised the Russians at Polotsk and, in an action lasting two hours, drove them back with a loss of 3,000 killed, plus 1,500 men and 14 guns captured. The French sustained casualties of 1,000 killed and wounded. Oudinot was gravely wounded on 17 August and Gouvion-St-Cyr, who took over, was also wounded on the 18th. He was rewarded with a marshal's baton. The Bavarian generals Count Deroy and Prince Karl von Wrede were both wounded, the former mortally.
Result: The immediate French objective was achieved. From the strategic point of view Napoleon, at Smolensk, was relieved of anxiety for his left flank.

POLOTSK II (USSR)   Napoleonic Wars/Europe   18 October 1812
Fought between the French and Bavarians under Marshal Marquis Laurent Gouvion-St-Cyr and the Russians under the Prince of Sayn-Wittgenstein-Ludwigsburg.
Strength: French/Bavarians 30,000; Russians 40,000.
Battle: The Russians surprised the French, defeating them and compelling them to evacuate Polotsk. St-Cyr was badly wounded in the foot.
Result: The capture of Polotsk threatened the route along which Napoleon was about to retreat via Smolensk and Borisov to Kovno.

PULTUSK II (Poland)   Napoleonic Wars/Europe   26 December 1806
Fought between the French under Marshal Jean Lannes and the Russians under General Count Bennigsen.
Strength: French 35,000; Russians 60,000 with 120 guns.
Aim: The French sought to corner the Russians at Pultusk, 25 miles north of Warsaw.
Battle: As part of his move against the mobilisation of the Russian army, Napoleon marched eastwards. Marshal Joachim Murat's cavalry reached Warsaw at the end of November while Napoleon, crossing the Vistula down-stream of the city, closed in towards Murat's left, thus boxing in the Russians under Bennigsen who continued his retreat steadily towards the Narew River. At this point Lannes attacked Pultusk which was held by Bennigsen's troops. Assaulting the Russian left, he attempted to pierce their ranks and cut them off from the town. In this the French did not succeed. On the Russian right, the French held their own but by nightfall little had been achieved. During the night the Russians retreated to Ostroleka and then Königsberg (Kaliningrad), claiming a major victory though their casualties were heavy, being 3,000 killed and wounded, as well as 2,000 captured along with many guns. Accounts of French casualties range from 1,500 to 8,000 killed and wounded. Marshal Lannes was among the wounded.
Result: The Russians avoided envelopment, but both sides went into winter quarters after the battle, so military operations were suspended.

QUATRE BRAS (Belgium)   Napoleonic Wars/Europe   16 June 1815
Fought between the left wing of the French Armée du Nord under Marshal Michel Ney, Prince de la Moskowa, and a part of the Duke of Wellington's Allied army.
Strength: French 25,000; Allies (initially Perponcher's Division, Dutch/Belgian and Nassauers) 8,000 men with 11 guns (rising to 36,000 men with 70 guns).
Aim: The French sought to capture the crossroads of Quatre Bras, near Brussels, and then to expose the left flank of the Prussian army at Ligny.
Battle: Wellington had been deceived by Napoleon's sudden advance. His army was spread out for administrative purposes, and it would be some time before it could concentrate. On 15 June Wellington ordered a concentration on Nivelle, 7 miles from Quatre Bras; he wanted the cross-roads at Quatre Bras to be held in order to keep communications open with the Prussians who were 8 miles to the east at Sombreffe. Prince Bernard of Saxe-Weimar, commanding a brigade of Nassauers in Dutch/Belgian pay in Lt-General Baron de Perponcher's Division, fought an action at Quatre Bras on the 15th, and held the French well to the south of the crossroads. On the 16th the Prince of Orange, Commander of the Dutch/Belgian troops, after consulting his Chief of Staff General Constant de Rebèque, and Perponcher, whose whole division was at Quatre Bras, decided to stand there. The position was strong but long–a rough half-circle with Quatre Bras in the centre. Wellington inspected and agreed the position before going on to Ligny to visit Field-Marshal Prince Blücher. Lt-General Sir Thomas Picton's Division also arrived to reinforce the Prince of Orange just before the first French attack.

Napoleon ordered Marshal Ney to capture Quatre Bras but failed to impress on him the need for speed. It was early afternoon before the French attacked the Allied left flank. Swiftly General Baron Bachelu's Division captured the farm of Piraumont. The Prince of Orange moved a militia battalion forward in support but it was scattered by General Comte Piré's cavalry. One brigade of General Maximilien Foy's Division seized Gismioncourt farm, and the whole left flank of the Allied line collapsed. Foy's other brigade attacked Saxe-Weimar's Brigade holding the Bossu wood on the Allied right, but failed to make progress. At 3pm Prince Jérôme Bonaparte's Division arrived and Ney sent it against the Pierrepont farm and Bossu wood. The farm was captured but the wood's defenders held on.

At this moment Wellington returned and new troops were arriving all the while. Picton deployed in front of the crossroads, and sent the 1/95th Rifles to recapture Piraumont. They failed to take it but held on nearby. The Prince of Orange sent his cavalry against Foy's right brigade but they were beaten off by Piré's lancers. Piré then attacked Picton's infantry, but although the 42nd Highlanders were overrun while trying to form square, the cavalry was beaten off. Ney now decided to force a decision. He ordered the cavalry of Baron L'Héritier's Division, under the command of General François-Etienne Kellermann, to charge the Allied centre. Although the 69th Foot was badly mauled, the charge failed.

It was now 6.30pm. Wellington took the offensive, launching two brigades into the Bossu wood and two more at Piraumont. The original Allied position was recaptured, and the action petered out as dusk fell. Allied casualties numbered 4,000 men, and French 4,000 men.

Result: The action resulted in a draw, for although Wellington held his position, he was unable to help Blücher at Ligny as he had hoped.

(See HUNDRED DAYS)

RAAB (SE Austria)   Napoleonic Wars/Europe   14 June 1809
Fought between the French under Prince Eugène de Beauharnais and the Austrians under the Archduke John of Austria.
Strength: French 44,000; Austrians 40,000.
Aim: The French sought to force the Austrian withdrawal, so they advanced from the Adige River. The Austrians, fearing to be cut off from the bulk of their army, withdrew eastwards.
Battle: Two Austrian rearguard actions at Kismeyger and Szabadhegy were unsuccessful, the French driving the Austrians out of both villages. Hearing of Napoleon's check at Aspern-Essling (qv), John made a stand at Raab, near Graz. De Beauharnais attacked, inflicting heavy casualties, although the Austrians held their ground until nightfall when they drew off and crossed the Danube to march up-stream towards Vienna. The Austrians sustained 3,000 casualties and had 2,500 taken prisoner. French casualties numbered 3,000 men.
Result: Although Archduke John had been beaten back into Hungary, he began to march towards Vienna. At Pressburg (Bratislava) he was again stopped by the French. De Beauharnais laid siege to Raab, which fell to him on 25 June whereupon he rejoined Napoleon in Vienna.

RASZYN (Poland)   Napoleonic Wars/Europe   19 April 1809
Fought between the Austrians under Archduke Ferdinand and the Poles, French and Saxons under Prince Josef Poniatowski.
Strength: Austrians 30,000; French/Poles 20,000.
Aim: The Poles sought to halt the Austrian march on Warsaw.
Battle: Poniatowski, who was defending Warsaw, came out of the city to meet the approaching Austrians. At Raszyn the two armies clashed and, after a stubborn conflict round the woods and marshes outside Raszyn, the Poles and French were driven back on Warsaw with casualties of 2,000 killed and wounded.
Result: Poniatowski surrendered to the Austrians a few days later to save Warsaw from bombardment.

RATISBON (REGENSBURG) (Bavaria, W Germany)   Napoleonic Wars/Europe   23 April 1809
Fought between the Austrians under Archduke Charles of Austria and a French army, comprising many different nationalities including Italian, Dutch, German as well as French, under Napoleon.
Strength: Austrians 80,000 (out of 186,000 in the area); French 76,000 (out of 176,000 in Germany).
Aim: On hearing that the Austrians, encouraged by French defeats in Spain, had decided to liberate Germany from French rule, Napoleon rushed back from Spain via Paris to Stuttgart, arriving on 16 April 1809. He found that his Chief of Staff, Marshal Louis Alexandre Berthier, whom he had left in charge, had not yet been able to concentrate his widely dispersed forces in order to recover the initiative after the

Austrians had invaded. Napoleon took over command and immediately decided to attack with the forces available.

Battle: Within a few days Napoleon fought and won the Battles of Abensberg (20 April), Landshut (21 April), Eckmühl (22 April) (qqv) and, in so doing, chased Archduke Charles north towards the Danube. Charles, in order to put the Danube between him and Napoleon's voracious forces, decided to defend the walled city of Ratisbon (Regensburg) to allow the rest of his forces to escape north over the river where they could recuperate safely and reform.

Napoleon's forces, utterly exhausted by the intensity of the fighting, the speed of the pursuit, and the heat of a central European summer, did not chase the Austrians with their usual energy. However, Marshal Louis-Nicolas Davout, using deliberate methods, fought his way into the town, but not before most of the Austrian army had escaped over the bridges. In an effort to urge his tired men on, Napoleon ventured too far forward and was slightly wounded.

In these four battles, all fought within a week, the Austrians suffered 26,000 casualties and had 4,000 men taken prisoner. French casualties numbered 15,000 men.

Result: These victories allowed Napoleon to enter Vienna unopposed on 13 May 1809. But he was to meet stubborn resistance in the northern suburbs of Aspern-Essling (qv), where he suffered his first defeat at the hands of the stubborn and resolute Austrians.

REIMS (France)   Napoleonic Wars/Europe   13 March 1814
Fought between the French, under Napoleon, and the Russians and Prussians under General St Priest.
Strength: French 30,000; Russians/Prussians 13,000.
Aim: Napoleon sought to drive the Allies out of Reims, which they had captured after the Battle of Laon (qv).
Battle: Napoleon, on hearing of the Allied occupation of Reims, marched across the front of Field-Marshal Blücher's army which was much larger than his own. His passage was uncontested and on 13 March he attacked the Allies in Reims and drove them out. French casualties were less than 1,000. Allied casualties numbered 6,000.
Result: The French reoccupied Reims, but Napoleon now had two Allied armies around his own and he was 83 miles from Paris.

RIPPACH (E Germany)   Napoleonic Wars/Europe   1 May 1813
Fought between the French under Napoleon and Allied forces.
On the eve of the Battle of Lützen (LÜTZEN II) there was a skirmish at Rippach, half-way between Weissenfels and Lützen, which was remarkable only for the death of Marshal Jean-Baptiste Bessières, who was killed outright by a cannon-ball.

SAALFELD (E Germany)   Napoleonic Wars/Europe   10 October 1806
Fought between the Prussian advanced guard under Prince Louis Frederick and the French under Marshal Jean Lannes.
Aim: The Prussians, whose orders were ambiguous, thought their mission was to hold the Saalfeld defile.
Strength: Prussians 8,300; French 14,000.
Battle: The French, advancing rapidly over the Thuringian Hills in three columns which formed a massive square with a 30-mile front, began to move round the Prussian left flank. Lannes's Corps, on the left side of the square, made an enveloping attack on Prince Louis Frederick's troops outside Saalfeld, south of Weimar. After bitter fighting, about midday, the Prussian-Saxon contingent fell back to the city walls where the Prince himself led five squadrons in a desperate cavalry charge which the French repulsed. The Prince refused quarter and was cut down by Quartermaster Guindé. Prussian casualties were 400 killed and wounded, and in addition 1,800 men were captured along with 33 guns. French casualties were 172 killed and wounded.
Result: The attack took the French into a position where they were closer to Berlin than the Prussians. This was the first action of the campaign, and as usual 'first blood' had an important moral effect.

SACILE (N Italy)   Napoleonic Wars/Europe   16 April 1809
Fought between an army of French and Italians under Prince Eugène de Beauharnais and the Austrians under Archduke John.
Strength: French/Italians 36,000; Austrians 40,000.

Aim: The French sought to force the Austrians to retreat into Hungary.
Battle: De Beauharnais attacked Archduke John at Sacile, but neither side displayed enough generalship to gain any advantage. The disorganised action was decided when an Austrian flanking movement threatened to cut off the French retreat, forcing de Beauharnais to withdraw. He fell back beyond the river Piave and then to the Adige.
Result: The French withdrawal gave the Austrians victory, but no further action took place until Napoleon captured Vienna.

SMOLENSK II (USSR)   Napoleonic Wars/Europe   17 August 1812
Fought between the French under Napoleon and the Russians under General Mikhail Barclay de Tolly.
Strength: French 50,000; Russians 60,000.
Aim: After the Russian defeat at Mogilev (qv) General Prince Petr Bagration linked with Barclay de Tolly at Smolensk, where the French army caught up with them. In order to continue their advance, the French sought to beat the Russians out of the town.
Battle: Smolensk was held by Bagration's Corps and was attacked during the afternoon of 17 August. By nightfall, after hard fighting, the French had penetrated the suburbs as far as the old city fortifications. Under cover of darkness the Russians fired the town and evacuated it, fearing that the French might initiate an offensive across the Dnieper and threaten Russian communications with Moscow. Russian casualties in the action were 10,000; French casualties 9,000.
Result: The French did not succeed in crushing the Russian armies as intended.

STETTIN (SZCZECIN) (Poland)   Napoleonic Wars/Europe   30 October 1806
The port of the Baltic, and capital of Prussian Pomerania, stands on the Oder, 17 miles above its entrance into the Stettener Haff. The fortress of Stettin (Szczecin) has the unusual, and unenviable, distinction of capitulating to a light cavalry brigade, having been infected by the panic which followed the Prussian defeat at Jena (JENA-AUERSTADT). General Antoine-Charles-Louis Lasalle, perhaps the greatest of all Napoleon's cavalry commanders, at the head of the 5th and 7th Hussars, bluffed the Governor into surrendering the fortress without the least resistance.

THREE EMPERORS, BATTLE OF THE   see AUSTERLITZ

TOLENTINO (N Italy)   Napoleon Wars/Europe   2–3 May 1815
Fought between a Neapolitan army under King Joachim I of Naples and an Austrian army under General Baron de Bianchi.
Strength: Neapolitans 28,000 (including 3,500 horse) with 35 guns; Austrian 11,000 (including 1,000 cavalry) with 28 guns.
Aim: The Austrians sought to eliminate Murat, who had attacked prematurely in support of Napoleon.
Battle: Murat declared war on the Allies on 15 March 1815, as soon as he heard of Napoleon's landing in France. His army was of poor quality but he at once took the offensive, sending a strong detachment to Rome, and marching up the Adriatic coast road with the majority of his forces. He tried to attack the Austrians in the flank as they moved up the Po valley towards France. At first he achieved some success, took Bologna, and pushed half-way to Mantua. But then he halted.

Soon he was forced to retreat, which upset his little army's morale. He turned at Tolentino, and attacked Bianchi on 2 May. The battle proceeded with fluctuating results until evening. Murat decided to attack again next day. The first attack had limited success, but an Austrian counter-attack broke his army, which fled. The Neopolitans sustained 4,000 casualties, and had many deserters. The Austrians had 800 casualties.
Result: The Austrians could now concentrate on Napoleon. Murat fled to France, but Napoleon, who was furious with Murat's premature attack, refused to employ him. After the fall of Napoleon Murat was captured and executed, on 15 October 1815.
(See HUNDRED DAYS)

TRAFALGAR (off Cádiz, Spain)   21 October 1805
Fought between the British fleet under Vice-Admiral Lord Nelson and a combined French and Spanish fleet under Vice-Admiral Pierre de Villeneuve. The Spaniards were commanded by Admiral Duque Federico Carlos de Gravina.

Strength: British 27 ships of the line; French/Spanish 33 ships of the line (French 18, Spanish 15) + 7 frigates.

Aim: Villeneuve was to sail to the Mediterranean to unite with other French ships and support Marshal André Masséna's Italian campaign. Nelson, hearing of the move, sailed out to stop them.

Battle: Nelson sighted Villeneuve at Cape Spartel, coming from Cádiz. The Franco-Spanish fleet, seeing the British, turned north once more and proceeded back towards Cádiz in an irregular line stretching 5 miles. At Cape Trafalgar, according to a prearranged plan, the British attacked the enemy fleet in two columns from the west, Nelson leading one division in *Victory* which attacked the front half of the fleet, and Vice-Admiral Cuthbert Collingwood leading the other in *Royal Sovereign* which attacked the rear of the combined fleet. Under the signal 'England expects every man will do his duty', the British attacked the Franco-Spanish fleet, breaking its column. In a five-hour battle, during which the accuracy of British gunnery was a dominant factor, 18 Franco-Spanish ships surrendered and 4 others were later taken off Corruna (La Coruña). The British lost no ships, but Nelson was mortally wounded. He died during the last stages of the battle when he knew that victory was certain. British casualties were 1,500 killed and wounded. The Franco-Spanish fleet had 7,000 killed and wounded, and 7,000 taken prisoner. Among the dead was the Spanish admiral Gravina.

Result: The immediate British objective was achieved, and only 11 ships of the Franco-Spanish fleet returned to Cádiz. British supremacy on the high seas was now assured, and French naval power destroyed in what had been the most decisive marine battle, both strategically and tactically, of history.

ULM (Bavaria, W Germany)   Napoleonic Wars/Europe   17 October 1805

Fought between the Austrians under General Baron Karl Mack von Leiberich and the French under Napoleon.

Strength: Austrians 72,000; French 180,000.

Aim: Napoleon sought to strike at and destroy the army of the Third Coalition.

Battle: At the time the Third Coalition was formed in 1805, Napoleon had massed 180,000 troops at Boulogne for an invasion of England. When Bavaria decided to side with France, he resolved to attack the Coalition from the south and withdrew his invasion force to Germany. Mack, expecting the arrival of a Russian army under General Mikhail Kutuzov and the appearance of Napoleon's army from the Black Forest, concentrated his army at Ulm. Napoleon, however, swung round Mack to cross the Danube down-stream of Ulm, thus cutting Mack off from Vienna and the approaching Russians. Mack, in turn, swung his army round to face the French, his left wing at Ulm and his right wing at Rain. Napoleon crossed the Danube at Neuburg and marched towards Ulm from the reverse direction with the bulk of his troops. Realising he was trapped, Mack tried to cut his way out by crossing the Danube at Gunzburg (qv), but he was repulsed by Marshal Michel Ney and returned to Ulm. At Elchingen (qv), Ney's 6 Corps held the bridge, enabling Napoleon to send more of his troops across the Danube. By the middle of October Mack was entirely surrounded. He surrendered with 30,000 men, 10,000 of whom were killed or wounded; 20,000 others escaped. French casualties were 6,000 killed and wounded.

Result: Having defeated the Austrians, the French were able to turn on the Russians. Mack was court-martialled and sentenced to twenty years' imprisonment.

VALUTINO (USSR)   Napoleonic Wars/Europe   19 August 1812

Fought between the French under Marshal Michel Ney and the Russians under General Mikhail Barclay de Tolly.

Strength: French 30,000; Russians 40,000.

Aim: The French pursued the retreating Russians in an effort to trap and crush them.

Battle: Ney's Corps attacked the Russian rearguard at Valutino, near Smolensk, which was posted in a strong position on marshy ground, protected by a stream. Despite the natural hazards, the French carried the position, losing General Comte Gudin de la Sablonnière, who was mortally wounded. Each side lost about 7,000 men. The Russian army retreated in good order.

Result: Although the French won the engagement, the Russians were able to draw off, thus evading the trap.

VIASMA (USSR)   Napoleonic Wars/Europe   3 November 1812

Fought between the Russians under Field-Marshal Prince Kutuzov and the French under Eugène de Beauharnais and Marshal Louis-Nicolas Davout.

Aim: The Russians sought to harass the French retreat from Moscow.
Battle: The corps of Eugène and Davout were attacked by Kutuzov during the retreat, and suffered a loss of 4,000 men.
Result: The Russians gained their objective.

WAGRAM (Austria)   Napoleonic Wars/Europe   6 July 1809
Fought between the French under Napoleon and the Austrians under Archduke Charles.
Strength: French 14,000 with 554 guns; Austrians 136,000 with 480 guns.
Aim: Napoleon sought to prevent the junction of the Archdukes Charles and John.
Battle: Once Eugène de Beauharnais had rejoined Napoleon, having driven the Austrians out of Italy, Napoleon began to cross the bulk of his army to Löbau Island, leaving the rest of his force to secure his line of communications. On the following night, 4/5 July, the French vanguard landed from Löbau on the east side of the Danube and began to push back the Austrians in order to widen their bridgehead. By 1pm on 5 July the French army was marching NE, driving Archduke Charles before it. The Austrians yielded the boggy Marchfeld and fell back on to the Wagram plateau, where the French attacked in the evening. Napoleon concentrated his efforts on the Austrian left wing in order to prevent Charles from moving eastward towards John. Archduke Charles, in turn, tried to force the French left and cut Napoleon off from his Danube bridgehead. Neither side achieved any positive results. The next day Archduke Charles renewed his attack on the French left, but was repulsed by Marshal André Masséna while Marshal Louis-Nicolas Davout's 2 Corps pushed back the Austrian left. During the day, the French left and centre gave ground when Napoleon brought up 488 guns and pounded the Austrian infantry in the greatest concentration of artillery thus far ever employed in a battle. At the same time, General Jacques Macdonald advanced in an oblong formation on the Austrian right and centre with three divisions. The French suffered many casualties but managed to break the Austrian line west of Wagram. Davout carried the heights on the Austrian left, outflanking them and rendering their position untenable. Archduke Charles's army was withdrawing to the north by 3pm and, later in the afternoon, Archduke John came up from Bratislava into the French rear but he was beaten back. The French sustained 32,000 casualties. Austrian casualties numbered 30,000 killed and wounded, while 9,000 were captured (including 12 generals) plus 20 guns. Marshal Jean-Baptiste Bessières was wounded in the battle, and General Comte Lasalle, perhaps the greatest of all Napoleon's cavalrymen, was struck down by almost the last shot of the day.
Result: Too tired to pursue Charles, the French slept on the field that night; but Charles, who had been slightly wounded in the battle, requested an armistice four days later. When the Treaty of Schönbrunn was signed only Britain, Portugal, Spain and Russia were left opposing Napoleon.
   Marshal Louis Alexandre Berthier was made Prince de Wagram.

WALTERSDORF (E Germany)   Napoleonic Wars/Europe   5 February 1807
Fought between the French under Marshal Michel Ney and the Prussians under General Anton Wilhelm Lestocq.
Strength: French 49,000; Prussians 10,000.
Aim: The French sought to prevent the Prussians joining the Russians at Eylau.
Battle: Lestocq's Corps was halted by the French and had 3,000 of its ranks killed, wounded or captured.
Result: The French were able to defeat, on 8 February, 67,000 Russians at Eylau (qv), the Prussians having arrived late on the field of battle.

WARTENBURG (E Germany)   Napoleonic Wars/Europe   3 October 1813
Fought between the Prussians under General Gebhard von Blücher and the French under Bertrand.
Strength: Prussians 60,000; French 16,000.
Aim: The Prussians sought to beat the French army back from their position between Dresden and Leipzig by harassment and attack.
Battle: The French were occupying a strong position behind a dyke and a swamp. The Prussians attacked, but the French held their ground for four hours until Blücher turned their right flank and drove them from their position. The Prussians sustained 5,000 casualties while the French admitted to 500.
Result: The French were forced to withdraw farther westward.

WATERLOO (Belgium)   Napoleonic Wars/Europe   18 June 1815
Fought between the French army under the Emperor Napoleon and an Allied army under the Duke of
Wellington with a Prussian army under Field-Marshal Prince Blücher von Wahlstadt.
Strength: French 71,947 (103 infantry battalions + 127 cavalry squadrons) with 246 guns; Allies 67,666
(49,608 infantry [85 battalions] + 12,412 cavalry [98 squadrons] + 5,646 artillery with 140 guns [British
23,991 with 78 guns, King's German Legion 5,829 with 18 guns, Hanoverians 11,220 with 12 guns,
Brunswickers 5,962 with 16 guns, Nassauers 2,880, Dutch/Belgians 17,784 with 32 guns]) with 156 guns,
Prussians 51,974 (41,283 infantry + 8,888 cavalry + 1,803 artillery with 104 guns) with 104 guns.
Aim: Napoleon sought to destroy Wellington's army before the Prussians could intervene.
Battle: After Ligny and Quatre Bras (qqv)–16 June 1815–an Allied retreat was necessary. As a result of
the slowness of the French pursuit Wellington was able, on 17 June, to withdraw under a cavalry and
artillery rearguard to his chosen position on the ridge of Mont St Jean, near Brussels, without difficulty.
While this retreat was going on, the weather broke with a thunderstorm and rain which continued into 18
June.

Wellington undertook to fight at Mont St Jean if the Prussians would promise to support him with one
army corps. In Blücher's absence Lt-General Graf von Gneisenau, the Chief of Staff of the Prussian army,
had chosen to retire upon Wavre (qv), which made such assistance possible, and Blücher promised to meet
Wellington's request. Wellington left 17,000 men of his army at Hal to cover his right flank, which he
regarded as vulnerable. The Waterloo position ran along a low ridge with a number of outposts on the
front of the ridge. These were, from west to east, the farm and wood of the Château de Hougoumont in
front of Wellington's right; the farm of La Haye Sainte in the centre; and the hamlets of La Haye,
Papelotte and Smohain in front of the left. Wellington garrisoned these outposts but withdrew almost all
his army, except Major-General van Bylandt's Dutch/Belgian brigade, on to the reverse slope.

After the rain the ground was sodden and thus, although the French army was in position on the evening
of the 17th, it was nearly noon before the French artillerymen felt it was dry enough to manoeuvre. At
about 11.30am the French attacked La Hougoumont, but the garrison, the light companies of the British
Guards, held on; and this action, which was eventually to draw in two complete French infantry divisions,
continued all day. At about 1.30pm the French artillery preparation began but, as most of the Allied
troops were hidden behind the ridge, only Bylandt's men suffered badly.

At 2pm the four divisions of General Comte Drouet d'Erlon's Corps moved forward, one directed on
the left-flank hamlets, the other three on the Allied left centre. Napoleon, whose physical condition was
poor on this day (he was suffering from haemorrhoids), was content to delegate much of the tactical
control to Marshal Michel Ney, who now made one of his major mistakes in the engagement. Ney chose to
deploy the three divisions into unwieldy columns, 200 men wide and from 24 to 27 ranks deep, thus
neutralising much of their potential fire-power. He also failed to co-ordinate the attack properly with his
cavalry. Bylandt's Dutch/Belgians were overrun, but General Sir Thomas Picton's Division behind the
ridge was able to repel the enemy, using its linear formation to develop greater fire-power. It then counter-
attacked, Picton being killed just as he had given the order to advance. The repulse of the French was
completed by the British heavy cavalry but, after this success, they went out of control and attempted to
charge the French guns, during which endeavour they were mown down.

There was then a pause, until Ney launched a great part of the French cavalry against the Allied centre.
This attack was also poorly co-ordinated and, although the Allied gun-line was overrun, the supporting
infantry squares held. Eventually the attackers were driven off, the Earl of Uxbridge, the Allied cavalry
commander, launching his cavalry to complete their defeat.

Time was now running out for the French, for a second battle was developing on the French right flank
as Blücher's army came on to the scene. At 4.30pm General Baron Friedrich von Bülow (4 Corps) began
his attack on Napoleon's right flank. Napoleon detached General Georges Mouton, Comte de Lobau's
Army Corps (6 Corps) to hold him off. Lobau attacked Bülow and cleared him out of Plancenoit. But
Blücher threw in more men against Lobau's right flank, and thereafter more and more French troops had
to be diverted from the main Waterloo battle to hold off this threat. Ney tried another cavalry attack
against Wellington's centre, this time using 9,000 cavalry, but again the French assault failed. After that he
again tried with infantry, but they were also beaten off.

Ney turned to attack La Haye Sainte, whose King's German Legion defenders were almost out of
ammunition. Ney's attack succeeded, only 42 of the defenders escaping. The crisis of the battle was now
reached. The French Old Guard was to be used in a final great effort. Wellington drew in reserves from his
wings to strengthen his centre. This was made possible because General Baron von Müffling, Blücher's

liaison officer on Wellington's staff, had persuaded Lt-General Graf von Zieten to commit his men in support of Wellington's left.

Napoleon sent two battalions of the Old Guard against the Prussians, and with the rest he attacked the British. This attack was beaten off, partly by the British Guards–the 1st Regiment of Foot Guards acquiring their title of Grenadiers for their part in defeating the Grenadiers of the Old Guard–and partly by Major-Generals Sir Frederick Adam's, Colin Halkett's and Lt-General Baron Chassé's Brigades. Having repulsed Napoleon's last throw, Wellington could now counter-attack, and soon the whole Allied line was on the move forward. The French army began to collapse and, although some battalions of the Guard stood their ground for a while, eventually the rout became general. Wellington and Blücher met at an inn called La Belle Alliance which had been Napoleon's headquarters, and it was decided to commit the pursuit to the Prussians who were fresher. French casualties numbered 37,000 men (including prisoners) and 250 guns. Allied casualties–killed, wounded and missing–totalled 22,790, made up as follows: (Wellington's army) British 6,826, King's German Legion 1,589, Hanoverians 2,007, Brunswickers 660, Nassauers 643, Dutch/Belgians 4,157 (total 15,882); Prussians 6,908.

Result: Napoleon's adventure was over. The French army broke up. Wellington and Blücher realised that the way to scotch any recovery was to move swiftly on Paris, and the two armies were to advance on parallel lines, the Prussians slightly ahead. At the same time the French fortress lines had to be cleared. Wellington blockaded and bypassed Valenciennes, and rushed Cambrai (24 June) and Peronne (26 June). Valenciennes surrendered on 26 June. Marshal Emmanuel de Grouchy, who had gathered a considerable army, fought Blücher indecisively on 27 and 28 June at Compiègne but was forced back into Paris on the 29th. Although Napoleon had abdicated (22 June), a French army of 70,000 had gathered to defend the capital, and Blücher ran into heavy fighting around Issy on 1–2 July. However, the Allies were ready to storm the capital and the French surrendered. Fighting actually continued until early October when certain minor fortresses surrendered. The Treaty of Paris was signed on 20 November 1815. France was occupied by an Allied army under Wellington from 1815 to 1818.

Napoleon left Malmaison on 29 June and, after attempting unsuccessfully to find a ship to take him to America, surrendered to Captain Frederick Lewis Maitland on HMS *Bellerophon* off Rochefort on 15 July. He was exiled to St Helena, where he died in 1821. Marshals Joachim Murat, Guillaume Brune and Ney, with some other French officers, were shot.

Wellington became a Tory politician and was Prime Minister of Great Britain from 1828 to 1830. He died at Walmer Castle, Kent, on 14 September 1852 aged eighty-three.

(See HUNDRED DAYS)

WAVRE (Belgium)   Napoleonic Wars/Europe   18–19 June 1815
Fought between the right wing of the French Armée du Nord under Marshal Emmanuel de Grouchy and the 3rd Army Corps of the Prussian army under Lt-General Freiherr von Thielemann.
Strength: French 25,473 infantry + 5,510 cavalry + 2,628 artillery and engineers + 96 guns; Prussians (14 June) 20,611 infantry + 2,405 cavalry + 964 artillery with 48 guns (less 1,000 men + 7 guns lost 16 June).
Aim: Thielemann was detailed to protect the rear of the Prussian army while it marched to help Wellington at Waterloo (qv). Grouchy was ordered to keep the Prussians away from their allies.
Battle: After Ligny (qv) the battered Prussian army retired northwards on Wavre, Thielemann's 3 Corps acting as rearguard. The pursuit was delayed by Napoleon's inexplicable unwillingness to issue orders. On the 17th the French had effectively lost contact. Their cavalry found a mass of fugitives fleeing towards Namur and Liège and, partly because that was where they expected and wanted the Prussians to go, assumed that that was where they were going. Even allowing for the uncertainty of his orders, Grouchy did not handle his men well. He continued until the evening of the 17th to believe that the Prussians were going to Liège and not northwards. It was only later that he found he was wrong. Grouchy was still in a position to intervene at Waterloo before the Prussians could do so, but he stuck to pursuing the Prussians without much sense of urgency.

General Thielemann, commanding the Prussian rearguard, was ordered by Field-Marshal Prince Blücher von Wahlstadt to stand his ground at all costs if he was heavily attacked. However, the French showed so little signs of attacking that Thielemenn began his own march towards Waterloo at 3.30pm on the 18th. But at 4pm the head of General Dominique-Joseph-René Vandamme's Corps appeared. The Prussian position was somewhat disorganised, and Major-General von Borcke's Brigade was still on the wrong side of the river Dyle. Borcke crossed at Basse Wavre, lined the left bank of the river from Basse

Wavre to Wavre with detachments, put two battalions into Wavre to support its existing garrison, and marched on with the remainder. This rearguard position was strong, for the Dyle was in flood.

Vandamme tried to storm Wavre. The suburb on the right bank was captured, but the assault on the bridge failed disastrously. Grouchy decided to support Vandamme by attacks on the flanks, which also failed. Napoleon's order to join him at Waterloo now arrived. These orders were too late for execution on the 18th, so Grouchy decided to send General Etienne Gérard's Corps to Waterloo via Limale, while again trying to storm Wavre with Vandamme's men. Pajol's cavalry rushed the Limale bridge, which had not been barricaded; but after thirteen attacks on Wavre had failed, although the Prussian right flank had been pushed back, fighting ended for the night.

Grouchy, unaware of the defeat of Napoleon at Waterloo, prepared to attack again on the 19th, surprising Thielemann, who did know. Thielemann saw his only chance was a pre-emptive strike but, with only ten battalions on his right against Grouchy's twenty-eight, and his own guns silenced by the superior French artillery, the attack swiftly stalled. Thielemann, therefore, began a temporary withdrawal. The French then learnt about Waterloo. They retreated in good order to France. Prussian casualties numbered 1,800 men, the French 2,500.

Result: The outnumbered Prussians had, on the 18th, held on with skill and courage, fulfilling Blücher's orders. Grouchy's handling of the battle drew him less credit. However, when he heard the outcome of Waterloo at 10.30am on 19 June, he promptly retreated–a manoeuvre he carried out with great ability. (See HUNDRED DAYS)

WINKOVO (USSR)   Napoleonic Wars/Europe   18 October 1812
Fought between the French under the King of Naples (formerly Marshal Joachim Murat) and the Russians under Field-Marshal Prince Kutuzov.
Strength: French 30,000; Russians 40,000.
Battle: General Count Denizov surprised the cavalry outposts of the Grande Armée which had emerged from Moscow and drove them from their position with a loss to the French of 2,500 men, plus 2,000 prisoners and 38 pieces of artillery, as well as baggage. Murat himself was wounded.
Result: This setback helped Napoleon to make up his mind to retreat from Moscow. But he had left it too late. Russian guerrillas, and Don Kuban Cossacks brought to the scene for the purpose, harried the retreating French day and night and caused far more French casualties in innumerable small actions than the Russian regular forces ever managed to do. These Partisans were mainly organised by Colonel Denis Davidov whose estates bordered the route of retreat. Davidov had been sent by Field-Marshal Kutuzov, at his own request, to the area for this special purpose.

ZNAIM (Austria)   Napoleonic Wars/Europe   14 July 1809
Fought between the French under Marshal André Masséna and the Austrians under the Prince of Reuss.
Strength: French 8,000; Austrians 30,000.
Aim: The French sought to beat back an Austrian counter-attack after Wagram (qv).
Battle: Masséna attacked the Prince of Reuss's troops as they moved forward and drove them back through Znaim, inflicting considerable loss and capturing 800 Austrians.
Result: The Austrians had already asked for an armistice and by the Treaty of Schönbrunn, which was signed between the Austrians and Napoleon on 14 October 1809, Austria ceded 32,000 square miles of territory to France and her satellites and agreed to join the continental blockade against Britain. Now the whole of Europe, apart from the Iberian Peninsula where the British and Portuguese armies, along with Spanish guerrillas, were maintaining the 'Spanish Ulcer', relapsed into an uneasy peace.

SECTION ELEVEN
NAPOLEONIC WARS/OUTSIDE EUROPE

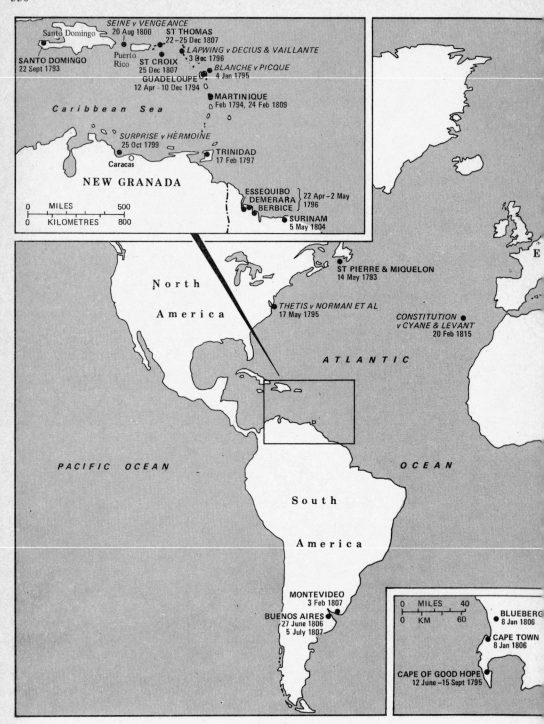

SEINE v VENGEANCE
20 Aug 1800

Santo Domingo

ST THOMAS
22–25 Dec 1807

SANTO DOMINGO
22 Sept 1793

Puerto
Rico

LAPWING v DECIUS & VAILLANTE
3 Dec 1796

ST CROIX
25 Dec 1807

BLANCHE v PICQUE
4 Jan 1795

GUADELOUPE
12 Apr – 10 Dec 1794

MARTINIQUE
Feb 1794, 24 Feb 1809

Caribbean Sea

SURPRISE v HERMOINE
25 Oct 1799

Caracas

TRINIDAD
17 Feb 1797

NEW GRANADA

ESSEQUIBO
DEMERARA
BERBICE
22 Apr – 2 May
1796

MILES   500
KILOMETRES   800

SURINAM
5 May 1804

North
America

ST PIERRE & MIQUELON
14 May 1793

THETIS v NORMAN ET AL
17 May 1795

CONSTITUTION
v CYANE & LEVANT
20 Feb 1815

ATLANTIC

PACIFIC   OCEAN

OCEAN

South

America

MONTEVIDEO
3 Feb 1807

BUENOS AIRES
27 June 1806
5 July 1807

MILES   40
KM   60

BLUEBERG
8 Jan 1806

CAPE TOWN
8 Jan 1806

CAPE OF GOOD HOPE
12 June –15 Sept 1795

24   The Napoleonic Wars: Outside Europe

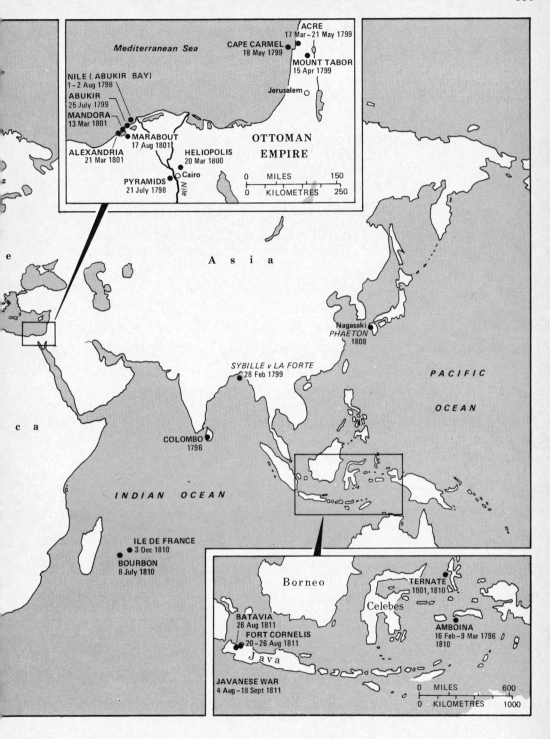

Mediterranean Sea

ACRE
17 Mar – 21 May 1799

CAPE CARMEL
18 May 1799

MOUNT TABOR
15 Apr 1799

Jerusalem

NILE (ABUKIR BAY)
1 – 2 Aug 1798

ABUKIR
25 July 1799

MANDORA
13 Mar 1801

MARABOUT
17 Aug 1801

ALEXANDRIA
21 Mar 1801

HELIOPOLIS
20 Mar 1800

OTTOMAN EMPIRE

Cairo

PYRAMIDS
21 July 1798

Nile

MILES   0   150
KILOMETRES   0   250

A s i a

Nagasaki
PHAETON
1808

SYBILLE v LA FORTE
28 Feb 1799

P A C I F I C

O C E A N

COLOMBO
1796

I N D I A N   O C E A N

ILE DE FRANCE
3 Dec 1810

BOURBON
8 July 1810

c a

e

Borneo

TERNATE
1801, 1810

Celebes

BATAVIA
26 Aug 1811

FORT CORNELIS
20 – 26 Aug 1811

AMBOINA
16 Feb – 9 Mar 1796
1810

Java

JAVANESE WAR
4 Aug – 18 Sept 1811

MILES   0   600
KILOMETRES   0   1000

ABUKIR (ABU QIR) (Egypt)   Napoleonic Wars/Outside Europe   25 July 1799
Fought between the French under Napoleon and the Turks under Ahmed Pasha (known as Djezzar—the Butcher), Mustafa Pasha IV.
Strength: French 7,700 with 18 guns + some siege guns; Turks 18,000 with 30 guns.
Aim: The Turks sought to invade Egypt, the French to prevent it.
Battle: Under British escort, the Turkish troops landed and entrenched at Abukir (Abu Qir). The French assaulted the outer of the Turks' two concentric positions and overpowered them. With the aid of an artillery barrage, they then attacked the inner defence and, though at first repulsed, they rolled up this second line, General Jean Lannes leading the assault with Marshal Auguste Murat at the head of the cavalry. Five thousand Turks surrendered, Mustafa Pasha among them. Altogether, two-thirds of the Turkish troops perished, 2,000 being killed and 11,000 being drowned whilst trying to escape. The French casualties were 900 men, including Murat and Lannes who were both wounded.
Result: The citadel of Abukir surrendered on 2 August.

ABUKIR (BAY)   see ALEXANDRIA III; also NILE

ACRE III (Israel)   Napoleonic Wars/Outside Europe   17 March–21 May 1799
Fought between the Turks under Ahmed Pasha (known as Djezzar—the butcher), Mustafa Pasha IV, with the British under Commodore Sir (William) Sidney Smith in support, and the French under Bonaparte.
Strength: Turks 5,000 with 250 guns, British HMS *Tigre* (80)–HMS *Theseus* (74); French 13,000 with 52 guns.
Aim: After the Battle of the Nile (qv) Bonaparte turned eastward towards Syria, on his way to capture Constantinople (Istanbul). The surrender of Acre could have led to French domination of Syria, which would then have been used as a base to defeat the Turks and take over the E Mediterranean.
Battle: Bonaparte invested the city on 17 March. An assault on the town was repulsed with loss. On the 18th the Royal Navy captured most of Bonaparte's siege train. A Syrian relief column was engaged at Mount Tabor, first by General Jean Kléber's Division and later by all the French under Bonaparte who temporarily raised the siege. On the resumption of the siege the French assaulted the town seventeen times without success and the defenders made eleven sallies from the town. Supported by a British naval squadron under Sidney Smith, the Turks had only to defend the three landward sides of the town. An epidemic of bubonic plague on the night of 20 May among the French troops forced Bonaparte to raise the siege and withdraw towards Egypt. French losses were 2,200 men, of whom 1,000 died of disease.
Result: Bonaparte's conquest of Syria was thwarted.

ALEXANDRIA III (Egypt)   Napoleonic Wars/Outside Europe   21 March 1801
Fought between the French under General Baron de Menou and the British expeditionary force under General Sir Ralph Abercromby.
Strength: French 10,000; British 14,000.
Aim: After General Jean Kléber's assassination (on 14 June 1800), the British, taking advantage of growing French weakness in Egypt, landed an expeditionary force at Abukir Bay and advanced towards Alexandria. Menou sought to halt the British advance.
Battle: The French attacked the British but were repulsed with a loss of 3,000 men. British losses were 1,400, Abercromby being mortally wounded. The action is also known as the Battle of Abukir.
Result: The defeat of the French proved to be the turning-point in their fortunes. Cairo surrendered in June, Alexandria in August, to the British commander General Sir John Hely-Hutchinson. Menou's force was sent back to France and Egypt was restored to the Turks under Selim III.
   France's reverses in Egypt were accelerated by the incompetence of Menou, who, it is of interest to note, had become a Moslem during his service in Egypt.

AMBOINA (AMBON) (Molucca Island, Indonesia)   Revolutionary and Napoleonic Wars/Outside Europe   1796; 1810
Fought between the Dutch and the British.
   When the Dutch became an ally of France, her East Indies possessions were opened to the French fleet. The British determined to remove this threat. In February 1796, with a squadron consisting of *Suffolk, Centurion, Resistance, Orpheus* and *Swift*, Admiral Peter Rainier sailed to Amboina. The Dutch surrendered immediately, and a small detachment of the Madras European Regiment under Major Vigors, involved in the capture, embarked with the squadron.

After the Peace of Amiens Amboina was restored to the Dutch along with her other East Indies possession, but in 1810 they were reoccupied when Captain Edward Tucker with *Doris, Cornwallis* and *Samarang* took 130 troops from the 1st Madras European Regiment, 50 troops of the Royal Artillery and some sepoys to the island. Four men were killed and 9 wounded during the occupation and a garrison was maintained until 1814, when the Treaty of Paris restored the island to the Dutch.

AMBOINA (AMBON)/BANDA ISLANDS (Molucca Islands, Indonesia)   Napoleonic Wars/Outside Europe   16 February–9 March 1796
Fought between the British under Admiral Peter Rainier and their former ally the Dutch.
On 16–18 February 1796 Admiral Rainier captured Amboina–capital of the Moluccas (the Spice Islands)–from the Dutch, whose garrison numbered 841 men. This capture gave Britain control of the bulk of the world's supply of cloves.
On 7 March Rainier reached the Banda Islands, a Dutch colony, occupying them on the 9th after some slight resistance. The garrison numbered 432, with no less than 260 cannon. Booty included 184,000 rix-dollars and vast quantities of spices. This was the basis of an immense personal fortune made by Rainier during his long sojourn in the East Indies.

BATAVIA (DJAKARTA) (Java, Indonesia)   Napoleonic Wars/Outside Europe   26 August 1811
Fought between the French and Dutch garrison and the British under General Sir Samuel Auchmuty.
Strength: French/Dutch 6,000; British 10,000.
Aim: The British sought to capture Batavia (Djakarta).
Battle: The town was taken on 26 August by the British, the garrison having abandoned it to occupy a stronger position at the neighbouring Fort Cornelis. The British then stormed the entrenchments there, the survivors laying down their arms. British casualties were 872 killed and wounded.
Result: The British objective was achieved.
On 17 September the Dutch were forced to sign the Capitulation of Semerang, the provisions of which ceded the islands of Java, Palembang, Timor and Macassar to the British in perpetuity. However, these islands were returned to the Dutch as part of the treaty-making in Vienna in 1816, at the end of the Napoleonic Wars.

BLANCHE v PIQUE (off Guadeloupe, West Indies)   Napoleonic Wars/Outside Europe   4 January 1795
Blanche (32) (Captain Robert Faulkner), cruising off Grande Terre in Guadeloupe (qv), sighted the French frigate *Pique* (32) (Conseil) at anchor off Pointe-à-Pitre. After some manoeuvring on both sides, *Pique* decided not to venture outside the cover of the shore batteries, which opened fired on *Blanche* at one juncture. Faulkner then decided to board an American schooner which had been sighted, took her in tow and proceeded. The next afternoon he discovered *Pique* about 6 miles astern. He cast off the tow, tacked and gave chase. The ships exchanged broadsides at about midnight and a spirited action, in which Faulkner was killed, continued with varying fortunes until 5am when *Pique* surrendered. The ships were evenly matched except that *Blanche* was short-handed as a result of releasing men to take away prizes.
Lieutenant Frederick Watkins, who took command after Faulkner's death, and Lieutenant David Milne were promoted to Commander as a result of the action.

BLUEBERG (BLUE MOUNTAIN) (Cape Province, S Africa)   Napoleonic Wars/Outside Europe   8 January 1806
Fought between the British under Lt-General Sir David Baird and the Dutch and French under General Jan Willems Janssens.
Strength: British 6,600; Dutch/French 1,000.
Battle: The force which landed at Saldanha Bay (qv) was attacked by the Dutch and French from Cape Town. The British gained a decisive victory for a loss of 204 casualties. Dutch and French casualties numbered about 300.
Result: Baird went on to occupy Cape Town (qv) on 10 January, Janssens surrendering on 18 January.

BOURBON (Réunion, Indian Ocean)   Napoleonic Wars/Outside Europe   8 July 1810
Fought between the French garrison and the British under Commodore Josias Rowley and Colonel Keatinge (56th Foot).

Aim: The British sought to capture the island of Bourbon, a French territorial possession.
Battle: With a squadron of 5 ships and a small detachment of troops, the British took the island on 8 July, at the expense of 16 killed and 67 wounded.
Result: The British objective was achieved, Bourbon remaining in British hands until the peace in 1814.

BUENOS AIRES I (Argentina)   Napoleonic Wars/Outside Europe   27 June 1806
Fought between the British under Colonel William Beresford (later Lord Beresford) and the Argentinians under General Jacques de Liniers.
Strength: British 2,500; Argentinians 20,000 (mostly militia).
Aim: In accordance with British policy to attack the overseas possessions of France and her allies wherever possible, Beresford sought to capture Buenos Aires, then held by the Spaniards.
Battle: Beresford and his men were landed by a small squadron under Commodore Sir Home Popham and took Buenos Aires. Before they could be reinforced, however, they were counter-attacked by the Argentinians under General Liniers, a French officer in the service of Charles IV. The British were forced to surrender, their casualties numbering 250 killed and wounded. The remainder were held in captivity.
Result: The British objective was not achieved and Popham, who had acted without orders, was later court-martialled for this débâcle, but two years later was promoted to Rear-Admiral.

BUENOS AIRES II (Argentina)   Napoleonic Wars/Outside Europe   5 July 1807
Fought between the British under General John Whitelocke and the Argentinians under General Jacques de Liniers.
Strength: British 10,000; Argentinians 30,000 militia, Partisans and guerrilleros.
Aim: The British sought to capture Buenos Aires.
Battle: Whitelocke, who had occupied Montevideo (qv) earlier in the year, moved against Buenos Aires. The city was assaulted, but casualties from sniper-fire were so great that in the end the British were forced to surrender.
Result: The British were forced to evacuate the Rio de la Plata area. The two attacks successfully repulsed by the Argentinians aroused national feeling to such an extent that direct Spanish rule was never fully restored there. Though the British military objective was not achieved, it may be said that the policy of the naval officers on the spot was successful in that the Spanish lost a colony, and the Argentinians ceased to support Spain.

CAPE CARMEL (Israel)   Napoleonic Wars/Outside Europe   18 May 1799
Fought between the British garrison of Acre under Captain Sir (William) Sidney Smith and a French fleet commanded by Rear-Admiral Perrée.
   The aim of the French fleet was to co-operate with Napoleon's land forces in an attack on Acre. This fleet, consisting of a flotilla of vessels with a battering train of artillery, ammunition, platforms, etc, and including *Marianne* (4), *La Négresse* (6), *La Fondre* (8), *La Dangereuse* (6), *La Maria Rose* (4), *La Dame de Grace* (4), *Les Deux Frères* (4) and *La Torrida* (2), were intercepted off Cape Carmel and captured by Sir Sidney Smith's flotilla, which included *Le Tigre* (80). This coup greatly reduced Napoleon's chances of capturing Acre and on 20 May Napoleon started to retreat. After continual harassment and losing command of the sea, he reached Cairo on 14 June having lost 2,200 men, half from disease.

CAPE OF GOOD HOPE (Cape Province, S Africa)   Napoleonic Wars/Outside Europe   12 June–15 September 1795
Fought between the British and the Dutch.
Strength: British 4 battalions + marines and seamen of the fleet; Dutch 800 regulars + 2,000 militia.
Aim: The British, after the collapse of the campaign in Holland, saw that it was vitally important to secure control of the Dutch overseas colonies to prevent their being used as bases for French commerce raiders. The most important of these was the colony at the Cape of Good Hope which stood astride the route to India, Australia and the Far East.
Battle: The Prince of Orange wrote a letter on 7 February 1795 to the governors of all Dutch colonies authorising them to admit British troops on condition that the colonies be returned at a general peace settlement. Commodore Blankett, RN, the senior naval authority in these areas, was sent with 4 ships and 500 men of the 2nd Battalion 78th Regiment of Foot under Major-General James Craig, to enforce this letter at the Cape. The ships were so crowded it proved impossible to carry any artillery. A second and

larger expedition, with three more battalions under Admiral Sir George Elphinstone and Major-General Alured Clarke, sailed a few days after Blankett's expedition. However, Elphinstone had orders to leave his soldiers at Bahia in Brazil until needed. He and Blankett arrived at the same time, and they asked for the surrender of the colony. This was rejected (12 June 1795).

Craig and Elphinstone soon realised force would be necessary and sent back for their troops. Craig, with only 1,600 soldiers, marines and seamen and without artillery, realised he could make no headway against the stronger Dutch garrison; but when Simonstown was abandoned by the Dutch, on 14 July, Craig moved in. On 7 August, with naval support, he began his advance on Cape Town. After a skirmish, in which he captured 5 guns, progress for the British was slow, since in outpost warfare the Boer irregulars excelled. On 3 September Craig, whose supplies were running out, decided on an all-out attack to coincide with the arrival of the fleet bearing Clarke's soldiers. On 15 October, after some more desultory fighting, the Governor agreed to surrender. British casualties were 4 killed and 60 wounded.
Result: Britain held the Cape until 1802, when it was returned under the Treaty of Amiens. It had to be recaptured in 1806 (CAPE TOWN).

CAPE TOWN (Cape Province, S Africa)   Napoleonic Wars/Outside Europe   8 January 1806
Fought between the British under Lt-General Sir David Baird and the Dutch.
Strength: British 6,000; Dutch 3,000.
Aim: Cape Town had been returned to the Dutch under the Treaty of Amiens in 1803. When the war against France and her allies was renewed, the British sent an expeditionary force against Cape Town, with the purpose of retaking it.
Battle: Baird landed his men at Saldanha Bay on the SW coast then, repulsing a combined French and Dutch counter-attack, secured the beachhead and went on to seize Cape Town.
Result: The British objective was achieved, and Cape Town remained in British hands after the end of hostilities in 1815.

COLOMBO (Sri Lanka/Ceylon)   Napoleonic Wars/Outside Europe   1796
Fought between the British, under Admiral Peter Rainier and Colonel James Stuart, and the Dutch under the Governor of Colombo, Van Anglebeck.

After Colonel Stuart of the Madras army had, with 1,100 British infantry and two Indian battalions, captured Trincomalee on 25 August 1795, the British sailed around the coast, escorted by 4 warships, capturing Fort Ostenburg, Batticaloa and Jaffnapatam, and landed at Negombo, 20 miles short of Colombo. On 7 February 1796 Stuart, after receiving reinforcements, started his march south on Colombo. In spite of easily defensible country the British met with no resistance until they were just outside Colombo where Colonel Raymond, a French officer, led a gallant attack with 300 Malay soldiers. These were easily defeated. The British had subverted a Swiss mercenary regiment, raised by the Comte de Meuron especially for the Dutch East India Company, for a price of £4,000. So, finding his most able soldiers had defected and the remainder unreliable, Van Anglebeck lost no time in capitulating, and on 16 February 1796 Stuart marched in.
Result: Prizes worth £300,000 were taken, including 173 brass guns and 187 iron guns, which compensated the British and Indian soldiery for their initiative and competence. In 1798 the independent King of Kandy recognised British suzerainty over the whole island, but further fighting and three wars were to be waged between the Kandyans and the British during the next twenty years, until 1818.

CONSTITUTION v CYANE and *LEVANT* (off Barbados, West Indies)   Napoleonic Wars/Outside Europe   20 February 1815 and 20 December 1815
On 14 January 1814 the US 44-gun frigate *Constitution*, now commanded by Commodore William Bainbridge, had evaded the British blockade and managed to escape from Boston. On 14 February, off Barbados, she captured and destroyed the 14-gun schooner *Picton*, and on 23 February while in the Mona Passage she fell in with the British 36-gun frigate *Pique* (Lieutenant the Hon Anthony Maitland). *Constitution* and *Pique* closed on each other, but by skilful manoeuvring kept out of range until in squally weather they finally lost sight of each other. Neither was keen to engage, but whereas Maitland had strict orders not to become embroiled with any of the big American frigates, there seems no reason why Bainbridge should have been so reluctant. *Constitution* then returned to Boston, where she remained for most of the rest of the year.

On 17 December 1814 *Constitution* slipped out again on a raiding cruise, and on 20 February 1815, 150 miles NE of Madeira, sighted the British 22-gun ship *Cyane* (Captain Gordon T. Falcon) and 20-gun ship *Levant* (Captain the Hon George Douglas). As there were several convoys sailing in that part of the Atlantic, the British captains decided to try and attack, hoping that together they might be able to make an impression on the much superior enemy. First *Cyane* was put out of action. Then *Levant*, whose masts and rigging had already been damaged and was drifting to leeward, tried to go to the assistance of *Cyane* and was knocked out. The *Constitution* captured both ships and crew.

DEMERARA, BERBICE AND ESSEQUIBO (Guyana, S America)   Napoleonic Wars/Outside Europe   22 April–2 May 1796
On 15 April 1796 a British expedition was mounted from Barbados to capture the Dutch settlements of Demerara, Berbice and Essequibo.
To achieve this objective, *Malabar* (54) (Captain John Parr) with some frigates and transports were detached from Rear-Admiral Sir John Laforey's squadron, embarking a force of 1,200 men commanded by Major-General John Whyte. The first two settlements surrendered peaceably on 22 April and the last-named on 2 May. The Dutch *Thetis* (24) and a cutter were captured at Demerara.

FORT CORNELIS (Java, Indonesia)   Napoleonic Wars/Outside Europe   20–6 August 1811
The British made an unopposed landing at Chillingcherry (4 August), Java, and after a sharp skirmish on 10 August, in which the advance guard under Colonel Rollo Gillespie ('the bravest of the brave') drove back the French, the British laid siege to Fort Cornelis. Admiral the Hon Robert Stopford landed a naval brigade with heavy guns, and on the 26th the fort was stormed.
Gillespie, a real fire-eater, again distinguished himself. He led the 22nd Light Dragoons in a 35-mile pursuit, captured 246 officers (including 2 generals), and took 6,000 other prisoners plus 280 guns. This bold attack led to the unconditional surrender of Java.

GUADELOUPE (Leeward Islands, West Indies)   Napoleonic Wars/Outside Europe   12 April–10 December 1794
After the capture of St Lucia, on 8 April Vice-Admiral Sir John Jervis sailed in *Boyne* (98) with some frigates and transports conveying a military force under General Sir Charles Grey for the Leeward Islands.
A force, including seamen and marines, was landed on Guadeloupe on 11 April, supported by *Winchelsea* (Captain Lord Garlies). The occupation of the island of Grande-Terre was completed by 12 April, and on the 14th the troops were re-embarked for an attack on Basse-Terre, another of the Leeward Islands. By 20 April the main garrison under General Collot surrendered Guadeloupe and with it the islands of Mariegolante, Descouda and Iles-des-Saintes. Leaving a garrison under Major-General Sir David Dundas, Jervis and Grey left Grande-Terre for St Christopher. However, on 3 June a French force consisting of 2 frigates, a corvette, 2 large ships armed 'en fluts', and 5 transports arrived off Gosier Bay. A number of skirmishes ensued, mostly to the disadvantage of the British, between the scattered British garrison and the French force, which eventually numbered 1,200–1,500.
Jervis and Grey arrived back on 7 June, when Grey landed at Basse-Terre. On the 8th Jervis in *Boyne* with 3 ships of the line arrived at Pointe-à-Pitre to find the French ships moored in the anchorage. Not until the 19th was Jervis able to muster sufficient transports to effect a landing against Grande-Terre. This landing included two battalions of seamen under the command of Captains Lewis Robertson (who was killed in the fighting) from *Veteran* and Charles Sawyer of *Vanguard*. A number of minor actions then took place with no great advantage to either side.
On 27 September, French reinforcements arrived and the whole of Guadeloupe was gradually recaptured. Fort Matilda was besieged and held out until 10 December, when the French recaptured the island and the garrison was evacuated by Captain Richard Bowen of *Terpsichore*, for which he was given a special commendation.
The island of Guadeloupe (discovered by Columbus in 1493) after brief British rule reverted to French sovereignty, which was confirmed in 1814.

HELIOPOLIS (Egypt)   Napoleonic Wars/Outside Europe   20 March 1800
Fought between the French under General Jean Kléber and the Turks under Ibrahim Bey.
Strength: French 35,000; Turks 70,000.

Aim: Kléber had made an agreement at the Convention of El Arish, in which Commodore Sir (William) Sidney Smith was involved, to evacuate Egypt in return for safe passage to France, but the British government disavowed the agreement and Kléber was forced to continue military operations.
Battle: The French attacked the Turks, routing them completely. Turkish losses amounted to several thousand men. The French sustained casualties of 300 killed and wounded.
Result: Kléber recovered Cairo, but was assassinated on 14 June 1800. He was succeeded by the incompetent General Baron de Menou.

ILE DE FRANCE (MAURITIUS) (Indian Ocean)   3 December 1810
Fought between the British, under Vice-Admiral Albemarle Bertie and Major-General the Hon John Abercromby (son of Sir Ralph Abercromby), and the French.
Strength: British 10,000 + 19 ships; French 4,000.
Aim: The British sought to capture the island of Mauritius.
Battle: Vice-Admiral Bertie commanded a fleet convoying 10,000 troops under General Abercromby. The island was taken with casualties of 167 killed, wounded and missing. French losses included 7 frigates, 10 sloops, 21 French merchantman and 3 captured British merchantmen.
Result: The British objective was achieved, and both Mauritius and Réunion (BOURBON) ceased to be bases for French privateers preying on British merchantmen in the Indian Ocean.

JAVANESE WAR   Napoleonic Wars/Outside Europe   4 August–18 September 1811
Fought between the British expeditionary force commanded by General Sir Samuel Achmuty and the Franco-Dutch forces under General Jan Willems Janssens.
Strength: British 5,344 Europeans + 5,777 sepoys (Madras army) + 839 lascars (camp followers); French/Dutch/Javanese 17,000 including 500 French voltigeurs.
Aim: In 1806 Napoleon established the kingdom of Holland under his brother Louis. The following year, one of his marshals, Herman Willem Daendals, the leader of the revolt which had unseated Prince William of Orange, was appointed Governor-General of Java, the colony established as far back as 1602 by the Dutch East India company. He strengthened Javanese defences against possible British aggression and raised an army of 17,000 men. He was replaced early in 1811 by General Janssens, a man of much lesser reputation and ability. In the pursuit of the war against French interests, Lord Minto, Governor-General of India, who had already occupied Mauritius, decided on the conquest of Java.

On 11 June 1811, the invasion fleet, comprising 57 transports and escorted by 33 warships commanded by Rear-Admiral the Hon R. Stopford, set sail for Malacca accompanied by Lord Minto in person. On 4 August the fleet arrived safely at Batavia, the Dutch capital, where the invasion force landed at Chillingcherry, about 10 miles to the east. Five days later, commanded by Colonel Rollo Gillespie ('the bravest of the brave'), the invading force occupied Batavia, which the Dutch evacuated without firing a shot, according to plan. Janssens had decided to oppose the invaders from a strongly fortified position in the hills at Cornelis, some 7 miles south of Batavia (with several redoubts and batteries totalling 280 guns). He also set up a strong outpost at Weltewreeden in front of his main position.
Battle: On 11 August, after a short engagement, the British drove out the Franco-Dutch forces from their entrenchments at Weltewreeden, inflicting casualties numbering 500 killed and wounded. The British then brought up heavy guns and mortars from the ships and, on 24 August, bombarded Cornelis, starting from a range of 800 yards. By this time sickness had reduced the defending force to 13,000 men and the British to only 8,000. A deserter from the Dutch led the way along a path to the flank of Janssens' position on the river Sloken and an assault party under Colonel Gillespie reached the enemy's lines before sunrise, unperceived. Gillespie's forces then charged, taking one redoubt after another. When the British main body joined in the attack, the Franco-Dutch army abandoned thier positions and fled–5,500 surrendered, after about 4,000 had been killed or wounded. General Janssens escaped with 600 men and fled to Samarang on the northern coast of Java, the remainder of his force dispersing to the hills. British losses during the whole campaign were 865 killed and wounded.
Result: On 10 September General Achmuty occupied Samarang without loss and, on 18 September, General Janssens formally surrendered. Lord Minto appointed Stamford Raffles, Lieutenant-Governor of Java and its dependencies, a position he held until 1816. After the fall of Napoleon the Indonesian territories were returned to Holland, but Raffles went on to develop the bleak, tiny, unpopulated island of Singapore as an alternative strategic outpost to guard Britain's shipping route to China.

LAPWING v DECIUS and *VAILLANTE* (off St Kitts, West Indies)   Napoleonic Wars/Outside Europe   3 December 1796
Lapwing (28) (Commander Robert Barton), at anchor off St Kitts, heard of an intended landing on Anguilla by French warships and troops. Barton decided to sail for Anguilla to prevent this, but he arrived too late the next day as the French force had landed and burned the town. However, the arrival of *Lapwing* decided the French commander to re-embark the invading troops on board the 20-gun ship *Decius* and brig *Vaillante*, which then stood out from the bay. They were chased by *Lapwing* and brought to action. The brig *Vaillante* bore away, subsequently ran aground and was destroyed by *Lapwing*'s guns. *Decius* surrendered.

Lapwing's casualties were slight (1 killed and 6 wounded), but those of *Decius*, overcrowded with troops, were heavy.

MANDORA (Egypt)   Napoleonic Wars/Outside Europe   13 March 1801
Fought between the British under General Sir Ralph Abercromby and the French.
Aim: The British sought to drive the French from Egypt and restore the country to the Turks, and also to safeguard Indian possessions which were threatened by Napoleon.
Battle: On 8 March the British expedition disembarked in Marmorice Bay under heavy fire, and, on the 13th, the march on Alexandria (ALEXANDRIA III) was begun. The troops moved in three columns, and at Mandora a numerically superior French force attacked the British, their cavalry spearheading the attack. The British corps leading the centre and left columns bore the brunt of the fighting, but it held well and gave the rest of the force time to deploy. The French were then driven back to their starting point and routed with loss. British casualties were 6 officers and 153 men killed and 66 officers and 1,936 men wounded.
Result: The overall British objective remained the same.

MARABOUT (N Egypt)   Napoleonic Wars/Outside Europe   17 August 1801
Fought between the British and the French under General Baron de Menou.
The 54th Regiment of the Dorsetshires was the force assigned to the assault on the French garrison at Fort Marabout, the tomb of a Moslem saint. The British carried a redoubt at the fort and Menou surrendered, being granted safe conduct for himself and his army to France, provided they did not serve against England for the rest of the war. After the surrender of Alexandria (see ALEXANDRIA III) the Treaty of Amiens was signed. But in 1803 the war was renewed which cancelled the terms of surrender. What was still left of the French army in Egypt was once again able to fight.

MARTINIQUE (Windward Island, West Indies)   Napoleonic Wars/Outside Europe   February 1794
On 5 February 1794 a British expedition, which had been fitted out at Barbados, arrived off Martinique. It consisted of a naval squadron of 5 ships of the line and several frigates commanded by Vice-Admiral Sir John Jervis in *Boyive* (98), and a military force under Lt-General Sir Charles Grey. Troops were landed at three points and the whole island, except for 2 forts, was in British hands by 16 March. Upwards of 200 seamen were landed, under Lieutenants Rogers and Rutherford, who distinguished themselves in the fighting and in dragging their cannon overland.

The forts were subsequently captured as a result of a boat attack, commanded by Lieutenant Richard Bowen of *Boyive*, and a landing supported by *Asia* (64) (Thompson) and the sloop *Zebra* (Captain Robert Faulkner). The French garrisons put up a gallant fight and sustained heavy losses, though British casualties were light. The French frigate *Bienvenue* was captured. She was renamed *Undaunted* and Faulkner was given command, being succeeded in *Zebra* by Lieutenant Bowen.

MARTINIQUE II (Windward Islands, West Indies)   Napoleonic Wars/Outside Europe   24 February 1809
Fought between the British, under Vice-Admiral Sir Alexander Cochrane and Lt-General Sir George Beckwith, and the French.
Aim: The British sought to take the island of Martinique.
Battle: Though the island had been restored to France under the Treaty of Amiens, the British retook it in 1809 with a combined naval and military force.
Result: The British objective was achieved. In 1814 Martinique was once more restored to France.

MONTEVIDEO (Uruguay)   Napoleonic Wars/Outside Europe   3 February 1807
Fought between the British under General John Whitelocke and a Spanish garrison led by Santiago de
Liniers y Brémont, the Viceroy.
Strength: British 8,000; Spanish 5,000.
Aim: The reduction by the British of the city of Montevideo to prevent its use as a base for enemy
privateers operating in the S Atlantic.
Battle: The city was assaulted by the British on 3 February, before which an action had taken place outside
the town. The Rifle Corps, later the Rifle Brigade, was prominent in the action. The city was taken with a
loss of about 600 British.
Result: The British immediate objective was achieved, but when Whitelocke's attempt to seize Buenos
Aires (BUENOS AIRES II) met with disaster in July of the same year, Montevideo was evacuated. Montevideo
became free from Spanish rule in 1814 and became capital of the Republic of Uruguay in 1828.

MOUNT TABOR (Israel)   Napoleonic Wars/Outside Europe   15 April 1799
Fought between the French, under Bonaparte and General Jean Kléber, and the Syrians.
Aim: The Syrians were on their way to relieve Acre. The French sought to prevent them from doing so.
Battle: Kléber, sent to stop the advance of the Syrian army, was surrounded by the enemy and was fighting
them in hollow square formation when Bonaparte came up, having temporarily raised the siege of Acre.
He in turn surrounded the Syrians, and the two French armies launched a two-sided attack which routed
and dispersed the enemy.
Result: Bonaparte was able to return to Acre, but the town, defended by Commodore Sir (William) Sidney
Smith, did not surrender and in the end he was forced to abandon the siege (ACRE III).

NILE (ABUKIR BAY) (Egypt)   Napoleonic Wars/Outside Europe   1–2 August 1798
Fought between the British fleet under Rear-Admiral Horatio Nelson and the French fleet under Vice-
Admiral François Brueys d'Aigalliers.
Strength: British 13 74-gun 2-decker ships of the line + 1 50-gun 2-deckers + 1 14-gun brig; French 1 120-
gun 3-decker + 3 80-gun 2-deckers + 9 74-gun 2-deckers + 4 frigates (1 × 48, 1 × 44, and 2 × 36) + 2
brigs + 3 bomb vessels and several gunboats in Alexandria. The French also had some land batteries
positioned to cover the flanks of their line.
   Nelson's squadron has been described as 'probably the finest fleet of 74s which was ever assembled'. The
French squadron was also of high quality, but not so good, nor nearly so experienced, as the British.
Certainly its leadership was inferior.
Aim: The British sought to destroy the French fleet and thus to isolate Bonaparte in Egypt and reopen the
Mediterranean to Britain. Admiral Brueys's squadron, having successfully escorted Bonaparte's army to
Egypt, was protecting his communications. His tactical aim was, by purely defensive methods, to preserve
his fleet intact. It seems he never considered the possibility of being attacked.
Battle: Nelson's fleet, returning to Egyptian waters for the second time, approached Alexandria about
noon on 1 August. Seeing no major warships in the harbour, Nelson kept on to the east when, at 2.45pm,
the French warships were sighted in Abukir Bay drawn up in line of battle. Nelson signalled 'Prepare for
Battle' and the long chase was over.
   The French fleet was drawn up in line astern, close into the shoals on the westward side of the bay.
Admiral Brueys assumed that he was close enough to prevent the British going round the head of his line,
and the battery sited on Abukir Island could provide additional protection. Also it was nearly dark by the
time the British fleet was close enough to attack. Three of Nelson's ships had been detached and would not
be able to get up until after dark. However, Nelson decided to attack–'it instantly struck his eager and
penetrating mind, that where there was room for an enemy's ship to swing, there was room for one of ours
to anchor'. Moreover, the leading French ship was too far from the 5-fathom line–thus allowing the
leading English ships to come inside the French line, while Nelson and the ships following him attacked
outside the French, thus concentrating his force against the French van. The French rear could not help
their van because of the direction of the wind. Gradually the British ships worked along the French line,
hammering their opponents in turn into submission. *Culloden* grounded on the tail of Abukir Island shoal,
but the other British ships kept up their attack. *Bellerophon* was put out of the action when she tackled the
much stronger French flagship *L'Orient* (120). However *L'Orient* caught fire and, at 10pm, exploded.
There was then a big pause before the battle resumed; but although the British ships continued to push
down the line, their crews were so exhausted that they could do little. The 3 rear French ships made sail,

together with the 2 surviving frigates, but one of them ran aground and was burnt by her crew. The battle petered out around midnight.

By dawn, of the 13 French ships of the line, 6 were in British hands; the seventh, *L'Orient*, had sunk; 4 were aground, and 2 escaped. British casualties were 288 killed and 677 wounded, French casualties were considerably higher–1,700 killed, 1,500 wounded, and 3,000 taken prisoner.
Result: This total British victory allowed Britain to isolate and eventually (1801) defeat the French army of Egypt. Control of the Mediterranean was regained.

This action is also known as the Battle of Abukir or Abukir Bay.

PHAETON (Nagasaki harbour, Japan)   Napoleonic Wars/Outside Europe   1808
In 1808 the British frigate HMS *Phaeton* sailed into Nagasaki harbour searching for Dutch ships to impound, Holland having entered the war on the side of Napoleon. Finding no Dutch ships the captain asked for supplies. On being refused he threatened to blow Nagasaki to smithereens so, as the Japanese defences were weak, the Governor complied, committing suicide that evening after *Phaeton* had sailed.

PYRAMIDS, THE (Egypt)   Napoleonic Wars/Outside Europe   21 July 1798
Fought between the French under Bonaparte and the Egyptians under Murad Bey.
Strength: French 25,000; Egyptians 21,000 (6,000 Mamelukes + 15,000 Fellahin).
Aim: When Bonaparte took Alexandria from the Mameluke ruler, Ibrahim Bey, Ibrahim crossed the Nile and prepared to flee to Syria. His military commander, Murad Bey, however, sought to block the French advance by occupying Embabeh on the left bank of the Nile.
Battle: Bonaparte advanced on the Egyptian position along the river while sending a flanking column to turn the enemy left. The Egyptian infantry, unused to organised warfare, took little part in the battle, but Murad, unwilling to be caught between the French and the river, launched cavalry attacks against the French, who had formed themselves into squares which repulsed the charges with great loss to the attackers. On the failure of this counter-attack, the Egyptian army collapsed, many being forced into the Nile.
Result: The French took Embabeh and many of the Egyptian infantry who were entrenched there. Murad fell back south unmolested. Bonaparte's casualties were only about 300. The day after the battle he occupied Cairo.

Bonaparte's preliminary exhortation deserves to be remembered: 'Forward! Remember that from these monuments forty centuries look down...'

ST CROIX (Virgin Islands, West Indies)   Napoleonic Wars/Outside Europe   25 December 1807
Fought between the British, under Admiral Sir Alexander Cochrane and General Bowyer, and the Danish garrison.
Aim: The British sought to capture the island of St Croix to use as a forward naval base.
Battle: The combined British military and naval force took the Caribbean island with little resistance.
Result: The British objective was achieved.

ST PIERRE AND MIQUELON (near Newfoundland)   Napoleonic Wars/Outside Europe   14 May 1793
Because of the importance of the fishing around St Pierre and Miquelon the British government decided to mount a small expedition from Halifax to clean up these French islands. On 14 May 1793 a British force of 310 all ranks from the 4th and 65th Regiments and artillery under Brigadier-General Ogilvie was landed from *Alligator* (William Affleck), *Diligente* and some river transports. The islands quickly surrendered.

ST THOMAS (Virgin Island, West Indies)   Napoleonic Wars/Outside Europe   22–25 December 1807
Fought between the British, under Admiral Sir Alexander Cochrane and General Henry Bowyer, and the Danish garrison.
Aim: The British sought to capture the island of St Thomas to prevent its occupation by the French.
Battle: Like St Croix, the island was captured by the British combined force of naval and military personnel.
Result: The British objective was gained.

SANTO DOMINGO (Dominican Republic, West Indies)   Napoleonic Wars/Outside Europe   22 September 1793
Acting on information from a M. Charmilly that some of the French settlements on Santo Domingo had Royalist sympathies and would welcome British occupation, a 1793 expedition sailed from Trinidad on 9 September. This consisted of *Trusty* (5) (Commodore John Ford) and some smaller vessels, embarking the 13th Regiment with two companies of the 49th Regiment and some artillery under Lt-Colonel John Whitelocke. They arrived off Jeremie on 19 September.

In order to cover the landing, a diversion was made to the south by *Penelope* (32) (Commander Josias Rowley), with *Iphigenia* and *Hermione*, with orders to capture or destroy the merchant ships there. Ten were brought back. A number of isolated French settlements were first occupied without oppostion, to be followed soon after by the whole of the French part of the island of Santo Domingo. During the five years of British occupation of Santo Domingo the British lost 20,000 men from disease, mainly yellow fever. The 96th Regiment perished to a man. Later the Negro slave Pierre Dominique Toussant l'Ouverture took control over the whole island.

SEINE v VENGEANCE (off Puerto Rico, West Indies)   Napoleonic Wars/Outside Europe   20 August 1800
Fought between the British and the French.

On 20 August 1800 *Seine* (38) (David Milne), in Mona Passage, sighted the French *Vengeance* (40) (S.L.M. Pichot) bound to French ports from Curaçao. *Seine* gave chase and engaged. After a long chase and a spirited running action, which continued into the next day, *Vengeance* was captured. The ships were evenly matched and losses were significant on both sides.

SURINAM (Guyana, S America)   Napoleonic Wars/Outside Europe   5 May 1804
Fought between the Dutch garrison and a British force of combined military and naval personnel under Commodore Samuel Hood and General Sir Charles Green.
Strength: Dutch 1,000 + some native militia; British naval squadron + 2,000.
Aim: The British sought to capture Surinam to control its rich timber and spices trade.
Battle: The British captured the garrison.
Result: The British objective was achieved with very little loss.

Shrapnel shell was used for the first time during this operation. Surinam was handed back to the Dutch in the 1815 peace treaty.

SURPRISE v HERMIONE (off Puerto Rico, West Indies)   Napoleonic Wars/Outside Europe   25 October 1799
On 22 September 1799 the frigate *Hermione* (32) had been cruising off Puerto Rico when the crew mutinied, killed the tyrannous captain, Hugh Pigot, and most of his officers, and then surrendered their ship to the Spanish at La Guayra on the north coast of South America. She was taken into the Spanish service as a 44-gun frigate.

Captain Edward Hamilton, with the 6 boats of his frigate, *Surprise* (28), cut out the *Hermione* at Puerto Cabello on the night of 24/5 October 1799. A sharp fight was decided when the surgeon, Mr John McMullen, boarded with 16 men from the gig. The Spanish had casualties of 119 killed and 97 wounded. British casualties numbered the captain, the gunner and 10 others wounded. *Hermione* was taken back into the Royal Navy as *Retribution*.

Hamilton was taken prisoner on his homeward voyage, but Bonaparte treated him with consideration and allowed him to be exchanged for 6 midshipmen. He was knighted and made a Freeman of the City of London, but he never fully recovered from his wounds.

SYBILLE v LA FORTE (off Bangladesh)   Napoleonic Wars/Outside Europe   28 February 1799
The *Sybille* (44) (Captain Edward Cooke), in a well-fought action of an hour and forty minutes, totally dismasted and took *La Forte* (50). Cooke was mortally wounded.

TERNATE (Molucca Islands, Indonesia)   Napoleonic Wars/Outside Europe   1801: 1810
Fought between the Dutch and the British.
Strength: Dutch 600; British 322.

One of the Molucca Islands, Ternate, was open to French ships when, at the outbreak of the French Revolutionary Wars, the Dutch became allies of Napoleon. Because the French vessels in the area attacked British vessels trading with China, it became necessary to reduce the ports which were owned by the Dutch. In 1801 a combined military and naval expedition was sent to Ternate under Colonel Burr and a siege of fifty-two days was endured before the Dutch Governor surrendered the island.

After the conclusion of peace the following year, the island was returned to the Dutch; but in 1811 hostilities broke out again and, after the reoccupation of Amboina (qv), a force under Captains Benjamin Tucker and Forbes sailed to the island, which surrendered after only slight resistance on 31 August.

The Dutch regained possession of the island under the terms of the Treaty of Paris in 1814.

THETIS v NORMAN et al (off Cape Henry, Chesapeake Bay, USA)   Napoleonic Wars/Outside Europe   17 May 1795
The British frigate *Thetis* (36) (Captain the Hon Alexander Cochrane–later Admiral Sir Alexander Cochrane) with another smaller frigate, the *Hussar* (28) (Captain–later Admiral–John Beresford), was stationed off Chesapeake Bay to intercept 3 French store ships.

At daybreak on 17 May Cochrane discovered 5 ships–*Norman, Trajan, Prévoyante, Theroux* and *Raison*–which, although large, had reduced armaments in order to act as transport, in line at the mouth of Chesapeake Bay. *Thetis* and *Hussar* attacked and all 5 ships were soon captured. British casualties were 8 killed and 12 wounded.

TRINIDAD (West Indies)   Napoleonic Wars/Outside Europe   17 February 1797
Fought between the British, under Rear-Admiral Sir Henry Harvey and General Sir Ralph Abercromby, and the Spanish.

An expedition consisting of 4 ships of the line, 2 sloops and boats under Rear-Admiral Harvey in *Prince of Wales*, joined later by 1 ship of the line, 2 frigates, 3 sloops and some transports, arrived off the island of Trinidad on 16 February. The troops were under the command of General Sir Ralph Abercromby. A Spanish squadron of 4 ships of the line and a frigate were found at anchor off Port of Spain under cover of shore batteries. Harvey anchored with 4 ships close by and sent the transports farther down the gulf. Early on the morning of 17 February the Spanish ships suddenly burst into flames and the shore batteries were found to have been abandoned. The island capitulated without opposition.

Trinidad was ceded to the British in the Treaty of Amiens 1802.

Select Bibliography

Alison, Archibald. *History of Europe*. London, 1935.
Allen and Muratoff. *Caucasian Battlefields*. Cambridge, 1953.
Almirante, J. (ed). *Bosquejo de la Historia Militar de Espana*. 3 vols, 1923.
Altamira, R. *Historia de España y de la Civilización Española*. 6 vols, 1900–30.
Anderson, M. S. *Europe in the 18th Century, 1713–1783*. London, 1961–7.
Andrews, Wayne. *A Concise Dictionary of American History*. New York, 1962.
Ballard, George. *Rulers of the Indian Ocean*. London, 1927.
Beatson, Brigadier-General F. C. *With Wellington in the Pyrenees*. London,
——*Wellington: The Bidassoa and Nivelle*. London, 1931.
——*Wellington: The Crossing of the Gaves and the Battle of Orthez*. London, 1925.
Becke, Major A. F. *Napoleon and Waterloo*. London, 1939.
Bence-Jones, Mark. *Clive of India*. London, 1974.
Bleiberg, German (ed). *Diccionario de Historia de España*. 1968.
Cassels, Lavender. *The Struggle for the Ottoman Empire, 1717–1780*. London, 1966.
Chandler, D. G. (ed). *A Traveller's Guide to the Battlefields of Europe*. 2 vols. 1965.
Chatterton, E. Keble. *Battles by Sea*. Wakefield, W Yorks, 1975.
Daniell, David Scott. *Sea Fights*. London,
Davies, D. W. *Sir John Moore's Peninsular Campaign, 1808–1809*. The Hague, 1974.
Denison, George T. *A History of Cavalry*. London, 1913.
Dictionary of National Biography.
Dupuy, R. E. and Dupuy, Trevor Nevitt. *The Encyclopaedia of Military History*. London, 1974.
Edwardes, Michael. *Battle of Plassey*. London, 1963.
——*Plassey: The Founding of an Empire*. London, 1969.
Elphinstone, Hon Mountstuart. *The History of India*. London, 1841.
Encyclopaedia Britannica. 1911 edition.
Esposito, Vincent J. (ed). *The West Point Atlas of American Wars*. New York, 1959.
Falls, Captain Cyril (ed). *Great Military Battles*. London, 1964.
Fisher, H. A. L. *A History of Europe*. London, 1936.
Forrest, Denys. *Tiger of Mysore*. London, 1970.
Fortescue, Hon John D. *A History of the British Army*. London, 1911.
Freeman-Grenville, G. S. P. *Chronology of World History*. Oxford, 1973.
Fuller, Major-General J. F. C. *The Decisive Battles of the Western World*. 2 vols. 1970.
Gibson, Charles. *The Clash of Fleets*.
Glover, Michael. *Britannia Sickens*. London, 1970.
——*The Peninsular War, 1807–1814: A Concise Military History*. Newton Abbot, 1974.
Glubb, Lt-General Sir John (Glubb Pasha). *Soldiers of Fortune: The Story of the Mamalukes*. London, 1973.
Grun, Bernard. *The Timetables of History*. 1975.
Hale, John Richard. *Famous Sea Fights*. 1911.
Hibbert, Christopher. *Corunna*. London, 1961.
Horward, Donald D. *The Battle of Bussaco*. Tallahassee, Fla, 1965.
Howarth, David. *A Near Run Thing*. London, 1968.
Jenkins, E. H. *History of the French Navy*. London, 1973.
Johnson, T. *The Oxford Companion to American History*. Oxford, 1966.
Kirkpatrick, F. A. *The Spanish Conquistadores*. 1934.
Lang, Andrew. *A History of Scotland* Vol IV. London, 1907.
Lawford, J. P., and Young, Brigadier Peter. *Wellington's Masterpiece*. London, 1973.
Lecky, W. E. H. *A History of Scotland in the 18th Century*, Vols IV-V. London, 1892.
MacMunn, Sir George. *Afghanistan*. London, 1929.
Malleson, G. B. *History of Afghanistan*. London, 1878.
Marcus, G. J. *The Formative Years: Naval History of England*, Vol 1. London, 1961.
——*The Age of Nelson: Naval History of England*, Vol 2. London, 1971.
Martin, K. L. and Lovett, C. H. *Encyclopaedia of Latin-American History*. 1964.
Montgomery, Field-Marshal the Viscount. *A History of Warfare*. London, 1968.
Mordal, Jacques. *25 Centuries of Sea Warfare*. London, 1959.
Morris, R. *Encyclopaedia of American History*. New York, 1976.
Napier, Sir W. F. P. *History of the War in the Peninsula and South of France*. 6 vols, various editions.
Norris, Sir A. H. *The Lines of Torres Vedras*. Lisbon, 1972.
Oman, Sir Charles. *A History of the Peninsular War*, 7 vols. Oxford, 1902–3.

346

Orme, Robert. *Military Transactions of the British Nation in Indostano*. 3 vols. Madras, 1861.

Rayner, R. M. *European History, 1648–1789*. London, 1949–64.

Reilly, Robin. *The British at the Gates*. London, 1976.

Richardson, H. E. *Tibet and its History*. 1962.

Sykes, P. M. *A History of Persia,* Vol II. London, 1915.

Story, Norah. *The Oxford Companion to Canadian History and Literature*. Oxford, 1967.

Warner, Oliver. *The Sea and the Sword*. London, 1965.

Webster's Biographical Dictionary. 1972 edition.

Williams, Henry Smith, (ed). *Historians History of the World*. 25 vols. London, 1907.

Winsor, Justin. *Narrative and Critical History of America,* Vol 6. New York and Boston, Mass, 1887.

Young, Brigadier Peter. *History of the British Army*. 1967.

INDEX

This Index includes all battles that appear as a heading in the text, together with the more prominent commanders.

Names and titles: because full names and titles, where known, are given in each entry of the text of the Dictionary, only surnames, with initials (or, where the forenames are unknown, title) are here given. Similarly the locations of battles are not supplied within the Index since these will be found next to the headings in the text.

Name order: persons from Arab countries or from the Indian sub-continent are indexed under their first names.

Typographical indications: textual headings are in capitals; names of ships and titles are in italics; map references, giving the page, and map number in brackets, are in bold type; a reference *not* preceded by an ampersand (&) indicates a battle or action.